PITTSBURGH BORN

PITTSBURGH BRED

Researched, written, and edited by

C. Prentiss Orr

Abby Mendelson   Tripp Clarke

With additional research and writing by

Marion Ahlers   Brian Butko   Chris Fletcher   Gregg Ramshaw

Emilia S. Boehm   Nicholas P. Ciotola   Rachel A. Colker   Sherrie Flick
David Grinnell   Arthur Humphrey   Norah A. Krakosky   Lisa Lazar   Anne P. Madarasz
Jennifer Pack   Edward J. Reis   Emily Ruby   Lauren Uhl   Lauren Zabelsky

THE OFFICIAL 250TH ANNIVERSARY EDITION

Published in cooperation with the Senator John Heinz History Center
Pittsburgh, Pennsylvania

Pittsburgh Born, Pittsburgh Bred
500 of the more famous people who have called
Pittsburgh home

Senator John Heinz History Center, Pittsburgh, PA 15222
www.pghhistory.org

© 2008 by C. Prentiss Orr

All Rights Reserved. Published 2008
First edition
Printed in the United States of America

05 04 03 02 01

ISBN 978-0-936340-16-6 (Trade Paper)
ISBN 978-0-936340-17-3 (Case Bound)

Library of Congress Cataloging-in-Publication Data

Orr, C. Prentiss., 1955-
   Pittsburgh born, Pittsburgh bred : 500 of the more
famous people who have called Pittsburgh home /
researched, written and edited by C. Prentiss Orr,
Abbott J. Mendelson, Tripp Clarke ; with additional
research and writing by Marion Ahlers ... [et al.]. --
The official 250th anniversary ed, 1st ed.
     p. cm.
   Includes bibliographical references and indexes.
   ISBN 978-0-936340-16-6 (trade paper : alk. paper) --
   ISBN 978-0-936340-17-3 (case bound : alk. paper)
   1. Pittsburgh (Pa.)--Biography. I. Mendelson, Abby. II.
Clarke, Tripp, 1961- III. Title.
   F159.P653A266 2008
   920.0748'8603--dc22
   [B]

                                          2008007279

Contents

Introduction

For more than two centuries, the Pittsburgh region has produced dreamers, creators, and innovators who have shaped the nation and the world. Some were born here; others came to study or worked for a time at one of the numerous industries that sprang up at the strategic confluence of the three rivers. Native people and soldiers wrangled over America's first western frontier; innovators created the materials and infrastructure that spanned the continent; visionary men and women pioneered the fields of medicine, railroad safety, and environmental health. Perhaps more than any other city or region, Pittsburgh shaped the commerce, industry, and artistry of our world. This book is a celebration of those people and this place.

Who are they? There was John Chapman, helping to secure the homesteads of Western Pennsylvania and Seneca Queen Aliquippa's quest to bring peace with settlers; Andrew Carnegie's sprawling steel industry and George Westinghouse's air brake and electrical empire; Willa Cather's news stories and David McCullough's sweeping historical narratives; Stephen Foster's songs of the South he never visited and Christina Aguilera's navel-baring pop; Mary Cassatt's paintings of mothers and children and Andy Warhol's silk screened soup cans; Rachel Carson's exposé on pollutants and Jonas Salk's polio vaccine; Roberto Clemente's heroics on and off the baseball field and the Rooney family's hands-on 75-year leadership of the Steelers; George Ferris' wheel in every amusement park and Jim Delligatti's billion-selling Big Mac; George Romero's zombie movies and Fred Rogers' neighborhood.

Other cities have been home to performers, writers, and artists who were inspired to invent, build, and create. But Western Pennsylvania has produced and nurtured an inordinate number of people who wanted to reach higher, to find a better way to do things, to explore new ideas that made the world a better place to live.

Along with the celebrities and renowned innovators, you'll find hundreds of people you don't know—astronauts, actors, activists; pioneers in so many fields that continue to give this region its reputation for hard work, integrity, and perseverance.

Over the years, thousands more have contributed to the Pittsburgh region's rich tradition of innovation—here are 500 you should know. H. J. Heinz was famous for saying that the key to success is to "do a common thing uncommonly well." Here in Pittsburgh, it seems people have come together to do uncommon things well, too.

Andrew E. Masich
President and CEO

Capitol Presents

BOZO AT THE CIRCUS

★ TALKING ANIMALS
★ THRILLING MUSIC
★ EXCITING SOUND EFFECTS

ICE CREAM KLONDIKES

The Biggest Bargain in Town!

6 for 1.49

28¢ EACH PLUS TAX

America's favorite ice cream bar . . . rich vanilla ice cream with a thick, tasty coating of chocolate. Choose plain or krispy.

From Klondikes, Chipped Ham, & Skyscraper Cones: The Story of Isaly's by Brian Butko

THE PARTRIDGE FAMILY

WORLD SERIES
NATIONAL LEAGUE vs AMERICAN LEAGUE

FORBES FIELD

GAME

7

FIRST FLOOR RESERVED
$7.70
Tax Included

Not Detach This Coupon RAIN CHECK.

1960 WORLD SERIES

NATIONAL LEAGUE — AMERICAN LEAGUE

FORBES FIELD — PITTSBURGH ATHLETIC CO., INC., Agent

RAIN CHECK

RETAIN THIS CHECK
Not Good If Detached
ADMIT ONE-Subject to the Conditions set forth on the back hereof.
Played Under the Supervision of FORD C. FRICK,
Commissioner of Baseball

SEC 19
ROW J
SEAT 8

FIRST FLOOR RESERVED

ENTER AT GATE 9

Pittsburgh's history is a flea market of great stories. From the introduction of Bozo the Clown on record albums composed and produced by two Pittsburghers to Pirates fans who still wax poetic about Mazeroski's home run in the 1960 World Series, our history is sweetened by the innovations, discoveries, and achievements of so many who have called Pittsburgh home.

Authors' Preface

It would seem, when it comes to fame, timing is everything.

Just like at Kennywood, not everyone gets to ride in the front seat of the Thunderbolt.

Not that the 500 people included in this book were just lucky or overly strategic in jostling to the front of the line, each really earned some small claim deserving of a fantastic ride.

Perhaps more prophetic than our own Andy Warhol exclaiming that, in the future, everyone would be famous for 15 minutes, was Marshall McLuhan (nope, not a Pittsburgher) declaring, "The medium is the message."

What we found fascinating is Pittsburgh's place in the evolution of "the medium." The greatest campfire stories of our nation began inside the barricades of Fort Duquesne. Some of the first great novels ever published were set (and typeset) downtown. The motion picture industry was founded here—not solely because of the success of a 96-seat theater, but because the same people who earned their first nickels here also created the studios of Hollywood. Radio? Yes, made commercially viable by a man who wanted only to amuse his children. Television? Not just one of the first TV stations or *the* first public education station; even the birth of the tube was incubated here.

If Pittsburgh didn't invent fame, we sure greased its wheels.

We, too, have had something of a thrill ride, discovering thousands of people whose stories have made headlines or whose achievements got buried behind more spectacular news. Let us state unequivocally that the rhyme and reason by which we compiled our list of 500 people is just as arbitrary as the final number. But while the ultimate decision of whom we would include rested squarely with us, many people—both affiliated with the History Center and not— tweaked our list a dozen times over, offering up hundreds of deserving candidates, many more than we could possibly write in time to celebrate our region's 250th Anniversary.

But of all the criteria we used to select our profiles, we included only those people—born here or bred here—for whom we had a great story to tell.

That is, after all, what Pittsburgh is all about: a treasured volume of colorful stories. And the timing to tell them could not be better.

C. Prentiss Orr
Abby Mendelson
Tripp Clarke

Key to the Cover

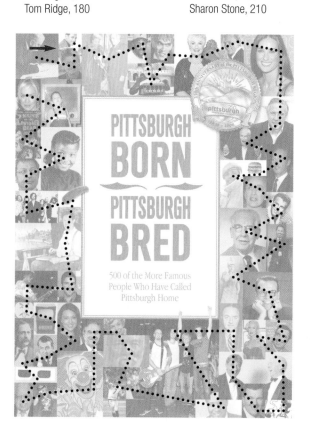

F. Murray Abraham

Born October 24, 1939—Pittsburgh

Aspiring screen actors everywhere know the risk of winning an Oscar.® If one wins the award for doing very significant work at a time when the public knows nothing of his career, he may be jinxed forever. Actors call it the F. Murray Abraham Syndrome. Within two years of winning the Best Actor Oscar for playing court composer Antonio Salieri in the screen adaptation of Peter Shaffer's *Amadeus*, Abraham's only credit was playing President Lincoln in a TV mini-series starring Richard Chamberlain.

Abraham was born in Pittsburgh—to a Syrian father, Fahrid, (from whence his F. comes) and an Italian-American mother, Josephine —but he moved to El Paso, TX, when he was an infant. There, Abraham eventually attended the University of Texas at Austin and followed his interests with dramatic instruction from Uta Hagen in New York City.

Like most actors, Abraham struggled. Between small screen roles in *The Sunshine Boys* and *All the President's Men*, and TV appearances on *All in the Family* and *Kojak*, Abraham even played the Fruit of the Loom Talking Fig Leaf in a 1975 ad campaign. He is proud to have fed his family working as an actor for 10 years before getting his big break. That came with the role of Al Capone in *Scarface* (Universal Studios, 1983), one year before *Amadeus*.

But few more significant roles have come his way. In 1998, he appeared as Ad'har Ru'afo in *Star Trek: Insurrection*. Said Abraham, "The Oscar is the single most important event of my career. I have dined with kings, shared equal billing with my idols, and lectured at Harvard and Columbia. If this is a jinx, I'll take two."

In 2007, Abraham was cheered by critics for his Broadway role in *Mauritius*.

Max Adkins

Born 1910
Died December 5, 1951—Los Angeles, CA

Maxwell Willis Adkins certainly had the credentials to be a great arranger and conductor. He studied with the legendary Cecil B. Leeson at the prestigious Interlocken Music Camp, and took conducting lessons from Vladimir Bakaleinikoff, one-time musical director of the Pittsburgh Symphony. But where Adkins really excelled was in developing the relationships he enjoyed with his pupils—students like Henry Mancini, Billy Strayhorn, Jerry Fielding, Billy May, Sammy Nestico, Maxine Sullivan and Erroll Garner.

In addition to teaching young jazz legends at Hammond's Music store downtown (as well as from his Shadyside home on South Aiken), Adkins was the pit conductor for the Stanley Theatre Orchestra and, for a time, the youngest conductor in the country. Adkins groomed his students to be the best in the business. When bandleaders came through town, they knew where to find the top notch musicians. In fact, bandleaders often left town with Adkins' protegees. It was Adkins who told his good friend Benny Goodman to let a young Henry Mancini write an arrangement for him; it was Adkins who arranged for a young Billy Strayhorn to give a recital for Duke Ellington; and, it was Adkins who arranged for a young Jerry Fielding to meet Alvino Rey.

Beyond his duties as orchestra pit leader and teacher, Adkins found time to serve as associate editor of *Orchestra World*, arrange orchestrations for the South Park County Fairs, conduct the orchestra for the annual Pitt Cap and Gown shows at the Nixon Theatre, and play in a five saxophone band he called the Saxamaniacs.

Adkins' reputation was national. He turned down an offer arranging for Guy Lombardo, and Warner Bros. courted him to arrange film scores.

Tragically, in the early morning hours of December 5, 1951, having just been elected board chairman of Local 60, Adkins died of euremic poisoning. He was just 41 years old.

Christina Aguilera

Born December 18, 1980—Staten Island, NY

Some of her earliest training was performing before Penguin and Steelers fans. Perhaps the violence and cheers, the adoration and taunts—the love-hate relationship she has often endured with her fans—have been the catalyst to this singer's most astounding career.

Born on Staten Island, NY, where her parents, Fausto and Shelly, separated when she was 6, Christina Aguilera and her mother moved into her maternal grandmother's home in Rochester, PA. She attended Rochester Area Elementary School. Her mother remarried, added three step-children to her two, and the new family settled in Wexford. Aguilera attended Marshall Middle School. Even then, her talents were lauded. Aguilera, with her four octave vocal range, performed locally in numerous talent events, often leaving her competitors wondering what had hit them.

At just 8 years of age Aguilera won an audition to compete on Ed McMahon's *Star Search* where, despite her rendition of "The Greatest Love of All," she lost in her juvenile category. More confident than before, she sang often in local venues, including Mellon Arena and Three Rivers Stadium. At 12, Aguilera landed a spot on Disney's *The New Mickey Mouse Club*, where she performed for two years with fellow rising stars Britney Spears and Justin Timberlake. When not taping in Orlando, Aguilera attended North Allegheny Intermediate, but her fame made it hard to create relationships with peers. She jumped schools often, eventually hiring a tutor.

Perhaps Aguilera's biggest break came next when she was chosen to sing a duet with Japanese singer Keizo Nakanishi,

the audition for which was recorded in a local Pittsburgh studio. The subsequent recording and tour were huge in Japan. Not surprisingly, Disney came calling again to ask her to sing "Reflection" in Disney's upcoming *Mulan*, the animated feature based on a Japanese legend. The performance won her a Golden Globe nomination, and within months her first hit "Genie in A Bottle" sold millions. So too, did her first album, *Christina Aguilera*, with eventual sales of more than eight million copies. That year, she won the 1999 Grammy® for Best New Artist. And she's won three more since. Aguilera continues to stay on the front line of pop.

Just one of 69 panels of Alexander's mural, *Apotheosis of Pittsburgh,* commissioned by Andrew Carnegie, c. 1904, Carnegie Institute of Pittsburgh

John White Alexander

Born October 7, 1856—North Side
Died May 31, 1915—New York, NY

The epitome of the stylish portraitist, John White Alexander gained international success in the 1890s painting beautiful women in stunning interiors. Employing provocative expressions and supple curves, Alexander lived to see his art celebrated worldwide.

Born in 1856 in Allegheny City (now the North Side), orphaned in infancy, John White Alexander started work as a 12-year-old telegraph messenger.

Noticeably talented, in 1875 at age 18, he moved to New York City, serving as a *Harper's Weekly* illustrator and political cartoonist.

Within two years, Alexander left to study in Europe. Four years later, in 1881, he had his own New York studio. He taught at Princeton, working as an illustrator, and published portraits in *The Century* of such notables as Oliver Wendell Holmes, Walt Whitman, and Robert Louis Stevenson.

In 1891 Alexander moved to Paris, where he exhibited with the Société Nationale des Beaux-Arts—and was elected a member. During his decade-long residence, through 1901, Alexander's 1893 Paris Salon was an enormous success. Named Chevalier of the Legion of Honor, he won a gold medal at the 1900 Paris Exposition—another at the 1904 St. Louis World's Fair, and a third at Pittsburgh's 1911 Carnegie International.

Retaining ties to America and Pittsburgh, in 1895 he was commissioned to paint a mural for the Library of Congress. A decade later, he received a similar commission for a Carnegie Institute mural. Working for 10 years, from 1905-15, Alexander created his version of Andrew Carnegie's philosophy of industry and democracy, *Apotheosis of Pittsburgh*, covering the three-story atrium walls.

Hailed as one of the period's great artists, Alexander's work hangs in collections from San Francisco to New York's Metropolitan Museum of Art, Philadelphia to Boston, the Smithsonian to the Carnegie Museum of Art.

Sally Alexander

Born October 17, 1943—Owensboro, KY

"I'd never be a writer," Sally Alexander says, "if I'd never been blind."

Turning a crippling disability into national-award-winning books selling in the six figures, "blindness," Alexander says, "improved me as a human being. And it gave me a voice."

Born Sarah Kay Hobart in 1943 in Owensboro, KY, raised in Conyngham, Eastern Pennsylvania, Alexander earned a Bucknell elementary education degree, then moved to Southern California to teach school in Orange County. Then, one day in the mid-1960s, she woke up and couldn't see so well.

Diagnosed with retinal hemorrhages for which there was no cure, she moved back home, then to Pittsburgh, to attend the Greater Pittsburgh Guild for the Blind, to learn Braille, then teach it.

By 1970 she had enrolled in graduate English studies at Pitt, then switched to social work, earning her MSW. Married, working as a youth counselor at Western Psych and St. Francis, she quit to be a stay-at-home mom for her two children. A decent storyteller, in 1981 she enrolled in a children's writing workshop—"as a diversion," she says.

Seven years, many drafts, and much frustration later, Alexander sold her first book— *Taking Hold: My Journey into Blindness*. Aimed at a young adult market, "at first," she says, "I didn't want to write autobiography, because an author exposes much more of herself than she wants. I finally gave in and wrote my story."

That book, and such later volumes as *On My Own: the Journey Continues*, *Mom Can't See Me*, and *Mom's Best Friend*, won high praise for Alexander's straightforward, non-self-pitying accounts of coping with disability.

Currently, Alexander divides her time between writing, teaching writing in Chatham University's MFA program, and leading writing groups in her Squirrel Hill home. "My message to anyone with or without disabilities is simple," she says. "If I can do it, you can, too."

Hervey Allen

Born December 8, 1889—Pittsburgh
Died December 28, 1949—Dade County, FL

When it finally appeared in 1933, after a five-year gestation period, the rambling historical novel was a meaty 1,200 pages and weighed nearly three pounds. Written by an obscure poet and English teacher with $30 in the bank, *Anthony Adverse* made its author Hervey Allen a literary star.

Born William Hervey Allen, Jr., the son of the inventor of an automatic blast furnace stoker, Allen went to Annapolis in 1910, but an injury led to his honorable discharge. Graduating from Pitt in 1915, he enlisted in the Pennsylvania National Guard the following year. Commissioned a second lieutenant, Allen served under Black Jack Pershing during the Pancho Villa raids, then in France during World War I. He was wounded at Fismes on the Western Front, then came back to fight in the Argonne.

Mustered out, by 1920 he was studying at Harvard, then taught English at Pitt, Columbia, and Vassar. Writing poetry since 1916, in 1926 he published *Israfel*, a biography of Edgar Allan Poe.

Mr. & Mrs. Allen aboard the *S.S. Normandie*, 1937

Then, living in Bermuda, Allen researched and wrote *Anthony Adverse*, the novel ranging from Napoleonic France to the American West. The book sold 2,000 copies a day—at $3.00 each in Depression-era dollars. Over the next dozen years, 1933-45, it sold more than a million copies and was translated into 19 languages. Made into a 1936 movie starring Frederic March, *Anthony Adverse* won four Academy Awards.

Although Allen sold three million books during his lifetime, he never repeated his initial success. Living in The Glades, a Florida plantation, Allen had a respectable career, embarking on a five-novel sequence, *The Disinherited*, about a young Pennsylvanian during Revolutionary America. Allen published three volumes; a fourth appeared posthumously.

Hervey Allen died of a heart attack at The Glades in 1949, age 60. He is buried in Arlington National Cemetery

Marty Allen

Born March 23, 1922—Squirrel Hill

Perhaps Pittsburgh's best answer to Jerry Lewis, Marty Allen was the combed-over, wild haired comic partner to singer Steve Rossi who, together as Allen & Rossi, appeared more times (45 according to Allen) on *The Ed Sullivan Show* than any other comedy team. He may have been the first celebrity to have a discernable Pittsburgh accent, too.

Born Morton Alpern in Squirrel Hill, Allen was the class clown at Taylor Allderdice where he graduated as president of his homeroom in 1940. Always the cut-up, Allen was popular as a jitterbug dancer having won the city championship sometime that year or earlier. In fact, one of his first jobs, after serving with the 484th Group of the Army Air Forces in Italy, was traveling door to door as a dance instructor. With records under one arm and a portable player under the other, he would ring doorbells and offer half-hour instructions to "the lady of the house" for $10. After the war, and while on the GI Bill to attend USC for a degree in journalism, Allen made extra cash by performing pantomimes and comic dance routines in local clubs. He discovered his calling, dropped out of college and soon traveled a circuit of small town theatres. "I was very popular in Beaver Falls, Ellwood City and Monongahela," he likes to report.

Allen gives credit to Nat "King" Cole for discovering him. While appearing at the Sands Hotel in Las Vegas, Cole called Allen to meet Steve Rossi, a nightclub singer in search of a bigger act. By all accounts, the duo became a sensation overnight. The year was 1959. By the early '60s they had appeared on just about every TV variety show produced by the big (and only) three networks. In 1966, they even starred in their own film, *The Last of the Secret Agents*, the world premiere of which was held at the Stanley Theatre downtown on May 19, 1966.

In October 1968, Allen & Rossi performed their last act together at the Riviera in Las Vegas. Or so they thought.

Allen left to entertain the troops in Vietnam, starting what became popular as his "Hello Dere" tours. In between tours, Allen was a frequent guest of Johnny Carson, Merv Griffin and Mike Douglas, a regular contestant on dozens of game shows, and he even garnered cameo appearances in dramatic series like *The Big Valley*, *Night Gallery*, and *Love American Style*.

In 1983, Allen & Rossi reunited in Atlantic City. After several years performing on cruise ships and doing one-nighters in New York City, they last played here at Montemurro's in Sharpsburg on May 24, 1986.

Queen Aliquippa

Born (date unknown)
Died December 23, 1754—Huntingdon Cty., PA

Known as a steelmaking town on the Ohio River, the borough of Aliquippa takes its name from an 18th-century Native American leader who was a strong ally of the British during the French and Indian War. Due to an absence of written information, relatively little is known about Queen Aliquippa's early life. In the 1740s, however, records show she was the leader of a migratory group of Seneca who resided in various locations along the four rivers of Western Pennsylvania—the Youghiogheny, Monongahela, Allegheny, and Ohio.

Honored as "Queen" by the British, Aliquippa demonstrated hospitality to many who traveled in Western

Pennsylvania during this time period, including Conrad Weiser the Indian agent for Pennsylvania and young George Washington, who met with her during his 1754 travels to the Pittsburgh region. In the Summer of 1754, Aliquippa traveled with her son and Seneca warriors to Fort Necessity to aid George Washington and the British in their defense of the site during the French and Indian War. Washington thought highly of her, and recommended that she be honored for her service and commitment to the British cause.

After the fall of Fort Necessity, the 80-year-old Queen moved to Huntingdon County and died by year's end. The borough of Aliquippa is named in her honor, most likely by the railroad company that first placed a station there.

Eric Andersen

Born March 23, 1922—Squirrel Hill

In the summer of 1970, a trainload of musicians traveled the Canadian countryside playing a legendary concert series called the Festival Express. Among the artists on that infamous train ride were Janis Joplin, The Grateful Dead, The Band, Buddy Guy, The Flying Burrito Brothers, and a singer-songwriter from Pittsburgh named Eric Andersen.

Eric Gallatin Andersen was born at West Penn Hospital in Pittsburgh in 1943. The family moved here from Cleveland when his father took a job with Mine Safety Appliances Company developing new technology for gas masks. They settled in Squirrel Hill and then in Oakdale. At a young age his family relocated to Buffalo, NY. After seeing Elvis and the Everly Brothers in neighborhood venues, he taught himself to play the guitar and piano. His musical tastes gravitated to the political songwriters of the day, like Woodie Guthrie and The Weavers, while his literary tastes gravitated to Kerouac and Ginsberg. However

as he began to write and perform, his songs reflected a departure from politics and social commentary and steered toward more romantic pursuits. At 20 years old, Andersen hitchhiked to the West Coast to immerse himself with like-minded youth in San Francisco

and Berkley. Folk singer Tom Paxton heard Andersen perform at the famous North Beach Beat hangout, the Coffee Gallery, and invited him to come to New York. Andersen was quickly embraced by the Greenwich Village folk scene, with contemporaries like Phil Ochs and Bob Dylan. Before long his songs were being covered by Judy Collins and Peter, Paul & Mary.

Andersen was asked to play the famed Newport Folk Festival in 1966 and later that year starred alongside Edie Sedgwick in Andy Warhol's film *Space*, after Warhol and Andersen had become good friends. In a close brush with destiny, Andersen was slated the following year to be signed by Beatles manager Brian Epstein who died before a contract was drawn. Several years later Andersen took off on the Festival Express between recording sessions. In 1972 he had his most successful recording to date, *Blue River*, which a 1992 *Rolling Stone* Album Guide called the "best example of the '70s singer-songwriter movement." In a cruel dose of fate, the master tapes of his heavily anticipated follow-up album, *Stages,* were lost. Mysteriously they reappeared 17 years later.

Over the years Andersen has performed with numerous musicians, from Bob Dylan and Joan Baez to The Band's Rick Danko and Richard Thompson. He has co-written songs with Townes Van Zandt and his songs have been covered by everyone from Johnny Cash to Bob Weir's band Ratdog. With a 40-year career and more than 20 albums under his belt, Eric Andersen is arguably America's first modern singer-songwriter.

Maxwell Anderson

Born December 19, 1888—Atlantic, PA
Died February 28, 1959—Stamford, CT

He wrote in longhand in wirebound notebooks, and refused to attend his plays' openings.

Pulitzer Prize winner and the 20th Century's most prolific American playwright, Maxwell Anderson eschewed all pretensions of the modern writer.

Born James Maxwell Anderson in 1888 on a farm in Atlantic, a tiny town near Meadville, the family moved to Ohio when he was three, later to Jamestown, ND, where Anderson graduated high school in 1908.

Graduating the University of North Dakota with a literature degree in 1911, Anderson earned a Stanford master's in 1914. In New

York and San Francisco, Anderson taught journalism.

In 1923, Anderson wrote his first play, *White Desert*, which ran 12 performances. His next play, however, was a huge hit. In 1924, *What Price Glory?* ran 433 performances on

Broadway and was made into a movie. It also made Anderson a literary star.

Equally adept at prose and blank verse drama, original screen plays and adaptations, Anderson toiled 35 years creating one of the century's most impressive resumes. His screen adaptations of *Death Takes a Holiday* and *All Quiet on the Western Front* (for which he received his only Academy Award nomination) are classics.

In 1935, Anderson wrote *Winterset*, based on the Sacco and Vanzetti case, which won the first New York Drama Critics Circle Award. The next year, 1936, Anderson won again for *High Tor*. Over the years he wrote *Knickerbocker Holiday* (1938), for which he also wrote lyrics, including "September Song"; *Key Largo* (1939), starring Paul Muni (later the Humphrey Bogart-Lauren Bacall film); *Lost in the Stars* (1949); *Bad Seed* (1954, made into the Patty McCormack film); and, *Both Your Houses* (1933), for which he won his only Pulitzer.

Kurt Angle

Born December 9, 1968—Mt. Lebanon, PA

When you're talking about wrestler Kurt Angle, it's hard to separate the hero from the hoopla, the beef from the baloney. But despite such nicknames as the Olympic Hero and the Extreme Machine, there's plenty of talent and achievement to go around.

First, the gold medal. Born in Pittsburgh in 1968, Kurt Steven Angle lettered in football and wrestled at Mt. Lebanon High, where, among other accolades, he was an all-state linebacker and the 1987 state heavyweight wrestling champion. 5'-10" and 250 pounds at Clarion University, Angle was NCAA Division I wrestling champion in 1990 and 1992, and a three-time NCAA Division I All-American. Graduating in 1993 with a degree in education (and a Clarion Golden Eagle tattooed on his back), Angle turned to the Olympics. Competing in the 1996 Olympic trials, Angle suffered severe neck injuries, two fractured cervical vertebrae, and two herniated discs. By the time of the Atlanta Olympics, though, Angle had healed sufficiently to compete—and win a gold medal. Although his injury was all-too-real, it led to Angle's braggadocios claim that he won his medal "with a broken freakin' neck!"

Next, the gold—and plenty of it. After a brief career as a Pittsburgh TV sportscaster, in 1998 Angle turned professional wrestler. Working through 2006 with the World Wrestling Federation, he became the sole Olympic gold medalist to enter the world of *SmackDown!* and moonsaults. Along the way to winning six world championships, and numerous other titles, Angle morphed into a consumer item, hawking T-shirts, hats, you name it. By 2007 a featured attraction of *Total Nonstop Action Wrestling*, his answer to his critics—"It's real, it's damn real!"—became both rallying cry and marketing slogan.

Angle is a 2001 National Wrestling Hall of Fame inductee. He lives in Pittsburgh with his wife and two children.

PHOTO COURTESY OF ANTI-FLAG

© 2008, AP PHOTO/MICHEL LIPCHITZ

Anti-Flag

Anti-Flag was formed in Glenshaw back in 1988 by Justin Greever (aka Justin Sane), Pat Thetic and a revolving door of various musicians including Sane's sister Lucy. The band first disbanded only to be resurrected in 1993, making their debut on CMU's radio station WRCT. Sane met Andy Wright (aka Andy Flag) when the two were forced by their mothers to attend a church function. Thetic, Flag, and Sane began playing local gigs and practicing relentlessly to hone their sound. After a couple of years, with little money but with lots of support from friends in the punk community, Anti-Flag hit the road on a self-booked U.S. tour in the summer of 1995. Their second tour, in the spring of 1996 was good for sustaining and building the band's momentum, but difficult on their friendships. The band's debut release "Die For The Government" came out in 1996 and by then, Andy Flag had had his fill of his fellow bandmates, deciding to call it quits.

The band's lineup would be rounded out when Chris Head, Jamie Cock, and Chris Barker (aka Chris #2) joined. Several solid releases and an invitation to participate in the Vans Warped Tour helped to fuel Anti-Flag's message against political corruption, racism,

homophobia, and fascism well beyond the confines of the three rivers.

Despite the rough and tumble reputation of the band, Pat Thetic had an opportunity to work with Fred Rogers during the last couple of seasons of *Mister Roger's Neighborhood* when he developed a real fondness for the children's TV icon. In an interview with *PopCulture-Madness.com*, Thetic told the story of Mr. Rogers joking with him once about creating a matronly puppet for him called "Auntie Flag."

They aren't just loud, angry, confrontational, and in-your-face. Anti-Flag is also involved, actively trying to get people to vote, actively helping to clean-up in Cameron Parish after hurricane Katrina, actively working with Amnesty International—even teaming up with Representative Jim McDermott to promote H.R. 2410, the Depleted Uranium Munitions Study Act.

Despite having a name that is often misunderstood, Anti-Flag is not anti-American; they just hold that the country has become militaristic, imperialistic, and intolerant. Anti-Flag has become a major force in the music of our youth, a sentiment recently confirmed by their signing with RCA Records—a move some view as too mainstream but others see as an opportunity to be heard by millions more.

Not your Disney-esque hero scattering free appleseeds, Chapman was more interested in sowing religious truth.

Johnny Chapman Appleseed

Born September 26, 1774—Leominster, MA
Died March 18, 1845—Ft. Wayne, IN

Drawn westward with settlers from New England by land developments in northwestern PA, John Chapman first settled near Warren, PA. By the mid-1790s he had traveled down the Allegheny River and is believed to have built a cabin on Grant's Hill in Pittsburgh. The land was then owned by James O'Hara who he is likely to have known. Here Chapman tended to an orchard, and is quoted as saying "The bees work without wages; why should I not do the same?"

Two encounters transformed Chapman into the folk-hero we know as Johnny Appleseed. Learning of cider mills run by German settlers along the banks of the Monongahela and Youghiogheny Rivers, near Belle Vernon and Smithton, PA, Chapman had the idea to save the seeds from the mill's pumice, and use them to plant nurseries along the banks of the Ohio and its tributaries. Rather than a charitable act, he developed this into a business to satisfy the settler's obligation to have a working orchard within three years of establishing their homesteads. Chapman sold seedlings from the nurseries he planted—for profit. He first set out from Pittsburgh in about 1802 in a canoe filled with seeds. He returned to Pittsburgh each fall to spend the winters and collect new seeds.

But it was Chapman's introduction to the Swedenborgian faith, here in western Pennsylvania, that molded him into the man of uncommon generosity that we know today. While on an errand to Greensburg in the late 1790s, he was introduced to the doctrines of Emmanuel Swedenborg by Judge John Young, also a likely acquaintance of O'Hara. Swedenborg (1688-1772) was a Swedish scientist who had experienced religious revelations and professed knowledge of the certainty of an afterlife. Young had been among the first American converts to this faith in Philadelphia around 1784. Two of the most important tenets of the Swedenborgian faith are **character** and **usefulness**, and Johnny set out to become not just a sower of seeds, but also a religious missionary who practiced these principles in his everyday life. In fact, one of the first Swedenborgian churches, built in Allegheny City, is what attracted Andrew Carnegie's father to emigrate to Pittsburgh.

John Armstrong

Born October 13, 1717—Ireland
Died March 9, 1795—Carlisle, PA

Although known as the "First Citizen of Carlisle," John Armstrong is closely associated with the county that bears his name. There, during the French and Indian War, Armstrong led a force of provincial troops to destroy an enemy Indian settlement at Kittanning. The apocryphal story goes that he brought the Indians a gift of blankets. A Trojan horse of infinite proportions, the blankets had been infected with small pox. Modern historians assert that Armstrong's shameless cunning was the first act of germ warfare on this continent.

In 1758, he participated in the Forbes expedition which forced the French to abandon and destroy Fort Duquesne. Armstrong later served with distinction in the Revolutionary War and as a Pennsylvania delegate to the Continental Congress. Armstrong County is named in his honor.

LaVar Arrington

Born June 20, 1978—Pittsburgh

Here's the all-time LaVar Arrington moment: the Nittany Lions are playing Illinois, fourth and short. Anticipating the snap, the Penn State linebacker, all 6'-3" and 257 pounds of him, simply leapt over the Illinois line, tackling the hapless ball carrier in his own backfield.

It was that kind of play—dubbed the

LaVar Leap—that landed the 21-year-old on the cover of *Sports Illustrated*, making him All Big-Ten, a first team All-American, and winner of the 1999 Chuck Bednarik and Dick Butkus awards.

Dubbed The Killa by his army of fans, LaVar RaShad Arrington was born in Pittsburgh in 1978. At North Hills High he ran track and field, and played basketball, the latter well enough to be recruited by Georgetown, UMass, and North Carolina, among others. But football was his game, on both sides of the ball, and as a senior linebacker and running back he was the 1996 *Parade* Player of the Year, the Bobby Dodd National Offensive Player of the Year, the Gatorade Player of the Year, and *USA Today* Pennsylvania Player of the Year.

After Penn State, Arrington was chosen by the Washington Redskins as the second pick of the first round in the 2000 NFL draft. A classic high-impact rookie, he racked up 44 tackles and four sacks. Career highs came with 82 tackles in 2001 and 11 sacks in 2002—two of his three consecutive Pro Bowl years.

Playing through 2005 for the 'Skins, a contract dispute, knee injuries, and charges that he wasn't playing the team game got Arrington his release. Jumping to the Giants in 2006, he suffered a ruptured Achilles tendon in week seven and missed the rest of the season.

Retiring in 2007, the brilliant, injury-riddled Arrington had 332 tackles and 23.5 sacks—a significant record by any standard.

Tom Atkins

Born November 13, 1938 —North Side

He debuted on Broadway in a short-lived comedy at the Plymouth Theatre. His co-stars were Maureen O'Sullivan, Patrick Magee, and Karen Black. He next appeared with Frank Sinatra, on film, in *The Detective*. Then, back on Broadway, with Blythe Danner and Robert Symonds in *Cyrano de Bergerac*. Followed closely by *The Front Page*, at the Ethel Barrymore, starring Robert Ryan. Then, winning the 1973 Drama Desk Award for Most Promising Performer, he played opposite John Lithgow in the premiere of *The Changing Room* at the Morosco.

For a 1965 graduate of Duquesne University's Red Masquers troupe, Tom Atkins' rise to recognition was no less meteoric than a Zambelli firework.

Raised in Knoxville, Atkins attended Rochelle Grade School, Knoxville Jr. High, and graduated from Carrick High School in 1956. Before earning a journalism degree from Duquesne, he served two years in the Navy.

Atkins wowed Pittsburgh audiences when he commanded the role of Randle P. McMurphy in *One Flew Over the Cuckoo's Nest* in the 1975 inaugural, sold-out season of the Pittsburgh Public Theater. Since then he has appeared in more than 10 PPT productions, most recently playing Art Rooney in Rob Zeller

and Gene Collier's one-man tour de force *The Chief*, a role he'll reprise in the fall of 2008.

Odd perhaps, he is better known to TV audiences and film buffs for playing dozens of roles as a Chief (of police) often in *Harry O.*, *The Rockford Files*, *Quincy M.E.,* and *The Equalizer*. As a cop, too, he was Frank McCae in *Maniac Cop*, Sgt. Fred Hardy in the Pittsburgh-filmed *Striking Distance*, Det. McCleary in George Romero's *Bruiser* and, his personal favorite, Det. Ray Cameron in the

cult classic, *Night of the Creeps*. But of his many film roles, he may best be known for his shortest, that of Michael Hunsaker, the businessman whose murdered daughter starts all the action in *Lethal Weapon*.

Atkins lives in Peters Township with his wife, Janis, their son Taylor, and Gus, the dog.

Austin performs at The Apollo Theater, Harlem, in 1959.

Chuck Austin

Born June 17, 1927—Ben Avon, PA

Every theater student is taught there are no small roles—just small actors. And every musician learns that a good conductor is only as good as the softest musician playing in his orchestra. Chuck Austin never played small.

A native of Ben Avon, Austin received his first trumpet on Christmas day when he was in the sixth grade. He immediately spent hours-upon-hours practicing. Within months he was the leader of a local dance band. Graduating from Avonworth High School in 1945, and after a tour of duty with the Navy, Austin polished his chops at the renowned Pittsburgh Music Institute. He joined Local 471, the black musician's union, and hit the local circuit, playing clubs like the Crawford Grill, where Austin served as house band leader alongside Horace Parlan, Art Nance, and Spider Lindsey. Among the early artists with whom he performed were vocalist Dakota Staton and bandleader Joe Westray.

New Orleans native Lloyd Price, famous for the Cajun-rock songs "Lawdy Miss Clawdy" and "Stagger Lee," caught wind of Austin's horn-blowing talents and booked him with his band for several years in the 1950s. Austin was on horns for Price's chart-topping hit "Personality" which propelled them to national fame, assisted immeasurably by an appearance on the *Ed Sullivan Show*. Austin's next gig was with The Apollos before getting a call from Ray Charles, whom he had befriended years earlier. Yet, like other local greats, Costa and Negri, Austin made the decision to stay home in Pittsburgh.

Over the years Austin has played with George Gee & His Make-Believe Ballroom Orchestra, The Balcony Big Band, Roger Humphries' Big Band, The Burg Band and for many years the Jack Purcell Orchestra. His passion for Pittsburgh's musical and cultural heritage has fueled another avocation. Austin is the co-founder and President of the African-American Jazz Preservation Society of Pittsburgh, which promotes an annual April jam and recognitions award.

Without great sidemen there wouldn't be great leaders. Austin, now in his seventh decade of jazz, is as good as they come.

Charles Avery

Born circa 1784—New York, NY
Died in 1858—Pittsburgh

Recognized as one of Pittsburgh's earliest philanthropists, Charles Avery was also known as an industrialist, church leader and abolitionist. Avery arrived in Pittsburgh around 1812 from New York at the age of 28. His intent was to establish himself as a druggist, a trade he had learned as an apprentice in New York City. In the 1830s he partnered with John and Thomas Arbuckle (famous for their coffee distributing interests) to form the Eagle Cotton Mill. Here he created the foundation of his wealth. However, Avery's later investment with Thomas Marshall Howe and Curtis G. Hussey in the Pittsburgh and Boston Mining Company provided him with enormous wealth. Until his death, he served as the president of this company that sank the famous Cliff Mine in Michigan's rich copper ore region.

Avery took very seriously the responsibility of his wealth. Inscribed on his monument is the Book of Matthew scripture "The tree be known by its fruit." Avery gave liberally to civic and religious organizations. He was one of the organizers of the Methodist Protestant Denomination. Avery was also very civic minded; he was one of the original incorporators of Al-

legheny Cemetery and he was active in the construction of bridges, the formation of the Monongahela Navigation Company, and the creation of a natural gas company.

Avery's activity as an abolitionist, however, is the role for which he is most remembered. Recognizing the intellectual equality of African Americans, Avery created the Allegheny Institute and Mission Church, later known as Avery College, to educate African Americans in North America. Upon his death, much of his estate was distributed as scholarship funds for African American students at many college and universities, including the University of Pittsburgh, Oberlin College and Wilberforce University.

Avery died in 1858 on the eve of the Civil War. Today, his monument in Allegheny Cemetery is not only a testament to his importance as an industrialist and civic leader, but to the political movements of his day. In his book, *Standing Soldier, Kneeling Slave*, Kirk Savage writes that the relief panel at the base of the Avery monument "is the first known instance of African American representation in marble or bronze."

Bob Babbitt

Born November 26, 1937—Mt. Washington

Bob Babbitt played on more #1 records than The Beatles, The Rolling Stones, Elvis Presley and The Beach Boys combined. He was a member of the legendary and brilliant Funk Brothers, the band that backed-up some of the greatest recording artists to swing through Hitsville, USA (aka Motown).

Originally from the West End, Babbitt was born Robert Kreiner to Hungarian parents. As a child, Gypsy music was a significant influence on his early musical development. He was introduced to the upright bass by his seventh grade choir teacher and began his classical training, which included spending three years playing with the Pittsburgh Symphony's Junior Orchestra. By his teens he had discovered the rhythm and blues of artists like Bill Doggett and King Curtis, in large part through Porky Chedwick at WHOD, and he would soon trade in his upright for a jazz bass. Babbitt cites among his influences Pittsburgh natives Ray Brown and Paul Chambers.

During his senior year in high school, his father passed away and Babbitt decided to forgo his scholarship to the University of Pittsburgh in order to support his family. An uncle persuaded Babbitt to relocate to Detroit and find work there. Working construction during the day, Babbitt began playing in clubs at night. He joined a band called the Royaltones and soon caught the attention of Michigan native Del Shannon and was enlisted as his touring band through the mid-1960s.

In 1967 Babbitt was called to fill in for legendary Motown Funk Brother bassist James Jamerson, who was having personal struggles. Although intimidating at first for Babbitt, the only white Funk Brother, he was embraced by his fellow musicians.

Babbitt became one of the most successful sidemen the music business has even seen, playing bass on countless classics, including "Cool Jerk" by the Capitols, "War" by Edwin Starr, "Signed, Sealed, Delivered" by Stevie Wonder, "Midnight Train To Georgia" by Gladys Knight and the Pips, "Mercy, Mercy Me" by Marvin Gaye, "Ball Of Confusion" by The Temptations, as well as the longest bass solo in Top 40 history on a song called "Scorpio" by Dennis Coffey.

When Motown moved to the West Coast Babbitt moved east, continuing his string of hits with artists like The Spinners, Bonnie Raitt, Frank Sinatra, Elton John and Jim Croce.

A mixture of entertainment news, interviews, and insider song tracks, *RadioScope* at its peak was enjoyed on more than 150 metro stations, and its attendant website, EURweb.com, now draws more than 10 million page views per month.

Benjamin Bakewell

Born in 1767—Derby, England
Died in 1844—Pittsburgh

Known by 1853 as the "father of the flint glass business" in the United States, Benjamin Bakewell played a key role in both establishing the glass industry in Pittsburgh and growing the city into a national center for innovation in the manufacture, design, and marketing of glass.

Bakewell began his career in 1781 as an apprentice in the retail trade. At 21, he went to work for a dry goods merchant in London; just a few years later, he opened his own establishment featuring goods imported from France. In 1793, when tensions between England and France and the events of the French

Revolution made acquiring goods difficult, Bakewell moved his business to New York. The business grew in size and complexity and involved oceangoing trade with France and Europe, the West Indies, and major U.S. port cities. The Embargo Act of 1807 shut the door on foreign trade and bankrupted Bakewell. Forced to sell his considerable real estate holdings to pay his creditors, he resigned himself to starting over (again) in business.

Pittsburgh offered this opportunity and in August 1808, Bakewell and his partners purchased a flint glass manufactory just built

Having spent his entire career behind the scenes, Babbitt and the Funk Brothers have received some recognition over the past several years. In 2002, the documentary *Standing In The Shadows of Motown*, which explored the legendary band responsible for creating so many hits, won a Grammy Award for Best Soundtrack. Additionally The Funk Brothers that same year won a Grammy for Best R&B Performance, and then in 2004 The Funk Brothers won the Grammy for Lifetime Achievement.

Over the course of his career, Babbitt has played on more than 200 Billboard Hot 100 Top 40 hits and has earned 25 Gold and Platinum records.

Lee Bailey

Born July 27, 1947—Moreland, GA

Even at 13, he had a voice so deep, so smooth and so passionate that friends five years his senior would ask him to call their girlfriends. That's the kind of power and influence Lee Bailey owned early on. And it was that voice that launched his career from vol-

Bailey and Gladys Knight, whose "Midnight Train" was recorded with Babbitt and the Funk Brothers, above.

unteering as a "go-fer" at WZUM to owning one of the largest and most successful syndicated radio programs in the country today.

Bailey grew up on a farm in Georgia with his grandparents, J.C. and Elvenia Bailey, but was brought up to Pittsburgh at 8 years of age to live with his once-estranged mother, Helen Smith, then newly remarried. Even on the farm, Bailey was captivated by radio, enjoying the "theater of the mind" experience that enthralled a young boy who had difficulty reading. Attending Latimer Junior High on the North Side, he was conscious of two personal problems: one, his real name was Harvey for which he was often ridiculed; and, two, his Georgian accent tended to distance himself from neighborhood friends. He decided at an early age to attend to his diction. While at Allegheny High School, Bailey hung out at Jimmy Pol's R&B station in Carnegie, popularly called ZOOM.

Once honorably discharged from the Air Force where he served in Sacramento, Bailey hosted his first radio show for KPOP from 10 to midnight. Filling the gap for soul music in the region, Bailey was nearly an overnight sensation. He earned his first class radio license and then jumped ship to afternoon drive jock in Stockton, CA. Climbing the airwaves along the West Coast, Bailey was recruited to Washington, D.C., then landed back in California at famed KUTE in Los Angeles. There, after several strong seasons, he had a falling out with radio personality Frankie Crocker, and was fired. That's when Bailey, known to millions of listeners as "The Voice," decided to clean out his garage and build a studio, producing voice-overs, national spots and, in 1983, the first urban entertainment series he titled *RadioScope*.

Bearden's *Pittsburgh Memories*, 1984, collage on board, H: 28 5/8 x W: 23 1/2 inches, Carnegie Museum of Art, Pittsburgh, Gift of Mr. and Mrs. Ronald R. Davenport and Mr. and Mrs. Milton A. Washington

here. Knowing nothing about glass, but well-schooled in establishing complex networks of trade and familiar with the finest goods available in England and France, Bakewell produced both everyday wares (such as bottles) and finer flint (lead) glass pieces. He garnered press for his enterprise by developing key clientele—Bakewell was the first U.S. maker to provide glass for use in the White House, for Madison, Monroe, and Jackson.

As one of the first factories to pioneer and adapt pressing technology, Bakewell led the industry into a new era of mass production, while having the foresight to retain the company's focus on high-end wares. Today, collectors still prize the finely made goods of Benjamin Bakewell's factory and recognize the impact they had on establishing the industry locally and in America.

William Ball

Born April 29, 1931—unknown
Died July 30, 1991—Los Angeles, CA

Of hundreds of actors, directors and theatre professionals who have distinguished themselves with degrees from Carnegie Tech or Carnegie Mellon, William Ball deserves special attention for having created ACT, the American Conservatory Theater, in Pittsburgh. Of course, ACT may have lasted only six months here, but once moved to San Francisco, the conservatory group soon became the benchmark of successful repertory theaters nationwide.

Originally a student of scenic design, Ball—always described as energetic and peculiar—graduated Carnegie Tech in 1956 with a Masters in Fine Arts. He appeared onstage in several Shakespeare Festivals and toured the country, eventually turning toward stage directing, mounting productions at some the country's newest and earliest resident theaters, like Washington D.C.'s Arena Stage, Houston's Alley Theater, and San Francisco's Actors' Workshop. His early successes in other cities led him to develop a new vision for a self-sustaining theatre complex. Working with two stages, producing multiple plays in rotation, while serving the interests of a university providing students who would learn from practical experience in theatre produc-

THE CURTIS THEATRE COLLECTION, UNIVERSITY OF PITTSBURGH LIBRARY

tion, design and acting, a professional repertory company could create theater of unprecedented artistic integrity and financial stability.

Ball launched ACT at the Pittsburgh Playhouse with his 1965 production of *Tartuffe*, starring fellow CMU alum Rene Auberjonois. The company was an instant success. Said the actor, "We had a spectacular season in two theaters. ...We did six months there. [But] I don't think Bill ever really intended for the company to stay in Pittsburgh, but that's how he could get it started."

The company left for San Francisco by year's end—some say, ironically, under a cloud of suspicion as to who and how the next season would be funded.

Two of ACT's productions, *Cyrano de Bergerac* and *The Taming of the Shrew* were filmed for PBS, and in 1979, Ball accepted a Tony Award for outstanding work in repertory theatre. Several years after resigning from ACT, Ball committed suicide in 1991.

Vince Barnett

Born July 4, 1902—Pittsburgh
Died August 10, 1977—Encino, CA

Even though Vince Barnett appeared in more than 350 films playing character or supporting roles to the likes of Gary Cooper, Jean Harlow and Spencer Tracy, he was most famous for his public pranks on famous newsmakers. Charles Lindbergh, George Bernard Shaw, President Franklin Roosevelt, and Henry Ford II all fell victim to his practical jokes, stories about which were circulated in the entertainment columns of his day.

Barnett grew up in Edgewood, graduated Edgewood High, attended Duquesne University's Prep School, and Carnegie Tech. As a young man, Barnett flew a mail plane between Pittsburgh and Cumberland, MD. But his father, Luke Barnett, a well-known banquet speaker, inspired his son to the dramatic arts. Within two years of his early aerial career, he was on Broadway appearing in George White's *Scandals of 1927*. Blessed with big ears, an early balding head and his trademark mustache, Barnett became familiar to thousands, making his eventual transition to the silver screen a cinch. His love of flying, in fact, helped him garner his first big role as *Scarface*'s secretary in the 1932 Howard Hughes' film. Other significant films include *Riff Raff, Springfield Rifle, The Virginian* and 1937's *A Star is Born* in which he took on the unaccredited role of "Otto, a photographer."

Of course, hundreds of his screen appearances show that he was the ever available bartender, doorman, crook or cabbie. And he appeared often in *Perry Mason, The Man from U.N.C.L.E., The Andy Griffith Show, Green Acres,* and *Mayberry R.F.D.*

Famously, he was known well by his pranks, often playing the bumbling waiter at large banquets, pretending to spill soup on the lap of Sir Winston Churchill, or losing Charles Lindbergh's last-minute speaking notes.

Perhaps because of his impish size relative to the stature of the dignitaries he teased, he was well liked by the press. In a 1972 interview by *Post-Gazette* critic George Anderson, Barnett said, "The secret is that [I] attacked the ego, not the person... I pretend to spill the soup and then wipe them off. But I never poured soup on anybody. That's not funny."

Barnett, Paul Muni, and an unknown hood appear in the 1932 gangster film, *Scarface,* directed by Howard Hawks and released by United Artists.

© BETTMANN/CORBIS

Romare Bearden

Born September 2, 1911—Charlotte, NC
Died March 12, 1988—New York, NY

It was in Pittsburgh that multi-talented, multi-faceted African-American artist Romare Bearden learned to draw.

And it was to Pittsburgh that he returned again and again, for inspiration and subject matter: African-American life, jazz, blues, and steel mill stories.

Born Romare Howard Bearden in 1911 in Charlotte, by 1915 his family had moved to Harlem. Regularly visiting his grandmother Carrie Banks' Penn Avenue rooming house, Bearden spent his fourth-grade year, 1920, in Pittsburgh. Returning in 1927 to work a U. S. Steel night shift, Bearden sat in the Lawrenceville parlor, and on the front steps, listening to steelworkers, finishing his last two years of high school, graduating from Peabody in 1929.

Studying at Lincoln, Boston, and New York Universities, by 1935 Bearden was painting and cartooning professionally. Two years after a 1940 New York exhibition he enlisted,

serving three years in the military. Mustered out, Bearden enjoyed three solo exhibitions, 1945-47.

Studying philosophy at the Sorbonne in Paris, 1950, making a living as a New York City social worker, Bearden excelled as a lyricist and writer as well as a serious artist. He experienced a career-altering breakthrough in 1964 when he began to work in collage; for the first time Bearden's work achieved widespread popularity. With his collages appearing in a variety of venues, including the covers of *Time* and *Fortune*, a 1971 Museum of Modern Art retrospective assured Bearden a place as one of America's great 20th-century artists.

Elected to the National Institute of Arts and Letters in 1972, he was awarded the National Medal of Arts in 1987.

Represented in virtually every major American collection, Bearden's smart, sensuous, gritty portraits of African-American life appear in a variety of media—cartoons, watercolors, gouache, oils, collages, even ceramic murals, as in the 12 X 70-foot mural in the Gateway Center T Station.

Cool Papa Bell

Born May 17, 1903—Starkville, MS
Died March 7, 1991—St. Louis, MO

"He was so fast," teammate and fellow Hall of Famer Josh Gibson liked to say, "that he could turn out the light and be in bed before the room got dark."

Well, maybe Cool Papa Bell wasn't that fast, but the speedster centerfielder moved quickly enough to be rated among baseball's top 100 players of the century.

Blessed with extraordinary durability, Bell played from 1922-50, often in the direst circumstances, never with any of the amenities contemporary athletes enjoy. Barred from the major leagues because of the color ban, James T. "Cool Papa" Bell's career was entirely in the Negro Leagues, including stints with Pittsburgh's two championship teams, the Pittsburgh Crawfords (1933-38) and the Homestead Grays (1932, 1943-46).

As a teenaged pitcher for the St. Louis Stars, young Jimmy Bell was so icy that he picked up the Cool tag, which followed him for the rest of his life. Although an adept pitcher, with his extraordinary speed—he could round the bases in an astounding 12 seconds—and hitting ability, the team wanted him in the lineup every day, making him the starting centerfielder in 1924.

Quick and daring, he was a feared base runner. One time, catching the fielders off

guard, and relying on his blazing speed, he scored from first on a sacrifice bunt. Although reliable records are rare, in all likelihood Bell stole 175 bases one season, hitting over .400 numerous times.

Playing for Gus Greenlee's perennial champion Crawfords, he enjoyed the company of four other future Hall of Famers. After jumping to the Mexican League, in 1942 Bell returned to Pittsburgh, joining the Homestead Grays, who won Negro League titles for the next three years.

By the late 1940s, Bell was playing and coaching for the Kansas City Monarchs where he tutored many future baseball stars, Jackie Robinson among them.

Elected to the Hall of Fame in 1974, he died at home, in St. Louis, in 1991.

Derrick Bell, Jr.

Born November 6, 1930—Hill District

The oldest of four children born to Derrick and Ada Bell in the Hill District, Derrick Albert Bell, Jr. assisted in his father's rubbish refuse company while attending Schenley High School, from which he graduated in 1948. The first of his family to attend college, he was offered a scholarship to Lincoln University, but chose Duquesne University instead, so he could continue to work with his father.

While at Duquesne he joined the ROTC and, upon graduation in 1952, under the wing of the U.S. Air Force, he was stationed in Louisiana. There he challenged a local, all-white Presbyterian church by demanding to sing in its choir. Reluctantly, he was accepted and, begrudgingly, he sang.

Returning to Pittsburgh after the Korean war, he was accepted to the Law School at Pitt, and excelled, graduating fourth in his class. In 1957 he accepted a position with the Civil Right Division of the Justice Department, but when questioned by his superiors for having joined the NAACP, he resigned his government job and took the position of first counsel in the NAACP's Legal Defense and Education Fund. There he worked with future Supreme Court Justice Thurgood Marshall, and litigated hundreds of desegregation cases in the South, most famously defending James Meredith's admission to the University of Mississippi.

Tired of the courtroom, but loving "center stage," Bell first taught law at USC. He applied twice to teach at Harvard, but not until the assassination of Martin Luther King, Jr. was Bell accepted at the venerable institution. Within several years, he became the school's first tenured black professor. His expertise has always centered on Constitutional Law, but as an active civil libertarian, Bell often stood up to his deans in protest over seemingly racist hiring practices. In 1981, he accepted the position of Dean of the University of Oregon Law School. His tenure was brief and disastrous; when an Asian-American was denied her tenure, Bell resigned.

However, he returned to Harvard in 1986. There he wrote many of his scholarly works, of which *Faces at the Bottom of the Well* (1992) proved to be one of his most successful. Shortly after its publication, Bell again resigned from Harvard—again over hiring practices.

Bell currently serves as a Visiting Professor of Law at NYU. His *Race, Racism and American Law*, published by Little, Brown in 2000, is considered by many to be *the* textbook for students of civil rights.

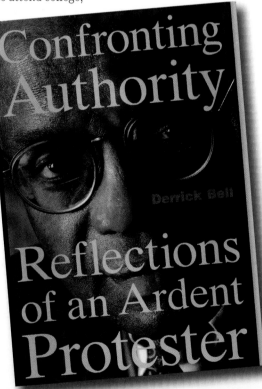

Bell's 1994 account of his dismissal from Harvard, as well as accounts of others who have confronted authority, was published by Beacon Press.

Thomas Bell

Born March 7, 1903—Braddock, PA
Died January 17, 1961—Santa Cruz, CA

The irony is that Thomas Bell never knew that he wrote a classic, his *Out of This Furnace* becoming the best-selling university press novel of all time.

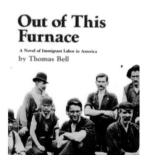

Born Adalbert Thomas Belejcak in Braddock, in 1903, Bell was the son of immigrant Ruthenian parents. Going into the Edgar Thomson works at 15 as an apprentice electrician, by 19, he moved to New York City, working as a mechanic, merchant seaman, and bookstore clerk.

Fulfilling his dream of writing, Bell's first novel, *The Breed of Basil*, was published in 1930. Bell went on to publish five more novels, *The Second Prince* (1935); *All Brides Are Beautiful* (1936), made into a 1946 film, *From This Day Forward*, starring Joan Fontaine; *Till I Come Back to You* (1943), which ran for nine performances on Broadway as *The World's Full of Girls*; and *There Comes a Time* (1946).

But it was 1941's *Out of This Furnace*, Bell's story of three generations of Braddock millhands, that brought him immortality. Covering a half-century, the novel follows Djuro Kracha's journey from Europe to Braddock, his daughter Mary's marriage to steelworker Mike Dobrejcak, and their son Dobie Dobrejcak's fight to unionize the mill.

Nevertheless, Bell never made much money as a writer, and by 1955 he had moved to California where he ran a Santa Cruz stationery store. Six years later, in 1961, Bell died from cancer at the age of 57. *In the Midst of Life*, his account of his illness, was published posthumously.

In all likelihood, Bell would have been forgotten had it not been for Carnegie Mellon English professor David Demarest, who convinced the late Fred Hetzel, editor of the University of Pittsburgh Press, to re-issue *Out of This Furnace* in 1976.

Since that time, the novel has been made a standard text in college curricula worldwide, selling more than 180,000 copies.

Michael Benedum

Born July 16, 1869—Bridgeport, WV
Died July 30, 1959—Pittsburgh

To capture the public's awe of Michael Benedum's inordinate success, one should open *Time* magazine's April 13, 1942, issue. Here, the story "Benedum Drills Again" con-

cerns his return to West Virginia to explore 200,000 acres optioned south of Sistersville: "To oilmen this move is something worth watching, for Mike Benedum is the luckiest wildcatter ever. With a $500 grubstake and more nerve than a circus trapezist, he got into the oil business in the '90s. In no time at all he made a killing in West Virginia oil, discovered the then huge Crawford Field in Illinois, lost most of his cash in Oklahoma mud. Then he whipped off again, struck the fabulous Caddo pool in Louisiana, moved on to drill in Mexico, Venezuela, Canada, Europe. Most spectacular was his discovery of the great Texas Yates pool, only 16 years ago. Although he owns about one-third of the $13,000,000 Plymouth Oil Co., has a large interest in tens of other companies, he always stayed an independent, was rarely listed as an

officer or director. But he profited. His fortune is estimated at around $70,000,000." Again, that was 1942.

The man who indeed became known as the "great wildcatter," had an earlier history, too. Born to Emmanuel and Caroline Benedum, farmers and general store proprietors in Bridgeville, WV, (for which Emmanuel also served as Mayor,) Benedum attended the local schoolhouse just four months of each of his ten years of education. He worked the farm, the store, and also sold milling equipment. Upon leaving the homestead to seek a more comfortable living, he had a lucky meeting on his way to Parkersburg, WV, with John Worthington, then president of the South Penn Oil Co. Worthington offered Benedum a starting position as a leasing agent. Legend suggests that Benedum learned his job well. So well, he had sufficient confidence to depart the company and form his own, in 1896, with petroleum engineer, Joseph Trees.

That same year, Benedum married Sarah Lantz and two years later they gave birth to their only child, Claude Worthington Benedum. The family moved to Pittsburgh and were lucky almost from the beginning. But with every great fortune comes sorrow.

At the age of 20, having been discharged from service in the Chemical Warfare Corps during World War I, Claude died in 1918. Whether the victim of a motorcycle accident, pneumonia, or the Spanish Influenza, no one today can say for certain.

For the rest of their lives, Michael and Sarah would commit their fortunes to memorializing their son. Just two years after his Sistersville gamble, Michael Benedum established the Claude Worthington Benedum Foundation. With 2006 year-end assets of $425,575,685, the Foundation, since its inception, has authorized grants totaling more than $316,000,000.

George Benson—See pages 22-23

Pandro S. Berman

Born March 28, 1905—Pittsburgh
Died July 13, 1996—Beverly Hills, CA

At the 1976 Oscar® Awards, Pandro S. Berman received the Irving G. Thalberg Memorial Award for his then 50 years of contribution to the motion picture industry. A producer who was employed by all the big studios—originally by Universal, then RKO and MGM—he was largely responsible for launching the careers of Bette Davis and Elizabeth Taylor, but was instrumental in accelerating the fame of Katherine Hepburn, Fred Astaire (who he first paired with Ginger Rogers,) Lana Turner, and Gene Kelly, too.

Born to early motion picture distributor Harry M. Berman, "Pan" Berman started working in the 1920s as a script clerk at Universal. He then rose to film editor there, but by 1931 found himself as an assistant director at RKO when Pittsburgher David O. Selznick took over the floundering studio. Selznick made him his assistant. His first film as a producer was *Bad Company*, a sure-fire sequel to an earlier gangster flick. Soon came many original choices he produced and, by 1933, Berman was on a roll. That year he produced his third film with Hepburn, *Morning Glory*, which won him his first nomination for Best Picture. The following year, he earned a second Best Picture nomination for *The Gay Divorcee* starring Astaire and Rogers, and an immediate third nomination for *Alice Adams*, starring Hepburn, that same year. By 1937, Berman was practically running RKO, and like Thalberg at MGM, he was recognized as the genius behind the scenes.

(CONTINUED PAGE 24)

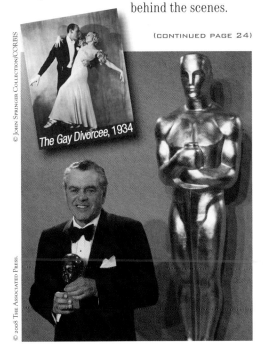

The Gay Divorcee, 1934

George Benson

Born March 26, 1946—Hill District

With all of the great jazz musicians to have come out of Pittsburgh, it should come as no surprise that one of the best-selling jazz albums of all time was the product of a local jazz legend.

"Little Georgie Benson" played a cigar-box ukulele on the street corners in the Hill District, singing songs for dimes and quarters when he was just 6 years old. By the time he was 7, Benson was doing local radio shows and selling ice cream and shoe polish on air. His stepfather, Thomas Collier, exposed him to artists like Charlie Parker and the great Charlie Christian, his first and favorite jazz guitarist. When his stepfather brought home an electric guitar from a pawnshop one night, his life would change forever.

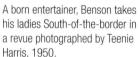

A born entertainer, Benson takes his ladies South-of-the-border in a revue photographed by Teenie Harris, 1950.

At night he would fall asleep with his ear pressed against the amplifier. A quick learner—"I've always had the ear," says Benson—he was soon offered as much as $40 a night to play the clubs of Pittsburgh. His mother, a nurse who earned only $35 every two weeks, urged her son to play on. And when one such club was raided by the cops, stepfather Collier served six months behind bars for breaking child labor laws.

Known for his great set of pipes, as well as for his slick guitar, Benson auditioned for jazz organist Jack McDuff who was in town for a show. Benson impressed McDuff so much that he asked Benson to join him on tour. A very popular jazz musician at the time, McDuff gave Benson an immediate following as well as the opportunity to play before crowds the size of which he had never

George Benson dominates the opening session of the Jazz Festival at Montreux, Switzerland, 2000. He plays with Ray Bryant, Tommy Campbell, Richie Cole, Dizzy Gillespie, James Moody, Jimmy Smith, and Phil Upchurch.

ASSOCIATED PRESS

seen. McDuff's band, however, was all-instrumental and he wouldn't permit Benson to stretch his vocal chords, reportedly telling Benson at one point "I don't want no singin' in my band."

Benson left McDuff in 1965 to form his own group. In Harlem he was soon discovered by legendary talent scout John Hammond, famous for launching the careers of artists like Billie Holiday, Bob Dylan, Stevie Ray Vaughn, and Charlie Christian—Benson's musical inspiration. Benson began recording with Herbie Hancock, Miles Davis, Ron Carter, and many others.

Wes Montgomery, another Benson favorite, died in 1968, leaving many to believe that Benson would become the unofficial successor to his throne. Yet Montgomery was often criticized, particularly in his later recordings, for uninspired playing. Benson garnered similar criticism when he signed with Creed Taylor's label, the same producer who had produced Wes Montgomery's later material.

But, in 1976, George Benson released the album *Breezin'*, the first jazz record to attain platinum sales. The breakout song on that release was Benson's cover of "Masquerade," which reached #1 on the pop, jazz, and R&B charts—the first song ever to achieve a hat trick. Ironically the song features Benson's unique scatting—a Benson "signature" that years earlier had been squelched by other record producers. "Masquerade" won the Grammy for Record of the Year and the title track "Breezin'" won Best Pop Instrumental Performance.

George Benson, winner of eight Grammys® over the years, was awarded an Honorary Doctorate Degree in Music from Berklee College of Music in 1990. Over the coming decades Benson's style would take on more of an R&B feel, but to millions of fans he is unquestionably one of the greatest jazz guitarists ever.

Photographer Teenie Harris captured WHOD disk jockey Mary Dee with Benson at a trade show, circa 1950.

© DERICK A. THOMAS; DAT'S JAZZ/CORBIS

Berman's list of producer credits is surpassed by only a rare few. In all, he produced more than 70 films for RKO and 60 for MGM, earning six Best Picture nominations (but never winning one) and receiving the David O. Selznick Lifetime Achievement Award in 1992, shortly before his death.

Harold Betters

Born March 21, 1928—Connellsville, PA

He's known as Mr. Trombone and the club where he spent so many great years playing became known as The House That Betters Built. His overwhelmingly jovial personality and his talent as a commanding trombonist have made Harold Betters a household name throughout Western Pennsylvania and beyond.

Betters grew up on North Eighth Street in Connellsville. His father was a carpenter and played a little violin, but both parents always encouraged their four boys to pursue their love of music. The trombone grabbed Better's attention in grade school where he began to play in the school band, as well as other local bands in Connellsville. The Betters family owned a bar in the area called the Betters Grill and soon Harold and his brother Jerry, who played drums at the time, were building a reputation gigging at their parent's establishment. The Betters brothers were soon recruited to play the Penn Albert Hotel in Greensburg, as the Jerry Betters Trio.

Steady gigs followed in Jeannette, then Turtle Creek and then a booking at the famed Pittsburgh club, the Midway Lounge, where greats like Dizzy Gillespie, Art Blakey's Jazz Messengers, and John Coltrane would play. After graduating from Connellsville High School, Betters decided to pursue a career in music education that took him to Ithaca College and the Conservatory of Music in Brooklyn, but the conflict in Korea forced Betters to march in the Army band.

Once back in Pittsburgh, Betters set off on a road to become the best among the best and to help open doors for many of his African-American brothers to play the "white clubs" throughout the area. Jerry Betters had decided to focus more on his singing and Harold decided it was time to branch out on his own. He formed the Harold Betters Quartet. His first engagement was at the Suburban Room in the South Hills. The Harold Betters Quartet became a staple at The Pink Cloud and then in the late '40s The Encore, aka The

House That Betters Built, where he remained for almost two decades. Pitt Pot, The Virginian Club in Ohio, South Hills Sheraton, The Holiday House, Pitt, WVU, Penn State, prisons, and Steeler games all became venues for Betters through the years. Additionally, Betters was the house band for comedian Dick Gregory, toured with Ray Charles for a couple of months, frequented the *Merv Griffin* and *Mike Douglas Shows,* and shared the stage with jazz giants Louis Armstrong, Maynard Ferguson, Urbie Green, Ramsey Lewis, Al Hirt, Pete Fountain and Pittsburgh native Slide Hampton to name just a few.

After 18 albums, six decades of entertaining, recognition as "Man of the Year" by the Pittsburgh Jaycees and accolades from the likes of *Downbeat* magazine to *Playboy*, Harold Betters stands among the ranks of true jazz giants of southwestern Pennsylvania.

Jerome Bettis

Born February 16, 1972—Detroit, MI

In sports, numbers never tell the entire story. They never measure the intangibles—desire, inspiration, leadership.

Certainly, Steeler running back Jerome Bettis used his powerful legs and incredibly quick feet to run to a certain berth in pro football's Hall of Fame. A star in high school and at Notre Dame, he was drafted by the St. Louis Rams, racked up yards for three years, and was traded to the Steelers in 1996. Wearing Pittsburgh black-and-gold for the next 10 years, Bettis ran for 10,000 yards, won multiple Steelers Most Valuable Player honors, and provided the leadership that led to victory in Super Bowl XL, in February 2006, their first championship in 26 years.

Nicknamed the Bus—because, as the man himself put it, "I've never been shy about

eating. They don't call me the Bus because I pass the plate." Coming to the Steelers was a dream come true, he once said. "It was a winning organization, a place that appreciated big running backs. I tried to be physical running the football. I tried to inflict punishment instead of taking it."

That kind of attitude—as well as Bettis' strong work ethic—made him "an inspiration," former Steelers coach Bill Cowher said. "He was a great leader."

Then came Bettis' last season, 2005. After 13 years in the NFL, more than 13,000 yards, more than all but four men in history, there was only one thing left: a championship ring. With Super Bowl XL being played in his home town, he asked his teammates to take the Bus home.

Then 7-5, the Steelers concocted an 8-0 miracle finish, playing—and winning—Super Bowl XL. "It's a dream come true," he said.

"You don't play for the money or the accolades," he said. "You play for the championship. Now that I have that, I feel complete."

Bettis gets a kiss from his most adoring fan, Mom.

Carl Betz

Born March 9, 1921—Pittsburgh
Died January 18, 1978—Los Angeles, CA

Best known to early television audiences as Dr. Stone, the physician-husband to Donna Reed, star of her eponymous show that aired on ABC from 1958 to 1966, Carl Betz was a ruggedly handsome man who discovered the theater at a very young age. Hollywood bios note that he performed plays in his grandmother's basement with childhood friends.

Betz won a four-year scholarship to Duquesne University, but graduated from the drama department of Carnegie Tech after taking several seasons off to do summer stock

Actors Paul Petersen, Donna Reed, Betz, and Shelley Fabares are grateful for their eight-year run on ABC's *The Donna Reed Show*.

Frank Bingaman

Born in 1875—Pittsburgh
Died in 1948—Pittsburgh

Shane Black

Born December 16, 1961—Pittsburgh

during the early 1940s. He served briefly in the Army, and returned to his hometown to work as a radio announcer on WTAE. Around the same time, he organized a Mt. Lebanon theater group, but then left to join East Coast stock companies.

Betz made his Broadway debut in 1952 with a flop, *The Long Watch*, and then toured with other na-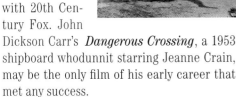tional produc-tions, mostly star vehicles, featuring Veronica Lake and Diana Barrymore, before landing his first film contract with 20th Century Fox. John Dickson Carr's *Dangerous Crossing*, a 1953 shipboard whodunnit starring Jeanne Crain, may be the only film of his early career that met any success.

Before earning national recognition as Donna Reed's husband, he played in the CBS soap, *Love of Life*. Following his eight-year stint as Dr. Stone, Betz appeared again on Broadway in Tennessee William's *Night of the Iguana*. And once again, he found himself being offered another TV contract, this time to play a flamboyant Texas lawyer, *Judd for the Defense*, for which he won an Emmy® as Best Actor in 1969, the same year the program was canceled.

Betz died at 57 from lung cancer.

There's a particularly appropriate photo-graph of Frank Bingaman perched on a tree stump some five feet in the air. Hat squarely on his head, in shirt sleeves, he's perfectly bal-anced, utterly focused. Gripping a huge Graphlex camera, he has no doubt he'll get the shot of the tent city before him. After all, he's Frank Bingaman, Pittsburgh's first great news photographer, and he'll get the shot.

Born in Pittsburgh in 1875, Frank E. Bingaman worked in his father-in-law's Wilkinsburg photography studio until, at the age of 29, he wanted to shoot the news.

It was 1904, and the world was changing at light speed. Joining the *Gazette-Times*, and then the *Chronicle-Telegraph*, using his tal-ent for portraiture, Bingaman drew such plum assignments as President Theodore Roosevelt, President William Howard Taft, and Belgian King Leopold. His 1914 portrait of Andrew Carnegie waving farewell to Pittsburgh re-mains a classic.

Nevertheless, Bingaman is remembered far less for his portraits than for his encyclopedic vision of Pitts-burgh. Seemingly everywhere at once during the first quarter of the 20th Century, Bingaman left more than 1,100 surviving Pitts-burgh prints, the most complete visual record of an era.

It is Pittsburgh's first, brawny vision of itself, steam-boats and arsenals, Pitt Pan-thers, and Mr. Carnegie's dinosaurs. Pirate Honus Wagner, nicknamed the Flying Dutchman, literally flying over the basepaths. The Chicago Cubs playing the Pi-rates, Exposition Park, 1906. In one exciting moment, three years later in brand-new Forbes Field, 1909, a couple of pros exchange World Series batting tips, Herr Wagner and the Georgia Peach, Detroit Tiger Tyrus Ray-mond Cobb. Some 27 years later, 1936, they'll be part of the first, highly exclusive class in the new baseball Hall of Fame.

But it's 1909, and they're still ballplayers, images of a time gone by, a time never to re-turn.

Frank Bingaman died in 1948 at age 73.

For a brief time in 1996, Shane Black held the all-time record for an original screen-play: a cool $4 million for *The Long Kiss Good-night*.

No matter that the actual film was pretty much a bust—pretty, apple-cheeked Geena Davis never really caught fire as an amnesiac assassin. Writer Shane Black was on top of the Hollywood heap.

Then, of course, he wasn't.

Born in 1961 in Pittsburgh, Black had considered writing as a child. As he puts it, "I wrote all the time, but the idea of doing it pro-fessionally seemed like pie in the sky. I grew up in Pittsburgh. It wasn't really a notion that a lot of people pursue."

His life changed radically when Black's family moved to Fullerton, CA, when Black was a high school student. After studying act-ing at UCLA, at 22 he wrote his first success-ful script, *Lethal Weapon*, in just six weeks. When it sold in three days for a quarter-million dollars Black's name became synonymous with wunderkind 1980s screenwriting. After the 1987 film became an enormous success, mak-ing Mel Gibson and Danny Glover major stars, Black became Hollywood royalty.

As a star writer, Black continued with smart-talking, male-oriented, large-scale ac-tion films. Penning three more *Lethal Weapon* scripts, Arnold Schwarzenegger's *The Last Ac-tion Hero*, and other films, Black became a mil-lionaire many times over. Taking a turn in front of the camera, he also acted in the 1987 thriller *Predator*, 1993's *RoboCop 3*, and other films. In 2005, Black sat in the director's chair for his own *Kiss Kiss Bang Bang*, a buddy-thriller with Robert Downey, Jr., and Val Kilmer.

Although since then Black has been on some-thing of a screen-writing hiatus, expressing displeasure with the limitations of the action-adventure genre, he has neverthe-less received major awards from the San Diego Film Critics Association and the Austin Film Festival.

Art Blakey

Born October 11, 1919—Hill District
Died October 16, 1990—New York, NY

A true jazz giant, Art Blakey chose his primary instrument when the owner of a Pittsburgh nightclub pointed a gun and ordered him off the piano and onto the drums. For the remainder of his career, drums would be his instrument of choice.

A tireless educator and perhaps jazz's fiercest drummer, Blakey taught himself to play the piano and, by 15, was leading his own big band. As the principal pianist he was soon displaced by another legendary Pittsburgh musician, Erroll Garner. Blakey became a student of famed jazz drummer "Chick" Webb, credited for discovering Ella Fitzgerald and popular for leading the house band at the Savoy Ballroom in Harlem.

It was a trip to Africa in the late '40s that was the catalyst for Blakey learning his signature polyrhythmic drumming technique.

Among the many musicians with whom Blakey played were Pittsburgh natives Mary Lou Williams, and Billy Eckstine.

Blakey was the driving force behind the hard bop movement of the '50s and his contributions to jazz go well beyond his skills as a master percussionist. Blakey helped bring drums to the forefront of music, making percussion an integral driver of the melody. A thunderous procession of rim shots, cymbal rides, and drum press rolls often elevated his soloists to another level of playing.

Through his famed Jazz Messengers, Blakey became a mentor and taskmaster to some of jazz's greatest stars, including Freddie Hubbard, Chuck Mangione, Wayne Shorter, Chick Corea, Keith Jarrett, Slide Hampton, Woody Shaw, Donald Byrd, and Branford and Wynton Marsalis.

About his upstart musicians Blakey said, "I'm always kicking them in the ass. It's as much as they can do to keep up with me. When they join, they're scared to death, and most of them grow up or die. When they join The Messengers, the bullshit's over. I'm not running a post-office. This is the Jazz Messengers."

Until his death in 1990, Blakey kept the message and the principles of the Jazz Messengers alive as an incubator of great talent. The inspiration and legacy of Art Blakey will long be heard in future generations of jazz musicians.

George Blanda

Born September 17, 1927—Youngwood, PA

It was 1970 when George Blanda became AFC Player of the Year.

That's when the 43-year-old replacement quarterback led Oakland to four wins and a tie in five games. Against his hometown Steelers, Blanda threw two touchdown passes and kicked a field goal for a 31-14 victory. A 48-yard field goal netted a 17-17 tie with Kansas City. Against Cleveland a touchdown pass and place kick produced a 23-20 win.

An 80-yard drive at Denver went for a 24-19 victory. After beating San Diego 20-17, Chiefs' owner Lamar Hunt joked, "this George Blanda is as good as his father, who used to play for Houston."

Poster boy for determination and endurance, Blanda became the primogenitor of the Western Pennsylvania quarterback. A coal miner's son, George Frederick Blanda was born in Youngwood in 1927. One of the first of some 50 professional quarterbacks from Greater Pittsburgh in the past 60 years, he played at 6'-2" and 215 pounds, going from Kentucky to the Chicago Bears as a 1949 backup quarterback and place kicker. Blanda enjoyed a 26-year, 340-game career, including stints with the Houston Oilers and Oakland Raiders. Leading the Oilers to the first two titles in AFL history, Blanda was 1961 AFL Player of the Year. In his last game, the 1976 AFC Championship game in Pittsburgh, the 48-year-old Blanda kicked a 41-yard field goal.

Elected to the Hall of Fame in 1981, Blanda had scored a then-record 2,002 points, throwing 1,911 completions, 26,920 yards, and 236 touchdowns.

Never without a sense of humor, Blanda once commented on a former teammate's claim that he had kicked a 75-yard field goal high on moccalino by saying, "I punted a ball 86 yards against Tennessee—high on Polish sausage."

Mel Blount

Born April 10,1948—Vidalia, GA

While it's rare for an athlete to achieve greatness, it's even more uncommon for an athlete to cause a rule change—but that's exactly what Steelers Hall of Fame cornerback Mel Blount did.

Born Melvin Cornell Blount in 1970, the youngest of 11 children, he grew up on a Vidalia, Georgia, dirt farm without plumbing or electricity. Starring in baseball, basketball, and track at Lyons High, Blount excelled in football. Accepting a scholarship to Baton Rouge's Southern University, he was an All-American defensive safety.

Picked by the Steelers in the third round of the 1970 draft, Blount played at 6'-3", 205 pounds, with extraordinary reach and uncanny speed. "He was the best ever to play the game," defensive coach Bud Carson claimed in the *Steelers' Official History*. "There's no one who comes close. With Blount's speed, anticipation, height, and reach, nobody could get away from him."

Missing only one game in 14 seasons, 1970-83, Blount earned five Pro Bowl berths, played in four victorious Super Bowls, and was 1975 NFL Defensive MVP. Snagging 57 interceptions—an all-time Steelers record—he returned the ball for 736 total yards and two touchdowns.

Playing when cornerbacks were permitted to hit open receivers, Blount was so devastating, and so fast, that the National Football League (NFL) changed the rule to prevent such hits.

After retiring, Blount became the NFL's Director of Player Relations, 1983-90; in 1983 he also founded the Mel Blount Youth Home, a shelter and Christian mission for victims of child abuse and neglect in Vidalia. In 1989, Blount opened a second youth home on 300 acres in Claysville, Washington County, near Pittsburgh.

Enshrined in the Pro Football Hall of Fame in 1989, Blount is also a member of the Louisiana and Georgia Sports Halls of Fame. Wearing his trademark white Stetson, Mel Blount lives in Claysville.

Nellie Bly

Born May 5, 1864—Cochran's Mills, PA
Died January 27, 1922—New York, NY

Tough, fearless, talented, journalist Nellie Bly lived in a madhouse, went around the world, and blazed a trail for women professionals of every kind.

Born Elizabeth Jane Cochran in Cochran's Mills, Armstrong County, in 1864, Pink, as she was called, and her family moved to Pittsburgh in 1880. When a column in the *Pittsburgh Dispatch* denounced women's roles, an incensed 18-year-old Pink wrote a passionate protest letter. The impressed *Dispatch* editor offered Pink a job.

Since women writers then used pen names, Pink Cochran became Nellie Bly, after the popular Stephen Foster song.

Focusing on working women, Bly went undercover to write about sweatshop life. Although the articles were highly successful, she was asked to cover fashion and society. Balking, Bly went to Mexico as a foreign correspondent.

Just 21, Bly spent six months in Mexico—until she ran afoul of dictator Porfirio Diaz. Threatened with arrest, Bly returned home.

Relegated again to soft stories, in 1887 Bly left for New York City. Landing a job on

Joseph Pulitzer's *New York World*, she wrote undercover assignments which brought her lasting fame. Successfully faking insanity, Bly reported on the horrific conditions at the Blackwell's Island Women's Lunatic Asylum. Published as *Ten Days in a Mad-House*, her reportage made Bly the most celebrated journalist in America.

As an encore, in 1889-90 she bested Jules Verne's *Around the World in Eighty Days*, circling the globe in a then-record 72 days. Her *Around the World in Seventy-Two Days* was an instant bestseller.

In 1895, at age 30, Bly married a millionaire industrialist and retired. After his death, Bly covered the 1913 women's suffrage convention, World War I, and other major events.

In 1922, the 57-year-old journalist died of pneumonia in New York City and was buried in the Bronx's Woodlawn Cemetery. In 2002, a postage stamp was issued in her honor.

David Blythe

Born May 9, 1815—East Liverpool, OH
Died May 15, 1865—Pittsburgh

Broken by the death of his wife, crushed by the failure of his career, deeply affected by the poverty and injustice he saw all around him, David Blythe painted to expose the world's evils.

Born in a log cabin in East Liverpool, Ohio, in 1815, David Gilmour Blythe moved 40 miles upriver to Pittsburgh at 16, to apprentice with James Woodwell, a master woodcarver. Tall, red-haired, unkempt, and habitually restless, within three years Blythe turned housepainter, then wandered the country and the Caribbean. Returning to the Ohio Valley, by 1840 he worked as an itinerant portrait painter. Settling in Uniontown, in 1846, Blythe married, carved an eight-foot wooden statue of Lafayette that adorned the Fayette County Courthouse, and painted *The Great Moving Panorama of the Allegheny Mountains*, a seven-foot-tall, 300-foot-long history of Western Pennsylvania.

But his young wife died, the panorama was seized for debt, and by 1856 Blythe had returned to Pittsburgh. Then 41, Blythe embarked on the most acerbic—and artistically productive—years of his career.

Seeing poverty, venality, and corruption all about him, Blythe's vision is encapsulated in his *Trial Scene*, a depiction of grotesque, shouting, lupine men. Painting every squalid

corner of society, he returned again and again to Pittsburgh's army of orphaned children.

Certainly, Blythe painted passionate, heroic figurations of President Abraham Lincoln. But more in keeping with his acidic views is his *Libby Prison*, a rendering of Richmond's notorious jail. Housing as many as 1,200 Union soldiers in six rooms, Blythe depicted Libby's unspeakable conditions.

As the Civil War raged Blythe painted obsessively—and drank heavily. Finally, a week after his 50th birthday in 1865, he died of acute alcoholism. As a legacy, his works have become part of the nation's finest collections: the Smithsonian, Metropolitan Museum of Art, Fine Arts Museums of San Francisco, and Carnegie Museum of Art.

Frank Bolden

Born in 1913—Washington, PA
Died August 28, 2003—Pittsburgh

It was a dark time in Pittsburgh, smoky, oppressive, and discriminatory. Faced with rampant racism, many marched, some spoke, while others wrote.

One of the more courageous writers was *Pittsburgh Courier* reporter Frank Bolden. A tireless champion of civil rights, Bolden wrote for nearly 30 years about the streets of Industrial America, pioneering the voice of independent African-American journalism.

The son of Washington PA's first black letter carrier, Bolden enrolled at Pitt in 1930 to study biology. He made extra money stringing for the *Courier*, and reporting full-time after graduation, covered Wylie Avenue, then the epicenter of Pittsburgh's black cultural life.

Bolden also followed the stars of the Negro National League.

During World War II, Bolden became one of only two accredited black war correspondents. "White America was convinced that Negro soldiers would be cowards and run," he said. "That's why I went over."

In the insect-riddled jungles of Burma, Bolden wrote of the black troops who died working on the Burma Road. In Europe, he covered the famed Buffalo Soldiers and the Tuskegee Airmen. He interviewed Stalin, Churchill, and Roosevelt at the Tehran Conference and pointedly told FDR that black people deserved better opportunities.

Returning to Pittsburgh in 1945, he spent the next 15 years working as a *Courier* writer and editor. By the early '60s he was in New York, at *The New York Times* and NBC's *Huntley-Brinkley Report*. By mid-decade he had returned home to a community relations post at the Pittsburgh Public Schools.

Dead at 90, in 2003, the much-awarded Bolden had become a true elder statesman of black Pittsburgh.

Barry Bonds

Born July 24, 1964—Riverside, CA

How much a single player can mean to a team is exemplified by all-time home-run king Barry Bonds, who in 1990-92 blossomed into a true major-league star. Bonds led the Pirates to the century's last National League East championship—and winning—season.

A scion of baseball royalty (his father was slugger Bobby Bonds, his godfather Hall of Famer Willie Mays), Barry Lamar Bonds attended San Mateo's Junípero Serra, where he was an All-America baseball player. Playing college ball at Arizona State, Bonds was similarly an All-American.

Chosen by the Pirates in the 1985 draft, he played in Pittsburgh for seven seasons, 1986-92. Starting in left field, standing 6'-1" and 200 pounds, Bonds began well, if not spectacularly, fueling speculation that despite his obvious talent he might not have long-term potential. Finishing sixth in the 1986 Rookie of the Year voting, Bonds hit 16 home runs and stole 36 bases. Al-

though his numbers improved, 1987-89—he hit 25, 24, and 19 home runs— they hardly presaged his exemplary play of the '90s.

From 1990-92, Bonds blossomed into a true star, the last great Pirate of the 20th Century. Twice hitting .300, slugging 33, 25, and 34 home runs, he led the Pirates to three consecutive National League East titles, winning two Most Valuable Player awards in '90 and '92, coming a close second in '91.

A free agent after 1992, Bonds returned to San Francisco with 176 Pirate home runs. His career continued to blossom and he became an unprecedented seven-time National League Most Valuable Player, in 2001 setting the single-season home run mark with 73.

In 2007, Bonds passed Henry Aaron's all-time home run record of 755, ending with 762. Yet that November he was indicted for perjury and obstruction of justice in a baseball steroid probe, a charge that might end his career.

In Pittsburgh, since Bond's last season the Pirates have failed to win a single title— or even to play .500 ball.

Robert Bork

Born March 1, 1927—Squirrel Hill

Best known for his arduous defeat at the hands of a Democratic congress, Robert Bork was denied the nomination for Supreme Court justice during Reagan's second term. His 1987 televised hearings amounted to one of the most heated debates between left and right wing foes whose media allocations amounted to an unprecedented $20 million. In question was his conservative stance against abortion and affirmative action, in particular, as well as more standard conservative issues relevant to constitutional adjudication, notably First Amendment rights and tort reform.

A then-standing federal appeals judge for the District of Columbia, Bork had made news some 13 years earlier when, as the Solicitor General for the Nixon Whitehouse, he fired special prosecutor Archibald Cox who demanded to have Nixon's Oval Office tapes released as part of his Watergate investigation. Both Attorney General Elliot Richardson and his Deputy Williams Ruckelshaus had resigned to save their political careers, but Bork did the firing as acting Attorney General before resigning himself to resume his earlier Justice position. The event became known as the Saturday Night Massacre, but it ultimately led to the hiring of Leon Jaworski as Special Prosecutor who famously obtained the tapes that brought about Nixon's resignation. From 1977 to 1979, Bork taught law at Yale, then served as an appeals judge until his Supreme Court nomination.

Self-described as a young radical, Bork attributes much of his intellect to late night debates with his mother, Elisabeth Kunkle Bork. His father, Harry, was a purchasing agent for Blaw-Knox Co. An only child, he grew up in Squirrel Hill, then Ben Avon, graduating from the preparatory Hotchkiss School when he was 17. After a brief stint at Pitt, Bork joined the Marine Corps, then attended the University of Chicago, before joining the Marines a second time. First a journalism major, he shifted to law upon his return to Chicago, practicing with several firms there. For two years he taught law at Yale before his sudden selection to serve as Solicitor General.

Bork's 1987 rejection was so contentious that his name is sometimes used as a verb. To bork someone means to ardently reject one's candidacy for position. Recently, upon George W. Bush's failed nomination of Harriet Miers for the Supreme Court, an MSNBC headlined his interview as "Bork Borks Miers."

A champion of tort reform over the years, in June of 2007 Bork sued the Yale Club of New York for $1 million after injuring himself climbing the dais to speak.

John Bowman

Born May 18, 1877—Davenport IA
Died December 2, 1962—Bedford, PA

Born into the world of academia, John Gabbert Bowman is most often remembered not for his scholarly achievements, nor his academic leadership, but for a single building to which he devoted most of his life. As chancellor of the University of Pittsburgh from 1921 until 1945, Bowman's dream and defining legacy is the Cathedral of Learning.

The son of the principal of Davenport High School, Bowman graduated under his father's watchful eye. He attended a first year at the University of Iowa, but had to excuse himself to work in hog sales and lumber rafting to earn his tuition for subsequent semesters. He graduated in 1899, spent a year as a reporter for the *Davenport Democrat*, then returned to his alma mater to earn a 1904 Masters. In 1906, after moving to New York to pursue post-graduate studies at Columbia, he was offered the job of Secretary of the Carnegie Foundation. He then became director of the American College of Surgeons, and in 1911 was chosen to serve as president of Iowa State, becoming then the youngest president of a university. He was just 33.

Ten years later, while speaking in Pittsburgh, he was offered the chancellorship of Pitt. In 1921, the school had a debt of $1 million, a fractured campus of ramshackle classrooms situated in former Army barracks, and a student population of less than 5,000. Bowman promptly impressed his industrialist trustees when he announced he would commit his presidency to building a singular skyscraper of 52 stories, and at a staggering cost of $10 million. Few doubted the money could be raised, but just as few knew how long it would take.

One of his first successes was in engaging the school's alumni; he hired Jock Sutherland to pull together a football team that would (and did) inspire unfathomable school spirit. But almost as quickly, autocrat Bowman's allegiance to his trustees commanded him to root out of his faculty a liberal mindset he felt contrary to his interests. In his first 12 years, Bowman fired some 25 professors, 59 in all resigning in protest. The American Association of University Professors blacklisted Pitt. Bowman's stoic response: "What of it?"

Yet, by 1937, Bowman had raised nearly $20 million and more than doubled the enrollment. And he had erected, with the aid of some 200,000 contributors—97,000 of whom were school children each donating a dime—a 42-story, 535 foot tall, 2,000 room monument to the aspirations of higher education.

William D. Boyce

Born June 16, 1858—Plum, PA
Died June 11, 1929—Ottawa, IL

Always thinking big, William Boyce offered congress $300 million in 1906 to privatize the U.S. Postal Service. Apparently, Boyce was not pleased with a proposed postage hike, and he believed that newspapers and magazines should be exempt from postage anyhow. Not surprisingly, at the time, he owned *The Saturday Blade*, the *Chicago Ledger*, *Chicago World,* and *Farming Business*. Their combined circulation was more than 500,000 and his readers all tended to live in rural areas of the country. Needless to say, Congress rejected his offer. And the proposed hike never happened.

Nevertheless, Boyce did have the support of 30,000 newsboys who delivered his illustrated weeklies for small change and smaller tips.

Always the adventurer—once famous for launching hot air balloons in East Africa to outdo Teddy Roosevelt's stories in competing papers—Boyce was on business in London when, according to legend, the fog was so thick, he asked the assistance of a young boy to help him cross the street. When the lad refused his tip, Boyce learned that his companion was "just doing a good deed" as a Scout, one of Lord Baden-Powell's aspiring youths. Eventually, Boyce met with the founder of the popular Scout Movement and returned to the states.

On February 8, 1910, W.D. Boyce incorporated the Boy Scouts of America.

The fledgling organization nearly failed within the first year, until YMCA Director Edgar Robinson and lawyer James West helped organize what Boyce was unable to do. Boyce had imbued the scout culture with American Indian lore and outdoor camping tips, and named himself Chief Totem. But West named himself Chief Scout Executive and eventually wrested the organization from Boyce, even erasing the founder's name from original documents.

Even though Boyce regularly supported the organization with personal funds, he launched an alternative movement, the Lone Scouts of America, to appeal to more rural boys who could not afford the uniforms and books required by the BSA. In 1924, however, the two scouting organizations merged. Today, the BSA boasts an active membership of more than three million scouts.

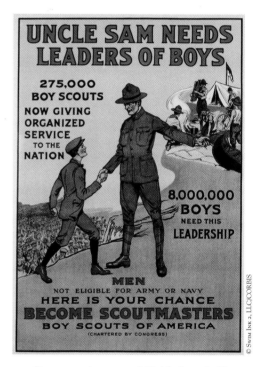

Boyce was born on a hillside farm in Plum where Boyce Park honors his homestead and legacy of outdoor adventure.

Hugh Henry Brackenridge

Born 1748—Kintyre, Scotland
Died June 25, 1816—Carlisle, PA

Politician, lawyer, judge, and author Hugh Henry Brackenridge was a true founding father of Allegheny County. While a legislator in the state assembly, Brackenridge championed the 1788 bill that created the county. At the same time, he pushed for legislation that created the Pittsburgh Academy, an institution of higher learning now known as the University of Pittsburgh. A fiery orator and prolific writer, Brackenridge was a key, yet controversial, figure in our region's history.

Brackenridge emigrated to America with his parents at age 5, and the family settled in York County, PA. At age 20 he enrolled in the College of New Jersey (now Princeton University), studying the classics and theology. There his powerful speeches and writings drew the attention of classmates, including future President James Madison and poet Philip Freneau. During the Revolutionary War, Brackenridge served as a chaplain in George Washington's army and delivered thundering, patriotic sermons to the troops.

Following a failed publishing enterprise in Philadelphia, Brackenridge obtained a law degree. Seeking a smaller community in which to begin his career, he crossed the Alleghenies and in 1781 opened a law practice in Pittsburgh. Writing later on the move, Brackenridge declared: "I had a strong interest to offer myself to that place. My object was to advance the country and thereby myself."

Brackenridge quickly distinguished himself in Pittsburgh and was elected to the state assembly. He was instrumental in the birth of the town's first newspaper, *The Pittsburgh Gazette* (still published today as the *Pittsburgh Post-Gazette*). However, his often erratic political views made him unpopular in the region. A muddled attempt to mediate the Whiskey Rebellion in 1794 left the outspoken Brackenridge with enemies on both sides of the skirmish, and the federal government considering trying him for treason. He was cleared following an interrogation by Secretary of the Treasury Alexander Hamilton.

After the scandal, Brackenridge returned to writing and the law. In 1799, he accepted an appointment to the Pennsylvania Supreme Court, and shortly thereafter moved to Carlisle. He died in 1816 and is buried in Carlisle's Old Graveyard. Brackenridge's only son, Henry Marie, also a judge and author, founded the city of Tarentum and is the namesake of Brackenridge borough.

Edward Braddock

Born circa 1695—Scotland
Died July 13, 1755—Braddock

The son of a general, Edward Braddock was destined for a career in the military. He entered the British army at the young age of 15 and moved steadily through the ranks. With the coming of the French and Indian War, he became Commander-in-Chief of British forces in North America. He arrived in Alexandria, VA, in 1755.

Charged with the task of capturing French-occupied Fort Duquesne, located at the confluence of the Monongahela and Allegheny rivers, Braddock embarked on his mission with a force of more than 2,000 British regular soldiers and colonial militia. The dense wilderness necessitated much clearing and construction to accommodate the passage of men and material. Known as Braddock's Road, the swath cut through the Pennsylvania wilderness by Braddock's force would later be used by thousands of settlers into Western Pennsylvania.

After making their second crossing of the Monongahela River on July 9, 1755, Braddock's advance guard was ambushed by a force of French and Indians under the command of Daniel Beaujeu. The British force was surprised and routed, sustaining over 1,000 casualties in the battle. After having four horses shot out from under him, General Braddock fell mortally wounded. The British retreat from the field of battle was overseen by young George Washington in what was an early test of his leadership mettle.

The borough of Braddock, located near the site of the ambush, is named in General Braddock's honor.

Terry Bradshaw

Born September 2, 1948—Shreveport, LA

Sometimes it's not how you play but how you end that matters most.

No one could deny that Terry Bradshaw was one of the greatest quarterbacks of all time—and certainly the greatest in Steelers history. Playing from 1970-83, gifted with a rifle arm and great on-field command, he established himself as one of the National Football League's premier passers.

By 1970 he had become the most desired football prospect, a national star for Louisiana Tech. Chosen by the Steelers with the nation's first draft pick, Bradshaw joined Chuck Noll's growing team of future Hall of Famers. In 1972, he proved himself a quarterback of destiny by throwing the pass that led to Franco Harris' Immaculate Reception.

At a time when quarterbacks called their own plays, Bradshaw's command of the field was unparalleled. When he retired, after 14 seasons, Bradshaw completed more than 2,000 passes for nearly 28,000 yards and 212 touchdowns—while rushing nearly 450 times for more than 2,200 yards and 32 touchdowns.

Then there were the Super Bowl victories—four of them in six years, IX, X, XIII, XIV, a record of achievement that many consider the finest in football history. In two of those victories—Super Bowls XIII and XIV—Bradshaw won MVP honors.

After retiring, Bradshaw enjoyed election to the College and Pro Football Halls of Fame, and success as a broadcaster, writer, spokesman, country singer, and actor. He also famously stayed away from Pittsburgh. Finally, he walked on the field, half-time, October 21,

2002, to have his #12 retired by the club. Standing at the 50-yardline, drinking in the ovation, he said, "I've missed you all terribly much. It's good to be home."

"Bessie Bramble"

Born circa 1837—Newcastle-on-Tyne, UK
Died circa 1910—Redlands, CA

A school teacher and mother of two, Elizabeth Wade used the pen name "Bessie Bramble" to critique Pittsburgh and the nation in the late 19th Century.

Born Elizabeth Angus Wilkinson, she came to Pittsburgh as a young girl. In a long and successful teaching career, she taught and served as assistant principal at Pittsburgh's Pike Street School and also at the Ralston Industrial School, where she eventually became principal. Elizabeth married banker Charles I. Wade in 1864, by which time she was already writing anonymous reviews for local newspapers. The Wades lived on Webster Avenue in the Hill District and later moved to Swissvale Avenue in Edgewood.

Writing as "Bessie Bramble"– a combination of her daughter's nickname and a prickly plant—Wade launched a prolific career in journalism. Mixing wit with biting criticism, "Bessie" offered candid observations on issues of her day. From politics and social events to

women's rights and education reform, her sharp pen targeted both local and national topics. While the author's true name remained the subject of great public speculation, her articles appeared in the leading Pittsburgh newspapers, including the *Leader, Dispatch,* and *Chronicle.* Even after Wade's identity was revealed in 1886 (following her retirement from public teaching) she continued to write as Bramble and defy the expected behavior of a woman of her stature.

Wade was the first president of the Women's Club of Pittsburgh (founded 1875) and a charter member of the Pittsburgh Woman's Press Club (1891). As the turn of the century approached, Bessie Bramble lost popularity, and Wade and her husband retired to the west coast.

Fred Brand, Sr.

Born in 1886—Carnoustie, Scotland
Died in 1946—Pittsburgh

Perhaps the most serendipitous thing ever to happen to Western Pennsylvania golf was the 1904 trip J. F. "Fritz" Byers took to Scotland. With golf growing in popularity, Byers went to famed golfing town Carnoustie looking for someone he could bring back to Pittsburgh to be the professional of the newly relocated Allegheny Country Club. Once on the North Side, by 1902 the links had been moved to their current Sewickley Heights aerie. The new course simply demanded someone to teach the game as it should be played.

In Carnoustie, where golf dates back to the early 16th Century, Byers spied an 18-year-old tournament player, a powerful young man who could hit the ball a fair country mile. When Byers convinced the Scotsman to become the new pro at the Allegheny Country Club, he changed Pittsburgh golf forever.

In the New World, Scottish pro Fred Brand, Sr., set the gold standard. Winning his first of four West Penn Opens the next year, 1905, stationed in his new digs below the 16th fairway, Brand was impatient, demanding, flinty.

With his German shepherd Jocko nestled by his side, standing near the 17th tee Brand would belt an even dozen balls—and heaven help the hapless caddie who brought back a paltry 'leven.

"Laddie," he'd say in his thick burr, "golf teaches trust and honesty. Golf," he'd say, "reveals character."

A founding member of the Tri-State PGA, Brand worked until his death of a diabetic stroke, in 1946, at age 60. Leaving a rich golf

heritage, his two sons became leaders of Western Pennsylvania golf. Fred Brand, Jr., 1910-98, won numerous titles and served as a golf executive and official, as did his brother Jack, 1919-2007. In 1954, they founded the Fred Brand Foursomes Championship, an annual trophied event in memory of their father.

John Brashear

Born November 24, 1840—Brownsville, PA
Died April 7, 1920—Pittsburgh

When, in 1900, Andrew Carnegie announced his intention to build the Carnegie Institute he made an example of John Brashear. "It is really astonishing how many of the world's foremost men have begun as manual laborers," Carnegie noted. "We have two notable examples of this in our own community, whose fame is world-wide. George Westinghouse was a mechanic; Professor Brashear, a millwright." Indeed, to three generations of Pittsburghers, "Uncle John" was a man who had followed his passions and achieved greatness.

John Brashear was born the eldest of seven children to Basil Brown Brashear, a saddler. His mother, Julia, had once worked in the cotton mill in which Carnegie first found employment. His maternal grandfather, Nathaniel Smith, was a tinker and traveling repairman who, with a friend, crafted a crude telescope—using glass from the recently burned Bakewell Glass Co.—sufficient at best to help outline constellations in the night sky. It was Grandfather Smith who excited his grandson's passion for astronomy when Brashear was just 8.

A bright child who was experienced in all manner of tooling, he earned a number of jobs as a mill mechanic. Married in 1862, he and his wife, Phoebe, built a house on the slopes (above 22nd Street) on the South Side where he worked at McKnight, Duncan & Co. After regularly long hours in the mills, at night he constructed a telescope of his own. Just grinding the glass took three years. His amateur interests in astronomy introduced him to the eminent Samuel P. Langley whose North Side observatory was also a nexus of the scientific community and of business leaders intrigued by new technologies. With assistance from Langley and a few rare books, Brashear developed a different and much improved means of silvering mirrors used in reflecting telescopes, and with this new skill, he offered up an ad in *Scientific American* magazine to sell telescope parts to other amateurs. A chance meeting with William Thaw, the railroad tycoon (and father of Harry,) allowed Brashear and his son-in-law to go into business to manufacture what was first intended to be expert optical lenses, but just as soon became an instrumentation shop, notably in spectrometers prized by scientists worldwide. Brashear took the path less traveled, quit his day job, and pursued his dream.

Among his countless achievements, Brashear lectured to international audiences, wrote dozens of scientific papers (as well as local newspaper columns, for which he was recognized as everyone's "Uncle John,") assisted Langley in developing his first flying machine, served as Acting Chancellor of Pitt (while concurrently serving on Carnegie's committee to found his new Technical School,) assumed sole responsibility of the H.C. Frick Educational Commission, toured China and Japan (where he was greeted by former Pittsburgh Mayor and then Ambassador, George Guthrie), and single-handedly raised more than $300,000 in 1905 to build the new Allegheny Observatory. His 75th birthday was a national day of honor. At 80, he died of complications from ptomaine poisoning.

Above, a somewhat distorted photograph of the moon captured through the lens of the Thaw telescope at the Allegheny Observatory on the North Side in 1915.

Michel Briere

Born October 21, 1949—Malartic, Quebec
Died April 13, 1971—Malartic, Quebec

The kid might have been a bit undersized, but what he lacked in physical presence he made up in smarts, skill, and swagger. Not yet 20, a skinny Junior League phenom, he wanted an extra $1,000 on top of his $5,000 Penguin signing bonus. When general manager Jack Riley balked, the kid just smiled.

"It's not really that much extra money," he said, "because I'll be playing for the Penguins for the next 20 years."

Sadly, it was not to be.

No one in the Penguins' brief history had blazed out of the Juniors like Michel Edouard Briere. Born in Malartic, Quebec, in 1949, and growing to only 5'10" and 165 pounds, his skating and stick-handling inspired comparisons with the best young players of the time. In just 100 Shawinigan Bruins games in his native Quebec, he'd scored a show-stopping 129 goals (75 his final year) and 191 assists. Selected 26th overall in the 1969 draft—relatively low because some thought he could not handle the rough-and-tumble NHL—he became the Penguins' original impact player.

At a time when players generally scored fewer goals than today, Briere's rookie totals were a respectable 12 goals and 44 points, good for third in team scoring. What those numbers don't reflect were his leadership, his ability to read a play, skate around defensemen as if they weren't there, and take a devastating shot. Leading the club to the playoffs, the Pens went to second round—and went to the off-season expecting more.

In his hometown of Malartic, Quebec, the car in which Briere was a passenger was in a horrific accident. Thrown from the backseat, Briere suffered irreparable brain damage. When he died eleven months later, in 1971, Michel Briere was just 21 years old.

As a tribute, the club retired his number, 21. A banner in his memory hangs from the roof of Mellon Arena today.

Don Brockett

Born January 30, 1930—Mt. Washington
Date May 2, 1995—Shadyside

Celebrating their "silver" anniversary as entertainers in 1985, Don Brockett and Barbara (Mazziotti) Russell, were well established at the Marriott Green Tree with a weekend revue show. Then, their material satirized the success of Michael Jackson, Madonna and Prince. But what audiences most loved were their comic winks and jabs at Pittsburgh's potholes and politicians. For another 10 years, still performing with Russell as Brockett & Barbara, Don Brockett was a Pittsburgh institution.

Always well known locally, the national media considered him more famous than Julia Child, for his 30-year recurring role as Chef Brockett on *Mister Rogers' Neighborhood.*

In addition to his TV work, Brockett appeared in some 34 films, most shot locally and many popular, like *Flashdance, Silence of the Lambs,* and *Hoffa.* They were all small roles, but as casting director Canice Kennedy once noted, "He always got cast because he was so totally unique. That wonderful face and, of

course, the voice and the walk and the everything. Directors fell in love with him."

His voice was wholly natural, gravelly even at two years of age. One critic commented that it seemed he had steel wool in his throat.

Brockett was born on Mt. Washington, the third child of Don and Regina. Dad sold stoves. Both parents dissuaded him from his love of theater. But at 16, while attending St. Mary's of the Mount, Brockett began suffering from slipped femoral epiphysis, a glandular condition that allowed his legs to detach from his hips. Brockett attended Duquesne University on crutches.

Ironically, Brockett started his career as a choreographer, notably at the Jennerstown Playhouse, where he first met Barbara Mazziotti, a sixth grade teacher. They became an instant duo, performing at the cast party for *Paint Your Wagon.* Soon, they developed the first of hundreds of musical revues and toured with other cast members. Brockett hit a loud chord with *Big Bad Burlesque* off-Broadway, but just as quickly made sour notes with *Sweet Feet,* a second revue. Brockett's financial success however was sustained by many annual industrial shows he wrote, staged and produced for companies like Clairol and Alcoa.

A Nantucket summer neighbor of Fred Rogers, Brockett joined the Neighborhood in 1966. There he taught Fred and his TV friends how to make healthy snack foods.

In his professional career, Brockett taught many aspiring actors to command the stage, including such notables as Lenora Nemetz, James Widdoes, Michael Keaton, Rob Marshall, and Patty Deutsch.

In 1995, while writing his fifth year of *Forbidden Pittsburgh,* Brockett died at home of a massive heart attack. He was just 65.

Charles Bronson

Born November 3, 1921—Ehrenfeld, PA
Died August 30, 2003—Los Angeles, CA

When you are one of 15 children born to a poor Lithuanian-American coal mining family in a town of only 230 residents just northeast of Johnstown, it matters not whether you were the ninth born or the 11th. Charles Buchinski was, however, the only family member to graduate from high school. Even still, he followed his father and six brothers into the mines of Ehrenfeld, earning $1 for every ton of coal they unearthed.

© BETTMANN/CORBIS

World War II may have saved him. He served as an Army Air Force gunner in Guam until 1946, and was discharged to Philadelphia. There he built stage sets in a local theater until he realized that actors got paid much more. In New York, waiting for the next audition, he shared an apartment with Jack Klugman. Small parts and short runs ensued. In 1949, he turned to California where he was discovered at the Pasadena Playhouse and was cast in the 1951 comedy, *You're in the Navy Now,* in which Lee Marvin also first appeared on screen. In his second film, *The People Against O'Hara,* he appeared with Pittsburgher John Hodiak. In 1952, he played "Pittsburgh Philo" in *Bloodhounds of Broadway.* He then pursued work in some of the very first TV shows, *Biff Baker U.S.A.* and *The Roy Rogers Show.* In 1953, using Bronson as his new stage name, he played Igor to Vincent Price's "Master" in *House of Wax,* one of few very successful 3-D extravaganzas. For the next seven years, his career flourished, alternating between TV roles as an Apache Indian, a gangster thug, tough hombre, bruised boxer, or Army sergeant.

"You know," said Bronson later in his career, "I don't look like someone who leans on a mantelpiece with a cocktail in my hand."

The ensemble action films of the '60s propelled him to fame. Successively, he appeared in feature roles in *The Magnificent Seven, The Great Escape, The Dirty Dozen,* and *Once Upon a Time in the West.*

What few Americans know, however, is that Bronson appeared as the leading action hero in dozens of Italian and French films after leaving Hollywood in 1968. In 1972, he shared the Golden Globe Henrietta Award for World Favorite Actor with Sean Connery.

In 1974, Bronson returned stateside to film the first of his legendary *Death Wish* films. Four sequels followed, as did memorable roles in *Telefon* and *The Valachi Papers.*

Married three times, the second iteration most famously to Jill Ireland, Bronson died at 81 in 2003.

Hallie Quinn Brown

Born in 1850—Pittsburgh
Died September 16, 1949—Wilberforce, OH

The daughter of freed slaves active in the Underground Railroad, educator, speaker, and writer Hallie Quinn Brown took her message of equality all over the world.

Born in Pittsburgh in 1850, Hallie Quinn Brown moved with her family to Chatham, Ontario in 1864. Six years later, she enrolled in Ohio's African-American Wilberforce University. Graduating in 1873, Brown went south, to teach in plantation and public schools in Mississippi and South Carolina. Working at South Carolina's Allen University, the Dayton public schools, and Tuskegee Institute (under Booker T. Washington), in 1893 Brown became professor of elocution at Wilberforce.

An elocutionist, she toured frequently, including Europe, notably Germany, Switzer-

land, and France, along with England, where she appeared twice before Queen Victoria. An advocate of women's rights, Brown was also an American representative at the 1899 International Congress of Women in London.

Tirelessly working for civil and women's rights, by 1920, when American women gained the right to vote, Brown had become a prominent member of the Republican Party. The first woman to speak from Presidential candidate Warren Harding's front porch, in 1924 she addressed the Republican National Convention.

Over more than a half-century, Brown published landmark works of African-American narrative, including *The Beautiful: A True Story of Slavery* (1924), *Our Women: Past, Present and Future* (1925), *Tales My Father Told* (1925), *Homespun Heroines and Other Women of Distinction* (1926), and *Pen Pictures of Pioneers of Wilberforce* (1937); her *Elocution and Physical Culture* (1910) and *First Lessons in Public Speaking* (1920) became standard texts.

In 1949, Hallie Quinn Brown at 99 died of

a coronary thrombosis in her Wilberforce home. She is buried in Xenia's Massies Creek Cemetery. St. Paul's Hallie Quinn Brown Community House and the Hallie Q. Brown Library at Ohio's Central State University are named in her memory.

Ray Brown

Born October 13, 1926—Pittsburgh
Died July 2, 2002—Indianapolis, IN

Within 24 hours of landing in New York to "make it big" he was introduced to the legendary Dizzy Gillespie. The next day he wasn't just jamming with him, he was in the band—along with Charlie Parker, Max Roach, and Bud Powell, four of the most influential jazz musicians of the day.

Ray Brown started off with fairly ordinary beginnings in the east end of Pittsburgh. He began his musical journey on piano, as his father had hopes of him playing like the legendary stride pianists Fats Waller and Art Tatum. He began taking lessons at 8 and by the time he was in high school had become quite an accomplished pianist. But, the piano didn't resonate with Brown and he found himself gravitating to the bass, quickly learning it by ear. He was able to use the loaner bass from school before they realized he was making money with it on the weekends.

After graduation from Schenley High School, he played throughout the area and developed a reputation as a hot bassist. But Brown was ready for greener pastures. He and three of his buddies all planned their exodus for New York, but on the eve of their break from Pittsburgh all but Brown chickened out. He met up with friend Hank Jones in New York who quickly introduced him to Gillespie.

Between 1946 and 1951, Brown played with Dizzy Gillespie's band, which also included among others, Pittsburgh's influential bop drummer Kenny Clarke. It was this group that eventually led to the creation of the Modern Jazz Quartet. Always looking for his next opportunity, Brown began a series of performances with JATP (Jazz at the Philharmonic). He met an up-and-coming singer named Ella Fitzgerald, who was touring with Dizzy. The two hit it off and married in 1947. Although the marriage would only last a few short years, it began a business and personal relationship that endured, including the adoption of a son, Ray Brown Jr.

It was during Brown's tenure with JATP that he met and teamed-up with the legendary Oscar Peterson. Worldwide tours and many recordings would follow for the next 15 years.

In the mid-1960s Brown quit the Oscar Peterson Trio. His deftness as a musician had him working with many of the great vocalists like Frank Sinatra, Tony Bennett, Nancy Wilson, and Pittsburgh's Billy Eckstine. Brown also composed the Grammy Award-winning song "Gravy Waltz," better known as the theme to the *Steve Allen Show*. He found time as well to manage several musicians (including a young Quincy Jones), open a nightclub, and help organize the Monterey Jazz Festival.

During the 1980s and 1990s Brown continued touring, recording, and mentoring many up-and-comers. Among his musical discoveries is contemporary jazz pianist Diana Krall. Always an avid golfer, in 2002, Brown died while napping after an afternoon round.

Felix R. Brunot

Born in 1822—Pittsburgh
Died in 1899—Pittsburgh

He was the grandson and namesake of his French immigrant grandfather, a physician who served in the Revolutionary War and later settled on what became Brunot's Island in the Ohio River just west of Pittsburgh. His wife, Mary Ann Hogg Brunot, grew up in the bustling river town of Brownsville,PA, but was educated in an elite girls' school in Philadelphia. Even at a young age, Mary Ann was quite certain of her support of temperance, the abolition of slavery, and her duty to spread the Gospel. Young Felix Brunot harbored the same notions while he worked in several industries, earning his fortune by investing in the steelmaking firm of Singer, Nimick and Company. Their marriage in 1846 lasted over

50 years, guided always by their devout faith as they worked to help runaway slaves, injured and dying Civil War soldiers, broken veterans and war widows, and even Native Americans far from Pittsburgh on the Western frontier.

The couple had no children but opened their otherwise empty mansion on Stockton Street in Allegheny City (North Side) to family, friends, and those in need—covertly using their home as a stop along the Underground Railroad. At the onset of the Civil War, Felix Brunot refused the opportunity to serve as an officer of the Union Army so that he could volunteer to aid wounded soldiers, traveling directly to the battlefields, delivering supplies and medical care. Brunot organized the Pittsburgh Sanitary Fair, an elaborate 18-day fundraising event that opened in June 1864, and yielded over $300,000 for aid to soldiers and the establishment of a convalescent home for returning veterans. After the war, Mrs. Brunot raised funds to establish a similar home in Pittsburgh for war widows and their children.

Felix Brunot's efforts were recognized by President Grant in 1868 when he was asked to head the U.S. Bureau of Indian Affairs. Brunot spent the next six years traveling to western states, negotiating tribal land rights. Mrs. Brunot continued her service work in Pittsburgh, helping to establish the Colored Children's Home and the Pittsburgh Y.W.C.A. Countless lives were saved and improved thanks to their generosity and kindness.

Kenneth Burke

Born May 5, 1897—Pittsburgh
Died November 19, 1993—Andover, NJ

Poet Howard Nemerov said that Kenneth Burke had a "mind which can't stop exploding."

Without a college degree, Burke became the most influential American literary thinker of the 20th Century. If nothing else, he seemed to have taught, befriended, influenced, or corresponded with virtually every major practitioner, including Malcolm Cowley (with whom he attended Peabody High), William Carlos Williams, Robert Penn Warren, Ralph Ellison, Katherine Anne Porter—even Susan Sontag and Edward Said. Add to the list his grandson, popular singer-songwriter Harry Chapin, who recorded Burke's song "One Light in a Dark Valley."

What unites this highly disparate list is Burke's lifelong interest in rhetoric, in how language affects not only thought, but also what he termed symbolic action. Focusing on the political and social power of symbols, Burke believed that an analysis of rhetoric could help elucidate the bases of conflict.

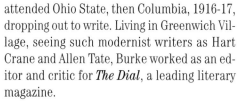

After Peabody, the man universally known as KB briefly attended Ohio State, then Columbia, 1916-17, dropping out to write. Living in Greenwich Village, seeing such modernist writers as Hart Crane and Allen Tate, Burke worked as an editor and critic for *The Dial*, a leading literary magazine.

By 1924 he published the first English translation of Thomas Mann's *Death in Venice*. A few years later, Burke built a small farmhouse—with neither electricity nor plumbing—in Andover, NJ, where he chopped wood for heat.

By the 1930s, Burke was publishing major works, beginning with *Counter-Statement*, 1931, and including *Attitudes Toward History*, 1937, and *The Philosophy of Literary Form*, 1939. His two most famous books, *A Grammar of Motives* and *A Rhetoric of Motives* came in 1945 and 1950.

Continuing to publish throughout his life, Burke left countless letters and other material, which scholars continue to catalogue, annotate, and publish.

Selma Burke

Born December 31, 1900—Mooresville, NC
Died August 29, 1995—New Hope, PA

It was a very bad time. The National Guard camped in Pitt Stadium, and tanks rolled down Fifth Avenue. For a time, people feared the city would simply tear itself apart.

More than anything, people needed hope, a vision that things could be better.

Into this cauldron stepped a 67-year-old woman, arguably the nation's greatest living African-American artist. A sculptor, educator, most of all a role model for decency and achievement, she came, in that frightening year of 1968, to dedicate an East Liberty arts center in her name. She was Selma Burke, and her Selma Burke Art Center changed Pittsburgh history.

No longer relegated to second-class status, African-American art could take its rightful place at center stage, as it does today.

Born Selma Hortense Burke in Mooresville, North Carolina, in 1900, the granddaughter of slaves was a talented sculptor when her parents, fearing that a black woman couldn't make a living as an artist, encouraged her to pursue a nursing degree.

Graduating in 1924, she moved to New York City, where she continued to study. A 1936 fellowship allowed Burke to travel to Europe; back home, she completed a Columbia master's degree in 1941. A doctorate followed some 30 years later.

Her most famous—and controversial -- moment came in 1943 when she won an international competition to sculpt a portrait of President Franklin Roosevelt. Unveiled in 1945, the 3.5-by-2.5-foot plaque still stands at Washington's Recorder of Deeds Building. Many observers, including Burke herself, believe this plaque served as John Sinnock's model for the Roosevelt dime.

A tireless educator, Burke taught art and sculpture at a variety of locations, including Pittsburgh. An A.W. Mellon Foundation consultant, 1967-76, Burke taught art and operated her Selma Burke Art Center until her 1982 retirement.

Frederick Burleigh

Born unknown—Boston, MA
Died unknown

Like most theatre companies, the Pittsburgh Playhouse started as a volunteer-led civic resource, accommodating the artistic needs of its amateur actors and directors as much as those of its audience. In 1934, with the stroke of a pen, the Playhouse Board registered for non-profit status. In 1936, it leased space on Craft Avenue in Oakland to renovate a former German Club into a new theatre. The next year, it hired Herbert Gellendre to serve as the company's director. His tenure, mottled with intellectual, artsy fare and professional actors brought in from New York, was short. And, in 1937, the Board replaced him with a young director from the Indianapolis Playhouse.

Frederick Burleigh was born in Boston and attended the high-brow Boston-Latin School, graduating in 1924. He came to the Pittsburgh Playhouse with the direction to lead the theatre into financial stability with the certain understanding that the best way for a theatre to sustain itself is by selling tickets. So Burleigh dumped the New York actors, invited seasoned amateurs to audition and staged plays that his audience might have read—or read about. Burleigh did stage some avant-garde pieces in the Spring, always a comedy in January, and almost every season a musical. By 1950, the Playhouse had 8,000 subscribers and three operating stages. In addition, the Playhouse conducted theatre and dance classes for students, as well as a two-year accredited course for those seeking professional careers. The Playhouse, in the days before television, was as much a part of the Pittsburgh community as any library, museum, or amusement park.

But the organization did not stop there. Under the Board's direction, aided of course

Above, Burleigh's 1952 production of *The Happy Time*, one of the first plays to be mounted on the new stage of the former Tree of Life Synagogue.

by Burleigh, the company added a Playhouse Junior, and in 1951, purchased the former Tree of Life Synagogue and refurbished it as the Craft Theatre. The Playhouse even added a restaurant and cocktail lounge.

So successful was the Playhouse that foundations sought out opportunities to enhance the thriving organization. And therein may have lied the end of Burleigh's tenure.

A remarkable artistic director, in his 28 years at the helm, Burleigh directed some 254 productions of the total 292 produced. By comparison, the director who would follow him, William Ball, produced only two.

Bill and Patti Burns

Bill: Born 1913—Houtzdale, PA
Died September 16, 1997—Pittsburgh

Patti: Born 1952—Mt. Lebanon
Died October 31, 2001—Pittsburgh

In the early days of television news, when men like Paul Long, Al McDowell, and Dave Murry appeared through the tiny black & white portal of the television set, good looks were not important. It would not be saying much that Bill Burns, among his peers, was arguably the more handsome of the local newscasters. In fact, he had an annoying command of proper diction. In a city filled with politicians by the last name of Flaherty, Burns made certain the name was pronounced with three distinct syllables.

Yet what made Burns stand out amongst

the legacies of Pittsburgh newscasters was his longevity. In 1978, he celebrated his 25th consecutive year on air, a milestone unprecedented by any newscaster of any major market. (And back then, Pittsburgh was among the top 10 broadcast markets). Furthermore, when his daughter Patti joined him as co-anchor in 1976, they enjoyed the highest ratings of any newscast of any market in their time. Not surprisingly, "Patti & Daddy," as devotees called the evening broadcast, were the only father and daughter news team in the country.

The first and only news reporter on WDTV (the Dumont Network affiliate that became KDKA-TV,) Burns had been hired from radio station KQV. Before his short tenure there, Burns had only recently arrived in Pittsburgh with his young bride, a newly hired school teacher. Born in Houtzdale, Clearfield County, PA, Burns attended Villanova, but

graduated from St. Joseph's College, before working at his hometown paper, *The Clearfield Progress*. While writing, he also drove a beer truck and sold typewriters. In 1946 he served in the 30th Infantry Division and was injured in France, where he stayed for more than a year recuperating from shrapnel lodged in his leg.

Burns' last broadcast on KDKA-TV was in 1989. He died of complications from pneumonia in 1997. That same year, Patti left the station and four years later died of cancer at 49.

Esther Bush

Born October 26, 1952—Hill District

Said Esther Bush about W.E.B. DuBois's prediction that race would dominate the issues of the 20th Century, "It appears that it will dominate the 21st Century as well."

Born the third child of Ola Mae and Willie Bush, who together founded the city's first black-owned trucking business, Clauzell Trucking, Esther Bush attended Westinghouse High School, graduating in 1969. She earned her B.A. at Morgan State College and an M.A. in Education from Johns Hopkins.

Bush began her career as a high school teacher. Starting in 1980 with the position of assistant director of the Labor Education Advancement Program for the National Urban League in New York City, she then served first as director of the New York Urban League Staten Island branch, next as Director of its Manhattan branch. Before returning to Pittsburgh in December 1994, Bush was president and chief executive officer of the Urban League of Greater Hartford.

Of her many accomplishments since helming the League's staff of 78 and administering its $6.1 million annual budget, she hosted the 2003 National Urban League Convention in Pittsburgh at which President George W. Bush spoke.

A much respected leader, she serves on more than a dozen different civic and cultural non-profit boards and is a perennial panelist on public forums addressing diversity, equal opportunity and justice. She resides in Highland Park.

Margaret Byington

Born in 1877
Died in 1952

At the turn of the 20th Century thousands of immigrants, a majority of them from Southern and Eastern Europe, poured into the United States with the hopes of making a better life for themselves and their families. Many found their way to the coal fields and steel mills of Western Pennsylvania. Consequently, some native-born Americans became

Lewis Hine's photographs of child laborers included many young miners. The year and location are unknown.

concerned with the conditions created by rapid urbanization and industrialization. The Progressive Era was characterized by these reform-minded individuals who attempted to alleviate some of the worst conditions of immigrant life through the application of the social sciences. In 1907 Pittsburgh, seen as a model industrial city, became the subject of one such study, spearheaded by reformer Paul F. Kellogg, and funded by the Russell Sage Foundation. What came to be known as *The Pittsburgh Survey*, published in 1907, employed social workers and reformers to document, through reports, photographs, and statistical analysis, the working and living conditions of Pittsburgh's immigrant community. Hopes were that widespread knowledge of the appalling conditions in Pittsburgh would be the catalyst for extensive reform.

Margaret Byington, a social worker and graduate of both Wellesley College and Columbia University, was hired as a part of this survey to examine living conditions in the steel town of Homestead, Pa., several miles up the Monongahela River from Pittsburgh. While the Survey examined everything from factory working conditions to the role of women in the workforce, Byington's study focused on the lives of African-American and immigrant families in Homestead. She wrote extensively on their daily budgets and rituals. Her report was highly critical of the local steel industry, which she blamed for much of the deplorable conditions she found in the neighborhood and within families. She highlighted the inadequate wages paid to the steelworkers that led to many women taking in boarders for supplemental income and the long hours, which kept the men from their families. In 1910 the results of Byington's study, *Homestead: The Households of a Mill Town*, were published as part of the six-volume survey.

After her work in Homestead, Byington continued her career as a reformer and social worker. She went on to become the director of both the American Association for Organizing Family Social Work and the American Red Cross. She died in 1952.

Virgil Cantini

Born in 1920—Italy

From gem-like jewelry to three-story installations, ceramics to metals, Virgil Cantini's stunning, ubiquitous sculptures have become an abstract mirror of how we see ourselves.

Born Virgil David Cantini in Italy in 1920, he emigrated to America a decade later. Coming to Pittsburgh as a Carnegie Tech student, he served in World War II, then returned to take a 1946 bachelor of fine arts and a Pitt master's degree two years later. Joining the Pitt faculty in 1952, Cantini rose to become a professor of fine arts and chair of the studio arts program.

An international star from 1953, when he was named one of *Time*'s Hundred Leaders of Tomorrow, Cantini's work has appeared in many venues, most notably the 1958 Brussels World's Fair.

The 1956 Pittsburgh Center for the Arts Artist of the Year, he has seen several pieces become Pittsburgh icons. For example, his *Joy of Life*, adjacent to the South Whitfield Presbyterian Church, East Liberty, has become the symbol of a resurgent neighborhood.

Prolifically represented on the Pitt campus, Cantini's wood-and-metal rendering of an arrow-pierced *St. Sebastian* adorns Hillman Library. In the Law Building's Teplitz Courtroom, his 24-by-36-foot mosaic, containing 126 porcelain-on-steel pieces, recalls the intricacy—and harmony—of our legal system.

Hanging in Posvar Hall (formerly Forbes Quadrangle), Cantini's *Skyscape*, an abstract of steel rods and multicolored glass, towers above passers-by.

Finally, his most famous—and most-viewed—piece is on the façade of Fifth Avenue's Parran Hall. *Man,* a three-story combination of bronze and steel, presents a

bronze skeletal man surrounded by upward-moving, randomly placed peaks of varying sizes. With close-set circular steel bands unifying the piece, *Man* is Cantini's ode to humankind's never-ending quest for knowledge.

Now a Pitt professor emeritus, Virgil Cantini lives and works in Pittsburgh.

Bill Cardille

Born in 1934—Sharon, PA

Chipped ham was to Isaly's as Chilly Billy was to Channel 11.

From the first day WIIC went on the air in 1957, Bill Cardille was behind the station microphone. A native of Sharon, PA, graduate of Indiana University of PA (IUP), and veteran of Erie radio, at just 23, he hosted live weekday shows like *Dance Party* and *Luncheon at the Ones* and delivered the weather report every night. On Saturday afternoons, he hosted *Studio Wrestling*, interviewing the honorables, like the great Bruno Sammartino or Jumpin' Johnny DeFazio as well as the no-goods, like Gorilla Monsoon or Professor Tanaka. Between rounds, Pirate legend Pie Traynor read live commercials for American Heating. *Studio Wrestling* was the number one rated show of the early NBC affiliate.

Yet in 1964, with his plate already full on Saturdays, station manager Sheldon Weaver asked Cardille to host a horror movie "after the weather."

"It cost the station $100 for each movie we aired," noted Cardille speaking at a recent fantest. "I'd announce the film, but after two weeks I got bored doing it straight. And I figured it was summertime, so I started messing around." "Chilly Billy," a name given him by sportscaster Red Donley's son, produced and

wrote his own material. The humor—mercifully unsupported by a laugh track—was oddly juxtaposed to the horror of the films shown. As the show's ratings climbed, Cardille cast a castle of characters to help play out short skits. The show's theme song, "Experiment in Terror," was a heavy sax riff taken from a film score written by Pittsburgher Henry Mancini.

Chiller Theater aired every Saturday night from September 19, 1964, to December 31, 1983.

George Romero cast Cardille as the news reporter in his cult classic *Night of the Living Dead*. Lori Cardille, his first born, starred in *Day of the Dead*.

Inducted into the PA Broadcasters Hall of Fame, Cardille is today the mid-day host of WJAS 1320.

Josie Carey

Born August 20, 1930—Butler, PA
Died May 28, 2004—Pittsburgh

"Why Hi, Don't I know you?" She did, of course, if you were a child in the early 1950s watching a black & white television set tuned to Channel 13 in Pittsburgh. Josie Carey was the animated, often giggling host of one of the first children's programs to air in the U.S. A pioneer in every sense—program host, children's author, lyricist, singer, and entertainer—Carey began working for the nation's first public television station, WQED, just six months before it went on the air in 1953.

Born in Butler, Josephine Vicari was the daughter of Anthony and Angeline Vicari, owners and operators of a local Italian restaurant. A 1947 graduate of Butler High School, she enrolled at Duff's College downtown to learn secretarial skills. And in 1953 she accepted a job as secretary to Dorothy Daniels, WQED's first station manager. Daniels soon truncated Miss Vicari's last name, asking her to work with the station's young program developer to create a children's program they would co-write and co-host together. Carey was "a natural" in front of the camera. Her co-host was more comfortable backstage, creating puppets and giving them life. One of the puppets, Daniel Striped Tiger, was named for the station manager. Daniel's puppeteer was Fred Rogers.

Together Carey and Rogers wrote some 68 songs—"Why Hi" was their theme song—and for seven years *The Children's Corner* was

renowned as one of the finest local educational children's programs on television, winning a 1955 national Sylvania Television award.

In 1961, Carey was asked to do a new show on KDKA television and, there, created three shows: *Funsville*, *Josie's Storyland*, and *Mr. Wrinkle* with Sterling Yates, featuring a silent, cigar-chomping pianist, known to kids as Indian Mary, but better remembered today as Johnny Costa.

From KDKA, she was hired away to South Carolina to host and produce *Wheee!* another local children's program on which Rick Sebak earned his television wings as an intern. She appeared in 473 half-hour shows there, before returning to her hometown, first living on Beechwood Boulevard in Squirrel Hill and, after being widowed to her first husband Henry Massucci, moving to Kennedy Township seven years later with her second husband, Joseph Franz.

Carey died in 2004, surviving Rogers, with whom she had had little contact after leaving WQED in the mid-'70s.

Max Carey

Born January 11, 1890—Terre Haute, IN
Died May 30, 1976—Miami, FL

"He played," the late Art McKennon, longtime Pirate announcer, recalled, "as if he were on springs."

Born Max Carnarius, in Terre Haute, IN, 1890, when the teenaged Lutheran divinity student could no longer afford school he turned to baseball. Quickly establishing himself as a star centerfielder and base stealer, Carey came to the Pirates as a 20-year-old in 1910, emerging as the team's brightest star over the next 17 seasons. A perennial National League top 10 player in nearly every offensive and defensive category, he led the Senior Circuit in runs once, triples and walks twice, and stolen bases 10 times. Hitting over .300 six times, in his one World Series—1925, when the Pirates bested Walter Johnson's Washington Senators—Carey pounded out 11 hits for a .458 average.

His 1925 high batting average of .343 remains the Pirates standard for switch hitters, and his 688 stolen bases are still the team high-water mark. Stealing home 33 times, in one game Carey scored five times without getting a hit—reaching first on an error and four walks. "He was harder to stop," opponent Joe Williams once quipped, "than a run in a silk stocking."

A dust-up with management in 1926 sent Carey to the Brooklyn Robins, as the Dodgers were then called. Retiring as a player in 1929 at age 39, he continued in baseball, briefly leading the Brooklyn club, later managing the Milwaukee Chicks and Fort Wayne Daisies of the All-American Girls Professional Baseball League. Scouting and managing in the minors, Carey retired in 1956 at age 66.

For his career, Carey's 738 steals rank ninth all-time, and his 2,665 hits stand 60th. Elected to baseball's Hall of Fame in 1961, he died in Miami in 1976.

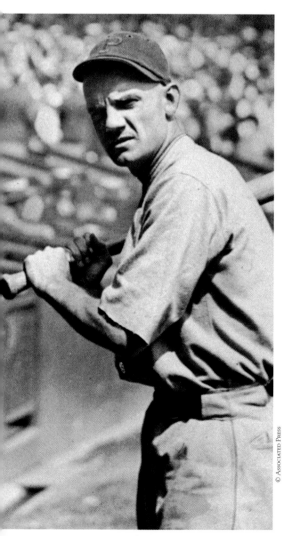

© Associated Press

Andrew Carnegie

Born November 25,1835—Dumferline, SCO
Died August 11, 1919—Lenox, MA

Andrew Carnegie is remembered as being both "overly proud of attainment and extremely fond of applause," two traits that guided his shrewd business acumen and his grand gestures of philanthropy. Known as the most successful steelmaker in the world, he amassed a fortune from his Pittsburgh companies throughout the late 19th Century and garnered unparalleled wealth and world-wide recognition for the great sums of money he later gave away.

Carnegie arrived in Allegheny City (the North Side) from Scotland when he was 13 along with his parents and younger brother, Thomas. While not formally educated in Pittsburgh, his early work as a boy in the telegraph business led him to a position with the Pennsylvania Railroad where he impressed the most powerful professional people of the time. They mentored the teen and taught him the art of big business as he moved up in the ranks, eventually serving as superintendent of the railroad's Pittsburgh Division from 1858 to 1865.

With railroad companies in mind, Carnegie and a few partners entered the iron business in 1863 making rails and bridges to meet the demands of the expanding network of trains that boomed after the Civil War. With a watchful eye on both the market and the emerging technologies of his industry, Carnegie moved away from iron production and constructed the first blast furnace in Pittsburgh and later a Bessemer furnace in Braddock in order to mass produce steel. When Carnegie sensed railroad expansion waning, he invested great sums in open-hearth furnaces at his Homestead Works, which produced steel well suited for the skyscrapers beginning to rise in urban areas around the world. Despite Carnegie's emerging philosophy to share his wealth with "the people" his focus at the mill was to keep production costs and wages low, resulting in the bloody Homestead Strike of 1892.

Carnegie earned over $225 million in 1901 after selling his mills to J.P. Morgan, who formed the U. S. Steel Corporation. At this time he was considered the richest man in the world. Pittsburgh's natural resources and immigrant labor provided him with the coal, coke, iron ore, rivers, and tremendous workforce required to build his empire. In return,

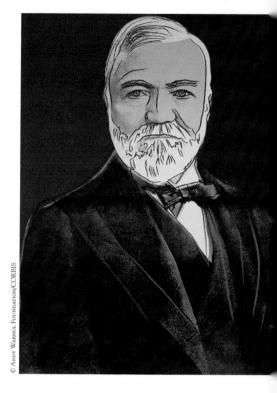

© Andy Warhol Foundation/CORBIS

Carnegie shared his wealth in Pittsburgh, establishing the first of his famous libraries here along with museums, schools, lecture halls, and pension funds.

John Dickson Carr

Born November 30, 1906—Uniontown, PA
Died February 27, 1977—Greenville, SC

The great Romantic poet Samuel Taylor Coleridge said that in order to appreciate literature a reader must have "a willing suspension of disbelief." If that's so, then readers  need a very large dollop for the 100-odd highly entertaining—and highly improbable—mysteries written by John Dickson Carr.

Born in 1906 in Uniontown, the son of a Congressman, Carr was a mediocre student at The Hill School, an exclusive Pottstown preparatory academy. Moving to England, Carr published his first detective novel at age 24 in 1930. Proving both popular and prolific, within five years, with the publication of his landmark *The Three Coffins*, Carr had become the acclaimed master of the locked-room puzzle, in which murders occur in a seemingly impenetrable room.

Living in England through 1948, setting most of his books there and in Europe, Carr

Above, Carr partnered with Arthur Conan Doyle's son, Adrian, right, to sustain the stories of Sherlock Holmes.

possessed a seemingly inexhaustible supply of plots, characters, detectives, even pseudonyms, publishing under his own name and Carr Dickson, Carter Dickson, and Roger Fairbairn.

Modeling his major detective, the corpulent lexicographer Dr. Gideon Fell, on fellow mystery writer G.K. Chesterton, Carr also created the Churchillian Sir Henry Merrivale, as well as Henri Bencolin and Colonel March.

A number of Carr stories were filmed, including the 1951 *The Man with a Cloak*, starring Joseph Cotton, Barbara Stanwyck, and a 20-year-old Leslie Caron. His 1953 film *Dangerous Crossing* starred Michael Rennie, Jeanne Crain, and Carl Betz.

Carr's 1949 biography of Sherlock Holmes creator Sir Arthur Conan Doyle won an Edgar, the Mystery Writers of America's top honor. Five years later, in 1954, Carr and Adrian Conan Doyle, Sir Arthur's son, published *The Exploits of Sherlock Holmes*, a book of original Holmes stories.

Elected a MWA Grand Master in 1963, Carr won a 1970 Edgar for his 40-year career.

In 1977, the 70-year-old Carr died of lung cancer in his Greenville, SC, home.

Rachel Carson—See pages 42-43

Mary Cassatt

Born May 22,1844—North Side
Died June 14,1926—Chat. de Beaufresne, France

She was the first great American woman painter, an integral part—and tireless promoter of—the new wave of Impressionism.

Born Mary Stevenson Cassatt in 1844 on the North Side, she grew up in more-than-comfortable circumstances. The daughter of a successful stockbroker, before Cassatt was 10 she had already toured Europe.

Leaving home at 17, in 1861, to study at Philadelphia's Pennsylvania Academy of Fine Arts, she stayed through 1865, then moved to Paris to pursue her art. Returning to Allegheny in 1870, at the outset of the Franco-Prussian War, Cassatt longed to return to Paris, which she did the following year.

Studying on her own, and with the great Camille Pissarro, by 1872 she had her first work accepted by the highly influential Paris Salon. Despite her success, Cassatt chafed under the Salon's formalism. Seeing Edgar Degas' new pastels in a dealer's window, she allied herself with Degas, becoming one of only three women—and the sole American—to be part of the original 1879 Paris Impressionist exhibition.

Although she continued to exhibit with the Impressionists—in 1880 and again in 1881—Cassatt's style and subject matter continued to evolve. By 1886, her last as an Impressionist, Cassatt had entered upon a series of tightly drawn, closely observed, and unsparing paintings of mothers and children.

A great proponent of the new French art, she convinced her brother Alexander—along with other serious American collectors—to collect such emerging French Masters as Manet, Monet, Renoir, and of course her friend Degas.

Awarded the French Legion of Honor in 1904, by 1915 Cassatt's own deteriorating eyesight caused her to stop painting. She died at age 82, in 1926 in Chateau de Beaufresne, near Paris, and was buried in the family vault at Mesnil-Theribus, France.

Ted Cassidy

Born July 31, 1932—Pittsburgh
Died January 16, 1979—Los Angeles, CA

He's creepy and he's kooky, mysterious and spooky, he's altogether ooky: *The Addams Family*'s butler, Lurch. Born in Pittsburgh, but a high school basketball star of Phillippi, WV, Theodore Crawford Cassidy moved two hours south of Pittsburgh as a young boy. There he excelled in sports, commanding both the gridiron and court with his 6' 9" stature. He attended West Virginia Wesleyan University, but graduated from Florida's Stetson University as a Speech Major in 1953.

Transplanted to Dallas, his early career offered him the role of "Creech," a space creature, on the local "Dialing for Dollars" program on WFAA-TV. Perhaps because of this

experience, he is credited in 1960 for lending his distinctive baritone voice to the Martian warning in the classic Sidney Pink sci-fi thriller, *The Angry Red Planet*. In 1963 Cassidy auditioned for *The Addams Family* and won the role for which he was forever associated. In fact, Lurch the butler, originally created by the popular *New Yorker* magazine cartoonist Charles Addams in his first iteration of the macabre genre, was not to have any spoken lines—just groans and moans. When Cassidy was first summoned by the noose-shaped bell pull in the Addams mansion, he answered, "You rang?" The producers loved it, and later wrote more dialogue for the Frankenstein-like servant.

Cassidy appeared in 38 episodes of the sitcom's two-year run on ABC. Cassidy's hands also played The Thing. Shot in black & white, the show was cancelled in 1966, presumably because of the prohibitive costs to convert the sets to color.

Cassidy's only significant film role was that of Harvey Logan, the threatening member of Butch Cassidy's Hole in the Wall gang who is kicked in the groin early in the film. For the next 10 years, Cassidy would be seen in tough-guy roles on a dozen popular prime-time shows, like *Bonanza* or *Mannix*, and more often heard in voice-overs for animations like *Space Ghost* or the opening credits of *The Incredible Hulk*.

He co-wrote the screenplay for 1972's *Charcoal Black* as well as 1973's *The Harrad Experiment*. But, in 1979, he died after open-heart surgery. True to his famously morbid TV character, Hollywood rumor has it that his cremated ashes are still buried in the backyard of his former Woodlawn Hills residence.

Rachel Carson

Born May 27, 1907—Springdale, PA
Died April 14, 1964—Silver Spring, MD

Carson's 1929 senior photograph
from Chatham College's yearbook

Odd that a child growing up along the banks of the Allegheny River would become one of the most respected authors of the natural life of oceanic fish and fowl. But Rachel Carson, writer, scientist, and ecologist, became so much more. A shy, retiring woman of short stature, she educated the public to the horrors of pesticides and forever redefined man's responsibility to his planet.

Born the youngest of three children to Robert Warden Carson and Maria McLean, she grew up in a farmhouse as a voracious reader, and as a young writer whose first works were published when she was just 11. Although her mother taught her principally about the natural ecology of Springdale's ponds and streams, she learned her three Rs at the local schoolhouse, among just 40 students. She attended Parnassus High School (now New Kensington) and matriculated to the Pennsylvania College for Women (now Chatham University.) There she studied English and writing, but switched her major to Biology. She then studied at the Woods Hole Marine Biological Laboratory, and received her MA in zoology from Johns Hopkins University in 1932.

During the Depression, she wrote seven-minute radio infomercials for the U.S. Bureau of Fisheries while also writing stories on natural history for the *Baltimore Sun*. She would later become editor-in-chief of all publications for the U. S. Fish and Wildlife Service.

In 1952 she published her first book, *The Sea Around Us*, and in 1955, her second, *The Edge of the Sea*, both of which earned her a large following of devoted naturalists. So popular were her first works, she resigned her government job to write full time.

Carson testifies before a Senate Government Operations Subcommittee in Washington, D.C. on June 4, 1963.

Students at Chatham College protest pesticides in the environment Friday, September. 27, 2002. The walk was part of the school's program commemorating the 40th anniversary of the publication of *Silent Spring* by alumna Rachel Carson.

In 1962 she published the book that would define a new generation of eco-friendly behavior. *Silent Spring* addressed the disastrous, long term effects of pesticides on America's farms and wetlands, and thus outlined a radical departure from government policy then in support of major chemical manufacturers like Dow, Monsanto, and the Stauffer Chemical Company, which at the time, was the world's largest producer of DDT. Carson railed against indiscriminate uses of pesticides but, in fact, held that certain practices were viable if well managed. Nevertheless, she was attacked mercilessly by the chemical industry whose arguments, in light of the chemical carnage of the Vietnam War, would never hold sway.

Carson died of breast cancer after a long and silent struggle in the Spring of 1964. In 2007, the 9th Street Bridge crossing the Allegheny River downtown was renamed in her honor.

Willa Cather

Born December 7, 1873—Winchester, VA
Died April 24, 1947—New York, NY

Willa Cather's prose was so powerful, her portrayal of prairie life so compelling, that in 1930, when fellow novelist Sinclair Lewis became the first American awarded the Nobel Prize for literature, he famously said that Cather should have received it instead.

The oldest of seven children, Wilella Sibert Cather was born in 1873 on a farm outside Winchester, Virginia. As a 9-year-old, her family moved to Nebraska, to Catherton, then to Red Cloud. In 1895, after graduating from the University of Nebraska, Lincoln, Cather returned home, then moved in 1896 to Pittsburgh, to edit the *Home Monthly* and write drama reviews for the *Daily Leader.*

By 1901, Cather was teaching English at Allegheny High School and writing poetry and short stories. With her early writing based in Pittsburgh, she used such settings as Carnegie Music Hall, Schenley Park, the Schenley Hotel, and the grand homes of Fifth Avenue and Old Allegheny. Crediting Pittsburgh with initiating her writing career, Cather published *April Twilights* (poetry, 1903) and *The Troll Garden* (short stories, 1905) here.

Having established herself, in 1906 Cather moved to New York City to work for *McClure's* magazine. Becoming a full-time novelist after the 1912 publication of *Alexander's Bridge*, of the books that followed three are masterpieces: *O Pioneers!* (1913), *My Antonia* (1918), and *Death Comes for the Archbishop* (1927). *One of Ours*, her 1922 novel about World War I, won a Pulitzer Prize.

A number of Cather's novels were filmed, including *A Lost Lady* (1934) with Barbara Stanwyck, and *O Pioneers!* (1992) with Jessica Lange.

Working up until her 1947 death, 73-year-old Willa Cather died of a cerebral hemorrhage in New York City. Buried in Jaffrey, New Hampshire, in 1973 a postage stamp was issued in her honor. In 1974, Cather was inducted into the National Cowboy Museum, and in 1986 into the National Cowgirl Hall of Fame.

Michael Chabon

Born May 24, 1963—Washington, D.C.

The Washington Post's distinguished book critic Jonathan Yardley has called Michael Chabon "the young star of American letters."

Living every writer's dream, enjoying enormous critical and commercial success, Chabon leapt from graduate school to six-figure contracts. One of the nation's rare celebrity writers, receiving literary plaudits while racking up popular sales, Chabon's wildly imaginative fiction blends pulp with verbal pyrotechnics, bends genres and genders, and stands smart, sassy, and Jewish.

Born Michael Chabon in Washington in 1963, as the child of divorced parents, he spent the school year with his mother in Columbia, MD, the summers with his father in Pittsburgh. Living on his bicycle, Chabon rode everywhere, notably to Oakland and Forbes Field, locations that later turn up in his fiction.

Coming back to Pittsburgh after high school, Chabon first chose Carnegie Mellon before transferring to Pitt, where he earned a 1984 B.A. Taking a passel of Pittsburgh memories, he attended the University of California, Irvine, for an MFA in creative writing. His master's thesis: *The Mysteries of Pittsburgh*.

Without telling Chabon, his professor, Donald Heiney (the writer MacDonald Harris,) sent the manuscript to his literary agent, who promptly set off a bidding war for the story of a sexually confused Pittsburgh college student. The result was a $155,000 advance, an unprecedented figure for an unknown writer's first novel. When *The Mysteries of Pittsburgh* was published in 1988, 25-year-old Michael Chabon became an instant celebrity. (Hating his new status, Chabon turned down such offers as Gap ads and a spot as one of *People* magazine's "50 Most Beautiful People.")

Working on a second novel, Chabon also published short stories, many in *The New Yorker*. A collection, *A Model World*, appeared in 1991; *Werewolves in Their Youth* in 1999.

In 1995, seven years and one enormous dead-end draft after his first novel, Chabon published *Wonder Boys*. Also set in Pittsburgh, also praised by pundits and purchased by people, the novel chronicles the foibles of an English professor who can't finish a bloated novel. Made into a successful Curtis Hanson film in 2000, *Wonder Boys*' all-star cast included Michael Douglas, Robert Downey, Jr., Frances McDormand and Tobey Maguire—

and featured the Academy Award®-winning Bob Dylan song "Things Have Changed."

In 2000, Chabon published *The Amazing Adventures of Kavalier & Clay*, a World War II-era novel about Jewish cousins who create a 1930s comic book. A *New York Times* best-seller, it netted Chabon a Pulitzer Prize.

In 2007, Chabon's fourth novel, *The Yiddish Policeman's Union*, set in a fictional Alaskan Jewish state, brought hard-boiled detective elements to Chabon's continuing examination of American Jewish life.

Expanding his work in genre fiction, Chabon has written children's literature (*Summerland*, 2002), comic books (*The Escapist*, 2004-06), and film scripts, although his *Kavalier and Clay* is long-stalled, a draft of 2004's *Spiderman 2* was heavily rewritten, and he was replaced on *Snow and the Seven*, a martial arts Snow White.

Chabon's first nonfiction book is scheduled for 2009, another novel in 2011. He lives with his wife and four children in Berkeley, California.

Paul Chambers

Born April 22, 1935—Pittsburgh
Died January 4, 1969—New York, NY

There are certain recordings that are held in such esteem as to be considered masterpieces. Paul Chambers, who John Coltrane called "one of the greatest bass players in jazz," was fortunate enough to take part in two of jazz's greatest recordings, Miles Davis' *Kind Of Blue* and John Coltrane's *Giant Steps*. Paul Chambers was one of the most sought-after bass players of the hard bop era.

He was born Paul Laurence Dunbar Chambers, Jr. After the death of his mother, Chambers moved to Detroit, where he would begin his musical adventures on the baritone horn, then the tuba. Tiring of lugging it in parades, Chambers switched to the upright bass. His early influences included Charlie Parker and Bud Powell, considered to be founding fathers of bebop, as well as Pittsburgh's revered jazz bassist, Ray Brown. He would eventually leave Detroit for New York and by the age of 20, Chambers earned a seat in Miles Davis' first quintet. At 21 he was awarded the "New Star" award from *Downbeat* magazine.

In addition to his several recordings as a leader, Chambers played alongside some of jazz's greatest, including Sonny Rollins, Cannonball Adderly, Red Garland, Donald Byrd, Bill Evans, and Pittsburgh's Art Blakey and Stanley Turrentine.

Like many of his peers, Chambers genius and talent would be overshadowed by heroin and alcohol abuse. By the age of 33, Paul Chambers had contracted tuberculosis and died a year later.

Oscar Charleston

Born October 14, 1896—Indianapolis, IN
Died October 5, 1954—Philadelphia, PA

He was called the Black Tris Speaker, the Black Ty Cobb, and, in his own right, the Hoosier Comet, a fleet and fierce centerfielder who played Hall-of-Fame-caliber baseball with some of the century's greatest Negro League talent.

Beginning in 1915, through the 1920s and '30s, before the major leagues were integrated, up to his 1954 death, the 6-foot, 190-pound Oscar Charleston played on and/or managed no less than 14 teams, reaching his zenith with Pittsburgh's Homestead Grays (1930-31) and Pittsburgh Crawfords (1932-38).

Born in Indianapolis in 1896, the seventh of 11 children, Oscar McKinley Charleston was a batboy for the Indianapolis ABCs before enlisting in the army at 14. Mustered out at 19, he joined his hometown ball team, establishing himself as a smart, strong hitter.

Considered by many the finest all-around player in Negro League history, the barrel-chested left-hander was famous for fighting with both players and umpires. Hitting for both average and power, he stole bases with abandon and played an extremely shallow center field. In 1921, for example, Charleston batted over .400, leading the Negro National League in doubles, triples, home runs, and stolen bases.

Feared by opponents, loved by his players, the tough, demanding Charleston came to Pittsburgh in 1930, playing on and managing teams with no fewer than five future Hall of Famers. Overall, his nine-year tenure produced two Negro League championships and three All Star appearances.

A lifetime .353 hitter, "Charleston could hit the ball a mile," observed Hall of Fame pitcher Dizzy Dean, who faced Charleston in exhibition games. "When he came up, we just threw the ball and hoped he wouldn't send it out of the park."

Dying in 1954 in Philadelphia of stroke-related injuries, nine days shy of his 58th birthday, Charleston's rightful tribute came 22 years later, with his 1976 election to the Baseball Hall of Fame.

Porky Chedwick

Born February 4, 1918—Homestead, PA

When Porky Chedwick hit the airwaves on WHOD back in 1948, his goal wasn't to defy the status quo, create new radio formats, or tear down racial barriers; his goal was to play good music. In the process, he did all of the above.

He was born George Jacob Chedwick to a steelworker father and a mother who died when he was a child. One of ten children, Chedwick grew-up in the poor and racially mixed Homestead neighborhood, delivering local newspapers for which he would later become a sports stringer. He became an announcer for local sporting events. And when local radio station WHOD, operating out of the back of a candy shop, placed an ad for announcers, Chedwick jumped at the opportunity. He was given just five minutes on Saturday afternoons to deliver sports commentary but then added music to his expanding show. What spoke to his soul was the music of gospel and rhythm & blues, also known at the time as "race" music—songs by black artists that were considered dirty and too provocative by much of mainstream America. Chedwick frequently played the B side, giving otherwise forgotten songs the spin they long deserved. Local youth fell in love with the "new" sound from artists like Little Anthony and the Imperials, Bo Didley, and Big Mama Thornton.

To help little 1,000 watt WHOD compete against local giants like KDKA, the disc jockeys created unique personalities to set them apart. Chedwick became the "Daddio of the Raddio," the "Platter Pushin' Papa," "The Bossman," and "Pork, The Tork." At the height of his popularity a crowd of 10,000 kids stormed the streets outside the Stanley Theatre during one of his live shows. When it was rumored that another 50,000 were on their way, the acting mayor had to come down and end the show.

Chedwick has had many homes on the radio dial for more than 60 years. In 1992, Chedwick's contributions to American culture were recognized when he was inducted into the Rock & Roll Hall of Fame.

Danny Chew

Born August 26, 1962—Squirrel Hill

It's good to have a goal, and cyclist Danny Chew's is modest. He just wants to peddle one million miles. "I'm already at 600,000," the Squirrel Hill native said. Born in 1962, engaging in serious riding since he was 6, Chew figures to break the tape when he's in his 70s. "Stationary riding or indoor miles do not count," he added. "I admit to being a cycling addict."

Six feet tall, 175 pounds of pure gristle, Daniel Paul Chew has doggedly pursued this goal since 1968, carefully recording every mile in hand-written journals. A leg up has been RAAM—the Race Across America. Taking different routes, RAAM varies its 3,000-mile west-east route every year. An eight-time competitor, Chew never finished lower than fourth. As a two-time national winner, in 1996 and 1999, Chew's best time was a breath-taking eight days, seven hours, 14 minutes. Sleeping no more than three hours a night, he spent a literal week in the saddle. "You have to be a little crazy," Chew said.

© RENÉE ROSENSTEEL

He's logged other endurance rides, too, such as a Pittsburgh-Savannah run in four days flat. His longest day's journey into night: an 800-mile ride to an Iowa race, then 500 miles in 24 hours to cop the crown. Such rides take their toll: he's been through 15 bicycles in 30 years.

When he can't ride, Chew cross-trains, cross-country skiing and stair-climbing Pitt's Cathedral of Learning. His record: 86 trips to the top in 12 hours, a vertical loft of 38,000 feet, or 9,000 higher than Everest.

"Fitness," Chew said, "is something that money can't buy. It has to be acquired through sweat."

Lou Christie

Born February 19, 1943—Glen Willard, PA

The list of songs banned by radio stations over the years is impressive, from "God Only Knows" by The Beach Boys to "Love Me Two Times" by The Doors. One such forbidden song was the product of a young man from Glen Willard, PA. His name: Lugee Alfredo Giovanni Sacco, better known as Lou Christie.

Christie was born in Pittsburgh to Polish and Italian parents. As a child he was known to spend much of his time singing, regardless of what he was doing around the house. He was a choirboy and attended Moon Township High School where he studied classical music and took voice training. In the late 1950s and early 1960s he cut a few records with some local labels. At 15 he befriended a woman named Twyla Herbert. Described as a "psychic gypsy," Twyla was a talented musician and songwriter who also happened to be more than twice Christie's age. They began a friendship and writing collaboration that would last through much of his career. He recorded locally under a couple of different names including The Classics and Lugee and the Lions. In 1963, Christie signed with local label, Co & Ce Records, owned by Herb Cohen and Nick Cenci, and released "The Gypsy Cried." Although the song never charted, it brought him to the attention of New York-based Roulette Records who re-released it.

All along Lou had been performing under his given name, but when Roulette signed him, they changed his name to Lou Christie. He was not happy. Despite his displeasure, in January 1963, "The Gypsy Cried" climbed to number 24 on *Billboard*'s charts and sold more than a million copies. Lou Christie became a superstar.

A year later he released "Two Faces Have I" which reached number 6 and then "How Many Teardrops" which peaked at number 46. Christie's unique singing style—switching effortlessly into a shrieking falsetto—hit a popular chord with America's youth. After recent recording successes, Christie was asked to join Dick Clark's *Caravan of Stars*. His rapid rise to the top would come to an abrupt halt when he was drafted into the Army. He served a brief time at Fort Knox, Kentucky. Without skipping a beat, Christie was out of the military and signed with MGM. His first release with the new label was the mega-hit "Lightnin' Strikes." In February 1966, on his 23rd birthday, "Lightnin' Strikes" landed at the number one spot in the nation, giving him his third gold single.

Christie released his follow-up single to much fanfare when some radio stations refused to play it because of its suggestive lyrics. The implications of something sexual happening in the backseat of a car to the rhythm of windshield wipers, and the furor surrounding it, caused "Rhapsody In The Rain" to be a another million selling success. In 1969, Christie scored his next and last top 10 hit in the U.S. with "I'm Gonna Make You Mine." As the times changed musically, Christie's style of music fell out of favor and he withdrew from music, fleeing personal demons, relocating to London.

One of Christie's childhood influences was Esther "Abbie" Neal, fiddler and country music entertainer, who performed throughout the Pittsburgh area, getting air time on KQV and WAMO. Their 20-year friendship may have been the inspiration behind Lou's comeback release, the critically acclaimed 1974 country-western release *Beyond The Blue Horizon*. One of the songs from that effort made its way into the 1988 film *Rainman*. The years following were spent on the Oldies circuit, with Christie touring continuously. And then in 1997 he released his first new material in more than twenty years called *Pledging My Love*.

Over his long and successful career, Lou Christie has shared the stage with some of the greatest performers in the business, from Diana Ross and the Supremes to The Rolling Stones. One of the first artists to write and perform his own material, he is said to have been a pivotol influence on John Lennon.

© PHOTO BY MICHAEL OCHS ARCHIVES/GETTY IMAGES

Samuel Harden Church

Born in 1858—Pittsburgh
Died in 1943—Pittsburgh

Like Oliver Cromwell, his hero and biographical subject, Samuel Harden Church was tough, tireless, a leader of men. And where the Lord Protector famously oversaw the trial and execution of a head of state, Church would have done the same—if only he'd been able to get his hands on the guy.

Born in 1858, Church worked his way up from Pennsylvania Railroad messenger boy to vice president. Taken with contemporary self-help thought, in 1881 he published *Horatio Plodgers, A Story of To-Day*.

Amassing a significant Cromwell library—some 75 volumes—Church added to the literature with *Oliver Cromwell, A History*, four editions, 1895-98.

Moving to historical romance, Church wrote *John Marmaduke: A Romance of the English Invasion of Ireland in 1649*, 1897, *Penruddock of the White Lambs: A Tale of Holland, England, and America*, 1902, and *Flames of Faith*, 1924, as well as a translation of *Beowulf*, 1901.

A Republican Party activist and Pennsylvania delegate to the 1904 convention, Church was a tireless pamphleteer, campaigning for American entry into World War I, against Prohibition, for and then against the New Deal. An ecumenicist, Church wrote a foreword to a collection of rabbinic sermons, and a 1903 pamphlet decrying Russian persecution of Jews. In honor of the city's 150th anniversary, Church published *A Short History of Pittsburgh* (1758-1908).

Tapped by Andrew Carnegie to become secretary of his Institute in 1909, Church became the longest-serving Board president, 1914-43, using his position to publish. In 1927, for example, he initiated the Institute's *Carnegie* magazine, which still exists today.

His most infamous moment came in 1940, when the octogenarian offered a $1 million reward for delivery of Adolf Hitler to the League of Nations.

Predeceasing Der Fuhrer by two years, in 1943, 85-year-old Samuel Harden Church suffered a massive heart attack at his desk, dying shortly thereafter in Shadyside Hospital.

Sonny Clark

Born July 21, 1931—Herminie, PA
Died January 13, 1963—New York, NY

A bebop jazz pianist whose career lasted less than a decade, Sonny Clark's immense talent has been elevated to a cult-like status among jazz aficionados worldwide. Like so many brilliant artists before him, Clark's struggles with heroin and alcohol cut short a life that was destined for greatness.

Born in the small Westmoreland County town of Herminie, Conrad Yeatis "Sonny" Clark was hitting the ivory at the age of 4. His family moved to Pittsburgh in the early 1940s and Clark, then 12, became active in his school band, on piano, vibes and standup bass. Musically his influences were jazz masters like Fats Waller, Art Tatum, Thelonious Monk, and Pittsburgh native Erroll Garner. When Clark turned 20, he and an older brother hit the West Coast. There, Clark befriended Wardell Gray, a tenor saxophonist (who coincidentally also died at a young age,)and the two headed for San Francisco to team-up with clarinetist Buddy DeFranco. Intending to stay only a brief time, Clark stayed five years. His last gig out West was in L.A. with the Lighthouse All-Stars, with whom he would tour the U.S. and Europe.

Longing to see his family in Pittsburgh and Dayton, OH, Clark joined Dinah Washington as an accompanist and headed back East, settling in New York. Considered a master composer, arranger and brilliant pianist, Clark was one of the most in-demand sidemen in jazz, playing on numerous Blue Note sessions with heavyweights such as John Coltrane, Sonny Rollins, Dexter Gordon, and Pittsburgh natives Stanley Turrentine and Paul Chambers. Clark led on several classic recordings including "Cool Struttin'," "Sonny's Crib" and, his final cut as a leader, "Leapin' and Lopin'," which featured Stanley's brother Tommy on trumpet.

Never able to kick his addictions, Clark died when he was just 31.

Caitlin Clarke

Born May 3, 1952—Sewickley, PA
Died September 9, 2004—Sewickley, PA

Not until she was 16, then attending Sewickley Academy, did Caitlin Clarke take to the stage. She played Marian the Librarian in *The Music Man* at the Edgewood Club. And then, not again until her sophomore year at Mt. Holyoke College did she join in a musical revue. A dabbler in the dramatic arts, she played two summers of stock in Vermont and then returned to her hometown. Here she took a job as house manager for the new Pittsburgh Public Theater, the city's first resident theater since the Playhouse had closed a decade and a half earlier.

Founded by Margaret Rieck and Joan Apt, the theater was first housed in the Hazlett Theater in Allegheny Center on the North Side. The seats were constructed of canvas stretched across scaffolding. If one heavy patron sat down hard in his seat, another five were sprung skyward like a trampoline. Fortunately, for both Clarke and the season's subscribers, so riveting were Virginia Mayo in *The Glass Menagerie*, Leonard Nimoy as Malvolio in *Twelfth Night*, or Tom Atkins' Randle P. McMurphy in *One Flew Over the Cuckoo's Nest*, there was little reason to leave one's seat.

For Clarke, the theater proved to be something more than just magical. In between dealing with the seats, scrubbing toilets, or cleaning the aisles, she got to play a small walk-on in *Cuckoo's Nest*.

Soon, she enrolled at Yale's School of Drama. Within two years of receiving her MFA, (and after a brief stint as an understudy in Joe Papp's Shakespeare in the Park,) Clarke landed the role of her brief lifetime, *Dragonslayer*, playing Valerian, a woman disguised as a boy. She starred opposite Sir Ralph Richardson and Peter MacNicol. The film was a huge success, and enjoys cult status today.

Although she appeared in two more films, including a scene as a hooker in *Crocodile*

Assistant manager, Clarke, (left), and Bill McKechnie, General Manager of the Pittsburgh Pirates, in 1926

Dundee, she regularly performed at the Goodman Theatre in Chicago, and then took turns on Broadway and in London. She played guest spots on TV shows like *Law & Order*, *Matlock*, and *Moonlighting*. Her last Broadway role was in *Titanic*.

Often returning to Pittsburgh to visit her family—her father, Charles is a physician, and mother, Cecelia, a nurse, (and one of her four sisters, Torie, was spokeswoman for the Pentagon until 2003,)—she taught acting at Ken Gargaro's Pittsburgh Musical Theatre. At 52, losing a four-year battle, she died of cervical cancer.

Fred Clarke

Born October 3, 1872—Winterset, IA
Died August 14, 1960—Winfield, KS

The very model of the modern player-manager, Fred Clarke's turn-of-the-20th-century Pirates won four National League pennants (1901-03) and the team's first World Series (1909), Clarke himself setting the pace in the Fall Classic by hitting both Pittsburgh home runs, leading both teams in home runs and RBIs.

Born on a farm in Iowa in 1872, at age two Fred Clifford Clarke's family joined a covered wagon caravan to Kansas. A talented ballplayer, Clarke played in Des Moines and Hastings, NE, quickly moving to Southern League teams in Montgomery and Savannah. Scouted by Louisville owner Barney Dreyfuss, the power-hitting leftfielder joined the Colonels in 1894 before his 22nd birthday. Quickly emerging as a team leader, Clarke was tapped to be player-manager in 1897 when he was only 24. To celebrate, he hit a career high of .390.

Dubbed the Boy Manager, Clarke played for the Colonels from 1894 to 1899, coming to Pittsburgh when the clubs merged in 1900. Playing 11 summers (with just 12 games in 1913-15), in his last season, at age 38, he hit

.324. In 18 campaigns, Clarke hit over .300 11 times, finishing with a robust 2,672 hits and a .315 batting average.

Even more impressive were his 1,602 managerial wins, his clubs finishing in the first division 14 times. In Pittsburgh, Clarke's 1,422 Pirate wins and .595 winning percentage are both high-water marks for any Buc skipper. In addition, his 110 wins in 1909 is an all-time club record, and his 1902 record of 36 losses has never been bested in the Major Leagues.

After 1915, when Clarke retired as manager, he stayed with the Pirates as a coach and in various front-office positions.

Elected to Hall of Fame in 1945, Clarke spent his last years on Little Pirate Ranch, his Winfield, KS, home, where he died at age 87, in 1960.

Kenny Clarke

Born January 9, 1914—Pittsburgh
Died January 26, 1985—Paris, France

Kenny Clarke may not be a household name, but for those who really love jazz, Clarke was more than just a great drummer; he just may be the father of bebop drumming.

Clarke changed the direction of jazz drumming by moving the responsibility for beat-carrying duties from the bass drum to the ride cymbal, freeing up the snare and the bass for punctuation. This rhythmic experimentation is credited for helping to give birth to what is known as modern jazz.

Born at Mercy Hospital, Kenneth Clarke Spearman was quickly exposed to dissident worlds, one of joyful music and the other of lonesome abandonment. As a child growing up on Wylie Avenue in the Hill District, Clarke's mom would teach him songs on the piano. Clarke's father abandoned the family while he was still a young boy and shortly thereafter his mother died.

He and his brother were placed in the Coleman Industrial Home For Colored Boys, an orphanage located downtown that eventually closed in 1947. It was there that a teacher recognized Clarke's musical talents. Clarke worked his way through several instruments and eventually landed on the snare drum as well as a role in the home's marching band. In and out of institutions and foster homes throughout the remainder of his childhood, at 16 he set out on his own to pursue his passion for jazz.

One of his earliest steady gigs was with a local group called the Leroy Bradley Band at a club called Derby Dan's. They played the Pittsburgh nightclub circuit as well as those in West Virginia and Ohio, where he began getting noticed by some of jazz's luminaries, including Pittsburgh's own Roy Eldridge, with whom he played for a time.

Clarke left for New York and was soon playing the famed Harlem club, Minton's. It is during this time that Clarke broke the mold of previous drummers by moving the time keeping away from the bass to the cymbal. With fellow musicians Thelonious Monk, Bud Powell, Charlie Christian, Dizzy Gillespie and others, Clarke soon became a critical component in the legendary improvisational jam sessions that would define bop.

Tiring of a musician's hectic life in New York, Clarke relocated to a town outside of Paris where he remained the rest of his career.

The Clarks

With an impressive array of alumni that includes an astronaut, numerous CEOs, and a Playboy playmate, Indiana University of Pennsylvania is also the proud alma mater of one of the most popular bands to ever play the Pittsburgh circuit, The Clarks.

Scott Blasey, Robert James, Greg Joseph and Dave Minarik all met while undergrads at IUP. Several of the members, all with ambitions of starting a rock band, met and formed a band called The Administration. They

(CONTINUED PAGE 52)

Roberto Clemente

Born August 18, 1934—Carolina, Puerto Rico
Died December 31, 1972—Off the coast of Puerto Rico

It was his showcase, and he was going to show the world something it had never before seen: Roberto Clemente

In the 1971 World Series against the Baltimore Orioles, the 37-year-old rightfielder demonstrated just how baseball should be played, fielding superbly, unleashing his rifle arm, hitting .414 with two doubles, a triple, and two home runs. Clemente played "something close to the level of absolute perfection," *The New Yorker*'s Roger Angell wrote, "as if it were a form of punishment for everyone else on the field."

Born Roberto Walker Clemente, in Carolina, Puerto Rico, in 1934, he played at 5'-11" and a muscular 175 pounds. A teenaged star for the Santurce Crabbers, he hit .356 in 1953, when the Brooklyn Dodgers signed him to a minor-league contract. Playing in Montreal in 1954, he attracted the Pirates' attention, who took him in a draft. In 1955, 20-year-old Roberto Clemente came to Pittsburgh for good.

From 1955 to 1972, if ever a player could be called the franchise, Roberto Clemente was it. Hitting .317 over 18 seasons, including 13 .300-plus years, he collected 3,000 hits, 12 Gold Gloves (a record for outfielders), four batting titles (1961, 1964-65, 1967), and one Most Valuable Player Award (1966).

Playing in both the 1960 and 1971 World Series, in the latter Clemente's performance won him the Series MVP. When presented with the trophy, Clemente had but two things to say. "I want everybody in the world to know," he said, "this is the way I play all the time. All season, every season." And in Spanish, he asked for his father's blessing. It was the sort of performance that made his teammates respect Clemente, and his army of fans—in Pittsburgh and across Latin America—adore him.

Fourteen months later, on December 31, 1972, Clemente was loading an airplane to take relief supplies to earthquake-torn Nicaragua. Hearing that other supplies were being stolen, he proclaimed that no one would steal from Roberto Clemente, and, against warnings that the old DC-7 was overloaded, he went aloft. Packed with five men and 16,000 pounds of supplies, the airplane pitched into the sea. It was never found.

The next summer, 1973, with the standard five-year waiting period waived, Clemente became the first Latin American player inducted into baseball's Hall of Fame. In addition, Major League Baseball renamed its annual

July 24, 1971, before pregame ceremonies at Three Rivers Stadium honoring the rightfielder, Clemente with his wife Vera and sons Roberto, Jr., and Luis, standing. On the left are his parents. Clemente bounces son Enrique on his knee.

humanitarian award for Clemente, recognizing his extensive charitable work, notably his efforts to build a sports-oriented youth city in Puerto Rico.

Accolades have continued. Numerous American and Puerto Rican streets, parks, and baseball stadiums have been named in his memory. In 1984, his likeness appeared on a United States postage stamp. In Pittsburgh, in 1994 his statue was unveiled at Three Rivers Stadium during the All Star Game festivities. (It now stands outside PNC Park.) The former Sixth Street Bridge, crossing the Allegheny River next to PNC Park, was renamed for him. Finally, the Allegheny River park running along the river's North Shore was re-named the Roberto Clemente Memorial Park in his honor.

Clemente receiving one of hundreds of awards, photographed by Teenie Harris, c. mid-1960s The two other men are unknown.

played local school parties as a cover band, covering many of the bands popular in the '80s. Thus began the slow but steady rolling snowball of a rock 'n roll band: dances, frat parties, club gigs, more frat parties, writing a few original songs, more clubs, and more original songs,all building favor with a growing legion of fans.

The Clarks went into the studio in 1988 and cut their first self-produced release entitled *I'll Tell You What Man* which launched the local hit "Help Me Out." Soon the band's momentum was making things really happen. They started their own publishing company—and label—called King Mouse Music. Their next release entitled *The Clarks* was another local hit and produced one of the band's moniker songs "Penny On The Floor." The Clarks added one more release under their belt when the big time came calling via MCA.

They say what glitters isn't always gold, and like a script for so many other great bands just beginning to take off, the support didn't materialize; the band was dropped from the label. They regrouped, recommitted and set off to reenergize their fans with a live album recorded in 1998 at Nick's Fat City.

The band's cache and fan base continued to rise locally with each new release. Nationally people were treated to The Clarks' tunes featured on *The Anna Nicole Show*, the Warner Bros. film *Summer Catch* and ESPN's *Cold Pizza*. Among The Clarks' more prominent appearances was in 2004 on *The Late Show With David Letterman*.

In 2006, The Clarks celebrated 20 years together. They're still favorites in Pittsburgh and Indiana, PA, and they've attracted legions of fans in cities as far as Milwaukee, Baltimore, and Chicago. The Clarks have also given back to their alma mater. In 2004 all four members received the IUP Distinguished Alumni Award.

Neil Cohen

Born January 15, 1943—Morningside
Died December 9, 2005—Aspinwall

All he and his wife Susan wanted was a way back home.

Peabody grad Neil Cohen had gone to Kent State, then in 1966 earned a master's in phys ed. at Western Michigan. After teaching for a year in greater Detroit, coaching track, cross-country, and wrestling, he was ready to come back to Pittsburgh.

It was 1967, and there was a new one-year-old junior college, the Community College of Allegheny County, housed in a few Ridge Avenue mansions on the North Side. Then, the students were using the Carrick High gym—and not doing well. Looking for a part-time gig, 24-year-old Cohen came for an interview. Fiery, energetic, the young man impressed the hiring committee. Well, they said, seeing how we're a tad short-handed, and you are very available, if we hire you...

My goal, he said, would be nothing short of building CCAC into a regional junior college athletic power. As it turned out, his accomplishments far outstripped his bold thinking. That's how Neil I. Cohen, born in 1943 in Morningside, became CCAC's athletic director, a job he held for the next 26 years, taking various CCAC teams to national junior college championships.

Building his teams from scratch, he transformed tiny CCAC into a regional power—and a national cross country powerhouse. With his team going an unapproachable 110-0-1, it claimed national junior college championships in 1973 and 1976-77. In all, CCAC teams won more than 60 championships during Cohen's 26-year tenure.

Inducted into the National Junior College Athletic Association Hall of Fame in 1990, Cohen also served on the track, field, and cross country coaches' advisory board for the Nike shoe company.

An accomplished photographer, Neil Cohen retired in 1993. He died in Pittsburgh in 2005.

Henry Steele Commager

Born October 25, 1902—Pittsburgh
Died March 2, 1998—Amherst, MA

Arguably America's most prolific historian, Henry Steele Commager's credo is best summed up by his own thoughts on education. "What every college must do," he said, "is hold up before the young the spectacle of greatness."

It was that spectacle of greatness that Commager ardently pursued, writing, co-writing, or editing some 40 books and more than 700 essays, articles, and reviews.

Born in 1902 in Pittsburgh, earning a University of Chicago Ph.D. by age 28, Commager was an expert on American history, politics, and Constitutional thought.

Teaching at New York University, Columbia, and Amherst (where he retired at age 89), Commager wrote a number of standard historical texts—any one of which could be considered a lifetime's work. In 1930, just 28 years old, Commager co-authored *The Growth of the American Republic* with Samuel Eliot Morison; in a half-century the book went through seven editions. Similarly, Commager's anthology *Documents of American History* ran to 10 editions.

Commager also wrote significant texts on the Civil War (*The Blue and the Gray*), the American Revolution (*The Spirit of Seventy-Six*), Woodrow Wilson and the Progressive Era, Franklin D. Roosevelt and the New Deal, and others.

Perhaps his most influential books were his 1950 *The American Mind: An Interpretation of American Character and Thought since the 1880s* and his 1977 *The Empire of Reason: How Europe Imagined and America Realized the Enlightenment*, both offering a piercing analysis of American intellectual history.

Never merely an ivory tower intellectual, Commager was a great popularizer of history, writing essays for such general-interest magazines as *Saturday Review*, *Atlantic*, *The New Republic*, *Harper's*—even *Senior Scholastic*, a high-school publication. Often appearing on public-affairs documentaries, he lent historical perspective to such events as the Apollo XI moon landing and Watergate.

In 1998, 95-year-old Henry Steele Commager died of pneumonia in his Amherst, Massachusetts, home.

Perry Como

Born May 18, 1912—Canonsburg, PA
Died May 12, 2001—Jupiter Inlet Colony, FL

Perry Como was a handsome, clean-cut, well-groomed crooner who had a reputation for being so mellow and laid back that his good friend Dean Martin commented once that he used to go see Perry to borrow a cup of sleep.

Born Pierino Ronald Como, he sang his way out of his humble coal mining town into the radios and televisions and hearts of fans the world over. Born into a family of 12 children, the son of a mill hand, Como got his start making money by sweeping the floors of the local barbershop when he was just 12 years old. Within a few years he was running the shop, snipping and shaving, and making more money than he ever had. What made the trip to the barber special for his customers was that Como would serenade and entertain them with his beautiful baritone voice. On the weekends Como would also perform at wedding receptions and local clubs, like the Sons of Italy.

In 1933, the same year that he married his childhood sweetheart, Roselle Belline, Como decided, while visiting Cleveland with friends, to audition for the Freddie Carlone Dance Band. To his surprise he was offered

Below, Como, boarding an Eastern Airlines flight to Palm Springs, 1961, with his wife Roselle and son Ronald

© ASSOCIATED PRESS

© BETTMANN/CORBIS

the job. (He almost turned it down because it wasn't as much money as he was making cutting hair). He worked with Carlone for the next five years until getting noticed by another band leader, Ted Weems, from Pitcairn, PA. Como toured with Weems for the next six years, skyrocketing his popularity and his reputation. Weems disbanded the group to serve in World War II. But before Como had a chance to sharpen his razor, RCA signed him to a recording contract and NBC offered him a spot on a radio show called the *Chesterfield Supper Club*.

The show made the transition to television in the late '40s and Como's visibility and star power continued to rise, making him one of the three hottest singing stars in the country alongside Frank Sinatra and his idol Bing Crosby. His signature cardigan sweater and low-keyed demeanor earned him the nicknames "Mr. Nice Guy" and "Mr. Class." Bing Crosby once called Perry Como "The man who invented casual."

Como enjoyed enormous popularity throughout the '40s and '50s, racking-up 42 Top 10 hits, starring in several feature films, hosting his own variety show, *The Perry Como Show,* and starting a Christmas tradition with his annual *Como Christmas Special* on ABC. It aired every year until 1987. "Hot Diggity," "Papa Loves Mambo," "Dream Along With Me" and countless other songs entertained scores of fans over the years. One in particular, "Catch A Falling Star," even won him a Grammy®. All told, this unassuming barber from Canonsburg sold more than 100 million records in his career.

Billy Conn

Born October 8, 1917—Pittsburgh
Died May 29, 1993—Pittsburgh

It was the Pittsburgh Kid versus the Brown Bomber.

On a steamy June night, 1941, in Manhattan's Polo Grounds, boxer Billy Conn came to take the heavyweight title from Joe Louis.

This was tough, feisty Billy Conn, who had battled his way up from high-school dropout to light heavyweight champion, then did something no one had ever done—resigned his two-year title just for a shot at Louis. Bigger, stronger, harder-hitting, Louis came into the ring outweighing underdog Conn by 30 pounds, 199 to 169.

But for 12 rounds Conn bested the champ. In a fight many consider the greatest of the century, Conn used his famous left, his jabs and hooks, keeping away from Louis' devastating right—the one that made him champ for a dozen years.

For 12 rounds, Billy Conn was the best boxer in the world.

But it was a 15-round fight, and virtually every one of the 54,487 in the house wanted Sweet William to hang on for three more rounds. Just nine minutes. The champ was tired, weary—everyone could see that. Everyone who had come to see East Liberty's Billy Conn, the Flower of the Monongahela, apply lessons in the sweet science.

But Conn wouldn't let himself take the title on points. Back home, his mother was dying of cancer, and Conn had promised her a knock out. So in the 13th round he went for the killer blow. A step here, a feint there, and Louis saw his opening. A paralyzing right to the jaw left Conn dazed. Then another, and a third. Counted out at 2:58, Conn was two seconds shy of the bell, six minutes away from the heavyweight crown.

Louis retained his title—and Conn went to Hollywood to star in *The Pittsburgh Kid*.

Born William David Conn, Jr., the oldest of five children to a Westinghouse mill hand, Conn left school to box for Depression prize money. Never an amateur, the 17-year-old,

142-pound welterweight made his professional debut in Fairmont, WV, in January of 1935. Conn's loser's share: $2.50.

But he learned fast, and the next year, 1936, Conn won every one of his 23 fights. By the time he was 21, Conn commanded matches with top opponents. By 1939 he was world light heavyweight champion.

Then came Joe Louis.

A 1942 rematch had been scheduled, but Conn broke his hand taking a swing at his father-in-law, former ball player "Greenfield" Jimmy Smith. By the time Billy healed, he was performing army goodwill tours.

The rematch came, but not until 1946, and Louis simply creamed the Kid. At Yankee Stadium Louis knocked out Conn, this time in the 8th round.

His record: winning 63 of 76 fights, 1935-48, including 14 knockouts, gave Conn a berth in the Boxing Hall of Fame.

After boxing, Conn retired, living with his wife and four children in the Squirrel Hill home bought after the first Louis fight. In 1993, pneumonia KO'd the 75-year-old Pittsburgh Kid. He is buried in Calvary Cemetery.

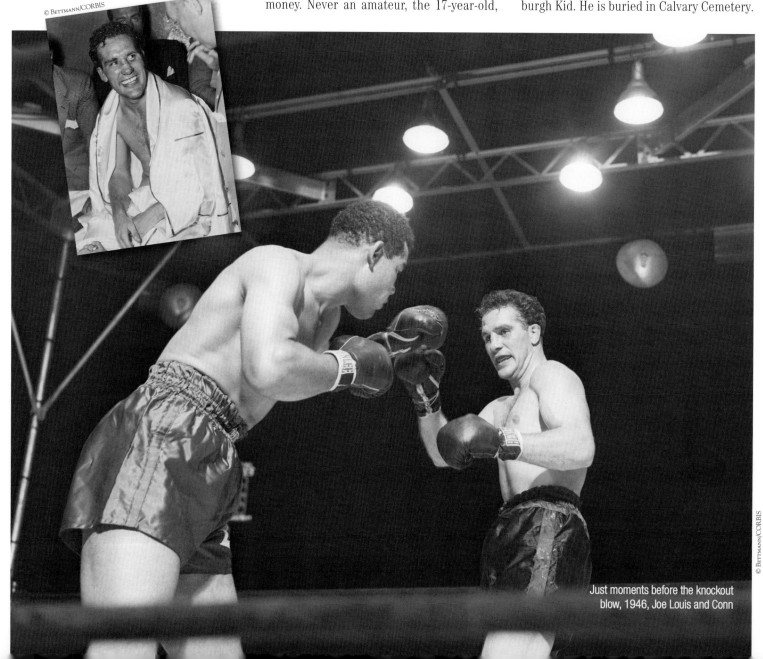

© BETTMANN/CORBIS

Just moments before the knockout blow, 1946, Joe Louis and Conn

1968, Connelly celebrates with Margalo Gillmore and Peggy Wood, early diners at the Algonquin Round Table.

Marc Connelly

Born December 13, 1890—McKeesport
Dies December 21, 1980—New York, NY

It's an irony that the man himself assuredly enjoyed: it took a white writer from McKeesport to put the first all-African-American cast on Broadway. Certainly, Marc Connelly enjoyed even more his *Green Pastures* winning him the 1930 Pulitzer Prize.

Born Marcus Cook Connelly, legend has it that by age five he was writing plays. What is certain is that Connelly's first published works appeared in the *Pittsburgh Sun*, where he worked as a reporter and columnist.

By 1915, 25-year-old Connelly had moved to New York City, where he was writing lyrics and stories for Broadway. By 1920, he was collaborating with fellow Pittsburgher George S. Kaufman on many successful Broadway comedies, including *Beggar on Horseback* (1924).

In 1930, Connelly adapted Roark Bradford's *Ol' Man Adam an' His Chillun*. Calling it *Green Pastures*, the play presented biblical scenes from an African-American child's point of view. An enduring hit, *Green Pastures* was revived twice on Broadway, in 1935 and 1951. In addition, Connelly adapted the play for the screen in 1936; for radio in 1940 and 1941; and for live television in 1957 and 1959.

Prolific and in demand, Connelly produced, directed, and wrote Broadway shows, also writing or adapting nearly three dozen films from 1920 to 1957, getting his sole Academy Award nomination for his adaptation of Rudyard Kipling's *Captains Courageous*. (The film won Spencer Tracy a best actor Oscar®). As an actor, Connelly enjoyed some two dozen film and television parts, *Tall Story* to *The Defenders* to George Bernard Shaw's *Don Juan in Hell.*

Contributing to *Life* and other magazines, Connelly was a member of the famous Algonquin Round Table, an informal group including George S. Kaufman, Dorothy Parker, Robert Benchley, Heywood Broun, and Harold Ross, that traded lunchtime barbs and bon mots at New York's Algonquin Hotel.

Charles Connick

Born September 27, 1875—Springboro, PA
Died December 28, 1945—Boston. MA

"Beauty can preach as very few men with bundles of words can preach," stained-glass artist Charles Connick wrote. "I want to make beautiful interiors for both churches and souls. I want people to hear my windows singing."

Sing they certainly do. Born Charles Jay Connick in 1875 in Springboro, Crawford County, America's greatest neo-medievalist trained and worked in Pittsburgh, and New York, before relocating to Boston in 1902. Working for other glass craftsmen, in 1910 Connick traveled to see the windows of the great French Chartres Cathedral. It changed his life.

Returning to Boston, within a year, 1912, Connick had set up his own studio at 9 Harcourt Street, Back Bay, where it remained past his 1945 death until 1986, when it finally closed—some 6,000 commissions later.

In the forefront of the movement that rediscovered 13th-century European stained glass, Connick's design skills, color choice, and architectural understanding established neo-Gothic as de rigeur American stained glass in the first half of the 20th Century.

Set in churches, hospitals, universities, and libraries, Washington to San Francisco, Boston to Chicago, Paris and beyond, Connick and his craftsmen employed clearly delineated places and character to tell their inspirational stories.

In Pittsburgh, Connick's masterpiece is Pitt's Heinz Chapel. With the chapel's 23 windows to-

1931 self-portrait by Connick

taling roughly 4,000 square feet, they contain nearly 250,000 individual pieces of glass. Employing 391 identifiable figures, plus a large, anonymous supporting cast, and an extensive variety of flora and fauna, Connick's iconography combines traditional religious figures with historic and cultural figures, the Bible through the 19th Century, Jesus and St. Francis through Beethoven and Chaucer.

Although Connick himself died in 1945, at age 70, for 41 succeeding years his studio remained open, his successors continuing to design windows in his style. By 1986, with an aging workforce, and the light irrevocably changed by Boston's ubiquitous highrises, Connick's workshop closed.

David Conrad

Born August 17, 1967—Edgewood, PA

Born the youngest of three sons to James and Margaret Conrad, an engineer and librarian, respectively, in Edgewood, where he attended school in Swissvale, then Woodland Hills High School and The Kiski School, David Conrad has made a name for himself, at a relatively young age, as a featured actor. He prides himself on his Pittsburgh roots and returns frequently for fundraisers and to perform at the Pittsburgh Public and Pittsburgh Irish & Classical Theatres.

Currently, he is best known for his recurring role as Jim Clancy on CBS's *Ghost Whisperer*, playing the supportive husband to Jennifer Love Hewitt whose character is supernaturally endowed with the ability to talk to the dead. His past TV roles have included starring in *Relativity* as Leo Roth and in the ill-fated *Miss Match*.

A graduate of Brown University and Julliard, Conrad has a very respectable resume of stage roles both on Broadway and in regional theatre. While performing in *Henry IV* at PICT, he broke his hand on stage. He has appeared playing opposite Blythe Danner and Edward Herrmann in Terence Rattigan's *The Deep Blue Sea*, and more recently performed in Tom Stoppard's *India Ink* in San Francisco, having played in Stoppard's *Arcadia* at the Pittsburgh Public. In 2007, he starred as *Henry V* at the New Jersey Shakespeare Festival.

Other television appearances include recurring roles on *Boston Public* and *Roswell High*. His film credits include *Men of Honor*, *The Weekend, Return to Paradise, Anything Else,* and *Navy Diver*.

For *Ghost Whisperer*, he auditioned for producer Kim Moses, a Donora native who was formerly married to Joe Montana.

With family roots dating back to 1840 in Pittsburgh, Conrad is the great-great grandson of radio pioneer Frank Conrad.

Frank Conrad

Born May 4, 1874—Pittsburgh
Died December 10, 1941—Miami

The highest academic degree he earned was graduating from his Seventh Grade class at Sterrett Grammar School in Point Breeze. His father, a railroad mechanic, believed that the best learning was hands-on. And, so, Frank Conrad, well trained in the use of tools, earned his first job as a bench hand at the original Westinghouse facility on Garrison Alley in the Strip District. He was just 16.

By the time he turned 23, Conrad had invented the glass-domed watt/hour meter, familiar to every homeowner who has ever read his own electric meter. Bright and curious, with full responsibility for the testing laboratory, Conrad also found time to pursue his personal interest in wireless telegraphy—or radio. (Nikola Tesla, then under contract to Westinghouse, had only recently received the U.S. patent). At the time, radio transmissions were exclusively used to send and receive Morse Code. Conrad would monitor Navy time signals, and by 1916 he received a license to operate as station 8XK

In 1918, Conrad enlisted in the war effort and created a new, wind-generated radio transmitter for aircraft. (He also invented a hand grenade). After the war, he continued his career with Westinghouse eventually amassing some 200 patents. But at night, and on weekends, he tinkered with his transmitter, adding vacuum tubes, and, for the amusement of his two musically inclined sons, Francis and Crawford, played phonograph records over the air. When he had played his collection, he accepted the offer of the Hamil-

ton Music Store in Wilkinsburg to play their records in exchange for promoting the store. The year, 1919—when only 400 people in Pittsburgh owned a radio receiver—marked the first commercial use of radio.

From his garage at Penn and Peebles Streets in Wilkinsburg, Conrad would play two hours of recorded music every Wednesday and Saturday night. When Joseph Horne's Department Store started advertising radios on which could be heard the "Conrad programs," his supervisor at Westinghouse, Dr. Harry P. Davis, determined that commercial radio was worth the company's investment. KDKA radio was soon launched in East Pittsburgh. On November 2, 1920, KDKA radio's first broadcast was the presidential election returns of Warren G. Harding.

Ironically, Conrad was not present, preferring "to standby" in his garage in case the broadcast equipment failed. Just as interesting perhaps, Westinghouse's interest in owning a station was not for the purpose of generating advertising revenues, but for selling radios, of which millions were sold within the next several years.

While vacationing in Florida, Conrad died from a heart attack just days after the bombing of Pearl Harbor.

Conrad's Wilkinsburg garage where he broadcast phonograph records and first plugged the record shop from whence they came.

K.C. Constantine

Born in 1934—McKees Rocks, PA

Creator of mysteries set in the Rust Belt town of Rocksburg, an amalgam of McKees Rocks, Greensburg, and Johnstown, K.C. Constantine's artistic credo is "I just type and revise it until it looks and sounds like it won't make me embarrassed to have my pen name on it."

Born Carl Constantine Kosak, he adopted a pseudonym to maintain what he believes is an acceptable level of privacy. Eschewing the cult of literary personality, Constantine never permits himself to be photographed, rarely allows interviews, and prefers to do his book signings in store rooms.

Having served in the Marines, taught English at Greensburg's Seton Hill University, and worked at the Greensburg *Tribune-Review*, Constantine was raised in Depression-era McKees Rocks. Adapting his home town's up-from-under attitude, he's published 17 novels over 31 years, *The Rocksburg Railroad Murders* (1972) through *Saving Room for Dessert* (2002). "I was born at the height of the Great Depression in an industrial town that nearly dried up and blew away as a result of it," Constantine has said, "and I'll never shake that experience."

With a down-at-the-heels cast of cops—rotund, wine-drinking police chief Mario Balzic; detective Ruggiero "Rugs" Carlucci; and beat cops William Rayford, Robert Canoza, and James Reseta—the novels concern less classic procedures and puzzles than people's passions and problems in a fading Western Pennsylvania town. "I think I'm trying to write books without plot because I'm thinking characters first, last, always," Constantine has said.

Prized by readers and reviewers, as the *Boston Globe* has said, "we read the Balzic novels for K.C. Constantine's ear, for the way people give themselves away when they talk, for his insider's knowledge of the way small towns work, for his understanding of people, his joy in the human comedy, and his compassion."

K.C. Constantine lives in Greensburg and writes full time.

Bob Cooper

Born December 6, 1925—Pittsburgh
Died August 5, 1993—Los Angeles, CA

Big band jazz leader Stan Kenton was one of the hottest musical acts during the 1940s and '50s. The band toured extensively and during one of their stops in Pittsburgh, Kenton's tenor sax player fell ill. A member of the band was friends with local musician Bob "Coop" Cooper, who was just 19 years old. The friend asked him to sit in for the engagement and Cooper remained with Stan Kenton for the next half dozen years, paving his way to becoming one of the leading figures of the West Coast "Cool Jazz" scene.

June Christy was the popular vocalist for Stan Kenton after the departure of Anita O'Day. Cooper and Christy met when he joined with the band on their stop in Pittsburgh. The two hit it off and soon got married. Cooper and Christie married in Washington, D.C. on January 14, 1947, and remained together until Christy's death in 1990. After leaving Kenton's band, Cooper settled in Los Angeles and became a key figure in the Lighthouse All-Stars, which included such notables as Maynard Ferguson, Shorty Rogers, and Bud Shank.

In addition to his signature tenor sax work, Cooper was known to solo with the oboe and English horn. After his stint with the All-Stars, Cooper began to take more work as a studio musician, in addition to arranging and composing works for film and television.

Coop was a respected sideman, arranger, composer, author, leader, and a considerable force on the West Coast jazz scene until his death in 1993.

Chuck Cooper

Born September 29, 1926—Pittsburgh
Died February 5, 1984—Pittsburgh

"Walter," an NBA owner objected on draft day, April 25, 1950, "don't you know he's a colored boy?"

"I don't care if he's striped or plaid or polka dot," Celtics owner Walter Brown snapped. "Boston takes Charles Cooper of Duquesne."

Which is how Pittsburgh's Chuck Cooper became the first African-American drafted by the National Basketball Association.

Charles Harrison Cooper was an all-city forward at Westinghouse High. A lanky 6'-5" and 210 pounds, Cooper went to West Virginia State before World War II took him into the Navy. After the war, he enrolled at Duquesne, where, as an All America player and team captain, Cooper led the Dukes to two NIT appearances in three seasons, 1947-50.

The first Duquesne player drafted by an NBA team, Cooper, according to his Hall of Fame coach Red Auerbach, "had to go through hell" as one of the first African-Americans in the sport. Only three years after Jackie Robinson integrated major-league athletics, owners of white-only hotels refused to rent Cooper rooms. Cooper stood tall. "Any black coming in after Jackie had it easy compared to the turmoil he lived through," he said.

Enjoying only a modest six-year NBA career, Cooper played four years with the Celtics before being traded to the Milwaukee Hawks, then finishing with the Fort Wayne Pistons. Playing 409 games, Cooper averaged less than seven points and six rebounds a game.

Cooper earned a master of social work from the University of Minnesota. Returning home, he served as city director of parks and recreation, later working as a supervisor at Pittsburgh National Bank.

The 57-year-old NBA pioneer died from cancer and is buried in Homewood Cemetery.

Myron Cope

Born January 23, 1929—Pittsburgh
Died February 27, 2008—Pittsburgh

He kept pretty good company, that Myron Cope. From the time he was on the masthead of *Sports Illustrated* next to George Plimpton, he became a broadcaster in the Pro Football Hall of Fame along with John Madden and Frank Gifford. The lone football voice in the Broadcasters Hall of Fame, Cope's cheek-to-jowl with Ed Murrow and Orson Welles. His Terrible Towel is surely the greatest-selling gimmick in sports history. The Steelers even retired his number, 35. Well, not his number, exactly, and not for playing. Instead, it represented his years of signal service in the broadcast booth, the longest in NFL history.

Born Myron Sidney Kopelman, distinguished Taylor Allderdice, Pitt, *Erie Times*, and *Post-Gazette* alumnus, Cope came to the Steelers in 1970, when the team moved to Three Rivers Stadium, working alongside the legendary Jack Fleming, then Bill Hillgrove. A throwback to a time when announcers were less corporate and more colorful, Cope was a

master of nicknames, of Jack Splat and the Emperor Chaz, of yoi! and double yoi!, of Cope's Cabana and the Cope-a-nuts. A spluttering dervish to the fans, insiders knew Cope as one of the best, most dedicated journalists in the business. "Nobody worked harder," commented retired Steelers publicity director Joe Gordon, a legend himself for hard work. "Nobody cared more. He had high standards and great creativity. He had great respect for athletes and coaches. Most of all, he had great respect for the fans."

By the end of 2004, Cope was not well. Throat surgery had shaken the little man with the big heart and the funny voice, and it was time to say goodbye—but not alone. At halftime on Halloween Night, 2005, a sold-out Heinz Field stood and cheered as Cope was presented his own black 35 jersey.

Corbin/Hanner

Pittsburgh's history of producing great songwriters dates back to the early 1800s when Stephen Collins Foster was writing songs that told of the American experience. More than 150 years later, the torch of local songwriting is now carried by two high school buddies from Ford City, Bob Corbin and Dave Hanner.

Corbin and Hanner met at Ford City High School in the eighth grade. Both lovers of music and the Beatles, they decided to form a band together. They hooked up with a producer who had worked with British sensation Chad & Jeremy (ala "A Summer Song,") and he named them Forever and Ever. It's still a sensitive subject almost 40 years later.

They cut an album on Jubilee Records but it didn't go beyond that. They assembled the rock band Gravel while Corbin was attending Alderson-Broaddus and Hanner was at IUP and they quickly became a popular draw throughout the tri-state area. Columbia Records caught on and was impressed enough to have them record a few singles for their label. With unimpressive sales, the band and the label went their separate ways.

In 1979 Gravel became the Corbin/Hanner Band, with a modified sound that leaned towards country, adding Al Snyder, Dave Freeland, and Kip Paxton to round out the sound. Corbin/Hanner became a regional success and beyond, contributing six singles to the Top 30 Country chart off their two releases, *Son Of America* and *For The Sake Of The Song.* The two headed to Nashville to drum up interest, hitting pay dirt when Mel Tillis signed them to his music publishing company and recorded their song "Blind In Love" which became a Top Ten Country hit for Tillis that same year. Back in

Pittsburgh Corbin/Hanner continued making the rounds at places like Johnny Dollars, Kretzler's Tavern and The Evergreen Hotel.

After a few years of playing the circuit, in 1984 Corbin and Hanner decided to give it a break. The two went their separate ways musically yet continued to collaborate as friends and occasionally as songwriters. Over the next half dozen years, Corbin and Hanner became two of the most sought after songwriters in country music. In all, over 50 artists have recorded their music, including George Jones, The Marshall Tucker Band, Hank Williams Jr. and Glen Campbell, plus several artists who took their songs to the number one position on the Country chart, including Mel Tillis, Alabama, The Oak Ridge Boys, and Don Williams.

Corbin and Hanner got back together in 1990 and have been writing songs since. Corbin produces artists (including local favorites, The Poverty Neck Hillbillies) and writes commercial jingles, clients of which include Pepsi, Doritos, Diet Sprite, Hi-C, Ford and Safeway Food Stores. Hanner, who co-wrote many of those jingles, is the former musical director for the North Star Kids, produces local acts from his home studio, and still finds time to get out with his long time friend Corbin to play a few sets.

Rege Cordic

Born May 15, 1926—Hazelwood, PA
Died Aril 16, 1999—Los Angeles, CA

When Rege Cordic left Pittsburgh in 1965 to take his talents to the airwaves of Los Angeles, it was not just one person who left town, but dozens. Characters like Carmen Monoxide, Baldwin McMoney, Lou the Garbageman, and a tiny visitor from Venus, Omicron, (though collectively voiced by Bob Trow, Karl Hardmann, Bob McCully and Sterling Yates) all departed, too. The host of Cordic & Co., he created lively, funny chatter, station visits by crazy characters, fictitious products, fake sports teams, and nearly mythological tales about hometown heroes. Cordic was a pioneer of the airwaves, born in the city that pioneered commercial radio, and is still revered by radio professionals today.

His father was employed by the P&LE Railroad. A graduate of Central Catholic High and a long-term resident of Northumberland Street where his third floor was a maze of Lionel trains running from one room to another, Cordic broke into radio when he was just 16.

His lucky break, after doing the midnight to 4:00 am shift on WCAE, (now WWSW or 3WS,) came when a morning DJ was dismissed. Cordic took over the slot in 1948 as a temporary fill-in but stayed there for six years, developing his eclectic assortment of characters, until the competition, KDKA, hired him away to more powerful airwaves. Eleven years and a generation of morning devotees later, he left Pittsburgh for L.A.. But not before creating such Pittsburgh favorites as Old Frothingslosh, "the stale, pale ale with the foam on the bottom" (eventually brewed and marketed by Pittsburgh Brewing Co.), or The Flying Fraction, a streetcar that ran Pittsburgh's longest route, 77/54, and for which the Pittsburgh Railways Co. (prior to PAT) christened a special car.

His company went on to find fame in other popular venues. Bob Trow was known to generations of kids as Bob Dog and Robert Troll on *Mister Rogers' Neighborhood*, Karl Hardmann became producer of George Romero's cult classic, *Night of the Living Dead,* Sterling Yates was already well known as "Mr. Wrinkle," and Bob McCully is still one of the funniest writers in town.

In L.A., Cordic's new morning show never garnered the attention it had here, but Cordic did find new opportunities to take his distinctive baritone to a host of popular TV shows. He had a recurring role as Karl Mauldin's doctor on *The Streets of San Francisco,* appeared

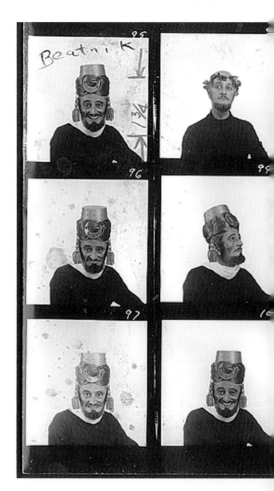

several times on *Gunsmoke* and was a regular villain on many Quinn Martin productions. He was also a popular host of *Sunday Afternoon at the Movies,* which aired here on WTAE, but was taped in Las Vegas.

Cordic died in L.A. in 1999.

Dan Cortese

Born September 14, 1967—Sewickley, PA

The youngest of four children who attended Quaker Valley High School where his father served as principal, Dan Cortese grew up in Sewickley, first attending Edgeworth Elementary. Upon graduating from University of North Carolina, Chapel Hill, where he played college football, he and his girlfriend (and future wife) Dee Dee Hemby drove across country to find work in Hollywood.

Cortese (pronounced Cor-TEZ) landed a small job at MTV as a production assistant. When his job was due to end, he tried out for the host of MTV Sports and surprisingly landed the job, though he had no prior experience in front of a camera, nor had he performed on any stage. The show had a popular run from 1992 to 1996, during which time Cortese had a small role in *Demolition Man* with Wesley Snipes and Sylvester Stallone. And he also launched a four-episode attempt

at playing a lead in the TV remake of *Route 66*. In 1994, his name and good looks were popularized when he played Elaine Benes' short-lived boyfriend on *Seinfeld* in an episode in which George Costanza has a "man-crush" and Jerry calls him a "mimbo" (for a male bimbo).

Although Cortese has made an apparent career of playing a hyper hunk on many teen targeted shows, like *Melrose Place, The Single Guy, 8 Simple Rules…* and *What I Like About You*, his greatest exposure on TV may have been as Dan Dan, The Whopper Man on more than 90 spots for Burger King in the 1990s.

Maurice & Dolores Costello

Maurice: Born February 22, 1877—Pittsburgh Died October 28, 1950—Los Angeles, CA

Dolores: Born September 17, 1903—Pittsburgh Died March 1, 1979—Fall Brooks, CA

Of the great theatrical families of the American stage and cinema, none has a longer legacy than that of the Barrymore's. When John Barrymore married his second wife Dolores Costello in 1928 he subrogated one of the greater family names of film fame then known.

Maurice Costello was, even by his own modest claim, the very first screen idol. Born to Thomas and Ellen Fitzgerald, he first served as a printer's apprentice and then as a messenger, learning to use his charms for extra tips. By 1894 he was singing and dancing Irish jigs on stage, and performed in many Harry Davis productions at his several theatres in Pittsburgh, before moving on to Brooklyn. There, he landed at the studios of Thomas Alva Edison. He made his first film in 1905. Soon nicknamed the Dimpled Darling, Maurice Costello was cranking out shorts at a frantic pace, so popular were his good looks. In fact, he is distinguished by legend as being the first "star" to refuse to lend a hand while others built the set. He was also one of the first actors to get screen credit. By the time he appeared in *The Man Who Couldn't Beat God*, the last film in which he was featured, in 1915, he had acted in some 200 (and directed another 75) films.

Having married stage actress Mae Altshuk in 1902, the couple welcomed their first child Helene that same year, and their second, in 1903, Dolores. Both girls followed in their parents' footsteps. Dolores appeared in her first film at the age of 6 playing a woodland nymph in *A Midsummer's Night Dream*. She played in many features with her father and sister, and by the '20s, also now trained as a fashion model, she landed a stage role in George White's *Scandals of 1924*. She was signed to her own contract by Warner Bros. that year, and moved to California, where she built a strong reputation both for her beauty and dignity.

In 1926, according to film lore, while on a Warner Bros. set, John Barrymore bumped into Dolores. He instantly exclaimed that she was "the most beautiful creature I have ever seen." And he just as quickly cast her as his co-star in 1926's *The Sea Beast*. They married in 1928. Soon she was known to flicker fans everywhere as The Goddess of the Silent Screen. In 1931, she gave birth to DeDe (Dolores) and, in 1932, to John Drew. Her husband, famous for his loose ways, began to show public displays of his hard drinking, and

by 1935, scandalized by his accusations that she had had affairs with her obstetrician (as well as producer David O. Selznick), they divorced.

Four years later she married her obstetrician, Dr. John Vruwink, and soon returned to the screen in several major releases, *Little Lord Fauntleroy* (1936) and *The Magnificent Ambersons* (1942). Her last film appearance was in *This Is The Army* (1943).

Owing to the ravages of harsh cosmetics used in her early film career, Dolores's face was forever damaged and she was forced to retire, moving to an avocado farm in Fallsbrook, CA. She died at the age of 75, one week after the birth of her granddaughter, Drew Barrymore, who was born on the same date, February 22, as Dolores' father, Maurice.

Johnny Costa

Born January 18, 1922—Arnold, PA
Died October 11, 1996—Arnold, PA

Any musician who knew Johnny Costa will tell you he was a man who could have had international fame—and fortune to boot. But being a native Pittsburgher who loved his family and his hometown, Johnny decided to make his neighborhood our neighborhood.

The son of Italian immigrants, Costa was born in Arnold, PA, about 20 miles north of WQED's Oakland studios where he spent almost 30 years of his professional career. At the age of 5, Costa took up the violin and by the age of 10 had moved on to the accordion. Wanting terribly to see that his son didn't have to work in the coal mines as he had, Costa's father encouraged his son to pursue music.

In high school Costa's music teacher and longtime friend, Frank Oliver, urged him to make the switch to piano. Costa enjoyed the energetic and rollicking sounds of Fats Waller and Art Tatum and soon was mastering Tatum's intricate arrangements. In 1948, Art Tatum visited a local nightclub and was introduced to Costa. Impressed with what he heard, he called Costa "The White Tatum."

Soon after graduating Arnold High, Costa was drafted into the military. After his discharge he enrolled at Carnegie Tech and continued his musical studies. In 1951, on the same day that Costa graduated, he was hired by KDKA-TV to play live music for all of the station's programs. For the next 16 years Costa wrote and performed for shows like *Meet Your Neighbor* and *Funsville*. Costa even had his own show for a while called *The Wonderful World of Johnny Costa*. He was traveling as well, playing various cities with his own trio. For a short time Costa even served as the music director on *The Mike Douglas Show*. Along the way, during the production of a show called *Children's Corner*, Costa met Josie Carey and Fred Rogers. Several years later, Rogers asked Costa to do 100 episodes of *Mister Rogers' Neighborhood* for $5,000, which just happened to be the exact amount Costa needed for his son's college tuition, and he accepted.

Costa has made several recordings with New York jazz label Chiaroscuro (who will release a posthumous two-CD set in 2008). To his legion of fans, however, his 1985 *Johnny Costa Plays Mister Rogers' Neighborhood*, produced by Family Communications, Inc., is enough to convince anyone of his genius.

Bill Cowher

Born May 8, 1957—Pittsburgh

Perhaps the best way to describe bright, hard-working Bill Cowher's 15-year tenure as Pittsburgh Steelers head coach is to say what went on around him. From 1992-2006, 105 NFL head coaches were hired. During the same time, the Steelers posted the NFL's best regular-season record, 149-90-1, a .623 winning percentage, the highest in team history. Making the play-offs 10 seasons, Cowher won eight division titles, played in six AFC championship games, and won one of two Super Bowls.

"History will look back on Bill Cowher as one of the great head coaches of his time," Steelers Chairman Dan Rooney said. "He led us through one of the most successful eras in franchise history and has my lasting respect and admiration."

Born in Pittsburgh in 1957, William Laird Cowher was raised in Crafton, starring in football, basketball, and track at Carlynton High. At North Carolina State, where Cowher played linebacker, he was team captain and MVP.

Graduating in 1979 with an education degree, Cowher played linebacker for Philadelphia (1979, 1983-84) and Cleveland (1980-82). A protégé of Marty Schottenheimer, Cowher began his coaching career in 1985 at age 28 as the Browns' special teams coach, 1985-86, and secondary coach, 1987-88, before following Schottenheimer to Kansas City in 1989 as defensive coordinator.

Tapped to replace Steelers Hall of Fame coach Chuck Noll in 1992, in just four years, at age 38 Cowher became the youngest coach to lead his team to a Super Bowl.

Eleven months after winning Super Bowl XL in 2006, Cowher retired, saying he wanted to spend more time with his wife and three daughters. Moving to Raleigh from Fox Chapel, Cowher joined Pittsburgh football great Dan Marino as a football analyst for CBS.

"Coach Cowher fit this team," Jerome Bettis commented. "He embodied the organization and the city: fiery and tough, not flashy."

Cowley is flanked by authors William Faulkner and John Dos Passos whose literary careers he molded with a sharp red pencil.

Malcolm Cowley

Born August 28, 1898—Belsano, PA
Died March 27, 1989—Milford, CT

In the history of American letters, no one ever had a better eye for the overlooked classic than Malcolm Cowley. Editor and encourager, without his guidance such luminaries as William Faulkner and Jack Kerouac may have been lost in obscurity.

Born in Belsano, Cambria County, Cowley was raised in Pittsburgh. Attending Peabody High School with future literary theorist Kenneth Burke, Cowley graduated in 1915, then went to Harvard. Driving World War I munitions trucks on the Western Front, he sent back dispatches to the *Pittsburgh Gazette*.

Graduating from Harvard in 1920, Cowley moved to Greenwich Village, publishing penny-a-word book reviews. Moving to Paris in 1921, he became part of the literary circle that included Scott Fitzgerald, Ernest Hemingway, and Gertrude Stein. His *Exile's Return*, 1934, chronicled the times.

Returning to America in 1923, Cowley moved back to Greenwich Village, writing advertising copy for *Sweet's Architectural Catalogue*. By decade's end, Cowley was *The New Republic*'s literary editor, a posting he held into the 1940s.

In 1948 Cowley went to Viking Press, a posting he held through 1985. An eminent literary critic, Cowley caused major re-evaluations of authors' works. Cowley's 1946 Introduction to Viking's *The Portable Faulkner* significantly improved Faulkner's reputation; three years later, in 1949, he won the Nobel Prize. Similarly, Cowley supported John Cheever and Sherwood Anderson.

Faced with a steamer trunk of a novel that had kicked around for six years, suffering multiple rejections, Cowley helped Jack Kerouac pare it down, re-titled it *On the Road*, and championed it. The novel became the prose anthem of the Beat movement.

Publishing widely in the 1950s and '60s, Cowley wrote landmark texts on Scott Fitzgerald and the Lost Generation, among others.

In 1989, 90-year-old Malcolm Cowley died of a heart attack at his Milford, CT, home. As a fitting tribute, *The Portable Malcolm Cowley* appeared in 1990.

Father James R. Cox

Born March 7, 1886—Lawrenceville
Died March 20, 1951—Pittsburgh

At the conclusion of World War I, Congress authorized a bonus of $1.25 per day to each soldier who fought overseas. The bonus, however, was a bond not to mature for 20 years. Of no help to the hundreds of thousands of veterans unemployed after the Crash of '29, by 1931, they wanted "their money" and they wanted it immediately. One man stepped forward to help resolve the situation. Father James R. Cox led the largest demonstration the country had then ever seen, rolling out 1,000 trucks and cars, and leading 25,000 unemployed to march on Washington.

Cox attended St. Mary's School, Duquesne University and St. Vincent's College where he was ordained in 1911. A part-time steelworker and taxicab supervisor, Cox served as a chaplain during World War I in Mongoson, France. Upon his return, he held increasingly responsible roles in the church,

until he was awarded the opportunity to lead St. Patrick's Church in the Strip District in 1924. He was then the youngest city priest in the diocese. When a cab strike was imminent, his former charges asked him to represent their interests. And when the impact of Wall Street's Crash trickled down to the ranks of his blue collar community, he stood up to defend their rights and honor.

Father Cox and an eight-mile long parade of hungry jobseekers marched into Washington the second week of January 1932. In fact, while many of his army were hoping they could convince Congress to issue them their bonus, Cox urged legislators to release $5 billion in public works jobs. Cox's Army was peaceful, but it inspired thousands more to descend on Washington until Hoover had to bring in the National Guard, with tanks, to clear the city.

A side note: then Secretary of the Treasury A.W. Mellon was accused of supporting Cox's Army. Some say he had Gulf Oil donate gasoline; others think he just bought train tickets to get the marchers home. Hoover asked for his resignation.

Cox that year became the presidential candidate of the new Jobless Party, but stepped down in deference to FDR's campaign. Cox was quoted as once saying, "There must be either a change or Communism." He is buried in Calvary Cemetery in Hazelwood.

Craig's empire was situated in the famous town on the Forks of the Ohio, depicted here in a map of 1796, the year before he opened his glassworks.

Isaac Craig

Born in 1742—County Downe, Ireland
Died in 1826—Pittsburgh

An Irishman by birth, Isaac Craig, like many other immigrants, became a staunch defender of his adopted nation during the Revolutionary War. His service during wartime brought him to Fort Pitt, where he settled in 1780. His leadership skills, honed in battle, were of great import to the newly formed community, where his legacy and name live on.

Born in Hillsboro, County Downe, Ireland, Craig grew up in a Protestant household. He apprenticed as a house carpenter, and at age 24, Craig sought opportunities in the New World. He settled in Philadelphia working first as a journeyman builder and then as a master carpenter. With war brewing in 1775, Craig joined the Navy as a First Lieutenant of Marines. Assigned to the *Andrew Doria*, he served 10 months. Promoted to captain, Craig was ordered to duty with the infantry in the army. He took part in the capture of the Hessians at Trenton on Christmas night 1776, and fought in the battles of Princeton, Brandywine (where he was wounded), and Germantown. By then a captain in the Regiment of Artillery, he suffered through the winter with his troops at Valley Forge. After a tour training at Carlisle in the preparation of munitions, Craig was sent to Fort Pitt with stores of military goods and artillery in 1780. He rarely left Pittsburgh after that, living in the area until his death in 1826.

After the war, Craig opened a mercantile business with a partner, Stephen Bayard. His military experience gave him both an understanding of the region and training in supply and distribution. In 1789, Craig was named the deputy quartermaster, responsible for supplying troops in the interior. He continued to develop and invest in new enterprises—mail boats on the Ohio River, the first glasshouse in the city of Pittsburgh, the Pittsburgh Glassworks, opened in 1797 with partner James O'Hara, and the building of ships for use by the U.S. government on the lower Mississippi against Spain. A trustee and original member of the First Presbyterian Church in Pittsburgh, Craig involved himself in the civic and religious life of his community and proved himself a leader of the young city.

Papa John Creach

Born May 28, 1917—Beaver Falls, PA
Died February 22, 1994—Los Angeles, CA

On the surface it was an odd pairing, a scrawny, middle-aged African-American gentleman, playing fiddle with a group of long-haired, psychedelic hippies from San Francisco. But it worked famously. As a result, John Henry Creach became one of the best known classically trained blues violinists in the world.

Papa John Creach, birth name John Henry Creach, was one of 10 children. He attended the Pittsburgh public schools and took a liking to the violin at a young age, when his uncle brought one around for him to play. His uncle showed him the fundamentals and Creach eventually was good enough to accompany his sister while she played the piano, mainly overtures.

Creach was serious about his music and at the age of 18 his family moved to Chicago in part so that he could pursue it professionally. He started out playing bars but was soon a guest artist with the Illinois Symphony Orchestra. His musical interests took him beyond just classical to jazz, blues, church music and R&B. In the late '30s and early '40s Creach had assembled a small trio making money playing hotels and cocktail lounges. A move to the West Coast and an official naming of The Johnny Creach Trio kept the band busy for many years playing various gigs throughout California, even a stint on a seacruiser.

In the late '60s, at a chance meeting in the local union hall, Creach met Joey Covington, then future drummer of the Jefferson Airplane. Joey was struck by Creach's gentlemanly charm, and being originally from Johnstown himself, the two native Pennsylvanians hit it off. Creach was asked several years later by Covington to play with the Airplane at a show at the Winterland Auditorium in San

Francisco in 1970, and the audience reaction to his playing was enough for the band to invite him on the tour. It was Covington who would become lifelong friends with Creach, and who gave him his nickname "Papa John."

Creach played with the Airplane, Hot Tuna (the side project with Jorma Kaukonen and Jack Cassidy) as well as Jefferson Starship, including a prominent role on their million-selling 1975 release *Red Octopus*. Creach left the Airplane to focus on a solo career, releasing works such as "I'm The Fiddle Man," "Rock Father" and "The Cat and the Fiddle." He made numerous appearances at the Montreaux Jazz Festival and even enlisted the talents of a young Keb Mo in one of his bands. Paul Kantner's Jefferson Starship Next Generation touring band in the early 1990s brought Creach out for a final round with the gang.

In January 1994, Papa John Creach suffered a heart attack and died a month later.

George Croghan

Born circa 1720—Dublin, Ireland
Died August 31, 1782—Passyunk, PA, now part of Philadelphia

Known as the "King of the Pennsylvania Traders," George Croghan was also an American Indian agent in Pennsylvania, Ohio, and Maryland throughout the second half of the 18th Century. With his business savvy and knowledge of Native American cultures, Croghan played a key role in the fate of Western Pennsylvania in the years leading up to the American Revolution.

Although details of his early life are obscure, in 1741, he immigrated to Pennsylvania where he entered the fur trade and by 1754, was one of the most successful British traders in North America. Instead of waiting for the American Indians to bring furs to his post, Croghan traded in their villages, gaining their respect and learning to appreciate the Native American way of life. Throughout the course of his career, he learned several Native American languages, including Delaware and Mohawk.

With the help of his Native American allies, Croghan expanded his trading sphere beyond the traditional boundaries of the time. His posts dotted the Pennsylvania landscape from Lake Erie to Sewickley Creek on the Youghiogheny River. Undeterred by angry French rivals, Croghan built a well-known

post near present-day Huntington, PA. After participating in Braddock's unsuccessful march to Fort Duquesne, he returned to Huntington and constructed Fort Shirley nearby, now present-day Shirleysburg, PA.

In addition to his booming fur trade business, Croghan was heavily involved in Native American and colonists' affairs. In 1756, he was named deputy Indian agent to Sir William Johnson, a well-respected diplomat who oversaw numerous treaties. For the next 16 years, Croghan worked with the Shawnees, Delawares, Miamis, Wyandots, and Ottawas, and was stationed at Fort Pitt for much of the French and Indian War (1754-1760). Once the war ended, he successfully secured the Native Americans' acceptance of British rule for the region and also negotiated the release of more than 300 British prisoners captured by the Indians at Fort Pitt.

Throughout his career, Croghan acquired large amounts of valuable Native American land, but as the Revolutionary War approached, Britain deemed relations with the Indians more important than western expansion, and Croghan found himself in financial ruin. He spent the rest of his life settling debts, and by the time he died in 1782 his personal property was estimated to be worth less than $100.

Sidney Crosby

Born August 7, 1987—Cole Harbour, Nova Scotia

As anyone in the sellout Penguin crowds can attest, nothing is as exciting as seeing Sidney Crosby charge over the blue line, skate around a defender as if he were standing still, then fire the puck by a stunned goalie.

At 5'-11" and 190 pounds, the hard-skating, left-handed center seems the very definition of Impact Player. Wearing 87—for his birthday, 8/7/87, in Cole Harbour, Nova Scotia—in 2005-06 Sidney Patrick Crosby became the youngest National Hockey League player ever to reach the 100-point mark, finishing with 102 points in 81 games. Leading the Penguins in goals, assists, and points, Crosby's sensational play accounted for the single largest spike in fan interest since Mario Lemieux's rookie season, 1984-85.

Not surprisingly, Crosby followed his first 100-point season with a second, consecutive 100-point season, 2006-07, becoming the youngest player to accomplish that feat.

Beginning his hockey career in his basement, shooting pucks into his mother's clothes dryer, Crosby learned to skate at

three. By seven he was giving interviews, and at 14 was on Canadian television—the same year he led the Dartmouth Subways to the national championships, taking both MVP and scoring honors.

After four years in the juniors, where he netted Rookie of the Year honors, and was twice named Player of the Year, he was taken by the Penguins as the first pick in the 2005 draft. Scoring 39 rookie goals, breaking Mario Lemieux's Penguin rookie record for assists, 63-57, Crosby's 102 points were two ahead of Lemieux's previous franchise rookie record. The result: Crosby became the youngest All Star in NHL history.

For an encore, 2006-07, the Penguins named the 19-year-old Crosby the youngest team captain in NHL history. Taking quadruple post-season honors, Crosby was named the NHL and players' MVP, won the league scoring title, and enjoyed another All Star berth.

Bill Cullen

Born February 18, 1920—South Side
Died July 7, 1990—Bel Air, CA

Anyone steeped in the popularity of game shows knows Bill Cullen. From the 1946 program *Winner Take All* on CBS radio to the last episodes of *$25,000 Pyramid* on which he appeared as a celebrity contestant, Cullen was host to more game shows, logged more broadcast hours hosting game shows, and appeared as a celebrity contestant on more game shows

(excluding, perhaps, Betty White) than any other personality in broadcast history.

Born at 20th and Mary Streets on the South Side, where his father ran a garage, Cullen was stricken with polio when just 18 months old. Although he was hospitalized for nine months following a near deadly car crash during his junior year at South High School, Cullen would limp his entire life from his polio affliction. Rarely, however, would television viewers see his physical challenge, if only because he stood behind a podium or was seated as a contestant.

Cullen's first broadcast job, for which he was paid $25 a week, was as an announcer on WWSW in 1939. Soon, he hosted the *1500 Club* overnight on the same station. He later earned more responsibilities as a radio host on KDKA while attending Pitt to earn a medical degree he apparently never did earn. New York beckoned. Cullen was hired by CBS on his first audition in 1944. And within two years of his employment, during which he wrote for celebrities like Arthur Godfrey and Milton Berle, he was signed to host *Winner Take All*, a radio game show which marked the first alliance of producers Mark Goodson and Bill Todman, with whom Cullen would associate for more than 40 years.

Cullen was the first host of *The Price is Right*, *Blockbusters*, *Winning Streak*, *Hot Potato*, and *Three on a Match*. Even in his busiest years, Cullen had a regular seat as a panelist on *To Tell the Truth*.

Reruns on the Game Show Network of such classics as *Child's Play*, *The Jokers Wild*, and *Password Plus* prove his easy-going patter and quick wit were unmatched. When a contestant tried to get his celebrity partner to guess the clue "Picasso" by picking his nose on camera, Cullen quipped, "Let's not go to the second syllable, please."

The Cynics

They harken back to the 1960s when four friends got together, picked up their guitars and headed to the garage to play Van Morrison's "Gloria" note for note. The Cynics, hailing from Canonsburg, led two waves of the garage rock revival, while ensuring that the genre's do-it-yourself sound would be distributed to a larger market.

Formed in 1983 by guitarist Gregg Kostelich, the band has gone through a number of personnel changes with lead singer Michael Kastelic being the one constant—the

Mick Jagger to Kostelich's Keith Richards. In fact, the Cynics have much in common with the early Rolling Stones, featuring a primal, wailing sound, with Kostelich's fuzzed, distorted guitar the perfect foil for Kastelic's moaning, screaming vocals. The young Kostelich came by his musical heritage by tagging along with his parents in the 1960s to hear legendary garage bands of the day like The Sonics and The Blues Magoos. It was a musical education rare for 7-year-olds.

Kostelich channeled those garage pioneers on the Cynics' debut album, 1986's *Blue Train Station*, now heralded as a classic by *Entertainment Weekly*'s Tom Sinclair who put it on a list of the most influential releases of its type. The album also gained notoriety at the time as a revival of what may be the first punk rock movement.

However, the album was not a big seller, prompting Kostelich to launch his own record label, Get Hip, from his Canonsburg bedroom. Not only did the fledgling label distribute Cynics releases, it also handled a number of other bands. But it was never a money-making venture, most years just breaking even.

The Cynics continued to refine their sound, even with periodic personnel changes. Albums like *Rock'n'Roll* and *Get Our Way* only cemented the band's near-cult status. The catalog included many originals combined with a sprinkling of covers from the first garage era. But internal pressures between Kostelich and Kastelic led to a four-year break up.

As the millennium began so did a new appreciation of the Cynics' music. They're frequently played on the nationally syndicated radio show, *Little Steven's Underground Garage*. Host Steven Van Zandt, also a guitarist for Bruce Springsteen's E-Street Band, is a fan. "I love them," he says. "They're a very important part of the contemporary garage movement." That movement is particularly strong in Spain, where the band has built a loyal following throughout the country.

It was that appreciation that led the band to reform in 2002 for what is often considered their best album, *Living Is The Best Revenge*. Plans are in the work for another album as the two collaborators have mended their relationship. They also continue to tour extensively. How long they ride the most recent wave of interest in garage music isn't important to Kostelich. "We have more gigs than we can do," he told the *Pittsburgh Post-Gazette*. "We're already working on new stuff. If things don't get any better than this, I'll be fine."

Iris Rainer Dart

Born in 1944—Squirrel Hill

She reached for the brass ring—and got it.

Living the golden dream, she moved to California, then hit it big—not once, but twice, in-demand TV writer, then bestselling novelist—most notably of *Beaches*.

Born Iris Ratner, she grew up in Squirrel Hill, the daughter of Yiddish-speaking immigrant parents who owned a landmark Murray Avenue hardware store. A child actress in local productions, she graduated Taylor Allderdice High School in 1962. An acting major at Carnegie Tech, her writing partner for two full-length musicals was Stephen Schwartz.

Graduating in 1966, Ratner planned to try her hand at Broadway, but a friend invited her to Hollywood. Picking up only small acting parts—she can be seen as a co-ed on "The Ivy Maze," a 1967 episode of *The Fugitive*—she turned to writing. When a manager suggested that she change her name, Ratner became Rainer. (Dart is her married name).

Writing for such hit '70s shows as *That Girl*, *The Sonny and Cher Show*, *Cher*, *Chico and the Man*, *The Odd Couple*, and *The John Davidson Show*, Rainer used her Hollywood experience for her first novel, 1978's *The Boys in the Mailroom*. Brassy, bold, and trashy, it was a huge bestseller.

Her next novel made her a household name.

The story of lifelong friends, based loosely on Dart and a cousin, 1985's *Beaches* was a three-hanky megahit. Made into a 1988 film with Bette Midler and Barbara Hershey, *Beaches* grossed more than $50 million.

Seven novels followed, 1987-2003, including *Til the Real Thing Comes Along*, *Beaches II: I'll Be There*, and *Some Kind of Miracle*. As she puts it of *Laughing Matters*, a musical that Dart hopes to premiere in 2008, "if you think you cried watching *Beaches*, you ain't seen nothing yet."

Iris Rainer Dart lives and works in Pebble Beach, California.

Marcia Davenport

Born June 9, 1903—New York, NY
Died January 15, 1996—Monterey, CA

Marcia Davenport is the greatest anomaly in Pittsburgh letters. Author of the seminal steel novel, *The Valley of Decision*, by turns she was a socialite, college drop-out, *New Yorker* writer, Mozart biographer, music critic, novelist—and Pittsburgher for all of two years.

Born Marcia Glick in 1903 in New York City, she was the daughter of Bernard Glick and Alma Gluck (born Reba Feirsohn), a world-renowned soprano. When her mother divorced Glick and married violinist Efrem Zimbalist, her daughter became Marcia Zimbalist; actor Efrem Zimbalist, Jr., is her younger half-brother.

Traveling in Europe and America, Marcia knew the great musicians of her time Gustav Mahler to George Gershwin. Dropping out of Wellesley in 1923 to marry Fred D. Clarke, she moved to Pittsburgh. However strong Marcia Clarke's reverence for the city's topogra-

phy, industry, and history, it could not save her marriage. Divorcing in 1925, she moved to New York City.

Taking an advertising copywriting job, in 1928 she joined *The New Yorker*. The following year, 1929, she married *Fortune* editor Russell Davenport. Encouraged by Scribner's editor Maxwell Perkins, she wrote an acclaimed 1932 Mozart biography, the first by an American.

Turning to fiction, she published *Of Lena Geyer* in 1936. Six years later, 1942, *The Valley of Decision* made her famous. An 800-page, multi-generation saga of mill and mine owners, the novel ranges from the Panic of 1873 until Pearl Harbor, encompassing the rise of industry, labor strife, and World War. A bestseller, it was revived in 1989 by the University of Pittsburgh Press. Filmed in part in Pittsburgh, the 1945 *The Valley of Decision* starred Greer Garson (who received an Academy Award nomination) and Gregory Peck.

Davenport's next novel, the 1947 *East Side, West Side*, starred Barbara Stanwyck and featured Nancy Davis—later First Lady Nancy Reagan.

Two novels followed, and an autobiography. In 1996, 92-year-old Marcia Davenport died in Monterey, CA.

John Davidson

December 13, 1941—Pittsburgh

Incredible as it may seem John Davidson learned to play the violin, cello, baritone horn, piano and guitar as a young child, the third of four boys born to a Baptist minister and homemaker. Just as incredible, he was a fraternity brother of Michael Eisner, yet appeared in only two Disney movies. Incredibly, too, he was the headliner at the Beverly Hills Supper Club, in Southgate, KY, on May 28, 1977, the night that 165 people perished in the infa-

© Associated Press

mous fire that also killed his musical director. Was it fate or fortune then that he became host, two years later, of the successful first "info-tainment" TV show, *That's Incredible*?

Always the clean-cut, dimple-cheeked "boy next door," Davidson has had a long and steady career as a singer, actor, musician and TV host. Born one week after the Japanese attack on Pearl Harbor, Davidson came into this world at Mercy Hospital. But he remembers very little of his childhood in Pittsburgh; his family moved to Warren, Pennsylvania, when he was a tot. Father Allie and mother Elizabeth hoped their son would pursue the ministry, but at Denison University, he discovered the theatre. Clearly, he had the good looks.

Indeed, he was soon cast in the Dolan-Mercer musical *Foxy* on Broadway, appearing with Bert Lahr in the title role, playing, of all things, a clergyman. The show ran for only two months, but he was spotted by TV producer Bob Banner and immediately cast in a new program, featuring Carol Burnett and Bob Newhart, called *The Entertainers*. In 1966 he moved to Hollywood to appear in a summer replacement variety show, and while there, was picked up by Disney for two unremark-

able family movies, *The Happiest Millionaire* and *The One and Only Original Genuine Family Band*.

By the mid-1970s with dozens of Las Vegas, Reno and Tahoe engagements and more than 12 albums to his name, Davidson was a popular talk show guest and a frequent substitute host for Johnny Carson. His fans are proud that he can claim the most hosting appearances on *The Tonight Show* of any singer.

In the 1980s he was awarded his own talk show, assuming Mike Douglas's time slot, while also appearing weekly on ABC, with Fran Tarkenton and Cathy Lee Crosby, in *That's Incredible*. The show, modeled after a Ripley's Believe It or Not roster of amazing human feats and re-enactments of bizarre coincidences, ran for five seasons.

Today, Davidson appears seasonally at the Surflight Theatre in Beach Haven, NJ, and tours regularly, performing often in Branson, MO.

Devra Davis

Born June 7, 1946—Washington, D.C.

"I'm a cancer orphan," epidemiologist Devra Davis says, having lost both her parents to the disease. "We have to prevent it. But we're fighting the wrong war with the wrong weapons against the wrong enemies."

Born Devra Lee Davis in Washington, D.C. in 1946, while her father served in the Army, she grew up in the Monongahela River town of Donora—where the infamous October 1948 air inversion killed 20 people outright, 50 more within a month, thousands within a decade.

Moving to Squirrel Hill at 14, she attended Taylor Allderdice High School, graduating in 1963. At Pitt, she earned a 1967 bachelor's degree in physiological psychology, then a master's in sociology. Moving to Chicago, she earned a University of Chicago Ph.D., then a master's in public health at Johns Hopkins.

Serving both the Carter and Clinton administrations, as well as the World Health Organization, Davis identified, tracked, and documented cancer-causing pollutants. Returning to Pittsburgh in 1999 to care for her ill parents and teach at Carnegie Mellon, she became the director of the Center for Environmental Oncology at Pitt's Cancer Institute and Professor of Epidemiology at the Graduate School of Public Health.

Her 2002 *When Smoke Ran Like Water* dissects Donora—as well as the 1952 London smog which killed thousands, Southern California's leaded gasoline smog (which she likens to World War I poison gas), and other chilling tales of environmental poisoning.

Her 2007 *The Secret History of the War on Cancer* documents public health studies made, data collected, conclusions drawn—only to be ignored, deleted, or covered up. We can no longer afford such misfeasance, she says.

"Toxic materials circulate globally," Davis says. "Pollutants don't need passports. We have to get smarter about predicting what will cause cancer—and ban them—rather than waiting for people to get sick or die."

Devra Davis lives in Shadyside.

November 3, 1948, the Donora Zinc Works of the American Steel and Wire Company is dimly seen through fume-laden smoke and fog believed to have caused the death of 50 people within two months.

© Bettmann/CORBIS

Harry Davis

Born in 1862—London, England
Died January 2, 1940—Oakland

At a time when Pittsburgh could boast having 12 skyscrapers (and New York City none), when iron and steel production attracted as many as 20,000 immigrants each year to its mills, and the typical ironworker sweated out 12-hour shifts, six days a week, Harry Davis, the son of an English millwright, owned three theatres, a pool hall, bowling alley, and several arcades downtown—all for the amusement of Pittsburghers. He was the city's greatest theatre impresario and, in 1905, created a single amusement venue that within two decades would be replicated in every neighborhood in the country, creating one of America's greatest contributions to world culture.

At 8 years of age, Davis landed in Pittsburgh in 1870 with his father John, mother Eleanor, and sister Eleanor, and attended the O'Hara Public School in the Twelfth Ward.

Three years later, a severe depression hit the country and he dropped out of school to work as a florist's helper, earning $1.50 a week. Soon he assisted his father in building several tinplate mills both in Leechburg, PA, and Wellsville, Ohio, returning to Pittsburgh to work in a grocery store. His father died in 1879, and Davis went into business for himself, selling stationery. His first attempt at show business was producing a schoolroom road show for a husband and wife team by the name of Schmiky. Davis lost his entire investment of $60. Again, he sold stationery, and also worked nights in a bowling alley. His association with the owner led him to create a museum, which in the 1880s were often leased rooms filled with strange curios, a freak show or an occasional vaudeville act. Davis eventually ran three Musee's, one of which was managed in Johnstown by John P. Harris, a man ten years his junior, who would later marry Davis's sister Eleanor in 1894.

Davis's moderate success in running three "theatres" earned him efficiencies in booking acts for his shows. He had, by design, created one of the first "circuits" to operate in Pennsylvania. By the turn of the century, Davis leased and managed both the Grand Opera House on Diamond Alley (now Forbes at Market Square) and the Avenue Theatre on Fifth. The two legitimate houses were back to back, between Wood and Smithfield Streets. The Avenue played vaudeville and motion pictures, while the Grand Opera played dramatic fare and, of course, operas. So profitable were his venues—with customary ticket prices at 25 cents to 50 cents—Davis seasonally refurbished and redecorated his palaces to draw more and more patrons to shows every season. (The New Grand Opera House eventually became the Warner Theatre.) And so successful was he, and so populated was the city, that many theatrical entrepreneurs regularly visited Pittsburgh to witness his latest productions. With their attention came more competition, and more theatres opened. Ever the competitor, Davis exploited State Senator Christopher Magee's scheme to create a trolley line, and built the Duquesne Gardens, at Craig Street and Ellsworth, the end of the line, in 1899.

In 1903, Davis established what might have been the first subscription package for theatre-goers. In 1904, he teamed with the Keith organization to own the Alvin Theatre. As his empire grew, so too did the competition. And, without means to book more shows more frequently, Davis invested heavily in real estate. Of the many properties he came to own, two were side by side at 433 and 435 Smithfield Street.

In 1905, he, his brother-in-law Harris, and theatre manager Harry Cohn renovated the store fronts of the new acquisition, hung up a white sheet inside, decorated the side walls with red velvet and placed 96 opera chairs in the otherwise open room. For a nickel each, patrons were admitted for 20 minutes to view a series of motion pictures projected on the sheet. Other than background melodies played on a phonograph, no other entertainment was offered. The idea was a simple one—and incredibly profitable. Davis earned as much as a $1,000 per week, packing in some 7,000 patrons a day. They called their movie house a Nickelodeon.

Davis opened three other Nickelodeons in the city within months, and soon operated hundreds in Ohio, New York and Pennsylvania. Though he did not create the movie industry, he whetted the appetite of its voracious audience, inspiring many local families, like the Warner Bros., and local jeweler, Lewis Selznick, father of David and Myron, to rethink their careers. Like others, Harry Cohn started his own film company, which would be called Metro Pictures, the forerunner of MGM.

Never married, in 1926, Davis had a stroke. Resigned to a wheelchair, he never spoke a word again. He died in 1940.

Opened to the public on January 23, 1899, the Duquesne Gardens was billed as the biggest skating rink in the world, with 26,000 square feet of skating surface. The two-story brick building was located at 110 N. Craig Street in Oakland.

Mary Cardwell Dawson

**Born in 1896—North Carolina
Died March 19, 1962—Munhall, PA**

History was made when Clarence Cameron White's opera *Ouanga* was performed for a Standing Room Only audience at the Metropolitan Opera House on May 27, 1956. It was not the first time the Met had had an SRO crowd, nor was it the first time White's opera was performed for a New York audience. But it was the first time an opera company, other than the Met's own, had permission to perform on its stage. The National Negro Opera Company, founded by Mary Cardwell Dawson 15 years earlier in Pittsburgh, premiered that night to thunderous applause.

Cardwell moved to Munhall with her parents Abraham and Elizabeth when she was quite young. Her father, a mill worker, purchased a house in Munhall, and later Cardwell graduated from Homestead High School. Recognized for her exceptional talents as a young member of the Park Place A.M.E. Church, she earned the opportunity to attend the New England Conservatory of Music where, between classes in voice and piano, she helped pay her tuition by working in a dentist's office. The only African-American in her class, she graduated in 1925 and two years later, returned to Pittsburgh with her new husband, Walter Dawson. They lived above his electrician's shop on Frankstown Avenue in Homewood.

Soon, she opened the Cardwell School of Music around the corner, at 7101 Apple Street. She recruited students and formed the Cardwell Dawson Choir. Among her early students were Ahmad Jamal and Robert McFerrin, father of vocalist Bobby. In 1939, she was elected President of the National Organization of Negro Musicians, and in 1941, to celebrate their convention in Pittsburgh, she organized the first assembly of the National Negro Opera Company. In all, there were four companies, one each for Pittsburgh, Chicago, New York and Washington, D.C.

A tireless, versatile and ever-optimistic dynamo—Madame Dawson was said to have been just 5 feet tall in her high heels—she sustained her opera companies for more than 20 years on prayers, donations and a very long shoe-string. The NNOC could not survive her death in 1962.

Wrote *Pittsburgh Courier* editor Frank Bolden in a personal memoir years later, "While others make a cult of finding a difficulty for every solution, Mme. Dawson appears to have a solution for every difficulty."

Bill Deasy

Born March 8, 1966—Pittsburgh

His song-writing could be considered the antidote to the blue-collar rustbelt rock and roll that often permeates the musical landscape of the northeastern United States. Bill Deasy is the real deal, reminding us that despite the tendencies toward "tough," there is a softer, more gentle way to sing about the same pains in life.

In 1991, Deasy's band Shiloh won the annual Graffiti Rock Challenge; Deasy was being touted as one of the local rising stars to watch. Within the next several years Deasy teamed up with producer and musician Dave Brown, with a little help from future Rusted Root percussionist Jim DiSpirito, to create the early stages of The Gathering Field. Their self-titled debut rolled out to rave reviews and overwhelming local fan and radio support. The song "Lost In America" became a regional radio hit and the Gathering Field seemed destined for Americana roots-rock fame. Several national labels showed interest in the band and Atlantic Records won the battle. But the band ultimately lost the war. Shortly after signing, and soon crowded out by other bands who had now diverted the label's attention, the Gathering Field fought to be released. Several tracks followed their 1996 debut and the Gathering Field decided to call it quits.

Deasy pushed on alone. His song writing talents were noticed by artists on a national stage, including Martina McBride, Howard Jones and Kim Richey, all of whom recorded songs of his. Additionally he began focusing on his solo work and recorded "Spring Lies Waiting" to favorable reviews and then in 2003 released *Good Day No Rain* once again to critical acclaim. Additionally, in 2001, during a trip to Nashville, Deasy co-wrote a song that was pitched to, and picked-up by, ABC for their morning show *Good Morning America*, called "Good Things Are Happening." The song that was intended for a 10 week run, ran for the next three and a half years. In 2005 Deasy released *Chasing Down A Spark* and followed it up in 2007 with *The Miles*.

In addition to his musical talents, Deasy is an award-winning author, who debuted his first novel *Ransom Seaborn* in 2006.

John DeFazio

Born October 30, 1940—Pittsburgh

Wearing white trunks, leaping over the ropes, facing the likes of Chet Walik and Jim Grabmire, he finished with his signature sunset flip, jumping on an opponent's back, flipping him, pinning him.

That move, and his steel-armed cradle, gave Jumpin' Johnny DeFazio his titles, fans, and solid-gold berth on cards all around the region—and on WIIC's hit Saturday afternoon show *Studio Wrestling*.

Trained by the legendary Zivko Kovacic, given his Jumpin' moniker by *Studio Wrestling* host Bill Cardille, John DeFazio was born in Pittsburgh, 1940. Raised on Mount Washington, a graduate of St. Justin's and South Hills High, DeFazio was working in the Jones & Laughlin Hazelwood mill and lifting weights in the Downtown YMCA when he met Kovacic. Training with him, practicing judo and karate, in 1961 the 21-year-old DeFazio was placed on his first Civic Arena card. Standing 5'-10" and 225 pounds, by 1967 DeFazio was World Wide Wrestling Federation Junior Heavyweight Champion, a title he never lost.

Teamed with Geeto Mongol (in real life a Nova Scotian named Newton Tattrie) in 1972, the pair beat Tarzan Tyler and Crazy Luke Graham to take the tag team title.

Although wrestling was his passion, DeFazio had never left steelworking, and at 29 was elected local representative. Going on staff with the United Steelworkers in 1976, DeFazio's union duties prevented him from traveling to defend his titles. Never defeated, his titles were officially vacated and given to others.

Retired from the ring, he returned in the late 1970s to face such national stars as Cowboy Bobby Duncum and Sgt. Slaughter. By 1980 he was gone for good.

In 2000 the Pennsylvania state USW representative ran in the inaugural race for County Council. Elected at-large, DeFazio was chosen to serve as its first president.

Living in Shaler, he is married with six children.

Martin Robinson Delany

Born May 6, 1812—Charles Town, VA
Died January 24, 1885—Wilberforce, OH

Martin Robinson Delany served as a major in the Civil War (the first African-American field officer in the U.S. Army), is considered the father of Black Nationalism, and published the first black newspaper west of the Alleghenies. But still, as W.E.B. DuBois remarked, "His was a magnificent life, and yet, how many of us have heard of him?"

Born in Charles Town, VA (now West Virginia), Delany grew up in a family that traced its lineage to African kings and queens. His parents, Samuel and Pati Peace Delany, prized education. At age 10, Martin's family moved to Chambersburg, PA, after Delany was

sent away by school officials for trying to enter a white classroom. In 1831, Delany came to Pittsburgh to attend the all-black school operated by Reverend Lewis Woodson. Hoping to be a doctor, he apprenticed under Dr. Andrew McDowell and later worked as a cupper and leecher, and was actively involved with reform movements. Convinced that education and knowledge were vital to attaining freedom, Delany founded the first black newspaper west of the Alleghenies, *The Mystery*, in 1843. He later ceased publication and worked as co-editor of Frederick Douglas' *The North Star*.

During the 1850s, Delany pursued both his personal desire to be a doctor and the cause of liberation for all African-Americans. Admitted to Harvard Medical School, he attended just one term before white students lobbied for his expulsion. Returning again to Pittsburgh, he published his landmark work: *The Condition, Elevation, Emigration, and*

Destiny of the Colored People of the United States, Politically Considered, which advocated that blacks should leave America and start a new nation. He dedicated himself to the cause of freedom, working as part of the Underground Railroad in Pittsburgh and in Canada, and traveling, lecturing, and writing. In 1865, Delany met with Abraham Lincoln, and a month later, the U.S. Army commissioned him a Major.

After the war, Delany served in politics in South Carolina. Eventually he settled in Wilberforce, OH, to be near his children. When he died on January 24, 1885, he was eulogized as, "a power in shaping events, especially where grave questions were to be met and decided."

Jim Delligatti

Born in 1918—Uniontown, PA

A one-time manager of an Isaly's store in Uniontown, Jim Delligatti dreamed of opening his own restaurant. He had a premonition that fast-food was the way to go, but he needed a model. So he attended a restaurant show in Chicago in 1956 and was introduced to a fledgling franchise, McDonald's Restaurants. In fact, Delligatti visited the first of Ray Kroc's hamburger stands which had opened in Des Plaines, IL, just the year before.

Delligatti opened his first McDonald's on McKnight Road in 1957. He built two more in the city, then opened his fourth in Uniontown. By 1965, he owned a dozen in the Pittsburgh area. "But I always thought something was missing," said Delligatti years later. "We needed a big sandwich."

Double-decker hamburgers were nothing new to Pittsburghers who had dined at any of 27 Eat'n Park restaurants opened by 1960. Originally known as Big Boys (but later renamed after a 1975 dispute with Elby's Big Boy Restaurants), Eat'n Park had a big seller. Delligatti's two all-beef patties had a special sauce that he hoped would make his sandwich a stand-out. Unfortunately, the corporate offices of McDonald's didn't like the sandwich—or the sauce. (Kroc was rumored to have preferred introducing a pineapple and cheese sandwich at the time). But Delligatti persevered, changing his recipe to use only ingredients already sold in his restaurants, and a new sauce—as well as a "center bun," added for stability—was introduced in his Uniontown McDonald's in 1967. He charged just 45 cents.

With more than 500 million Big Macs sold each year, in August of 2007, the Delligattis, who still own 18 franchises in the region, opened the Big Mac Museum Restaurant in Huntingdon, PA.

The Del Vikings

The Del Viking's story is one of the more interesting (and most confusing) in the history of rock. They began as five African-American singers from various parts of the country who met while stationed as members of the Air Force at the old Greater Pittsburgh Airport. Their beautiful singing harmonies won them numerous talent contests. Among their earlier songs was an original a capella number called "Come Go With Me." But just as they were beginning to jell as a group, two of the members were transferred to Germany.

Of the two members that replaced them, one was black and one was white. The group caught the attention of local Pittsburgh DJ Barry Kaye and producer Joe Averback who recorded a number of their songs at George Heid Productions. The demo was shopped around but one record company after another turned it down. So Joe Averback signed the group to his own label, Fee Bee Records, and he then recorded another version of "Come Go With Me," this time with musical accompaniment. The song hit #4 on the national charts.

The Del Vikings became the first interracial band to chart a top 10 hit.

Success was imminent, but four of the musicians were then under 21. Their contract was disputed when an opportunistic manager pirated the teens to a better deal with Mercury Records. The one legal contract singer stayed with Fee Bee. But with "Come Go With Me" making such a splash, Mercury took the name Del Vikings. So Fee Bee called their band The Dell Vikings. The double-L Dells

recorded "Whispering Bells." It hit number 9 on the national charts. Meanwhile, the Del Vikings, on Mercury, released "Cool Shake." Needless to say, DJ's were confused. Mercury sued, winning the rights to the name Del

The second set of Del Vikings (l to r): Dave Lerchey, "Kripp" Johnson, Norman Wright, Gus Backus and Clarence Quick.

Vikings and any variation of it. Legal wranglings and military duty kept the Del Vikings from taking advantage of the usual music tours to which such stars were accustomed.

When the various members had either been released from their contracts or discharged from the military, the Del Vikings made their rounds with Dick Clark and Alan Freed, as well as on variety shows such as *The Tonight Show* and *The Ed Sullivan Show*. Future releases never achieved the success of their early material and by the mid-1960s the Del Vikings had disbanded, only to regroup in the early 1970s just long enough to re-record their classics for Scepter Records.

The band once again resurfaced in 1980 and a version of The Del Vikings has been active ever since.

Ebenezer Denny

Born in 1764—Carlisle, PA
Died in 1822 —Pittsburgh

It was considered the bloodiest battle and most devastating defeat for American troops on the Western frontier, and Ebenezer Denny survived it. In November 1791, Shawnee and Miami Indians outside of Fort Washington, near what is now Cincinnati, attacked and killed nearly 700 troops, however Denny, a seasoned major in the U.S. Army, escaped the slaughter, writing in his journal, "My friends at Pittsburgh ... seem to view me as escaped from the dead ... but all this will

1781, Yorktown, British General Cornwallis surrenders to General George Washington. Denny was there to witness it.

soon be forgotten." He was, however, revered as a wartime hero by settlers in the region and after a distinguished military career, entered local politics and became in 1816 the growing city's first mayor.

As a 13-year-old boy, the eldest son of William and Agnes Denny, he traveled alone over the Allegheny Mountains from his home in Carlisle, PA, to deliver messages to troops stationed at Fort Pitt. He ran dispatches for the military (a dangerous job) to help support the family. His bravery and earnestness impressed his officers, and he was soon granted the rank of ensign in the First Pennsylvania Regiment as the Continental Army prepared to battle for independence in the American Revolution. He was present at many critical conflicts including the surrender of Lord Cornwallis in 1781 at Yorktown, Virginia. After the Revolution, Denny served as an aid-decamp of General Arthur St. Clair and later as a captain in and around Pittsburgh to secure lands from Indian and foreign threats.

Two years before his retirement from the army in 1795, Denny married Nancy Wilkins (1776-1806), and they settled first on a farm in Streets Run and then moved a few miles up the Monongahela River to Pittsburgh. Denny worked as a merchant and entered local politics as county treasurer and later the first director of the Pittsburgh branch of the Bank of Pennsylvania. He only served as mayor for a year, resigning due to poor health. Denny helped forge the commerce, industry, and government of a new city that took hold in a region he had spent so many years defending.

Patti Deutsch

Born December 16, 1945—Pittsburgh

In the 1970s, TV game shows were king.

They even began airing at night, especially when featuring celebrity panelists. *Match Game 73* was one of the first game shows that Mark Goodson and Bill Todman revived from an earlier format, adding risqué humor and double-entendres to the questions. Premiering a week late because of the Watergate hearings, *Match Game 73* ran to *Match Game 79*. Patti Deutsch was a regular panelist.

Daughter of Mr. & Mrs. Bernard Deutsch, Patti has said of her childhood, "I was a really ugly kid—very thick glasses, and me very thin. I was the kind of kid about whom people would say, 'she has nice teeth.' I didn't talk to people until I was 12." Deutsch graduated from Taylor Allderdice and then attended

Carnegie Tech "about four times," she admitted. A student of playwriting, she was introduced to Don Brockett. From 1963 to 1967, she performed in dozens of Brockett shows at Beck's Charter Oaks and Bill Kramer's Back Room. And then she went to New York with another Brockett show, *Hello, Tourista,* that closed soon after. Deutsch stayed in the Big Apple and married playwright and comedy writer Donald Ross.

She appeared on *The Dick Cavett Show*, and soon became a darling of the evening talk shows—most often on *Merv Griffin*, but frequently on the *The Tonight Show* and *Mike Douglas Show*, too—for her wry sense of humor, and an oddly nasal voice. With Fred Willard and three other comedians, she founded The Ace Trucking Company, performing ensemble comedy sketches regularly on *The Tom Jones Show* and often on *The Tonight Show.*

In 1973, she became a regular on *Rowan & Martin's Laugh-In*. That year, too, she was tapped for *Match Game*. In more recent years, her distinctive voice has helped create many animated characters, most notably for Disney's *Monsters, Inc.* and *The Emperor's New Groove*.

Dena Dietrich

Born December 4, 1928—Pittsburgh

The very nature of good acting is to fool the audience into believing that that which is not real, seems wholly natural. For more than nine years in the '70s, Dena Dietrich fooled TV audiences into believing that a tub of margarine could taste as natural as real butter.

The CLIO-winning actress who made famous the ad phrase, "It's not nice to fool Mother Nature!" Dietrich is the daughter of Mahlon Lloyd and Helen Frances Dietrich, both actors who appeared often at the Pittsburgh Playhouse. Young Dena graduated from Westminster College in 1950 and followed her muse to New York City where she studied with Uta Hagen for two years. A versatile actress who has a long resume of performances on stage and screen, she is well known, in addition to her Chiffon commercial, for recurring roles on sitcoms and soaps like *Adams Rib, All My Children, Boy Meets World, Mad About You,* and *Murphy Brown*.

She currently works regularly in Hollywood, teaching acting, performing voice-overs, and appearing often in regional theaters.

Annie Dillard

Born April 30, 1945—Point Breeze

"When everything else has gone from my brain," Annie Dillard writes in *An American Childhood*, her brilliant, impeccably described 1987 memoir of growing up in Pittsburgh, "the President's name, the state capitals, the neighborhoods where I lived, and then my own name and what it was on earth I sought, and at length the faces of my friends, and finally the faces of my family—when all this has dissolved, what will be left, I believe, is topology: the dreaming memory of land as it lay this way and that."

Writing with astonishing clarity, Dillard's 1955 Pittsburgh resounds with the bustle of men going to work, piano lessons and dance classes, the natural world, the stacks at the Carnegie Library. Throughout, she molds the mundane into quintessential American life and art.

Born Meta Ann Doak in Pittsburgh in 1945, she grew up in the East End, attending The Ellis School, cribbing cigarettes and drag-racing, reading everything from Emerson to Kerouac. Off to Virginia's Hollins College, as a 20-year-old sophomore she married her writing professor, poet Richard Dillard. Earning

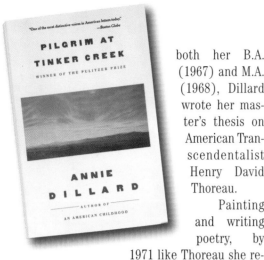

both her B.A. (1967) and M.A. (1968), Dillard wrote her master's thesis on American Transcendentalist Henry David Thoreau.

Painting and writing poetry, by 1971 like Thoreau she retreated into nature, a cabin at Tinker Creek, in Virginia's Blue Ridge Mountains. Keeping a reading journal, which ran to 20 volumes, Dillard transposed her thoughts onto notecards, then stitched them together into a book. Often writing 15 hours a day, living largely on coffee and Coca-Cola, after eight months she had lost some 30 pounds—and had written *Pilgrim at Tinker Creek*, an extended meditation on solitude, nature, and the Divine.

It was 1974. Save for a slender book of poetry, *Tickets for a Prayer Wheel*, Annie Dillard was an entirely unknown 29-year-old writer. Then she won the Pulitzer Prize.

Suddenly famous, and not liking it, like Thoreau she retreated even further—from Tinker Creek to a Puget Sound cabin. Tempted to write travel pieces, to go to "wonderful places," she said, and write about them, instead Dillard chose teaching, first in Washington, then at Wesleyan, in Connecticut. "I loved college," she has said. "The minute I got there I thought, 'this is for me.' I decided I was going to stay at college for the rest of my life, and I have."

There was a second marriage, to anthropologist Gary Clevidence, and a daughter, and time spent on Cape Cod.

There was writing, too, including such highly regarded non-fiction as *Holy the Firm* (1977), *Living by Fiction* (1982), *Teaching a Stone to Talk* (1982), *The Writing Life* (1989), and *For the Time Being* (1999). A second volume of poetry, *Mornings Like This*, appeared in 1995, along with two novels, *The Living* (1992), and *The Maytrees* (2007), the latter her first book in eight years.

Sparked by a mutual interest in Henry David Thoreau, of whom he had written a biography, she met and married her third husband, historian Robert D. Richardson, Jr. They live and work in Middletown, CT.

Mike Ditka

Born October 18, 1939—Carnegie, PA

Iron Mike. The name says it all.

"Pain," he famously said, "never really bothered me."

A three letter athlete at Aliquippa High—baseball, basketball, and football—All America at Pitt, Super Bowl champion as player and coach, Mike Ditka stands as one of the most successful football players in Pittsburgh history.

Michael Keller Ditka, Jr., was a heavily recruited scholastic star who chose hometown Pitt over Penn State and Notre Dame. Tough blocker, superb receiver, Ditka played tight end, leading the Panthers in receptions three consecutive years, 1958-60.

© Associated Press

Taken by the Chicago Bears in the first round of the 1961 draft, Ditka was an immediate high-impact player who hauled in 56 passes—and took NFL Rookie of the Year honors. A perennial All Pro, his six-year stint with the Bears included 84 consecutive starts—as well as a berth on the 1963 NFL Championship team.

Ditka was traded to Philadelphia in 1967 and spent two seasons with the Eagles before ending his career with the Dallas Cowboys, 1969-72, where he scored a touchdown to cement the Super Bowl VI championship.

Hired by the Cowboys as an assistant coach, 1973-81, Ditka helped steer the team to six division titles, three NFC Championships, and victory in Super Bowl XII.

In 1982, Ditka became the Chicago Bears' head coach for 11 years, winning Super Bowl XX in 1985.

In 1992, Ditka became a football broadcaster, returning to the sidelines in 1997 for a three-year stint with the New Orleans Saints.

Retired from football since 2000, he was enshrined in the College Football Hall of Fame and became the first tight end in the Pro Football Hall of Fame. The father of four, Ditka continues broadcasting as well as operating Mike Ditka's Restaurant in Chicago.

Jack Dodson

Born June 16, 1931—Pittsburgh
Died September 16, 1994—Los Angeles, CA

If any character actor owned the role of the mama's-boy nerd, it was Jack Dodson. Recognized by generations of TV viewers as county clerk Howard Sprague, Dodson enjoyed tenure with CBS on *The Andy Griffith Show*, and then *Mayberry R.F.D.*, for more than six years, first appearing in 1966 as an insurance salesman, and then returning as one of Mayberry's regular quirky townsfolk.

Not surprisingly, Dodson was an established stage actor, who shared the limelight on many of the great experimental New York stages in the 1960s. Appearing at the Circle in the Square often, in such classic plays as *Our Town*, *The Balcony*, *Under Milkwood,* and *The Quare Fellow*, he was "discovered" by Andy Griffith in 1964 while performing in a two character drama on Broadway, playing opposite Jason Robards in Eugene O'Neill's *Hughie.*

Son of John M. and Margaret S. Dodson, Jack graduated from Carnegie Tech in 1953, before serving in the Army as a sergeant. In 1959, he married fellow Carnegie Tech grad Mary Weaver, a production designer, who is Fritz Weaver's older sister.

Following his popular run as Howard Sprague, Dodson appeared often in similar character-type on TV sitcoms, as well as in a few TV-inspired films, like *Munster, Go Home*, and *Angel in My Pocket*, also with Andy Griffith. Dodson also appeared in a few Sam Peckinpah flicks, notably with Steve McQueen in *The Getaway,* and with James Coburn and Jason Robards in *Pat Garrity and Billy The Kid*. In the 1980s still often playing the nerd, he was seen as

Ralph Malph's optometrist father on *Happy Days*. In 1983, he appeared on Broadway for an extended run in George S. Kaufman's *You Can't Take it With You*, and, in 1984, he reprised his early Broadway success with Jason Robards in *Hughie*, which was then made for TV.

Tony Dorsett

Born April 7, 1954—Rochester, PA

They called him the Hawk, which aptly summarized his talent as the finest breakaway runner Pittsburgh ever produced.

Born Anthony Drew Dorsett, one of seven children, Tony Dorsett was raised in Aliquippa. A linebacker at Hopewell High , Coach Butch Ross recognized the 5'-11" 185-pound Dorsett's extraordinary speed and maneuverability. Switching the youngster to halfback, as the position was then called, the move paid off immediately; Dorsett gained more than 1,000 yards as a junior.

Playing at Pitt, 1973-76, Dorsett became the greatest running back in Panther history. The first college back to gain 1,000 or more yards in each of four seasons, Dorsett racked up an NCAA record 6,082 yards. A three-time All America, and Heisman Trophy winner in his senior year, Dorsett led the Panthers to the team's first national championship since Jock Sutherland's team took the 1937 title.

Drafted second in the nation in 1977 by the Dallas Cowboys, Dorsett rushed for more than 1,000 yards, won Rookie of the Year, and led his team to victory in Super Bowl XII. The following year, he ran for more than 1,300 yards—all the way to Super Bowl XIII—where the Cowboys lost to Dorsett's hometown Steelers.

Running for 1,000 or more yards eight of his first nine seasons, the four-time Pro Bowler played 11 seasons in Texas, 1977-87, gaining more than 12,000 rushing yards.

Traded to Denver in 1988, he was set to return in 1989 until a knee injury forced his retirement.

The Dorsett dossier: 12 years, 12,739 rushing yards and 77 rushing touchdowns—16,326 yards total, 91 touchdowns, making him one of the top running backs of all time.

Elected to both the Pro Football Hall of Fame and the College Football Hall of Fame in 1994, Dorsett saw his defensive back son Anthony play in the NFL 1996-2003.

Herb Douglas

Born March 9, 1922—Pittsburgh

In 1936, 14-year-old Herb Douglas met Jesse Owens when the Olympic gold medalist took a victory swing through Pittsburgh's Hill District. "He was my hero," Douglas recalled nearly 70 years later. "Even today he inspires me."

Little did the budding track and field star know that a dozen years later he would follow his hero by also winning an Olympic medal.

Born Herbert Paul Douglas, Jr., in Pittsburgh in 1922, raised at 160 Hazelwood Avenue, he attended Gladstone School, then Taylor Allderdice High, where he lettered in four sports. Douglas' training regimen was racing up and down the nearly vertical—and seemingly endless—Hazelwood Avenue.

Going to Xavier, in New Orleans, where he competed nationally in track and field, a family illness forced Douglas to leave school and go to work. After serving honorably in World War II, in 1945 he enrolled in Pitt, where he followed Jimmy Joe Robinson to become the second African-American on the Panthers' varsity football squad.

Nevertheless, track and field—the 100-yard dash and the long jump—were Douglas' main sports. Setting a Pitt long-jump record that stood for 23 years, Douglas took three national AAU championships and five intercollegiate championships.

Then came summer, 1948, in London, a city still scarred by World War II's relentless blitz. After a hiatus of a dozen years, the Olympics were held once again. And once again, as in 1936, an African-American excelled in track and field: 26-year-old Herb Douglas leapt 24 feet 9 inches to win the bronze medal.

Earning a 1948 bachelor of science and a 1950 master of education, in 1980 Douglas founded the International Amateur Athletic Association (IAAA), establishing the Jesse Owens International Trophy.

Inducted into the New York Athletic Club Hall of Fame, the Pennsylvania Sports Hall of Fame, and the African American-Ethnic Sports of Hall of Fame, Herb Douglas lives in Philadelphia.

In Pioneer Run, PA, derricks of the Shoe & Leather Petroleum Company and the Foster Farm Oil Company cover a hillside in 1895.

Edwin Drake

Born in 1819—Greenville, NY
Died in 1880—Bethlehem, PA

In 1859, Edwin L. Drake's oil well struck "black gold" in the small town of Titusville, PA, ushering in the age of oil. Although the presence of oil was known, its potential as an energy source had not been fully utilized, largely because no one had found a reliable way of extracting it from the ground. Little did Drake realize how his oil well would change the course of history and influence world politics.

Before his oil prospecting days, Drake spent time as a clerk, express agent, and railroad conductor. In the late 1850s he was hired by James Townsend, an agent of the Seneca Oil Company, to investigate the possibility of large oil deposits near Titusville. He decided that drilling was the best method to extract oil from the ground and spent some time observing salt well drilling in the area. After spending months acquiring a borer and the parts to build the well, he started drilling in May 1859. During this time his contract with the Seneca Oil Company ran out—they had already invested $2,000 in the project and declined to send Drake more funds. Townsend provided $500 more from his own pocket, and after six weeks of drilling, hitting bedrock, and engineering a flood-proof drill, Drake's patience was rewarded. "Crazy Drake," as he was dubbed by locals, had finally struck oil on August 28, 1859.

Within months Pennsylvania's oil rush was under way. Because he failed to patent his drill, Drake saw little of the oil industry's wealth. Only a few years later John D. Rockefeller would enter the business and build one of the largest oil monopolies in history. In 1873 the state of Pennsylvania voted to offer Drake an annuity of $1,500, which he collected until his 1880 death in Bethlehem, PA.

© Associated Press

Barney Dreyfuss

**Born February 23, 1865—Freiburg, Germany
Died February 5, 1932—New York, NY**

A small man who ran away from the Kaiser's army, he changed the way Americans experience sports—and left a Pittsburgh legacy that has lasted a century.

Bernhard "Barney" Dreyfuss emigrated to America to avoid military conscription. Joining family members in Kentucky, he got involved in the new, growing field of spectator sports, notably baseball.

Although the Pirates had been in Pittsburgh since 1887, they were a sub-par team with weak spectator support. Then the unexpected occurred: in 1900, when the National League slimmed down from 12 to eight teams, Dreyfuss folded his Louisville Colonels and moved 14 of his top players to Pittsburgh. Led by future Hall of Famers Honus Wagner and Fred Clarke, the Pirates leapt from seventh in '99 to National League pennants, 1901-03.

Finishing first wasn't enough for Dreyfuss. While many cursed the new American League—as Dreyfuss himself might have, having lost a number of stars who jumped ship—he proposed a post-season contest between the two rivals. Calling it the World Series, his 1903 Pirates played Boston. Although Pittsburgh lost, Dreyfuss won; post-season championships reshaped professional sports forever.

In addition, unhappy with old wooden Exposition Park on Pittsburgh's North Side, Dreyfuss wanted a better ballpark. Following the advice of his friend Andrew Carnegie, who pointed out vacant land near his new Oakland Institute, in 1909 Dreyfuss built Forbes Field. Using new technology—steel frame and poured concrete—and looking out on Schenley Park, Forbes Field was hailed as the most beautiful ballpark in America.

Through it all, Dreyfuss did not neglect his team. Establishing the Pittsburgh tradition of excellence, for the next 20 years, until his 1932 death in New York City, the Pirates were perennial contenders, winning the World Series in 1909 and 1925, losing in 1927 to Babe Ruth's New York Yankees.

He was inducted posthumously into baseball's Hall of Fame in 2008.

Billy Eckstine

**Born July 8, 1914—Highland Park
Died March 8, 1993—Pittsburgh**

Highland Park native Billy Eckstine was much more than a well-dressed, suave, handsome hit-making balladeer; he was an astute mentor of emerging talent and a pioneer in challenging and breaking racial barriers and stereotypes.

At the peak of his career in 1950, Billy Eckstine, or "Mr. B" as he was better known, rivaled Frank Sinatra in popularity and was even referred to as "the sepia Sinatra."

Born to William and Charlotte Eckstine, he began singing as a young boy in his East End neighborhood and made his singing debut at the age of 11 at a church bazaar. As a teenager he won a local talent contest when he imitated the great entertainer and jazz singer Cab Calloway—it was clear that his talents were solid. He attended Peabody High School and loved football almost as much as he loved music. If Eckstine was torn which to pursue, a broken collarbone made the decision easy. After graduation he competed in a talent contest in Washington, D.C. where he attended Howard University, making his decision to pursue music rather than an academic career an easy one. He left school and headed to Chicago.

For a short while, at the suggestion of a club owner, Eckstine changed the spelling of his name to Billy X. Stine, because his real name was thought to sound too Jewish. In 1939, Eckstine was asked to join Pittsburgher Earl "Fatha" Hines' Grand Terrace Orchestra as a soloist. In 1943 Eckstine left Hines to form his own band, the first bop big band. The musicians whom he brought under his fold would turn out to be some of the greatest in jazz, including Pittsburgher Art Blakey, Charlie Parker, Dexter Gordon, Sonny Stitt, Dizzy Gillespie, Fats Navarro, Kenny Dorham, Sarah Vaughan, and arranger Tadd Dameron. It was seeing the Billy Eckstine Orchestra as a child that Miles Davis would later remark was what made him sure he wanted to be a musician.

© Bettmann/CORBIS

Davis would later join Eckstine's band replacing Navarro.

All along, Eckstine had been performing solo work as well, and quite successfully, scoring million sellers with both "Cottage For Sale" and "Prisoner Of Love" in 1945. After several years of touring, in 1947 Eckstine disbanded the group and set out on his own as a solo performer, focusing more on his balladry. As one of the first signings to the newly formed MGM Records, Eckstine began churning out numerous hits like "My Foolish Heart," "I Apologize," "Everything I Have Is Yours," "Blue Moon," and "Caravan." By 1949 Eckstine was the Top Male Vocalist and the Most Pop-

ular Singer in *Metronome* and *Down Beat* magazines, respectively, and by 1950 was MGM's top-selling singer, drawing record-breaking crowds in Los Angeles and New York. Additionally, Eckstine created a fashion craze with his narrow ties, loose-fitting suits and his trademark Mr. B. Collar, a look that was popular with both hipsters and mobsters. Eckstine appeared on numerous variety shows, including *The Ed Sullivan Show*, *The Tonight Show*, *The Joey Bishop Show*, and *The Flip Wilson Show*. He even had a cameo on *Sanford & Son*. *Life* magazine featured Eckstine in a story, the first time a black singer would grace the cover.

Eckstine continued to tour and record as a singer and multi-instrumentalist for decades. His final recording was the Grammy-nominated *Billy Eckstine Sings With Benny Carter* in 1986.

Throughout his career, even at its peak, Eckstine frequently returned to Pittsburgh to play the local clubs that were once the most important jazz scenes in the world. Eckstine died in Pittsburgh in 1993.

Goldie Edwards

Born January 14, 1934—Auckland, NZ

Some athletes seem to defy pain. Others, gravity.

For nearly a half-century, Goldie Edwards seemed to defy time itself. Playing squash, she held a national title longer than any athlete in Pittsburgh history—25 years.

Born in 1934 in Auckland, New Zealand, Dr. Marigold A. Edwards played competitive, winning sports for nearly 50 years: field hockey, 1952-59; badminton, 1960-64; tennis 1960-62; squash, 1968-2000.

Armed with a New Zealand college degree, she was touring the world when she got a 1962 call from Pitt: could she join them in the emerging field of exercise physiology? Thirty-seven years later, she retired.

Developing such courses as healthy lifestyle, stress management, and good nutrition—then revolutionary, now standard—she also served as a special consultant to the President's Council on Physical Fitness and Sports, earning her master's and Ph.D. in exercise physiology.

Switching to squash in 1968—at age 34, far above the starting point for any serious player—she played three hours a day, seven days a week, "and did better at it than I had at anything else," she recalls.

A former national Senior Singles Squash Champion, 1974-98, Edwards' list of awards, championships, and gold medals seems endless. Ranked in the top 10 by the United States Squash Racquets Association in all but two years, 1968-93, and in the top four, 1969-90, Edwards twice won the Canadian Ladies Single Championship, 1970-71. Decades later she was still winning gold medals. In 1996, for

example, at the inaugural International Senior Games in Bermuda, and the World Masters Games in 1998. Her last win came in 2000 at age 66; her last competition the following year.

The first woman inducted into the Pennsylvania Sports Hall of Fame, Western Pennsylvania chapter, she retired in Pittsburgh. Still in shape, Edwards bicycles, walks, and hikes the New Zealand mountains, where she returns annually.

Roy Eldridge

Born January 30, 1911—Pittsburgh
Died February 26, 1989—Paris, France

Roy David "Little Jazz" Eldridge was a standout in the jazz world, not merely for his energetic and superb trumpet playing but for also being among the first African-Americans in an all-white jazz band.

A student of Louis Armstrong's style of playing, Eldridge, during the 1930s would later be regarded by many as technically superior to Armstrong. He began playing drums at the age of 6 and got his first formal training on the trumpet from older brother Joe, who played saxophone. He led a local band for a while and then at just 16 began performing with a touring carnival where he would mimic intricate solos by esteemed artists such as Coleman Hawkins. Eldridge spent time playing throughout the Midwest before landing in New York.

Eldridge's highly competitive nature pushed him constantly to out-play fellow musicians, especially during late night "cutting contests." It was Eldridge's speed and timing that became a major influence on Dizzy Gillespie, who was so instrumental in the formation of bop.

In 1941, Eldridge was asked to join legendary drummer Gene Krupa's band. Among the first occasion in which a black musician would become a regular member of a white band, frequent episodes of discrimination were a painful reality for Eldridge. Once, at the Valencia Ballroom in York, PA, Krupa was arrested for punching out the club owner for refusing to admit Eldridge to play.

He moved to Paris for a period of time and produced some of the finest recordings of his career. Returning stateside in the early '50s, he became a fixture in the jazz world, playing with artists like Benny Carter and Ella Fitzgerald. Eldridge continued performing through the next several decades until he suffered a stroke which hampered his trumpet playing. Not to be held back, Eldridge pressed ahead as a singer and pianist until his death in 1989.

Esteban

Born June 26, 1948—Bethel Park, PA

Sandwiched between Library Road and West Liberty Avenue sits Seton LaSalle, the result of a merger between South Hills Catholic and Elizabeth Seton High Schools, which has graduated such local down-home guys as the Honorable Judge Jack Bova, sportscaster John Steigerwald and... Esteban. Yeah, the Zorro-looking guy in the dark sunglasses and bolero hat. That Esteban.

Stephen M. Paul grew up in Bethel Park. His father Ed was a steelworker and his mother Marian, a homemaker. His love—obsession really—for the guitar began at the age of 8 when his uncle George from Squirrel Hill bought him his first acoustic guitar. It never left his hands. Paul taught himself to play and was deeply influenced by his uncle who would expose him to everything from Benny Goodman to Vicente Gomez. By 12, he was giving other kids guitar lessons and cleaning-up on the talent show circuit. He attended Carnegie Mellon where he double-majored in Music and English Literature.

Between his studies and gigs at local nightclubs, Paul honed his playing skills and immersed himself in the stylings of the father of modern classical guitar, Andre Segovia. Relentless in his drive to study with Segovia, Paul essentially began stalking him, sending hundreds of notes inscribed, "My life is meaningless unless I study with you." Segovia eventually gave in and soon Paul was in Spain on what was to turn into a four-year instructional sabbatical with Segovia. It was here that Stephen Paul would become Esteban, the Spanish translation of Stephen and the name that the maestro Segovia gave to his student.

In 1978, Esteban returned to the states and began touring. Just two years later, he was in a near-fatal car crash and suffered broken ribs, lost a number of teeth, developed a light-sensitive eye (the reason for the omnipresent sunglasses) and suffered nerve damage to his left arm and hand, rendering him unable to play the guitar. Esteban resorted to sales work to feed his family. After ten years of therapeutic acupuncture, he began to regain feeling in his fingers and he resumed playing.

He regained his former skill level and found work playing guitar in the lobby of a Hyatt Regency in Scottsdale, Arizona. A hit with patrons, an album under his belt and adoration from many fans, Esteban played the Hyatt for the next 11 years. In 1999, Esteban came to the attention of the inventor of the Miracle Mop and was invited to play on QVC, launching the Flamenco guitar instruction tour de force that the world has come to know. Moving to HSN, Esteban sold 132,000 CDs after two appearances and his albums rapidly climbed *Billboard*'s charts. In 2000, Esteban left his job at the Hyatt Regency.

The subject of frequent ridicule, and never at a loss for detractors, Esteban is now marketing his instructional DVDs and American Legacy Guitar line. He has sold millions of CDs, performing all over the world, including several stints in Las Vegas. Frequently he tops *Billboard*'s New Age chart. He has appeared on *The Late Show with David Letterman*, has been parodied on *South Park*, and was featured in *The Wall Street Journal* and *People* magazine. More recently, he starred in a Geiko Insurance television spot.

PHOTO COURTESY OF ESTEBAN, ESTEBANMUSIC.COM, AND PAUL SCHNEIDER

William Eythe

Born April 7, 1918—Mars, PA
Died January 26, 1957—Los Angeles, CA

Good timing may be everything to a comedian, but it can make or break actors, too. William Eythe started his professional career performing in *Lend An Ear* at the Pittsburgh Playhouse, soon after graduating from Carnegie Tech in 1941. Perhaps ironically, within two years, while playing the role of a Nazi in Steinbeck's *The Moon is Down* on Broadway, he ruptured his ear drum, and was thus, forever disqualified for active military duty. With most every young man heading off to World War II, he was discovered as one of very few male leads available for work in Hollywood.

© ASSOCIATED PRESS

His first screen role, though a small part, was played in *The Ox-Bow Incident*. And shortly thereafter, he took on lead roles in *Wing and a Prayer, The Eve of St. Mark, The House on 92nd Street,* and *A Royal Scandal*. Just 27 years old, he returned to Pittsburgh to be feted at the William Penn Hotel, visit his drama teacher, Marry Morris, and stay with his parents, Mr. & Mrs. Carl S. Eythe (he, a successful contractor) still residing in his boyhood home in Mars, PA.

As a student at Mars High School and as an undergraduate at Carnegie Tech, Eythe held many odd jobs. "And believe me, they were odd," he once said. He was a rote lecturer of astronomy at the Buhl Planetarium, worked in a dairy store, and launched with fellow Carnegie Tech students the Fox Chapel Players, a theatrical company that apparently lasted but one performance.

Perhaps Eythe was most famous for his final scene in his second film ever, 1943's *The Song of Bernadette*. Eythe played opposite Jennifer Jones. Of course, many film credits followed. He also later produced *Lend An Ear* on Broadway, featuring a very young Carol Channing.

In January of 1957, at the age of 38, Eythe died of complications from hepatitis, and is buried in St. Peter's Cemetery in Butler.

Above, Eythe dances with June Haver on the dance floor of the Hollywood Mocambo, December 29, 1944.

Roy Face

Born February 20, 1928—Stephentown, NY

A three-time All Star, 1959-61, from 1953-69 Roy Face was one of the National League's premier relief pitchers—and a Pirate bullpen mainstay. Elroy Leon Face had remarkable strength and consistency—especially for a man who stood but 5'-8" and played at 155 pounds.

One of the first modern relief specialists to develop a trademark pitch, Face relied on a devastating forkball—a pitch jammed between the index and middle fingers, which, thrown like a fastball, breaks sharply at the plate. During a career that lasted from 1953-68 for the Pirates, there were years that the rubber-armed Face was virtually unbeatable. From 1956-63, for example, he never finished out of the National League's top six in games pitched, taking first place twice. During his career, Face placed in the top five in saves 10 times, including three first-place finishes. Recording 96 career relief wins, and 193 saves, Face still holds the major-league record for most relief wins in a season, 18 (17 consecutive)— matched by only one defeat. That year, 1959, his 18-1 record, or .947, remains the major-league benchmark.

Although many of Face's records have been eclipsed, he still holds the National League career mark for games finished (574) and games pitched for one club (802—all for the Pirates).

Always dependable in high-stakes situations, in the 1960 World Series against the New York Yankees, Face saved three of the Pirates' four wins. Pitching until he was a gray-bearded 41, in mid-'68 he went to the Detroit Tigers, then played his last season (1969) with the Montreal Expos. Strong, sentient, never sore-armed, Face crediting his extraordinary durability to his off-season work as a carpenter. "I always kept my arm in shape," he said, "by putting in people's game rooms."

Scott Fahlman

Born March 21, 1948—Medina, Ohio

The problem that 33-year-old Scott Fahlman solved at his research job at CMU was not a joke.

In the early days of bulletin board or bboard communications, where professors and students would discuss subjects of enormous complexity via simple text screen typing, one student might mistake a professor's sense of humor as sarcasm or indifference. "After all," noted Fahlman years later, "when using text-based online communication, we lack the body language or tone-of-voice cues that convey this information when we talk in person or on the phone." Fahlman would know; his entire academic life, beginning with his undergraduate years at MIT, was devoted to developing digital languages.

Earning both his B.S. and M.S. in electrical engineering and computer science from the Massachusetts Institute of Technology in 1973, he received his Ph.D. in artificial intelligence from the same institution in 1977. By July of the following year, he was employed at CMU as a research computer scientist. And for nearly forty years he has led the development of CMU Common Lisp, an extensive programming environment, as well as co-writing two programming languages for Apple. Fahlman also shares a patent, titled "Method for transforming message containing sensitive information."

Back in 1982, human sensitivity irked him more. When fellow communicators on his bboard wouldn't get a joke—or worse, went into a tirade or "flamed" the discussion board—Fahlman knew that he needed to add a visual marker. Wrote Fahlman on September 19, 1982:

From: Scott E Fahlman <Fahlman at Cmu-20c> I propose that the following character sequence for joke markers: :-) Read it sideways. Actually, it is probably more economical to mark things that are NOT jokes, given current trends. For this, use :-(

The lasting impact of Fahlman's "smileys"—or emoticons (for emotion icons)—is found in both AOL and Microsoft languages which recognize the combined keystrokes and deliver a wholly new graphic character. ☺

Barbara Feldon

Born March 12, 1932—Butler, PA

Long before being cast in the supporting role as Agent 99, in Mel Brooks and Buck Henry's long running TV comedy, *Get Smart!*, Barbara Feldon had claimed two distinctions in her young career. First, she was a *$64,000 Question* winner for knowing her Shakespeare, and secondly she had captured the American male's ego when, in a memorable commercial for Top Brass dandruff cream, she stretched out on a tiger rug, growled, and coaxed her men to "Sic 'em, Tiger."

Barbara Hall took ballet classes as a young girl, attended Bethel Park High School, and graduated from Carnegie Tech in 1955. For several years, she appeared in productions at the William Penn Playhouse, (now the Little Lake,) White Barn and Pittsburgh Playhouse. By 1957, while on the New York stage in *Ziegfeld's Follies*, she met photographer's agent, Lucien Feldon. Together they opened an art gallery in New York City while she sought work as a model and commercial actress. Her big break came when Top Brass aired her sultry persona, and she was suggested as a co-star to Don Adams. Although much taller than Maxwell Smart, Agent 99 rarely wore shoes on the set, so as not to upstage the bumbling spy. Feldon appeared in 131 episodes of *Get Smart!* from 1965 to 1970.

Feldon also appeared in a few movies, notably *Fitzwilly* with Dick Van Dyke, and was featured on many sitcoms after the run of *Get Smart!*. Divorced from Lucien Feldon, she married Burt Nodella, *Get Smart!*'s producer, but then, too, divorced seven years later. Today, living in New York City, she is an advocate for women's rights, author of *Living Alone and Loving It*, and is still called on often for her sultry voice and sexy growl.

George Ferris

Born in 1859—Galesburg, IL
Died in 1896—Pittsburgh

A fair just wouldn't be a fair without a Ferris Wheel. The well-loved revolving ride was invented more than 100 years ago by Pittsburgh engineer George Washington Gale Ferris. His giant observation ride was one of the most popular attractions at the 1893 Chicago World's Fair, and today, Ferris Wheels of various sizes make their rounds all over the world.

Ferris was born in Illinois, and lived in both Nevada and California as a child. In 1881, he received an engineering degree from Rensselaer Polytechnic Institute in New York. Eventually, the young engineer moved to Pittsburgh and started his own business, G.W.G. Ferris & Co., Inspecting Engineers, testing metals for bridges and railroads. He called the Steel City home for the remainder of his life.

When organizers of the 1893 Chicago World's Fair searched for a signature structure that would outshine the Eiffel Tower, Ferris stepped forward with a novel idea for a large revolving observation attraction reminiscent of a bicycle wheel. At first, the fair directors dismissed his idea as impossible, but they eventually agreed to let him build the daring ride.

Ferris' wheel was more than 250 feet tall and powered by two 1,000-horsepower steam engines. The wheel's axle was the largest piece of steel forged at the time, weighing 46-1/2 tons. The ride boasted 36 railroad car-sized gondolas, each carrying up to 60 passengers, allowing the wheel to accommodate more than 2,000 people per ride.

The Ferris Wheel carried its first riders on June 21, 1893. Fairgoers paid 50 cents for two revolutions and breathtaking views of the famous Chicago fairgrounds, also known as the White City. Ferris' invention was dubbed the "mechanical wonder of the fair," and it astounded visitors from around the globe.

The Ferris Wheel was reused at the St. Louis World's Fair in 1904 but was dismantled shortly afterward.

Until recently, the London Eye, a gigantic observation ride on the banks of the River Thames in London, was the tallest Ferris Wheel in the world. The famous landmark was outdone, however, by China's Star of Nanchang in 2006, which stands more than 520 feet tall.

Jerry Fielding

Born June 17, 1922—Pittsburgh
Died February 17, 1980—Toronto, Canada

Best known for his macho film scores, Jerry Fielding was one of the most successful and more experimental composers in Hollywood during the '60s and '70s.

He was born Joshua Feldman. Captivated as a teen by swing and sophisticated musical arrangements by the likes of Academy Award-winning composer Bernard Herrmann, he was given formal musical instruction by Max Adkins. He became proficient at piano, clarinet and saxophone, and before long, Fielding was writing arrangements for the Stanley Theatre's pit orchestra where Adkins served as conductor. Just 17 and still in high school, Fielding was introduced to guitar swing great Alvino Rey and the King Sisters, and with them, he hit the road.

He began writing arrangements for Tommy Dorsey, Charlie Barnet, Claude Thornhill, Kay Kyser, and one of his greatest influences, bandleader Jimmy Lunceford. His work brought him to the attention of Hollywood and Fielding was hired as the musical director for *The Jack Parr Show*. Forming his own orchestra in 1952, Fielding then conducted the house band for Groucho Marx's popular game show, *You Bet Your Life*. Fielding's hiring of African-American musicians, and his leftist affiliations, brought him to the attention of Senator Joe McCarthy and the House Un-American Activities Committee. When asked to testify, and to implicate Marx, Fielding took the Fifth. But Groucho fired him anyway. "That I bowed to sponsors' demands is one of the greatest regrets of my life," Marx would later write.

Blacklisted and out of work, Fielding headed for the lights of Las Vegas and rapidly found work with stars such as Eddie Fisher, Debbie Reynolds, and Abbott and Costello. He returned to Hollywood in 1962 and began writing music for television, most notably the theme to *Hogan's Heroes*. More significantly he began a successful run scoring some of Hollywood's biggest films in the decade of the '70s. Among his scores are *The Wild Bunch* and *Straw Dogs* (both of which earned Academy Award® nominations), *The Gauntlet*, *The Enforcer*, *Escape From Alcatraz*, and *The Outlaw Josie Wales* (which also earned an Oscar® nomination).

In 1980, while working in Canada, Fielding died of a heart attack. He was only 57.

Regina Fisher

Born in 1923—Pittsburgh

"Film is cheap," Roy Stryker told the young woman in June, 1951, "but your time is not. Use as much as you want."

Directed to photograph inner-city playgrounds, 28-year-old Regina Fisher's shot behind the Bloomfield swimming pool made her famous. Her image of two boys playing in an abstract landscape of concrete culvert and monkey bars won her $400 from *Life* magazine—and got her picture on the cover, young and pretty and hopeful, November 26, 1951.

The Allegheny Conference-funded Pittsburgh Photographic Library, which had begun the year before, in 1950, was to document the emerging Pittsburgh Renaissance—a brawny, human city on the move. Stryker, who had directed photography projects for the Farm Securities Administration and Standard Oil of New Jersey, hired a number of veteran photographers, including Harold Corsini, Esther Bubley, and Clyde "Red" Hare. Although Stryker resigned in the fall of 1951, PPL continued, eventually creating some 18,000 images, now in the Carnegie Library. (A representative sampling appears in *Witness to the Fifties*, University of Pittsburgh Press, 1999).

Fisher, the only PPL member born in Pittsburgh, 1923, was raised in Wilkinsburg and Irwin, and studied studio art at Carnegie Tech. Working for a New York photographer, she took classes at the New School. One night, Stryker spoke to Fisher's pictorial journalism class. Hoping to get work, Fisher tried to contact Stryker, only to find he had gone to her hometown to direct the PPL project.

Returning herself, Fisher contacted Stryker. Agreeing to take her for a few weeks, Stryker sent Fisher to Pittsburgh's neighborhoods.

After Stryker's resignation, Fisher rejoined PPL twice, in May, 1952, and March, 1953, contributing some of the PPL's strongest images—worn, weathered people presented with enormous compassion.

Joseph Fitzpatrick

Born in 1909—Williamstown, PA
Died in 1994—St. Marys, PA

Then there was the time that Joe Fitzpatrick told Frank Lloyd Wright how beautiful Pittsburgh was.

The Master, however, wanted none of it. "It would be easier to tear it down," he growled, "than improve it."

That's when Fitzpatrick gave Wright a piece of his mind, telling America's most famous architect how ungrateful he was, how he lacked an appreciation of real beauty.

"Wright was taken aback," Fitzpatrick remembered years later. "Nobody ever talked to him like that."

Nobody, except Joe Fitzpatrick, who never backed off from the truth, be it about art or his adopted home, Pittsburgh.

Arguably the city's greatest 20th-century art teacher, for more than 30 years he influenced literally thousands of students, Philip Pearlstein to Andy Warhol, Jonathan Borofsky to Annie Dillard.

Born Joseph C. Fitzpatrick, in Williamstown, Dauphin County, in 1909, he came west, to Edinboro State College, taking a 1931 art teaching degree. After a 1934 master's from Columbia, Fitzpatrick moved to Pittsburgh, to paint, to teach.

A tall man with white hair, he taught at Schenley High School, later supervised the Pittsburgh Public Schools' art curriculum. On Saturdays, Fitzpatrick taught at the Carnegie Institute, in the Tam O'Shanter and Saturday Palette classes. Endlessly encouraging, Fitzpatrick joyfully inspired generations of Pittsburgh artists to do well—then do better. "Look to see to remember to enjoy," he'd enjoin them, and they did.

A talented artist in his own right, Fitzpatrick was the one-time president of Pittsburgh's Associated Artists. Hosting WQED-TV's syndicated *World of Art* in 1957, in 1973 he was named the Pittsburgh Center for the Arts Artist of the Year.

Retiring from the Pittsburgh Public Schools in 1974, Fitzpatrick remained in Pittsburgh, living in his Fifth Avenue row house, walking everywhere.

Moved to the Elk Haven Nursing Home in St. Marys, Fitzpatrick died of congestive heart failure at age 85, in 1994.

Joe Flaherty

Born June 21, 1941—Pittsburgh

Pittsburgh is famous for its Flahertys, but Joseph O'Flaherty may be the best known of the lot. For seven seasons he was an ensemble comedic star of *SCTV* wherein he created dozens of immortal characters, one clearly modeled after his hometown's own Chilly Billy.

A student of Central Catholic and Westinghouse High, he joined the Air Force, then attended Point Park College on the G.I. Bill. After but one year, hanging out at the Pittsburgh Playhouse, he was hired by a small Chicago improv group to hang lights. But he wound up on stage. After seven years appearing almost nightly on stage, fellow Second Citizens John Candy, Eugene Levy, Andrea Martin, Harold Ramis and Dave Thomas created a concept for a low-budget TV show, one that satirized television by showing the underbelly of a small town TV station. *SCTV* premiered one year after *Saturday Night Live*.

Flaherty played Guy Caballero, the independent station's wheelchair-bound general manger; Floyd Robertson, the slick newscaster; Count Floyd, host of Monster Chiller Horror Theater; and, Sammy Maudlin, the smarmy host of a self-adoring talk show. Unlike *SNL*, Flaherty and his co-stars actually wrote all of their own material. Flaherty won two Emmys® for comedy writing. In small parts, Flaherty's younger brother Paul also wrote and appeared in Count Floyd segments as the Pittsburgh Midget—close shades of Bill Cardille's castle of characters.

In more recent years, Flaherty has had many recurring roles in TV sitcoms, playing Commander Helfilfinger on *Police Academy: The Series*, the father Harold Weir on *Freaks & Geeks*, and Father McAndrew on the *King of Queens*. To cult fans, he is also well known for his small bit as the heckler in the Adam Sandler film, *Happy Gilmore*.

Stephen Flaherty

Born September 18, 1960—Dormont

He improvised piano accompaniment for Sister Judith Kenaan's production of *Peter Pan* at St. Bernard's School in Mt. Lebanon when he was 12, and he has been writing musicals ever since. Born in Dormont, Stephen Flaherty is the Tony Award®-winning composer of *Lucky Stiff, Once On This Island, My Favorite Year, Ragtime, Seussical,* and *The Glorious Ones* which premiered at the Pittsburgh Public Theater and debuted on Broadway in October, 2007.

A graduate of South Hills High School ('78) and the Cincinnati College Conservatory ('82,) Flaherty has worked with lyricist Lynn Ahrens since 1983. A former ad copywriter responsible for writing many of the songs of ABC's *Schoolhouse Rock*, Ahrens also wrote the jingle for "What Would You do For a Klondike Bar?" Their first collaboration, *Lucky Stiff,* ran Off-Broadway and helped cement the team name Flaherty & Ahrens—not unlike Rodgers & Hammerstein—within New York circles. The production was also choreographed by Graciela Danielle who directed their most recent Broadway production, *The Glorious Ones*.

Perhaps their most significant achievement is *Ragtime*, E.L. Doctorow's epic novel, turned stage play by Terrence McNally, which covers the popular history of early 20th century New York, focusing on Evelyn Nesbit's courtship by rival suitors Harry Thaw and Stanford White. Following Flaherty's Tony Award for Best Composer, the team collaborated on *Seussical*, which struggled for life on Broadway, but is today one of the most produced high school musicals in the country. So, too, is *Once On This Island,* a romantic, tear jerking musical of Carribean culture.

In 2007, Flaherty returned home—which he does often to visit his large family—to help stage the world premiere of *The Glorious Ones*. In October the production debuted at The Lincoln Center to promising reviews.

Sharon Flake

Born December 24, 1955—N. Philadelphia, PA

The e-mail to Sharon Flake came from an Alabama high-school librarian. It seemed that all these teenaged white boys were reserving her 1998 young-adult book *The Skin I'm In*—and why was that? Skin?—something about sex?

A peek inside told the librarian that this tale of a misfit African-American girl had struck a chord with all adolescents. And therein lies the secret of Flake's success—a success that runs to sales in the serious six figures.

Born Sharon Geraldine Flake, she never wrote before moving to Pittsburgh. "I didn't think I had talent," she says.

Coming to Pitt to study medicine, she switched to English writing. After graduating, and working with troubled youth at McIntyre Shelter, she came back to the university, working in public relations for 18 years. Spurred by an article in *Essence* magazine, Flake began to write a young adult novel. By 1998 she was ready to show it around.

Six titles later—*The Skin I'm In* (1998), *Money Hungry* (2002), *Begging for Change* (2003), *Who Am I Without Him?* (2004), *Bang!* (2005), and *The Broken Bike Boy and the Queen of 33rd Street* (2007)—Flake has won numerous awards and sold a half-million books.

With her fiction used in public and private schools around the nation, Flake is also college-level required reading for students in education, child development, and children's literature. In addition, her work is favored by adult book clubs.

Working from her modest Stanton Heights home, Flake is happy that her novels have found multiple audiences—not only among young African-American women, but among people of all ages and races. "They're all connecting at the same place," she says. "Especially kids. There's a vulnerability in my characters that all people can connect to. My characters are very direct and blunt—and that's very real."

John Forbes

Born September 5, 1707—Scotland
Died March 11, 1759—Philadelphia, PA

The lengthy thoroughfare running though Pittsburgh's East End and the classic baseball stadium the Pirates called home from 1909 to 1970 were named for John Forbes, a military officer whose campaign against the French-held Fort Duquesne brought him to the Pittsburgh region.

After an early military career in Europe, which included service with distinction in the War for Austrian Succession, Forbes traveled to the New World in 1757 during the French and Indian War. The British Secretary of State William Pitt selected Forbes to mount a campaign against Fort Duquesne, a French outpost located at the confluence of the Allegheny and Monongahela rivers. Only several years earlier British General Edward Braddock had been charged with the same

task but was ambushed and defeated. In 1758, General Forbes departed Philadelphia for Fort Duquesne. He opted not to advance along Braddock's original route, instead choosing a different path westward, making sure to stop periodically in order to establish supply depots and defensive posts along the way. His campaign route was later named Forbes Road.

As he advanced on Fort Duquesne, Forbes divided his force into three brigades—one commanded by George Washington—in order to best assault the French garrison. On November 25, 1758, however, Forbes succeeded in capturing Fort Duquesne without a fight. Entering the burned and abandoned French outpost, he promptly erected a British flag and renamed it Fort Pitt in honor of William Pitt. The name "Pittsboro"—later, Pittsburgh—has endured for 250 years.

Walter Forward

Born January 24, 1786—East Granby, CT
Died November 24, 1852—Squirrel Hill

Walter Forward came to Pittsburgh a penniless 16-year-old with no formal schooling. Some accounts even say he traded a lucky horseshoe found during his travels for ferry passage across the river into town. These meager beginnings did not deter the ambitious Forward, however, and after a serendipitous meeting with his mentor, the prominent lawyer Henry Baldwin, he found his way to becoming one of Pittsburgh's community leaders in law and politics.

For the first few years in Pittsburgh, Forward worked closely with Baldwin to learn law. At age 19, he was the editor of the Jeffersonian newspaper *Tree of Liberty* and one year later was admitted to the Pittsburgh Bar. He married in 1808 and settled his family on Hays Row near Penn Avenue.

Forward became known for his strong moral character, oration skills, and his no nonsense approach to trial work. In 1817, he was elected to the state legislature and after the retirement of Baldwin, was elected to replace him in Congress from 1822 -1825.

Forward was a man of the people and fought on their behalf for better roads and river navigation. In 1837, he was part of the Constitutional Convention and played a prominent role in reforming Pennsylvania's public school system. It was during this time he moved his wife and six children to a larger homestead in Pebbles Township, now Squirrel Hill.

Forward's political career peaked in 1841 when he was offered the position of U.S. district attorney under President William Henry Harrison. He declined the offer, only to accept the appointment of comptroller of currency a few months later. After Harrison's death, Forward was named Secretary of the Treasury under President Tyler; he resigned in 1843 to return to his legal roots in Pittsburgh. By 1851, Forward was serving as president judge of the District Court of Allegheny County. One year later he took ill on the bench and died at age 66. Forward Avenue in Squirrel Hill is named for him. He is buried in Allegheny Cemetery.

Stephen Foster

Born July 4, 1826—Lawrenceville
Died January 13, 1864—New York, NY

"Dear Friends and Gentle Hearts" read the small note found in the pocket of the destitute 37-year-old Stephen Collins Foster upon his untimely death in New York City. Perhaps this was the beginning of another song for the prolific composer of "Oh Susanna," "Camptown Races," and "My Old Kentucky Home." Considered America's first composer and musician, Foster wrote popular lyrics and harmonies for over 200 songs with both minstrel shows and parlor parties in mind, feeding the growing mid-19th-century appetite for a distinctly American musical style.

The youngest of four, Foster was born in Lawrenceville where his father owned a stately home and sizeable tracts of land, but struggled to keep them. The battle ended when Foster was 3, and the family was evicted. They remained downwardly mobile for the rest of his childhood, bouncing from Allegheny City to Pittsburgh to Youngstown, OH. In later years, Stephen's older, more successful brothers helped him with a formal education and business opportunities in Cincinnati, neither of which he pursued with enthusiasm. Instead, Foster's early aptitude for music preoccupied his time and when his first song sold in 1842 he'd found his livelihood. Some say a longing for "home" pervades his lyrics because of his childhood upheavals. The death of his musically inclined older sister Charlotte also greatly affected him. She is said to be the inspiration for his 1848 success: "Oh, Susanna." (Susanna being Charlotte's middle name.) Foster never earned much money despite the popularity of his work due to both his own inept business savvy and his fondness for drink and merriment.

Although the tunes remain catchy and timeless, some of his most popular songs, written in dialect for minstrel shows where singers performed in blackface, have what would be considered today racist lyrics. His melodies and "doo-dah" lyrics evoked a simpler life, which resonated with Americans in the 1840s and 1850s when rapid expansion and growing commerce, and the institution of slavery divided the country. Pittsburgh is never mentioned, rather lands of the South and the West, some of which he never visited.

Innovations in mass printing and distribution helped his songs reach audiences throughout the United States, creating a wildly popular, American music with themes that have been adored for more than a century. Foster is buried in Allegheny Cemetery.

Bill Fralic

Born October 31, 1962—Penn Hills

There was tackle Bill Fralic, an eighth-grader, invited to work out with the Penn Hills varsity before the season. As it happened, a college scout spotted him. Ignoring all the juniors and seniors, he asked coach Bill Urbanic about the 13-year-old who just happened to be 6'-4" and 235 pounds.

Born William P. Fralic, Jr., he had an astonishing 20-year football run as an offensive lineman. Beginning at age 11 playing for the Morningside Bulldogs against teen-aged players, Fralic was already fully grown in high school, Penn Hills, Class of 1981. Standing 6'-5" and 260 pounds, he could bench press more than 400. During his four-year varsity tenure, Penn Hills lost just three games, while taking three Associated Press state champion polls.

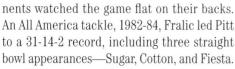

Parade's 1980 National Player of the Year, Fralic chose Pitt for college, 1981-85. Putting on 25 more pounds, the four-letter letterman's hits were so shattering that the term pancake block was invented for him, meaning opponents watched the game flat on their backs. An All America tackle, 1982-84, Fralic led Pitt to a 31-14-2 record, including three straight bowl appearances—Sugar, Cotton, and Fiesta.

Drafted second in the nation by the Atlanta Falcons in 1985, Fralic was a four-time Pro Bowler, 1986-89, and a two-time team MVP. Playing in Atlanta through 1992, Fralic's final year was with the Detroit Lions, 1993.

A veteran of *WrestleMania 2*, 1986, when he and other NFL stars took on Andre the Giant, Fralic was elected to the College Football Hall of Fame in 1999.

While Fralic and his family live in Atlanta, where he owns Bill Fralic Insurance Services, he serves as Pitt football color commentator. Having created the William P. Fralic Foundation in 1992 to help Pittsburgh-area youth athletic programs, he runs the Bill Fralic Golf Classic, an annual fundraiser.

John Frank

Born April 17, 1962—Pittsburgh

What is rarer in sports than to be a college MVP, enjoy a championship pro career, then return to your alma mater for an MD?

It all happened to Mt. Lebanon's John Frank.

Frank played Big Ten football at Ohio State. Standing 6'-3" and 225, starting at tight end 1981-83, Frank was a three-time Academic All America, two-time All-Big Ten, and Ohio State MVP.

For good reason. In 1981, Frank caught 45 passes for 449 yards as the Buckeyes took a share of the Big Ten title. The following year, OSU went to the Holiday Bowl, Frank taking All-Big Ten honors. Finally, in his senior year, 1983, as Frank was team MVP and again All-Big Ten, the Buckeyes went to the Fiesta Bowl, where Frank's four catches for 57 yards iced a 28-23 victory over the Pitt Panthers.

Finishing as the all-time Ohio State tight end, in 1988 OSU inducted him into the school's Hall of Fame.

Drafted by the San Francisco '49s in 1984, Frank joined fellow Pittsburgher Joe Montana as a member of one of the most devastating offenses in NFL history. Again playing tight end, Frank helped his team win two Super Bowls—XIX (1984 season) and XXIII (1988 season).

Retiring after five seasons, 1984-88, earning two Super Bowl rings, Frank returned to Ohio State to purse a medical degree, which he earned in 1992.

Yet his sports career was not over. In 2002 Frank co-created a bobsled team to compete in the Winter Olympics—for Israel, a country with virtually no snow. Practicing in Canada, the team entered world-class events. However, their times were not sufficient to warrant a seed at the 2006 Turin Olympics.

A surgeon in New York and San Francisco, in 2006 John Frank was inducted into the National Jewish Sports Hall of Fame.

Chris Frantz

Born May 8, 1951—Fort Campbell, KY

Who would have guessed that when The Lost Chords played a gig at the Fox Chapel Presbyterian Church back in the late 1960s, that it would be a stepping stone to the famed CBGB's club that produced some of the hottest bands of the late '70s. It was for Lost Chords drummer Chris Frantz less than a decade later when his band The Talking Heads became one of the biggest bands in the land.

Charton Christopher Frantz, a military brat, was born at Fort Campbell, Kentucky. His father had earned a law degree in the Army and while remaining in the Army Reserve, he moved the family to the North Hills so that he could take a job with a downtown law firm.

Frantz's musical exploits began at about 10 years old when he tried his hand at the trumpet, then the trombone, and eventually settled in on the drums. Frantz attended Berkeley Hills Elementary School, where he was a drummer in the school band, and then the family moved to O'Hara and enrolled their young drummer at Kerr Elementary and then Aspinwall Junior High School. Frantz graduated from Shady Side Academy and enrolled at The Rhode Island School of Design (RISD), where he would meet Tina Weymouth and David Byrne.

While at RISD, Frantz and Weymouth became an item and moved to New York. In need of a bassist, Weymouth took up the instrument and the three began collaborating in preparation for what was to become a landmark debut at CBGB's—opening for The Ramones.

The Talking Heads quickly became part of the New York club scene, along with bands like Blondie, Television and The Ramones. The trio was rounded out by Jerry Harrison, former keyboardist with Jonathan Richman's band The Modern Lovers. With heavy rotation on MTV and as part of the exploding "new wave" scene, The Talking Heads became a mainstay, appearing on everything from *Saturday Night Live* to *David Letterman*.

In 1981 the band took a hiatus and Frantz and Weymouth, who were now married, embarked on a side project they called The Tom Tom Club. They produced something that the Talking Heads had not done—a gold record. "Genius Of Love" became one of the most sampled songs in music history.

The Talking Heads reunited and produced some of their most successful recordings until 1991 when David Byrne announced to the *L.A. Times* that the band was calling it quits. Frantz and Weymouth continued with the Tom Tom Club, which still records today. Additionally, Frantz has been active in other projects throughout the years, producing and recording with various emerging bands, including adding drums and vocals to the hip hop band The Gorillaz. Frantz and his wife Weymouth have also produced recordings for Ziggy Marley, The Happy Mondays, Los Fabulosos Cadillacs, and Angelfish.

Left, wife Tina Weymouth and Frantz appear in the limelight of The Talking Heads in 1980.

Henry Clay Frick

Born December 19, 1849—West Overton, PA
Died December 2, 1919—New York, NY

At age 21, Henry Clay Frick entered the coal and coke business; in 10 years he would be a millionaire. A controversial figure from Pittsburgh's turn-of-the-last-century industrial history, Frick built his fortune providing coke to the nation's iron and steel works, and as an executive for the Carnegie Steel Corporation. Frick became a renowned art collector and philanthropist whose legacy is visible in the region today.

Born in West Overton, Westmoreland County, Frick was determined to make his fortune from a young age. As a young man he entered a mining partnership with two cousins and canvassed southwestern Pennsylvania, securing customers for the firm. A meticulous manager with a keen financial mind, Frick purchased more land and built coke ovens across the region. Soon, Frick had coke orders from across the country and fulfilled his wish of being a millionaire by age 30. In 1881, Frick married Adelaide Howard Childs, daughter of prominent Pittsburgh shoe merchants. The couple would settle into Clayton, a mansion at the corner of Penn and Homewood Avenues in the fashionable Point Breeze neighborhood. There the Fricks raised three children: Childs, Martha (who died at age 5), and Helen.

Frick's rapidly expanding coke empire caught the attention of Andrew Carnegie, whose iron and steel works needed coke by the tons. The two magnates would enter a tumultuous but highly lucrative relationship in 1881, when Carnegie unexpectedly announced their partnership at a luncheon in New York City.

Though Frick's anti-union leanings led to several clashes with labor in his career, he is most remembered for his involvement in the infamous Homestead Steel Strike of 1892. Homestead became national news after striking employees from Carnegie's Homestead Steel Works clashed with Pinkerton detectives hired by Frick, leaving 10 dead and scores injured. Frick's role in the ordeal left him vilified in the press and despised by labor advocates. Labor unions would not establish themselves at Homestead for another 44 years.

Plagued by poor health throughout his life, Frick suffered from debilitating attacks of inflammatory rheumatism. He died in New York, where he lived for the last 15 years of his life, shortly before his 70th birthday.

Albert Gallatin

Born January 29, 1761—Switzerland
Died August 12, 1849—Astoria, NY

When Meriwether Lewis traveled west of Pittsburgh on August 31, 1803, his map was compiled from information provided by Albert Gallatin. A close friend of Thomas Jefferson, Gallatin (who had strongly supported the Louisiana Purchase in his position as Secretary of the Treasury) recognized the potential

of lands west. An ardent map collector, he had special interest in the regions drained by the Missouri River saying, "The future destinies of the Missouri country are of vast importance to the future of the U.S."

Gallatin's life and work before 1803 demonstrated his understanding of the significance of the interior to the growing nation's future prospects. A Swiss immigrant, Gallatin came to this country when he was 18. In 1784 he journeyed to Western Pennsylvania to examine a tract of land he owned. He built a small log structure on the property, sited at the junction of the Monongahela River and Georges Creek in Fayette County. Four years later he purchased a nearby estate, Friendship Hill, which became his home. Though often away in Washington D.C. on business (Gallatin served first in the U.S. Senate and then from 1795 to 1801, in the House of Representatives) he continued to buy and develop property in this region and the Ohio Valley. In 1795, in partnership with four other men, Gallatin expanded his holdings to a site with access to both the river and major overland routes. With three mills already in business, the site seemed ripe for commercial development. The partners added a retail business and made efforts to establish a viable town, naming it New Geneva in honor of Gallatin's Swiss heritage. In 1797, they opened a window and bottle glass factory, one of the first two to open that year in the region. Named Secretary of the Treasury in 1801, Gallatin reduced the public debt and argued for free trade.

After the War of 1812, Gallatin participated in peace negotiations, and then served as minister first to France (1816-23) and then Britain (1826-27). After retiring from politics, he lived the rest of his life in New York where he was instrumental in the founding of the American Ethnological Society.

Chip Ganassi

Born May 24, 1958—Pittsburgh

Barely 24, Chip Ganassi broke into national auto racing at the 1982 Indianapolis 500, where, as the fastest rookie qualifier, he finished 15th.

Born Floyd R. Ganassi, Jr., in 1958 in Pittsburgh, growing up in Fox Chapel, Chip Ganassi was set for life when his father paved a go-kart track for him. With a boyhood spent on go-karts and dirt bikes, it was a short jump to weekend work on Formula Fords and Formula Super Vees as a Duquesne University undergraduate.

Armed with a 1982 business degree, Ganassi went right to the Brickyard, competing in five straight Indy 500s, 1982-86, his best finish coming in '83, a solid 8th.

At the time his racing future seemed assured. The next year, however, Ganassi was in what could have been a life-threatening accident at a Michigan track. Unconscious for 12 hours, he spent a week in the hospital. Although his most serious injury was a broken wrist, Ganassi nevertheless was away from racing for six months. When he returned— to two more Indys, some 30 races in all—he had lost the champion's edge.

Leaving competitive driving in 1987, the following year Ganassi turned to ownership, buying an interest in a racing team. By 1990, he went on his own.

Now, Chip Ganassi Racing has grown to include 10 cars in five different series. Proud possessor of an unprecedented four consecutive CART championships, 1996-99, in 2000 a Ganassi car won the Indianapolis 500. All told, Ganassi cars have seven championships and more than 75 wins. A developer of racing talent, in 2003 Ganassi became the first owner to have three drivers take rookie of the year honors.

Headquartered in Pittsburgh, Ganassi owns facilities in Indianapolis and Concord, North Carolina. A part-owner of the Pittsburgh Pirates and a supporter of St. Jude Children's Hospital, Chip Ganassi still lives in Fox Chapel.

Erroll Garner

Born June 15, 1921—Pittsburgh
Died January 2, 1977—Los Angeles, CA

Physically he was not a big man. In fact, he needed to sit on a telephone book to get his required angle on the keys. But what he lacked in height jazz pianist Erroll Garner more than made up in talent.

He was born Erroll Louis Garner. By the age of 3, Garner was already playing piano with both hands. He was surrounded by music as a child. His mother, who graduated from Avery College, played recordings for the children before going to bed. The following morning young Erroll would dash to the piano where he could play the tune he had heard the night before. Erroll's father was a trumpeter, his older brother Linton played piano, and all three of his sisters were musicians as well. At the age of 7, Erroll began playing on KDKA radio as part of *Kan-D Kids*, a program which showcased talented young musicians. Among his musical influences were Fats Waller and Earl "Fatha" Hines.

Garner attended Westinghouse High School but dropped out to join local saxophonist Leroy Brown's orchestra. After several years with Brown's outfit, Garner made the obligatory exodus all aspiring jazz musicians take—to New York City. His first big gig there was with Slam Stewart, the famous humming bass player. His stint with Slam only lasted a couple of years before he broke out on his own, achieving success in the nightclubs of New York. In 1947, Erroll Garner backed Charlie Parker on his famous "Cool Blues" session during a brief relocation to California.

Over the course of the next 30 years, Erroll Garner enjoyed enormous popularity, from his numerous concert appearances to his frequent television appearances, including *The Tonight Show*, to his classic hit "Misty," the title subject of Clint Eastwood's 1971 film *Play Misty For Me*. He was an ambidextrous master of all 88 keys who was respected and well-liked inside jazz circles, and he was accessible to and enjoyed by the jazz-loving public. His live recording, "Concert By The Sea," was one of the best selling jazz albums of all-time.

In the mid-'70s Erroll Garner enjoyed sold out concerts around the world, even playing a season with the National Symphony in Washington. Poor health forced him to stop touring when he was diagnosed with lung cancer. Erroll Garner passed away in 1977 at the age of 55.

Henry Highland Garnet

**Born December 23, 1815—New Market, MD
Died February 12, 1882—Liberia**

Few people could stir the souls of Northern abolitionists like Henry Highland Garnet, an educator and minister whose eloquent speeches and impassioned work of the mid-1800s galvanized the anti-slavery movement and advocated for the basic human rights of black Americans. By the time he came to Pittsburgh in 1869 to direct Avery College—a small school for black students in Allegheny City—he held a national reputation for his ministry, his involvement in the Underground Railroad, and his council on Reconstruction after the Civil War. Over a century later, black civil rights leaders such as Malcolm X and Martin Luther King, Jr., turned to his ideas on freedom and black empowerment to help lay the foundation for their own important work.

Garnet's family, enslaved in Maryland, escaped to New York City in 1824. His father established a cobbler shop, and the young Garnet was introduced to formal education and the powerful presence of the well-established black churches.

In 1843 Garnet was ordained a Presbyterian minister and that same year delivered a controversial speech to an all-black convention that called slaves into action: "If you must bleed, let it all come at once—rather die free men than live to be slaves. Let your motto be resistance, resistance, resistance!" These powerful words, considered too radical by some, brought Garnet to the attention of prominent abolitionists and politicians, and

in 1865 he was the first black American to deliver a sermon to the U.S. Congress.

Garnet's stay in Pittsburgh from 1869 to 1872, established Avery College as a more rigorous academic institution. At this time he also founded the still-active Grace Memorial Presbyterian Church, the first black Presbyterian church west of Philadelphia, in Pittsburgh's Hill District.

In 1881, he arrived in Liberia as U.S. Ambassador, but died just two months later. Although brief, his time in Africa was a kind of homecoming, a fitting culmination to his life's work, which called for a world without slavery that embraced the basic freedoms and rights of blacks everywhere.

Josh Gibson

**Born December 21, 1911—Buena Vista, GA
Died January 20, 1947—Pittsburgh**

When it comes to Negro League slugger Josh Gibson, it's hard to separate fact from fiction. While some things are questionable, this much is known:

Born in 1911 in Buena Vista, Georgia, 13-year-old Joshua Gibson's family moved to Pittsburgh when his father took a steel mill job. By the time Gibson was in his middle teens he was a standout sandlot/semi-pro ballplayer, playing for the Gimbel Brothers and Westinghouse Airbrake teams, even for an

early version of the Pittsburgh Crawfords, 1927-29. By 1930, 18-year-old Gibson was so well known that when the Homestead Grays catcher was injured during a game at Forbes Field, player-coach Judy Johnson came into the stands to ask Gibson if he'd take the injured man's place.

A prodigious slugger, high-average hitter, and passable catcher, Josh Gibson became one of the Negro Leagues' greatest drawing cards. Playing at 6'-1," his weight fluctuating between 215 and 256, he played for the Crawfords, 1930-36, then the Grays for the rest of his career, 1937-46.

Although there are questions about Gibson's records, since accurate statistics were not kept, Gibson did win four Negro League batting and nine home run titles. While his often-cited career total of 800 home runs is debatable, Gibson's Negro League output of some 200 was in keeping with major stars of his day. A power hitter par excellence, one Monessen shot was measured at 575 feet, while a Yankee Stadium homer hit the centerfield wall—580 feet away.

Also hitting for high average, Gibson's Negro League lifetime batting average is believed to be .362.

Plagued by a brain tumor, Gibson died of a stroke at 35, on January 20, 1947. Inducted into baseball's Hall of Fame in 1972, Josh Gibson is buried in Allegheny Cemetery, Lawrenceville.

August 13, 1944, during the East-West game of the National Negro Leagues, Gibson slides home.

Christopher Gist

Born in 1706—Maryland
Died in 1759—unknown

Christopher Gist was a surveyor and frontiersman who explored Western Pennsylvania for the British. Perhaps due to his early experience as a mapmaker, Gist was chosen by the Ohio Company to explore lands west of the Allegheny Mountains. He made his first survey of the region in 1750. This seven-month-long journey took him through what is today the city of Pittsburgh and then into Ohio and Kentucky.

In 1751, Gist's second survey for the Ohio Company had him traversing present-day Fayette and Washington Counties and ultimately West Virginia. After these travels, Gist moved his family to a plantation in Western Pennsylvania. Gist lived there during a period of rising tensions between the British and French military forces in North America, which later evolved into the French and Indian War.

In the fall of 1753, Gist served as guide for young George Washington in his travels to the French-occupied Fort LeBoeuf, in Erie County. During this expedition, Gist is reported to have saved George Washington's life on two occasions. Once, during an attempted assassination when Gist subdued the would-be murderer and, second, when he pulled Washington from the icy waters of the Allegheny River at a site near present-day Washington's Landing.

In 1755, Gist served as a guide for British General Edward Braddock in his expedition to French-occupied Fort Duquesne. Before reaching their objective at the confluence of the Allegheny and Monongahela Rivers, the French and their Indian allies ambushed the British forces. General Braddock was mortally wounded, but Gist and other members of his force, including George Washington, escaped.

After a later career as an Indian agent, Gist died of smallpox in 1759. During his lifetime, he was highly regarded by his contemporaries as a mapmaker, woodsman, and frontier guide. His travels through Western Pennsylvania and into Ohio and Kentucky predated those of the better-known Daniel Boone and served as important early steps in the movement of British colonists westward. His detailed journals are an important resource for early descriptions of Western Pennsylvania.

© BETTMANN/CORBIS

Scott Glenn

Born January 26, 1941—Churchill

Although debilitated by a childhood fever at age 9, he learned to conquer his limp. Although left handed, he learned to write with his right hand for dramatic authenticity. Although a high-paid actor, he often insisted on performing his own stunts. His good friend, Gary Busey, calls him "an adrenaline junkie." Indeed, Theodore Scott Glenn's movie career is an impressive demonstration of high action-adventure work for which he trains constantly.

Father Theodore, a salesman and later an executive for Snap-On Tools, and mother Elizabeth lived on Churchill Road when Glenn was born the eldest of three children. The family moved to Philadelphia when Glenn was 12. He graduated with an English major from William and Mary College in 1963 and enlisted in an elite corps of the Marines, touring Viet Nam before the height of the war. Determined to be a writer—his family is supposed to have descended from Lord Byron—Glenn sought work as a journalist, but while writing a play, he took acting lessons to learn the craft.

As early as 1966, Glenn was performing with the La MaMa Experimental Theatre Club in New York. For physical training, he learned martial arts. And in 1968, he joined The Actors Studio where he met James Bridges who later cast Glenn in his first film, *The Baby Maker* (1970). Glenn moved to Los Angeles for seven of the "most miserable years of my life," finding little work while his new wife Christina supported them. Always active, training and playing bit parts on episodic TV shows like *Ironside, Baretta,* and *The Rock-*

ford Files, he quit the Hollywood hustle and moved to Ketchum, Idaho.

There, tabloids report, he took outdoor work as a hunting guide and mountain ranger, while Christina took up pottery—offering lessons to neighbor Demi Moore, who later used her skills to sensual effect in *Ghost*. Again, James Bridges called with a casting offer; Glenn would play the nemesis to John Travolta's *Urban Cowboy*. The year was 1980. His career was launched.

Immediately, Glenn appeared as the rugged type in a string of hit films, like *The Right Stuff* as Alan Shepherd, *The River* as Joe Wade, *Silverado* as Emmet, *The Hunt for Red October* as Commander Mancuso and, no where near done, as FBI agent Jack Crawford, mentor to Jodie Foster's FBI assistant, in *Silence of the Lambs*, filmed in Pittsburgh.

Inspired by *The Right Stuff* and deep in the lore of NASA, astronauts often still quote the prayer delivered by Glenn so ineloquently, "Dear Lord, please don't let me f**k up."

Jeff Goldblum

Born October 22, 1952—West Homestead, PA

Perhaps most famous for landing supporting roles as the quirky intellect in two of the highest-grossing films of the 1990s, *Independence Day* (1996) and *Jurassic Park* (1997), Jeff Goldblum's latest starring role is in the independent film, *Pittsburgh* (2006). Now released since headlining the 5th Annual Tribeca Film Festival, the comic mockumentary follows the frantic rehearsals and offstage antics of Goldblum after he's arrived in Pittsburgh (actually, two years earlier) to play the lead role in the 2004 CLO production of *The Music Man*.

Some 40 years earlier, Goldblum appeared in *Guys & Dolls, 42nd Street*, and *Sweet Bird of Youth* at Mifflin High School. At 17, rebelling against his disciplinarian father, he made haste for New York, and first appeared on the professional stage as a guard in a New York Shakespeare Festival production of *Two Gentlemen of Verona*. At 22, he appeared in his first film, as a mugger, in *Death Wish*, starring Johnstown's own Charles Bronson. And, at 25, he delivered one of the stand out lines of Woody Allen's *Annie Hall* when, as a befuddled party guests, he realizes, "I've lost my mantra." From that one scene, many title roles followed. He displayed memorable turns in 1983's yuppie drama *The Big Chill*, met his one-time wife Geena Davis while filming *Transylvania 6-5000*, created the title character in the cult classic *The Adventures of Buckaroo Bonzai Across the 8th Dimension* (1984), and withstood five-hour make-up sessions for David Cronenberg's 1986 remake of *The Fly*.

Since repeating his role as Dr. Ian Malcom in Stephen Spielberg's *Jurassic Park* sequel, *The Lost World*, more recent roles have included surprising performances in *Igby Goes Down* (2002) and Wes Anderson's *The Life Aquatic with Steve Zissou* (2004).

The third of four children, Jeff took early lessons from jazz pianist Frank Cunimondo and still plays jazz gigs with friend Peter Weller when in Hollywood. His brother Lee is a local realtor and mother Shirley Tyson, who lives in Pittsburgh, appeared as herself in *Pittsburgh*.

Malvin & Mary Dee Goode

**Mal: Born February 13, 1908—White Plains, VA
Died September 12, 1995—Pittsburgh**

**Mary Dee: Born in 1905—White Plains, VA
Died unknown**

In a special CNN broadcast by Bernard Shaw upon the death of his friend Mal Goode, the Washington anchorman said, "Goode certified himself as a man of the universe when he answered the question: How do you want to be remembered? Goode responded, 'I'd like to be remembered as someone who tried to do something to make life better for someone, not better for black people, not better for Afro Americans, not better for white people, but better for humanity.'"

More than 30 years earlier, in 1962, Goode became the first black news correspondent hired by any of the three major TV networks. For ABC, he covered the United Nations. No sooner had he been hired than the Cuban Missile crisis became the top story around the world.

His sister, Mary "Dee" Dudley Goode, was the first African-American woman ever to host her own radio show. In fact, Mal and Mary "Dee" co-hosted the morning news on WHOD for six years. Mary Dee made WHOD one of the top stations in the east—the "Station of Nations"—with a diverse program featuring the talents of many young musicians, including George Benson. The Homestead station is now known as WAMO.

Both brother and sister grew up in Homestead. Both graduated Homestead High School. Mal went on to graduate from Pitt in 1931, while Mary Dee, just three years younger, attended Howard University, but did not graduate.

Mal Goode's early career started in the local mill. But five years after earning his degree, he worked for the Juvenile Court through the Centre Avenue YMCA; then, for six years, with the Housing Authority. In 1948, he became a reporter for the *Pittsburgh Courier*, then the largest circulated black newspaper in the country. Eventually, he started brief news shows on KQV before switching to WHOD.

In 1971, long before his retirement 10 years later, Goode was named the first black member of the National Association of Radio and Television News Directors.

Television .. At Long Last ..

GOODE AND HAGERTY—Mal Goode, former Courier staffer, is shown in a conference with James Hagerty, the American Broadcasting Co.'s news chief. Mr. Goode last week became the first Negro TV network news correspondent, when ABC TV appointed him to United Nations coverage.

Siblings who shared duties delivering local news and weather on WHOD, Mal later covered the United Nations and Mary Dee promoted the "Station of Nations." Below, a young Porky Chedwick confers with Mary Dee.

Frank Gorshin

Born April 5, 1933—Garfield
Died May 17, 2005—Burbank, CA

While attending Peabody High, Frank Gorshin got a job as an usher at the Sheridan Square Theatre, just blocks away, in East Liberty. There, watching his screen idols, he learned to do impressions—so well, apparently, he won a talent contest. The prize was a week-long gig at the Carousel Nightclub. Whether a good comic or not, his timing was impeccable; Alan King was headlining at the time and helped launch his career. He entertained nights, attending Carnegie Tech by day.

After a brief stint in the Army, serving three years in the entertainment troupe, he was introduced to Hollywood agents and landed roles in a number of B films, pictures like *Invasion of the Saucer Men*, *Hot Rod Girl,* and its presumed sequel *Dragstrip Girl*. In 1957, however, he was cast in a meatier role in *The Bells are Ringing* with Dean Martin.

In between sporadic shoots, Gorshin enjoyed bookings at the better clubs in Las Vegas and the best variety shows on TV.

Again, his timing could not have been better. On the February 9, 1964, *Ed Sullivan Show*, Gorshin followed the Beatles' first telecast. When asked by the AP how it felt to be the unlucky performer, he said, "I looked out the window of my dressing room and said, 'Look at all the kids that came to see me!'"

In 1966, Gorshin won his most memorable role ever, that of The Riddler on *Batman*. "I could feel the impact overnight," Frank recalled later. His fame gave him headline status in Las Vegas and it was there, legend says, that he taught Sammy Davis Jr. and others how to do impersonations. His career never peaked higher.

Starring as George Burns in the 2002 Broadway-launched, one-man show, *Say Goodnight, Gracie*, Frank toured the production for several years, appearing in Pittsburgh on the last leg of its tour. He died of lung cancer in 2005.

Aaron Gorson

Born June 2, 1872—Kovno, Lithuania
Died October 11, 1933—New York, NY

It was the interplay of light and dark that made painter Aaron Gorson love Pittsburgh so much.

"Bountifully endowed by nature with scenes of grandeur and enthralling picturesqueness," Pittsburgh, he said, was beautiful in "the way in which the muddy river water catches the gleam of the dying light and becomes transformed into running gold."

Although a sufficiently gifted portrait painter to secure commissions from such luminaries as Mellon and Carnegie, Gorson was drawn to the Pittsburgh landscape, to massive mills, open hearths burning in the night, coke fires reflected in blackened rivers.

Born in Kovno, Lithuania, in 1872, 16-year-old Aaron Harry Gorson emigrated to America in 1888. Working with a brother in a Philadelphia textile factory, he studied art—and came under the wing of Rabbi Leonard Levy, who in 1899 arranged for Gorson to study in Paris.

Returning to Philadelphia, Gorson had portraits accepted at the 1902 Pennsylvania Academy of Fine Arts exhibition—the same year he exhibited at Chicago's Art Institute.

Moving to Pittsburgh in 1903, when his patron accepted a position at Oakland's Rodef Shalom Congregation, Gorson opened his own studio. Over the next 18 years, Gorson produced a body of work unmatched in Pittsburgh history. Widely collected and exhibited, Gorson's stunning landscapes re-cast the way the world looked at Pittsburgh's industrial might.

Within a year of his return, Gorson had a landscape accepted at the Carnegie International. Between 1908 and 1921, he exhibited nine paintings at seven Internationals. As a measure of Gorson's stature, his 1921 *Nocturne* was placed beside works by Mary Cassatt, Childe Hassam, Claude Monet, Camille Pissarro, and John Singer Sargent.

But exhibitions did not necessarily mean sales, and that year Gorson moved to New York City, where he painted the Manhattan skyline and the Hudson River.

Aaron Gorson died at age 61, in 1933, in New York City.

Gorson's *Pittsburgh at Night,* 1926, oil on canvas, H: 34 1/4 x W: 36 1/4 inches, Carnegie Museum of Art, Pittsburgh, Gift of Barbara M. Lawson in memory of Roswell Miller, Jr.

Martha Graham

Born May 11, 1894—North Side
Died April 1, 1991—Barcelona, Spain

Like so many artists whose prodigious works have been acclaimed over many decades, Martha Graham achieved a persona that superceded any single contribution to the world of dance. She was a gaunt figure, hair pulled tightly back, high cheek bones and startling lips painted bright red. And she was considered to have the kind of body—short of stature, disproportionately shorter legs and thinner arms—that betrayed the form of the model ballerina. Yet, Graham will be forever honored as the Mother of American Dance.

Andy Warhol unveils *The Kick* presented to Graham at the Martha Graham Dance Center in May 1986.

Born before the turn of the century in Allegheny (the North Side,) the first of three daughters of a Presbyterian physician who specialized in mental health, George Graham, and of Jane Beers, said to have been a direct descendant of Miles Standish, Graham was raised in a strict Calvinist home. She did attend theater as a child, however, and watched Ruth St. Denis (once a "Leg Dancer" discovered by theater impresario David Belasco and then a serious solo performer of "interpretive" dance) perform. Legend says that this performance changed Graham's life. But not until her father's death was she permitted to follow her passion. And in that same year, 1916, having moved with her family to Los Angeles eight years earlier, Graham enrolled in the Denishawn School to learn dance from Ruth St. Denis herself. Graham was then 22.

By today's standards, Graham would have been 10 years too old to be considered a likely success.

After seven years of instruction and another move—to New York City—Graham performed recitals and modeled fashions, while she gave classes to up-and-coming thespians. She was said to have taught Bette Davis, Gregory Peck and Richard Boone how to move gracefully on stage. In 1929, she launched her own dance company.

And by the 1940s she had developed a short repertoire of dances that were remarkable as much for their symbolism as they were for their music compositions.

In 1944, Graham's commission of Aaron Copland's *Appalachian Spring* became an instant classic, a modern dance interpretation of a pioneer wedding, supposedly drawn from Graham's Pennsylvania roots. In 1947, Graham premiered *Cave of the Heart*, set to music composed by Samuel Barber, reinterpreting Greek mythology with a sense of modern horror. Famously, Graham astounded her public by playing Medea who eats her entrails.

Her contributions to the evolution of dance were many. Critics noted that her work was physically grounded, not always aerial as was the expectation, that she focused more on the human passions expressed through internal movements, rather than external, and that she eschewed rigid ballet stances for more flexible and "more human" composure.

Even with the success of her company, and that of the many students she trained, Graham insisted on performing as a principal for more than 50 years. She was 76 when she last danced on stage. And, even at 93, she was premiering new works. In all, she created 177 choreographies, more than any other contemporary master like George Balanchine, Agnes De Mille or her famous students, Merce Cunningham and Paul Taylor.

Harry Greb

Born June 6, 1894—Garfield
Died October 22, 1926—Atlantic City, NJ

In the ring the aptly nicknamed Human Windmill did everything but bite his opponents, throwing non-stop punches at breathtaking speed from virtually every angle. Fighting his way to Roaring Twenties light heavyweight and middleweight titles, Harry Greb racked up an incredible 178 consecutive fights without a loss, 1916-23, winning 260 of 299 career fights, 1913-26.

Born Edward Henry Greb, by 1913 he had turned professional. Variously called the Garfield Goer and the Pittsburgh Wildcat, Greb fought at 5'-8" and 138-158 pounds, depending on weight class (middleweight and light heavyweight). Punching in such Pittsburgh palaces as Exposition Park, Duquesne Garden, Forbes Field, and Motor Square Garden, Greb was as tireless as he was successful. In 1919 alone he fought 45 times.

Suffering a detached retina in a 1921 fight, Greb fought one-eyed for the rest of his career. Boxing against some 18 champions, Greb's greatest bouts came against light heavyweight title holder Gene Tunney. At Madison Square Garden, May 23, 1922, Greb copped the crown, handing the Fighting Marine the sole defeat of his career. As legendary sportswriter Grantland Rice saw it, "Harry handled Gene like a butcher hammering a Swiss steak."

The following year, Greb lost the title back to Tunney, but took the middleweight crown at the Polo Grounds. Holding the title through 1926, 32-year-old Greb lost a title fight, lost the re-match, and retired.

Although Greb sparred numerous times with Jack Dempsey, he never fought the Manassa Mauler. Visiting Dempsey in Atlantic City, Greb refused to get in the ring, preferring elective surgery to repair boxing-related facial damage. Never recovering from the anesthetic, Greb died of a heart attack at age 32.

Elected to the Boxing Hall of Fame in 1955, Greb was buried in Pittsburgh's Calvary Cemetery—where one of his pallbearers was his five-time opponent Gene Tunney.

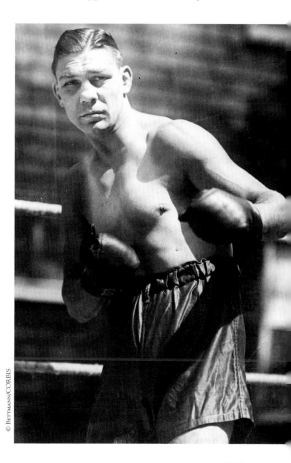

© BETTMANN/CORBIS

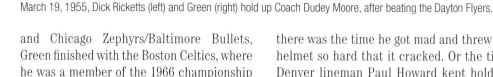
March 19, 1955, Dick Ricketts (left) and Green (right) hold up Coach Dudey Moore, after beating the Dayton Flyers.

Sihugo Green

Born August 20, 1933—New York, NY
Died October 4, 1980—Pittsburgh

The year was 1955. Dwight Eisenhower was in the White House. Fans rioted to see Elvis Presley in Jacksonville. And Duquesne University won its sole national championship in basketball.

Before the NCAA became the premier national college basketball showcase, it was the province of the National Invitational Tournament. In 1955, it was all Duquesne—led by spindly 6'2", 185-pound guard Sihugo Green.

Born in New York City in 1933, a product of the famed Brooklyn Boys High, Si Green came to Duquesne possessed of dazzlingly quick moves—so good, an assistant coach remembered, that he could tell an opponent which way he would go and still get around him. Averaging 19.8 points and 11.5 rebounds a game in his three varsity years, 1953-56, Green's great skills made him the only two-time consensus All-American in Duquesne history. During Green's varsity tenure the Dukes went 65-17, including three NIT appearances.

In 1955, Green led an undersized Dukes squad to top 10 rankings in the polls—sixth in Associated Press, seventh in United Press International. Carrying a 22-4 record, on March 20, 1955, the Dukes marched into New York's Madison Square Garden. Before a sellout crowd of 18,496, the Dukes out-shot, out-played the Dayton Flyers, 70-58, Green doing a masterful job of guarding a Dayton forward nearly a foot taller.

It was that kind of performance that caused Green to be the nation's number one choice in the 1956 NBA draft—before sure-fire star Bill Russell. Sadly, as future Hall-of-Famer Russell's career sizzled, Green's fizzled. Playing nine NBA seasons, for the Rochester/Cincinnati Royals, St. Louis Hawks,

and Chicago Zephyrs/Baltimore Bullets, Green finished with the Boston Celtics, where he was a member of the 1966 championship team.

Returning to Pittsburgh after his NBA career, Green managed a linen company. He died of cancer at age 47, 1980.

Joe Greene

Born September 24, 1946—Temple, TX

Sometimes the difference a single person makes can be enormous. For the Steelers, the team's rise to greatness begins with the first pick of coach Chuck Noll's first draft: future Pro Football Hall of Famer Joe Greene.

Born Charles Edward Greene in 1946 in Temple, TX, Mean Joe—a nickname he picked up in college and always despised—played at little-known North Texas State. Normally, playing at such a school may have caused Greene to be overlooked in the pro draft. However, Chuck Noll, as a Baltimore Colts assistant coach, had scouted Greene—and knew his strength, ferocity, and leadership. "He never lost a battle," Noll remembered.

He never did for the Steelers, either. Standing 6'-4" and weighing 275, Joe Greene played 181 games as left tackle on the Steel Curtain defense, 1969-81. "Joe Greene was unrelenting," linebacker Andy Russell recalled. "He made huge plays when they had to be made."

Like the time he singlehandedly saved one playoff game by sacking Houston Oilers quarterback Dan Pastorini six times. Then

there was the time he got mad and threw his helmet so hard that it cracked. Or the time Denver lineman Paul Howard kept holding Greene—until Mean Joe simply decked him. The league fined Greene, but the Steeler Nation loved him all the more.

Defensive Rookie of the Year in 1969, Greene also took Defensive Player of the Year honors in 1972 and '74. Playing in 10 Pro Bowls, six AFC title games, and four victorious Super Bowls, Greene recorded a career 66 sacks and 16 fumble recoveries.

Today, despite a brilliant playing career, Joe Greene is most remembered for the Coca-Cola® commercial where he downs a bottle of the product then tosses his jersey to a dewy-eyed lad.

All that aside, Dan Rooney said, "he was the best leader I've ever seen."

"Losing," the man himself said, "was not something I tolerated."

Gus Greenlee

Born December 26, 1893—Marion, NC
Died July 7, 1952—Pittsburgh

He was big, noticeably big, 6'-3" and over 200 pounds, and was generally found chomping a cigar and sitting in his legendary Crawford Grill No.1, holding court with a crowd of fans and admirers from all walks of life.

He was William Augustus "Gus" Greenlee. His Crawford Grill No. 1 (established in 1931) and Crawford Grill No. 2 (established in 1942 with Joe Robinson) attracted top-flight entertainers and musicians, both national and local. Greenlee also owned one of the great-

© ASSOCIATED PRESS

est teams in Negro Leagues history and built the first African-American-owned and -operated baseball park.

Born in Marion, NC, in 1893, Greenlee moved to Pittsburgh's Hill District in 1916. Driving a taxi—and selling Prohibition-era bootleg liquor—he graduated to selling daily numbers. By 1930 the man known as Mr. Big bought a sandlot baseball team, the Pittsburgh Crawfords.

Using his enormous gambling revenues—estimated as high as $25,000 daily—Greenlee signed the era's brightest Negro League stars—Satchel Paige, Cool Papa Bell, Josh Gibson, and others. After 1931, when his team was denied use of Forbes Field dressing rooms, he built Greenlee Field—the nation's first African-American-owned baseball park.

Greenlee dines with an unknown acquaintance in this Teenie Harris shot. Greenlee was a close friend of Harris.

Opened in 1932 at a reported cost of $100,000, Greenlee's 7,500-seat park hosted what many consider to be the greatest team in Negro Leagues history. Perennial champions, the 1932-36 Crawfords were stocked with future Hall of Famers.

To help ensure revenues, in 1933 Greenlee organized the Negro National League, the most stable Negro Leagues organization in history. In addition, he initiated the East-West Classic, a Chicago-based all-star game.

But in 1937, Dominican dictator Rafael Trujillo decided to import championship baseball and raided the Crawfords. With much of Greenlee's talent gone, the Crawford's last two years, 1937-38, were poor indeed. In December 1938, Greenlee tore down his ballpark, selling the franchise to Toledo in 1939.

Denied a berth in baseball's Hall of Fame, Gus Greenlee died in Pittsburgh of a stroke in 1952 and was buried in Allegheny Cemetery.

"Mean" Joe Greene and child actor Tommy Okon appear in this memorable 1979 Coca-Cola® TV commercial.

Grace Greenwood

Born September 23, 1823—Pompey, NY
Died April 20, 1904—Squirrel Hill

Grace Greenwood, born Sara Jane Clarke, was a popular writer, poet, and correspondent in the mid-19th century. Born in Pompey, NY, near Rochester, Sara was the youngest of 11 children. Her father, a physician, moved the family and his practice to New Brighton, PA, in 1842. There Sara attended the Greenwood Institute, an academy for young women, which likely inspired her pen name.

Grace began composing poems while still living in New York; several were published in the local Rochester newspapers and magazines. After moving to Pennsylvania, she wrote for the popular magazine *Godey's Lady's Book* and the abolitionist newspaper *National Era*. When her anti-slavery views caused resentment among Southern readers of *Godey's*, she left the magazine and in 1850 moved to Washington D.C. to continue her work with the *Era*, and she became a correspondent for the *Saturday Evening Post*.

An extended trip overseas resulted in her most popular book *Haps and Mishaps of a Tour in Europe*. Shortly after her return to the U.S., Grace married Leander K. Lippincott, a dashing, unreliable, and unfaithful young man from Philadelphia. Together they published *The Little Pilgrim*, a popular magazine for children blending stories, poems, and puzzles. They had one daughter, Annie. A reformer at heart, Grace was interested in abolition, women's suffrage, prison reform, and other causes to better humanity. While Annie was still a small child, Grace went on the lecture circuit sharing her vision of the world in messages such as "The Heroic in Common Life."

Grace accompanied Annie, a talented singer, to Europe to pursue a musical education. While there she continued to write articles on a wide range of topics—medical studies, political demonstrations, interviews—always eager to share her experiences. In the late 1880s Grace returned to the states and began a series of articles for the *Independent* on her "Reminiscences of Washington Before and During the War." She continued to write until the very end, penning her last article a few months before her death at age 81. Although she had lived away from New Brighton since her late 20s, Grace was buried in Grove Cemetery next to her parents.

Ken Griffey Sr. & Jr.

Sr.: Born April 10, 1950—Donora, PA
Jr.: Born November 21, 1969—Donora, PA

The perfect baseball trivia question is: what's the only father-son combination to play in the majors in the same year, 1989?

Two clues: The following year, 1990, they played together on the same team.

Then they hit back-to-back home runs.

The only correct answer is: the Ken Griffeys, Senior and Junior, of Donora.

One was very good, playing for 19 seasons, 1973-91, including two World Champions. The other is one of the greatest ballplayers of all time, a certain Hall of Famer.

Born in 1950, George Kenneth Griffey, Sr., joined the Cincinnati Reds as a 23-year-old outfielder. Member of two World Champions, 1975-76, Senior was a cog in the Big Red Machine, a Yankee, Brave, and Mariner. Playing at 6' and 200 pounds, Senior topped .300 eight times, ending with a lifetime .296.

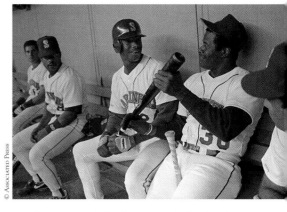

By contrast, Junior seemed destined to rewrite the record books. Born in 1969, playing at 6'-3" and 205 pounds, George Kenneth Griffey, Jr., joined the Seattle Mariners as a 20-year-old phenom. With a swing many considered the best of its era, and extraordinary fielding ability, Junior's rookie season set the pace for his brilliant, injury-plagued career.

Batting over .300 seven times in the '90s, Junior also belted more than 400 home runs. Simply awe-inspiring in center field, he made spectacular diving plays and impossible grabs of balls hit over the wall. The 1997 AL MVP, he hit .304 and 56 home runs. As his celebrity waxed, Junior was featured on a Wheaties box and had his own Nike sneaker line.

Moving to his father's team, the Reds, in 2000, Junior grew incredibly fragile, suffering season-ending injuries in 2002-04.

Only Barry Bonds and Sammy Sosa, among active players, have hit more homers.

Robert Griffing

Born June 9, 1940—Linesville, PA

The White Man came, with his muskets and his wars, with his lies and his insatiable desire for land, and, faced with an overwhelming, implacable foe, the Native Americans knew that their time would soon be past. "I focus on their struggle in the face of European invasion," painter Robert Griffing says, "and how they were able to survive. My work is about how they maintained their pride and dignity in the face of extreme change."

Born in 1940, growing up in Linesville, Northwestern Pennsylvania, Griffing walked the Native American trails near his home, believing that he might find a painted tree, one where the original inhabitants might have left tales of battle—or warnings to outsiders.

He left the woods, and Lake Pymatuning, to attend Pittsburgh's Art Institute. Enjoying a 30-year career in commercial advertising, Griffing's most memorable moment was designing Arby's cowboy-hat logo. Working daily on illustration, design, and layout, "I learned to work with models and fine-tune my sense of composition," he says. "I could never have achieved success as a painter without the benefit of that experience."

Retiring in 1992, Griffing returned to painting, creating historically accurate representations of Native American and Colonial life. In a Griffing painting the clothing, weapons—even the leaves on the trees—are all authentic. He paints on site, using his own library of historical papers and journals to insure that every detail is correct. In addition, Griffing uses re-enactors and Native American models—many from the tribes he depicts.

Aside from his strong sensitive rendering of Native American life, Griffing has also painted many historical places and events, including Fort Duquesne, Fort Pitt, the Battle of Bushy Run—all told, some three dozen scenes.

Robert Griffing lives and works in Gibsonia.

Dick Groat

Born November 4, 1930—Wilkinsburg

"It's the greatest thrill in sports," former Pirates shortstop Dick Groat said, "to win a World Championship in your own home town."

Born in Wilkinsburg in 1930, Richard Morrow Groat grew up playing baseball and basketball at Swissvale High. Graduating in 1948, Groat went to Duke University, primarily as a basketball player. Standing six feet and 180 pounds, he was a back-to-back All-American, 1951-52, then played for the National Basketball Association Fort Wayne Pistons.

Yet Groat was also an All-American shortstop, 1951-52, and was drafted by Pittsburgh. The rare ballplayer who never played in the minor leagues, Groat joined the Pirates right out of college. Playing 95 games his rookie year, 1952, the 21-year-old shortstop hit .284.

Drafted into the army, 1953-54, Groat rejoined the Pirates in 1955. Establishing himself as one of the league's premier shortstops, he broke the .300 mark in hitting in 1957 (the year he made the last putout in New York's Polo Grounds) and '58. Leading the league in putouts and double plays, 1958-59, in 1959 Groat was elected to his first of five All Star teams.

As Pirate captain in 1960, Groat had his single greatest year, hitting .325, good for the batting title, winning the Most Valuable Player award, and leading the Pirates to their first World Series in 33 years—and first victory in 35.

Traded to the St. Louis Cardinals in 1963, Groat hit .319; in 1964 he made his last All Star appearance, then collected another World Series ring.

Finishing with the Phillies and Giants, Groat retired in 1967. His 14-year totals: a .286 average and 2,138 hits.

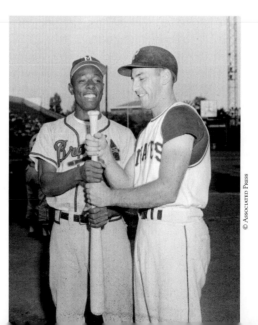

Hank Aaron, left, Milwaukee Braves centerfielder, and Pirates' shortstop, Groat, grip bat on August 21, 1957.

A 2007 inductee into the National Collegiate Basketball Hall of Fame, Dick Groat still lives in Swissvale, serves as a Pitt basketball radio analyst, and with fellow former Pirate Jerry Lynch owns Ligonier's Champion Lakes Golf Course and Bed and Breakfast.

Charles Grodin

Born April 2, 1935—Highland Park

Most recently appearing as a commentator on *60 Minutes II*, or as host of his eponymous cable talk show, Charles Grodin has never been short for words. Indeed, as a kid growing up in Highland Park and attending Fulton Elementary School, he was often sent to principal Bower's office because he questioned his teachers' skills or debated the injustice of school rules. For six years in a row, Grodin was elected his class President.

Raised in a small six-room house on North St. Clair Street, Grodin's childhood was spent among hours of Hebrew School, working in his father's dry good store, and playing sandlot football. Living so close to the Pittsburgh Zoo, Grodin, in his 1989 autobiography, *It Would Be So Nice If You Weren't Here*, related "Some nights I would lie in bed [and] would try to entertain myself by thinking of jokes I could finish telling just before the next hyena laugh." While preparing to be Bar Mitzvahed at the Margaretta Street synagogue, he caught his first glimpse of a stage. That same year, 1948, he starred in his Fulton School production of *Getting Gracie Graduated*. During his teen years at Peabody High, he never once took to the stage, rather organizing school dances that were held during lunch hour.

In 1952, following a long depression set by his father's death, Grodin attended the University of Miami as a drama major, but never graduated. He took a leap to New York and trained with Uta Hagen at HB studios and, persevering hundreds of auditions, landed his first Broadway role in *Tchin, Tchin*, starring Anthony Quinn. The production ran for 222 performances, yet did little to establish his career. Dozens of small TV roles followed, another shorter run on Broadway in *Absence of a Cello*, a short-run Broadway gig, directing *Lovers & Other Strangers*, and, in 1970, Grodin was cast as Captain Aarfy Aardvark in *Catch 22*. Despite the film's success, Grodin again searched for work. Two years later, Grodin landed the lead in Neil Simon's film *The Heartbreak Kid*. Were his career assured with this success, his next film, *11 Harrow-house*, a box office bomb, dashed all hopes. But Grodin, ever tenacious, was cast in 1976's *King Kong* and 1977's *Thieves*, landing him his first hosting role on *Saturday Night Live*. It was his last, too. Written and staged to make it seem as though Grodin had missed every rehearsal for the newly popular live show, Grodin was so off-kilter, he was banned from appearing ever again.

Success came again, most notably in his lead role, opposite Robert DeNiro, in *Midnight Run*. Then followed several lackluster films, noticeably Universal Studio's *Beethoven* dog films. In 1994, he took on the commentary segment of *60 Minutes II* and the next year hosted his own MSNBC cable program. But with a newborn son to his second wife, Grodin decided to be a stay-at-home Dad, and in 1995 dropped out of the scene. Returning to his long-fought profession in 2007, several new Grodin films are now in post-production.

The author of several books, mostly autobiographical, Grodin's ultimate legacy may be his learned advice to would-be actors. "Don't," he has said. "The acting profession is something like making a living selling poetry door-to-door."

Joe Grushecky

Born May 6, 1948—Greensburg, PA

In 2005, *Esquire* magazine rated Pittsburgh as "The #1 City That Rocks." And so, it's only fitting that Pittsburgh would also claim one of the greatest rock bands ever in The Iron City Houserockers.

The late 1970s and early 1980s were great times to be a rocker in Pittsburgh, and The Iron City Houserockers came to define the sound of the city during that period. Their anthemic song "Pumpin' Iron (Sweatin' Steel)," from their *Have A Good Time But Get Out Alive* release, celebrated the blue collar, rowdy rock with which Pittsburgh had come to be associated.

The Iron City Houserockers started out as the Brick Alley Band in the late '70s and eventually took the name The Iron City Houserockers. Their sound resonated with the crowds who piled into the Decade on weekends to hear their brand of Heartland rock. Their sound resonated with people in the record industry as well and the band was put under the management of Steve Popovich, famous for signing bands such as Ted Nugent, Boston, Cheap Trick, and Michael Jackson. Their debut release in 1979 *Love's So Tough* received favorable reviews from critics, also earning the "Debut Record of the Year" title from *Rolling Stone*. The band's second release *Have A Good Time But Get Out Alive* received the careful production attention of three industry heavy weights: Ian Hunter (Mott The Hoople), Mick Ronson (Mott The Hoople, David Bowie and Lou Reed), and Steven Van Zandt (Southside Johnny and The E Street Band). The release was a critical darling and received accolades from industry publications like *Creem*, *Billboard*, and *Rolling Stone*. Their next album, now as The Houserockers, included the production input of legendary Southern Soul guitarist Jeff Beck, and Blues Brothers band member, Steve Cropper. Once again their release garnered favorable reviews. Despite the strength of the recordings, its revenues never measured up to anyone's expectations. In 1984 the Iron City Houserockers called it quits.

Founding Iron City Houserockers band member Joe Grushecky grew up in a working class family, the son of a coal miner. His writing has always reflected the work ethic and attitude of the middle class—hard work, tough love and fading dreams. Over the past couple of decades he has continued to write and

record some of his best material. In 2005 a song which he co-wrote with good friend Bruce Springsteen, "Code Of Silence," helped Bruce win a Grammy© for Best Solo Rock Vocal Performance.

In addition to his decades of music contribution, for the past twenty years Grushecky has worked as a special education teacher, currently in the Sto-Rox School District. Deep down, he's still a regular Joe with a big heart and a bad-assed guitar.

Jack Ham

Born December 23, 1948—Johnstown, PA

Hall of Fame Steeler quarterback Terry Bradshaw summed up the Steel Curtain linebackers. "Andy Russell, Jack Ham, and Jack Lambert were all 220 pounds, ran 4.5 forties, and were smart as all get-out. Those were the kind of people Hall of Fame coach Chuck Noll wanted. Because smart people don't make mistakes. They may lack a little bit physically, but they make up for it. They're always in the right position."

How smart was Jack Ham? "Jack Ham was brilliant," fellow linebacker Andy Russell said. "He didn't make mistakes, knew the game, and anticipated well. Plus he was an explosive talent, probably the fastest Steeler in

© Associated Press

five yards. He made it look easy, but it was astounding how good he was. He was the best linebacker I ever saw—absolutely unbeatable."

"Jack Ham was so good," added long-time Steelers coach Dick Hoak, "that teams wouldn't throw the ball to his side."

Born in Johnstown in 1948, Hall of Fame outside linebacker Jack Raphael Ham, Jr., went from the famed Penn State football program to play 12 seasons for the Steelers, 1971-82. The eight-time Pro Bowler recorded an impressive 25 1/2 sacks, 21 recovered fumbles, and 32 interceptions. Inducted into the Pro Football Hall of Fame in 1988 and the College Football Hall of Fame in 1990, Ham played in five AFC championship games and Super Bowls IX, X, and XIII. (An injury sidelined him from Super Bowl XIV).

But records don't tell the entire story. A quiet, thoughtful man, as the *Steelers' Official History* puts it Ham "played so well and so calmly that it seemed as if he had already seen that game's film and was merely following the script."

Slide Hampton

Born April 21, 1932—Jeannette, PA

Locksley Wellington Hampton, aka "Slide," was not so much born into a musical family as he was into a family band. With a mother and father who played instruments, as well as four sisters and five brothers who also played, there was one instrument missing from the family—the trombone. Slide Hampton became the First Trombonist for the Hampton Family Band.

Although he spent the majority of his formative years in Indianapolis, Hampton was

born in Jeannette, PA. His father was a self-taught musician and didn't know the difference when he purchased a left-handed trombone for his right-handed son. Hampton adapted and eventually went on the road with his family, playing Carnegie Hall, the Savoy Ballroom and the Apollo. Smitten with New York, Hampton had set his sights to get back to the big city as soon as he was old enough.

R&B pianist Buddy Johnson heard Hampton play and invited him to join his band in the mid-1950s. The move elevated his profile and afforded him greater recognition to arrange and play with the likes of Max Roach, Dizzy Gillespie and Pittsburgh's Art Blakey. He joined Lionel Hampton's band for a time but shortly thereafter teamed-up with Maynard Ferguson. Deciding to lead his own gig, Hampton formed his own octet, while simultaneously acting as music director for New Orleans R&B singer Lloyd Price. As the 1960s ushered in an appetite for rock and what Hampton felt was apathy for jazz, he took his arranging and directing talents to Motown, where he would work with Stevie Wonder and The Four Tops. In 1968 Hampton headed to Europe with the great swing clarinetist Woody Herman. There he would decide to take up residency for the next eight years. In the late 1970s Hampton returned to the states and formed the World of Trombones.

Slide Hampton continues to play gigs, and in 2005, was recognized by the National Endowment for the Arts with their Jazz Master Award, the organization's highest accolade.

© Nancy Kaszerman/ZUMA/Corbis

Terry Hanratty

Born January 19, 1948—Butler, PA

In athletics as in life, timing is everything. Nowhere more than in the National Football League.

Perhaps no one in the past half-century seemed more assured of having a golden professional career than Butler native Terry Hanratty. Born in 1948, Terrence Hugh Hanratty was a star quarterback at Butler High, an All-American at Notre Dame, where his Fighting Irish were national champions.

© Associated Press

Playing at 6'-1" and 190 pounds, featured on the covers of *Time* and *Sports Illustrated*, Hanratty seemed bound for glory. Taken by the Steelers in the second round of the 1969 draft, he was right in the middle of Chuck Noll's freshman rebuilding effort.

But that '69 squad, stocked with has-beens and never-weres, went 1-13, and Hanratty never got to strut his stuff. "It was the longest year I ever spent in football," he recalled. "Going back to grade school, I never lost more than one or two games in any season."

The next year, the Steelers drafted a young fellow from Louisiana named Bradshaw, and Terry Hanratty spent the next six years, 1970-75, holding a clipboard, charting plays. "You just couldn't go in and say, 'I want to be traded,'" he said. "It just didn't happen. You had to bite the bullet."

Bite he did, finally moving on to Tampa Bay in 1976, for a year of backing up Steve Spurrier. Then he was gone.

Although Hanratty earned two Super Bowl rings for being on the 1974-75 Steelers, he never wears them. A New York stockbroker, he became philosophical about his football career—or the lack thereof. "Life is timing," Hanratty agreed, "and I've had good timing for the better part of my life. If that small portion is all the bad timing I'll ever have, I can live with that."

Clyde Hare

Born July 11, 1927—Bloomington, IN

It was October, 1950, when the 23-year-old photographer saw Pittsburgh for the first time. Dazzled by the lights, the buildings, steel mills, and rivers, the young Hoosier was awestruck. "Boy," "Red" Hare muttered, "this is my city."

And so it was.

Born Clyde William Hare, son of a furniture manufacturer, he was discharged from the Navy in 1946, before enrolling at Indiana University, His elective courses in photography changed his life. Shooting pictures for Indiana newspapers, he met Roy Stryker. Told of the Pittsburgh Photographic Library project, Hare borrowed $500—and his father's car—and drove east.

Starting at $50 a week, Hare worked from October, 1950 through April, 1953—the entire life of the project. Focusing on the city's enormous physical changes, Hare captured Downtown, notably the Point redevelopment, as well as such changing Pittsburgh neighborhoods as the North and South Sides.

Hare's *Nun and Billboard,* 1950, gelatin silver print, H: 9 7/16 x W: 9 1/2 inches, Carnegie Museum of Art, Pittsburgh, Gift of the Carnegie Library of Pittsburgh

Prolific and fearless, Hare (and fellow PPL photographer Harold Corsini) stayed when the project ended. Working on Stryker's next project, Hare documented Jones & Laughlin steelmaking, 1952-56. Two years later, in 1958, he became the first photographer honored with a one-man show at the Carnegie Museum of Art.

Working as a freelance photographer, Hare enjoyed assignments from *Life*, *Fortune*, and *Time*. For *National Geographic*, Hare again photographed his adopted city. "I made up my mind," he said, "to take one great photograph each day, one that would live, would be simple, would have something to say."

Hare saw many of those images collected in *Clyde Hare's Pittsburgh: Four Decades of Pittsburgh, Frozen in Light*, published by Pittsburgh History and Landmarks, 1994.

Walt Harper

Born unknown—Schenley Heights
Died October 25, 2006—Pittsburgh

Of course, "Satin Doll" is the jazz classic written by Duke Ellington and Billy Strayhorn. But to Pittsburgh jazz lovers, it may as well have been Walt Harper's composition. "Satin Doll" was his oft-embellished theme song.

Walt Harper, grew up in Schenley Heights, an area considered the Upper Hill. His father, Charles, owned a contracting business and his mother, Lucinda, operated a beauty shop in their home on Clarissa Street, near Herron Hill Park. Walt was one of eight children and was encouraged to pursue music as a child. Older brother Ernie was a pianist and younger brother Nate played saxophone.

Even as a child, Walt played the valve trombone with the Swinging Five, a group that included bass player Ray Brown, a close friend of Harper's for many years. When Harper and Brown were kids they would play hooky from school and go to Erroll Garner's to listen to him practice piano.

After graduating from Schenley High, Harper attended the Pittsburgh Musical Institute, the same school that legendary composer and pianist Billy Strayhorn had attended. Harper also spent two years studying at the University of Pittsburgh before hitting the road with his brother Nate from 1949 to 1954. Walt grew weary of life on the road and headed back home. He soon garnered the nickname "Prom King" for his many frat and society gigs. He played often at the Crawford Grill and much of the college crowd would go hear him, integrating the popular club on Wylie Avenue. Harper stayed at the Crawford Grill until 1969 when he opened Walt Harper's Jazz Attic in Market Square, downtown. His reputation and friendships in the jazz community helped attract some of the hottest local, and biggest national acts like Cannonball Adderley, Billy Taylor and the Modern Jazz Quartet, turning Market Square into one of the most happening spots in the city. After seven years Walt sold The Attic and moved on. It was about this time that Dan Rooney hired Walt Harper's band to perform at every Steelers home game, which they did until 2002.

Walt then opened Harper's Jazz Club in One Oxford Center downtown. Harper's also drew big name jazz acts like Dave Brubeck, Nancy Wilson, and a young Wynton Marsalis. Harper's remained one of the marquee jazz clubs until its closing in 1988.

Those who knew Walt were charmed by his radiant smile, impressed by his ability to remember everyone's name and are forever grateful he chose to make his career in Pittsburgh. After more than 50 years of entertaining, Walt Harper died of a heart attack in 2006.

Beaver Harris

Born April 20, 1936—Pittsburgh
Died December 22, 1991—New York, NY

The rich lineage of great drummers from Pittsburgh that includes Art Blakey, Kenny Clarke and Jeff "Tain" Watts, also includes Beaver Harris, one of the more underappreciated leaders in the free jazz movement.

Born William Godvin Harris, he was a well-rounded athlete and musician. He played clarinet and alto sax before he found his way to the drum kit sometime in his 20s. An excellent baseball player, Harris played for the Negro Leagues and was even scouted by the Brooklyn Dodgers and New York Giants. But he chose to pursue the drums. Sonny Rollins, Thelonious Monk, Larry Coryell, Sonny Stitt, Maxine Sullivan, and Chet Baker are just a few of the greats with which Harris performed. In the mid-'60s Harris teamed-up with Archie Shepp to record and tour throughout Europe.

In addition to his ability to play straight-ahead jazz, Harris became a major figure in the avant-garde free jazz movement in the 1960s and 1970s. Harris also participated in numerous drumming clinics with Max Roach and Kenny Clarke.

At just 55, Harris died of prostate cancer.

Harris stands in front of his studio at 2128 Centre Avenue, Hill District, holding his familiar camera.

Charles Teenie Harris

Born June 26(?), 1908—Hill District
Died June 12, 1998—Pittsburgh

"Teenie" Harris was accorded a rare double measure of respect. First, Pittsburgh Mayor David Lawrence, notoriously impatient, invariably deferred to Harris, waiting while the *Pittsburgh Courier* photographer took just the right photo. "One Shot," he called Harris, because that's all Harris needed to get the perfect image of Pittsburgh's great political boss.

Second, as fellow Pittsburgh photographer Greg Lanier has said, Harris saw black people with dignity. "There's a reason he had all the access that he did. People trusted him. They knew they would be portrayed in a warm and caring light."

Born Charles Harris in Pittsburgh's Hill District in 1908, a cousin from Detroit gave him his lifelong nickname when he was a baby. "Teenie Little Lover," she called him. As Harris grew—young and strong, a dapper dresser and sandlot baseball player—the Little Lover sobriquet slipped away. He was Teenie, for life.

Harris was the son of hoteliers, owners of Wylie Avenue's Masio Hotel. After graduating Watt (now Robert L. Vann) School, Harris

took his eighth-grade education into work as a mechanic, chauffeur, and numbers runner. But by 1929 Harris wanted a different life, telling his brother William "Woogie" Harris that he'd like to become a photographer. When Woogie countered that Teenie was crazy, that he couldn't make money shooting pictures, Teenie's riposte was "you give me $350, and I'll show you what I can do."

Thus challenged, Woogie, who also owned Wylie Avenue's Crystal Barber Shop, loaned Teenie the money for a camera—and a place for his darkroom.

At first, Harris freelanced for the Washington-based magazine *Flash!*, taking pictures of celebrities in Pittsburgh—athletes, musicians, and politicians.

With his work increasingly popular, and noticed, by 1936 he had joined the *Courier*—at $35 a week, plus $10 for supplies. Working for the next 40 years, Harris' portraits of the full spectrum of African-American life—barbers and beauticians, baseball players and balladeers—are simply unparalleled. Indeed, Harris' 80,000 images form America's most complete chronicle of the black urban experience, evoking the depth of humanity and spirit of an era, the Depression through World War II to the Civil Rights Movement.

A tireless, prolific photographer, Harris often worked around the clock. As *Courier* city editor Frank Bolden recalled, when Harris was assigned to cover a baseball game, he came back not only with photos of the athletes, but also with pictures of people in the stands, on the field, in clubs after the game. "He had a better instinct for people than some of my reporters," Bolden said. "He always had a news story in that camera."

By 1938, Harris had become such a local celebrity that he opened his own photographic studio at 2128 Centre Avenue. Operating it to great profit, after 15 years he closed it, 1953. In 1975 he retired from the *Courier*.

Always well dressed, driving his own signature Cadillac, Teenie Harris died in 1998, two weeks before his 90th birthday. He is buried in Homewood Cemetery.

Harris's *Group Portrait,* 1948, Ansco Safety film, H: 4 x W: 5 inches, Carnegie Museum of Art, Pittsburgh, Gift of the Heinz Family Fund

Harris captured Earl "Fatha" Hines, Mary Lou Williams, Erroll Garner, Billy Eckstine, and Maxine Sullivan in one shot.

Franco Harris

Born March 7, 1950—Fort Dix, NJ

Simply, it is the most famous play in football history. The Steelers, who had not won anything in 40 years, were losing—again.

December 23, 1972, with 22 seconds left in the game, Terry Bradshaw's 4th down pass intended for "Frenchy" Fuqua is immaculately received by Harris for the TD.

Down to their last 22 seconds of 1972, so bleak were their hopes of a winning season that even the Chief had given up. Head hung, shoulders slumped, he left before the denouement, prepared to give his troops his 40th consecutive "nice-try, men" speech.

What he missed made history—the jewel in the diadem of a Hall of Fame career. "I always looked for something," Franco Harris recalled. "Play the situation. Make something happen. Make the big play."

Big is an understatement. With the Steelers losing to the Raiders 7-6, fourth and 10 on the Steelers 40, a desperate Terry Bradshaw fired one of his patented armor-piercing passes to Frenchy Fuqua, which instead hit Raider strong safety Jack Tatum. The ball fell and fell and—seemingly out of nowhere rookie Franco Harris, who had run his route and trailed the play as he had done at Penn State, scooped up the ball and raced for the end zone. As pandemonium erupted in Three Rivers Stadium, Pittsburgh won 13-7. "The play," Harris said, "just gets bigger every year."

Dubbed The Immaculate Reception, it became Chuck Noll's all-time favorite Steeler moment. "Up until that point," he recalled, "I was the one who believed this was a good football team. That play was a sign that this was a team of destiny."

So was its happy participant. Born in 1950 in Fort Dix, New Jersey, power back Franco Harris played at Rancocas Valley High, in Mount Holly, New Jersey, then joined Penn State's vaunted football program, primarily blocking for All-American running back Lydell Mitchell. Nevertheless, the Steelers liked the smart, strong Harris, taking him as the #1 draft pick in 1972.

Playing at 6'-2" and 230 pounds, at first Harris seemed slow and tentative—until the pre-season game in Atlanta when he turned away from a botched play at full speed, galloping 75 yards for a touchdown.

Playing for the Steelers for the next 12 years, 1972-83, when the club won four championships, Harris, Dan Rooney says, "was the soul of this team." "He was the single most important guy," Joe Greene adds, "who got us that rough first down, who kept the ball when we needed it, the guy the team rallied around."

A perennial 1,000-yard rusher, Harris did it eight times, racking up 47 100-yard games. An eight-time Pro Bowler, his 158 yards in Super Bowl IX netted him most valuable player honors. In his 13 seasons (the last with Seattle), Harris gained more than 12,000 yards and scored 91 touchdowns on nearly 3,000 carries. "I had vision and anticipation," he recalls. "My strong suit was reading—I could read situations quickly and react."

The Steelers' first celebrity player, he inspired Franco's Italian Army, a loose conglomeration of fans which included Frank Sinatra.

Enshrined in the Pro Football Hall of Fame in 1990, Harris owns Pittsburgh-based Super Bakery.

Harris on drums with Hosea Taylor on saxophone and Gordon Jackson on piano, c. 1945, by Teenie Harris.

Joe Harris

Born in December 1926—North Side

The Manchester resident has played some of the most important gigs in jazz, working with Dizzy Gillespie in his teens to serving as the drummer-in-residence at Harlem's famed Apollo Theater.

By age 14, Harris proved to be a shrewd negotiator. He ran errands and did odd jobs around a downtown music store in exchange for one drum lesson a week. Those lessons provided Harris with an advantage over many other jazz drummers—he could read music. It earned him the nickname the "Professor."

It was Ray Brown who introduced him to Gillespie, and the young percussionist joined Dizzy's band. A nasty dispute about overtime pay in 1947 led to Harris' firing from the band, yet he still managed to find work with the likes of Ella Fitzgerald, Sarah Vaughan, Billie Holiday, and Dinah Washington.

His musical travels eventually brought him to Sweden in the mid-1950s, which would have a profound effect on his career. He formed and led numerous integrated jazz bands and helped to popularize jazz in Sweden. He also played with famed saxophonist Sonny Rollins and toured with Quincy Jones. He married in Sweden, but when the relationship soured he left the country and found work with Uncle Sam as part of Radio Free Berlin's band.

By the mid-1960s, Harris was ready to return to the United States. His friend Nathan Davis, who headed up jazz studies at the University of Pittsburgh, invited him to teach. For 14 years Harris juggled teaching and touring.

In 1992, people danced to his beat in a different form. Harris was the subject—and star of—*Clean Drums,* a play based upon his life staged at the Kuntu Repertory Theatre, written by Rob Penny. The title refers to Harris' disciplined drumming style, a clear contradiction to the flashier style of lesser artists.

John H. Harris

Born July 9, 1898—McKees Rocks
Died February 12, 1969—Los Angeles, CA

John H. Harris, the eldest son of John P. Harris, was General Manager of his father's Amusement Company when his father, then serving as a State Senator in Harrisburg, died. The younger Harris, born on George Street, attended Crafton High and graduated from Georgetown University with a law degree before working in the movie theatre industry full time. In 1930, Harris Amusement Company sold 40 of its theatres to Warner Bros., and Harris, employed now by Warner Bros., entered into a five-year non-compete contract. But movies weren't the only amusement the Harris family promoted. The company had interests in sporting venues, too, like the Duquesne Gardens where, in 1925, the Pittsburgh Yellow Jackets, a semi-pro hockey team, became the city's first NHL team and was renamed the Pittsburgh Pirates.

In 1932, John H. Harris bought the team, which had moved previously to Philadelphia, floundered, and re-emerged, again, as the Pittsburgh Yellow Jackets. He also leased the Duquesne Gardens and introduced rodeos, boxing matches and dance

contests for the amusement of Depression-era audiences. Always the promoter, Harris learned that hockey alone wasn't always sufficient to draw a crowd, and he started to introduce entertainment between periods. In 1936, he hired three-time Olympic Gold medal winner Sonja Henie to perform on his ice and so realized a new opportunity for popular amusement. He called it the Ice Capades.

In 1940, with a chorus of lavishly costumed beauties, Harris introduced one of the first Ziegfeldian revues on ice. He hired jugglers, bicyclists, comedians and clowns to create a touring "ice carnival" which would appear in cities across America. Former Olympic skaters interpreted Tchaikovsky or Gershwin in fluid ballets, and in every show the chorus girls, whom he labeled Ice Ca-Pets, would revolve in an ever-extending straight line as the youngest and best of the Ca-Pets had to skate faster and faster to catch up to the last position. Perennial favorite skaters were Bobby Specht and Donna Atwood (to whom Harris was married for nine years and with whom he had three children). Even in 1949, the Ice Capades paid homage to Walt Disney's films, featuring Snow White and her Seven Dwarfs. Today, Disney on Ice still tours, but after several failed ownerships (including 700 Club evangelist Pat Robertson,) the Ice Capades ceased skating in 1996.

the Harris Musee in McKeesport and, thus started his own theatrical enterprise separate from Davis. But their relationship must have been close. In addition to sharing Eleanor, Harris' eldest brother Denis joined Davis' stock company of actors, who performed regularly at the Avenue Theatre which Davis leased and where Harris was also General Manager. (Mt. Lebanon's Denis Theatre was named for Harris' brother).

Although by 1900, motion pictures were often featured in many of Davis' several theatres, Harris is today credited with the idea of opening a storefront on Smithfield Street where the only entertainment—continuously running from 8:00 am to midnight—were one-reel films. A phonograph played background music. So popular was the 96-seat venue named the Nickelodeon—Nickel for the admission, and Odeon, Greek for theatre—Davis and Harris were pulling in $1,000 a week.

Harris, like Davis, quickly launched dozens of Nickelodeons in both downtown Pittsburgh and in many other cities. The Harris Amusement Company was similarly incorporated in several states to manage their many movie theatres. But Harris also built eponymous theatrical stages in Pittsburgh and in McKeesport.

John P. Harris

Born December 4, 1871—Hill District
Died January 26, 1926—Harrisburg, PA

Born on Cliff Street in the once uptown neighborhood lost to the flattening of Grant's Hill, John P. Harris was the third son of John and Bridget Harris, natives of Blackburn, England. As a boy, he sold newspapers. His father, once a school teacher, then a cigar manufacturer, co-founded the firm of Harris and Willoughby, and among other uncertain amusements, may have engaged hot air balloonists performing daring aerial acrobatics. It's also as likely the younger Harris hawked his papers to audiences exiting the several entertainment halls downtown. Either way, Harris was introduced to "showbiz"at an early age.

History is more certain that Harris worked as a ticket seller for Harry Davis in the late 1880s, when Davis was the owner of the Eden Musee on Fifth Avenue near Market Square. As its name implies, The Musee was more museum than entertainment, but typical venues of its kind led patrons from viewing freakish curios to standing in front of a stage where simple vaudeville acts performed. Admission was 10 cents.

No doubt, the venue was profitable and Harris shared in those profits. As Davis invested his earnings into leasing more legitimate theatre space downtown, Harris invested in opening other musees elsewhere. Harris served as Davis' treasurer.

Harris married Davis's only sibling, Eleanor, in 1894. A year later, Harris opened

In 1922, filling the incomplete term of a state senator, Harris took office in Harrisburg and was re-elected in 1924 as a Republican representative of the Pittsburgh area. He died on the senate floor of a heart attack in 1926. In addition to his wife, Harris was survived by his five children, John H., Nellie, Mary, Harry D. and Geneva, and by his father John, who died a year later.

Orrin Hatch

Born March 22, 1934—Homestead, PA

Born to Mormon parents, Jesse and Helen Hatch, Orrin was one of five children who grew up in a two-story house built by his father in a once-wooded area above the Homestead Works. The family, like many in the early 1930s, struggled to make ends meet, but his father's income as a wall lather furnished enough disposable income that Orrin and his siblings could subscribe to student seats at the Pittsburgh Symphony Orchestra in Oakland. His early years were committed to learning the piano and playing basketball. Eventually he became accomplished on the violin and organ, which he played for his church. He became captain of his basketball team at Baldwin High School, from which he graduated in 1954.

As a missionary for the Church of Jesus Christ of Latter Day Saints, he spent two years in Ohio and Indiana spreading the gospel before heading on to Brigham Young University where he graduated in 1959. There he had met Elaine Hanson whom he wed in 1957. They returned to Pittsburgh and Orrin studied law at Pitt, earning his J.D. in 1962. To pay his tuition, he worked as a janitor and, like his father, a union metal lather. He then worked at the firm of Pringle, Bredin and Martin (now Thomson, Rhodes & Cowie P.C.) for seven years. In 1969, the Hatch family moved to Salt Lake City.

In 1977, challenging incumbent Senator Frank Moss in his first-ever run at political office, he won the junior seat for Utah. Hatch now serves as the eighth-most senior member of the Senate and the fourth highest-ranking Republican, serving as the Chairman of the Senate Judiciary Committee twice since 1995.

In 2000, he ran for President, losing the nomination, of course, to George W. Bush. In more recent news, the conservative Hatch fought for the failed passage of the Children Health Insurance Program, and was often discussed as a viable replacement to Alberto Gonzales as Attorney General. A composer of some repute, some of his songs have been recorded by Gladys Knight, Donny Osmond, Brooks and Dunn, and Natalie Grant.

Connie Hawkins

Born July 17, 1942—Brooklyn, NY

There's never an ill wind that doesn't blow somebody some good.

Which is how Pittsburgh won its only professional basketball championship.

The story begins in the Bedford-Stuyvesant neighborhood of Brooklyn, in 1942, with the birth of Cornelius L. "Connie" Hawkins. A neighborhood basketball legend as a child, by age 11 he could dunk. And then he got better.

Leading the famed Boys High School to back-to-back City League championships, 1959-60, Hawkins was named a *Parade* high school All American. Going to Iowa for college ball, he was named—and later completely exonerated—in a point-shaving scandal. Ex-

pelled, barred by the NCAA from playing at any other college, and banned by the NBA, in 1961 the 19-year-old Hawkins came to Pittsburgh to play for the Rens (for Renaissance) in the new American Basketball League.

Standing 6'-8" and a whip-thin 215 pounds, Hawkins was spectacular. Professional basketball's first great showman, he easily earned his nickname Hawk, jumping, soaring, dunking the ball in ways not previously seen—but widely imitated. Named ABL Most Valuable Player, Hawkins stayed with the team until the league disbanded, in late 1962.

Joining the Harlem Globetrotters, Hawkins toured the world before returning to Pittsburgh in 1967 to join another new league, the American Basketball Association. Playing for the Pittsburgh Pipers, Hawkins took the

April 25, 1986, Hawkins (42) of the Pittsburgh Pipers watches his own shot go over the basket.

scoring title, was named ABA MVP, and led the team to Pittsburgh's sole professional basketball championship in 1968.

When the franchise moved to Minnesota the following season, Hawkins went with it—for a time. Cleared of all gambling charges, he jumped to the NBA—as a 27-year-old rookie.

Playing in the NBA for seven years, 1969-76, for the Suns, Lakers, and Hawks, Hawkins became a member of the Basketball Hall of Fame in 1992. Now living in Phoenix, he works as a community relations representative.

Ernie Hawkins

Born September 22, 1947—Point Breeze

Ernie Hawkins, who began his guitar-playing days at hangouts like Shady Grove Coffee House and Loaves & Fishes, is considered to be one of the great guitarists carrying the torch of the Piedmont-style of blues.

Ernest Leroy Hawkins was born in the East End. He attended Linden Elementary and began playing guitar at the age of 13. As a teenager he happened to hear an old tune by the legendary Piedmont blues guitarist Blind Reverend Gary Davis called "Let Us Get Together." If ever there was a moment of artistic awakening, it was Hawkins' epiphany to the Reverend's renditions of Piedmont blues. Hawkins graduated from Taylor Allderdice High School with the sole purpose of finding and studying with Reverend Davis, who by now was in his late '60s and living in New York. After learning from his idol for a year, Hawkins returned home and enrolled at Pitt, earning a degree in philosophy. During those years back home, Ernie and his wife Annie brought the legendary blues musician to play various venues throughout the area. In the early 1970s Hawkins moved to Dallas to study the blues. There and elsewhere he played with some of the great blues artists, including Son

House, Mississippi Fred McDowell, and Mance Lipscomb.

Again Hawkins returned to Pittsburgh and spent 10 years with The Blue Bombers, working the clubs throughout town. As a student of the blues he began to pass on his vast knowledge through workshops, instructional videos, and personal lessons, at home and around the world. Hawkin's renown as a world-class guitarist has also earned him appearances on *Mountain Stage, Woodsongs Old-Time Radio Hour,* and *A Prairie Home Companion.*

Sara Henderson Hay

Born November 13, 1906—Pittsburgh
Died July 7, 1987—Squirrel Hill

An adept, award-winning poet, Sara Henderson Hay wrote wry, modern stories filled with compassion, irony, and humor. Who else would have re-cast *Little Red Riding Hood,* having granny invite the wolf inside for a warm bed and a well-gnawed bone?

As a child her family moved to Anniston, AL. Publishing poetry at age 10—a poem about golf appeared in *Judge* magazine—she returned to Pittsburgh, attending Squirrel Hill's Wightman School, graduating eighth grade in 1921. As a high school student, she published in the *Anniston Star*.

After her 1929 graduation from Columbia University, Hay took a secretarial job at Scribner's. Within two years, 1931, she was publishing in such prestigious journals as *The Atlantic Monthly* and *The New Yorker*. In 1933, she published her first of six books of poetry, *Field of Honor*.

In 1935, as secretary to syndicated columnist Gladys Baker, Hay traveled to Europe, meeting Pope Pius XI, Benito Mussolini, and Turkish president Mustafa Kemal Ataturk, among others.

Back in New York, Hay wrote poetry and reviews for the *Saturday Review*, and in 1939 published *This, My Letter*. Twelve years later, 1951, she published *The Delicate Balance*, which won the Poetry Society of America's Edna St. Vincent Millay Memorial Award.

Her late-1950s marriage to Russian-American composer Nicolai Lopatnikoff, a Carnegie Mellon professor, brought her back to Pittsburgh. In 1960, Hay published the multiple award-winning *The Stone and the Shell*. In 1963, she published *Story Hour*—and became a Distinguished Daughter of Pennsylvania. In 1966, she published her sixth and final book, *A Footing on This Earth*.

In 1987, 80-year-old Sara Henderson Hay died in her Beacon Street home.

Michael Hayden

Born March 17, 1945—North Side

© Roger Wollenberg/Pool/epa/Corbis

Born to Harry and Sadie Hayden in the neighborhood razed for Three Rivers Stadium, Michael Hayden played junior football under coach Dan Rooney. He was an Honors student at North Catholic High School, where he served on the Student Council. At Duquesne University, he earned his B.A. in history in 1967 and a masters in American history two years later, all while enlisted in Duquesne's ROTC program from which he was commissioned as a 2nd Lieutenant in the Air Force.

Hayden served in the Air Force for 36 years, three of which in the U.S. Embassy in Bulgaria. He was appointed Director of the National Security Agency from 1999 to 2005, serving as the top intelligence officer during 9/11. On April 22, 2005, he was given the rank of General, becoming the highest-ranking intelligence officer in the armed forces. He was appointed to the position of Deputy Director of the new Department of National Intelligence under then first-ever Director John Negroponte. In 2006, when Porter Goss, then head of the CIA, suddenly resigned (without explanation), President George W. Bush appointed Hayden as the new and current top officer of the agency.

Surely, any more personal information about Hayden is now classified.

Alexander Hays

Born July 8, 1819—Franklin, PA
Died May 6, 1864—Battle of the Wilderness

Among the several monuments to famous military figures at Allegheny Cemetery, one stands out among all the rest—that of a much celebrated Gettysburg commander, General Alexander Hays.

Born in Venango County, Hays was the son of a member of Congress and general in the Pennsylvania militia. He attended Venango Academy, Mercer Academy, and Allegheny College in Meadville, where he left in his senior year to enter West Point. No scholar, Hays graduated 20th out of 25 students in his class of 1844.

Hays' military career began during the Mexican War where he served in several battles, none of which distinguished him for heroic measures. He resigned in 1848 and returned to Franklin to take up business in the iron trade. A failed businessman, he left for California to seek a fortune in gold and, fleeing destitution there, returned to Pittsburgh to apply his skills as an engineer and bridge builder. Some believe he helped name the Mexican War Streets on the North Side.

At the outbreak of the Civil War, he reentered the military, first as a private, but soon as Colonel of the 63rd Pennsylvania Volunteers. His first campaign was in combat at Seven Pines. A month later, Hays directed a bayonet charge during the Seven Days' Battle and was injured in his left arm. A month later, in August of 1862, he took up a charge at Second Bull Run and shattered his leg. While convalescing, he was promoted to Brigadier General and, by sole virtue of his seniority, was promoted again to lead the Third Division, Second Corp, just three days before the Battle of Gettysburg.

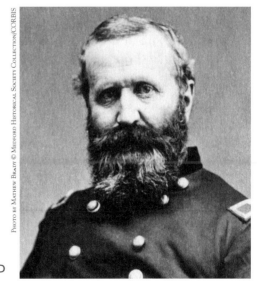
Photo by Mathew Brady © Medford Historical Society Collection/CORBIS

According to Civil War historian Larry Tagg in his much-respected account of Hays' actions on Cemetery Hill, "Hays, always an emotional fighter, had a special intensity at Gettysburg. On July 3, 1863, under the terrific cannonade that preceded Pickett's Charge, Hays suddenly appeared and had his men gather up all discarded rifles, clean them, load them and have them handy." Apparently, Hays suspected that the next assault would come from Confederate infantry. With his men each equipped with as many as four loaded rifles, Hays' instincts proved dead on.

"When the smoke cleared, Hays, who was unhurt but had had two horses shot out from under him, kissed his aide in the exhilaration of the moment." His division had broken the final charge of Pickett's men at Gettysburg,

At the Battle of the Wilderness, in the Spring of 1864, Hays was killed by a single bullet to the head.

Theodore Hazlett

Born in late 1918—Pittsburgh
Died July 8, 1979—Pittsburgh

It's hard to imagine Ted Hazlett recasting Pittsburgh while playing ping-pong, but as a young attorney just out of Harvard Law School that's what he did. Working—and playing—with many of the most powerful Pittsburgh people of the 1940s, Hazlett changed the face of this city—and many others worldwide.

For some three dozen years, Theodore Lyle Hazlett, Jr., was among the region's most influential men, serving the Allegheny Conference, Pittsburgh's Urban Redevelopment Authority, and Andrew W. Mellon Educational and Charitable Trust, among others. Ted to his friends, he was a man of extraordinary vision and boundless energy, seemingly everywhere when it mattered most.

Born in Pittsburgh in 1918, the Fox Chapel resident began by serving as Allegheny Conference solicitor. Just three years out of Harvard Law School, Hazlett drafted what became known as the Pittsburgh Package—the nation's first modern redevelopment laws. Tackling such issues as smoke control, blight, and eminent domain, Hazlett's legal skill helped transform Pittsburgh into a clean, attractive, world-class city.

Epitomizing Pittsburgh's public-private partnership, Hazlett simultaneously served as Urban Redevelopment Authority general counsel. Using his legal skill, he helped create the nation's first modern redevelopment project, the Point and Gateway Center, and first modern industrial redevelopment project, at the former Jones & Laughlin steel site.

By 1965 Hazlett had became A.W. Mellon Educational and Charitable Trust president, devoting endless time—and some $20 million over the next 15 years—to launching or sustaining many area arts organizations.

After a long battle with cancer, he died at age 60 in 1979, survived by his wife and four children.

As a tribute, in 1980 the North Side's former Carnegie Hall, which he had helped transform into the first home of Pittsburgh Public Theater, was renamed the Theodore L. Hazlett Theater, recast in 2004 as the New Hazlett Theater.

Sam Hazo

Born July 19, 1928—Pittsburgh

"Ask me where I was born," poet Sam Hazo wrote in the 1998 edition of *The Pittsburgh That Stays Within You*, "and I will say the place exists no more except within me, literally inside of me. Where else is history but there in each of us? Tens of thousands of Pittsburghs (each dawn reveals a similarly different city) have come into existence since I arrived on the scene. And many thousands will follow...[There is] the desire within us to get rid of the no longer functional or beautiful or serviceable and replace it with something else—hopefully but certainly not always something better."

With something better Hazo's goal, he is by turns poet, novelist, essayist, playwright, Duquesne University professor, and International Poetry Forum founder and director.

Born Samuel John Hazo in 1928 in Pittsburgh, he began writing poems as a Notre Dame undergraduate. After earning a 1948 English B.A., Hazo enlisted in the marines, rising to the rank of captain. Returning to Pittsburgh, he earned a 1955 Duquesne M.A. and a 1957 Pitt Ph.D. Teaching English at Duquesne since the mid-1950s, a half-century later he is a McAnulty Distinguished Professor Emeritus.

The author of some 30 books of poetry, Hazo's work has appeared in countless newspapers, magazines, and anthologies. Often writing about family, suffering, and the mysteries of life, his work is marked by sharply observed details and an ability to express wonder.

Little wonder, since for Hazo poetry is "a time when suddenly things come into focus, and you work under the imperative of some impulse, something you did not will into being, that came to you, and you must work it out in words that are just now coming to you, that are making you put everything that you have at that moment right on the line."

As if that weren't fit work for a lifetime, in 1966 Hazo founded the International Poetry Forum, which he still directs. Drawing Nobel Laureates, Pulitzer Prize winners, even Academy Award winners, IPF has hosted the best of poetry and performance—Chinua Achebe and W.H. Auden, Saul Bellow and Jorge Luis Borges, Robert Penn Warren and Yevgeny Yevtushenko; Jane Alexander and Judith Anderson, Princess Grace and Julie Harris, James Earl Jones and Gregory Peck.

Summarizing his multiple successes, the fourth edition of Hazo's *The Pittsburgh That Stays Within You* contains his poet's call-to-arms:

"The visions of writers and artists are crucial to the life of any city," Hazo wrote in 2003, "and woe unto the city that derides or banishes or otherwise stultifies them. If intellectual conformity is the dominant 'ism' of our time, it is the arts that stand for intellectual and spiritual individuality and independence. They exist to remind us of who we really are. They mirror us to ourselves whether we like what we see or not, and they tell us what we truly know but which we sometimes forget."

Hardly banished, in 1993 Hazo was named Pennsylvania's first Poet Laureate. Father of award-winning composer Samuel Robert Hazo, Sam Hazo lives and works in Pittsburgh.

George Heid, Sr.

Born October 8, 1902—Brooklyn, NY

Dave Garroway, primogenitor of *The Today Show* for NBC, once said of George Heid, "He's the most versatile, creative man I know in show business." After mastering numerous facets of the entertainment industry—and helping to pioneer some of them—Heid became one of the shining stars of Pittsburgh's entertainment scene.

George Herman Heid was born in Brooklyn, New York. A love of music and theater, at age 12, George sang and danced on street corners for pennies, launching a singing and performing career: first in Nickelodeons and vaudeville, then in legitimate theater and Light Opera. After a successful decade on stage, he entered the young radio industry as program director of KPO in San Francisco.

Around 1934, his good friend Dale Jackson encouraged Heid to move to Pittsburgh where he was offered the position of program director at KQV. He was soon lured over to KDKA.

During the 1930s and 1940s, he produced and hosted many beloved radio shows, including a Pittsburgh favorite, Al Marsico's *Memory Time.* He also produced music programs, such as *The Big Swing to Isaly's,* with Max Adkins' Orchestra at the Stanley Theater. Another favorite was *Dimling's Candy Kids.* It was on this program that Heid gave the then-11-year-old child prodigy Erroll Garner his first professional gig. Additionally, Heid was producing live radio programs for WCAE, WJAS, and WWSW.

He started Pittsburgh's first recording studio, George Heid Productions, in the mid-1930s. Using bulky on-location equipment, he made the first recordings of the Pittsburgh Symphony Orchestra. He recorded early pivotal music career dates for Billy Strayhorn, Mary Lou Williams, Henry Mancini, Erroll Garner, George Benson, and Fred Rogers. Additionally, he founded the George Heid School of Radio and Television Arts in 1948. Acclaimed graduates of his school include Ray Scott, Dick Stockton, Stan Wall, Henry Debecco, Perry Marshall, Marie Torre, Eleanor Schano, Nick Perry, and Ray Lehman.

In 1948, he moved his recording studio to larger, state-of-the-art facilities on the Club Floor of the William Penn Hotel. George Heid Productions became the place to record music. Many of Pittsburgh's finest artists became regulars at the studio. Johnny Costa, Joe Negri, Lorin Maazel, Walt Harper, Shirley Jones, Dodo Marmarosa, Eddie Jefferson, George Benson, the Skyliners, the Marcels, and the Del Vikings made memorable and historic recordings there.

Perhaps it was his fine baritone voice that led him to his most enduring and memorable roll, playing Santa Claus. His first-rate "Ho, Ho, Ho," his warm smile and sparkling eyes, and his sincere love of children made him Pittsburgh's most beloved Santa. For many years, he played Santa on Paul Shannon's *Adventure Time.* But it was the volunteer charity work of playing Santa to hundreds of handicapped children that brought him his greatest joy. Many witnessed and would recall seeing a tear in his eye as he sang, with heartfelt love, "Toyland," to all those children's beaming smiles.

H. J. Heinz

Born October 11, 1844—South Side
Died May 14, 1919—Pittsburgh

If at first you don't succeed, learn from the man whose horseradish got him in a pickle.

Born in Birmingham (now the South Side,) but whose father owned a brickyard in Sharpsburg, young Henry John Heinz plowed the family's vegetable garden as a young boy. His disdain for then-bottled produce, laden with "fillers," inspired him to bottle his own horseradish in clear glass, so that all could see his product was pure. With partner L. Clarence Noble, Heinz & Noble was born in 1869. But by 1875, the company went under; H.J. learned then not to buy produce on contract, but to be selective and wary of abundant harvests. A year later he reorganized the business with his brother John and, at great risk, founded the F&J Heinz Company. The company, like's it product lines, grew rapidly and by 1888, H.J. was able to buy out his brother and other (retrospectively unfortunate) investors. In that same year, he started construction on his factory along the Allegheny River, sewed up contracts with wholesalers in the UK, and hired more staff to process his highly-acclaimed prepared foods. In fact, perhaps more than having raised consumers' expectations of quality, Heinz also began to raise the level of workers' care and compensation. His new facility on the North Side would become a model in the Industrial Age. So proud was H.J. of his factory, he was the first to offer public tours.

Heinz also believed strongly in the magic of marketing and the power of public relations. His many delivery trucks bore over-sized pickles upon their roofs, and public trolleys, both here and abroad, proudly advertised his many products. His were some of the first billboards ever erected. And, even when he decided that the Heinz label should declare "57 Varieties," he had many more than 57 to sell. (Apparently, he just liked the number). The birth of the pickle pin came at the Columbian Exposition in Chicago, 1893, when the free gherkin was an instant crowd charmer. A pure competitor, too, Heinz was instrumental in passing one of the first consumer protection laws when, in 1906, the Pure Food and Drug Act was enacted by Congress.

Married in 1869, H.J. and Sarah Sloan Young had four children: Irene, Howard, Clarence and Clifford.

Howard inherited his father's work ethic, as well as the top seat of the company, starting first by working on the pickling lines. He graduated from Yale in 1900, and only then worked in company management. Under his tenure, the company grew to greater profitability, expanding sales while opening new markets across Europe.

In 1906, Howard married Elizabeth Granger Rust who gave birth to two heirs, Jack and Rust. In 1941, following failed surgery, Howard died from a stroke. His will thus created the Howard Heinz Endowments.

Jack Heinz

Born July 10, 1908—Pittsburgh
Died February 23, 1987—Hobe Sound, FL

Like his father Howard, Jack spent summers in the factory. He grew up on Morewood Heights, attended the Choate School, Yale and Cambridge Universities, and joined the company sales team in England. While he would take over the top desk in 1942 and build the company's monumental brand, Jack Heinz's real legacy was in building Pittsburgh.

Jack married aviatrix Joan Diehl in 1935 and moved into a new family estate, Rosemont, in Fox Chapel. Three years later they gave birth to their only child, H.J. "John" Heinz III. But, in 1941, all hell broke loose: Howard died unexpectedly, Jack was ascended to the top office, and Jack and Joan divorced. Jack took the reins at a time of in-

credible stress; America was at war, Europe was in dire straits, and food rationing became a point of national duty. Of course, the Heinz Company did its part to alleviate hunger in Europe, and, at home, Jack chaired the United War Fund. On the North Side, the company even secretly retooled its factory to manufacture glider planes.

After the war not much changed in Pittsburgh. The skies were thick with smoke as the steel mills belched and moaned, keeping up with domestic demand. It was at this time that Richard King Mellon invited the city's CEOs to a secret lunch at the Duquesne Club. (No president was allowed to send a vice president). Mellon, one by one, tapped his cohorts for their support in cleaning up the skies, diversifying its industries, and building the city for tomorrow. The lunch helped solidify the formation of the Allegheny Conference on

Heinz ketchup is found in four out of five U.S. restaurants. Each year, it sells a whopping 11.4 billion portion-control packets, introduced under Jack Heinz's tenure.

Community Development. Attending, of course, was Jack Heinz.

As Chair of the Pittsburgh Symphony, then performing in Oakland's Syria Mosque, Heinz committed his resources to moving the orchestra to the lower Hill District, where, by the late 1950s, plans were drawn to build something much like an acropolis of cultural venues. Those plans became the Civic Arena, then the world's largest dome. But Heinz wanted to locate his beloved symphony in something grander. When visiting the shabby Loew's Penn Theatre in 1966, he envisioned a

more suitable home. And with an investment of $850,000 for the building, and another $7 million for restoration, Heinz Hall opened on September 10, 1971.

But Heinz didn't stop there. His vision was clearly something of greater scope. He envisioned an entire district of cultural venues and new office towers sharing parks and parking garages, and attracting a newfound diversity of retail interests to the Golden Triangle. In 1984, Heinz created the Pittsburgh Cultural Trust to steer, among dozens of projects, a $43 million restoration of the Stanley Theatre. The old movie house would become the Benedum Center. The former Fulton Theatre

would reappear as the Byham. And a wholly new O'Reilly Theatre, by 1999, would emerge as the home of the Pittsburgh Public Theater.

Heinz died just months before the opening of the Benedum in 1987. His widow, Drue Maher Heinz, whom he married in 1953, lives now in Manhattan.

In 1969, the former Loew's Penn Theatre undergoes a dramatic transformation into the city's signature venue for the performing arts.

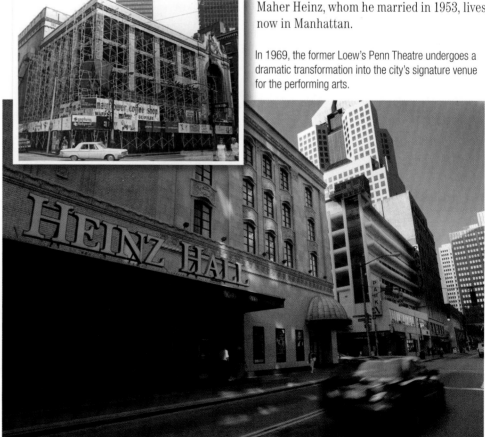

Sen. John Heinz III

Born October 23, 1938—Pittsburgh
Died April 4, 1991—Lower Merion Twp., PA

The only child of H. J. "Jack" Heinz II and Joan Diehl, John Heinz grew up primarily in San Francisco when his mother, divorced in 1942, moved to the Bay Area. His stepfather, C.C. Monty McCauley, a U.S. Naval Aviator, shared the joy of flying with Joan. John, too, learned to fly, and had his own pilot's license at the time of his tragic death on April 4, 1991, when the plane he chartered, but which he was not flying, collided with a helicopter above a playground outside of Philadelphia.

John attended the Town School for Boys in San Francisco, graduating from Phillips Exeter Academy in 1956, and Yale in 1960. Before earning a master's degree in business from Harvard in 1963, Heinz worked in Sydney, Australia, for International Harvester. In 1963, he enlisted in the Air Force Reserves and also served as a legislative assistant to Senator Hugh Scott of Pennsylvania. While traveling through Switzerland, he met Teresa Simoes-Ferreira, a Mozambique-born professional interpreter. They were married in 1966.

Although employed by his grandfather's vast corporation, many of Heinz's early years in Pittsburgh were devoted to working with his father on civic development downtown.

December 10, 1975, Heinz III announces his bid for the senatorial seat of Hugh Scott, accompanied by his wife Teresa and three sons, John, Christopher and Andre.

But, in 1971, he ran for political office, winning the Republican nomination from Ernest Buckman, and defeating Democratic challenger John Connelly for the 18th District seat left vacant by the death of Congressman Robert Corbett. He won re-elections in 1972 and 1974, and then ran for Senator of Pennsylvania in 1976. He represented Pennsylvania in Congress for more than 20 years.

Heinz's legacy in Washington was well earned for his legislation on health care, the elderly, foreign trade and environmental issues. He was a leading advocate of Project 88, an innovative policy that encouraged the profitable practice of recycling newspapers, oil and other household wastes, and he re-instituted economically feasible regulations for clean air. Heinz was also well regarded for proactively meeting with his constituents. Not just a frequent campaigner, Heinz hosted more than 500 town meetings in his short career and, in fact, was scheduled to attend a similar event in Media, PA, the evening of his tragic death.

Anna B. Heldman

Born January 15, 1873—Castle Shannon, PA
Died March 15, 1940—Castle Shannon, PA

Historians of social health can debate in what American city the mission of Visiting Nurses began, but certainly Pittsburgh was one of the first to adopt the innovative community service. And the pioneer of this health movement, known to Pittsburghers as "the angel of the Hill," was Anna B. Heldman.

One of five daughters born to Louis and Anna (Vetter) Heldman of Castle Shannon, young Anna grew up attending the Scott Township public school and matriculating at Duquesne College. Although her father enrolled her in a business school to learn secretarial skills, Anna wished to be a nurse and, so graduated from the Nurses' Training School of the South Side Hospital in 1897. Employed as a private nurse for several months, she volunteered to serve in the Spanish-American War and was assigned to the Capt. Alfred Hunt Post No. 1 until the war concluded in 1898.

Again, she returned to private nursing but was not pleased with her singular responsibilities. Preferring a more active role in public health, she interviewed for a new position at the Columbian Council School and Settlement. The community center was established in 1895 by the Council of Jewish Women to offer classes in English and Citizenship to the many immigrant Jews who settled in the Hill district. The Settlement also offered summer daycare, a library and health clinics. Heldman started work on October 1, 1902. Her job was to go into the community, seek out the ill and infirmed, and offer her aid. After her first month, she could find no more than 11 people wanting her services. After her second

month—no longer a stranger—she found herself in need of an assistant.

In her first five years on the job, Heldman marched to Harrisburg to advocate for state laws requiring professional nurse registration, enacted the first public school health inspections, established new protocols for the County Child Welfare Division, and organized the Typhoid Study for the 1906 Pittsburgh Survey.

F10630 A Glimpse of Miss Heldman and the Personal Service Dept. Jan. 1936

By 1909, with a gift from Henry and Emma Kaufmann to memorialize their daughter, the Settlement became the Irene Kaufmann Settlement.

In 1917, when the U.S. entered World War I, a pandemic of influenza killed tens of thousands of Pittsburghers. Heldman nursed more than 1,000 patients in the course of just 42 days.

At the IKS, Heldman initiated dozens of innovative health programs, including the "Milk Well" program for new mothers, then the "Better Baby Clinic," both programs of which became models duplicated in scores of U.S. cities after the war.

Upon her sudden death at 67, Heldman, a Christian, was eulogized by Rabbi B. A. Lichter and buried in Zion Cemetery.

© British Medical Journal, BMJ, Inc.

Philip Showalter Hench

Born February 28, 1896—Pittsburgh
Died March 30, 1965—Ocho Rios, Jamaica

A co-winner of the 1950 Nobel Prize for Medicine, Philip Hench, then Chief of Rheumatology at the Mayo Clinic in Rochester, Minnesota, earned $10,571 as his share of the prize. He discovered, along with chemist Edward Kendall, and predecessor Tadeus Reichstein of Switzerland, the active hormone now commonly known as cortisone.

Hench, born to Clara Showalter and Jacob Bixler Hench, a school administrator, lived on Kentucky Avenue and attended Shady Side Academy, graduating in 1912. He enrolled at Pitt, but was enlisted shortly thereafter in the U.S. Army Medical Corps during the outbreak of World War I. Put on reserve, he then enrolled at Lafayette College, earned his B.S. in 1916, then returned to Pitt for his M.D. in 1920. He first interned at St. Francis Hospital. In 1923 he served as an assistant at the Mayo Clinic and by 1926 was named Head of the Department of Rheumatic Diseases. Seeking higher knowledge in a field of study about which arthritis sufferers believed that whisky and aspirin were the only known relief, Hench studied abroad at Freiburg University and at the von Muller Clinic in Munich.

In 1929 Hench first addressed his observations that patients with arthritis suffered less pain when they had jaundice. He noticed too that pregnant women seemed not to suffer, and he conjectured that a hormone from the adrenal glands might serve as an anti-rheumatic steroid. Although he always insisted that his work was oriented to research, the compound he extracted (actually from bile) enabled long-suffering patients to dance and, in one story, leave their hospital bed to go shopping.

Married in 1927, and with four children, Hench devoted his spare time to historical research. Fascinated by the story of Walter Reed, Jesse Lazear and the Yellow Fever Commission, he collected every relevant scrap of information about the public health story. His extensive archive is housed at the University of Virginia.

Never afforded the time to write his book about Yellow Fever, he died of pneumonia under a diabetic coma while on vacation.

Victor Herbert

Born February 1, 1859—Dublin, Ireland
Died May 26, 1924—New York, NY

Victor August Herbert conducted the Pittsburgh Symphony from 1898 until 1902. Under Herbert's direction, the Pittsburgh Symphony evolved into one of the premier American ensembles, with performance schedules in many major U.S. cities.

His father died when Herbert was a child so he moved in with his grandfather, who encouraged the young boy in the ways of music. It was his grandfather who exposed Herbert

© Bettmann/CORBIS

© Bettmann/CORBIS

to the great Italian cellist Alfredo Carlo Piatti, inspiring him to perform and write at a young age. He began his studies in Germany at the Stuttgart Conservatory and by his late teens Herbert, an astonishing cellist, soloed with major orchestras. His career included a stint in the orchestra of the brother of waltz king Johann Stauss.

In 1886 he married soprano Theresa Herbert-Foster. Foster was offered a position with the Metropolitan Opera and the two moved to the United States. The Pittsburgh Symphony hired Herbert, to the audience's delight and some critic's dismay, and propelled the young symphony to national prominence. In just its second season under the leadership of Herbert, The Pittsburgh Symphony was invited to perform at Carnegie Hall in New York City, financed by Andrew Carnegie.

Among his numerous works were operas, choral compositions, a cantata, operettas, and many popular songs. Some of his best known works include *Naughty Marietta*, *The Fortune Teller* and *Babes In Toyland,* a fantasy that is said to have inspired Frank L. Baum to write *The Wonderful Wizard Of Oz*. Herbert was one of the first to record his music, a result of his friendship with Thomas Edison.

In addition to being one of the best known figures in American music, Herbert was also a founder of ASCAP (American Society of Composers, Authors, and Publishers), an organization which, still to this day, protects copyrights and collects royalties on behalf of musicians and songwriters.

Above, Jeannette MacDonald and Nelson Eddy played the parts of the countess and the captain in the 1935 movie version of Herbert's *Naughty Marietta*. The television roles were played by Patrice Munsel and Alfred Drake (right) in a NBC TV special which aired on January 15, 1955.

Elsie Hillman

Born December 9, 1925—Squirrel Hill

Her basement wall is covered with friends, acquaintances and political allies. What is more remarkable than the diversity of photographs that parade five former U.S. Presidents, golf gatherings with Greg Norman and Arnie Palmer, award accolades to and from local legends, and costumed capades on ice and stage, is the consistency of the laughing, loving smiles of Elsie Hilliard Hillman. One of the most revered private citizens of Pittsburgh, she has made more things happen here than anyone will ever know.

She was born on Aylesboro Avenue and "had loads of fun" playing with her friends while otherwise studying at The Ellis School. While this was during World War II, her first community service was as a volunteer at the Eye and Ear Hospital where she prepped patients prior to surgery. Graduating from the

Ethel Walker School in 1944, she attended Westminster Choir College in Princeton for one year. She married Henry Hillman in May of 1945 while he flew for the United States Navy. After a few months in Dallas, he was discharged and they returned to Pittsburgh. Living for two years at the Schenley Apartments, they moved to Squirrel Hill where they have lived ever since.

In 1952, Elsie entered the world of politics, stumping for Ike. Asked to help get out the labor vote, she soon recognized the disconnect between the African-American community and the opportunities that white- and blue collar workers were afforded in an era of great productivity. She worked with Wendell Freeland to help found Hill House. She worked tirelessly with Frieda Shapira and Art Edmonds to build the Urban League Chapter.

She worked with Nate Smith to help train his unemployed "brothers." And she worked with a young Jesse Jackson, through Smith, who then helped her raise minority interest for candidates like Dick Thornburgh and John Tabor. And that's just the first decade of her community activism.

By 1974, Elsie was the County Chair of the Republican Committee, and a year later she was appointed to the State Committee. From 1975 until her retirement in 1996, she served on the National Executive Committee, getting to know personally every Republican candidate and every President—former, hopeful, Democratic or current—from Ike to Dub-ya. One of her biggest thrills in politics was sleeping in the White House (not in Lin-

coln's bedroom, but the Queen's). And to squelch the hearsay that she is Barbara Bush's kin, she succinctly reports, "My first cousin, Louise Walker, married George H.W. Bush's uncle."

A list of non-profit boards on which she has served, being too long to cite, would omit the least and most deserving of organizations for which she has deeply cared. On the other hand, a short list of favorite musicians with whom she has played is illuminating: Walt Harper, Victor Borge, William Steinberg, Johnny Costa and Henry Hillman.

Above left, Reporter Harold Hayes, Hillman and President George H.W. Bush meet at the Pittsburgh Airport.

Above, ever youthful, Hillman awards WQED thanks with Tinkerbell, WQED President George Miles.

Left, Hillman, Urban League president Art Edmonds, and Frieda Shapira proclaim promising changes in Pittsburgh.

Below, Hillman upstages an original Burton Morris variety.

Henry Hillman

Born December 25, 1918—Morewood Heights

From the Christmas Day on which he was born, Henry Hillman's life has been about Pittsburgh. While his business activities are necessarily diverse geographically, his lifelong commitments to family, philanthropy, and civic responsibility have been focused on the city of his birth.

Attending Shady Side Academy, Taft School and Princeton University ('41), he entered the Navy, coincidentally, on December 7, 1941, Pearl Harbor Day. He served as a Naval Aviator until the end of World War II. In 1945 he married Elsie Mead Hilliard, with whom he has enjoyed 63 years of "wonderful marriage," off-springing four children, nine grandchildren and four great-grandchildren.

In business, he started as a trainee at a small industrial company, Pittsburgh Coke and Chemical, becoming President in 1955. He later took the company private, selling off all of its lagging, old-economy, industrial operations, and refocusing them in more promising ways.

After his father's death in 1959, he became President of J.H. Hillman & Sons, later renamed The Hillman Company. Hillman made the founding investment in Kleiner Perkins, which has continued to be a leader in Silicon Valley. He later was the founding investor in Kohlberg, Kravis & Roberts, which became the most prominent leveraged buyout firm. (Today The Hillman Company is largely a highly diversified investment company). Hillman also served on the board of directors of General Electric, Chemical Bank, Merck, Cummins Engine, and PNC.

Since returning to Pittsburgh after the War, he has served his community as President/Chairman of the Allegheny Conference, a member of the Urban Redevelopment Authority, and director of Action Housing and the Pittsburgh Regional Planning Association. He has served many years as a trustee of Children's Hospital, Pitt, and the Carnegie Museums of Pittsburgh.

Philanthropy has been a constant focus of his life. A number of grants from the Henry L. Hillman Foundation and the Hillman Foundation have resulted in the Hillman Cancer Center (UPMC), Hall of Minerals and Gems (Carnegie), Center for Performing Arts (Shady Side), Pediatric Transplantation Center (Children's) and, earlier, the Hillman Library (Pitt). And he plans to continue his philanthropic focus on Pittsburgh.

In spite of his active participation in many areas, he still finds time to play golf and the piano, and to read voraciously. Never enjoying publicity, his motto has always been "The whale gets harpooned only when it spouts."

Earl "Fatha" Hines

Born December 28, 1903—Duquesne, PA
Died April 22, 1983—Oakland, CA

He has been called "the first modern jazz pianist" and at the height of his career played under the heavy hand of Chicago mafia boss Al Capone.

Truly one of the all-time great pianists, Earl "Fatha" Hines started out on the cornet. Although he studied the wind instrument with his father, a professional cornetist, he switched to the piano. Maybe because his mother played the church organ, he took to the keyboards. Either way, he was classically trained on the piano. By the age of 11 he was playing Chopin preludes and performing on concert stages. He moved into the city with his Aunt when he was 14 and soon began to study jazz while attending Schenley High School. His first professional performance was in 1918 with Pittsburgh singer Lois Deppe, with whom he first recorded. And in 1921, Hines and Deppe became the first African-Americans to perform live on radio, Westinghouse's KDKA. In 1924 Hines took the advice of a fellow musician and moved to Chicago. There, he began a long friendship with Louis Armstrong and recorded a number of revered jazz classics.

Conflicting stories surround how Hines got his nickname. One story says he picked-up the nickname "Fatha" after reportedly offering some "fatherly" advice about excessive drinking to a show MC. Another story says Hines "fathered" a style of jazz piano that until then had been predominantly orchestral in nature. Hine's skill at the piano was so remarkable that it was rumored he had made a pact with the devil, cutting the webs between his fingers so he could get the stretch that only he seemed able.

In 1940 Pittsburgh native and vocalist Billy Eckstine joined forces with Hines, as did other jazz greats including Charlie Parker, Dizzy Gillespie and Sarah Vaughan. Unfortunately, due to a musician's union dispute, none of those sessions were ever recorded.

Hines and Armstrong joined forces again in the late 1940s before Hines left for the West Coast. There, for the next decade, Hines recorded only sporadically, and he fell off the radar of mainstream jazz. Then in 1964 Hines was invited to play a series of shows in New York which resurrected his career and fueled a renewed popularity until his death at 79.

Margaret Hodges

Born July 26, 1911—Indianapolis, IN
Died December 13, 2005—Pittsburgh

Sometimes a person's true calling comes later in life. At age 47, Margaret Hodges published her first children's book, then spent nearly a half-century publishing some 50 more.

Born Sarah Margaret Moore, she grew up on books—Beatrix Potter, Lewis Carroll, and Louisa May Alcott. Earning a 1932 Vassar B.A., she married Fletcher Hodges, then came to Pittsburgh in 1937 when he became Pitt's Stephen Foster Memorial curator.

Living in Shadyside, raising three sons, in 1953 Hodges—Peggy to everyone—went to work as a Carnegie Library children's librarian. Her readings to children were so lively that they were broadcast on WQED-radio as *Let's Tell a Story*.

Hodges trained as a librarian at Carnegie Tech and received her Master of Library Science in 1958, the same year she published her first book, *One Little Drum*. Based on the lives of her sons, Hodges followed with more stories about her children.

By 1964, she had moved over to television on WQED's *Tell Me a Story*, taping through 1976. Serving as a Pitt lecturer for the Graduate School of Library and Information Science, Hodges made assistant professor in 1968. Rising through the ranks to full professor in 1975, she became an emeritus professor in 1978.

Her all-engaging stories fall into three categories—fictionalized tales of her children; biographies of Queen Anne, Joan of Arc, and others; and re-tellings of works of English, Greek, even Russian literature. An inveterate traveler, her visits to the British Isles, Europe, and the Orient found their way into her books as well.

A multiple award-winner, her top honor was the 1985 Caldecott Medal for *Saint George and the Dragon*, her version of Edmund Spenser's *Faerie Queene*, Book I.

Named a 1970 Distinguished Daughter of Pennsylvania, 94-year-old Margaret Hodges died in 2005 in her Oakmont home.

John Hodiak

Born April 16, 1914—Pittsburgh
Died October 19, 1955—Tarzana, CA

Born of Ukranian-Polish parents, Walter and Anna Hodiak, John Hodiak bucked all odds. He took diction lessons to mask his immigrant dialect, kept his birth name, declined an offer to play for the St. Louis Cardinal's farm team, and became one of Hollywood's better known "tough guys" in a string of war films. He even married a Hollywood starlet. His career was consistent, rewarding and secured by studio contracts. But he died young.

As a child, his family moved to Detroit where he first performed in his Ukranian Church. Itching to work in radio, his early auditions failed when he was told to "lose the accent." A stock boy for Chevrolet, he cleaned up his diction and found character work in radio, eventually creating the voice of popular comic strip character Lil Abner.

Rejected from enlisting in the war effort due to hypertension, Hodiak was one of few fresh male faces in Hollywood when he signed a contract with MGM in 1942. With a few small parts under his belt, Alfred Hitchcock booked him to play the subversive engineer in Steinbeck's *Lifeboat*, starring Tallulah Bankhead, Hume Cronyn, and William Bendix. The following year, appearing again with Bendix, Hodiak was cast as the Army major responsible for cleaning up the war torn town in *A Bell for Adano*. His career was now assured.

In more than 20 of his next films, Hodiak would play the tough, no-nonsense platoon leader, cavalry commander or square-jawed detective. In1946, while filming *Somewhere in the Night*, Hodiak married Ann Baxter, a young supporting actress who would later achieve acclaim for *The Magnificent Ambersons* and star as not one, but two villainesses in TV's *Batman*.

In 1953, Hodiak took a successful turn on Broadway in the gripping court drama, *The Caine Mutiny Court Martial*.

Two years divorced from Baxter, back in Tarzana, CA, in 1955, Hodiak died suddenly of cardiac thrombosis. He was just 41.

John Hoerr

Born December 12, 1930—McKeesport, PA

"I can make no pretense of objectivity," John Hoerr wrote in his 1988 *And the Wolf Finally Came*, his authoritative, exhaustive, highly personal, 600-page examination of its subtitle: *The Decline of the American Steel Industry*. "This is my home. I was born in the valley, grew up here, went to school, played, worked, and was part of a family here, and I dread the sight of silent mills and dying mill towns...I can see that an immense tragedy is unfolding."

To recreate that tragedy, Hoerr dissects with a journalist's skill—and a patriot's heart—people and places he knows, shortsightedness and sell-outs, the destruction of a 46-mile world-class riverside production line that he calls "swift and brutal."

Graduating McKeesport High in 1948, the year his uncle Harry Davenport took a seat in Congress, by 1960 Hoerr was a labor reporter for *United Press International*, *The Daily Tribune*, and *Business Week*. Covering the quickening collapse of the steel industry, and encouraged by the University of Pittsburgh Press' late Fred Hetzel, Hoerr's *And the Wolf Finally Came* is an enormous diorama, the creation of Big Steel through the landmark 1959 116-day strike to the 1982 market collapse.

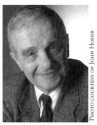

Following his first book, Hoerr's *We Can't Eat Prestige: The Women Who Organized Harvard*, examines union activities in that Ivy League school.

Third in his trilogy is his 2005 *Harry, Tom and Father Rice: Accusation and Betrayal in America's Cold War*. Examining his Congressman uncle Harry Davenport, United Electrical Workers' Tom Quinn, and labor priest Father Charles Owen Rice, the book looks at Pittsburgh's home-grown McCarthyism and three lives, friends then foes.

A frequent visitor to his White Oak family, John Hoerr lives and works in New Jersey.

Jane Holmes

Born in 1805—Ireland
Died in 1885

A dying girl, ailing from tuberculosis, was found on the steps of Jane Holmes' house on Sherman Avenue, Allegheny City, in 1883. Indigent, she sought "Bountiful Jane," the kind and wealthy women known throughout the city as a friend to those in need. Holmes took the girl into her home and cared for her after area hospitals had turned her away. This event inspired the elderly Holmes to convert her family's Lawrenceville summer house along Penn Avenue into the Protestant Home for Incurables, a facility that later became the Holmes House and continued for almost 100 years.

Born in Ireland, Holmes came to Pittsburgh with her parents as a young girl in 1807. Her father Nathaniel established a successful banking and brokerage firm that brought tremendous wealth to the family and a sizable inheritance to Jane and her four brothers. Considered one of Pittsburgh's earliest philanthropists, Holmes used her family's fortune to establish and endow scores of charitable homes and organizations, many of which continue today. Known as "Pittsburgh Jane" (not to be confused with her cousin "Baltimore Jane," who hailed from Maryland and led a similar charitable life in Pittsburgh) she championed the needs of the sick and the poor regardless of race or religion with particular attention to women and children.

At a time when few social services were available, Holmes helped fund homes, schools, and hospitals including the Protestant Home for Children (later Pressley Ridge), the Home for Colored Children (now Three Rivers Youth), Western Pennsylvania Humane Society, the Western Pennsylvania School for Blind Children, and the Western Pennsylvania School for the Deaf. As a generous benefactor, giving away over $1 million in her lifetime, and a crusader for the underserved, she used her family's wealth to transform the lives of those less fortunate.

Hedda Hopper

Born May 2, 1885—Hollidaysburg, PA
Died February 1, 1966—Hollywood, CA

Money was tight for the butcher's daughter from Altoona, but for Elda Furry the exorbitant $10 she paid a numerologist to determine the name that would lead her to success, it was the investment of a lifetime. That name was Hedda, and when paired with the last name of her husband, matinee idol DeWolf Hopper, that name became synonymous with fame and style, dirt and cruelty.

Hedda Hopper dropped out of the Carter Conservatory of Music in Pittsburgh to begin her career in New York as a chorus girl on Broadway. Ambition carried her west. She decided in 1915 that Hollywood needed her more as a silent film actress. Indeed, she starred in more than 120 films, earning the distinction as "Queen of the Quickies." What she demonstrated in volume, however, she lacked in talent, and as her movie career predictably waned in the 1930s, her true calling emerged as she turned to writing newspaper columns as a means of quick cash. Soon the money she made with insider gossip eclipsed any salary she had earned as an actress. With a growing power to make or break up-and-coming stars, Hedda ensured her own fame was a given.

How she knew what she knew few dared to ask. Hedda answered to no one save her column, which was replete with Tinsel Town divorces, affairs and who left town under the cover of night and why. Though frequently wrong, her tidbits routinely trumped competing scandalmongers, including the famed Louella Parsons, a onetime friend turned lifetime rival.

Professional rivalry, however, was nothing compared to the sheer hatred and invective Hedda invited as she enthusiastically named names of those she suspected of communism during the advent and reign of the Hollywood Blacklist. With FBI director Herbert Hoover as her personal "informed source," she used her daily columns to expose those deemed anti-American, permanently ruining many talents in the process.

She literally wrote until her death in 1966 of double pneumonia. She returned home a final time and is buried in Altoona.

Lena Horne

Born June 30, 1917—Brooklyn, NY

One of the most glamorous and sophisticated ladies of jazz, Lena Horne was married, had two children and spent several of her formative years here in Pittsburgh. Horne was a powerful voice, not just in jazz, but for the causes of black Americans during a time of great social indifference.

Horne's father left the family when Lena was just three. Her mother was an actress who traveled frequently, leaving Lena's upbringing to Horne's grandparents. Her father would eventually settle in Pittsburgh, where he was active in the numbers business. Horne was shuffled between many homes as a child but retained an interest in dancing and performing. At just 16 years old she was hired as a chorus dancer at the Cotton Club in Harlem. She continued to get work acting and singing but derailed her career in 1937 when she was introduced to, and then married, Pittsburgher Louis Jones, a clerk in the County Coroner's office. Their brief marriage bore Horne and

Jones two children, Gail and Teddy (who died in 1970 from a kidney disease).

Settling on Milwaukee Street in the Hill District, Horne would occasionally sing in the homes of wealthy Pittsburgh families to earn money, and she would frequent the Crawford Grill No.1, where she would pass time with Gus Greenlee, entrepreneur William "Woogie" Harris and famed Pittsburgh journalist Frank Bolden. In the fall of 1940, Horne and Jones called it quits and Horne moved back to New York to restart her career.

She was soon singing with bandleader and saxophonist Charlie Barnet, one of the first bandleaders to integrate his act. Nightclub singing, radio work and acting jobs were abundant for Horne by now. She became the first African-American performer to sign a long-term Hollywood studio contract and at one point was the highest paid African-American artist in the country. Despite her success, Horne suffered gross discrimination; often filmed standing alone in her many movie appearances, her scenes were easily edited out for distribution to southern movie houses. Segregated experiences like these were likely the catalyst for her lifelong contributions to the Civil Rights movement, attending the March on Washington in 1963, her active participation in the NAACP and her efforts on anti-lynching legislation. During World War II Horne also used her own money to travel and entertain the troops.

A very private individual, Horne has seen years of great publicity and years of great reclusiveness. Among her latest comebacks was to honor her dear friend, Billy Strayhorn, whom she referred to as "… brilliant but gentle and loving… the only man I really loved."

Beyond her legendary voice and numerous accomplishments, Lena Horne has been a humanitarian and champion of racial and social injustice her entire life.

Above, Teenie Harris captured a radiant Horne in town for a 1944 performance at the Stanley Theatre.

Roger Humphries

Born January 30, 1944—North Side

Much like the Steelers are known for linebackers, Pittsburgh's jazz pantheon has built an impressive array of drummers–from Art Blakey to Jeff "Tain" Watts. Smack dab in the middle is Roger Humphries, whose drumming moves effortlessly from delivering a driving background to riffing the refrain with imaginative solos.

Humphries was a child prodigy whose informal musical education began on Pittsburgh's North Side. The youngest of 10 siblings, he came from a musical family tht provided him an introduction to some of the area's best jazz players. In fact, before he was born, Art Blakey and Billy Eckstine used to rehearse at his grandmother's house. Another influence came from the church services he attended growing up. He learned the rhythms of the drums in the form of the preacher and the choir. Humphries took that education and turned it into a doctorate at the Hill District's legendary homes of jazz, the Crawford Grill and the Hurricane.

At the urging of his brother, Norman, Humphries picked up the drum sticks. By the time he was 12, Roger began sitting in at the clubs. Then he met his idol, Blakey, who invited him to play. Humphries recalls that night: "He set me up there with Lee Morgan and Hank Mobley. And when I went home I had to lay on the couch for three hours because my stomach had a muscle spasm. I was full of nerves."

After graduating from high school, Humphries hit the road with another Pittsburgher, Stanley Turrentine and his then-wife Shirley Scott. That gig put Humphries on the jazz fast track, building his reputation for versatility, creativity, and musicianship. He often described his drumming as "telling a story and delivering a message." Soon other musicians were getting the message that another great Pittsburgh drummer was on the scene. Humphries landed jobs playing with Horace Silver (a four-year partnership that produced the classic *Song For My Father* album), Coleman Hawkins, Dizzy Gillespie, Lee Morgan and Ray Charles.

But Humphries decided to return to Pittsburgh, and in 1969 formed his own band, R.H. Factor, which played the local circuit. As Blakey had done for him, Humphries also took it upon himself to help young musicians. He joined the faculty at the Creative and Per-

forming Arts High School as a teacher of jazz and orchestral percussion. He also continued to play at clubs around town and frequently performed at the James Street Tavern on the North Side.

In 1998, Humphries headlined the Mellon Jazz Festival, a recognition for his continued excellence. For his contributions to jazz in Pittsburgh, Humphries has been honored with a tile in the Mellon Jazz Festival honoree walkway at the Senator John Heinz History Center.

Cy Hungerford

Born in 1889—Manilla, IN
Died May 25, 1983—Wexford, PA

How old-school was Cy Hungerford? Old-school enough to wear his hat in the *Post-Gazette* city room.

But Hungerford didn't wear his trademark fedora as a fashion statement. Or because he fancied himself a tough guy. No, Cy Hungerford wore his hat for protection.

It seems that to seek inspiration, the legendary editorial cartoonist often kept odd hours—and sometimes fell asleep at his desk. To celebrate the occasion, one wag drew a smiley face on Hungerford's bald dome.

Hungerford never went hatless again.

And for him, again was a very long time.

Dean of Pittsburgh's editorial cartoonists, the man with the most recognizable cast of characters and longest tenure in city history, Cyrus Cotton Hungerford was born in 1889 on a farm in Manilla, IN. Moving as an infant to Parkersburg, WV, where his father took a job selling farm equipment, Hungerford passed a placid childhood copying newspaper cartoons. By the time he was 14, in 1903, he had placed his first cartoon in the *Parkersburg Sentinel*.

Graduating to the *Wheeling Register*, Hungerford moved to Pittsburgh in 1912 to join the *Sun* staff, where for a decade, 1915-25, he drew Snoodles, a syndicated daily comic strip. By 1927, he shifted to the *Post-Gazette*, the job Hungerford held for the next half-century. There, his strong-lined, gently humorous cartoons—notably his rotund, colonial-style Pa Pitt—helped define the city's image of itself. During World War II, Hungerford also contributed to the war effort, drawing defense posters.

"The idea that comes quick is the true one," Hungerford once said of his considerable—and incredibly prolific—art. "Make people smile—and think while they're smiling."

A multiple award-winner, Hungerford's material was reprinted in many national outlets—and was collected by many of his subjects. Retiring in 1977 at age 89, Cy Hungerford died in Wexford six years later, in 1983.

Phyllis Hyman

Born July 6, 1949—Philadelphia
Died June 30, 1995—New York

She was a local girl with a voice on par with Anita Baker and Whitney Houston. Booked for a series of shows at the famed Apollo Theater, she mentioned to a friend that this would be her last. To the horror of her adoring family and friends, police confirmed the afternoon of June 30th, 1995, that it in fact was.

Phyllis Hyman was born in Philadelphia , the oldest of seven children, but moved to Pittsburgh before she was a year old. Growing up in the rough St. Clair Village in Mount Oliver, singing came naturally to her. She at-

tended Philip Murray Elementary School where she caught the attention of her third grade teacher, Mrs. Eleanora Lesesne, who gave the young girl voice lessons.

She moved on to Knoxville Junior High, then Carrick High School where she would begin to explore the local music circuit. After graduation she attended Robert Morris College where she set her sights on a career as a legal secretary. Working odd jobs throughout the area, including Westinghouse and Neighborhood Legal Services, Hyman continued to sing in area clubs, including an occasional set with Walt Harper's All That Jazz.

In 1971 she was asked to tour with the Florida-based band All The People. Her repertoire of styles was diverse and her reputation as a rock solid singer was growing. She even appeared in the film *Lenny*, starring Dustin Hoffman. New York was her next stop. Working some of the hottest clubs in New York, she was a favorite of regulars like Stevie Wonder, Al Jarreau, Roberta Flack and George Benson.

Hyman signed with Buddah Records and released her self-titled *Phyllis Hyman* in 1977. But it was with Arista Records that Hyman made her mark when "Somewhere In My Lifetime" and "You Know How To Love Me" cracked the Billboard R&B top 20. Soon after, "Can't We Fall In Love Again," a duet with Michael Henderson, became a top 10 hit. Simultaneously, Hyman was on Broadway in *Sophisticated Ladies*, a tribute to Duke Ellington, which she performed for almost three years, earning a Tony® Award nomination.

© JACQUES M. CHENET/CORBIS

Hyman's 1983 release *Goddess Of Love*, was only a moderate success, yet she appeared on numerous releases of other artists, toured extensively, appeared in several television commercials and was even in Spike Lee's film *School Daze*. In 1986, Hyman signed to the Philadelphia International label where she recorded some of her best music in years, including several Top 10 R&B hits and her 1991 song "Don't Wanna Change The World," her only #1 R&B hit.

Beset with personal struggles including, depression, alcoholism, bipolar disorder and grief from the loss of her mother, grandmother and a close friend who all died within a month of one another, Hyman slipped into deep despair. On June 30th 1995, Phyllis Hyman committed suicide with sleeping pills. Found by her side was a note that read "I'm tired. I'm tired. Those of you that I love know who you are. May God bless you."

Donnie Iris

Born February 28, 1943—Ellwood City, PA

It's rare for any musician or band to have a number one hit and it's almost unheard of for a musician to have a number one hit with two separate bands. Lightning struck for Ellwood City native Dominic Ierace, aka Donnie Iris, in 1970 and again in 1976 with the bands "The Jaggerz" and "Wild Cherry," respectively.

Donnie Iris's mother taught him to sing at a young age, while she accompanied him on the piano. While still under the age of 10 he was a guest on local radio programs and competed in various talent shows. His musical journey really took off at Slippery Rock University in the early 1960s. Donnie had formed a band called Donnie and the Donnells with some of his fellow classmates. Primarily a cover band they played mostly frat parties. Another local band was losing one of their singers and called Donnie to fill the void. The band was Gary and the Jeweltones. The band would eventually take the name The Jaggerz, named not after Mick, but rather the prickly things that get on your clothes only when you run through the woods of southwestern PA; not burrs or stickseeds—Jaggerz.

The Jaggerz were primarily an R&B and classic rock cover band emulating the sounds of The Temptations to the Kinks. The work got good enough that Donnie eventually quit college to play music full time. They wrote a number of original songs; one of them about

how guys hit on girls or "rap." Under the management of Joe Rock, the South Side native responsible for the success of The Skyliners, The Jaggerz released "The Rapper" and it immediately took off. In 1970, "The Rapper" made it to number one on *Record World*'s top 100 list and number two on *Billboard*, earning the band their first and only gold record. Sales eventually reached over five million copies.

The Jaggerz would break up several years later. Then Iris met his next collaborator, Mark Avsec with the band Wild Cherry. Fresh off their hit "Play That Funky Music," Wild Cherry's staying power was weak, so Iris and Avsec decided to try going it on their own. The two put together a rock outfit called Donnie Iris and The Cruisers and in 1980 released a song locally called "Ah Leah." With the support of radio play from stations such as WDVE, the song was an immediate success. MCA signed The Cruisers to a contract and released *Back On The Streets*, recorded in Beaver Falls. "Ah Leah" climbed the national charts settling in at number 29.

During the early 1980s, on the heels of the success of "Ah Leah," Donnie Iris and the Cruisers toured with a who's who of 1980s bands including Foreigner, Journey, The Romantics, and Cleveland-based The Michael Stanley Band. Their second release *King Cool* spawned a couple more hits including "Love Is Like A Rock" and "My Girl" (which actually climbed higher on the charts than "Ah Leah"). Three years and three releases after their debut release, MCA dropped The Cruisers.

Despite the setbacks, Donnie Iris and The Cruisers continue to release new material, like their 2006 *Ellwood City*, named, of course, for Iris' hometown. The band still tours and is a popular draw in the region.

K. Leroy Irvis

Born December 27, 1919—Saugerties, NY
Died March 16, 2006—Pittsburgh

Fifteen-term state representative, of which the last 11 years of his 30-year tenure in Harrisburg were served as Speaker of the House, K. Leroy Irvis was an indisputable champion of civil rights, fair housing, equal opportunity and higher education for all Pennsylvanians. Of more than 850 singular pieces of legislation sponsored by Irvis, 264 were made into state law.

Born just north of Albany, NY, Irvis graduated summa cum laude from Albany's Teacher College in 1938 with a master in education and left to teach in Baltimore. He found his job through the acquaintance of Daisy Lampkin. When war broke out, Irvis was a civilan employee of the War Department hired to teach women how to cut and rivet aluminum for Martin bombers. Married to Katharyne Ann Jones in 1945, they moved to Pittsburgh where Irvis was first employed by the Urban League as a public relations manager. Irvis staged a protest against unfair hiring practices in front of a downtown department store, and was fired. His wife opened a hot dog stand in the Hill District and he worked as a chipper in the steel mills along the Strip District. Almost killed in the mill, Irvis immediately applied to Pitt's Law School and subsequently received a scholarship. He graduated fourth in his class and before clerking for the Court of Common Pleas, worked briefly as a broadcaster. He also served as a radio broadcaster for WILY, later known as WEEP.

From 1954 to 1956, he was the *Pittsburgh Courier*'s "High Noon Reporter."

In 1958, he ran for state rep of the Hill District and won the seat he held for 30 consecutive years. Irvis is best known for his roles in founding community colleges, the Pennsylvania Higher Education Assistance Agency, Act 101, the Minority Business Development Authority, and the Pennsylvania Council on the Arts.

Irvis married Cathryn Edwards in 1973. An avid wood sculptor and model airplane enthusiast, Irvis also published a book of poetry in 1988. He died in his Reynolds Street home in 2006, having served for more than a decade as the first African-American Speaker of the House of any state in the country.

Henry Isaly

Born August 13, 1905—Mansfield, OH
Died August 11, 1961—Pittsburgh

Klondike ice cream bars may be Isaly's most notable contribution to America's eating habits, but it's the company's dairy stores, chipped ham and Skyscraper cones that locals lovingly remember.

Isaly's was named for the Swiss family who founded the chain. At its peak in the mid-20th Century, Isaly's was the world's largest family-owned dairy company. Plants stretched from Pittsburgh to Iowa, and some 400 stores blanketed Western Pennsylvania, Ohio, and northern West Virginia. Their success came from owning both dairy plants and retail stores, thereby eliminating distributors and assuring consistency and freshness.

The family traces its dairy roots to Christian and Verena Iseli (the original spelling), who brought their family and cheese kettle to America in 1833. Grandson William founded the company in 1902 by purchasing milk delivery routes

in Mansfield, Ohio. He expanded into ice cream and began offering it right at the plant: swift sales of then-new cones led to the company's first Isaly's store. Plants followed in Marion and Youngstown, each run by a son of William.

While the Depression reversed many corporate expansions, Isaly's broached Pittsburgh, building a fabulous art deco plant on the Boulevard of the Allies and six initial stores. Henry Isaly, youngest of the brothers, was put in charge, but first, he got a job at Donahue's downtown market to get to know the city's people. He became legendary for his gentle, paternal ways, roaming the plant, asking about products and families, regularly eating in the employee cafeteria. Other managers may have kept the company on track business-wise, but it was Henry's caring leadership that endeared Isaly's to tens of thousands of workers and customers, even to this day.

Henry suffered a heart attack on the way home from a Pirates game in 1961. By then, the industry was changing: customers wanted suburban supermarkets, convenience stores, and soft serve stands. The Isaly family sold their business in 1972. A few stores remain, and a descendant company continues to license the name to ice cream, chipped ham, barbecue sauce, and other deli products, but it's the 5-cent Skyscrapers, and memories of a magnanimous company and leader, that still inspire devotion in Western Pennsylvania.

Anne Jackson

Born September 3, 1926—Millvale, PA

The youngest sister of three, Anne Jackson lived a rather happy, although poor childhood. Her father John was born in Croatia and worked as a barber and hairdresser, moving his family from Millvale to Harmarville when Anne was four, and then to Job's Hill, near

Tarentum, where he opened his Scientific Beauty Shop just prior to the Depression. Jackson attended elementary school in Natrona Heights. At an early age, she often performed skits with her sisters, and imitated the great film stars of the silent screen. When the economy crashed, the family moved to Brooklyn for better opportunities.

A particularly bright and attractive redhead, Jackson earned a scholarship to study acting with Herb Berghof before he opened his famed studio to train students in the Stanislavsky method of acting. Jackson won a national audition, and was granted another scholarship to study with Sandy Meisner at the Neighborhood Playhouse where Jackson also took classes from dance instructor Martha Graham.

In 1945 she debuted in Chekhov's *The Cherry Orchard* and toured with the production for several months. At the Hudson Street Library, while auditioning for Tennessee William's *This Property is Condemned*, Jackson met Eli Wallach, fresh from the Army, who also auditioned. That same year they appeared on Broadway together in three productions of the American Repertory Theatre. Three years later they married and, quite famously, have been married ever since.

Often performing together, they share 13 Broadway credits, including successful runs in *Rhinoceros, Promenade All, Waltz of the Toreadors,* and *Twice Around the Park*. Their shared television credits run into the hundreds, but they have only a few films in common. Jackson's more popular films include *The Tiger Makes Out, Lovers and Other Strangers, The Bell Jar,* and *The Shining*. Together they have a daughter, Roberta, who also acts. All three have appeared on *Law & Order*, but not in the same episode.

Jaromir Jagr

Born February 15, 1972—Kladno, Czechoslovakia

With speed, style, and his trademark salute, Czech star Jaromir Jagr was the perfect complement to Mario Lemieux in the Penguins' back-to-back Stanley Cup championships, 1991-92.

Born in what is now the Czech Republic, Jagr, on the ice at three, a national star at 16, had but one goal—"to play in the NHL," he said, "because that is the best hockey in the world."

Coming of age after the Velvet Revolution, Jagr became the first Czech who did not have to defect to play in the National Hockey League. Drafted by the Penguins in 1990, he played right wing at a bruising 6'-3" and 245 pounds. Wearing 68 in honor of the Prague Spring rebellion, and in memory of his grandfather who died that year, Jagr was just 19 when he scored his first goal in the Stanley Cup finals, the youngest NHL player ever to do so.

Seemingly unstoppable in his 11 seasons as a Penguin, in 1995 Jagr became the first European to win the Art Ross Trophy, leading the league in scoring, a feat which he repeated as a Penguin four times in a row, 1998-2001. A perennial All Star, and Hart Trophy winner in 1999 as the league's most valuable player, Jagr also took the Lester Pearson Award as the league's outstanding player (as judged by the players) twice as a Penguin, 1999, 2000. His highest point-total season came in 1995-96, when he had 62 goals and set league right-wing records with 87 assists and 149 points—only to lose the scoring title to teammate Lemieux.

Penguin captain, Olympic gold medal winner, certain Hall of Famer, Jagr was traded to the Washington Capitols after the 2001 season. After two-and-a-half seasons, he moved on to the New York Rangers, where he continues his record-breaking career.

Ahmad Jamal

Born July 2, 1930—Pittsburgh

Born Frederick Russell Jones in 1930, it was a couple of decades later before "Fritz," as he was known, would convert to Islam and take the name that the jazz world has come to revere—Ahmad Jamal.

Like so many great pianists, Jamal took to his instrument at a very early age. In Jamal's case, he was just 3 years old. At 7 his mother arranged for him to begin formal training under the direction of both Mary Cardwell Dawson, the founder of the National Negro Opera Company, and pianist James Miller. One of Jamal's first jobs was running a newspaper route, delivering papers, coincidentally, to another Pittsburgh virtuoso, Billy Strayhorn.

By the age of 11, Jamal was skilled enough to play at local clubs. He attended Westinghouse High School and excelled academically while furthering his training in both classical and jazz. Although influenced by the likes of Art Tatum, Roy Eldridge, Earl Hines and Duke Ellington, Jamal counts Erroll Garner as the one single most inspirational artist on his playing style. In fact, Jamal's playing was at times compared to that of Garner's, yet

often considered more complex.

Jamal joined the local musician's union, Local 471, when he was just 14 years old. After graduating from Westinghouse, he joined the George Hudson Orchestra and set out on a national tour. A year later Jamal teamed up with his friend and fellow Pittsburgher, Joe Kennedy Jr., who played jazz violin, as part of The Four Strings. In 1950, Jamal formed his own group with Pittsburgh guitarist Ray Crawford and Eddie Calhoun when they were discovered by the legendary John Hammond and

signed to Okeh Records. Jamal's trio would later record the influential *Chamber Music of New Jazz* and gain the attention and admiration of Miles Davis. The group then set-up shop in Chicago, at the Pershing Hotel, as the the house band. In 1958, the group recorded a live album, *Ahmad Jamal at The Pershing: But Not For Me* which produced what would become Jamal's signature song "Poinciana." The album remained at the top of the Billboard charts for over 100 weeks.

Jamal recorded and toured extensively throughout the late 1950s and 1960s. His recording continued through the coming decades and in 1989 he recorded an album entitled *Pittsburgh,* a tribute to his late mother and his hometown. Ahmad Jamal continues to record, perform and inspire generations of jazz musicians.

Tommy James & The Shondells

Tommy: Born April 29, 1947—Dayton, OH

Like most artists who eventually "make it," Thomas Gregory Jackson started playing in bands at a very young age. Not even in his teens, he formed his first band called Tom and the Tornadoes and developed a loyal following throughout the Niles, MI area.

At 17, Jackson and his band recorded four songs for a small regional label called Snap Records and decided to call themselves The Shondells. One of the singles they recorded was a song originally recorded by The Raindrops, as a B Side, called "Hanky Panky." Released as a single, the song did well on local stations in the Niles and South Bend areas but failed to break into the larger markets of Chicago or Detroit. By then, Jackson had graduated high school and, with the failure of any single to get national attention, he and the Shondells went their separate ways.

Jackson, out of work, living at home, then got a phone call from Mike Metrovich, aka KDKA's "Mad Mike." He had found the two-year-old single and was playing it on his show. When another Pittsburgh DJ heard the song and began spinning it at local dances, the song was met with wild enthusiasm. Then a local bootlegger taped the single over the radio and pressed 80,000 copies to sell to anxious fans. Realizing the sensation "Hanky Panky" was stirring, Mad Mike had called Jackson to invite him to Pittsburgh.

Jackson headed east, but, without his Shondells, he had to recruit new ones, whom he found, in part, through a local bar band then known as The Raconteurs. New York's Roulette Records then signed the band and by the summer of 1966, under the new name of Tommy James and The Shondells, "Hanky Panky" was the number one song in the nation.

"Hanky Panky" was quickly followed by two more million-selling records, "Say I Am" and "It's Only Love." A string of successful hits ensued over the next several years, including "I Think We're Alone Now," "Mony Mony," "Crimson and Clover," and "Crystal Blue Persuasion."

After the Shondells, Tommy James had a successful solo career with hits like "Three Times In Love" and his top 5 hit "Draggin' The Line." To date, Tommy James has sold over a million records, achieved 23 gold singles and 9 gold and platinum albums. And he continues to tour and record, thanks in no small part to a Pittsburgh DJ and a local audience with an ear for a hit.

Robinson Jeffers

Born January 10, 1887—Pittsburgh
Died January 20, 1962—Carmel, CA

It's somehow fitting that Robinson Jeffers, the quintessential California poet, was born in Pittsburgh.

John Robinson Jeffers was the son of a Bible professor at Western Theology Seminary, forerunner of Pittsburgh Theological Seminary, then located in Allegheny. With his father tutoring him, Jeffers—called Robin throughout his life—learned Greek at five. When his family toured Europe, Jeffers attended schools in Zurich, Leipzig, and Geneva. Back in Pittsburgh in 1902, fluent in French, German, Latin, and Greek, 15-year-old Jeffers entered the University of Western Pennsylvania, now Pitt, also in Allegheny.

The following year, 1903, 16-year-old Jeffers' family moved to California, where he enrolled in Occidental College as a junior, graduating two years later, 1905, at age 18.

© BETTMANN/CORBIS

Attending the University of Southern California, in literature and medicine, he married in 1913 and moved to Carmel. Beginning to publish poetry as early as 1912, at first Jeffers was relatively obscure. By the 1920s, however, he had acquired a national following for his blend of Greek tragedy, individualism, and nature. *Tamar* (1924), *The Women at Point Sur* (1927), and *Give Your Heart to the Hawks* (1933), among his many volumes, cemented Jeffers' reputation.

Beginning in 1920, Jeffers wrote in the morning, then in the afternoon built Tor House, his granite home on the Carmel cliffs. Lit until 1949 by oil lamps and candles, it was an important stop on the West Coast cultural map, hosting such luminaries as George Gershwin and Charlie Chaplin, among others. Often photographed, Jeffers was captured by Edward Weston and was a rare human subject for nature master Ansel Adams.

On Broadway, Jeffers' 1947 adaptation of Euripides' *Medea*, starring Judith Anderson and John Gielgud ran for seven months.

In 1962, 75-year-old Robinson Jeffers died at his Carmel home. In 1973 a postage stamp was issued in his honor.

Eddie Jefferson

Born August 3, 1918—Pittsburgh
Died May 9, 1979—Detroit, MI

Rap has roots in Pittsburgh. The music style known as vocalese—scatting lyrics to famous instrumental solos—was pioneered by Eddie Jefferson.

He started out as a tap dancer and became an adept multi-instrumentalist, as well, playing the tuba, drums, and guitar. His father, also an entertainer, naturally steered his son in a similar direction. By his early twenties he was writing lyrics, singing—and yet using his voice to do something be-bopish and different.

The first time Jefferson was captured singing vocalese was during a live performance singing "Moody's Mood for Love" in 1949 (recorded on Spotlite Records) several years before King Pleasure's hit of the same name (the song for which Pleasure is often, but incorrectly, cited for originating the style).

Jefferson recorded his first session in Pittsburgh when New York label Hi Lo Records came to town. He began his association with saxophonist James Moody in 1953. But for the next several years Jefferson was little heard from as jazz vocalists Lambert, Hendricks and Ross took the style and ran with it. He would work again with James Moody in the late 1960s and then spend time performing with sax player Richie Cole.

By 1978, Jefferson had caught the attention of The Manhattan Transfer when he was commissioned by them to set lyrics to the song "Birdland."

Jefferson was never able to complete the request. He was murdered outside of Baker's Keyboard Lounge in Detroit, Michigan, on May 9th, 1979.

PHOTOGRAPH © 2008 CARNEGIE MUSEUM OF ART, PITTSBURGH

Patricia Prattis Jennings

Born July 16, 1941—Lincoln-Larimer

She broke new ground for the Pittsburgh Symphony Orchestra as its first African-American player and became a voice for black classical musicians worldwide.

Born in Pittsburgh's Lincoln-Larimer section, she started studying the piano at age 6 and the violin at age 8. She knew from an early age that classical music was her career path—the only question being which instrument to play. In 1954, then 13-year-old Jennings wrote in a school report, "I would very much like to become a concert pianist." It would prove to be prophetic as her debut came a year later when she was invited to perform Mozart's "Coronation Concerto" with the PSO under the direction of William Steinberg.

COURTESY PITTSBURGH SYMPHONY © MICHAEL SAHAIDA

She studied with Harry Franklin at Carnegie Mellon University, graduating with a degree in piano performance, mastering the piano, organ, harpsichord, and celesta.

Jennings joined the symphony for good in 1964, a significant cultural achievement in the mostly male, mostly white world of classical music. From the beginning, her play—particularly her phrasing—elicited stellar reviews. *The London Daily Telegraph* praised her as a "dazzling performer."

She was often a featured player as her reputation and that of the PSO grew. She helped export the orchestra, starring in many high-profile performances. Music Director Andre Previn chose her to perform four-hand Mozart sonatas on the debut of the PBS series *Previn and the Pittsburgh,* a landmark television program that introduced much of the nation to the PSO. When the orchestra toured the Far East in 1987, she was the featured soloist on Gershwin's "Concerto in F." Her skills interpreting Gershwin were also recognized when she was selected to play "Rhapsody in Blue" with Benny Goodman and his jazz band toward the end of the famed band leader's career.

But Jennings sought to make more of an impact in music than just performing well. "Getting up there on stage and playing, that's showing off," she told the *Pittsburgh Press*. "It pleases me to know that I bring pleasure and enjoyment to people who listen, but it's not useful." To increase that sense of "usefulness" she then turned her attention to helping other musicians share in the opportunities she was fortunate enough to have.

In 1988, she launched Symphonium, a newsletter that provided information for and about professional African-American classical musicians. Jennings also served as a mentor for black musicians through her work with the Music Assistance Fund, and she was instrumental in the launch of music programs at Manchester's Bidwell Center.

Her commitment to music was recognized in 1999 when she was named a Distinguished Daughter of Pennsylvania. She remains active in musical education and serves as a freelance writer about chamber and classical music when she is not performing.

Shirley Jones

Born March 31, 1934—Charleroi, PA

When an actress so successfully spans several generations of American pop culture, she becomes good fodder for trivia buffs. From getting a chorus role in *South Pacific* to playing Mrs. Partridge on the iconic family sitcom of the 1970s, Shirley Jones is one celebrity about whom everyone—especially a Pittsburgher—knows some trivia.

For example, everyone assumes she was born in Smithton, PA, where her father "rolled out the Stoney's." But she was actually born in Charleroi. Many adamantly believe she earned an Academy Award for her all-American, wholesome role as Marian the Librarian in MGM's *The Music Man*. But, in fact, she won her only Oscar®—for Best Supporting Actress—for playing a prostitute in *Elmer Gantry*. Of course, real trivia buffs will argue that, not since Ozzie & Harriet, had a TV Mom starred with her son in a wildly popular sitcom. Well, not quite; David Cassidy, with whom she starred in *The Partridge Family*, is her stepson. However, Shirley Jones is the first leading actress to appear on Broadway with a leading son, Patrick, who teamed up with her in 2004's revival of *42nd Street*.

She was named for Shirley Temple. Born the only child to Paul and Marjorie Jones, she

was singing for her family at four, started formal training at 12, attended classes at the Pittsburgh Playhouse while a student (and majorette) at South Huntingdon High, and was named Miss Pittsburgh in 1952. She made her Pittsburgh Civic Light Opera debut in 1953 in *Lady in the Dark*, when the company performed in the open air at Pitt Stadium.

Success then came quickly. While heading to college, she auditioned for Richard Rodgers during rehearsals for *South Pacific*. When the composer asked her to wait to meet his partner, she answered, "I will. And, who are you?" She was placed in the chorus, except legend says that Rodgers, impressed with her soprano, knew she would be ideal for the lead in *Oklahoma!*, which was yet not finished. She then hit the touring circuit with *Me and Juliet*, before being cast to take the film lead in *Oklahoma!*, playing Laurey opposite

Gordon MacRae's Curley. She was not yet 21 when she came home to Smithton to celebrate her success before returning to Hollywood to film *Carousel*, again with Gordon MacRae.

Ready to take on more ambitious projects, she found herself to be typecast. So, in 1956, she played an alcoholic in the 1956 *Playhouse 90* production *The Big Slide,* opposite Red Skelton. The part got the attention of Burt Lancaster, as well as an Emmy nomination, and he paved the way for her 1961 Oscar win in *Elmer Gantry*.

Married to Jack Cassidy in 1956, she was pregnant with her second son, Patrick, while on the set for *The Music Man* in 1962. Once again, her image became wholesome and, with the increasingly prohibitive costs of movie musicals, Jones found herself flourishing but fallow in many early TV shows.

That, of course, would change with the "fan"-tastic run of 51 episodes of ABC's *The Partridge Family*. Playing the hip, cool, widowed mother to five kids who toured their pop-rock band in a mod school bus, Jones has said, "The show killed my movie career, [but] I had done 25 motion pictures prior to The Partridge Family and nobody knew my name."

She divorced Cassidy in 1974, before his tragic death in an apartment fire. She's been married to comic Marty Ingels since 1977. In 2007, she appeared again in *Oklahoma!* with the CLO, at Heinz Hall, playing the elderly role of Aunt Eller.

John Kane

**Born August 19, 1860—West Caldor, Scotland
Died August 10, 1934—Pittsburgh**

If John Kane weren't real, Pittsburgh would have to invent him. Unsentimental, unschooled, in some ways he was Pittsburgh's perfect painter. Pure-blood blue-collar, Kane created our enduring image of the city: bold, honest, clear.

His is a story of physical labor, economic necessity, and wanderlust. Born in 1860 in an Irish family that had emigrated to West Caldor, Scotland, looking for work, John Cain (an Akron bank clerk mistakenly misspelled his name, and the quixotic Kane let it stick) grew up like most children of his time: at age 9 he took his third-grade education into a Scottish shale mine. Emigrating to Braddock at 19, by turns Kane worked as a bricklayer, coal miner, street paver, carpenter, railroad man, and steelworker.

Cutting across a train yard one night in 1891 cost him his left leg, and, unable to perform heavy labor, Kane worked as a watchman and railcar painter. Painting boxcar landscapes during lunch breaks, Kane used only primary colors, mixing them with black and white, a method he maintained all of his life.

Married, Kane fathered two daughters, then, in 1904, a son, who died of typhoid fever. Kane took it hard—hard enough to take to the bottle. Hard enough to leave home for the next 23 years.

Picking up odd jobs, he painted Pittsburgh landscapes on discarded beaverboard, his earliest surviving paintings dating from around 1910. Considering art school, Kane couldn't afford the tuition. Instead, he painted—portraits, religious subjects, Pittsburgh landscapes, Scotland. Spending hours in the library copying art books, in 1925 and 1926 Kane submitted paintings to the Carnegie International Exhibition, then America's most important salon of international contemporary art. Rejected, he was told that the International accepted only original works.

Kane's third time was the proverbial charm. In 1927 his *Scene in the Scottish Highlands* was accepted, exhibited, purchased. Today, it is hard to imagine what a revolution that was, for it marked the first time that a living, self-taught artist—a housepainter and handyman—had been recognized by the art establishment.

American Primitive! the cognoscenti hailed. After nearly seven decades the self-taught, self-schooled Kane—and his flat-perspectived, brightly colored, highly detailed paintings—were an overnight sensation.

With his simple, fresh approach to everyday subject matter, Kane's success came in part because of the Modernist interest in primitive and folk art. In quick succession, Kane became a member of the Associated Artists of Pittsburgh, seeing his paintings exhibited at Harvard, in Philadelphia, the New York's Whitney. The flat, meticulously detailed *Larimer Avenue Bridge*, in the Carnegie Museum of Art, is typical of Kane's work, as his stern, angular *Self-portrait*, in New York's Museum of Modern Art.

For the next seven years, Kane painted more than 150 oils. But both Depression and disease hit Pittsburgh hard, and in August 1934, nine days short of his 77th birthday, John Kane died of tuberculosis, knowing that his paintings continued as mainstays in art collections the world over.

Kane's *Touching Up, c.* 1931, oil on canvas, H: 20 3/4 x W: 27 inches, Carnegie Museum of Art, Pittsburgh, Gift of Thomas Mellon Evans

Milton Katselas

Born December 22, 1933—East Pittsburgh

His 1969 Tony© Award nomination for directing *Butterflies Are Free*, starring Blythe Danner, Eileen Heckart and Keir Dullea, so impressed the critics that he directed the 1972 film version with Goldie Hawn and Edward Albert. Eileen Heckart, reprising her stage role, won an Academy Award. The play's theme tells us "none are so blind as those who won't see." It is a fitting lesson for those who have steeped Milton Katselas—director, actor, painter and sculptor—in a long controversy over his devotion to L. Ron Hubbard and the Church of Scientology.

At the Beverly Hills Playhouse, which he purchased in 1970 and where, in 1978, he founded his acting studio, Katselas has taught many of the great film stars of recent years: Michelle Pfeiffer, George Clooney, Tyne Daly, Jeffrey Tambor, Jenna Elfman, Tom Selleck, and Anne Archer. He is often lauded by his students and alumni as being the very best in the industry, and his 1996 self-help book, *Dreams Into Action*, sat on the *New York Times* best seller list for many months. The book is filled with admonitions, observations, and pithy remarks Katselas has culled from his years of training actors to get in touch with their inner-selves. Many of his students are Scientologists, and because of Katselas's insistence that his students buy his books, attend his gallery openings, and use their free time for his aggrandizement, he is often suspected of evangelizing Scientology among the Hollywood elite.

Katselas was born to Greek parents who operated a three-booth, 12-stool diner outside of the Westinghouse Electric plant in East Pittsburgh. His father performed in a small theatre with Greek friends, and Katselas followed along by working with the Sherwood Forest Theatre of New Kensington, where

Johnny Costa also played and Don Brockett developed early revues. When he was 14, his father purchased the Frederick Theatre, where the young Katselas often watched the same film "as many as 15 times." Katselas graduated from Carnegie Tech in 1954, and went to New York where he apprenticed for Elia Kazan, while taking acting classes from Lee Strasburg. In 1960, he debuted off-Broadway in Edward Albee's *The Zoo Story*.

Allegedly a one time metamphetamine addict, Katselas kicked the habit cold-turkey before going on to direct *Camino Real* and *The Rose Tattoo* on Broadway, and *The Seagull*, *Romeo & Juliet* and *Streamers* in L.A., for each of which he won the L.A. Drama Critics Circle Award.

Katselas is the younger brother of prominent Pittsburgh architect, Tasso Katselas.

George S. Kaufman

Born November 16, 1889—Shadyside
Died June 2, 1961—New York, NY

George S. Kaufman, arguably the funniest, all-time most successful playwright, director, and producer in American theater history, winner of two Pulitzer Prizes, got his start at Pittsburgh's Congregation Rodef Sholom.

Born George Kaufman—he added the middle initial in memory of his grandfather, Simon—in Pittsburgh in 1889, he grew up on Walnut Street in Shadyside, attended Liberty School, and worshiped at Rodef Sholom Congregation, the Fifth Avenue synagogue that his grandfather had co-founded in 1848.

With his acting applauded in Rodef Shalom plays, and at Central High, even his rabbi felt Kaufman had a future in the theater.

Choosing law at first, he enrolled in Western University of Pennsylvania (as Pitt was known). Leaving due to illness, for two years Kaufman worked as a surveyor, stenographer, and tax clerk.

By his early 20s he was off to New York City, first to write criticism, ending up as *New York Times* drama editor, then on Broadway. Although his first play, 1918's *Someone in the House*, was a flop, the die was cast.

Nicknamed the Great Collaborator, Kaufman always worked with others—George and Ira Gershwin, the Marx Brothers (*The Cocoanuts* and *Animal Crackers* made them Broadway stars), Marc Connelly, Ring Lardner, and Moss Hart, among others. In an un-

© Bettmann/CORBIS

matched record, from 1921 through '58, every Broadway season had at least one Kaufman-written, -directed, or -produced play.

In Hollywood, Kaufman penned the Marx Brothers' screenplay, *A Night at the Opera*, writing much of Groucho Marx's witty dialogue.

Much awarded, Kaufman won his first Pulitzer Prize in 1931 for *Of Thee I Sing*, the first musical so honored, and again in 1937 for *You Can't Take It With You*. (The movie version won two Academy Awards the following year).

A member of the Algonquin Round Table, George S. Kaufman died in New York City, age 71, in 1961.

The Kaufmann Brothers

Jacob: Born in 1849—Viernheim, Germany
Died November 1, 1905—Philadelphia, PA

Isaac: Born May 15, 1851– Viernheim
Died July 18, 1921—Pittsburgh

Morris: Born in 1858– Viernheim
Died August 6, 1917—Lancaster, PA

Henry: Born July 12, 1860—Viernheim
Died March 1955—New York, NY

To generations of Western Pennsylvanians, the phrase "Meet me under the Kaufmann's clock" stirs memories of shopping trips to the massive Pittsburgh department store at Fifth Avenue and Smithfield Street, but the Kaufmann's empire began with a modest tailoring business founded by four German Jewish immigrants, brothers Jacob, Isaac, Morris, and Henry Kaufmann.

The Kaufmann brothers were born in

Germany to cattle farmer Abraham Kaufmann and his wife Sara. Jacob was the first to emigrate to America, arriving in 1868; Isaac met him in Pittsburgh soon after and in 1871 they opened J. Kaufmann & Brother at 1916 Carson Street. Primarily a tailoring establishment, Kaufmann's also carried a small selection of men's wear. As the store expanded, Morris and Henry joined the venture. By 1880, J. Kaufmann and Brothers closed their South Side and North Side locations (the latter opened about 1875) and opened for business on Smithfield Street.

The store continued to grow and thrive under the Kaufmanns' direction, adding women's clothing, house wares, and shoes to their sales in 1888. The brothers advanced business practices radical for the time, such as printing the price of merchandise on a card accompanying each item. Through marketing mottos such as "fair dealings, one price to all" the Kaufmanns earned the trust of their customers and laid the foundation for the store's many years of popular and commercial success. The descendants of the four founding brothers would oversee Kaufmann's acquisition by the May Company in 2005, turning the Pittsburgh-born business into a nationally-known chain.

Made millionaires from their department store, the Kaufmann brothers gave back to the region through a tremendous record of philanthropy. The legacy of the Emma Kaufmann Camp, endowed by Isaac and Morris, is still felt today, as is that of the Irene Kaufmann Settlement (IKS). Led by Henry, who gave over $3 million to the institution during his lifetime, the Kaufmanns were generous supporters of the IKS, which provided social and cultural services to thousands of immigrants. The IKS continues today in the work of the Jewish Community Center of Greater Pittsburgh.

Each of the Kaufmann brothers were members of the Rodef Sholom Congregation. Jacob, Isaac, and Morris Kaufmann are buried in Pittsburgh's West View Cemetery; Henry is buried in New York City.

Michael Keaton

Born September 5, 1951—Robinson Twp., PA

For a young actor with no formal training, who once derided the notion that acting could be taught—whose first exposure to being on camera came from having been *behind* the camera while working for *Mister Rogers' Neighborhood*—Michael Keaton became one of the hottest actors ever lauded in Hollywood.

Born the youngest of seven children to George and Leona Douglas in the once rural neighborhood of Forest Grove in Robinson Township, Michael Douglas was a rambunctious and precocious kid. To entertain his parents' friends, he'd tear strips from a Hershey bar wrapper, lick and stick them to his cheeks, and parade around the living room doing Elvis impersonations. Surely, Michael was not the only funny kid in his close-knit family.

He attended Montour High, then majored in Speech at Kent State. But he dropped out. After driving a cab, working as a Good Humor man, and trying his luck at stand-up comedy, he became a production assistant at Family Communications, Inc., sometimes operating Picture, Picture for Fred Rogers. In one segment, he entertained King Friday on camera as a flying Zucchini Brother.

With a great deal of pluck, Douglas moved to L.A. and joined the Second City comedy troupe while auditioning for, and winning bit parts on, *Maude, The Tony Randall Show, All's Fair*, and the *Mary Tyler Moore Hour*. His first regular gig was with James Belushi in the short-lived sitcom *Working Stiffs*. Then came his big break when he was cast by Ron Howard to play the enterprising morgue attendant opposite straight man Henry Winkler in the box office hit, *Night Shift*. The year was

1982, and in his first film, he got title credit. In fact, Keaton would never again appear in any film without top billing.

The next year, he was *Mr. Mom* and clinched his spot on the A-list of young comedic actors. Many critics claim Keaton, who changed his name not to emulate the comic Buster, but the more contemporary Diane, paved the way for other soft-hearted talents like Tom Hanks.

But from 1984 to 1988, Keaton's career flat-lined. Films like *Johnny Dangerously, Touch and Go, The Squeeze*, and even Ron Howard's *Gung Ho!*, filmed in McKeesport, did little to advance his star power. In fact, Keaton was first cast in Woody Allen's *The Purple Rose of Cairo*, but got dumped for an unknown Jeff Daniels.

Along came Tim Burton and his over-the-top black comedy, *Beetlejuice*. Keaton wowed the critics and fans alike, earning a box office gross of $73 million. As if the year wasn't already successful, Keaton next starred in *Clean & Sober*, demonstrating his ability to command a dramatic role. The juxtaposition of characters was barely sufficient to convince Warner Bros. executives—despite a huge outcry from prospective filmgoers—that Keaton could carry himself as millionaire Bruce Wayne. Tim Burton's *Batman* earned an unprecedented $251 million in 1989.

As if the opportunity would ever again exist, Keaton has not since achieved greater fame. From his astonishing psychopathic role in *Pacific Heights* (1990) to Disney's recent *Herbie Fully Loaded*, Keaton has offered an extraordinary diversity of dramatic talent.

Formerly married to Caroline McWilliams with whom he shares a son, Sean, Keaton has regularly returned to Pittsburgh to help benefit the Parental Stress Center. In addition, five of Keaton's siblings, Joyce, Paul, Pam, Diane, and George, Jr. live in the region still.

Rick Kehoe

Born July 15, 1951—Windsor, Ontario

The picture of steady, consistent play, a fine shooter with excellent timing and a deadly wrist shot, all-star right winger Rick Kehoe brought grace, stability, and good sense to the Penguins organization for 32 years both on and off the ice.

Born in 1951 in Windsor, Ontario, Rick Thomas Kehoe was drafted high by the Toronto Maple Leafs. After leading the club in goals, however, he was traded in 1974 to the Penguins, where he served as a player, scout, assistant coach, and head coach, becoming a charter member of the Penguins Hall of Fame.

A notably clean player—he had a scant 120 penalty minutes over 14 seasons—Kehoe won the Lady Byng Trophy for gentlemanly play in 1980-1981, the same season he scored a career-high 55 goals.

Playing at a lithe 5'-11" and 180 pounds, Kehoe put in 10 full seasons in a Penguin jersey, leading the team in both goals and points three times. Scoring 25 or more goals in nine of his 10 Penguin seasons, he topped the 30 mark five times. Retiring in 1985 as the club's career scoring leader, he saw his own records eclipsed by Mario Lemieux and Jaromir Jagr. Now the third all-time Penguin scorer with 636 points, Kehoe also stands fourth all-time with 722 Penguin games and 312 goals.

Moving from the ice into scouting and coaching, Kehoe became the Penguins director of pro scouting and an assistant coach in 1986, serving in those positions for 14 years. Named head coach in 2001, he led the team for two seasons, through 2003. After as dismal 55-81-14 record, when the Penguins failed to make the playoffs, Kehoe returned to scouting, finally moving to the New York Rangers in 2006.

Fred Kelly

Born June 29, 1916—Highland Park
Died March 15, 2000—Tucson, AZ

Three years younger than his more famous brother, Fred Kelly was the child that his parents James and Harriet Kelly deemed the most likely to succeed. At age 3, taking dance lessons with his four siblings, Fred was the one child who said he truly loved to dance. And perform, too. At 8 years of age, Kelly was earning as much as $50 a week tap dancing in local shows. From the age of 11 to 17, Fred was the host and star of his own show, *Kelly's Kiddie Kaper*, at the Warner Theatre in downtown Pittsburgh. He danced, emceed, performed magic, and played sidekick to a number of guest performers.

By the age of 18, Kelly was touring with the large riverboats, leaving Pittsburgh for New Orleans, doing nightly shows. And, in between gigs, with his brother, he taught thousands of students—often in long assembly line classes of 20-minute durations—in a free room provided by Beth Shalom, at a charge of 25 cents per leg.

Pinky Lee and Martha Stewart fall in step with Kelly, 1952.

The family admits that Fred taught Gene how to tap.

When Gene was given the title role in *Pal Joey*, Kelly followed his brother in the long run of William Saroyan's *The Time of Your Life*, earning him three Donaldson Awards (precursors to the Tonys). But producers soon saw that the younger Kelly could offer much more as a choreographer and director than as a featured performer. In fact, the Army discovered his directorial talents, too. When he enlisted in December 1941, he was attached almost immediately to one of the Corps' entertainment units, and ultimately sent to Camp Upton on Long Island to work with Irving Berlin in creating the 300-member cast production of *This Is The Army*. The show opened on Broadway, but not before Kelly married his childhood sweetheart, Dottie Greenwalt, with whom he had grown up on Kensington Street. Without a honeymoon, the two toured 13 cities, ending up in Hollywood where *This Is The Army* was soon prepared for film production.

Though clearly never reaching the star power that Gene earned, Fred had many great credits. He was an early TV variety show director, particularly of the *Colgate Palmolive Hour*, and he later directed more than 1,000 hours of *The Steve Allen Show*. He choreographed John H. Harris' Ice Capades for three years. He taught the royal princesses Margaret and Elizabeth to dance. He popularized the Mambo in the Latin Quarter of New York, and he alone created the Cha-Cha, modeled after the popular Lindy Hop, under the alias Frederico Calais.

He appears only once on film with Gene, in the musical *Deep In My Heart*, doing the quirky number, "I Love to Go Swimmin' with Women."

For 30 years, before retiring to Tucson, Fred instructed thousand of children at his Cloister, NJ, studio. To more modern audiences, he is most famously credited for having taught a young John Travolta to dance.

Gene Kelly

Born August 23, 1912—Highland Park
Died February 2, 1996—Beverly Hills, CA

For the past 17 years, students from the Pittsburgh region have flocked to the Benedum Theatre downtown to reprise a single number from their Spring musical. The night is an electric event, staged by Pittsburgh CLO, underwritten by the University of Pittsburgh, and it sells out every year, so that parents and family members have to stand outside—some years in the rain—watching their kids sing and dance on the Jumbo-tron overhanging Katz Plaza.

Today, the Kelly homestead on Kensington in Pittsburgh's East End.

In 1955, Betsy Blair, married to Kelly at 17, divorced at 32, was a film star in her own right. Kerry is their only child.

The Gene Kelly Awards were established in 1991, five years before Pittsburgh's legendary dancer, actor, choreographer and director died at the age of 83 in 1996.

Eugene Curran Kelly was the third child of five born to James and Harriet Kelly on Portland Street at Bryant near Highland Park. Canadian-born James was a traveling salesman for the Columbia Phonograph Company and Harriet, daughter of a saloon keeper, occasionally performed in amateur revues. Both were keen on popular music and so they made certain their children—James Jr., Joan (or "J"), Eugene, Louise and Fred—learned music and dance. The Five Kellys, as they were sometimes billed, all attended St. Raphael's Academy on Chislett Street.

Excited most by gymnastics and hockey, Kelly excelled as an athlete, though he continued dance lessons even through his years at Peabody High. He attended Penn State but the Depression made tuition money scarce. While his mother worked as a receptionist for the Bolton School of Dance, the company went bankrupt. Harriet however paid the school's debts and purchased her right to run it herself. Kelly returned to Pittsburgh to teach dance, eventually earning a degree in economics from Pitt. Though the Depression ensued, the film industry flourished, offering escape from the hardships of daily life. Kelly's dance studios flourished too as hundreds of little girls in curls came to learn tap, just like Shirley Temple.

The Kellys then moved to Kensington Street, a dead end street abutting Frick Park. The Gene Kelly Studio of the Dance was on Munhall Road, off Beacon Avenue, in Squirrel Hill.

By 1938, after several years of choreographing shows like *Hold Your Hats* at the Pittsburgh Playhouse, Kelly left for New York and soon debuted on Broadway in *Leave It To Me*. Then came a dramatic role, albeit as a hoofer, in William Saroyan's *The Time of Your Life*. When he left the show a full year later, he gave the role to his younger brother Fred. His big break came when he was cast in the title role of Rodgers and Hart's *Pal Joey*. Not only did the stage critics go wild, but

GENE KELLY   FRANK SINATRA
BETTY GARRETT   ANN MILLER

M's Big CHNICOLOR usical!

THEY PAINT THE TOWN WITH JOY!

ON THE TOWN

JULES MUNSHIN · VERA-ELLEN ·

SCREEN PLAY BY ADOLPH GREEN... BETTY COMDEN... BASED UPON THE MUSICAL PLAY
Directed by GENE KELLY and STANLEY DONEN Produced by ARTHUR FREED
A METRO-GOLDWYN-MAYER PICTURE

© Associated Press

Pittsburgh innovation strikes again when Kelly insists on shooting *On The Town* on the actual streets of NYC. It had never been done before—at least not with mega-stars, music, and choreography.

Discovered by Pittsburgh's own David O. Selznick, Kelly is paired with Judy Garland in *For Me and My Gal*. Unlike their dance routines, the plot is lame.

© Associated Press

David O. Selznick signed him to a seven-year film contract which, though not unprecedented for an up-and-comer, was all the more amazing in that Selznick had no musicals waiting for Kelly. In fact, he was loaned straight out to MGM to co-star with Judy Garland in Busby Berkeley's *For Me and My Gal*. The film was a modest hit, if only because Garland was still considered a juvenile.

As World War II ensued, Kelly was cast in several war films, but made his next significant career move when he starred in—and choreographed—*Cover Girl* with Rita Hayward, the darling of GIs everywhere. Now, he was more than just a dancer who could act; he had creative clout. When he lobbied hard to dance with an animated mouse in *Anchors Aweigh*, (and pulled it off at great expense to the studio), Kelly earned true star power. Soon he teamed with Director Stanley Donen in *On The Town* and convinced the studio to shoot outdoor dance numbers on the real streets of Manhattan. That had never been done before. Nor had any film musical risked its romantic plot to a climactic modern ballet, as Kelly insisted, dancing with Leslie Caron in *An American in Paris*. Another Pittsburgher, Oscar Levant, took his turn in that film, too.

Though 30 films followed, *Singin' in The Rain* is the classic for which Kelly is most remembered. Said Kelly years later, "…I tried to do things uniquely cinematic, that you couldn't do on a stage. Call it 'cine-dancing,' or whatever, but I tried to invent the dance to fit the camera and its movements." Few other films capture the euphoria of love as well as Kelly's innocent stomping in the puddled streets of the American dream.

© Sunset Boulevard/Corbis

Jim Kelly

Born February 14, 1960—East Brady, PA

Fearless on the field, blessed with a rifle arm, East Brady's Jim Kelly quarterbacked his Buffalo Bills to four consecutive Super Bowl appearances—and celebrated his record-breaking career with a niche in the Pro Football Hall of Fame.

© Associated Press

Born James Edward Kelly, he played championship basketball and all-state football at East Brady High. Choosing Miami-Florida for college ball, Kelly led the Hurricanes to a 1980 Peach Bowl appearance.

The Buffalo Bills' first-round pick in the 1983 NFL draft, Kelly instead played for the Houston Gamblers in the fledgling United States Football League, 1984-85. Standing 6'-3" and 225 pounds, Kelly had 16 300-yard passing games, three 400-yard games, and one incredible 574-yard game. Throwing for more than 9,000 yards, and named All-USFL in both seasons, Kelly is widely considered the single greatest player in the league's brief history.

After the USFL folded, Kelly signed with the Bills, playing 11 seasons, 1986-96. Using the no-huddle K-Gun offense, Kelly helped make the Bills one of the strongest NFL teams of the 1990s. Leading Buffalo to playoff berths eight times, including four consecutive Super Bowls, XXV-XXVIII, 1990-93, Kelly passed for more than 3,000 yards in a season eight times, passing for more than 300 yards in a game 26 times—once for more than 400. Finishing with some 2,800 completions, Kelly threw for more than 35,000 yards.

Inducted in the Pro Football Hall of Fame in 2002, Kelly has been a leader in charitable causes. Founding the Kelly for Kids Foundation in 1987, Kelly helps raise money for children's charities in western New York, where he still lives with his family. In 1997, when his son Hunter was diagnosed with Globoid-Cell Leukodystrophy (Krabbe disease) shortly after his birth, Kelly established Hunter's Hope to raise awareness about the disease—that took his son's life in 2005.

Marie Kelly

Born in 1917—Pittsburgh
Died December 29, 2000—Pittsburgh

Perhaps it was being a stay-at-home mother to her three sons that gave Marie Kelly's incredibly eclectic art its spontaneous, nearly childlike glee. From horses to madonnas to explosively colorful abstracts, in painting, sculpture, fiber, ceramics, silkscreen, and paper, Kelly's work inevitably exudes a boundless optimism, an ineffable joie de vivre.

Born Marie Tuicillo, Kelly grew up learning fine needlework from her mother and grandmother. Attending Carnegie Tech, she studied art with famed instructors Samuel Rosenberg and Robert Lepper.

Married and the mother of three sons, Kelly painted and drew during the day, worked on tapestries at night.

Blurring the lines between high art and folk art, between art and craft, there was virtually no local honor that Kelly did not receive. By 1952, for example, she had placed a painting in the Carnegie International. The 1961 Pittsburgh Center for the Arts Artist of the Year, she also regularly exhibited in the Associated Artists shows at the Carnegie Museum of Art. A member of the prestigious Three Rivers Arts Festival 10-For-10 show, she was one of the artists who'd been juried into

the festival each of its initial 10 years.

As an instructor at the now-defunct Ivy School and at the Manchester Craftsmen's Guild, Kelly was greatly admired—and remembered as a very serious teacher.

Continuing working in her Oakland studio into her 80s, Kelly died in 2000 at age 83, not long after a Pittsburgh Center for the Arts exhibition honoring her—and all other former Artists of the Year. In March, 2001 the Society for Contemporary Craft held a major retrospective of her work.

With her art in numerous permanent museum collections, including the Carnegie and the Philadelphia Museum of Art, Kelly's work is prized by local collectors—as well as by such national names as Walter Cronkite, Barbra Streisand, and Ralph Lauren.

Samuel Kier

Born July 19, 1813—Indiana County, PA
Died October 6, 1874—Pittsburgh

He made small fortunes in managing canal boats, forging wrought iron, transporting coal, and trading salt, but he is most remembered for selling snake-oil—and failing. If ever there was a patron saint of blind perseverance, his name was Samuel Kier.

Born along the Connemaugh River near Livermore, PA, Kier, the son of a salt manufac-

turer, first moved to Pittsburgh to work as a forwarding merchant. In the Crash of 1837, he went bankrupt. He turned to running the Mechanics Line of boats on the Pennsylvania Canal, and quite successfully repaid his debts, while also investing in a new line of amphibious boats to cross the Alleghenies. When the Pennsylvania Railroad forged west in 1854, Kier was out of business again. By that time, however, he had irrevocably changed the world.

Returning to his father's Tarentum salt mines in 1846, while boring for water, Kier encountered a slimy ground oil—so much of it, in fact, that dumping it into a nearby canal cost more than the value of the salt he could save. So he bottled it, and sold it as Kier's Rock Oil, a "remedy of wonderful efficacy."

Kelly's *Picnic A Fiesole* demonstrates her fresh whimsy.

Quite the salesman, Kier had dozens of gold and red wagons hawking his product at 50 cents per half-pint. For all of its promises—"the lame, through its instrumentality, were made to walk; the blind to see"—Kier's Rock Oil couldn't cure a hangnail, and so it failed.

Legend says that one day, a salt miner tossed a burning ember on the oil-laden canal, and "bang!," the idea was born. In 1850, Kier experimented with the oil, not as a fuel or an explosive, but as a household illuminant. (whale oil, the only common lamp oil, was by now a considerable expense). Though the oil smoked, and the odor was no less offensive than whale oil, Kier knew he could improve its qualities. By 1854, he operated a five-barrel distillery, the first oil-refining plant in America, at Grant and Seventh Streets in downtown Pittsburgh. Kier also tinkered with and improved upon the benefits of oil lamps for home and business. Demand followed, and Kier's fortune was ensured.

Except that he forgot to do one thing: register his patents. Within a few years, his claims were lost to others. And, inexplicably, he never sank wells dedicated to extract more oil.

He died, the father of four, not so poor as he was proud. Kier is buried in Allegheny Cemetery.

Ralph Kiner

Born October 27, 1922—Santa Rita, NM

From April 16, 1946 through June, 4, 1953, fans came to Forbes Field for one reason: to see Pirate outfielder Ralph Kiner hit home runs. Doing so with great regularity, Kiner became the only player to lead the National League in homers for seven consecutive seasons, 1946-52.

Born in Santa Rita, New Mexico, Kiner grew to be a powerful righthander. Although the Pirates signed Kiner out of high school in 1940, a couple of years in the minors and a hitch in the Navy delayed his arrival in Pittsburgh until 1946. He hit only 23 round trippers that year, but it was good enough, as the 24-year-old became the first rookie in 40 years to lead the league.

In 1947 Kiner graduated to the 50-homer club, hitting 51 for the title. And so on, year after year. Although the Pirates had the most dreadful teams in club history, in 1947 the Pirates broke one million in attendance for the first time, double the previous year, the first of four straight million-plus seasons.

When future Hall of Fame executive Branch Rickey came, his plan was to bring up minor-leaguers and trade veterans, Kiner included. About the 1953 10-player swap that sent Kiner to the Chicago Cubs, Rickey reportedly said, "we finished [last] with you. We can finish [last] without you."

But when Kiner left so did the fans. Pirate attendance fell to a half-million in 1953, staying below that figure for two more years.

All told, he hit 369 home runs (301 as a Pirate), one homer for every 14.1 at-bats, a ratio behind only Babe Ruth and Mark McGuire. In 1975 he was elected to the Hall of Fame. "It certainly wasn't strength or bulk muscle," Kiner said. "I happened to have that kind of swing."

Alive and well and living in the Big Apple, Ralph Kiner has enjoyed a long, distinguished career as a New York Mets broadcaster.

Roger Kingdom

Born August 26, 1962—Vienna, GA

For four years, he was the fastest man in the world.

Born in Vienna, Georgia, in 1962, Roger Kingdom was a scholastic track and field star. Georgia state champion in high jump, discus, and 110-meter hurdles—which he ran in a world-class 13.7 seconds—in 1980-81 at Vienna High, Kingdom was so multi-talented that he considered training for the decathlon. Standing 6'-1" and 180 pounds, he came to Pitt in 1981 on a football/track scholarship. Yet after winning the 1983 NCAA 110-meter hurdles, to go with a gold medal at the Pan-Amer-

ican Games, and the 1984 NCAA 55-meter hurdles, Kingdom abandoned his studies to enter the world of competitive running.

Training extensively in the 110-meter hurdles, he won the Olympic Gold Medal in Los Angeles, 1984. Four years later, in Seoul, 1988, Kingdom repeated his achievement—one of only two hurdlers to notch consecutive gold-medal victories in Olympic history. In Seoul, Kingdom's time of 12.98 seconds not only shattered the 13-second barrier, it also stood as an Olympic record for eight years.

The following year, 1989, in the World Games in Zurich, Kingdom set a new world record of 12.92 seconds, a mark which stood for four years.

Aside from his Olympic records, before retiring in 1998 Kingdom took five US Outdoor championships (1985, 1988-90, 1995), two Gold Medals at the Pan Am Games (1983, 1995), a World Cup gold medal (1989), and a Gold Medal at the World University Games (1989). After competitive running, Kingdom, who was ranked number one in the world five times (1984-85, 1988-90) returned to Pitt, where he finished his degree in 2002.

A 2005 inductee in the Track and Field Hall of Fame, Kingdom lives with his family in suburban Pittsburgh. Since 2004 he has coached track and field at California University of Pennsylvania, assuming head coaching duties in 2006.

Billy Knight

Born June 9, 1952—Braddock, PA

Braddock's all-time favorite son, and the single greatest basketball player in Pitt history, Billy Knight led the 1973-74 Panthers to a 25-4 record and a berth in the NCAA Elite Eight, the team's all-time highest ranking.

Born William R. Knight in Braddock in 1952, 6'-6", 195-pound Billy Knight went from Braddock High to Pitt, where, over his three-year varsity career, 1971-74, Knight scored more than 1,700 points—and became Pitt's first consensus All-American.

In Knight's junior year, 1972-73, the Panthers were nationally ranked for the first time. The following season, 1973-74, Knight led the Panthers on a 22-game win streak. Then, in the NCAA Tournament, scoring 34 points, Knight led the Panthers to an 81-78 victory over Furman, setting up an East Region Final against North Carolina State—which went on to take the national title.

The only player in Pitt history to average more than 20 points and 10 rebounds a game, Knight was one of only four Panthers to record more than 1,000 points, 600 rebounds, and 200 assists.

Pitt's first-ever first-round draft pick, Knight was taken in the 1974 American Basketball Association draft by the Indiana Pacers. An ABA and later NBA All Star—a Panther first—Knight's 11-year professional career, 1974-85, was the longest for any Pitt grad. Primarily playing for the Pacers, where he continues to rank among the team's all-time players, Knight also saw action with Buffalo, Boston, Kansas City, and San Antonio.

After retiring from playing, Knight became an executive with the Pacers, later moving to the Vancouver/ Memphis Grizzlies. In 2002, Knight joined the Atlanta Hawks, where he is Executive Vice President and General Manager, coordinating the team's basketball operations.

In 1989, Pitt retired Knight's number 34, one of only three players to be so honored. Billy Knight lives in Atlanta with his wife and two daughters.

Philander Knox

Born May 6, 1853—Brownsville, PA
Died October 12, 1921—Washington, DC

Attorney General Philander Knox famously told Theodore Roosevelt about the Panama Canal, "Mr. President, do not let so great an achievement suffer from any taint of legality."

Instrumental in bringing the Canal to Panama—resulting in an enormous contract for his benefactor, Andrew Carnegie—Knox was Pittsburgh's first great Washington insider and consummate power broker.

The turn-of-the-20th-Century Canal fight was hard-fought and fractious. Having seen the French fail, the new Republic was determined to construct a path between the seas. But how? And where?

Some favored Nicaragua. Others favored a sea-level route. Clearly, the most difficult, and dangerous, and costly, was cutting through Panama. So why go that way?

One reason was steel. Panama's overland route required six massive locks. In the Senate, millionaire lawyer Philander Knox made the case. Two days later, the Senate voted approval. And U.S. Steel got the contract.

Born Philander Chase Knox, he attended Ohio's Mount Union College, where he met future President William McKinley, who advised Knox to read law. Admitted to the Pittsburgh bar in 1875, within a year Knox was an Assistant United States Attorney.

Forming Knox and Reed (later Reed Smith), he became Andrew Carnegie's corporate counsel. Offered the post of U.S. Attorney General in 1899 by President McKinley, Knox declined, being heavily involved in the creation of U. S. Steel. That finished, Knox took up the President on his offer.

After McKinley's 1901 assassination, Knox continued under Roosevelt. Appointed in June, 1904, to fill a vacant Senate seat, Knox served through 1909. Serving as President Taft's Secretary of State, 1909-13, as Taft's confidante Knox was widely considered the most powerful man in the Administration. At State, Knox practiced so-called Dollar Diplomacy, encouraging and protecting American investments abroad.

Elected again to the Senate, Knox served from 1917 until his death, age 68. He is buried in Washington Memorial Cemetery, Valley Forge.

Henry Koenig

Born July 14, 1891—Springdale, PA
Died May 20, 1934—Denver, CO

More astounding than the lethal effects of radium—first produced commercially in Pittsburgh at the Standard Chemical Company in Oakland—was its market price. A single gram, requiring 500 tons of carnotite ore and six months to reduce, cost $120,000 in 1920. So valuable was this much studied and "most promising" element that Madame Marie Curie sailed to the states in 1921 to receive a gift of one gram of radium from President Warren G. Harding. Because the gram was produced here (well, actually reduced at the company's facility in Canonsburg,) she also visited Pittsburgh.

It is likely, though not certain, that Henry Koenig was in Pittsburgh to greet Madame Curie. As the chief radium chemist for Standard Chemical, the two were well acquainted, most likely from his pioneering work in Brussels. There he had just perfected an extraction process for the ore, thus almost doubling the world's supply of radium.

Koenig, whose father died when he was 7, graduated from Tarentum High in 1908, and pursued his Bachelor of Science at Pitt, graduating in 1912. Upon completing graduate work at both Princeton and Columbia, he began his career at Standard Chemical Company. Along with associates Charles Viol and Glenn Kammer, he is credited with crystallizing over half the radium produced in the world before 1920. The demand had been created by false claims that radium would cure cancer. Many health-conscious A-types would drink radium tonics and those afflicted by gout, arthritis, and a hundred common maladies would ingest toxic doses to cure their ills. Not just sold for medicinal purposes, radium-painted watches became quite the fad, as did its application to fish bait, lamp pulls, and theater seats—because it glowed in the dark.

Exclaimed as the world's most renowned radium scientist, second only to Madame Curie, Koenig eventually worked in her Paris laboratory for three months.

At the age of 42, he died of bone cancer just two months before Curie. He was the last of her dedicated staff to suffer the devastating effects of radiation.

In 1986, his body was exhumed from Homewood Cemetery for research purposes.

Henry Koerner

Born in 1915—Vienna, Austria
Died July 7, 1991—St. Polten, Austria

He was Viennese after all, a man of infinite charm and palpable brilliance, whose 7,000 works of art—from his exquisite portraits to his painful post-Holocaust paintings, his 65 covers for *Time* magazine to his playful, phantasmagoric representations of Pittsburgh—were never less than colorful, representational, often shocking and erotic, but always visionary.

Born in 1915 in Vienna, Henry Koerner trained as a graphic designer. Following the 1938 Nazi annexation of Austria, the 23-year-old Jewish Koerner fled, emigrating to the United States. At first designing book jackets in New York, in 1942-43 he drew award-winning posters for the Office of War Information. Drafted into the army in 1943, Koerner worked for the Office of Strategic Services. In 1945, he was sent to Berlin as a Nuremberg trials court artist. Following his 1946 discharge, Koerner returned to Austria to discover that his entire family, including his parents and brother, were Holocaust victims.

Painting his own pain and family tragedy, in 1947 Koerner had his first, acclaimed solo exhibition in Berlin. Returning to New York, Koerner held his first American exhibition and subsequently had his work included in the Whitney Museum's 1949 annual show.

Moving to Pittsburgh in 1952 to serve as artist-in-residence at Chatham College, Koerner lived close by, on Negley Avenue. Painting a wide variety of people, narrative ideas, and landscapes, Koerner never lost the skilled detail of his graphic training—or his survivor's sense that the world could disappear in an instant.

For *Time*, his 1950-60s cover portraits—Phillies' Hall of Fame pitcher Robin Roberts, diva Maria Callas, Senator John Kennedy—are inevitably colorful, pensive, always telling a story.

Retiring in the 1980s, given major shows at the Carnegie and in Vienna, in 1991, then 75, Koerner was bicycling outside Vienna when he was hit by a car. He died three weeks later.

Kathryn Kuhlman

Born May 9, 1907—Concordia, MO
Died February 20, 1976—Los Angeles, CA

She believed in miracles, because she believed in God.

Kathryn Kuhlman was not the first nationally-known evangelist, but her twinkling eyes, beaming smile and charismatic passion drew millions to her weekly broadcasts every Friday night from Carnegie Hall on the North Side.

Kuhlman was the second daughter born to Joseph and Emma Kuhlman on their Missouri farm. "Born again" when she was 10, she later followed her older sister Myrtle and evangelical brother-in-law Everrette Parrott to Oregon when she had just graduated from 10th grade. For five years, estranged from her parents, she learned the power and influence of organizing revival meetings in rural America, traveling to Boise in 1928 (where she first preached a sermon), to Pueblo, Colorado, (where she witnessed her first healing), then to Denver where, attracting crowds to a Montgomery Ward store on Sundays, she also broadcast her first radio show.

In 1937, she accepted Iowan evangelist Burroughs A. Waltrip's hand in marriage, when, no sooner had she walked down the aisle, she publicly acknowledged that Waltrip had just dumped his former wife, leaving behind two children. The scandal of their marriage dogged the two spiritual leaders as long as they were together, which was all of four years.

Miss Kuhlman, reclaiming her maiden name, accepted an invitation to preach in Franklin, PA, where, returning often, she attracted a new following in her Gospel Tabernacle. Soon, she was broadcasting her own radio show on WKRZ in Oil City, and just as soon, she was heard in Pittsburgh on station WPGH. Her audience grew quickly, her charitable largess swelled, and the demands of her ministry required new headquarters—in Pittsburgh. Here, she leased Carnegie Hall at Allegheny Center and occupied the sixth floor of the Carlton House with staff sufficient to run her growing foundation. For 20 years she hosted a weekly revival on the North Side, and for eight years more at the First Presbyterian Church Downtown. She lived in Fox Chapel, but never learned to drive. Every day she was heard on more than 50 radio stations, and once a week seen on her national TV program, *I Believe in Miracles*, taped in Television City. She lifted the spirits of American and Canadian Christians reaching out for her healing spirit.

Beloved by millions, Kuhlman died from complications of an enlarged heart. Her eponymous foundation still offers videos, prayers and a Pittsburgh address for those who believe.

Jack Lambert

Born July 8, 1952—Mantua, OH

He came across the middle, glaring, missing teeth, a wraith in black and gold. "Lambert may have had the image of a wild man," fellow Steeler linebacker Andy Russell recalled. "But he killed you with his precision."

"He was the most focused individual I ever had," added Chuck Noll, his Hall of Fame coach.

Playing at a pencil-thin 6'-4" and 220 pounds, for 11 years, 1974-84, middle linebacker Jack Lambert was a quarterback's worst nightmare. Riding previously unimaginable intensity, captaining the vaunted Steel Curtain defense, he was elected to the Pro Football Hall of Fame in 1990.

John Harold Lambert was considered by many as too small to be a successful National Football League linebacker. Taken in the second round of legendary 1974 Steeler draft that produced four future Hall of Famers, Lambert celebrated by reporting immediately to watch game films.

Quickly developing into what his Hall of Fame profile aptly reports as the "prototype middle linebacker -- intense, intelligent, fast, quick, durable. Noted for vicious tackling, great range, and superior pass defense, he was a two-time NFL Defensive Player of Year and an All-Pro eight times."

Playing in six AFC championship games and four Super Bowls, Lambert notched 28 career interceptions and 17 fumble recoveries. Yet for his many great plays, perhaps Lambert's most famous moment came between whistles in Super Bowl X. When Dallas Cowboy Cliff Harris taunted Steeler kicker Roy Gerela for missing a field goal, Lambert threw Harris to the ground.

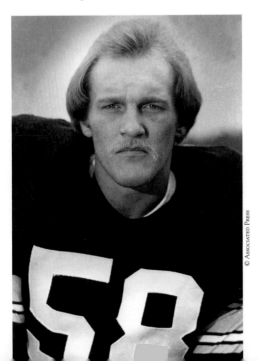

© Associated Press

"How fortunate I was to play for the Pittsburgh fans," Lambert said in his 1990 Hall of Fame speech, "a proud and hard-working people who love their football and their players. If I could start my life all over again, I would be a professional football player. And you damn well better believe I would be a Pittsburgh Steeler!"

Daisy Lampkin

Born August 8, 1883—Reading, PA
Died March 10, 1965—Pittsburgh

Forceful might not be strong enough, but Daisy Lampkin was that. The first national vice president of the NAACP, and a Field Director of the organization, her charge was to raise money. Recalled Robert Lavelle, founder and president of the Dwelling House Savings Company upon his first week of work as a teen at the *Pittsburgh Courier* in 1935, "I had worked about 80 hours… and I was elated to have this 10 dollars and went out the door. And there was Daisy Lampkin. She said, 'Wait a minute, young man. Give me a dollar.' I said, 'A dollar? What for?' 'NAACP membership.' I became a rabid NAACP member. I mean—they took one-tenth of my salary!"

Lampkin was also a stockholder of the *Pittsburgh Courier*, as well as a columnist and a vice president. The story goes that in 1918 she won a sales contest for the nationally-acclaimed black paper, but the company couldn't pay the prize. So Lampkin took stock.

Born in Reading, PA, Daisy Elizabeth Adams moved to Pittsburgh in 1909 to marry her husband, William Lampkin. Although she gladly took his name, she was an early member of the Lucy Stone League, a suffrage group, founded in 1920, which advocated the retention of women's real names. From her early work for women's rights, she developed a reputation for getting things done. Soon she organized the first chapter of the American Red Cross for African-American women. Active, too, in politics, she was twice nominated to serve as an alternate delegate at National Republican Conventions in the 1920s.

She is credited by some for having recruited Thurgood Marshall to the legal defense team of the NAACP. During World War II, she raised more than $2 million in Liberty Bonds, principally from the African-American community. And, in 1964, just before her death, she was named the first recipient of the highest award of the National Council of Negro Women. She died before receiving the formal honor.

Posthumously, in 1983, a plaque was mounted outside her home at 2519 Webster Avenue, the first such marker honoring an African-American woman in Pennsylvania's history.

Charles "Teenie" Harris Collection, Gift of Heinz Family Fund © 2008 Carnegie Museum of Art

Samuel Langley

Born August 22, 1834—Roxbury, MA
Died February 27, 1906—Aiken, SC

Just nine days after he launched his latest iteration of a manned flying machine, the Wright Brothers convinced the world that they had rightfully earned claim to the first

© University Archives, University of Pittsburgh

successful demonstration of sustained, powered flight. It's a shame for Pittsburgh, because much of Samuel Pierpont Langley's early studies of wind, weather, and birds were conducted as Director of the Allegheny Observatory.

Born in Roxbury, MA, Langley graduated from the Boston Latin School and was hired as an assistant at the Harvard Observatory. With no apparent academic degree, he became Dean of Mathematics at the United States Naval Academy where he also devoted his free time to servicing the campus observatory. For this experience, he was then hired to teach astrophysics at Pitt and serve as the director of the Allegheny Observatory, the lat-

ter to which he committed his greater energies. It was here on the North Side that Langley made the acquaintance of many of the city's more powerful industrialists and endeared them to his scientific interests. By acquisition of a transit telescope, Langley was able to record accurate time which he sold as a service to business, telegraphing the information twice daily. Here, too, is where Langley invented the bolometer, a device capable of measuring within one one-hundredths of a degree the intensity of the sun's radiant heat. Here, also, is where Langley mentored a young John Brashear who would later assume the directorship of the Observatory.

Langley's fascination with the sun's effect on weather patterns brought him to study wind and birds—and flight. Langley's first calculations of aerodynamics were drawn at the Observatory. His work caught the attention of the Smithsonian Institution and he was hired as its third president. But he remained in Pittsburgh, pursuing his interests in solar energy.

Ultimately, Langley took his drawings for a heavier-than-air flying machine to test from the top of a house boat on the Potomac River. Many aeronautical engineers believe the sixth model of his flying machine, which he called an aerodrome, might have flown had the catapult worked properly on December 8, 1903.

David Lawrence—See pages 130-131

Jesse Lazear

Born May 2, 1866—Baltimore County, MD
Died September 25, 1900—Quemados, Cuba

Although born in Maryland, Jesse Lazear traveled often to Pittsburgh with his brother and father—both Williams—for purposes of transporting dry goods sold through his family's grocery stores in both Pittsburgh and Baltimore. The younger Lazear attended Washington & Jefferson College and after two years, was accepted to study at Johns Hopkins in 1887. There he applied his skills in physics and chemistry, and pursued a medical degree from Columbia University. Upon graduation in 1889, he studied overseas at the University of Edinburgh, returned to Pittsburgh and then was married to his wife Mabel in 1896 before

joining the medical staff at Johns Hopkins. His specialty was in clinical pathology and so, in support of the U.S. military operations in Panama, he joined Dr. Walter Reed to study the Yellow Fever pandemic and to help identify the "germ" that had killed thousands of workers then digging the Great Canal.

Rather than setting up shop in the infected country, he was sent to Cuba to work with Dr. Carlos Juan Finlay to isolate the germ.

There are varying accounts of Lazear's heroism. Some say he alone followed a different path, deciding that mosquitoes may be the means of transmission for the germ. Some say, he allowed an errant mosquito to sting him so as not to upset a delicate procedure he was then performing. Others say he purposefully injected himself to determine the incubation period of the dreaded disease. Whichever the truth, the import of Lazear's sacrifice to science was the proof that, despite conventional wisdom, indeed mosquitoes were the culprits. Lazear died within 11 days of his experiment, leaving behind a wife, a son, and a daughter he never met. He is buried in Allegheny Cemetery. A Chemistry Hall at Washington & Jefferson is named in his honor.

David Leavitt

Born June 23, 1961—Pittsburgh

"I am totally out," David Leavitt told *Newsweek*. "I am a very outspoken gay man. But," he added, "I think it's also important, particularly for writers, that we not be imprisoned within a limiting identity. It's really important to get beyond the point where you are a gay writer."

Born David Adam Leavitt in Pittsburgh in 1961, he spent a very short five years here while his father, Harold J. Leavitt, taught at Carnegie Tech. Moving to Palo Alto in 1966 when his father took a job at Stanford, Leavitt went to Yale, where he majored in English and established himself as a wunderkind writer. Publishing the short story "Territory" in *The New Yorker* at age 20, at 23 Leavitt published his first story collection, *Family Dancing* (1984). Nominated for both the National Book Critics Circle Award and the PEN/Faulkner Award, *Family Dancing* placed gay concerns in the context of American life.

Hailed by the *New York Times* as a writer of "great talent," within two years of his debut volume, Leavitt's first novel, *The Lost Language of Cranes* (1986), told of a young New Yorker increasingly open about his sexuality. In quick succession Leavitt produced the novels *Equal Affections* (1989), *While England Sleeps* (1993), *The Page Turner* (1998), *Martin Bauman* (2000), *Florence* (2002), *The Body of Jonah Boyd* (2004), and *The Indian Clerk* (2007); as well as three story collections: *A Place I've Never Been* (1990), *Arkansas* (1997), and *The Marble Quilt* (2001).

Author of books about Italy, in 2005 Leavitt wrote *The Man Who Knew Too Much: Alan Turing and the Invention of the Computer*, the tragic story of the brilliant gay Englishman whose scientific contributions literally changed the world.

Leavitt currently serves as an English professor at the University of Florida.

David Lawrence

Born June 18, 1889—North Side
Died November 21, 1966—Pittsburgh

Impatient, imperious, long-visioned and short-tempered, David Lawrence was the most popular mayor in Pittsburgh history. Impeccably dressed, banging his large ring on the table to signal that meetings were over, he was a classic political boss who treated the Democratic Party as his personal fiefdom. Elected a record four times, Lawrence created the role of the activist-mayor, inaugurating social and economic development programs that would change Pittsburgh forever.

Born David Leo Lawrence in 1889 in the First Ward, now Gateway Center, son of a working-class Irish Catholic family, as a teenager Lawrence clerked for Pittsburgh attorney William Brennan, then chairman of the local Democratic Party.

Without either a college education or social standing, the young Lawrence seemed destined to be little more than another party apparatchik—in what was then a party without power. Nevertheless, the canny, driven Lawrence, by dint of hard-work and endless attention to detail—to party regulars, rallies, hospital visits, even wakes—built a power base of people intensely loyal to the Democratic Party and to him personally.

Elected Allegheny County Democratic Party chairman in 1919, Lawrence reaped his first patronage job in 1933, when new Democratic President Franklin Roosevelt appointed him U.S. Collector of Internal Revenue for Western Pennsylvania. The following year, Lawrence helped elect George Earle Pennsylvania's first 20th-century Democratic governor. Returning the favor, Earle appointed Lawrence Commonwealth Secretary; in the same year, 1934, Lawrence became Democratic Party state chairman.

Eleven years later, in 1945, Lawrence was elected Mayor. Serving 1946-59, Lawrence forged an unprecedented partnership with the corporate community to redevelop Pittsburgh. Working with Richard King Mellon to create Pittsburgh's first Renaissance, Lawrence's extraordinary changes include clearing the skies of smoke and transforming more than a quarter of Downtown to create Point State Park, Gateway Center, Mellon Square, the Civic Arena, and others.

Initially reluctant to run for Pennsylvania governor in 1958 because of his age—Lawrence was nearing 70—he nevertheless ran and won, becoming Pennsylvania's first Catholic governor. Bringing his customary activism to Harrisburg, Lawrence initiated environmental protection laws, fair housing laws, and historical preservation initiatives.

Lawrence served until 1963, limited to a single term, then became Chairman of the President's Committee on Equal Opportunities in Housing for Presidents John Kennedy and Lyndon Johnson.

Collapsing during a late 1966 political rally, Lawrence died 17 days later of heart failure at age 77. He was buried in Calvary Cemetery.

With no less than three Pittsburgh buildings named in his memory, including the David L. Lawrence Convention Center, he is fittingly remembered by a 1956 speech he gave at Harvard. "Our grand design in Pittsburgh," he said, "has been the acceptance of a belief that a city is worth saving." Of his own role he added, "I am only a very practical and prosaic mayor of a large city, which I love, and which I want to see become more serviceable to its region and more livable for its inhabitants. My effort must go, not into architectural and planning critiques, but into the limited, tedious, persevering work of making things happen."

April 27, 1946, Lawrence speaks to CIO laborers to help settle a union dispute.

POINT BASE BALL TEAM — SUMMER, 1905.
REAR ROW LEFT TO RIGHT: THOMAS TOOLE, PATRICK KEADY, THOMAS DONNORS,
JOHN O. FLAHERTY, ALEX McGREW, JOSEPH FLAHERTY.
THIRD ROW: WILLIAM HERST, WALTER FISHER, RAY EARLE, MARTIN RILEY,
FRANK CONNORS, BIGGS SNYDER, DAVID LAWRENCE.
SECOND ROW: JOSEPH SULLIVAN, CARL FISHER, WILLIAM T. KEADY, HARRY EARLE,

Both as a youth and a politician, Lawrence learned how to take a
swing at his competition. Below, Pittsburgh's African-American
community gets behind the wheel of Lawrence's gubernatorial drive.

Mario Lemieux

Born October 5, 1965—Montreal, Quebec

In his native French, Penguin center Mario Lemieux's name means "the best," and he certainly was.

One of the greatest National Hockey League players of all time, Lemieux stands as the Penguins' all-time Number One Star. The club's leading scorer, captain of two Stanley Cup championship teams, 1991-92, Hall of Famer Lemieux achieved greatness despite being plagued by severe injuries and life-threatening illnesses. "The best, most complete player I've seen," summed up hockey legend Scotty Bowman, Lemieux's one-time coach.

Born in 1965 in Montreal, Lemieux grew up playing on a rink his father built on his front lawn. As a teen in junior hockey, Lemieux set a record for points in a season: 282 points in 70 games. His remarkable three-year totals: 247 goals, 562 points.

Drafted first overall by the Penguins in 1984, Lemieux played at 6'-4" and 235 pounds. With an astounding ability to skate around other players as if they were standing still, his extraordinary reach, balance, and shooting left opposing players—as well as his league-wide legion of fans—wondering how he did everything so well while making it appear so effortless.

On October 11, 1984, on his first shift of his first game, Lemieux scored a goal on his first shot—and never looked back. By the end of the year, he had scored 100 points and was named Rookie of the Year—as well as Most Valuable Player in the All Star Game, the only rookie ever to be so honored.

While it is impossible to re-state all of Lemieux's extraordinary feats, one game—in an extraordinary season—will suffice. On New Year's Eve 1988, Lemieux had what many consider the greatest game in NHL history, scoring five goals five different ways: even-strength, power play, shorthanded, penalty shot, and empty net. That season, 1988-89, his 85 goals and 199 points—both career highs—led the league.

A multiple award winner over 17 seasons, 1984-2006 separated by a severe back injury and Hodgkin's lymphoma, he won six Art Ross (scoring) trophies, three Hart (most valuable player) trophies, four Lester Pearson (league's outstanding player judged by the players) awards, and two Conn Smythe (playoff MVP) trophies. A three-time All Star Game MVP, elected to the Hall of Fame in 1997, his career totals include 915 games, 690 goals, 1,033 assists, and 1,723 points. Summed up fellow Penguin Jaromir Jagr, "he was the best player I've ever seen. He was the most gifted at everything—size, strength, skill, how smart he was. There is no other player like him."

All that would be sufficient to remember Lemieux, but there are two more aspects of his life. First, in 1999 when the Penguins fell into bankruptcy, with the certainty of leaving Pittsburgh, Lemieux formed an investors' group to save the franchise. Acting as president, chairman, and CEO, Lemieux became the first player to become majority owner of his team.

Finally, after he was diagnosed with lymphoma in 1993 he created the Mario Lemieux Foundation, making generous gifts to many health-care institutions, establishing the Mario Lemieux Centers for Patient Care and Research. A tireless fundraiser, organizer of highly successful celebrity golf tournaments, he lives in Sewickley with his wife and four children.

The Lettermen

Tony Butala: Born November 20, 1940—Sharon, PA

It's hard to believe that just a few miles west on U.S. Route 62 from Mercer, PA. where industrial rocker Trent Reznor of Nine Inch Nails was born, is the hometown of a founding member of one of the most amiable pop vocal groups in history, The Lettermen. A greater dichotomy of sounds does not exist.

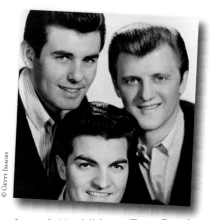

One of 11 children, Tony Butala was reared by musical parents John, a Westinghouse laborer who sang in the church choir, and Mary, who played the organ. Many hours were spent on the front porch of their Sharon home singing and harmonizing as a family.

Butala began performing in local clubs, like the Elks Lodge and Knights of Columbus, and in local musical revues. In 1948, he was featured in *Starlets On Parade* on KDKA radio. At the invitation of a cousin living in California, Butala auditioned for a seat in the famed Robert Mitchell Boys Choir in Hollywood. Singing for the next several years, he eventually became the assistant director, while finding other work in film and television, including the classics *White Christmas* and *Lassie.*

In the late 1950s Butala was asked to join Mike Barnett's band called The Lettermen. Barnett and the other members left soon after and Butala recruited two vocalists, Jim Pike and Bob Engemann, and reformed the trio. Of course, vocal groups were all the rage in the pre-British Invasion days of 1961; The Lettermen caught the ear of Capitol Records. (A studio vacancy left by The Four Preps allowed The Lettermen to be heard by record execs). Capitol signed The Lettermen to what would become a 24 year relationship with the label, producing such hits as "When I Fall In Love," "Theme From A Summer Place," "Put Your Head On My Shoulder," "Shangri-La," and

"Going Out Of My Head/Can't Take My Eyes Off Of You," (first performed in front of an audience at Penn State University).

The Lettermen have amassed 11 Gold records and five Grammy nominations and have performed on *The Tonight Show*, the *Dinah Shore* and *Mike Douglas Shows*, as well as with Frank Sinatra, Bing Crosby, Dean Martin, Sammy Davis Jr., and Sam Cooke.

Despite many personnel changes over the years, the one constant and remaining member of the band is Sharon-native Tony Butala, who still keeps the band actively touring.

Oscar Levant

Born December 27, 1906—Hill District
Died August 14, 1972—Beverly Hills, CA

His one-liners could fill a swimming pool but his demons could fill an ocean. He was a gifted musician, composer, writer, and sideman whose self-destructive and unpredictable nature made him a favorite among fans for decades.

Oscar Levant was raised in a strict and sometimes abusive household. His father Max had immigrated at the turn of the century, making his home in Pittsburgh at 1420 Fifth Avenue. A watchmaker by trade, his family lived in cramped quarters in the rear. A Russian Orthodox jew, Max insisted on much from his children: discipline always and respect above all. He even insisted on musical educa-tion for his children, but warned that pursuing a professional career in music was strictly forbidden. Oscar's mother at times resorted to tying the young Levant to a piano bench to get him to practice. And so he learned to play.

As a child, baseball was Levant's first love and he had dreams of playing for the Pirates at Forbes Field. At the age of 12 he was awestruck when hearing a performance by George Gershwin. He attended Forbes Elementary School. His prowess on the piano was evident and as a child he would play Chopin and Beethoven at family gatherings. While in his junior year at Fifth Avenue High School, his father died. Then, just 15, he and his mother escaped to New York to pursue his musical training. A week later, she left him. Levant never got over his feelings of abandonment.

In Manhattan Levant began playing the nightclubs and speakeasies along Broadway. His humor and talent helped him ascend into higher New York social circles, which also opened doors to Hollywood where he met and befriended George Gershwin. His admiration bordered on idolatry and after Gershwin's death, Levant became one of the most prolific interpreter's of Gershwin's compositions.

As a brilliant pianist and musician, Levant was at one point one of the highest paid performers on the circuit, leading numerous orchestras, including the Pittsburgh Symphony in November, 1939, at the age of 32. As his stock and involvement in other projects rose, so did his mental illnesses, his hypochondria, his sardonic demeanor, his drug addictions, and his smoking (at one point as much as five packs a day).

A master of the one-liner and the quickest of wits, Levant was a regular panelist on *Information Please*, a popular radio game show. He also hosted his own television program aired locally in Los Angeles.

In the mid 1940s, Levant appeared in a number of Hollywood musicals, notably playing the piano in the Gershwin biopic *Rhapsody in Blue*, and acting in two Fred Astaire films, *The Barkleys of Broadway* and *The Band Wagon*.

Later in his career he became a staple on *The Jack Parr Show*. Most of his appearances were live and, given his volatility and unpredictable character, he was always a treat for audiences.

Oscar Levant died at the age of 64. Never at a loss for wit, his epitaph was inscribed "I told them I was ill."

Jay and Alan Livingston

Jay: Born March 28, 1915—McDonald, PA
Died October 17, 2001– Los Angeles, CA

Alan: Born October 15, 1917—McDonald, PA

Brothers Jay and Alan Livingston (born Levison) grew up in McDonald, PA, a once flourishing oil town where their father, Maurice, owned Levison's Shoe Store. Both brothers were encouraged in the ways of music by their mother Rose, and every Saturday they would ride the train into Pittsburgh to take music lessons at Volkwein's. Jay's musical aptitude proved useful while attending McDonald High School; in fact, he penned the school's Alma Mater before graduating in 1933. Jay went on to the Wharton School at the University of Pennsylvania. While there, he befriended Ray Evans, who would become a best friend and lifelong collaborator.

Upon graduation Jay and Ray went to New York to become songwriters. There Jay arranged music for NBC and, together, they wrote for the theatre. After World War II, in Hollywood, they would write some of their most successful work, including "Buttons and Bows," Oscar-winner "Mona Lisa," the number one hit "Que Sera, Sera," and "Tinkle Bells." (The song was re-titled "Silver Bells" and sold over 140 million recordings). Additionally the two collaborated on television scores, writing theme songs to the successful series *Bonanza* (which Jay's brother Alan created) and the

Jack Buchanan as Jeffrey Cordova, Fred Astaire as Tony Hunter, Nanette Fabray as Lily Marton, and Levant as Lester Marton in the 1953 musical comedy film *The Band Wagon,* c. 1953. Pittsburgher Smoki Whitfield had a role, too.

ever popular *Mr. Ed* in which Jay's vocals are immortalized for those who have now heard of a talking horse, of course.

Considered by many to be the last of the great Hollywood songwriters, Jay Livingston and Ray Evans contributed songs to more than 80 films, won three Academy Awards and worked with some of the great composers including Percy Faith, Sammy Cahn, and Max Steiner.

Jay's younger brother Alan also graduated from McDonald High School, went on to attend Wharton and, after an advertising stint in New York, moved west. Hired by Capitol Records, his first success was the creation of the record-reader concept that included a fictional character he named Bozo The Clown. (Coincidentally the music was arranged by Billy May). A huge success for Capitol, Livingston went on to produce other children's recordings for Walt Disney, Walter Lantz (of Woody Woodpecker fame) and Warner Bros., writing the classic "I Taut I Taw A Puddy Tat."

Alan moved into adult-oriented music and was made a vice president. One of the first artists he was responsible for signing was Frank Sinatra—at the time in a career slump. Livingston's contract with Sinatra paired him with Nelson Riddle, rekindling "Swoonatra's" charm. Livingston left Capitol but was rehired several years later as President where he engineered contracts with evermore contemporary rock artists, like Steve Miller, The Beach Boys, and The Band (whom he helped name). And, in 1963, Alan took a leap of faith and signed a relatively unknown group from England named The Beatles. He brought home a "45" and played it for his wife. Livingston recalled, "She looked at me and said, 'I Want To Hold Your Hand'? Are you kidding?' I said, 'God, maybe I made a mistake!'"

Never forgetting their roots, the Livingston Brothers often attended their McDonald High School reunions.

Maurice Lucas

Born February 18, 1952—Hill District

Some athletes enjoy charmed lives, always having great teammates, always playing on championship teams.

So it was with basketball star Maurice Lucas.

Soft-spoken off the court, hard-hitting on it, Lucas was born in Pittsburgh in 1952. Standing 6'-9" and 215-pounds, Lucas grew up in the Hill District, playing on a scholastic team among the greatest in Pennsylvania history. With Lucas and legendary co-stars Jeep Kelly and Ricky Coleman, the 1971 Schenley squad took the State Championship, beating Norristown 77-60.

Recruited for basketball power Marquette, Lucas led the Warriors to the 1974 NCAA championship game. Although Marquette did not win, Lucas established himself as a national star, playing a full 40 minutes, leading his team with 21 points and 13 rebounds.

Joining the American Basketball Association's Spirit of St. Louis after his junior year, Lucas was traded to the Kentucky Colonels, where he became an All Star in his second season, 1975-76.

When the ABA merged with the NBA in 1976, and Lucas fell to the dispersal draft, the Portland Trail Blazers made him the second overall pick. Paying immediate dividends, Lucas led the Trail Blazers in virtually every category—scoring, minutes played, field goals, free throws, and rebounds. Not only did the Trail Blazers make the playoffs for the first time, but Lucas and teammate Bill Walton also led the squad past Los Angeles and Philadelphia to take the 1977 NBA title.

A three-time All Star for the Trail Blazers, Lucas was traded to New Jersey in 1980. Later playing for New York, Phoenix, Los Angeles, and Seattle, Lucas returned to Portland for his 14th and final season, 1987-88.

Serving as a Trail Blazers assistant coach in 1988-89, then as NBA Players Association vice president, in 2005 Lucas rejoined the Trail Blazers as an assistant coach. He lives in Portland with wife and three children.

Barbara Luderowski

Born January 26, 1930—Flushing, NY

Transforming a derelict factory into an international showplace, she changed the landscape of Pittsburgh art. In rehabilitating nine neighborhood buildings, she changed the perception of what was possible in the inner city.

By any yardstick, Barbara Luderowski's story is remarkable: how a widowed artist-sculptor came to town, created the Mattress Factory, which she still heads as Executive/Artistic Director, and assumed control of the long-dormant 10-property Garden Square North.

Born Barbara Simpson in Flushing, New York, in 1930, raised in Connecticut, Luderowski briefly attended Carnegie Tech before studying at New York's Art Students League

and Michigan's Cranbrook Academy of Art. A one-time General Motors designer, in 1972 she left her rural Michigan home to drive east. Passing through Pittsburgh, Luderowski had no intention of staying. However, she recalls, "there was something about the Mexican War Streets. It was a racially mixed community. The real estate values were good. I could take apart a building and put it back together. It all added up to a challenge—and an opportunity."

Three years after buying her home, she acquired a former Stearns and Foster mattress warehouse, inviting fellow artists to move in. By 1977, Luderowski had incorporated the Mattress Factory as a nonprofit museum, using its half-dozen stories and vast open spaces to accommodate hard-to-hang installation art. Because it not only offered great space, but also a hands-off approach to art, the Mattress Factory became a major stop on the arts circuit. In 30 years, more than 100 artists have created original installations, with the institution supporting some 200 more in residency programs—causing some to call the Mattress Factory the world's foremost enabler of installation art.

In 1994 the Mattress Factory was named development partner of Garden Square North, which Luderowski plans to make a magnet for arts, retail, and residency. "This," she says, "is an even greater opportunity."

Lucas of the Trail Blazers is mobbed by well-wishers as he returns to Portland early Saturday, June 4, 1977.

Gene Ludwig

Born September 4, 1937—Twin Rocks, PA

The flip of a coin was the deciding factor in whether he would continue to pursue his job in construction or whether he would pursue his real passion, music. Good thing for his legions of fans worldwide that whatever side ended up, it wasn't the one that would have sidelined one of the most talented jazz organists ever.

Gene Ludwig was born in the tiny coal-mining town of Twin Rocks, PA, about 15 miles north of Johnstown. When he was four years old his family moved to Swissvale when his father was hired at Westinghouse. He began taking piano lessons at an early age and soon found a real love for the music he was hearing over the radio. In particular, he loved the jazzy rhythm and blues numbers he heard Porky Chedwick spinning on WHOD in Homestead—artists like Bill Doggett and Wild Bill Davis. Despite 12 years of piano, and a mother who had hopes of her son becoming a classical pianist, it was the organ that would grab his attention and never let go. A frequent patron of area jazz clubs, like the Crawford Grill and The HiHat, Ludwig would get a chance to see first hand some of jazz's greatest talents, many of whom were natives, like Ray Brown and Ahmad Jamal. But it was an evening at the famed Hurricane where Ludwig saw jazz organist Jimmy Smith play and he was so taken by the playing of Smith that it was at that moment he decided the organ was what he wanted to play.

Ludwig assembled an organ combo with saxophonist Sonny Stanton that played in clubs around town. The gigs began to take him to towns outside of Pittsburgh and eventually on the road to places like St. Louis and Indianapolis. Recording dates soon followed and one of Ludwig's songs "Sticks and Stones," an instrumental version of the Titus Turner classic, received some airplay on local radio. In 1969 Ludwig got the chance to record with Sonny Stitt, an opportunity that he still reflects back on as one of the more important in his career.

Ludwig returned to Pittsburgh after his stint with Stitt and was a regular in places like The Balcony, The Crawford Grill and The James Street Tavern. He also was popular on the jazz festival circuit, appearing at the famed Montreaux Jazz festival in Switzerland, as well as playing Birdland in NYC and the San Francisco Jazz Festival.

In a career that has lasted in excess of 45 years, Gene Ludwig is highly regarded as a consummate professional, a master on the Hammond and an all around nice guy.

Lorin Maazel

Born March 6, 1930—Neuilly-sur-Seine, France

Like the old commercial says, "We accomplish more before 9:00 a.m. than most people do in an entire day." Lorin Maazel accomplished more by the age of 12 than most conductors do in an entire lifetime. Maestro Maazel made his conducting debut with the New York Philharmonic before he even turned 13, a post that he returned to four decades later and still holds today.

Lorin Maazel was born in France to American parents. At a very young age the family moved to Los Angeles. Music always filled the air in the Maazel household and young Lorin began to show signs of his prodigious talents as early as 8 months, when he would hum Brahm's "Lullaby." It is said that Maazel was discovered to have perfect pitch and a photographic memory at the age of 4.

His parents started him on violin lessons when he was 5 and conducting lessons at 7 with conductor and composer Vladimir Bakaleinikoff. When Bakaleinikoff accepted a position with the Pittsburgh Symphony as an associate conductor in 1939, the Maazel family followed and settled down in the East End of Pittsburgh. Over the course of the next several years, Maazel would conduct the Los Angeles Philharmonic, the NBC Symphony, and many other major American orchestras—all leading up to his New York Philharmonic debut at age 12.

Maazel enrolled at the University of Pittsburgh in 1947 where he studied philosophy, mathematics and languages. Concurrently, Maazel was a violinist with the Pittsburgh Symphony and served as an apprentice conductor. After Pitt, Maazel traveled to Italy to further his studies, and in 1953 made his European conducting debut. In 1960, Maazel became the first American to conduct at Bayreuth, the famed home of Richard Wagner. From there, Maazel conducted in Berlin, Cleveland, and Vienna, until 1988 when he was invited back to Pittsburgh to conduct the Pittsburgh Symphony Orchestra, solidifying the PSO's standing as a world class symphony. Maazel held his post as the music director of the Pittsburgh Symphony through 1996.

In the years following, Maazel has conducted in virtually all of the world's leading orchestras, has made over 300 recordings (including the complete works of Beethoven, Mahler, Tchaikovsky, Strauss, Brahms, Debussy, Schubert, and Rachmaninoff) and has received countless awards and distinctions. Additionally, Maestro Maazel is involved as a mentor to aspiring young musicians and is committed to various environmental and humanitarian causes.

Christopher Lyman Magee & William Flinn

Magee: Born April 14, 1848—Pittsburgh
Died March 8, 1901—Pittsburgh

Flinn: Born May 26, 1851—Manchester, UK
Died February 19, 1924—St. Petersburg, FL

Christopher Magee and William Flinn were Republican Party bosses active in Pittsburgh politics and business in the late 1800s. As a secretive team, they represent the closest thing to the notorious Tammany Hall of New York that Pittsburgh may ever have seen.

Magee's family was involved in the street car industry, and Magee served as president of the Consolidated Traction Company. He became active in politics through his uncle Squire Thomas Steele, the city controller, who served on the boards of several banks. Magee became city treasurer at just 21. He is most widely remembered as organizing the Republican Party machine and serving as its boss.

Flinn, who owned and operated a contracting business, received many of the city construction contracts in those years. His company built the Liberty Tunnels, Wabash Tunnels, and Armstrong Tunnels as well as the Holland Tunnel in New York City. He also served on the Pennsylvania General Assembly, was a state senator, and, as chairman of the local Party, was a delegate to the Republican National convention for almost 30 years.

In 1879, Flinn and Magee struck up a mutually beneficial partnership that helped Flinn win his seat in the General Assembly and quiet some of Magee's political enemies. Together they worked to change the city charter to grant more power to department heads and fuel Pittsburgh's post-Civil War industrial growth. Their partnership was exposed in Lincoln Steffens' 1903 book *The Shame of Cities* and eventually ended with Magee's death in 1901 and Flinn's loss to the Citizens Party, which passed several reforms to curb the Republican machine.

Flinn retired to his home north of Pittsburgh called Beechwood Farm, now Beechwood Farm Nature Reserve. His daughter's home, Hartwood, eventually became Hartwood Acres Park. Despite their reputations as political bosses, they are also remembered for developing the Pittsburgh Zoo, which was a gift from Magee to the city, and Magee Women's Hospital in Oakland which began as a maternity hospital in his home.

George Magovern

Born November 17, 1923—Brooklyn, NY

It is impossible to imagine modern cardiothoracic surgery without Allegheny General Hospital's Dr. George Magovern. In 1959, when he came to Pittsburgh, coronary artery bypass surgery and heart transplantation had never been done. Nuclear-powered pacemakers were inconceivable. Due to his efforts, that is no longer the case.

George J. Magovern attended Manhattan and Union Colleges, then Marquette University's medical school, 1943-47. Training in Kings County Hospital, St. Vincent's Hospital, New York Medical Center (Downstate), and George Washington University, by 1961 he made medical history by performing Pittsburgh's first heart valve replacement. The following year, 1962, Magovern performed the world's second lung transplant.

Always searching for better cardiothoracic solutions, spending countless hours in research, in the 1970s he helped develop a high-volume, low-pressure endotracheal tube, the Lanz Device, and in 1980 successfully pioneered the clinical use of small centrifugal pumps as left/right ventricular assist devices. That same year he performed the nation's first cardiomyoplasty procedure, in which back muscle is wrapped around the heart and trained to beat for it.

A dedicated educator, Magovern served as program director for Allegheny General's thoracic surgery residency program, teaching and advising thoracic surgery residents for some 30 years. A role model for students, Magovern also inspired his two sons, George Magovern Jr. and the late James Magovern, to join him as AGH cardiothoracic surgeons.

A scholar as well as a teacher, Magovern has written more than 200 scientific articles and, as holder of some two dozen academic appointments, has made countless presentations at a wide variety of medical conferences.

Johnny Majors

Born May 21, 1935—Lynchburg, TN

No one in Pittsburgh sports history had a more sudden, more profound impact than Pitt football coach Johnny Majors.

Although from 1955-63 the Panthers finished in the top ten six times, 1964-72 did not produce a single winning season. An exercise in futility, the Panthers finished 1-9 three times, then dropped to 1-10 in 1972.

To turn around the program, Pitt hired a proven winner, a scion of bona fide football royalty—who not only took the Panthers to a bowl game in his first year, but produced the team's first National Champion in four decades.

John Terrill Majors was the son of famed high school and Sewanee college coach Shirley Majors. One of five ball-playing brothers, Johnny Majors' high-school team won the 1951 Tennessee state championship. An All-American tailback at Tennessee in 1956, Majors' career netted him Hall of Fame honors in 1987. As coach at Iowa State, 1968-72, Majors took a perpetual loser to the team's first-ever bowl appearances in his final two seasons.

Coming to Pitt in 1973, Majors transformed a perpetual loser into a Top 20 ranking and a trip to the Fiesta Bowl—Pitt's first postseason appearance in 17 years. The following year, 1974, his 7-4 Panthers were ranked number 8. In 1975, his team went to the Sun Bowl. Finally, in 1976, Majors' 12-0 team trounced Georgia 27-3 in the Sugar Bowl to take Pitt's first—and only—National Championship since Jock Sutherland's Depression-era Panthers.

Returning to Tennessee to coach his alma mater, from 1977-92 Majors' Volunteers went to 11 bowls and took three SEC championships.

In 1993, back at Pitt, Majors coached the Panthers for four seasons, 1993-96, but failed to notch even a single winning season.

Henry Mancini

Born April 16, 1924—Cleveland, OH
Died June 14, 1994—Beverly Hills, CA

As a child he had learned to play a variety of instruments and as a teen he was already arranging and composing. With the help of his teacher Max Adkins, he sent one of his compositions off to his idol Benny Goodman. Goodman replied with an encouraging word, but candidly told the young Mancini he wasn't quite ready for the big time. Ironically, a little more than a decade later, it was Mancini who would score the music for the film *The Benny Goodman Story*.

Enrico Nicola Mancini was born in Cleveland, Ohio, but moved to the small town of West Aliquippa when he was still young. His Italian immigrant parents were insistent that Henry develop a talent and an appreciation for music. Exposing his son to the works of great Italian composers like Rossini and Puccini, his father Quinto, who labored as a steel worker, wanted to give his son a talent that could broaden his opportunities beyond the steel industry. Henry Mancini began taking piccolo lessons at 8 under the strict direction of his father, who would "whack" his son with the wooden perch from the bird cage whenever he played the wrong note.

His professional calling would become clear when on his 12th birthday his father took him to the Stanley Theatre to see Cecil B. DeMille's *The Crusades*. He was so captivated by the integral part that the music played in the action of the movie that he knew he wanted to write music for films. He assuredly would.

By the age of 14, now playing the piano, Mancini fell in love with the big band sounds of Benny Goodman, Artie Shaw, and his favorite, Glenn Miller. After graduating Aliquippa High School in 1942, Mancini studied for a brief time at Carnegie Institute of Technology before receiving a scholarship to the world-renowned Julliard School of Music. World War II cut short his studies. When he received his draft notice to join the Air Corp, he was directed to play in Major Glen Miller's 28th Air Force Band. (Sadly, Mancini never did play with Miller whose plane went missing). Upon his discharge, Mancini was hired to play piano for the Glen Miller Band, now led by Tex Beneke. It was during this time that Mancini met his wife-to-be Ginny O'Connor, who was a back-up singer with Mel Torme's band. The two moved to Los Angeles and were married. Mancini got some part-time work with Universal Studios that turned into a six-year run. From there, Mancini went on to compose and arrange some of the most beautiful and successful film scores Hollywood ever released, including *Breakfast At Tiffany's, The Days of Wine and Roses, Experiment In Terror, The Great Race, Victor/Victoria,* and *The Pink Panther*. He also composed work for television series, including the theme songs to *The Thorn Birds*, *Newhart, Remington Steele,* and *Peter Gunn*. He even composed the "Viewer Mail" theme for *Late Night With David Letterman*.

Mancini's body of work is by any measure astounding. He was nominated for 72 Grammy® Awards and won 20, nominated for 18 Academy Awards® and won 4, won a Golden Globe, and was nominated for two Emmys®. He recorded over 90 albums in all, of which eight were certified gold. And he conducted some of the world's greatest symphony orchestras.

Henry Mancini died at the age of 70, but his wife and three children have made certain his legacy lives on in Western Pennsylvania through the Geneva College annual Henry Mancini Musical Theater Award and the Henry Mancini Arts Academy at the Lincoln Park Performing Arts Center in Beaver County.

© Bettmann/CORBIS

Pete Maravich

Born June 22, 1947—Aliquippa, PA
Died January 5, 1988—Pasadena, CA

For pure ballhandling, passing, and shooting ability, many consider Pistol Pete Maravich the greatest offensive basketball player of all time.

Born in Aliquippa in 1947, Peter Press Maravich was the son of Press Maravich, a basketball coach and former player. Training from age 7, young Pete spent 10-hour days dribbling, passing, shooting—which he used to great effect as a scholastic, collegiate, and professional star.

Moving out of Pittsburgh as a pre-teen, Maravich grew to 6'5" and 198 pounds. Entering Louisiana State University in 1966, where his father was coach, in three varsity seasons, 1967-70, Maravich simply rewrote the NCAA record book. Averaging 43.8, 44.2, and 44.5 points per game, leading the  nation in scoring each year, during his senior year alone Maravich scored 50 or more points in 10 of LSU's 31 games. Named College Player of the Year in 1970, among other accolades, Maravich holds virtually every NCAA scoring record, including most career points (3,667), highest career scoring average (44.2 ppg), most field goals made (1,387), and most career 50-point games (28).

Picked third in the 1970 NBA draft by the Atlanta Hawks, Maravich averaged 23.2 points per game his rookie season. After four years in Atlanta, 1970-74, Maravich was traded to the New Orleans Jazz, where he led the league in scoring, 1976-77. Playing with the New Orleans-Utah Jazz, 1974-80, and Boston Celtics, 1980, after 10 seasons knee injuries forced Maravich's retirement. Overall, the five-time All-Star scored 19,948 points in 658 games, a 24.2 points per game average, good for 15th all-time.

Inducted into the Basketball Hall of Fame in 1987, the youngest player ever to receive that honor, Pistol Pete Maravich died of a congenital heart defect during a pick-up basketball game in Pasadena, 1988. Just 40 years old, he was buried in Baton Rouge, LA.

© Associated Press

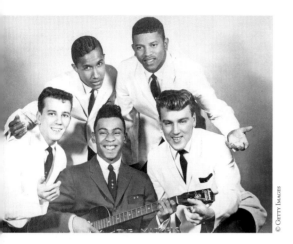

The Marcels

In the early 1960s a local singing group that honed its skills at Oliver-Allegheny High School on the North Side, recorded an unexpected smash hit which knocked Elvis Presley out of the number one spot on the charts.

Their name was taken from a popular hairstyle of the day called the Marcelle. The racially integrated quintet—(pictured from left clockwise) Richard Knauss, Fred Johnson, Gene Bricker, Bingo Monday, and Cornelius Harp—caught the ear of Colpix producer Stu Philips, when he received a blind demo tape. Philips invited the young men to New York to do some recording, despite not having any original material of their own. During the session on February 15, 1961, someone suggested singing the Rodgers & Hart standard "Blue Moon," but with a reworked intro. The "bompa-bomp, danga-danga ding-dong" cut was released. Famous New York disc jockey "Murray The K" got ahold of the single and reportedly played it 26 times during a single show. The reaction was overwhelming and within four weeks of its release the single had marched to the top spot on both the pop and R&B charts.

The Marcels followed their smash hit with a reworked Gershwin tune called "Summertime," barely cracking the Hot 100. Hollywood soon came calling and The Marcels were cast to perform their smash hit in *Twist Around The Clock* starring Chubby Checker and Dion. Their follow-up hit was also their last, a song called "Heartaches" which peaked at number seven on the charts.

Despite being in the limelight for a shorter period than they may have deserved, The Marcels are considered by many to be among the best vocal groups of all-time. Their hit "Blue Moon" is immortalized in the Rock & Roll Hall of Fame as one of the 500 Songs That Shaped Rock & Roll.

Dan Marino

Born September 15, 1961—Oakland

He was 23 and had nothing but time. Playing for the Miami Dolphins in Super Bowl XIX, 1985, future Hall of Fame quarterback Dan Marino faced Pittsburgh-area rival Joe Montana, leading the San Francisco 49ers. That day, the 'Phins were good, but the 'Niners were better—a lot better. Losing 38-16, Marino was not happy, but, as the youngest quarterback ever to take his team to the Show, "I felt I'd have more opportunities," he recalled. "But I never got back."

Daniel Constantine Marino, Jr., played 17 stellar NFL seasons, none better than the record-setting 1984 campaign in which he was the league's Most Valuable Player, throwing for more than 5,000 yards and 48 touchdowns.

Drafted in the first round, 1983, he came with all the credentials for greatness. Born in Oakland, 1961, and raised within walking distance of Central Catholic, he was a *Parade* All-American and a good enough baseball player to be drafted by the Kansas City Royals in 1979. But football was his passion, and his destiny, and he went to Pitt, 1979-82, where he was also an All-American. As a junior, in 1982, he led the Panthers to a last-minute Sugar Bowl victory over Georgia, throwing the game-winning touchdown pass with less than a minute to play. In four stellar seasons, Marino racked up numerous records, including throwing for more than 8,000 yards, with 79 touchdowns. Seeing the post-season every year, he led the Panthers to four major bowl appearances: Fiesta, Gator, Sugar, and Cotton.

Blessed with a powerful, accurate arm and incredibly quick release—his 1.9 seconds has been judged the single fastest in NFL history—from 1983-99 his Dolphins reached the post-season 10 of 17 seasons. Selected to the Pro Bowl in his rookie year, his first of nine appearances, he was the first rookie quarterback to start. Upon his retirement, Marino held virtually every NFL passing record, including most career touchdown passes (420) and most points scored (2,574). Perhaps the most astounding is his 61,361 career passing yards—the equivalent of passing a football across the entire state of Rhode Island.

Ben Roethlisberger, left, meets Hall of Fame Marino after taping an interview Tuesday, Nov. 2, 2004, in Pittsburgh.

After his retirement at 39, both Minnesota and Pittsburgh made him offers, but Marino, citing age, injuries, and family considerations, declined. Post-playing honors included the Dolphins retiring his number, 13, and erecting a statue in his honor at Miami's Pro Player Stadium. In 2003, he was inducted into the College Football Hall of Fame, and two years later into the Pro Football Hall of Fame.

Floridian, broadcaster, restaurateur, husband, and father of six, Marino has turned his celebrity status into a tool for helping children. Heading The Dan Marino Foundation, which he established in 1992 after a son was diagnosed with autism, he's raised millions of dollars for research, services, and treatment programs for children with neuro-developmental disabilities. The related Dan Marino Center, which opened in 1995 for the diagnosis and treatment of children at risk for developmental and psychological problems, treats nearly 50,000 children a year. "I'm in a unique position to help others," Marino has said. "I can help raise a lot of money. That's one of the reasons we started the foundation, as a vehicle through which we could channel that money to worthwhile causes."

Dodo Marmarosa

Born December, 1925—Larimer
Died September 17, 2002—Lincoln-Lemington

Michael "Dodo" Marmarosa was one of the finest bop pianists in jazz history. Having once pushed a piano off a third floor balcony to hear what chord it would make when it hit the ground, he was equally as enigmatic as he was talented.

Dodo Marmarosa grew-up on Paulson Avenue in the city's Larimer section, where he was buddies with another jazz legend-to-be, Erroll Garner. He was given the nickname Dodo because of his large head and his small body. Marmarosa was a child prodigy and a classically trained pianist who eventually turned his interests to jazz. One of his early inspirations was the extraordinary jazz pianist Art Tatum.

At the age of just 15, he was asked to sit in as the piano player for the Johnny "Scat" Davis Orchestra. He had developed a reputation as a solid player and his ability to read music made him even more of a hot item. Although his gig with Davis was short-lived, over the course of the next several years Marmarosa played with greats such as Gene Krupa, Tommy Dorsey (where he played alongside Buddy Rich), Charlie Barnet and Artie Shaw (where he played alongside fellow Pittsburgher and trumpet player Roy Eldridge). Shaw once described Marmarosa as "the best white modern jazz pianist of his time."

In his late teens, Marmarosa and a friend, musician Buddy DeFranco, were badly beaten up by a gang of soldiers who mistook them for draft dodgers, leaving Dodo in a coma for days. The event appears to have had a lasting impact that Marmarosa was never quite able to shake. His playing continued at high levels, but he was a changed man, fragile and troubled.

Marmarosa's immense talents didn't go unnoticed. In 1947 *Esquire* magazine published its annual jazz poll and listed Dodo Marmarosa, at just 21 years old, as its rising star. The list included such other jazz luminaries as Sarah Vaughan, Miles Davis and Pittsburgh bassist Ray Brown.

Marmarosa served briefly in the army in 1954, but was discharged after spending several months in the hospital with "emotional issues." He reportedly received electro-shock therapy whileunder care. Because of his poor health and emotional frailty, he returned to

Pittsburgh where he played an occasional set at The Colony Restaurant in Scott Township. His final performances were for the residents of the VA Medical hospital in Lincoln-Lemington, where he, too, resided. Dodo Marmarosa died in September of 2002.

George C. Marshall

Born December 31, 1880—Uniontown, PA
Died October 16, 1959—Washington, D.C.

Excluding Commanders in Chief, and thus Presidents Woodrow Wilson and Jimmy Carter, George C. Marshall is the only U.S. military officer to have won the Nobel Peace Prize. He was so honored in 1953, having served as Chief of Staff, as well as Secretary of State, for his economic recovery plan of Europe, the chapter in world history most students know today as the Marshall Plan.

A no-nonsense, soft-spoken leader, Marshall was born the son of a wealthy coal baron, George Marshall, who by the time of his son's enrollment in the Virginia Military Institute in 1897, was ruined by failed investments. Young Marshall showed early leadership po-

tential, if not academic prowess (he was just better than an average student,) by claiming the titles of top cadet, first corporal, first sergeant and first captain in each of his successive years of military training.

In February 1902, he entered the military as a second lieutenant of infantry, shipping off to the Philippines for his first command. Before returning there in 1914, Marshall proved his mettle as a staff officer in a number of U.S. posts, principally at Ft. Leavenworth. While in command in the Philippines again, he was recognized by General John Pershing for whom he would later serve five years as his aide. At the outset of World War II, Marshall managed the transfer of some 400,000 foreign troops, a mere fraction of the eight million men he would manage during the war.

In fact, Marshall may be credited best for increasing US military troops and capabilities prior to Pearl Harbor, at which time he then served as Deputy Chief, then Chief of Staff to FDR. Until 1945, Marshall was President Roosevelt's "go to" man in most every decision of the war. Intending to retire, Marshall was called to negotiate between warring interests in early Communist China, and dutifully followed President Truman's assignment to serve as Secretary of State. From 1947 to 1949, Marshall reorganized the State Department, represented the U.S. in the Council of Foreign Ministers, and laid the groundwork for his historic European Recovery Program. Never tiring, even after the removal of a kidney, he then served as Secretary of Defense, evading political suicide when he supported Truman's 1951 dismissal of General MacArthur from Korea. Incredulously, Marshall was also brought before Senator Joe McCarthy's "witch trials" for being soft on communism.

A five-star general upon his 1951 retirement, Marshall is buried in Arlington National Cemetery.

July 5, 1950, Marshall confers with Ike outside a senate subcommittee considering a bipartisan bill designed to set up a "Marshall Plan of Ideas" to halt Communism.

© BETTMANN/CORBIS

Rob & Kathleen Marshall

**Rob: Born October 17, 1960—Madison, WI
Kathleen: Born in 1962—Madison, WI**

Born in Wisconsin, but brought as toddlers to Pittsburgh by parents Bob and Anne, both Pitt professors, the three Marshall kids, Rob, twin Maura and little sister Kathleen, grew up on Beechwood Boulevard in Squirrel Hill. They all attended Falk School where they once filmed a spoof of *The Brady Bunch* as a class project. Introduced to the theatre by their parents, and inspired by Lenora Nemetz (for whom they created the Lenora Nemetz fan club,) the three Marshalls won their first-ever auditions and appeared as Von Trapps in the 1973 CLO production of *The Sound of Music*. They continued the following season in two CLO productions, *The King and I* and *South Pacific*, the latter featuring Lenora Nemetz and Don Brockett. For several summer seasons, Rob also apprenticed at the Odd Chair Playhouse in Bethel Park.

Rob and Kathleen both attended Taylor Allderdice. Rob went onto Carnegie Mellon and Kathleen to Smith College. Before graduating CMU in 1982, Rob toured in the national company of *A Chorus Line*. Kathleen returned often to the CLO where she earned her Equity

card, and then, upon graduation, followed her brother in the national tour of *Cats*. Rob herniated a disc during the run and decided then to work as a choreographer and director. He earned his first Broadway gig choreographing Chita Rivera in *Kiss of the Spiderwoman*, and brought his younger sister on as a dance assistant. They collaborated again in staging *She Loves Me*, then *Damn Yankees* with Jerry Lewis. When Rob went on to stage *Company* for the Roundabout Theatre, Kathleen earned her first show, choreographing *Swinging on a Star* in New Jersey, which later arrived on Broadway. Both had now found independent acceptance in the small world of Broadway's producers and directors.

In more recent years, Rob has earned significant fame for bringing musical theatre back to film, having won the Best Picture Oscar® in 2004 for *Chicago*. His next film musical is *Nine*. Meanwhile, Kathleen has triumphed on Broadway and television, translating the success of *The Music Man*, with Matthew Broderick, for ABC/Disney, and staging *Wonderful Town* on Broadway for a surprising run and a 2004 Tony© for Best Choreography. She also won a 2006 Tony® for choreographing *The Pajama Game* with Harry Connick, Jr. Sister Maura is an architect and designer, married with kids, in Washington, D.C.

Curtis Martin

Born May 1, 1973—Homewood

It must be the all-time oddest path to the Pro Football Hall of Fame, where he's a 2011 certainty.

As a boy, Curtis Martin never watched football, never went out for the football team. Growing up in Homewood, attending Taylor Allderdice, it was only after his mother pressed him to find an extra-curricular activity that Martin reluctantly chose football—as a senior. By the end of the Dragons' season, Martin had garnered a Pitt scholarship offer.

Unmemorable for his first two Panther years, Martin rushed for more than 1,000 yards as a junior—and seemed destined to be a first-round draft choice. After an ankle injury hobbled his senior year, in 1995 Martin was taken by New England in the third round—a distant 74th.

Then came the unexpected. As a rookie, playing at 5'-11" and 210 pounds, Martin rushed for more than 1,400 yards, was named

Offensive Rookie of the Year, and took his first of five trips to the Pro Bowl. The next year, Martin went to his second Pro Bowl—and ran the Pats to Super Bowl XXXI.

A free agent after 1997, Martin jumped to the New York Jets, where, playing for seven years, Martin earned three more Pro Bowl berths and helped make the Jets perennial play-off contenders. Taking the NFL rushing title in 2004, with nearly 1,700 yards, he tied the record of 10 straight 1,000-yard seasons.

In 2005, on track to be the first running back to lodge 11 straight 1,000-yard seasons, Martin was sidelined with a career-ending knee injury.

The fourth all-time NFL rusher with 14,101 yards, Martin also has more than 3,300 yards receiving and is one of only 16 players to score 100 or more touchdowns.

Currently living in Garden City, Long Island, Martin is highly active in charitable and Christian activities.

Hilary Masters

Born February 3, 1928—Kansas City, MO

Coming to Pittsburgh in 1983 to join one of the nation's premiere university creative writing programs, Hilary Masters brought unprecedented talent and boundless dedication to the lives and careers of his students.

Born Hilary Thomas Masters, he is the son of Edgar Lee Masters, sometime law partner of Clarence Darrow and the astonishingly prolific author of the 1915 classic *Spoon River Anthology*, as well as a dozen plays, 20 other volumes of poetry, six novels, and six biographies, including Lincoln and Mark Twain.

Raised by his maternal grandparents, Masters attended Kansas City public schools, then graduated from New Hampshire's Brewster Free Academy, 1944.

Enrolling in North Carolina's Davidson College, two years later he enlisted in the Navy. Discharged, Masters worked at a Washington newspaper before going to Brown University, graduating in 1952.

He moved to New York City and worked

for a press agency whose clients included Martha Graham, Jose Limon, and the Ballet Monte Carlo. Establishing his own agency, handling Off-Broadway theatres, in 1956 Masters founded *The Hyde Park Record*, a weekly newspaper.

By 1959 he had turned to full-time writing. Often concerned with abandonment—physical, spiritual, and moral—Masters' first novel, *The Common Pasture*, was published in 1967. Seven more novels followed, the last in 2006, plus two collections of short fiction, and two volumes of essays.

Masters' best-known—and best-received—work is his *Last Stands: Notes from Memory*, published in 1982 and 2004. A rich family history, the book's apex describes Edgar Lee Masters' last, nearly destitute years living in New York City's Chelsea Hotel.

Beginning college teaching in 1975, by 1983 Masters had come to Carnegie Mellon, where for a quarter-century his productivity, dignity, and leadership have inspired generations of emerging writers.

Living in the North Side's Mexican War Streets, Hilary Masters continues to write and teach in Pittsburgh.

Peter Matz

Born November 6, 1928—Pittsburgh
Died August 9, 2002—Los Angeles, CA

The two words most often used to describe Peter Matz's career are prolific and legendary. Matz arranged, composed, and conducted for some of the entertainment industry's greatest names, including Tony Bennett, Lena Horne, Peggy Lee, Carol Burnett, and most famously, Barbra Streisand.

Peter Matz was born in Pittsburgh, son of Louis N. and Alice Matz. Despite an education that steered him toward a career in chemical engineering, which Matz described as a result of his "terribly misguided youth," upon graduation from UCLA he immediately set out on the path of his illustrious career. He left for Paris where he would engage in an intense two-year music apprenticeship and immerse

himself in the lively Parisian music scene. In 1954 he returned to the states and settled in New York where he studied piano and music theory. His first work was as a rehearsal pianist for the Broadway production of *House Of Flowers,* starring Diahann Carroll and scored by the great American composer Harold Arlen (famous for the classic "Over The Rainbow.") His next project for Arlen was the show *Jamaica* starring Lena Horne. Arlen became a mentor to Matz and, as a result, his reputation and experience grew exponentially. He went on to do substantial work with Noel Coward before breaking off into the emerging medium of television where he composed and arranged the music for such popular hits as *The Jimmy Dean Show, The Kraft Music Hall*, and *Hullabaloo*.

The film industry beckoned and Matz began composing for some of Hollywood's biggest talents. His most important work of this period was with Barbra Streisand. His long association with Streisand included scoring her 1975 film *Funny Lady,* as well as arranging her 1964 album *People*, her 1965 TV special "My Name Is Barbra," her first five albums for Columbia Records, and her platinum recording *The Broadway Album*. Matz's other truly significant work was as composer, arranger, and conductor for *The Carol Burnett Show*, which ran for eight years and earned him an Emmy and three additional nominations.

In all, Matz's television credits included scoring more than 40 movies and serving as musical director on hundreds of specials as wide ranging as The Presidential Inaugural Gala to *The Muppets In Hollywood*. Some celebrities for whom he directed television specials include George Burns, Lily Tomlin, Bette Midler, and Dolly Parton.

Billy May

Born November 10, 1916—Lawrenceville
Died January 22, 2004—San Juan Capistrano, CA

Edward William May, the son of a roofer, played tuba in the Schenley High School band. May credits his doctor (who assumed that the tuba would be good therapy for his asthma) for recommending an instrument that afforded him so much down-time he could learn the art of composition while waiting out his turn to play. May however switched to the trumpet. After graduation, he wrote an arrangement for bandleader Charlie Barnet,

then on tour. Barnet so much liked the arrangement he fetched the young talent to play trumpet and write arrangements for his band. Then May's arrangement of the song "Cherokee" became a major hit during the swing era, as well as the signature song of Barnet's band.

During the 1940s May arranged and played trumpet for the bands of Glenn Miller and Les Brown before going to work for NBC's radio network. By the 1950s Capitol Records had hired him for a series of children's records. For the next couple of decades, May arranged music for many of the great recording stars of his day, helping to produce hits like "Walkin' My Baby Back Home" with Nat "King" Cole, "The Boy From Ipanema" with Peggy Lee and "Come Fly With Me" by Frank Sinatra. Additionally May arranged for Sammy Davis Jr., Nancy Wilson, Bobby Darin, Vic Damone, and in 1959, he won the Grammy® Award for Best Performance by an Orchestra for his "Billy May's Big Fat Brass." (That same year Pittsburghers Henry Mancini and Perry Como won Grammys for Album of The Year for *Peter Gunn* and Best Vocal Performance by a Male for "Catch A Falling Star," respectively). The "attacking" brass and the "slurping" saxophone were the signature sounds of many of May's arrangements.

As the big band sound fell out of favor, May diverted his attention to working in television and film, composing such memorable scores as the theme to *Emergency, The Mod Squad,* and *The Green Hornet*. Many of Billy May's arrangements can be found on the popular Ultra-Lounge CD series.

Bill Mazeroski

Born September 5, 1936—Wheeling, WV

"I was always a high fastball hitter," Bill Mazeroski said.

That's what he got from Yankee hurler Ralph Terry.

The irony is that baseball's biggest home run, ending the 1960 World Series, came from a lifetime .260 hitter who made the Hall of Fame for his defensive prowess.

© Associated Press

Born in Wheeling in 1936, William Stanley Mazeroski played varsity baseball for Warren Consolidated High, Tiltonsville, OH, as a 14-year-old. Earning the nickname "No Touch" for the incredible speed with which he turned the double play, Maz came up to the majors as a 19-year-old in 1956, played at 5"-11" and 180, and stayed for 17 seasons. A 10-time All Star, eight-time Gold Glover, he bagged 2,016 hits in 2,163 games, still holds the all-time single-season double play record, 161, and the all-time double play record with more than 1,700.

Retiring after the 1972 season, Mazeroski's incredible agility is reason enough to remember him. But it is for one swing of the bat on October 13, 1960, that he makes the Pittsburgh sports pantheon.

In the wildest World Series ever, the underdog Pirates played the lordly New York Yankees. Facing a team stocked with future Hall of Famers, including Whitey Ford, Mickey Mantle, and Yogi Berra, the Yankees simply crushed the Pirates—16-3, 10-0, 12-0. But the Pirates won the close ones, 6-4, 3-2, 5-2.

Game Seven, Forbes Field. With the game tied in the bottom of the ninth, 9-9, Mazeroski parked the second pitch over the left field wall, becoming the first player ever to end a World Series on a home run. The Pirates had been outscored 55-27, out-hit 91-60, but took the Series 4-3.

In 2001, the Veterans Committee finally recognized Mazeroski for his all-time defensive skills, inducting him into baseball's Hall of Fame. Retired, he and his wife live in Panama City, Florida.

Marian McCargo

Born March 18, 1932—Squirrel Hill
Died April 7, 2004—Santa Monica, CA

A Squirrel Hill native who lived on Bennington Avenue and attended The Ellis School, graduating in 1949, Marian McCargo was a young tennis star who defeated Maureen "Little Mo" O'Connor at Forest Hills for the Wightman Cup in 1950. But her fame was founded on playing supporting roles in early television series like *Perry Mason, The Man from U.N.C.L.E., Mannix,* and even *Gomer Pyle, U.S.M.C.*

In 1951, she married ad executive Richard Moses, a Yale Whiff n'Poof, in Los Angeles. They had four sons, Graham, William, Harry, and Rick. She divorced Moses in 1963 and found work as an actress by employing her natural beauty, which was often compared to that of Grace Kelly.

A single mom, she first appeared in *The Rogues*, a short-lived TV series with David Niven and Charles Boyer, in 1964. After a few more episodes of *Perry Mason*, she got her first film role in the 1966 *Dead Heat on a Merry Go Round*, starring James Coburn, and in which Harrison Ford had his first screen appearance. The film was forgettable. In 1968, she played Peter Lawford's wife in the Gina Lollobrigida vehicle, *Buona Sera, Mrs. Campbell*, and the following year, played Rock Hudson's wife in the successful *The Undefeated*, starring John Wayne. Her last film role was in *The Doctors' Wives* in 1971.

She married Alphonzo Bell, Jr., a widower with three sons of his own who would later serve eight terms as California's U.S. Representative. McCargo gave up pursuing the limelight to attend to his political career.

But in 1981, she landed the one role for which she is most remembered, that of Harriet Roberts, mother to Jordan, played by Morgan Fairchild, on *Falcon Crest*. Her real-life son, William R. Moses, played the role of Cole Gioberti in 140 episodes.

James McClelland, Jr., M.D.

Born May 20, 1845—Pittsburgh
Died November 14, 1913—Pittsburgh

A colleague once said James McClelland "gave himself unselfishly to the cause which he knew would bring much good to the whole world." He was devoted to the development of medicine and determined to bring advancements to Pittsburgh, including modern hospital facilities, new surgical techniques, and classes for the future nurses of Allegheny County.

One of 11 children, McClelland was born to Scottish-Irish parents who immigrated to Pittsburgh in 1816. After attending Western University of Pennsylvania, at the behest of his family physician, he followed his passion and studied medicine at Hahnemann Medical College. After graduation in 1867, McClelland returned to Pittsburgh as a surgeon for Pittsburgh Homeopathic Medical and Surgical Hospital. Soon after his appointment, he was elected to the board in 1869 and served as secretary, before becoming chairman in 1882. During his tenure, he performed complicated surgeries including amputations, tumor removals, and brain surgeries.

McClelland also devoted much of his time to improving the standard of care in Pittsburgh. He started

the Training School for Nurses in 1876 at Pittsburgh Hospital, the first of its kind west of the Alleghenies, and also helped establish the Homeopathic Hospital on Second Avenue in 1884. Although a precursor to the larger and more modern Homeopathic Hospital built in 1907 on Centre Avenue, which is now Shadyside Hospital, this institution was the first of its kind to offer state-of-the-art care accessible to the entire community.

Although his efforts were mainly local, McClelland gave guest lectures at Boston University School of Medicine and was Professor of Surgery at his alma Mater, Hahnemann Medical College from 1876-1879.

McClelland passed away in Pittsburgh, leaving behind his daughters, Sarah and Rachel, and his wife May at Sunnyledge, his estate on Fifth Avenue, which still survives today as a hotel and tea room.

Suzie McConnell-Serio

Born July 29, 1966—Brookline

By the time she was 22, Suzie McConnell Serio had an Olympic Gold Medal.

By the time she was 40, her name had become synonymous with the highest-level women's basketball—scholastic, collegiate, professional.

Even as a grade-schooler growing up on Dunster Street in Brookline, Suzie McConnell was a champion. Before her 14th birthday, her team at Our Lady of Loreto had taken a 1980 state championship.

Playing scholastic ball at Seton-LaSalle Catholic High School, McConnell led the Lady Rebels to a 35-1 record in 1984—and a PIAA State Championship.

At Penn State from 1984-88, playing at 5'-5" and 125 pounds the quintessential play-making point guard, McConnell led the Lady Lions to a 95-33 four-year record, four consecutive NCAA tournament appearances, and two Atlantic 10 Tournament championships (1985-86). A four-time All-Atlantic 10 Conference player, she still owns the top four assist-per-game seasons in Atlantic 10 history, ranks 10th nationwide in career points (1,897), second in steals (507), and first in assists (1,307)—the most assists ever by a college basketball player, man or woman. Before she graduated in 1988, McConnell was named the first First-Team All-American in Penn State women's basketball history.

After graduation, McConnell joined the 1988 U.S. Olympic team. Competing in Seoul, McConnell directed the offense, scored 8.4 points a game, and led her team to a Gold Medal victory. Four years later, in Barcelona, McConnell again served as point guard—as the Americans took a second medal, this one

bronze. She also played on a Gold Medal team at the 1991 World University Games.

By then, the two-time Olympian had returned to scholastic ball—as the highly successful girls basketball coach at Pittsburgh's Central Catholic High School. Head coach for 13 seasons, 1991-2003, McConnell-Serio led her teams to three PIAA state championships (1993, 2001-03), two runners-up (2000-2002), and five consecutive district championships (1999-2003). Reaching her 300th win in December 2002, she finished her high school coaching career with a 321-86 record, including a 120-10 record her last four seasons.

At age 32 she accepted an offer from the WNBA Cleveland Rockers, playing guard for three seasons, 1998-2000, taking Newcomer of the Year and All-WNBA First Team honors as she led her team to the playoffs.

After resigning from Central Catholic in January 2003, McConnell-Serio returned to the WNBA as head coach of the Minnesota Lynx. Taking a team that had finished 10-22 in the previous season, she led the Lynx to a best-ever 18-16 record and first-ever playoff appearance. The next season, 2004, she took a team picked to finish last and made a return trip to the playoffs—a success that netted her WNBA Coach of the Year honors.

However, the Lynx struggled in 2005-06. McConnell-Serio resigned mid-season, 2006.

Back in Pittsburgh, in April 2007 she was named head coach of the women's basketball program at Duquesne University.

Married to Brookline's Pete Serio, Suzie McConnell-Serio lives in Pittsburgh with her husband and four children.

David McCullough

Born July 7, 1933—Point Breeze

"If nations appointed historians laureate," the *Washington Post* wrote, "David McCullough would surely be ours."

The contemporary voice of American history—and the measured, mellifluous voice of PBS' *Smithsonian World*, *The American Experience*, Ken Burns' *The Civil War*, and many others—was born David Gaub McCullough in Pittsburgh in 1933. Raised on Glen Arden Drive, in a house that his father, Hax McCullough, co-founder of McCullough Electric, built in 1929, young David attended nearby Linden School, then Fox Chapel's Shady Side Academy. Spending Saturdays at Carnegie Institute, "I got a great sense of history from

growing up in Pittsburgh," he said.

Graduating in 1951, McCullough's father hoped that David would attend Pitt or Carnegie Tech, but his mother Ruth would have none of it. Believing that it was integral to the college experience to leave home, she sent McCullough—and his three brothers—to Yale.

Considering portrait painting, McCullough came under the tutelage of Pulitzer Prize winner Thornton Wilder. Often lunching with the author of *Our Town* and *The Skin of Our Teeth* (as well as *The Matchmaker*, later adapted into *Hello, Dolly!*), McCullough instead pursued literature, taking a 1955 honors degree.

After graduating, McCullough moved to New York to work at *Sports Illustrated*. McCullough then moved to Washington in the early 1960s to edit a United States Information Agency magazine; by 1964, he was writing for *American Heritage*. Finding Library of Congress photos of the horrific 1889 Johnstown Flood, he began to research the event. With a $5,000 book advance, McCullough, working nights and weekends, finished the book in three years. His 1968 *The Johnstown Flood*, compellingly told and meticulously researched, established him as a historian.

McCullough then cast about for a sophomore edition and recalled that a friend had wondered about the history of the Brooklyn Bridge, which McCullough had often walked across when in New York.

Interested, he first discovered a Pittsburgh connection: John Roebling, the bridge's designer, had settled in Saxonburg, Butler County, and had designed the first metal Smithfield Street Bridge. Second, there was no book-length study of the Brooklyn Bridge. Thus, McCullough's second project, 1972's *The Great Bridge*, was born.

Five years later, his 1977 *The Path Between the Seas*, the exhaustive study of the Panama Canal, made McCullough a national star. Hitting bookstores just as the Senate was debating the Panama Canal treaty, McCullough wound up testifying before a Senate committee and consulting with President Carter. He also won his first National Book Award.

Turning to biography, his 1981 *Mornings on Horseback* chronicled the life of the young Theodore Roosevelt; it, too, won a National Book Award.

After publishing a series of biographical sketches, *Brave Companions*, in 1992, his monumental *Truman* appeared in 1993, netting McCullough his first Pulitzer Prize.

Nine years later, his 2002 *John Adams* sold more than two million copies, spent a solid year as a *New York Times* bestseller, and brought McCullough his second Pulitzer.

His year in the life of the Republic, *1776*, was published in 2005.

David McCullough lives and works in West Tisbury, Martha's Vineyard.

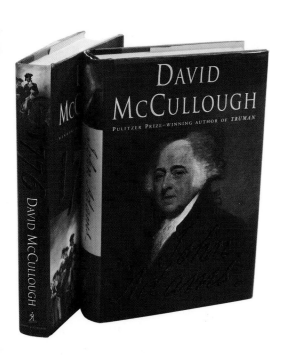

Frances McDormand

Born June 23, 1957—Chicago, IL

Most famous for her turn as Marge Gunderson in the Coen Brothers' instant classic, *Fargo*, Frances McDormand, who won an Oscar® for the role, is an actress whose love of acting can be attributed directly to the auditorium of Monessen High School. Mrs. Davies, her English teacher, was well aware that the shy, quiet girl hiding behind her glasses and long hair harbored a passion for Shakespeare. Her first performance was as Lady MacBeth.

Born in Chicago, she was adopted by Vernon and Noreen McDormand, a Disciples of Christ pastor and registered nurse, respectively. Charged with restoring faith in ailing churches, the family, including adopted daughter Dorothy, moved often, but landed in Monessen at the First Christian Church. McDormand was an outsider, a late-comer and different. About her high school theatre, she said in a *New Yorker* interview, "You can either play the lead girl or you can play the girl who wears a cowgirl outfit and sings a song. For me, there was no choice. It had to be the cowgirl."

McDormand was the only theatre major of her 1979 Bethany College graduating class. She went right on to the Yale School of Drama ('82) and then roomed with classmate Holly Hunter in NYC while waiting tables. She met Joel and Ethan Coen when they cast Holly for the lead role in *Blood Simple*. But Hunter had a conflict, and so they cast McDormand. The film was well received. The Coens then wrote and produced *Raising Arizona*, starring Hunter and Nicolas Cage, and featuring McDormand. Some forgettable TV work later, McDormand awoke critics with *Mississippi Burning*, another Coen success, for which she was nominated for an Oscar®. And, as though one nod was not enough, she was nominated for a Tony® the same year (1988,) for her Broadway role as Stella Kowalski in *A Streetcar Named Desire.*

After a slew of films directed by the Coens, Robert Altman, Tim Robbins, and Tommy Lee Jones—some flops, some made for TV, and some applauded—she married Joel Coen in 1992, and two years later, don'tcha know, she won her Oscar for *Fargo*.

One of the best character actresses of her generation, McDormand's more recent work includes Michael Chabon's *Wonder Boys*, filmed in Pittsburgh in 2000, and *Something's Gotta Give*, with Jack Nicholson, in 2003. She will star in the title role of *Miss Pettigrew Lives for a Day* in 2008.

Margaret McFarland

Born July 3, 1905—Oakmont
Died September 12, 1988—New York, NY

She was in many ways the woman behind the famed cardigan. Dr. McFarland, a child psychologist at the University of Pittsburgh, served as mentor and consultant to Fred Rogers in creating the content of the groundbreaking *Mister Rogers' Neighborhood* television series. In fact, Rogers would say that his approach to the show was based on the teachings of McFarland, with an important central message: in teaching, attitude matters above all.

McFarland's effect on child psychology was not solely based on the tube. In addition to writing numerous papers, she helped establish the department of child development and child care within the department of psychiatry at the University of Pittsburgh's School of Medicine. She also was a co-founder along with famed psychologist Dr. Benjamin Spock and Erik Erikson of the Arsenal Family and Children's Center in 1953. She served as its director until 1971.

But it was while at Pitt that she met Rogers, who was studying child development in preparation for developing his children's show. The two struck up a personal and working relationship, McFarland noting that Rogers was "more in touch with his childhood than anyone I have ever known." From McFarland, Rogers picked up an important mantra: "Attitudes aren't taught, they're caught."

Joanne Rogers remembers the relationship between her husband and McFarland. "For as long she lived, he had sessions with her every week," she recalls. "He worked with her a lot so he was always learning. They worked on scripts together, and she was able to tell him—in a clinical way—what was going on in the inner lives of children he was communicating with."

The two continued working together even though McFarland accepted a position as associate professor of psychology in Columbia University's psychiatry department, where she also earned a master's degree and doctorate. She died in 1988 at the age of 83 after a long illness. However, her contributions to the field continue to be recognized. Historian David McCullough called her "one of the most influential teachers of the past 50 years."

Colleen McKenna

Born May 31, 1948—Springfield, IL

It was in the mid-1980s when little Collette McKenna, just five years old, wailed at her mother Colleen, who had just given birth to Collette's third younger sibling, "we've got too many McKennas!" that an idea—and a franchise—was born.

Transforming her four madcap McKenna kids into the troublesome, all-too-human Murphys, Colleen McKenna was on her way to selling some three million children's books.

Born Ruth Colleen O'Shaughnessy, she moved to Pittsburgh as a four-year-old. First setting her sights on writing as a shy eighth-grader at Fort Couch Middle School, she sent three scripts to the television hit *Bonanza*. No sale, although McKenna did receive a treasured rejection letter.

Off to Slippery Rock for a 1970 elementary education degree, she taught at Bethel Park—and loved it. Finding herself with 36 noisy kids, she wrote plays to keep them quiet. Married in 1972, McKenna retired to raise a family. Living in Shadyside, within a decade, she was looking for a diversion. Encouraged to take Marilyn Hollinshead's famed children's book writing workshop at her Shadyside-based Pinocchio Bookstore, by 1987 McKenna turned out three manuscripts, which Hollinshead passed on to Scholastic Books. When *Too Many Murphys* hit bookstores, McKenna's career was made.

Turning out roughly two books a year over the last 20, McKenna has continued to use her children—and now her six grandchildren—as models for her characters. Known to be quick and adept, she was also tapped to pen two young-adult *Dr. Quinn, Medicine Woman* novels, based on the award-winning Jane Seymour television series.

Inaugurating a new series in 2001 with *Third Grade Stinks*, McKenna includes a multi-cultural cast. "I wish I had known at 40 what I knew in third grade," she says, "what's funny and good about the world."

Colleen McKenna continues to live and write in O'Hara Township.

Andrew Mellon

Born March 24, 1855—Pittsburgh
Died August 26, 1937—Southampton, NY

The sixth child of Judge Thomas Mellon, founder of the banking empire now merged with the Bank of New York, is responsible, if only by an age difference of three years from that of his brother Richard B. Mellon, for amassing the incredible wealth of industrial fortunes that are Pittsburgh's legacy.

Long before he inherited his position in his father's new bank, both Andrew (A.W.) and Richard (R.B.) were entrusted to build businesses in the region—their first a lumberyard in Carnegie, PA. Each was assigned important duties as young men. Even at just 17, Andrew was sent to Philadelphia to wrest control of a theatre from its owner (then in arrears to the judge,) as well as to recruit a new and more suitable owner for the venue.

Andrew, like his father, was introverted, calculating and tireless in his work ethic. But he valued his younger brother's more outgoing persona, and, once in full control of the bank, gave up half of it to Richard. Almost immediately, they diversified their financial holdings and created the Union Trust Company. Together, they championed controlling interests in fledgling start-ups like the Aluminum Company of America, Carborundum Company, Koppers Coke and Coal, dozens of smaller specialty steel firms, and, early in the 20th Century, the Spindletop Oil gusher, which became Gulf Oil Corporation.

Uncompromisingly formal—it is said he always addressed his good friend as "Mr. Frick"—he quite suddenly fell head over heels for a young British lady while on a transatlantic cruise and implored her to marry him within the year, 1898. Two years later, his one marriage to Nora McMullen, gave them two children, Ailsa and Paul, but ended in a bitter and costly divorce in 1911. Mellon was said to have influenced the opportune passing of Pennsylvania divorce laws just prior to his public trial.

Ever the influential financier, in 1921, A.W. was appointed Secretary of the Treasury and he served in good favor with three Presidents—Harding, Coolidge, and Hoover—reducing the national debt by half and imposing the first Republican taxation scheme for trickle-down economics. But the public, much poorer for the Crash of 1929, distrusted his capitalist ways, and Mellon resigned his post in 1932, accepting instead the Ambassadorship to the UK. He served in that post for just one year.

Before his sudden death (while on a rare vacation to visit his daughter on Long Island,) A.W., along with R.B., had created the Mellon Institute, and proposed the gift of his vast art holdings to a national repository.

Nephew Richard King Mellon and son Paul flank the former Secretary of the Treasury and U.S. Ambassador, year unknown.

Paul Mellon

Born June 11, 1907—Pittsburgh
Died February 1, 1999—Upperville, VA

"I have been an amateur in every phase of my life," he wrote in his autobiography *Reflections in a Silver Spoon*, including, "an amateur connoisseur of art" and "an amateur museum executive."

For an amateur, a man who never lifted a brush or held a chisel, Paul Mellon changed the face of American art, raising the bar for philanthropy, and, with his family, creating and endowing America's greatest public art museum, Washington's National Gallery of Art.

Born in Pittsburgh in 1907, scion of the great banking family, after attending Choate, Yale, and Cambridge, Mellon returned to Pittsburgh to work for the bank. By 1935, however, he had relocated to Virginia, where he spent the rest of his life.

Son of the great philanthropist Andrew W. Mellon, Paul Mellon followed his father into collecting—and donating. Shortly before his father's 1937 death, construction began on the new National Gallery, for which Andrew Mellon had provided both construction funds as well as a significant art collection. Four years later, 1941, Paul Mellon presented the nation both the magnificently designed building and 115 paintings.

Mellon served on the museum's board for more than four decades. Commissioning I.M. Pei's design of the new East Wing in the 1970s, Mellon also provided funds for its construction. By the time of his death, Mellon had also donated more than 1,000 art works, including some by such masters as Vincent van Gogh, Paul Gauguin, Winslow Homer, Edgar Degas, Auguste Renoir, and Pablo Picasso.

In addition, Mellon donated his extensive collection of British art to Yale University, along with funds sufficient to create the Louis Kahn-designed museum to house it. To the Virginia Museum of Fine Arts, Mellon also gave more than 2,000 art works.

Thomas Mellon

Born February 3, 1813—Castletown, County Tyrone, Northern Ireland
Died February 3, 1908—Pittsburgh

Born Thomas Alexander Mellon, Jr., on a farm near Ulster, he emigrated to Baltimore at the age of five with his parents, Andrew and Rebecca. Here, in Westmoreland County, his grandparents had already settled. The Mellons were all farmers. But at the age of fourteen, inspired by the words of Benjamin Franklin, Thomas Mellon chose not to work the land, but his mind. He enrolled in the Western University (Pitt) and graduated when he was but 19. Mellon entered law and built a solid reputation for himself, first working for the County Prothonotary, and then starting his own firm in 1838.

He was married on August 22, 1834, to Sarah Jane Negley (also born on February 3), a woman considerably above his station, which caused some parental consternation in their courtship. However, they were blessed with a growing income, as well as eight children, of whom Andrew and Richard were the two youngest surviving children. (A younger brother George died at nine, and their two immediately older sisters died in infancy).

In 1859, Thomas Mellon was elected to the Court of Common Pleas. He would forever be known as "the Judge," but after 10 years on the bench, with a small fortune amassed from real estate ventures, he chose to open a banking house at 514 Smithfield Street. Just above the shingle announcing the enterprise of T.

Mellon & Sons, was perched a bust of Benjamin Franklin.

From the start, January 2, 1870, Andrew (or A.W.) and Richard (or R.B) worked for their father in the banking business. Their timing might not have been better; with fewer assets and younger clients, the bank survived one of the country's more devastating crashes, the collapse of 1873, when more than 50 of the 90 banks in the region failed. It was at this time, too, that a young Henry Clay Frick, seeking a loan of $20,000, first made the acquaintance of both the judge and young A.W., with whom he would remain good friends throughout his career. In 1882, the judge handed the bank over to his son A.W., who within the same year, gave up half to his brother. Together they would create one of the largest banking institutions in the U.S., Mellon Bank.

Ever serious, devout, and frugal, Judge Mellon died on his birthday in his Calvinist home, one renowned for its absence of light, color, or warmth.

Adolphe Menjou

Born February 18, 1890—Hill District
Died October 29, 1963—Beverly Hills, CA

Born at 75 Elm Street in the Hill, an address that no longer exists, and raised in the Café Royale, a long-lost restaurant managed by his parents, on Fifth Avenue between Smithfield and Wood, Adolphe Menjou was reared by his French grandmother in the heart of downtown Pittsburgh. Known for his suave and debonair manner, his impeccable European tastes, and a sartorial splendor unmatched on-screen or off—he was said to have owned more than 200 different overcoats—Menjou appeared in as many films and was the epitome of Hollywood's European chic for many years.

Actress Celeste Holm shares a "cuppa" with Mesta, 1958.

"I started this best-dressed-man business as a deliberate stunt when I first came to Hollywood in 1920," he once told a reporter. Educated at Culver Military Academy and Cornell University, Menjou knew what he was doing when first he left home to try his fortunes on Broadway. Within a month, however, he was farming on Long Island. But then he tried again, getting a bit part in a silent film at Vitagraph Studios in New York. Several films followed. Then World War I broke out. Menjou was captain of an ambulance squad in France.

Upon his return, he headed out to Los Angeles and plied his trade in several silent films until he got his big break. In 1921, he landed significant roles in three major movies: *The Sheik* starring Rudolph Valentino, *Through the Back Door* starring Mary Pickford, and *The Three Musketeers* starring Pickford's husband, Douglas Fairbanks.

Then came stardom. Producing a feature to be titled *A Woman of Paris,* Charlie Chaplin was seeking a debonair Frenchman to take the romantic lead. Menjou fit the bill.

In 1931, he was nominated for Best Actor in *The Front Page*, playing Walter Burns in last minute casting. Soon after, classics like *A Farewell to Arms* (1932), *Forbidden* (1932), *Little Miss Marker* (1934), *Morning Glory* (1933), *A Star Is Born* (1937), *Stage Door* (1937), and *Golden Boy* (1939) were added to his credits.

Menjou's career was never as consistent as his fashionable persona or the trim of his trademark mustache. In the 1940s, he led the ranks of the right-wing elite, supporting Senator Joe McCarthy's Communist paranoia, but never "outed" fellow actors.

His last film role, played purposely against type, was as a rumpled curmudgeon in Disney's *Pollyana*.

Perle Mesta

Born October 12, 1889—Sturgis, MI
Died March 16, 1975—Oklahoma City, OK

Known as the "Hostess with the Mostess" after the Irving Berlin song of the same name, Pearl Skirvin Mesta was born in Sturgis, MI, a daughter of Oklahoma oil and real estate tycoon William Skirvin. She moved to New York City in 1915 and met George Mesta, owner of Mesta Machine Company at a dinner party hosted by her aunt. They married in 1917 and settled into the Mesta Mansion in West Homestead.

Perle (she changed the spelling in 1944) quickly immersed herself in the welfare and social concerns of the Mesta employees. Through her efforts, George started a cafeteria and hospital at the plant and established a program to provide two hours of schooling with pay each day for young apprentices. George's death in 1925 left Perle in charge of the company for a time.

In 1949, President Truman appointed her Minister to Luxembourg, and she used her legendary party skills as a tool for solving diplomatic problems. Her later years were devoted to lecturing, writing, and entertaining. She died in Oklahoma City in 1975 and is buried in the Mesta mausoleum in Homewood Cemetery.

Mary Lou Metzger

Born November 13, 1950—Pittsburgh

Pittsburgh can lay claim to two marvelous contributions to the "wunnerful, wunnerful" world created by Lawrence Welk and his musical family. Host, conductor, and sometime accordionist of *The Lawrence Welk Show* from 1955 to 1982 (not including another 10-plus years of repackaged reruns on PBS stations across the country,) Lawrence Welk was to squeaky-clean entertainment as Marcel Marceau was to mime, but without all the controversy.

In preparation for Lawrence Welk's band scheduled to play the 17th floor ballroom of the William Penn, in 1938 hotel engineer Ludwig Dernoshek created a nifty little machine, made from a simple fan and a clock motor with soldered wands, which blew soap bubbles into the air. Lawrence Welk, whose lively repertoire was often promoted as "champagne music," loved the device so much he toured with the "bubble machine," later incorporating the device in his first broadcasts in 1955.

Pittsburgh's other great contribution to the show is Mary Lou Metzger. Born the only child of Helen and Ernie Metzger, Mary Lou was singing and dancing on the Steel Pier in Atlantic City when she was just 7. Cast in a few community theatre productions, she was spotted while performing in *The Crucible* and auditioned for the part of Amarylis for the touring production of *The Music Man*. 299 performances later, she returned to her family who had moved to Philadelphia. She attended Temple University, won a music competition at Drexel, and went to L.A. to tape the *All American College Show*. While there, she was auditioned by Lawrence Welk in front of a live audience and hired to sing and dance with his musical family. Metzger, first appearing on the Mother's Day show in 1970, was often Welk's dance partner in the closing number of another 12 years of shows. (In all, the Lawrence Welk Show aired weekly for 26 years, and since 1987 has been a re-run staple of PBS).

In 1973, Metzger married the show's tuba player, Richard Maloof. Today, Metzger is an associate producer of the Welk Organization's many theatrical and television specials. She conducts many of the interviews of Welk alumni seen on repackaged shows most every Saturday night on WQED.

Long-time Lawrence Welk executive producer Bob Allen and Metzger make precious memories for a 2005 show.

Bret Michaels

Born March 15, 1963—Lyndora, PA

One has to wonder how a menacing figure like Hall of Fame Steeler Jack Lambert had any relationship to the former lead singer of a 1980s big-hair glam band. But it was Lambert's tenacity and willpower to win that gave Bret Michaels' his drive to succeed in the music industry at all costs.

Born in Lyndora, PA, right outside of Butler, Bret Michael Sychak has been a mainstay on the rock scene for more than 20 years, primarily as the former lead singer for the rock band Poison. His family relocated to Mechanicsburg, outside of Harrisburg, when Michaels was young. After graduating from Mechanicsburg High School, Michaels found work busing tables. On the side he formed a band called Paris and played the Harrisburg club scene. In 1985, Michaels took his tip money, bought a used ambulance for $700, and headed out to L.A. Once there., the band, now calling themselves Poison, became a hot ticket along the famed Sunset Strip playing clubs like The Roxy and Pandora's box—clubs that spawned rockers like Van Halen, Motley Crue, and Guns N' Roses. Poison was among the glam rock set, with big hair, lipstick, eye shadow, and a reputation for wild stage shows.

© CORBIS

In 1986 the band was signed to Enigma Records and released their debut album *Look What The Cat Dragged In*. Sales were good for the band's debut, but it was their follow-up release *Open Up And Say… Ah!* that would sell over eight million copies and produce their biggest hit "Every Rose Has Its Thorn." The band's third release went multi-platinum and their momentum appeared to be unstoppable.

Tensions within the band began to mount and their lead guitarist C.C. DeVille was kicked out following an altercation with Michaels backstage at the 1991 MTV Video Awards. Sales of the band's fifth release were disappointing and then in May 1994, Michaels was involved in an auto accident and badly injured. The band continued to record and tour and even saw the reunification of Michaels and DeVille.

A lifelong diehard Steelers fan, Michaels stopped in at Three Rivers Stadium on December 3, 2000, to sing the national anthem before a packed home crowd. In 2006 Poison celebrated its 20th anniversary together with a tour that was among the most successful of the summer and then in 2007 VH1 announced plans for a Bret Michaels reality show called *Rock Of Love With Bret Michaels*.

Poison has had 10 Top 40 singles and sold in excess of 25 million albums.

Delvin Miller

Born July 5, 1913—Woodland, CA
Died 1996—Meadow Lands, PA

He came up as a high school racer in the era of county fairs and back-lot contests. Following his grandfather to the harness track, he became an internationally known—and revered—breeder, trainer, driver, owner, and executive. From 1929 until his 1996 death, Delvin Miller transformed a farm boy's love of horses into an eight-decade, Hall of Fame career. Wearing his trademark brown-and-gold racing silks, the slight, small-boned man notched more than 2,400 wins—and took home $11 million in prize money.

With an innate decency and sunny personality that caused him to be universally known as Harness Racing's Goodwill Ambassador, Delvin G. Miller was born of Pennsylvania stock in Woodland, CA. As a child, his family moved back to the Avella farm that had been Miller land since 1795. Just 5'-6"—perfect for a racing sulky—he played hooky from high school to compete in his first race at the Burgettstown Fair. Miller's first purse: $8.00.

A three-sport letterman in high school, Miller briefly attended Penn State, considering veterinary science, but returned home instead to go in the horse business. Spending the Depression racing throughout the region, Miller ran horses on Pittsburgh tracks in Schenley and South Parks, along with dozens throughout West Virginia, Ohio, and New York. Called Little Pennsylvania by the touts, Miller's skilled horse handling led him to win such prestigious races as the Hambletonian, Little Brown Jug, and Kentucky Futurity. Training and driving countless standardbred horses, the horse with whom Miller is most associated, Adios, was born in 1940 in Indiana. Acquiring the multiple world champion in 1948, Miller turned him out to stud. Arguably

the greatest stud in harness racing history, Adios sired some 589 offspring, including eight Little Brown Jug winners. In addition, two of Adios' sons, Adios Butler and Bret Hanover, won harness racing's Triple Crown.

Two years after Adios' 1965 death, Miller named an annual race in his memory. Now the Coors Delvin Miller Adios, it is Pennsylvania's richest harness race for three-year-olds. The $1 million, week-long August event takes place at The Meadows, Pennsylvania's first pari-mutuel harness racing track, which Miller opened in 1963 close by his own Meadow Lands farm. (Ironically, although he competed in the Adios, Miller never won the race).

Competing on six continents, winner of innumerable awards, at 75 Miller was still breaking records—and was still racing three months before his death. Inducted into the Harness Racing Hall of Fame in 1968, the U.S. Trotting Association also named Miller racing's Man of the Century. A man who gave out honors as well, in 1985 he formed the Delvin Miller Amateur Drivers Association to promote the sport among amateurs; he also created the Harness Tracks of America Red Smith award to honor outstanding horse caretakers.

Dedicated to this region's past, in 1969 Miller joined his brother Albert in opening the Meadowcroft Museum of Rural Life.

A year after his 1996 death, at age 83, New Jersey's Meadowlands created the Delvin Miller Memorial Race in his memory.

Dennis Miller

Born November 3, 1953—Castle Shannon

The oldest of three boys and a sister whose father disappeared when he was 7, Dennis Miller was by some accounts a shy and nondescript kid at St. Anne's Elementary in Castle Shannon. Not until he attended Keystone Oaks High School, (which was then brand new), did his penchant for ranting sardonic diatribes come forth. His comic comments were heard not in the classroom, but at the dinner table among many welcoming families for whom the Miller boys were regular guests. Hardworking Mom, Norma Miller, was busy as a dietician at the Baptist Home.

Miller graduated from Keystone Oaks in

1971 and attended Point Park College, graduating with a degree in journalism in 1976. Among his many early jobs was writing sports commentary for the *South Hills Record*, driving a flower truck and working the deli counter in Kennedy Township's Giant Eagle.

His local break came when KDKA's *Evening Magazine* toured a few nightclubs to highlight local talent. Miller was doing stand-up at Brandy's in Oakland. (He had already crafted his show while first working at the Oaks Lounge in Castle Shannon). Miller was asked to do a few taped segments for KDKA and was then offered the job of providing audience warm-ups for Patrice King Brown's live afternoon talk show, *Pittsburgh 2Day*. Within the year, Miller was host of *Punch Line*, KDKA's short-lived attempt at a teen show, which in 1981, occasionally introduced a new music video. Miller's quip: "And, now, Flock of Seagulls—not your average polka band."

His national break came when Lorne Michaels caught his act at Budd Friedman's Improv in L.A. and hired him for the *SNL* news desk, a job he commanded for six years. Few know today that Miller was invited to the Improv by Jay Leno, who was as yet "undiscovered." And fewer know that Miller's two brothers also worked there—Rich as a bouncer, and Jimmy, backstage, building a clientele of young talent. Today, Jimmy is one of the hottest agents in L.A., having guided Jim Carrey and Jennifer Lopez to fame. Rich also runs his own artist management company.

Though known to millions as the literary, quick-tongued, and equally fast-thinking comic, Miller's career is still evolving. From *Saturday Night Live* to his own late-night *Dennis Miller Show* (which was pulled after only six months) to serving as the most un-

likely host of *Monday Night Football* to his current XM Satellite radio show, Miller has appeared on countless talk shows, a few movies and is, for many, a resolute voice of the right-of-center. Some know him, too, as a solid family man, married to former model Ali Epsley and as a father of two sons, Holden and Marlon. Of marriage, Miller has said, "I'm sure of two things—first, never wallpaper together, and second, you'll need two bathrooms... both for her. The rest is a mystery, but a mystery I love to be involved in."

Ming-Na

Born November 20, 1963—Macau, China

If Pittsburgh has a Chinatown, it is a single restaurant downtown, favored for more than 60 years by mayors, members of city council, lawyers, and business associates, called appropriately, The Chinatown Inn. Once owned by her step-grandfather, and now managed by her half-brother, Jonathan, and his wife Wei Yee, The Chinatown Inn offers a wall of honor to Ming-Na Wen, but not because she was a waitress there. Unlike most actors, she will admit she was not a good waitress.

Born on Coloane Island, Macau, Ming-Na and her mother Lin Chan, a nurse, immigrated to New York, landing briefly, before she met Soo Lim Yee, remarried, and settled in Pittsburgh to help run the family's restaurant. Ming-Na, which roughly translates to "enlightenment," was 9 at the time. She went to Mt. Lebanon High School. "I was the only Asian. I got into fights all the time. I'd rebel, skip school, and go to the movies. At the same time, I was an A student." She graduated in 1981, having performed in many school productions. "I'm one of those people," said the actress, "who always knew what I wanted to do."

She attended CMU and received her BFA in theatre arts in 1986. Two years and dozens of off-off-Broadway productions later, she was cast as Lien Hughes on CBS's *As The World Turns*, playing the first Asian-American character ever on a soap. In 1993, she was cast by Director Wayne Wang to play June in the film adaptation of Amy Tan's *The Joy Luck Club*. And, in 1995, she took on the recurring role of Dr. Deb Chen in the John Wells NBC production of *ER*. The role was not written for an Asian woman, but Ming-Na auditioned anyway and changed the producers' minds. She appeared in the first season, then returned for seasons six through 11.

From 1995-97, she played Trudy Sloane in the sitcom, *The Single Guy*. Cast against type again, she played Wesley Snipe's wife in *One Night Stand*.

In 1998, she lent her voice to Disney for the title role of *Mulan*. And, that same year, appeared on Broadway in David Henry Hwang's *Golden Child* which won a 1998 Tony® nomination for best play.

Married in 1995 to Eric Michael Zee, a screenwriter, the couple have two children, and, until 2006, they co-managed an Asian a capella boy band, At Last.

Grover Mitchell

Born March 17, 1930—Whatley, AL
Died August 7, 2003—New York, NY

Raised in Pittsburgh's fertile jazz environment, Grover Mitchell earned his musical chops here before making the move to big band music, landing one of the ultimate gigs—lead trombonist for Count Basie's Orchestra.

Mitchell's family moved to Pittsburgh in 1938. Soon he expressed an interest in playing an instrument and enrolled in his school's

free-instrument program, with hopes of learning to play the trumpet. However, it was the height of the Depression and there weren't enough trumpets to go around, so he settled for the trombone instead.

The young Mitchell was surrounded by talent. His neighborhood was literally dotted with future jazz superstars. Erroll Garner lived around the corner. His school orchestra included the likes of Dakota Staton and Ahmad Jamal. Upon graduation, he enlisted in the Marines, playing big band music as part of the Corps' military band. He later said, "That's where I got my first picture of what would probably be required if I went in that [big band] direction."

After the Marines, Mitchell moved to San Francisco in search of his big break. He subbed with Lionel Hampton's band and even played "saxophone" for Duke Ellington (he transposed the sax parts so that they could be played on the trombone). His versatility and talent caught the attention of Count Basie who invited Mitchell to come aboard in 1962. Mitchell eventually made his way to the first trombone chair, where his playing was captured on the album *On My Way And Shoutin' Again*. He also served as a companion and caretaker for Basie toward the end of his life. He played for such notables as Henry Mancini, Nelson Riddle, Paul Weston and Frank DeVol.

With Basie's passing, Mitchell launched a band of his own—a 12-piece orchestra that owed much to his jazz upbringing. The band produced five albums, including 1990's classic *Hip Shakin'*.

Gwendolyn Mitchell

Born December 27, 1955—Pittsburgh

"The introspection and quietude brings us back again to Gwendolyn Mitchell's achievement," the poet Hoke S. Glover III wrote of her 2002 *House of Women*, poetic tales of African-American women's tragedies and triumphs. "She succeeds in remembering, in a calm and settled way, the pictures of our lives. These images give birth to questions and contemplations. They make readers focus and look more closely at the women and the houses of their own lives."

In the vanguard of independent African-American poetry and publishing, editor and poet Gwendolyn Ann Mitchell was born in 1955 in Pittsburgh. The daughter of a teacher and a police commander, she attended Lemington School and Westinghouse High before graduating from Taylor Allderdice in 1973. Moving to Dallas, she worked at Neiman Mar-

cus before returning to Penn State, earning a 1988 bachelor of arts in political science and a 1991 master of fine arts in poetry. Five years later, in 1996, Mitchell earned a certificate in arts management from the University of Massachusetts, Amherst.

Teaching in Penn State's English and Women's Studies departments, Mitchell also worked as a staff assistant in Senator Harris Wofford's Pittsburgh office. After working for Youth Enrichment Services and the Pennsylvania Council for the Arts, in 1997 she moved to Chicago to serve as editor of Third World Press, a leading independent African-American publisher, where she has co-edited anthologies of creative writing.

As a poet, Mitchell's work tends to the lyrical, vignettes in which women sing of love, solidarity, and sisterhood. Author of the powerful *Veins and Rivers*, which she wrote at Penn State; *Ain't I Black*, a book-length monologue; and *House of Women*, which closely examines everyday life, takes experience to the threshold of history, and renders understanding into the mythos of an entire people.

Gwendolyn Mitchell lives and works in Chicago.

Joe Montana

Born June 11, 1956—New Eagle, PA

A two-time NFL MVP, three-time Super Bowl MVP, eight-time Pro Bowler, and holder of countless NFL records, Monongahela's Joe Montana stands among the premiere quarterbacks of all time.

Born Joseph Clifford Montana, he started peewee football a year early, at 8 years old. A three-letter man at Ringgold High School, Montana was a *Parade* All-American in his senior year.

Choosing perennial champion Notre Dame, he found his stride as a 6'-2", 200-pound sophomore, staging what became his trademark: dramatic come-from-behind victories. He led the Fighting Irish to a 1977 National Championship, beating heavily favored Texas—the first of two consecutive Cotton Bowl victories.

While scouts believed in the Montana Magic, they asked if the Comeback Kid could play in the NFL. As such, Montana was chosen by San Francisco in the third round of the 1979 draft. He was the nation's 82nd pick.

Finally starting late in 1980, his sophomore season, Montana staged the first of 31 fourth-quarter comebacks.

The following year, 1981, Montana's 49ers rolled to Super Bowl XVI. In quick succession, they racked up victories in Super Bowls XIX (1984), XXIII (1988), XXIV (1989)—Montana never throwing an interception or giving up a fumble. Two Super Bowl ironies: Montana, who shares four-time Super Bowl champ status with the Steelers' Terry Bradshaw, defeated Dolphins' wunderkind Danny Marino in his only Super Bowl appearance.

After injuries limited his playing time, 1991-92, Montana spent the final two years of his career, 1993-94, with the Kansas City Chiefs. Over 16 years, he threw more than 3,400 completions for 273 touchdowns and more than 40,000 yards.

Above, Montana and fiancee Jennifer Wallace, and his parents, Theresa and Joe, Sr., January 1985

Inducted into the Pro Football Hall of Fame in 2000, Montana lives near Oakland, CA, with his wife and children. A horse owner and vintner, he manages private equity funds.

Demi Moore

Born November 11, 1962—Roswell, NM

Demetria was born to Virginia and Danny Guynes (pronounced gu-Wines) in a trailer park in New Mexico, but her real father was Charles Harmon who fled Roswell months before her birth. Traveling often with stepfather Danny, a smalltown newspaper ad salesman, Demi spent most of her formative years in Glencannon and Rogers Manor, PA, both in Washington County. She attended Borland Manor Elementary (North Strabane,) Canon-McMillan Junior High, and Charleroi High School.

Demi was, by her own admission, an ugly duckling—with a family as dysfunctional as that of the fairy tale. Her mother was often troubled by alcohol, and her stepfather, who she believed to be her real father until she was 13, committed suicide in 1979. Long before then, however, she and her mother had moved to West Hollywood where Demi was enrolled in Fairfax High School.

Her first professional job was posing provocatively for *Oui* magazine. Hanging out in the rock club scene, she met and married Freddy Moore of The Kats. The marriage lasted three years, during which time Demi partied with the young Hollywood set. Despite having no training as an actor, she landed a regular job playing Jackie Templeton on *General Hospital*. The steady gig got her roles in two 1982 B movies, *Young Doctors in Love* and *Choices*. She was then cast in *Parasite*, a blatant rip-off of Ronald Shusett's *Alien*, and was subsequently offered her first leading role, with Jon Cryer, in 1984's *No Small Affair*. Within the year, she was cast in Karl Curlander's first screenplay, *St. Elmo's Fire*, along with a new breed of hard-partying young actors, branded forever as the Brat Pack. Demi and co-star Emelio Estevez were engaged to marry, but never walked down the aisle.

With a career fully promoted by tabloid journalism, a well-publicized marriage to Bruce Willis, and publicity stunts (like her pregnant and nude cover shot in *Vanity Fair*) staged as much to expose her "true" character as to mask her failed films, Demi Moore became the highest-paid actress in Hollywood, sustained by a long string of profitable, though less triumphant films. Today, she is married to Ashton Kutcher with whom she appeared most recently in *Bobby*, the 2006 film written and directed by former lover, Emelio Estevez.

Natalie Moorhead

Born July 27, 1898—Squirrel Hill
Died October 6, 1991—Montecito, CA

There is very little to be said of the unremarkable film career of Natalie Moorhead other than that she appeared in supporting roles to some of the greatest of Hollywood stars, many of whom were just claiming their first leads. Actors like Clark Gable, Joan Crawford, Fay Wray, Pittsburgh's William Powell ,and Myrna Loy all knew Moorhead well, but the archives of celebrity gossip have little to say. If any claim to fame, she might best be credited for being one of Hollywood's first platinum blonde vamps.

Her childhood may be more interesting. Born with the name Nathalian to wealthy parents Mr. & Mrs. James Vincent Moorhead, she was raised in a large house on Eldridge Street in Squirrol Hill. Hor fathor was an executive of the U. S. Steel Company. She attended St. John's School, Peabody High School, and Scton Hill College.

At a young age, her father subscribed to a season box at the Alvin Theater downtown and, though the theater was no pursuit for a lady of society, Moorhead fell in love with the idea of acting. But her father died when she was about 10. And her mother had to abandon the estate and move her family to Arsenal where they lived at 39th Street.

A trip to New York to window shop with friends found her being "accosted by a casting director," seeking her interest in playing a bit part on Broadway in *Abie's Irish Rose*. She accepted immediately for a grand salary of $25 a week, which, even in 1922 was hardly sufficient for room and board. After a month, she returned to Pittsburgh, but soon convinced her mother to afford her the opportunity to join a stock company in Plainfield, New Jersey. From there, her star rose.

Moorhead appeared in more than 65 films from the 1930s to the mid-1940s, playing the often-blonde show girl or mysterious vamp in films like *Show Girl in Hollywood*, *The Office Wife*, *Hook, Line and Sinker*, and, in 1934, *The Thin Man*. A brief clip of her hoofing in the 1931 film, *Dance, Fools, Dance* is included in MGM's *That's Entertainment*.

Burton Morris

Born March 25, 1964—Pittsburgh

More than a soupçon of credit for Burton Morris' meteoric Pop Art career must go to Belgian artist Pierre Alechinsky. Visiting the 1977 Carnegie International at the Museum of Art, the 13-year-old Morris was taken by the enormous playful paintings that resembled outsized comic strips. The die was cast.

Born in Pittsburgh in 1964, Morris earned a 1986 Carnegie Mellon fine arts degree, then hopped the bus Downtown to work in advertising and commercial art. Talented, creative, and agreeable, Morris seemed a natural. But there was always Alechinsky; there was always something more.

In 1990, he opened Burton Morris Studios, and began turning out bright, colorful art, firmly in the Pop tradition of Roy Lichtenstein—and fellow Pittsburgher and CMU grad Andy Warhol. Creating a cornucopia of

the first players to rush for 1,000 yards each in a 14-game season. Back-to-back Super Bowl Champs, 1972-73, the Dolphins went 32-2.

Playing his eighth and last season, 1976, in San Diego, injuries forced Morris to retire.

Financially and physically devastated, within six years Morris was a cocaine addict who, in 1982, was convicted of trafficking. Sentenced to 20 years in prison, in 1986 Morris' conviction was overturned.

Clean and sober, in 1988 Morris published *Against the Grain,* his account of turning around his life. Since that time, he has told his story on such major media outlets as *Nightline, The Today Show, The Larry King Show, Good Morning America, The Oprah Winfrey Show, 48 Hours,* and many others. A regular guest host on *CNBC's Talk Live,* as part of *Sports Stars USA* Morris also works as a motivational speaker. Married, the father of six, Mercury Morris lives in Princeton, FL.

Americana, Morris painted icons as well as everyday life—the Statue of Liberty to popcorn boxes, Absolut Vodka to steaming coffee cups.

An immediate hit in the corporate world, Morris received commissions from such blue-chip outlets as AT&T, Perrier, Microsoft, Sony, Heinz, Coors, and Gallo. Embraced by Hollywood as well, where some of his collectors include Brad Pitt, Jennifer Aniston, Tim Allen, and John Travolta, for 10 seasons Morris' eye-catching designs appeared in the hit TV show *Friends'* Central Perk Café.

Branching out to mass markets, and major events, Morris completed 36 paintings on the spirit of the Olympic Games, exhibited at the International Olympic Museum in Lausanne, Switzerland, during the 2004 Athens summer games. In the same year, Morris produced the signature image for the 76th Academy Awards, a striking, light-exploding camera. In addition, he has created posters for the 38th Montreux Jazz Festival and Major League Baseball's 2006 All-Star Game—held in Pittsburgh.

Having had a Shadyside home and studio, Morris has relocated to Los Angeles, where he continues as a working artist.

Mercury Morris

Born January 5, 1947—Pittsburgh

In one of the most remarkable stories in Pittsburgh sports history, Mercury Morris went from Super Bowls to penury, prison to media star and motivational speaker.

Born Eugene Edward Morris, he played football at Avonworth High and West Texas A&M, where he was an All-American running back, 1967-68. Picking up the nickname Mercury, Morris set collegiate rushing records— in one game, for example, he carried 35 times for 341 yards and four touchdowns.

Standing 5'-10" and 190 pounds, he was taken by Miami in the 1969 draft. Playing seven seasons for the Dolphins, 1969-75, Morris went to three Pro Bowls and Super Bowls VI, VII, VIII, 1971-73. Part of the famed 1972 Perfect Team, the undefeated Dolphins are widely considered one of the greatest NFL squads of all time—in part because Morris, along with co-running back Jim Kiick, were

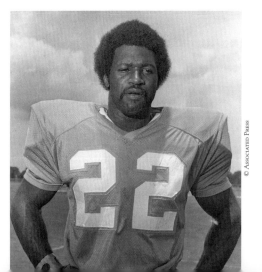

Thad Mosley

Born 1926—New Castle, PA

It was the late 1940s, and Thad Mosley came face-to-face with something that would change his life forever: African sculpture. "I quickly grew from being interested in it," he told artist-architect David Lewis, "to being exhilarated by the energy and inventiveness of those countless objects."

That's all it took. The self-taught Thaddeus Mosley took a turn in the Navy, earned a Pitt English degree, and went to work in the post office. By the mid-1950s he was a postal worker by day, sculptor by night.

Initially showing anywhere that would have him—churches, garages, even gas stations—by 1963 Mosley was sufficiently established to join the Society of Sculptors. More prestigious placements followed, including shows at the Carnegie Museum, as did such accolades as 1978 Pittsburgh Center for the Arts' Artist of the Year and 1999 Pennsylvania Artist of the Year.

Creator of strong, immediately recognizable pieces—including his signature 14-foot cedar Phoenix, Centre Avenue and Dinwiddie Street, and the limestone Mountaintop, Martin Luther King, Jr. Library, both in the Hill District—Mosley works in cherry, walnut, and sycamore, woods often given to him by tree surgeons and the city's forestry department; sandstone and limestone; even found objects—scrap steel, bolts, wire.

Listening to jazz as he works, Mosley never pre-sketches his sculptures. Instead, he says, "I draw with a hammer and chisel. It's a sculptural improvisation, a journey. I channel my mental energies into a sculptural focus: materials, form, rhythm, surface, relation to earth, capacity to soar."

As an African-American sculptor, he freely draws on both traditions: one day, reading a poem by Stephen Crane and listening to a song by John Coltrane, he created the sculpture Trane to Crane, blending both traditions.

Celebrated sculptor, father of six, Thad Mosley lives and works on the North Side.

Bill Moushey

Born January 15, 1954—Canton, OH

Justin Kirkwood was glad *Pittsburgh Post-Gazette* investigative reporter Bill Moushey was on his case.

Spending two years in prison for a 2003 New Castle robbery he didn't commit, Kirkwood might have remained in SCI Somerset had not Moushey, also the director of Point Park University's Innocence Institute, published the story "Sight Unseen," which was instrumental in uncovering phone records proving Kirkwood's innocence.

Ditto Drew Whitley, who spent 18 years in prison for a Kennywood-area murder he did not do. Another of the 11 convictions overturned because of Moushey's investigative work, Whitley, freed after DNA tests proved he was not the killer, singled out the Innocence Institute, which investigated his claims for five years. "Bill Moushey," he said as the court freed him, "you are my hero. Thank you."

Born William Moushey in Canton, Ohio, he earned a 1976 journalism B.A. at Kent State, then came to Pittsburgh three years later, first to work on a magazine, then on television. Moving to the *Post-Gazette* in 1985, he quickly established himself as the newspaper's top investigative reporter, primarily in the field of criminal justice.

A 1997 Pulitzer Prize finalist for his exposé of the witness protection program, Moushey's 1998 "Win at all Costs" series about prosecutorial misconduct won multiple journalism awards.

Following the lead of numerous American legal clinics, in 2001 Moushey began one of the nation's first—and still one of the few—journalism-centered Innocence Institutes. As a Point Park professor, Moushey enlists Innocence Institute students to work on questionable cases, seeking to re-open or overturn Pittsburgh-area wrongful convictions. If the results are publishable, stories carry student by-lines—rare in professional journalism.

To hone his own skills, Moushey earned a 2004 Point Park criminal justice administration degree.

A 2006 Golden Quill Lifetime Service awardee, Pittsburgh's highest journalism honor, Bill Moushey lives in Pittsburgh.

Robert Munsch

Born June 11, 1945—Pittsburgh

For Robert Munsch, the road to becoming Canada's best-selling author, selling some 30 million books—including the 1994 classic *Love You Forever*—was entirely unplanned, but highly rewarding.

As a high schooler he considered becoming a Catholic priest. Studying with the Jesuits, he earned a 1969 Fordham history B.A., and a 1971 Boston University anthropology M.A., finally opting for work with children, earning a 1973 Tufts child studies M.E.

Moving to Ontario in 1975 to work at the University of Guelph preschool, Munsch began telling children stories to quiet them down.

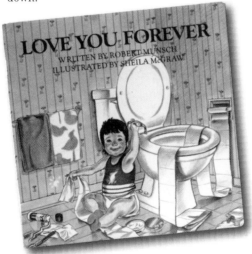

Discovering that he could invent moving children's fare on the spot, Munsch never gave it a second thought. "For 10 years," he says, "I did this without thinking I had any special skill."

Encouraged to publish by people who heard him, in the late 1970s Munsch took off two months, wrote 10 stories, and sent them to 10 different publishers. With nine rejections in hand, the 10th publisher brought out *Mud Puddle* in 1979. When it sold 3,000 copies, Munsch was on his way.

Selling well in Canada in the early 1980s, Munch was still relatively unknown in his native country. Then in 1986 he published *Love You Forever*, a memorial for his two stillborn babies, 1979-80. By decade's end, it had sold more than a million copies. By the mid-1990s, it had sold more than eight million.

Generally publishing two books a year, Munsch's more than 40 books are notable for their use of real children, characters taken from life, plots often defeating expectations, and endings that are not always happy.

Still a regular storyteller, Munsch works festivals—as well as schools and daycares, often simply showing up, introducing himself with a letter a class has written to him.

Robert Munsch continues to live and work in Guelph, Ontario.

Philip Murray

Born May 25, 1886—Blantyre, Scotland
Died November 9, 1952—San Francisco, CA

He became a union leader the hard way. After fighting with a foreman who he thought was cheating him, Murray was fired from his mining job. When 600 of his co-workers went on strike in support of his rehiring, Murray, his father, stepmother, and seven siblings were evicted from their house and sent to the streets.

That wasn't what the Murray clan, including 16-year-old Philip, had anticipated upon their arrival from Ireland to United States in 1902. Lured by the promise of prosperity in America, Murray soon saw that unionization was necessary after his firing. He formed a local of United Mine Workers (UMW) in 1905 in Horning, PA. It was there that he developed his famed negotiating skills while taking correspondence courses in English, math, and science.

He rose through the ranks of the union, gaining attention as a more moderate voice in the labor movement. He was elected president of UMW District 5 in 1917, using that position to lobby for the national ascendancy of John L. Lewis. In return, Lewis selected Murray as his right-hand man, whose job was to work closely with the membership. It was a strong working relationship that lasted 20 years, including the formation of the Congress of Industrial Organizations (CIO).

The two would split over politics in 1938. Murray was in charge of the CIO's Steel Workers Organizing Committee and had led successful labor actions and argued his cases before the fledgling National Labor Relations Board. His SWOC had successfully chartered more than 1,000 local unions. But his decision to support Franklin D. Roosevelt's re-election campaign along with FDR's efforts to bring America into the war led to a lifelong schism between Murray and Lewis—something Murray would later call "heartbreaking."

He replaced Lewis as president of the CIO, and Murray was instrumental in keeping production for America's war effort by making a no-strike pledge for his unions (nonetheless, he managed to secure gains for the membership). Remembering being at the mercy of the mining company in his youth, Murray fought for set minimum wages, worker pensions, and lobbied to make permanent the Fair Employment Practice Commission.

The final part of his career saw Murray, who headed both the CIO and the United Steelworkers, squarely in the fight over Communism, expelling several members of his union who supported third-party Communist candidate Henry Wallace in the 1948 presidential election. He also continued to push for social and economic advances of his membership. Murray died of a heart attack shortly after leading a steel-industry strike, leaving behind the legacy of being one of the most accomplished figures in the rise of organized labor.

Danny Murtaugh

Born October 8, 1917—Chester, PA
Died December 2, 1976—Chester, PA

He'd go to Forbes Field early, before his players, to sit in his rocking chair and play the upcoming game in his mind. Then, when the

Pirates came, Danny Murtaugh was ready to mold them into champions.

The only four-time manager in Pittsburgh history, by the time Daniel Edward Murtaugh retired he had joined the exclusive 1,000-victory club—and notched two World Championships.

Born in 1917 in Chester, PA, Murtaugh came to the major leagues as a 23-year old second baseman for the Phillies. Standing just 5'-9" and 165 pounds, he played 1941-51 for Philadelphia, Boston, and Pittsburgh. Staying in the Pirate system, he managed the minor-league New Orleans Pelicans before taking over the parent club in mid-1957.

Calm, patient, an excellent judge of talent, by 1958 Murtaugh led Pittsburgh to a second-place finish, its highest since 1944. Two years later, 1960, he piloted the Pirates to their first National League Pennant since 1927, then led them to a World Championship over the Yankees. Out scored 55-27, including losing three games 38-3, Murtaugh kept the Pirates focused—and took home the trophy.

After four more seasons, in 1964 Murtaugh retired for the first of four times. Three years later, mid-1967, he was back, leaving again when the season was over.

Back in 1970, he oversaw the move to Three Rivers Stadium, then managed the Bucs to their first first-place finish in a decade. An NL East winner again the following year, 1971, Murtaugh took the title from the reigning World Champion Baltimore Orioles.

Retiring a third time, by the end of 1973 he returned, steering the Pirates to two more first-place finishes, 1974-75.

Retiring the fourth and last time after the 1976 season, he returned to Chester. Just two months later, Murtaugh suffered a fatal stroke. He was 59 years old.

Stan Musial

Born November 21, 1920—Donora, PA

It was a leather-lunged Ebbets Field rooter that gave him his memorable nickname. As St. Louis Cardinal Stan Musial strode to the plate, the Brooklyn man bellowed, "here comes that man!"

Holder of 17 major league, 29 National League, and nine All Star records when he retired after 22 years, in 1963, Donora's Stan "The Man" Musial stands as one of the greatest baseball players of all time. A three-time National League MVP, seven-time batting champion, and Hall of Fame inductee, Musial was, in the words of baseball commissioner Ford Frick, "baseball's perfect knight."

Born Stanislaw Franciszek Musial, later anglicized to Stanley Frank Musial, in 1920, he came up to the Cardinals as a 20-year-old rookie in 1941. A failed minor-league pitcher re-made into an outfielder, Musial used an unorthodox corkscrew batting stance to hit .300 or more 17 times, and 475 home runs, for a .331 lifetime batting average.

Leading the Cardinals to three World Championships, all in the 1940s, he amassed 3,630 hits, making him the National League's all-time leader when he retired. Batting with a machine-like consistency, Musial hit .336 at home, .326 on the road; .340 in day games, .320 at night; 1,815 hits at home, 1,815 on the road.

"I consciously memorized the speed at which every pitcher in the league threw his fastball, curve, and slider," Musial explained. "I'd pick up the speed of the ball in the first

30 feet of its flight and knew how it would move once it had crossed the plate."

"All Musial represents," sportscaster Bob Costas said, "is more than two decades of sustained excellence and complete decency as a human being."

Marrying his high-school sweetheart at age 19, the father of four, Stan Musial lives in St. Louis, a successful businessman and restaurateur.

Michael Musmanno

**Born April 7, 1897—Pittsburgh
Died October 12, 1968—Pittsburgh**

In the darkest days of America's 20th-century labor wars, Pittsburgh legislator Michael Musmanno's play *Black Fury* helped bring about necessary, life-saving reforms.

Born Michael Angelo Musmanno, he was by turns an attorney, legislator, author, jurist, and naval officer. An appellate attorney for Sacco and Vanzetti, Musmanno also debated Clarence Darrow and was a witness against Adolf Eichmann in Jerusalem.

A Pennsylvania legislator concerned with workers rights, Musmanno fought to dismantle the infamous Coal and Iron Police, a private army that, in one notorious case, beat a coal miner to death. *Black Fury*, Musmanno's play based on the incident, was so powerful that it helped get the strike-breaking armies banned. Turned into a 1935 film (and later Musmanno's own novel), it starred Paul Muni, who received a rare write-in nomination for a best actor Academy Award.

Elected Common Pleas judge in 1934, by World War II Musmanno was exempt from military duty. Enlisting in the Navy, he rose to rear admiral, serving as a naval aide to General Mark Clark. Musmanno received the Distinguished Service Cross for action under fire, and also served as a military governor in Italy.

After the war, Musmanno was appointed to serve as a judge at the Nuremberg Trials, including one concerning the Einsatzgruppen, the notorious S.S. mobile killing squads responsible for murdering more than 1.4 million people.

Returning to Common Pleas Court, in 1952 Musmanno took a seat on the State Supreme Court, a post he held until his death.

Author of 16 books, his *Ten Days to Die* recounted Hitler's last days, which Musmanno had personally investigated in Europe. Among his other scrupulously researched titles were the *Eichmann Kommandos*, a Lincoln biography, and *Columbus Was First*, his defense of America's European discoverer.

Ironically, 71-year-old Michael Musmanno died in Pittsburgh on Columbus Day, 1968, and is buried in Arlington National Cemetery.

Burt Mustin

**Born February 8, 1884—Pittsburgh
Died January 28, 1977—Glendale, CA**

Burt Mustin was one of those great TV characters actors who—eternally old but loveable—could turn up anywhere. And often he did. First, regularly, as Gus the Fireman in

Leave it To Beaver, then as Jud Crowley on *The Andy Griffith Show*, next as Grandpa Jensen on *Petticoat Junction*, and just as often, 20 years later—no older and no different—as Mr. Quigley on *All in the Family*.

But he *was* old. Born in 1884, Mustin grew up the son of an early bondbroker. At 15, he went off to the Pennsylvania Military Academy (now Widener University in Chester, PA) where he excelled in sports and served as yearbook editor before graduating in 1903. Despite the "rich man's panic of 1904" that ruined his father's firm, he found work selling newfangled automobiles, which allowed him evenings to rehearse and perform with the Pittsburgh Savoyards. A member of the Pittsburgh Athletic Club, the Musicians Club of Pittsburgh, and as one of the first announcers on radio station KDKA in 1921, Mustin often performed in amateur theatre.

Mustin and his wife Robina moved to Tucson, AZ, where, ever keen to the stage, he was discovered playing the janitor in *Detective Story*, a play that was then soon to be made into a film, starring Kirk Douglas. He was hired to play the film role and he moved to Hollywood.

Described once as someone who looked like a baby chick after a bad hatch, Mustin was easily cast in dozens of films as the "old coot." Mustin in fact often called himself the "They Went That-a Way" guy, a role that could only be played by someone who appeared trusting, wise, and slow. With the advent of TV, Mustin's career was certain. Indeed, there are only a handful of classic sitcom's—certainly none loved or re-aired—in which Mustin did not appear.

His last TV appearance was in a starring role on *Phyllis*. In 1976, his character, Arthur Lanson, married Mother Dexter, played by Judith Lowry. Lowry died a few days before the program aired. Mustin died two weeks later, at 92, of natural causes.

Joe Namath

Born May 11, 1943—Beaver Falls, PA

The title of his first autobiography sums up Hall of Fame quarterback Joe Namath's customary bravado: *I Can't Wait Until Tomorrow 'Cause I Get Better Looking Every Day*.

Known equally for his on-field heroics and off-field antics, Joseph William Namath went from Beaver Falls to Broadway, toast of New York and the NFL. Famously guaranteeing a win in Super Bowl III over the heavily favored Baltimore Colts, he made the boast stand up—and made himself a star.

Born in 1943, a multi-talented athlete at Beaver Falls High, Namath turned down six professional baseball offers, and college football at Penn State, Ohio State, and Notre Dame, to play for legendary coach Paul "Bear" Bryant at Alabama. On the varsity 1962-64, in his senior year Namath led the Crimson Tide to a National Championship.

A 6'-2", 200-pound first round draft pick,

(CONTINUED PAGE 158)

© ASSOCIATED PRESS

NASA Astronauts

It may not be a huge stretch—or long span—to credit John Roebling, engineer of great bridges, with man's first steps toward conquering space. His wire cable made it possible for Langley to build his first airplanes, and for Calbraith Rodgers to fly across the continent, inspiring a new generation to look beyond the clouds. Here are four distinguished men from Pittsburgh who orbited above them.

Irwin rides shotgun, David Scott drives, and Alfred Worden stands-by for a publicity shot on Earth, April, 1971.

James Irwin

Born March 17, 1930—Beechview
Died August 8, 1991—Glenwood Springs, CO

He was the eighth man to walk on the moon. As a team member of Apollo 15 in July 1971, Irwin was part of the fourth mission to the moon, the first to employ a lunar Rover and the first to explore the Apennines Mountains located in the lunar Sea of Rains. Later, he would search more famous mountains—on earth—pursuing his quest to discover Noah's Ark.

The eldest son of a plumber who was employed by the Carnegie Institute in Oakland, Irwin grew up on Palm Beach Avenue in Beechview, attending Holy Trinity Lutheran Church before moving, at age 11, to Florida briefly, then to Salt Lake City where he graduated from East High School. Graduating from the Naval Academy in 1951, he was commissioned in the Air Force, took flight training at Hondo Air Base, joined the F-12 Test Force at Edwards Air Force Base, and was selected in 1966 as one of 19 astronauts to join NASA.

Upon orbiting the earth in Apollo 15, he was transfixed to a religious calling, uttering the words of the Psalm, "I'll look unto the hills from whence cometh my help," adding, " but of course we get quite a bit of help from Houston, too." Among other events recorded by his flight, Irwin experienced irregular heart rhythms perhaps due to the strain of the mission. After splashing down in the Pacific on August 7, 1971, he remained earthbound for the rest of his career.

Soon thereafter, he was urged by the Reverend Dr. Billy Graham to form an evangelical organization, High Flight, to preach about his epiphany in space. Speaking to thousands of school children—and once to an audience of 50,000 in the Houston Astrodome—Irwin toured the country, while penning his autobiography, *To Rule the Night*.

Standing fourth from right, Irwin prepares to climb Ararat.

In the early 1980s, Irwin also led two missions, one by land and one by flight, to search for Noah's Ark atop Mount Ararat in Turkey. While descending the mountain on his first attempt, he was severely injured in a fall, breaking both of his legs. Irwin died of a heart attack at just 61 years of age.

Jay Apt

Born April 28, 1949—Springfield, MA

He thinks his first interests in outer space were realized when he built dozens of Estes® Rockets in the family's glass house on Woodland Road. His mother, Joan, (who with Margaret Rieck co-founded the Pittsburgh Public Theater in 1975), believes her son was first entranced with physics when they would visit the Foucault pendulum at the old Buhl Planetarium on the North Side. Certainly both experiences helped launch the boy's career as one of NASA's most devoted astronauts.

Graduating from Shady Side Academy in 1967, Apt attended Harvard, affording flying lessons by tutoring other students, and graduated Magna Cum Laude in 1971. No slouch, he earned his Ph.D in laser physics from MIT in 1975. Twice he applied to NASA's Space Program and twice was rejected. While working as a staff member at the Center for Earth & Planetary Physics at Harvard, he created temperature maps of Venus. Then, as an assistant director of Harvard's Division of Applied Sciences from 1978 to 1980, he applied to NASA for a third time, and was accepted, first serving at the Jet Propulsion Laboratory, then managing payload operations at the Johnson Space Center.

In July 1986, he was qualified as an astronaut. Apt's first mission was on the space shuttle *Atlantis* launched from Kennedy Space Center on April 5, 1991. He helped deploy the Gamma Ray Observatory (by which he studied vast forms of distant radiation) and took one of the first-ever unscheduled space walks to help unfold the observatory's large radio antennae. Apt next flew *Endeavor* in September 1992, serving as a flight engineer. Two more missions followed, his last on *Atlantis* in 1996, when the craft docked with the Russian Mir space station. In all, Apt logged over 35 days in space, including two space walks.

In May 1997, Apt accepted the title of director of Carnegie Institute's Museum of Natural History. At just 48 years old, he became its 11th director and engaged in a hard-fought, but short-lived battle to add greater interactive technology to its hallowed halls. He resigned in February 2000, and today is a CMU Tepper School professor and executive director of its Electricity Industry Center.

Mike Fincke

Born March 4, 1967—Emsworth

Born Edward Michael Fincke, the eldest of the nine children of Edward and Alma Fincke of Emsworth, PA, young Mike was so bright and studious, he earned a scholarship to Sewickley Academy. So, too, did his eight younger siblings, all of whom are today inordinately successful in their chosen careers. None, however, took quite the path that Mike did—to the International Space Station where he orbited the earth for 187 days, 21 hours and, to be precise, 17 minutes.

Upon graduation from the Academy in 1985, Fincke attended MIT on an Air Force ROTC scholarship, graduating with dual degrees in astronautics and planetary sciences in 1989. In 1990, he earned his Masters in aeronautics and astronautics from Stanford University. Somehow, in his spare time that intervening summer, he also studied Cosmonautics with the Moscow Aviation Institute. No doubt a challenge to most aspiring astronauts, speaking Russian was relatively easy for Fincke who had the foresight to study Russian while at MIT. In fact, when the eldest Fincke had applied for admission to Sewickley Academy, he declared then that he would someday become an astronaut.

On April 18, 2004, Expedition-9 was launched from the Baikonur Cosmodrome, Kazakhstan. Fincke and cosmonaut Gennady Padalka took command of the International Space Station on April 21, 2004, working for just nine days with two other returning astronauts. The Expedition-9 mission concluded with undocking from the station and a safe landing back in Kazakhstan on Oct. 23, 2004. During his six months on board, Fincke conducted four separate space-walks.

Said Fincke in a 2004 *Post-Gazette* interview, "One never truly leaves home in one's heart. Traveling at 17,000 mph, I could see the pyramids, the Amazon River, Mount Kilimanjaro—and the Ohio River!"

In February 2007, NASA announced that Fincke will return to space as commander of Expedition-18.

Dick Scobee, George Nelson, James van Hoften, Hart, and Robert Crippen, repaired the Solar Max, April 14, 1984.

Terry Hart

Born October 27, 1946—Mt. Lebanon

Currently professor of aerospace engineering at Lehigh University, where he graduated with a B.S. in 1968, Terry Hart logged 168 hours in space when he lifted off on the space shuttle Challenger on April 6, 1984. His mission was responsible for retrieving and repairing the Solar Maximum Satellite. In addition, his flight was one of the first to film planet earth with the IMAX Camera System.

Hurricane Frances as photographed by Fincke in 2004

MIT President Charles M. Vest, left, applauds as Fincke, evidently via satellite, greets members of his 15-year reunion class at MIT from aboard the International Space Station, Saturday, June 5, 2004.

Just before his 11th birthday, he remembers watching the early evening sky to see Sputnik orbit outside his home. A 1964 graduate of Mt. Lebanon High School, he attended Lehigh for his mechanical engineering degree, and earned a Masters from MIT in 1969. After joining the Air Force Reserves, he worked with Bell Laboratories earning two patents for communications systems, while also logging some 3,200 hours flying F-106 interceptors up and down the New Jersey coast.

Following his NASA career, Hart became president of Loral Skynet, part of the Telstar satellite network, just recently merged with Telesat Canada.

With two daughters from a previous marriage, Hart married Mary Jane McKeever, a Pittsburgh native who graduated from Pitt in 1979. McKeever enjoyed a 23-year career in government relations with AT&T. In 1994, she was general manager of Skynet for AT&T, and sold the division to Loral Corporation. She now serves on the Advisory Board for Lehigh's College of Education. Together they have a son and both work in Bethlehem, PA, when not enjoying their Delaware beach house.

Namath signed for a then-record $400,000 with the New York Jets. The only quarterback to throw for 4,000 yards in a 14-game season, he did it on knees that often were drained of fluid during half-time. Playing 13 years with the Jets, 1965-76, and Los Angeles Rams, 1977, Namath was a two-time AFL MVP, Super Bowl MVP, and five-time Pro Bowler.

Aka Joe Willie, aka Broadway Joe, Namath also made headlines by wearing full-length fur coats, posing for pantyhose ads, and growing football's first Fu Manchu mustache. When ordered to shave, he did so—on television, for a fee of $10,000.

Elected to the Pro Football Hall of Fame in 1985, Namath followed football with film. Seemingly everywhere, Namath appeared on *The Brady Bunch*, *Laugh-In*, and many other shows, even substituting for Johnny Carson on *The Tonight Show*.

Now living in Tequesta, FL, Namath owns bars in New York and Tuscaloosa, staying in the public eye with celebrity interviews and a second autobiography, *Namath*, published in 2006.

Joe Negri

Born June 10, 1930—Pittsburgh

There was a time early in his career, shortly after being discharged from the Army, when Negri had an opportunity to join legendary jazz clarinetist Woody Herman's band. Instead, he chose to return to his family and pursue his career in Pittsburgh.

Growing up on Mount Washington, he wanted more than anything to be a sports announcer. His musical talents however were more apparent than his broadcasting abilities.

Negri began playing the ukulele at just 4 years old and by 5 was singing weekly on KDKA's *The Uncle Henry Radio Show*. He then formed a vaudeville song-and-dance troupe called Joe Negri and the Rhythm Boys, which included his brother Bobby and cousin Mutzy, and performed at schools and various venues locally. Story is that the boys were so good that Gene Kelly asked Rose Negri, Joe and Bobby's mom, if they would be allowed to tour. Rose wouldn't hear of it.

Like so many local youngsters, Negri took guitar lessons at Volkwein's downtown. His influences included guitar greats Les Paul, Charlie Christian, and Django Reinhardt. He was so accomplished by his mid-teens that band leader Shep Fields asked him to join his touring swing band, where he would stay for the next couple of years. He returned to Pittsburgh and enrolled at Carnegie Tech—at the recommendation of Johnny Costa—to further his musical studies. By now Negri and his wife Joni had decided that pursuing a professional music career anywhere but Pittsburgh was not an option. They wanted to stay here.

Negri made his leap into television, first at KDKA, then at WTAE as a regular on Paul Shannon's *Adventure Time* and as station musical director. Additionally Negri appeared in the role that made him famous with children all over the world—as Handyman Negri on *Mister Rogers' Neighborhood*.

Joe Negri, an accomplished composer, has played with the Pittsburgh Symphony, written a guitar instructional book, taught at the University of Pittsburgh, CMU, and Duquesne, recorded 4 CDs, and has performed with countless world-class musicians from Yo Yo Ma and Wynton Marsalis to Tony Bennett and Andy Williams. He is one of Pittsburgh's most cherished neighbors.

Lenora Nemetz

Born November 11, 1949—North Side

Pigeon-toed, knock-kneed, and known to her dance instructors Maurice and Andrea Sabatier as "little monster," Lenora Nemetz was just four when she would trudge up Monument Hill with her grandmother to attend dance lessons. Mother Helen was a busy seamstress for Steiner Drapery and Dad Nick traveled for Allis Chalmers. An only child, she lived in a "huge brownstone" at 844 Reedsdale with her parents, Grandma Katherine, and many cousins. Friends Joanie Zoff,

Susan Orr, and Keith Trudy would put on plays in the backyard of the Garden Café, drinking Squirt paid for by silver dollars their neighbor "Mr. Rooney" would hand out on the street.

She got her first laugh on stage at the Pittsburgh Grotto when, during a dance recital, she crossed the stage off-cue and mugged for the audience. "I remember, too, sitting on my Dad's lap watching Gwen Verdon perform a routine on Ed Sullivan." Quite prophetically, she told her father, "Hey, I can do that."

The Nemetzes moved to 1468 Rydal Street when construction for Three Rivers Stadium claimed their neighborhood. She attended Schaeffer Elementary and Langley High School and sang, danced, and acted her way to New York. While playing "the rear end of a cow" in *Gypsy* at Club Benet in New Jersey, she auditioned for three Broadway musicals on the same day and was cast in the 1968 chorus of *Cabaret*. She was just 18.

By the time she turned 23, Lenora was headlining. She understudied the role of Roxie Hart in Bob Fosse's *Chicago* and within a month replaced Chita Rivera as Velma Kelly. Famously, within a year, she replaced her idol Gwen Verdon as Roxie. Next came *Working*, the Studs Terkel inspired musical, written and directed by Stephen Schwartz, and for which Nemetz was nominated for a 1978 Drama Desk Award as Outstanding Featured Actress in a Musical. The following year she headlined with Peter Allen in *Up In One*, and in 1984 understudied for Liza Minnelli in *The Rink*, a production also noted for its dance routines captained by a young Robby Marshall, the self-proclaimed President of the Lenora Nemetz Fan Club.

Never estranged from her hometown, Nemetz has starred often and regularly with the CLO, at City Theatre, and most recently with the Pittsburgh Public Theater, playing Fraulein Kost in 2007's *Cabaret*. One of the greatest "triple-threats" to hit the Great White Way, Nemetz generously teaches singing, dancing, and acting to young children whenever her schedule permits.

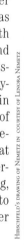

Evelyn Nesbit

Born December 25, 1884—Tarentum, PA
Died January 17, 1967—Santa Monica, CA

Born on Christmas Day in Tarentum, the little girl's beauty was said to be obvious even at birth. Later, she would turn heads, crush hearts, inspire art, and incite murder.

Upon her father's death when Evelyn Florence Nesbit was 8, Mrs. Winfield Scott Nesbit showcased her child to portraitists and photographers to earn modeling fees. So profitable was her portfolio, they moved to New York City. Among dozens of studios, Evelyn was drawn by Charles Dana Gibson, and became one of the most cherished of Gibson Girls.

The public fascination earned her a role in *Florodora* on Broadway. And that appearance attracted the lust of the city's most wealthy gentlemen, chief among them Stanford White, the famed architect of Madison Square Garden, and Harry Kendall Thaw, a ne'er do well trust fund junkie from Pittsburgh.

Visiting White's studio one evening, unchaperoned, Evelyn was deflowered after famously cavorting on his red velvet swing and quaffing champagne. She was just 16. Their relationship was short-lived, if only because of the advances of John Barrymore, the famous actor. A none too dire bout of "appendicitis" landed her in a secluded hospital room. And there Nesbit began receiving gifts of flowers and candies from Thaw.

Harry inherited vast fortunes from his railroad and coal baron father, but was allowed only $200 a month until his widowed mother, bowing to Harry's regular tantrums, increased his annual allowance to $80,000.

Thaw, now a morphine and cocaine addict, was a big shot in the Big City. He insisted on courting Miss Nesbit, and with her mother,

he treated them to a year in Paris. There, he asked for her hand in marriage, but when Evelyn refused, Thaw had a fit, sent mother Nesbit home, then raped and abused her throughout Europe. Some say he used a dog whip at times, but Nesbit, with no money, had no means of escape.

They returned to New York and Evelyn had a second attack of "appendicitis." In an effort to rid herself of Thaw, Evelyn divulged the horrid details of her one night tryst with White. The plan backfired. She would be "saved from certain ruin" by marrying the possessive Thaw in 1905.

A year later, while attending a cabaret on the rooftop of Madison Square Garden, Harry Thaw—his beautiful bride in attendance – marched up to Stanford White and shot him three times in the face. The murder was so inexplicably brazen that insanity could be his only defense. Thaw was tried once in front of a hung jury, then again for what became known as the crime of the century. He was jailed in a low security sanatorium, and walked away months later.

Evelyn, too, became addicted to drugs, had a son, Russell William Thaw, in 1910, and married dancer Jack Clifford in 1916. They separated two years later. Famously, both *The Girl in the Red Velvet Swing* (1955) and *Ragtime*, E.L. Doctorow's 1975 epic novel turned film, are classics of America's culture of wealth.

Sammy Nestico

Born February 6, 1924—Pittsburgh

A world-class arranger, Sammy Nestico has written and arranged music for everybody from President Johnson and Pat Boone to Goldie Hawn and *Gomer Pyle*, not to mention his 14-year tenure as arranger for the world-famous Count Basie Orchestra.

He was a typical youngster—had a paper route, played pick-up football and baseball in his North Side neighborhood—specifically playing on the cow pasture next to the old Himmelstein's dairy. In his early teens he began playing trombone in the beginner's orchestra at Oliver High School. His mom would encourage him to put down the instrument and go out to play with his friends, but his love of music, especially swing, kept him inside. He spent his Saturdays at the Stanley Theatre, mesmerized by Max Adkins' pit orchestra and particularly by his trombonist, Matty Shiner.

In the 10th grade he was playing a nightclub gig at Balconades along Route 51. After graduating from Oliver High School, Nestico was hired as the 2nd trombonist for the WCAE staff orchestra, the ABC affiliate radio station in Pittsburgh. After several years in the service, Nestico headed to Chicago to play with the Charlie Barnet orchestra. He returned to Pittsburgh to WCAE and earned a degree in music education from Duquesne University. He taught briefly at Wilmerding High School. Nestico became the arranger for the newly formed Air Force Glenn Miller Orchestra, renamed the Airmen of Note. As the leader, he traveled extensively, returning from Europe to arrange for the Air Force Symphony Orchestra and then the Marine Band in 1965, serving also as the director of the White House Orchestra.

Within a year Nestico was hired as the composer/arranger for the legendary Count Basie orchestra, where he would remain for 17 years. With Basie, Nestico directed four Grammy® winning recordings and with various labels collaborated with numerous artists including Frank Sinatra, Barbra Streisand, Sarah Vaughan, and Nancy Wilson. Over the course of the next several decades, Nestico wrote for TV, films, and numerous orchestras. Just a sampling of his TV shows include *The Mary Tyler Moore Show*, *M*A*S*H*, *The Mod Squad*, *Gomer Pyle*, *The Bob Newhart Show*, *The Streets of San Francisco*, and *Charlie's Angels*.

In 1993, Nestico added published author to his long list of credits for his textbook, *The Complete Arranger*.

Ethelbert Nevin

Born November 25, 1862—Edgeworth
Died February 17, 1901—New Haven, CT

Born near Sewickley, Ethelbert Nevin was an American composer and pianist. His composition "The Rosary" would become one of the best selling and most cherished songs during the early 1900s. Sales of the song were handsome, but not enough to support the lavish lifestyle and drinking that would eventu-

ally consume his life at the young age of 37.

Nevin was a gifted musician whose first composition was published when he was 12. He attended Western University (now The University of Pittsburgh) but dropped out after his first year for musical pursuits in Boston and then in Germany. In 1886 he debuted his work professionally in Pittsburgh to much critical acclaim.

Popular songs such as "Water Scenes," "Mighty Lak A Rose," "Narcissus," and "The Rosary" brought Nevin notoriety and significant wealth. His lifestyle however kept him in constant debt and alcohol began to ravage him physically and mentally. After fleeing to Italy for inspiration, he soon found an audience with Andrew Carnegie, who was so taken by his music that he coaxed Nevin to return.

Nevin relocated to New York in 1897 and then a few years later settled in New Haven where his years of alcoholism would finally claim his life.

Nevin's widow teamed-up with John Phillip Sousa to lobby Congress to enact intellectual property rights that would protect her husband's work as well as other American composers, actions which led to the formation of ASCAP (American Society of Composers, Authors, and Publishers).

Greg Nicotero

Born March 15, 1963—North Hills

It's just creepy how many Pittsburgh celebrities found fame because they loved Chilly Billy Cardille. Greg Nicotero was just such a kid, making the occasional Aurora® plastic model of the Wolfman, Dracula or Frankenstein, reading gory monster magazines, but always staying up late on Saturday nights to watch Bill Cardille on WIIC (now WPXI), when he discovered what it was he wanted to do most in this strange world.

The son of parents who loved the movies, and whose father performed in a number of local theaters, Nicotero grew up in the North Hills, attending Sewickley Academy.

He didn't know George Romero when the first of his cult classics, *Night of the Living Dead*, was released in 1968. But he knew who George Romero was—knew him so well as a fan, in fact—he recognized the director in a restaurant in Rome. "I walk up to him and say 'Hey, you're George Romero. My uncle was in 'The Crazies' and we ultimately sort of struck up a conversation and became friends. So I went to visit sets of films that he was working on. I remember I went to the mall where they were shooting 'Dawn of the Dead.' I went to the set when they were shooting 'Creepshow' and, lo and behold, that was when I became friends with Tom Savini."

In 1984, Nicotero got his first professional

job as a make-up assistant to Savini on the set of Romero's third zombie feature, *Day of the Dead*. Many films followed. In 1988, joining as the middle "N" between Robert Kurtzman and Howard Berger, KNB EFX Group was formed. Their list of films is astounding to those who are fans of horror flicks like *The Texas Chain Saw Massacre, Halloween 5, A Nightmare on Elm Street 5, Phantasm II, The Haunting* (1999), George Romero's *Land of the Dead,* and Romero's latest, *Diary of the Dead* (2007).

Nicotero was instrumental, too, as make-up and special effects artist on films like *Dances with Wolves, The Green Mile, Mulholland Drive, The Chronicles of Narnia, Vanilla Sky,* and both of Quentin Tarantino's Volumes of *Kill Bill.*

Chuck Noll

Born January 5, 1932—Cleveland, OH

To understand Steelers head coach Chuck Noll's greatness, you must cast your mind's eye back to the bad old days, 1933-68, when the Same Old Steelers were perennial laughingstocks. Louts and losers, they had had a dozen head coaches and never won a thing.

Then came a young Baltimore assistant named Chuck Noll, whom Vince Lombardi predicted would be the next great coach. He was, for 23 years, 1969-91, becoming the only NFL coach to win four Super Bowls.

Charles Henry Noll began as an all-state running back at Cleveland's Benedictine High. After captaining the University of Dayton squad, he was drafted by the Cleveland Browns in 1953. Standing 6'-1" and 218, Noll played seven seasons for Paul Brown. A linebacker and messenger guard, Noll ran in the plays from the bench, learning first-hand how the Hall of Fame coach thought.

Retiring as a player, age 27 in 1959, Noll became an assistant coach, first for the Chargers, then the Colts, specializing in defense. In 1969, after nine years as an assistant, Noll took the Steelers helm.

Noll believed that the key to building a successful team began in the draft. His first pick was defensive star Joe Greene. The next five drafts netted quarterback Terry Bradshaw, running back Franco Harris, wide receiver Lynn Swann, linebackers Jack Lambert, and Jack Ham, and more—all Hall of Famers.

Combining the power running of Harris with the Steel Curtain defense, within four years the Steelers were AFC Central Champions. Two years later, the team won its first Super Bowl, IX, on the way to three more (X, XIII, XIV) over six years, 1974-79, a record unmatched. Overall, the Steelers had 13 consecutive winning seasons, 1972-84.

Retiring in 1991 with a record of 209-156-1, Chuck Noll was elected to the Hall of Fame in 1993.

Bill Nunn, Jr.

Born October 20, 1953—Sugartop

Famous father-child legacies are rife in Pittsburgh's history. But few are as astounding as the Nunn family's. Bill Nunn, Sr., was for more than 15 years the managing editor of the *Pittsburgh Courier*, once the country's most widely circulated black newspaper. The daily, with circulation running as high as 200,000, championed many social causes, among them boldly protesting the mis-

representation of African-Americans by the mass media in popular culture. His son, Bill Nunn became sports editor of the *Courier*, then managing editor, but is equally revered by generations of football fans for being one of the better scouts of the Pittsburgh Steelers. He is credited for having discovered Stallworth, Blount, and Schell. Bill Nunn, Jr., as though fitting fate to his grandfather's early editorials, is one of mainstream film and television's more active character actors.

Born in the Sugartop neighborhood above Schenley Farms, Nunn, Jr., went to Madison Elementary, graduated from Schenley High, and entered Morehouse College in 1970. While there, he studied English and creative writing.

"I thought I wanted to be a writer," he recalled in a 1992 *Courier* interview, "but I finally realized that writers have to write, and I wasn't doing the work." While accompanying a friend to an audition, with no intent of doing so himself, he was cast in four roles of the same play. Nunn later confessed that what gravitated him to the theater was not the spotlight, but the camaraderie of actors. He found his calling.

After graduation, he auditioned for fellow Morehouse alum, Spike Lee, who cast him in both of their first films, *School Daze*. Then came two more Lee films, *Do The Right Thing* in which he played the pivotal role of Radio Raheem, and *Mo Better Blues*. Immediately following, he starred in Mario Van Peebles' *Now Jack City*. Then his career potential soared, when cast opposite his type, he played the physical therapist to Harrison Ford in *Regarding Henry*. Amazingly, his next film was an even bigger hit, *Sister Act* in which he

plays the huggable cop charged with protecting Whoopi Goldberg.

Never having moved to L.A. or NYC—he is happiest living in Atlanta with his wife and two daughters—his career is remarkably strong. In 2007, he completed his third recurring role as Robbie Robertson in *Spiderman III*.

Madalyn Murray O'Hair

Born April 13, 1919—Beechview
Died September, 1995—Real County, TX

Life magazine called her "the woman most hated in America" when, after her 1960 lawsuit (Murray v. Curlett) was brought to the Supreme Court, she monopolized the voice of the atheistic movement, removing all prayer from public schools. Years later, her body and that of her youngest son and granddaughter were found hacked to pieces and buried on a Texas ranch, a victim not of religious conservatives, but of an ex-con she had hired to manage her office.

Madalyn Mays was born on Palm Sunday to John, a steel contractor, and Lena Mays in Beechview. Said O'Hair in a taped interview in the '70s, "I had handsome parents, a brother, and was born into a family of considerable affluence. We couldn't have been more WASP if we tried." An intelligent child, she skipped third, fifth, and seventh grades at Beechwood Elementary. When the Depression hit, the family moved to Madison, OH, where Madalyn attended Rossford High. Her yearbook professes that she would "Serve God for the Betterment of Man." She earned many degrees, including a Ph.D. in philosophy and religion, and a Doctor of Jurisprudence from South Texas College of Law. "I wasted an

awful lot of time in colleges and universities."

In 1941, she married John Roths. World War II broke out and each went their separate way, Madalyn serving as a cryptologist in Italy, where she had an affair with William J. Murray, Jr., and gave birth to her first son, William. They never married, but Madalyn dropped her married name for Murray. In 1954, she gave birth to a second son, Jon Garth Murray, whose father is unknown.

While living in Baltimore, struggling as a single parent, she took her elder son out of a private, suburban school to attend the closer public school. Madalyn did not like what she saw in the way of an ineffectual, bureaucratic administration, and as an inherently argumentative person, fought the state statute that permitted the reading of Bible lessons and the Lord's Prayer in the classroom. Her lawsuit was joined with a Pennsylvania argument, Abington v. Schempp, before the Supreme Court ruled in her favor in 1963.

Unlike other proponents in her cause, Madalyn captivated the media. She was Phil Donahue's first TV guest, and she appeared often on other shows debating religious leaders and confronting public opinion. She founded the American Atheists organization, garnering donations in the millions.

In 1965, she married ex-Marine Richard O'Hair. In 1980, her son William was "born again" in a South Dallas Baptist Church, and is today the President of the Religious Freedom Coalition. William and his mother never spoke again, but William's first child, Robin, lived with her grandmother until 1995 when she, Madalyn and her uncle Jon were abducted by office manager David Roland Waters and murdered. Said O'Hair in one of her many diatribes, "No god ever gave man anything, nor ever answered any prayer at any time—nor ever will."

Judy Oliver

Born October 3, 1947—Pittsburgh
Died September 10, 2002—Sewickley

At the end, she was far more than a gifted amateur golfer. At the end, the gracious woman who made it all look so easy was a true profile in courage.

Born in Pittsburgh in 1947, Sewickley's Judy Johnson grew up playing basketball and field hockey at The Ellis School. But as the daughter of champion amateur golfer Evelyn St. Clair Moreland, Johnson, who married fellow Sewickleyite John Oliver in 1972, seemed programmed to follow her famous mother onto the links.

A graceful player with a superb short game, at age 23 she won her first amateur championship the same year she graduated New York's Briarcliffe College. At 27, Johnson won the 1974 Broadmoor Invitational—her first national championship. In 1976, she won the Women's Eastern Amateur and the Harder-Hall. By the time she was 30 Oliver had won Western Pennsylvania women's titles, had appeared in the U.S. Women's Open, and had one overriding desire: to play on a U. S. Curtis Cup team, the women's amateur version of the Ryder Cup, pitting Americans against their British counterparts. "It's the only thing I wanted to do," Oliver said. "That was my goal."

In 1978, she got her wish, and again in 1980 and 1982. A decade later, she was asked to captain the 1992 Curtis Cup team. "It was more fun than anything I'd ever won," Oliver said. "It was better than playing."

By 2002, she was battling the lung cancer that took her life. Tapped to be the first-ever Curtis Cup honorary captain, in August she was released from Allegheny General Hospital, walking arm-in-arm with the captains of the American and British teams during the opening and closing ceremonies.

A month later, 54-year-old Judy Oliver died.

A fitting tribute came two years later, in 2004, when the Western Pennsylvania Golf Association's Women's Amateur Championship trophy, which she had last won in 1999, was re-named in her memory.

Stewart O'Nan

Born February 4, 1961—Point Breeze

Award-winning novelist Stewart O'Nan took a boyhood love of horror literature and transformed it into terrifying narratives of desperate, stunted people in lives that go terribly wrong.

O'Nan grew up in Point Breeze, delivering the *Post-Gazette* and relishing George Romero films. After graduating Taylor Allderdice High in 1979, he earned a 1983 bachelor of science at Boston University. Taking a job as a test engineer at Grumman Aerospace, on Long Island, 1984-88, O'Nan left to enroll in Cornell's writing program, graduating in 1992. He began teaching at both the University of Central Oklahoma and the University of New Mexico. Writing short stories, publishing them in literary magazines, in 1993 he entered the University of Pittsburgh Press' Drue Heinz competition—and won. His collection *In the Walled City* was published to virtually universal acclaim for its taut portrayals of unraveling lives.

The following year, 1994, O'Nan's *Snow Angels*, his novel about a Butler-area disintegrating marriage, won a national award. (It has since been made into a film starring Kate Beckinsale and Sam Rockwell).

A year later, in 1995, O'Nan and his family moved to Avon, CT, where they still live, when he became writer-in-residence at Trinity College, a position he held for two years.

Named by Granta as one of America's best young novelists in 1996, O'Nan continues to publish regularly. His novel *The Names of the Dead* (1996) measures the terrible after-effects of Vietnam; *The Speed Queen* (1997) is narrated by a spree killer on death row; *A Prayer for the Dying* (1999) centers around a Civil War-era epidemic; and *Everybody People* (2001), set in East Liberty, reports the tragedies visited on inner city people.

Author of five other novels, O'Nan's nonfiction includes *Faithful*, an account of the historic 2004 Boston Red Sox World Championship, co-written with Stephen King.

O'Nan's latest work is *Last Night at the Lobster*, published in November 2007.

Satchel Paige

Born July 7, 1906—Mobile, AL
Died June 8, 1982—Kansas City, MO

"Don't look back," he famously instructed, "something might be gaining on you."

Apparently heeding his own advice, Satchel Paige enjoyed a 40-year baseball career, beginning on semi-professional Alabama sandlots and ending in Cooperstown's Hall of Fame.

Along the way, using a blazing fastball and pinpoint control, he pitched for Gus Greenlee's 1930s Pittsburgh Crawfords, helping make them the greatest Negro League team of the era.

Born Leroy Robert Page—the family later changed the spelling of its last name—in Mobile in 1906, Paige picked up his nickname as a youthful railroad bag handler. Pitching for the semi-pro Mobile Tigers at age 18, Paige moved to the Negro Leagues fulltime in 1926. Playing at a beanpole-thin 6'-4" and 180 pounds, by 1931 Paige was recognized as one of the stars of Negro League baseball.

As Pittsburgh's Gus Greenlee began to stock his Crawfords with talent, he went after Paige—who, for the princely sum of $250/month, was available. A great showman, master of a multitude of baffling pitches, including his hesitation pitch, midnight rider, and four-day creeper, Paige often deliberately loaded the bases, called in his outfielders, then struck out the side.

Throwing a no-hitter in July 1932, Paige followed it with many stellar starts, none greater than his July 4th no-hitter, 1934, against the crosstown-rival Homestead Grays—a brilliantly pitched, 17-strikeout performance that many consider among the best in Negro League history.

Performing near-perfectly, Paige's record was 32-7 in 1932, 31-4 in 1933, 10-1 in 1934, and 24-3 in 1936. (Due to a salary dispute Paige missed much of 1935—pitching instead in Bismarck, ND).

Leaving in 1937, when Dominican leader Rafael Trujillo imported many Negro Leaguers, Paige, unlike many former Crawfords, never again played for a Pittsburgh team.

However, his extraordinary career was hardly over. Playing for a dozen different teams, including Mexico and Puerto Rico, Paige pitched the Kansas City Monarchs to four consecutive Negro American League pennants, 1939-1942, and a fifth in 1946.

Considered a prime candidate to integrate the Major Leagues, he was passed over because of his age—41 in 1947—in favor of the younger Jackie Robinson.

Trailing Robinson by just one season, Paige arrived in the majors in 1948 at age 42—baseball's all-time oldest rookie. Pitching for the Cleveland Indians, Paige ended the year with a 6-1 record, 2.48 ERA, two shutouts, and 43 strikeouts—and a World Series ring.

Pitching with the Indians again in 1949, and St. Louis Browns 1951-53, Paige made a last appearance for the Kansas City Athletics in 1965, age 59, the oldest man ever to pitch in the major leagues.

Going Hollywood, Paige appeared in the 1960 Robert Mitchum oatburner *The Wonderful Country*. Publishing his autobiography *Maybe I'll Pitch Forever* in 1962, he became the first Negro Leaguer inducted into the Hall of Fame in 1971.

Paige was portrayed by Louis Gossett, Jr., and Delroy Lindo in biopics. He died of a heart attack at his Kansas City home in 1982, a month short of his 76th birthday.

Arnold Palmer

Born September 10, 1929—Latrobe, PA

It was an Arnold Palmer moment. At the 18th hole of a Florida invitational tournament, the golfing legend stood more than 200 yards from the green. Famous for his go-for-broke playing style, Palmer sized up the lie, then used his driver to power the ball onto the green. Palmer danced in glee.

His loyal fans—Arnie's Army—went wild. Arnold Palmer was 74 years old.

It was just that sort of play, and outsized emotion, combined with good looks, easy demeanor, and humble background, that made Arnold Palmer the most popular golfer in history.

Arnold Daniel Palmer learned golf literally from the ground up. Son of Milfred J. "Deacon" Palmer, who had risen from groundskeeper to professional at Latrobe Country Club, Arnold was a golf prodigy. Playing at 4, notching competitive scores by 7, caddying at 11, Palmer won his first of five West Penn Amateur Championships at 17 and was Pennsylvania high school champion twice.

Attending Wake Forest University, Palmer was first seed on the golf team. He won the U.S. Amateur Championship in 1954, and his first major professional tournament the following year—the 1955 Canadian Open.

Playing at 5'-10" and 185 pounds, over 50 years Palmer won more than 90 major tournaments, including 62 on the PGA circuit. Taking seven major championships—The Masters (1958, 1960, 1962, 1964), the U.S. Open (1960), and the British Open (1961-62)—he also won in Australia, France, and Spain.

Golf's first $1 million winner, Palmer's best years were 1960-63, when he took an incredible 29 PGA events. Playing on six Ryder Cup teams (1961-73), Palmer joined the Senior PGA Tour at its 1980 inaugural season, winning 10 times.

Since retiring in 2006, he has been awarded countless honors, including the 2004 Presidential Medal of Freedom. A charter member of the World Golf Hall of Fame, he is also enshrined in both the American Golf and PGA Halls of Fame.

Off the links, working with pioneering sports entrepreneur Mark McCormack, he established Arnold Palmer Enterprises in 1961. With his signature multicolored golf umbrella on clothing, stationery, and golf equipment,

Palmer is a sought-after spokesman, endorsing such prestigious names as GlaxoSmithKline, Encore Bank, Pennzoil, and Rolex.

In addition, Palmer owns Latrobe Country Club and Orlando's Bay Hill Club and Lodge, including the Arnold Palmer Golf Academy. His Arnold Palmer Design Company has designed more than 250 golf courses in 20 countries. There is also Arnold Palmer's Restaurant in La Quinta, CA.

Publisher of *Kingdom*, a golf magazine, Palmer has also authored nine golf books and videos, has his own signature wine, and co-founded The Golf Channel.

Palmer also founded Orlando's Arnold Palmer Hospital for Children, Latrobe's UPMC Arnold Palmer Pavilion, and La Quinta's Arnold Palmer Prostate Center.

Dividing his time among Latrobe, Orlando, and La Quinta, Palmer remains such an icon that in 2007 he was invited to the White House for dinner with Queen Elizabeth II—and had his signature iced tea/lemonade drink mentioned on *The Sopranos*.

Perry Como and Bob Hope give Palmer a few pointers at a charity outting, May 24, 1967.

Malcolm Parcell

Born January 1, 1896—Claysville, PA
Died March 25, 1987—Washington, PA

Malcolm Parcell was such a famed artist that the Barrymores—John, Ethel, and Lionel—wanted him to come to Hollywood to paint their portrait. But Parcell so loved home, the green, rolling hills of Washington County, that, while not adverse to traveling for commissions, he turned down the Barrymores—and the klieg lights of Hollywood.

Born New Year's Day, 1896, in Claysville, Washington County, son of the pastor of the Broad Street Baptist Church, Malcolm Stevens Parcell was introduced to painting by his father, who had studied art before entering the ministry.

Commuting daily by trolley and train to Carnegie Tech, Parcell earned a 1918 degree in fine arts, joined the Associated Artists, and turned professional. Moving to New York, which he despised, Parcell quickly achieved both artistic and commercial success, including placing a portrait as a *Town and Country* magazine cover.

Despite his burgeoning career, including an offer of cover work by the *Saturday Evening Post*, Parcell returned home. Nevertheless, to find portrait work he traveled to Cleveland and Chicago, even Boston and New York. Staying up to four weeks in hotels, advertising in local newspapers, Parcell painted portraits, seven or eight sittings for each subject, two hours a sitting.

Considered by many the most skilled portrait painter of the era, Parcell also excelled at Washington County landscapes. Between the two genres, he placed 30 paintings in an unprecedented 30 Carnegie Internationals, 1920-50, a number unmatched by any other artist.

Parcell's *Return to the Village*, c. 1925, oil on canvas, H: 41 1/8 x W: 48 1/4 inches, Carnegie Museum of Art, Pittsburgh, Purchase; gift of the H. J. Heinz II Charitable and Family Trust

Moving in 1963 to a 14-acre farm near Prosperity which he called Moon Lorn, for its tree-obstructed views, Parcell and his wife lived in a remodeled log cabin. Wearing a skullcap cut from women's felt hats, painting in an adjacent A-frame, in his lifetime he created some 2,000 paintings.

In 1987, at age 91, Parcell died of heart failure in Washington Hospital.

Barry Paris

Born February 6, 1948—Pittsburgh

A chance encounter in Wichita made screen biographer Barry Paris' career—and changed serious American screen studies.

Born in Pittsburgh in 1948, Barry Paris took a 1969 Columbia University degree and  set off to write about movies, first at Munich's Institute for the Study of the USSR, where his *Russian Cinema and the Soviet Film Industry* was one of the world's first thorough studies on the subject, then in this country, at Wichita's *Prairie Journal*, 1972-74. Discovering a treasure trove of original material on the silent screen icon—and cult figure—Louise Brooks, a Wichita native, Paris spent years doggedly pursuing his reclusive subject.

Moving to the *Miami Herald*, and seeing two tours of duty at the *Pittsburgh Post-Gazette*, Paris' 1989 *Louise Brooks* became an instant classic. Receiving universal praise for its measured tone, stunning prose, and scrupulous research, no less a film avatar than Leonard Maltin named *Louise Brooks* his Film Book of the Year. Paris also scripted the 1998 Emmy-nominated documentary *Louise Brooks: Looking for Lulu*.

Established as the pre-eminent screen biographer of his time, Paris followed with *Tony Curtis: The Autobiography* (1993), *Garbo* (1995), which developed another screen icon with Brooks-like depth, and *Audrey Hepburn* (1996). A literary scholar as well as biographer and critic, Paris also edited and wrote the preface to *Stella Adler on Ibsen, Strindberg, and Chekhov*, a 1999 collection of talks by the great drama teacher.

Away from stage and screen, his remarkable, inspirational 2000 *Song of Haiti: The Lives of Dr. Larimer and Gwen Mellon at the Albert Schweitzer Hospital of Deschapelles* documented how Paul Mellon's youngest son and his wife moved to one of the most isolated and impoverished sections of Haiti, building and staffing a hospital themselves.

Still writing film criticism for the *Pittsburgh Post-Gazette*, Barry Paris lives and works in Pittsburgh.

Horace Parlan

Born January 19, 1931—Pittsburgh

Horace Parlan became an accomplished jazz pianist who recorded with some of the industry's most respected musicians. He was able to accomplish this in spite of a physical disability that rendered two of his fingers on his right hand virtually useless and the entire right side of his body partially paralyzed.

Parlan grew up in East Liberty. He developed polio as a child but he began playing piano at the request of his parents who thought it might be good therapy for his ailment. The piano lessons did help but he gave them up. It wasn't until he was almost ten when he rediscovered the piano with the help of teacher James Miller, also known for teaching a young Ahmad Jamal.

Gospel music became a major influence on Parlan, the son of a minister. He graduated from Peabody High School in 1949. As a teenager his musical cravings would move towards jazz and by the early1950s he was a busy musician working clubs like the Crawford Grill and the Midway Lounge, jamming with some of the greatest musicians in the business. It was during this time that he met musical mentors Tommy Turrentine and Charles Mingus who invited him to New York to play with his band.

Parlan may have been a good balance to Mingus's volatile and abrupt demeanor. Mingus was an abrasive, yet well respected artist who demanded a great deal from his band. Parlan's time with Mingus's Jazz Workshop was rewarding for both musicians. During the next several years Parlan played with a who's who of the New York jazz scene. For a while he was even a member of the house band for the famed Harlem club, Minton's Playhouse. By the late 1960s the New York scene had become less appealing to Parlan; the violence, the drugs, the work all began to take their toll. Parlan had played a brief engagement in Copenhagen and, enamored with the jazz scene and relaxed environment there, departed for Denmark.

Parlan worked and recorded steadily over the next decades and was popular internationally, but didn't get quite the same attention in the states. Among his many recordings were two critically acclaimed releases that he recorded with Archie Shepp, the fiery hard bop saxophonist. Parlan did make one brief trip back to the continent in 1999 for the Montreal Jazz Festival, where he made an appearance once again with Shepp.

Horace Parlan still lives in the Danish countryside.

Joe Pass

Born January 13. 1929—New Brunswick, NJ
Died May 23, 1994—Los Angeles. CA

Joe Pass experienced the depths of drug abuse and the heights of virtuosity as one of the greatest guitarists in jazz.

Joseph Anthony Jacobi Passalaqua, though born in New Jersey, moved to Johnstown, PA with his family as a toddler. Pass's father worked in the steel mills and saw to it that his children learned a skill so proficiently that they wouldn't have to do the same dirty work he did day in and day out. As a young boy Pass was mesmerized by "The Singing Cow-

boy," Gene Autry, and got his first guitar when he was 9. His father required him to practice eight hours a day: two hours before he went to school, two hours after school and four hours before he went to bed. Wishing he were out playing ball instead, Pass submitted to the regimen until he was in his mid-teens. He started working with small groups, playing parties and dances, occasionally making more money gigging than his father made in the mill.

Bandleader Charlie Barnet employed the young guitarist and he eagerly hit the road to New York. There, caught-up in the jazz scene and fueled with a desire to rebel against his father, Pass slid into a world of alcohol and heroin. The next decade was spent in various cities, in and out of prison, on drugs, off drugs, personally and musically in a state of decay. In 1960, Pass checked into Synanon, the famed and controversial drug and alcohol treatment center in California. Two years later Pass, accompanied by fellow patients and using a borrowed guitar, recorded his landmark release *The Sounds of Synanon*. From then on, Pass conquered the world of jazz with his virtuosity, winning a Grammy© with Oscar Peterson, working as a sideman for the likes of Frank Sinatra, Johnny Mathis, Sarah Vaughan, and Della Reese. He accompanied greats like Ella Fitzgerald, Duke Ellington, Count Basie, Dizzy Gillespie, and Pittsburgh-natives Ray Brown and Roy Eldridge, and he worked on numerous TV shows from Johnny Carson to Merv Griffin. For a period during the 1970s and 1980s Joe Pass was one of the most recorded jazz guitarists in the world. Despite his stature as an elite musician, Pass had an equal reputation as being one of the kindest, most down-to-earth people in the business.

In 1992, Pass was diagnosed with liver cancer. On May 7, 1994, at a club in L.A., Pass turned to a fellow musician and, with a tear in his eye, said he could no longer perform. Just two weeks later Joe Pass died.

William Passavant

Born October 9, 1821– Zelienople, PA
Died June 3, 1894—Pittsburgh

William Alfred Passavant was a Lutheran clergyman, writer, and founder of numerous hospitals and orphanages. Born and bred in Western Pennsylvania, his influence and his many surviving ministries continue to help people across the country.

Born in Zelienople to wealthy immigrant parents, Passavant was influenced by the Lutheran faith from an early age. After graduating in 1840 from Jefferson College in Canonsburg, he studied to become a pastor at the Lutheran Seminary in Gettysburg. Passavant was ordained in 1843 by the Maryland Synod and was soon assigned to his first small parish in Canton, MD.

Early in his career, Passavant became interested in writing and editing religious periodicals. He served as an assistant at the *Lutheran Observer*, a publication that endorsed a relaxed version of Lutheranism. He was soon drawn back to a more conservative approach to his religion, however, and founded his own publication, the *Missionary*, in 1848.

In addition to his writing career, Passavant was the pastor of the First English Lutheran Church of Pittsburgh from 1844 to 1855. It was during this time that he seriously focused his attention toward those in need. Passavant used his good reputation to gather funds and supplies for Lutheran settlers headed out west.

By 1849, Passavant garnered enough support to open the first Protestant hospital in the United States. Located in Pittsburgh, the hospital was initially understaffed, and Passavant and one young colleague were the only people on hand to care for the facility's patients, injured soldiers from the Mexican War. Passavant was sometimes criticized for caring for those dying of highly infectious diseases like cholera and smallpox, but the pastor would not turn patients away.

Over the next 30 years, Passavant founded hospitals in cities such as Milwaukee and Chicago and orphanages in Rochester and Boston. Today, several Pittsburgh area hospitals, including UPMC Passavant in the North Hills, pay homage to the generous pastor by using his name. Passionate about higher education, Passavant established several schools, including Thiel College in Greenville and the Chicago Lutheran Seminary.

Passavant died of natural causes in 1894 at age 73. Today, he is honored as an inspiring religious leader and a fearless provider for those in need.

The Rev. Leroy Patrick

Born November 17, 1915—Charleston, SC
Died January 12, 2006—Pittsburgh

No sooner had he arrived in Pittsburgh to lead the Bethesda United Presbyterian Church of Homewood than he jumped into a pool—specifically, the Highland Park city pool—but more figuratively the frigid waters of Jim Crow segregation. In July 1951, the Rev. LeRoy Patrick, wrapping up a hot day with kids from both his church and those from East Liberty Presbyterian, joined arms to take a swim in the mostly white neighborhood, prompting vicious racial epithets.

The following summer, Patrick's crusade against segregated pools included 25 more visits with kids. Attorney Wendell Freeland joined him on several occasions, as did city police to keep the peace. The perceived audacity of his campaign, three years before Rosa Parks' refusal to move to the back of her bus, did not escape fellow black clergy, some urging him to stop, others joining him later at pools all around the county.

In the early 1950s, Patrick became chairman of the Public Accommodation Committee of the NAACP as well as the chairman of the Race Relations Department of the Pittsburgh Presbytery.

Patrick was also instrumental in creating the Bethesda Center, one of the city's first social services agencies, founded from his church. A graduate of Union Theological Seminary in 1942, he had graduated from Lincoln University in 1939.

For 35 years, he presided as pastor at Bethesda, of which 10 he also served as Moderator of his 226-church Presbytery. Patrick also served on the boards of the Pittsburgh NAACP and the Pennsylvania Historical and Museum Commission. Tall, thin, eloquent and always dressed in a full dark suit—unless ready to jump into a pool—Patrick died in his Oakland apartment at the age of 90.

Ron Paul

Born August 20, 1935—Green Tree

It is all too possible, given the mercurial nature of U.S. politics, that Ron Paul may one day become President of the United States. Of course, as Horton told the Who, anything is possible. Ever convinced, Ron Paul has campaigned for the office since 1988.

Born the third of five boys on his parents' Green Tree Dairy, he drove a milk truck as soon as he was able to drive. Paul graduated from Dormont High in 1953, and paid his way through Gettysburg College where he received a B.S. in biology in 1957. That same year he married Carol Wells in Dormont. In 1961, after serving two years in the Air Force during the Cuban Missile Crisis, he earned a medical degree from Duke University, then returned to active duty as a flight surgeon. Returning home to Pittsburgh, he later served his residency in obstetrics and gynecology at Magee-Women's Hospital from 1965 to 1968. The family moved to Surfside, TX, and he opened his practice.

Politics loomed bright in 1974 when Paul first ran for Congress—as a Republican—and lost. Two years later he won the seat of his former opponent and, for all but one term, represented the 22nd congressional district until 1985 when he lost to a young upstart, Tom DeLay. In 1988, he beat out contender Frank Zappa for the Libertarian nomination for President. Defeated, he returned to his medical practice.

Again in 1996, he ran for Congress, defeating Charles "Lefty" Morris, and is currently congressman for Texas' 14th District.

Paul's platform is to work "tirelessly for limited constitutional government, lower taxes, free markets, and a return to sound monetary policies."

Michelle Pawk

Born November 16, 1961—Renfrew, PA

Michelle Pawk grew up in Renfrew where her parents Michael and Sandy ran the Lyndora Hotel and Natilli's Italian restaurant. Although her siblings, Laura, Matthew, and Michael still work in the Pittsburgh region, none might have suspected then that Michelle, a small, slim dark-haired dancer, (who had considered pursuing a degree in anthropology at Allegheny College,) harbored a talent that would launch her to a full-bodied career on the musical stage.

Pawk, who earned her Equity card from playing in the chorus of the CLO 1986 season, debuted on Broadway in the long forgotten *Mail*, an ensemble musical that ran barely a month in 1988. She left for Los Angeles and got by with small parts on TV shows like, *Golden Girls, L.A. Law,* and *Dear John.* Then, in 1991, while in Pittsburgh for her brother's wedding, she got a call for auditions in L.A. She flew instead to NYC. There she won the East Coast chance to play the role for which she was first considered in L.A. And, within, three months, she opened in the smash hit *Crazy For You,* which ran an astounding 1,622 performances. She played the role of the rich bitch Irene and commanded the stage with her rendition of Gershwin's "Naughty Baby" for which she was nominated for the 1992 Drama Desk Award for Outstanding Featured Actress in a Musical. Not bad for a 32-year-old in just her second run on Broadway.

Featured in dozens of new musicals and revivals following her first big success, she got a second crack at fame in *Seussical*, creating the original role of Mayzie LaBird. And then it happened again. Pawk won the lead in *Hollywood Arms*, playing alongside Linda Lavin. She won the 2003 Tony® for Best Featured Actress in a Play.

Twice married, working in regional theatres and on Broadway tours, never having considered that her early school productions at Knoch High in Saxonburg would amount to very much, Pawk performs often and regularly.

Philip Pearlstein

Born 1924—Pittsburgh

Carnegie Tech classmate of Andy Warhol, creator of outsized, somnambulant nudes, he has been called a pioneer of post-abstract expressionism, the leading contemporary American realist, the man who singlehandedly created new opportunities for representational art.

Born in Pittsburgh in 1924, the son of a surgeon, Philip Pearlstein attended Taylor Allderdice High School. He attended Saturday art classes at Carnegie Institute during high school and enrolled full-time after his 1942 graduation. Drafted into the Army after his freshman year, 1943, Pearlstein worked as an artist, first in the United States, then in Italy.

In many ways, the war provided an unparalleled educational opportunity for Pearlstein, who, apart from the art techniques he learned at his various postings, made regular visits to Venice, Milan, and Florence, among other cities, to study classic art and architecture first-hand.

Returning home in 1946, he re-enrolled at Carnegie Tech, where he was a classmate—as well as a studio-mate—of Andy Warhol. Earning a bachelor of fine arts in 1949, marrying fellow art student Dorothy Cantor in 1950, Pearlstein moved to New York.

Painting—largely landscapes, principally rocks and eroding cliffs—and studying at New York University, by 1954 Pearlstein was selected for an Emerging Talent show at the prestigious Kootz Gallery. The following year, 1955, Pearlstein enjoyed his first one-man exhibition at New York's Tanager Gallery; that same year he received a master of fine arts

from New York University. In 1956, Pearlstein was included in a Whitney Museum show, his first of 10 such postings through 1973.

Making a living as a graphic designer, including a stint at *Life* magazine, a 1957-58 Fulbright Fellowship took Pearlstein back to Italy. On his return, he took a job as an instructor at Brooklyn's Pratt Institute; in 1963 he moved over to Brooklyn College, from which he retired a quarter-century later, in 1988.

It was at the same time that Pearlstein found his signature style—and lifelong subject matter: carefully drawn, nearly super-realistic watercolors and oils of studio nudes, the lighting flat, the colors harshly intense.

Exclusively painting living models, taking up to two months of weekly sessions in a studio perched atop his New York home, Pearlstein begins by making careful pencil drawings, then lays in foundation washes, finally refining every detail. With the women invariably appearing bored or fatigued, and the nudes deliberately non-erotic, Pearlstein achieves an acute emotional distance between the viewer and the work. This is blunt sexuality, not voyeuristic, salacious, or earthy. It offers nothing and never attempts to be inviting.

As his technique has changed over the past five decades, more extraneous material has entered Pearlstein's paintings, the nudes posed with folk art, kimonos, rugs, and sculpture, much of it Pearlstein's own.

With his work now part of more than five dozen major American museum collections, including Chicago's Art Institute, Washington's Corcoran Galley, and New York's Metropolitan Museum of Art, Pearlstein is a recognized American master, multiple award winner, and holder of three honorary doctorates.

Philip Pearlstein still lives and works in New York City.

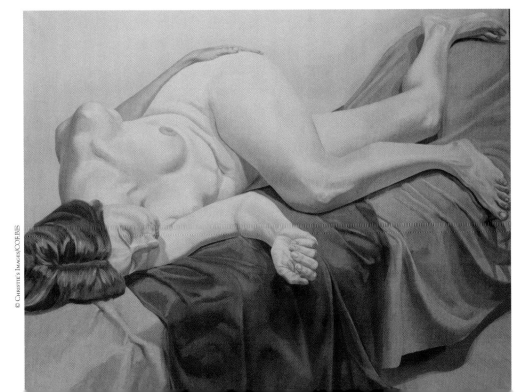

Robert Peary

Born May 6, 1856—Cresson, PA
Died February 20, 1920—Washington, D.C.

His father, Charles Peary, had been a "successful builder of barrelheads and staves," most likely for the adventurers and settlers heading west from Pittsburgh on the Ohio River. So when Charles died suddenly of pneumonia in 1859—as Civil War fever began to spread across the nation—his wife, Mary Wiley Peary, took their 3-year-old son Robert from the family homestead in Cresson, PA, and headed to Maine.

At age 8, Peary went to boarding school, then attended high school in Portland, and won a scholarship to Bowdoin College. He sought and accepted a commission as a civil engineering officer in the U.S. Navy in 1881. Having lived with his mother all his life until that time, Peary once wrote his mother, "I shall not be satisfied until my name is known from one end of the world to the other… I must have fame."

Author Bruce Henderson writes in his book, *True North: Peary, Cook and the Race to the Pole*, that Peary was raised as a mamma's boy. She even made him wear sun bonnets to shield his delicate skin from sunburn. It forced him to prove his manliness in fistfights growing up. That delicate image is in sharp contrast to the powerful six-foot figure photographed in fur and animal skins and sporting a bushy walrus moustache, who withstood some of the most perilous elements known to man.

In his lifetime, Peary made seven expeditions to the Arctic. He claimed that on one of those treks, in 1909, he set foot on the true North Pole, a point, he insisted, as accurate as could be determined on a moving ice cap with relatively primitive navigational instruments of that day. That claim was disputed by Dr. Frederick Cook, a fellow explorer, who claimed he'd found true north a year earlier in 1908. Their conflicting claims, intense rivalry, and bitter feud lasted their lifetimes. Since each man claimed to have reached the pole by himself, without witnesses, neither could offer absolute proof of his achievement. In 1988, *National Geographic*, having reviewed Peary's long-suppressed diary and notes, published an article concluding Peary had actually missed the North Pole by perhaps as much as 80 miles.

When Peary retired from his explorations, he returned to live on Eagle Island in Freeport, Maine, appropriately perhaps, the home of outfitter L. L. Bean. Peary is buried in Arlington National Cemetery.

Rob Penny

Born August 6, 1941—Opelika, AL
Died March 16, 2003—Pittsburgh

The assasination of Martin Luther King, Jr., in 1968 provoked outrage and violence from coast to coast, including Pittsburgh.

Playwright Rob Penny reacted, too. Working with his anger, and his angst—and his hope—he and his friend August Wilson co-founded the Black Horizon Theater.

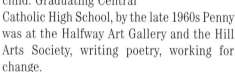

Born Robert Lee Penny, he moved to Pittsburgh's Hill District as a child. Graduating Central Catholic High School, by the late 1960s Penny was at the Halfway Art Gallery and the Hill Arts Society, writing poetry, working for change.

Then came the riots, and Pittsburgh's first sustained African-American theatre. Although Black Horizon lasted only three years, closing in 1971, its impact was profound. Touring to places that had never seen all-black productions, Black Horizon placed African-American culture squarely in the city's forefront.

Writing some 30 plays over a 40-year career—including such standouts as *Nefertari Rising, Diane's Heart, Clean Drums*, and *Sun Rising on the Hill District*—Penny's work attacked injustice. Railing against racism, his themes range from personal spirituality to family relationships, women's liberation to substance abuse. Penny's venues stretched to Chicago's ETA Performing Arts Foundation, Brooklyn's Billie Holiday Theater, and New York's New Federal Theater, at the latter, the *New York Times* praised Penny's *Who Loves the Dancer* for its "inherent honesty"—an apt description of all his work.

Becoming a Pitt professor of Africana Studies in 1969, he chaired the department, 1978-84. A lifelong proponent of African culture, intimates called him Brother Oba—Yoruba for king.

With Pitt's Kuntu Repertory Theatre created in 1974 to showcase Penny's work, where he served as playwright-in-residence, in 1976 he founded the Kuntu Writers Workshop, a project he led until his death.

In 2003, the 61-year-old Rob Penny died of a heart attack in his Hill District home.

Nick Perry

Born 1916—Morningside
Died April 22, 2003—Pittsburgh

Nicholas Pericles Katsafanas graduated from Peabody High and Duquesne University knowing that he wanted to be a radio announcer. In 1939, however, he had a tough time getting a job, winding up at a small station in Charleston, WV, to start his career. Eventually, he was hired at the new WDTV, the forerunner of KDKA-TV, and later switched to WTAE-TV on the day its studio doors first opened.

For more than 22 years, Perry was a staple at the station, announcing , and more popularly, hosting *Dialing for Dollars* and *Bowling for Dollars*, two shows that were common local fare for many stations filling afternoon time slots before the advent of syndicated programming. Perry might have retired in this role, but, on April 24, 1980, the Pennsylvania Daily Lottery numbers came up 666, and his life changed dramatically thereafter. Perry had been the evening host of the Daily Numbers drawing for two years.

Although he denied guilt in the "fix" up until his death in 2003, he was always suspect. The story goes like this. In alleged association with Peter and Jack Maragos, two brothers who operated a vending machine business in

McKees Rocks, Perry conspired with a lottery official and his station's art director to have lottery balls switched in the machine. The fake balls—that is, all but the 4s and 6s—were filled with trace amounts of white latex paint, adding just enough weight to prevent them from being drawn up the vacuum display. Meanwhile, the Maragos brothers traveled the state playing as much as $1.6 million at various machines and on various combinations of fours and sixes.

Ironically, state lottery officials only became suspicious when local bookies announced they would not pay out on the 666 win. There was a "buzz" on the streets. WTAE-TV took an active role in the investigation, proving through stop-frame review of the broadcast that, indeed, only the four and six balls were jumping on that fated evening.

Perry was convicted and spent two years in prison and, just blocks from where he was born in Morningside, he spent an additional year in a half-way house.

In 2000, John Travolta and Lisa Kudrow starred in *Lucky Numbers*, a film loosely based on the incident.

Nathaniel Philbrick

Born June 11, 1956—Boston, MA

America's premiere contemporary seafaring stories—true-life yarns of bold victories and incalculable disasters—trace their origins to a child's bedroom in Pittsburgh's East End.

That was where Thomas Philbrick, a distinguished Pitt professor of American literature, told his young son Nathaniel bedtime stories. One of them, about the whaleship *Essex*, the real-life model for Melville's doomed Pequod in *Moby Dick*, particularly thrilled the young child—so much so that he turned it into a bestseller and National Book Award winner.

Born Nathaniel Philbrick in Boston in 1956, he attended Linden School and Taylor Allderdice. After a B.A. from Brown, where he was that school's first All-American sailor, and a Duke M.A., Philbrick wrote for *Sailing World* magazine, then wrote and edited several sailing books, including *Yaahting: A Par-*

ody and *The Passionate Sailor.*

Moving to Nantucket, Philbrick wrote the 1994 *Away Off Shore: Nantucket Island and Its People*, a thorough island history, and the 1998 *Abram's Eyes: The Native American Legacy of Nantucket Island*.

Philbrick's masterpiece came two years later, in 2000, with *In the Heart of the Sea: The Tragedy of the Whaleship Essex*. Winner of the National Book Award, 40 weeks a *New York Times* bestseller, the book is a terrifying account of the ship's destruction by a giant whale, unspeakable conditions, and cannibalism. Philbrick also re-told the story in the 2003 *Revenge of the Whale*, a young reader's version, and *The Loss of the Ship Essex, Sunk by a Whale: First-Person Accounts*, co-edited by his father.

In 2003, Philbrick followed with *Sea of Glory: America's Voyage of Discovery—The U.S. Exploring Expedition, 1838-1842*, the attempt to map the Pacific—and the discovery of Antarctica; and the 2006 *Mayflower: A Story of Courage, Community, and War*. The dark tale of disease and death was a 2007 Pulitzer finalist.

Nathaniel Philbrick lives, writes, and sails on Nantucket Island.

Deacon Phillippe

Born May 23, 1872—Rural Retreat, VA
Died March 30, 1952—Avalon, PA

"Phil, Phil, Phillippe, Phil," chanted the Pittsburgh fans, "he can win, and you know he will."

Sadly, it would not be so.

Charles Louis "Deacon" Phillippe was big for his day, 6 feet and 180 pounds. A righthanded pitcher, he played 13 seasons, winning 189 games.

Coming to the Louisville Colonels in 1899, Phillippe won 21 games. Playing 1900-11 in Pittsburgh, Phillippe notched four consecutive 20-win seasons, 1900-03, the Pirates taking three National League titles.

In 1903, when Phillippe won a career-high 25 games, owner Barney Dreyfuss created the World Series, a nine-game championship against the American League. Handed the ball for Game One against the Boston Pilgrims, Phillippe bested Denton

True "Cy" Young—Cy for cyclone, for the fastball that netted him a record 511 wins. Starting and winning games three and four, Phillippe had done the impossible—up 3-1, it seemed the Pirates would coast to victory.

Shelled in game five, snuffed in game six, the Series was suddenly tied 3-3. With the weather bad, and the Pirate arms worse, the Deacon was the only man standing. Pitching well—very well, in fact—he nevertheless lost game seven to Young and game eight—and the Series—to Bill Dinneen.

The Pirates may have lost, but Deacon Phillippe's achievements will never be equaled: five World Series decisions, five complete games, 44 innings pitched.

Often injured over the next seven years, he won 20 in 1905, but in the 1909 World Series pitched just six innings. After three 1911 appearances, he retired.

The following year, 1912, Phillippe managed the Pittsburgh Filipinos in the short-lived United States League. In 1913 he managed the Federal League's Pittsburgh Stogies.

Working as a court tipstaff in his later years, Deacon Phillippe died in suburban Avalon in 1952.

Duncan Phillips

Born June 26, 1886—Pittsburgh
Died May 9, 1966—Washington, D.C.

In discussing the influence of art collector and curator Duncan Phillips, no less a prestigious journal than *The New Criterion* commented on "the power that an individual sensibility can wield in forming and enhancing public taste."

In 20th-century art, Phillips's power was extraordinary—perhaps unmatched.

The grandson of James Laughlin, a banker and co-founder of Jones and Laughlin Stool, Phillips and his family moved to Washington, D.C. in 1895, when Duncan was 9. Evincing an early interest in art, as a Yale undergraduate he published a 1907 essay "The Need of Art at Yale."

Duncan, left, with his father Major Duncan Phillips (seated) and his brother, James, right, ca. 1900

By the century's second decade Phillips was a noted collector and critic, one of the first Americans to embrace and support impressionist and modern art both here and abroad. After his father and brother died within 13 months of each other, 1917-18, Phillips wanted art to be their memorial. Buying extensively in 1919-20, in 1921 Phillips, along with his mother Eliza Laughlin Phillips (for whom the South Oakland J&L steel mill was named), opened the Phillips Memorial Art Gallery in a specially built, skylighted room in their 1897 Georgian Revival home, 1600 21st Street, Washington, D.C. Also offering art classes, Phillips initiated an ambitious publication program, many of the catalogues including his own contributions.

By 1930, when the collection grew to more than 600 works, Phillips turned the entire DuPont Circle residence into a museum. What began as America's first collection of modern paintings grew into the country's foremost collection of modern art, featuring such masters as Renoir, van Gogh, Monet, Degas, Cézanne, Braque, Picasso, Matisse, and Klee—along with Winslow Homer, Thomas Eakins, James McNeill Whistler, Georgia O'Keeffe, Mark Rothko, and Richard Diebenkorn—many discovered, supported, and publicized by Phillips himself.

Although 80-year-old Duncan Phillips died in 1966, his Phillips Collection survives him, featuring a permanent collection of some 2,500 works.

Irving Pichel

Born June 24, 1891—Pittsburgh
Died July 13, 1954—Hollywood, CA

Irving Pichel (rhymes with Mitchell) grew up in Shadyside, attended Rodef Sholom, and was best friends with George S. Kaufman who, at 14, organized a drama league at the Oakland synagogue. Kaufman, whose greatest comedic plays were all written with others, first collaborated with Pichel to write *The Failure*. It was. But its two actor/authors proved time and again that success is born from determination.

A 1910 graduate of South Side's Bedford School, Pichel went to Harvard and there joined the once-famed "47 Workshop," a playwriting practicum (Professor Baker listed his course as English 47) that also bred the talents of George Abbott, S.N. Behrman, and Eugene O'Neill. Blessed with a more remarkable stage voice than literary, Pichel embraced the stage and, upon graduation, headed west to Chicago, then Pasadena, to act and direct under the tutelage of Gilmor Brown, the founder of the Pasadena Playhouse. Pichel, along with Brown, became early founders of the Little Theatre movement that, representative of the Pittsburgh Playhouse, relied heavily on semi-professional, but absolutely dedicated artists. It was the Pasadena Playhouse where early silent film stars were sent to train for the "talkies."

Soon, Hollywood returned the favor, and in 1931, Pichel was signed to Paramount to act and direct. He debuted in front of the camera in 1930's *The Right To Love*, and behind the camera in 1932's *The Most Dangerous Game*. In 1931, however, he was almost cast as the original *Dr. Jekyl & Mr. Hyde*, until director Rouben Mamoulien famously exclaimed, "He's more like Mr. Hyde & Mr. Hyde." In 1933 he received mixed reviews playing Fagin opposite Dickie Moore in Monogram Picture's *Oliver Twist*. From then on, Pichel's career as a director soared in reverse proportion to his acting credits.

His more famous directorial triumphs include *The Miracle of the Bells*, starring Fred MacMurray and Frank Sinatra (1947), and *Mr. Peabody & The Mermaid*, starring William Powell (1948). To movie trivia fans, he is revered for narrating John Ford's classic *She Wore a Yellow Ribbon* (1949) as well as for directing Robert Heinlein's *Destination Moon* for which he won a 1951 Oscar® for Special Effects.

Sidney Pink

Born March 6, 1916—Pittsburgh
Died October 12, 2002—Pompano Beach, FL

With the advancing popularity of television, in 1952 movie studios looked to innovative technology to get patrons back into neighborhood theaters. One new system required two reels of film to be projected simultaneously on the same screen. The idea was to replicate human vision by offering a stereoscopic difference between what the right eye and left eye saw. Of course, theater patrons had to wear special glasses. The system was called "Natural Vision" but is more widely known today as "3-D."

One Hollywood producer, born in Pittsburgh (and whose wife just happened to own a chain of theaters here) knew well what 3-D could do for the future of films. Native son and Pitt graduate Sidney Pink is credited as the first producer to bring a feature-length 3-D movie to the general public. *Bwana Devil,* upon its release on November 22, 1952, was an instant success. Said its star, Robert Stack, "Over the titles, they had a train that made a long, circling turn and then came directly to the camera. …People began to scream and jumped out of their seats and ran out of the theater. I remember one of the guys saying, 'Son of a gun, it really works!'"

So successful was the film, other studios jumped at the technology. 1953 was the year of 3-D movies and by far the most successful was *House of Wax,* starring Vincent Price and featuring, as Igor, a young Charles Bronson.

Later that year, Pink would bring his second 3-D feature to the screen, *I Was a Burlesque Queen*, which was a catastrophic fusion of poor writing and too few 3-D effects.

Yet, Pink had tasted the sweet success of

innovation and, undaunted, looked for newer techniques. With the Cold War raging, producers turned to the chilling plot opportunities of Sci-Fi and, in 1959, Pink produced his second big hit, *The Angry Red Planet*, a film shot with a technique he called Cinemagic. Though the film is today a cult classic, Cinemagic, which amounted to shooting scenes through a colorizing filter, was a laugh.

Pink moved his production crew to Denmark, and there he wrote, filmed, and produced *Reptilicus* in 1961. Always looking to do things on the cheap, Pink was also one of the first spaghetti-western producers. *Finger on the Trigger*, starring Rory Calhoun, was one of his first, but his most famous may be *Madigan's Millions* for which he cast a young and unknown Dustin Hoffman.

In all, Pink made more than 50 films before he died at the age of 86.

Jimmy Ponder

Born May 10, 1946—Pittsburgh

When he was in his mid-teens, a young guitar-playing Jimmy Ponder was told that there were clubs on the North Side of Pittsburgh where he'd be beat-up if he didn't play to the crowd's liking. He took the gigs anyway and is now recognized as one of the most accomplished—and underrated—jazz musicians in the world.

He began playing at the age of 11, barely big enough to hold a guitar. Ponder grew up in the Beltzhoover area of the city and attended Knoxville High School. Even at his young age he would spend up to six hours a day practicing, which could help explain how he was able to win area talent shows. He performed locally in doo-wop and R&B groups. Jimmy only had one lesson in his career,

studying the stylings of his hero, Wes Montgomery. Ponder even replicated his strumming style, choosing to play with his thumb rather than a pick. Additionally, the music that he heard on local station WAMO exposed him to a wide variety of jazz styles. Ponder had only been playing guitar several years when he was offered a job by soul-jazz organist Charles Earland who was playing a date at The Hurricane in the Hill District. Two years later, after graduatng from South Hills High School, Ponder followed Earland to Philadelphia.

Ponder played extensively as a sideman for artists such as Donald Byrd, Dizzy Gillespie, and Pittsburgh's own Stanley Turrentine. Ponder even led his own band on a number of occasions. In the late 1980s Ponder returned to Pittsburgh and appeared regularly at local jazz establishments like James Street Tavern and Gullifty's.

What may be the finest compliment ever paid to a student by his teacher was a message relayed to Jimmy Ponder after Wes Montgomery passed away in 1968. The story is that Montgomery told a good friend that Jimmy Ponder would carry on his legacy.

Billy Porter

Born September 21, 1969—North Side

W. Ellis Porter started singing at age 4 in his Baptist Church on Manhattan Street on Pittsburgh's North Side, and wound up singing in Manhattan on Broadway. In the early 1990s, Billy Porter was cast in original roles in both *Miss Saigon* and *Five Guys Named Moe*. But he garnered the most attention for appearing as a replacement in *Smokey Joe's Café* and as a soloist in Rosie O'Donnell's revival of *Grease*.

Born on the North Side, Billy was a self-confessed sissy whose mother decided that he needed "man lessons" as a child. At 13, he had an artistic epiphany when he watched Jennifer Holliday perform "Dreamgirls" on the 1982 Tony® Awards.

And from that moment on, he relates in his musical life story, *Ghetto Superstar*, he knew he would one day become a "Black Broadway Bitch." "I sing like a black woman, you know," exclaims Porter.

A 1987 graduate of Pittsburgh's High School for the Creative and Performing Arts and 1991 graduate of Carnegie Mellon University, Porter's first step to fame came when he won the $100,000 male vocalist grand prize on Ed McMahon's 1992 *Star Search*.

Since his first performance on Broadway, he has appeared in three films (*Noel*, *The Broken Hearts Club,* and *Interns*), recorded two albums (A&M's *Untitled* and *At the Corner of Broadway & Soul* for Sh-K-Boom Records),

performed for Symphony Pops concerts across the U.S., sung at the White House, and acted in dozens of Off-Broadway and regional theatres.

His dramatic role as Booth in *Topdog/Underdog* during the 2004 City Theatre season won him Best Performer of the Year by Chris Rawson of the *Post-Gazette*.

Edwin S. Porter

Born April 21, 1870—Connellsville, PA
Died April 30, 1940—New York, NY

Born in Connellsville, PA, the town from which Frick would amass his fortunes producing coke, Edward Stanton Porter was the fourth of seven children born to Thomas R. and Mary Clark Porter. For whatever reason, he was nicknamed "Betty" as a kid. The family earned their income from furniture and cabinet making and mortuary services. His was the town's one funeral home.

Porter did not attend school for long, yet he was bright enough to earn his wages in many endeavors, first as a telegraph operator at the age of 14, then as a gas line plumber and, when the town's gas supplies were depleted, as an electrician helping to string power lines to stores and offices. With a friend, he designed and patented an early regulator for D/C current, allowing Edison's light bulbs to dim if too bright. His older cousin Byron Porter, a photographer, was manager of the town's new Newmyer Opera House, and there Edwin Porter was employed in various jobs, as were many of his cousins. For indis-

cernible reasons, Porter also ran a tailor's shop that went bankrupt. In 1895, Porter fled Connellsville and joined the Navy.

In 1898 he landed in New York and was employed as the projectionist at the popular Eden Musee. Although many theaters were playing short films between vaudeville acts, the Eden prided itself in producing and shooting its own. Porter was among the crew that would travel far and wide to shoot what were called "actualities," real-life scenes of boxing matches or armies on parade, all of which were patented by Edison under his special license. Always a technician, Porter departed the company to make and sell his own equipment, but a fire destroyed his small factory. Porter then applied to the Edison Company as an operator and cameraman. He was soon employed as a technician in a sparkling new glass-enclosed studio in New York at 41 E. 21st Street. Although the company was now famous for its Black Maria studio in E. Orange, NJ, Edison's success in asserting his patent rights assured the demand for more motion pictures. And it would be here that he could shoot any number of staged comedies and dramatic shorts to meet the demand.

Although Porter would shoot hundreds of "actualities" over the next several years, he stepped behind the camera to discover new techniques in shooting features that visualized the narrative form of a story. His most basic revelation was that, unlike a stage play that employs a series of scenes, the basic unit of a film is the single shot. For example, he could inter-cut an exterior shot with an interior one, suggesting both dramatic irony as well as a new reality of time. His camera could give focus to details with a close-up that stage scenes never could. And he could pan his camera to capture the enormity of a scene to

heighten its dramatic impact. In *The Life of an American Fireman*, Porter edited actual footage of a fire brigade with staged dramatics of a rescue. His most enduring masterpiece,

1903's *The Great Train Robbery*, employed camera motions, editing, and special effects that, some critics say, advanced the art of film-making more than any other movie of its time.

Porter resigned from Edison's studios in 1909 and he eventually became the principal director of Adolph Zukor's Famous Player Pictures. His directorial efforts never eclipsed the innovations of his earlier successes. He invested his fortunes in the Precision Machine Company in 1915, where he later became president, but lost everything to the Crash of '29. He died in obscurity.

Cumberland Posey

Born June 20, 1890—Homestead
Died March 28, 1946—Pittsburgh

He was a college basketball player when the game was in its infancy, a semi-pro outfielder, and a man who enjoyed a 35-year career in sports, in the process transforming a mill-hand baseball team into the strongest, most successful Negro League franchise in history.

Born in 1890 in Homestead, the Homestead Grays' Cumberland Willis Posey, Jr., was by turns player, manager, owner, and league executive. A strong athlete at Homestead High, he attended Penn State, Pitt, and Duquesne, studying chemistry and pharmacy.

Always a ballplayer, Posey joined the semi-pro Grays before his 21st birthday in 1911. By the following year, 1912, his skills at talent-spotting and game-booking had propelled the team from strictly semi-pro to full-time professional.

Standing 5'-9" and 145 pounds, Cum Posey became player-manager in 1916, owner in 1920. An aggressive recruiter, he had the financial prowess to stay solvent, especially during the Depression when many Negro League teams—and two leagues—fell to bankruptcy.

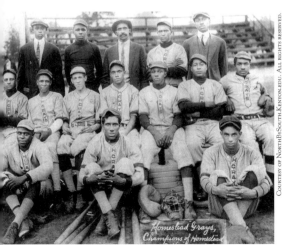

Posey, third from left, second row, seated with the Homestead Grays in 1913

A co-creator of the East-West League in 1932, Posey survived its demise, and raids of some of his finest talent by cross-town rival Gus Greenlee, to re-constitute the Negro National League. As club owner and league official, Posey guided the Grays to an unmatched eight of nine pennants, 1937-1945, including three world titles.

As the best-drawing Negro League team, the Grays played regularly at both Pittsburgh's Forbes Field and Washington's Griffith Stadium, with crowds of 30,000 a game coming to see such future Hall-of-Famers as Oscar Charleston, Josh Gibson, Buck Leonard, Judy Johnson, and Cool Papa Bell.

The man whom *Pittsburgh Courier* sportswriter Wendell Smith once called "the smartest man in Negro baseball and certainly the most successful" was elected to baseball's Hall of Fame in 2006. Some 60 years earlier, in 1946 at age 55, Cum Posey died of lung cancer in Pittsburgh and was buried in Homestead Cemetery.

William Powell

Born July 29, 1892—North Side
Died March 5, 1984—Palm Springs, CA

Were it not for a loan of $700 from his aunt, Mrs. Elizabeth E. Haywood of Sharon, PA, William Powell might never have become the mega-star of his day. Forever identified through his film career as Philo Vance, Nick Charles, or Godfrey (the Butler,) Powell was one of the best paid actors under contract at MGM. He was adored by fans both for his suave demeanor on stage as, as well as for his personal sorrow when Jean Harlow, whom he had dated for two years, died suddenly.

Born on Federal Street on the North Side, Powell knew that, even while attending the Sixth Ward School, he was to become a lawyer. His father, a public accountant, moved the family to Kansas City before William started high school, and there, Powell got his first taste of the stage. Upon graduation, he informed his parents that he would rather attend the Academy of Dramatic Arts in New York than go to an ordinary college and, so, to settle matters, he was told to find a job and pay the tuition himself. After several months working as a telephone company clerk by day, and theater usher by night, he drafted a 23-page letter to his wealthy aunt back in Pennsylvania, pleading for help. She replied with the loan.

Powell starved for many years while sharing an East Side room with Ralph Barton, later to become a well-known magazine illustrator. He finally got his first part in *The Ne'er Do Well* in 1912 and was propelled into the theater circuit without much fanfare. Then, in 1922, he got his first silent film role, playing Jury Forman to John Barrymore's *Sherlock Holmes*. Years of playing villains followed, then talkies became popular, and so too did Powell, unlike many of his contemporaries.

Powell became famous for the six films in which he played the top-hatted detective Philo Vance, then more famous for his role opposite Myrna Loy in *The Thin Man* series, and then even more famous for playing *My Man Godfrey*, sharing top billing with his ex-wife, Carole Lombard, to whom he had once been married for two years. The latter two films earned him Oscar® nominations.

In 1937, Jean Harlow died, and Powell was said to have placed two dozen roses on her gravesite each week for many years. Sorrow ensued. His only child, William, born to his first wife, Eileen Wilson, committed suicide.

In 1947, Powell was nominated for his third Oscar® for *Life with Father*. His final screen appearance was in 1955, playing the ship's doctor in *Mr. Roberts*, with James Cagney, Henry Fonda and Jack Lemmon.

Powell, having married a third time, to Diana Lewis in 1940, retired to Palm Springs and, in 1984, died of old age.

Billy Price

Born November 10, 1949—Fairlawn, NJ

If you spent any time in Shadyside during the 1970s at the Fox Café, you likely received a good old-school soul preachin' from Pittsburgh's own blue-eyed soul man Billy Price.

His real name is William Pollak. Although both of his parents dabbled with musical instruments, Billy's passion for the blues and soul was cultivated as a youngster listening to the sounds of artists like the Coasters, Sam Cooke, Fats Domino, and Otis Redding. He was influenced as well by Gospel and the sounds of the Deep South. He took to singing, trying to emulate his soulful heroes. At 12 he had his first band, The Thunderbirds, and in high school it was Billy and the Uptights. During a trip with his brother to an all-black club outside of New York, Billy was goaded into competing in an amateur contest, and won. When the club manager asked him his name, Billy summoned the surname of his hero, Lloyd Price. His stage name stuck.

In 1967 Price became a Nittany Lion, enrolling at Penn State University. His first band at State College was the Respectables, where needless to say they played plenty of frat parties and school concerts. He would eventually form his own band called the Rhythm Kings, the band that joined him in Pittsburgh.

COURTESY OF BILLY PRICE

When Billy and the Rhythm Kings came to town, Walnut Street was wild and bustling with places like Mardis Gras, Taylors, and the Encore. Billy and his boys booked a gig at the Fox Café and remained there as the undisputed heavy weight champs of Pittsburgh Rhythm & Blues for the next year. One of the many fans that frequented the Fox Café was the business manager for world class blues guitarist Roy Buchanan. He was greatly admired for his guitar playing prowess but lacked strong singing abilities. Buchanan's manager felt that Billy Price's strong soulful voice was just the combination needed to take both artists to the next level. Price agreed, left Pittsburgh—and the Rhythm Kings—and joined Roy Buchanan's band, immediately launching him into a national spotlight. On paper, the combination looked great; in reality Roy's fans were there to hear Roy play and Price felt as though his singing merely filled the gaps between Buchanan's guitar solos. He recorded two CDs with Roy, *That's What I'm Here For* and *Live Stock,* and called it quits.

Back in Pittsburgh, Price put together the Keystone Rhythm Band and, for the next decade, they played in and around Pittsburgh and all along the East Coast, stopping for extended runs in places like New Orleans and Austin. The Keystone Rhythm Band said goodbye to their Pittsburgh fans with a two night, sold-out engagement at the old Graffiti.

Various iterations of Price's band continue to record and play throughout the area. In addition to his preachy croons, Billy fills his days working at the Software Engineering Institute of Carnegie Mellon University, where he received his M.A. in professional writing.

Bob Prince

Born July 1, 1916—Los Angeles, CA
Died June 10, 1985—Pittsburgh

Famous for his colorful wardrobe and even more colorful vocabulary, gravel-voiced broadcaster Bob Prince simply was the Pittsburgh Pirates for generations of baseball fans.

Born Robert F. Prince on July 1, 1916, in Los Angeles, he graduated from Schenley High and attended Pitt, where he was a varsity swimmer. Beginning his broadcasting career in 1941 on WJAS' "Case of Sports," by 1948 he had joined Pirate pioneer broadcaster Rosey Rowswell, becoming the Voice of the Pirates upon Rowswell's 1955 death.

Working with a number of partners over the next 21 seasons, fellow broadcaster Jim Woods tagged Prince as "The Gunner" for his staccato style.

Tirelessly rooting for the Pirates, he called for a "hoover" (double play) or "a bloop and a blast" (base hit and home run), among others. Fans waited to hear Prince say, "Kiss it goodbye" (home run) or "we had 'em all the way (victory).

Master of clever marketing gimmicks, Prince's 1966 Green Weenie—a plastic hot dog filled with pebbles—and his 1974 Babushka Power were wildly popular.

After the 1975 season Prince, and his co-announcer, former Pirate pitcher Nellie King, were abruptly fired—Prince after 28 years.

COURTESY OF THE PITTSBURGH PIRATES

A decade later—after 10 years of broadcasting the Houston Astros, *ABC Monday Night Baseball*, even the Pittsburgh Penguins—he was back with the Pirates.

Suffering from cancer, barely able to croak out a few innings, he nevertheless received standing ovations at Three Rivers Stadium. Broadcasting just a handful of games, he fell victim to pneumonia, lapsed into a coma, and died just five weeks later. Bob Prince was 68 years old.

The following year, 1986, he was given the Ford Frick Award by baseball's Hall of Fame, its highest honor for a writer or broadcaster.

Jean Pronovost

Born December 18, 1945—Shawinigan Falls, Quebec

The epitome of the dedicated, hard-working athlete, Penguin right-winger Jean Pronovost was the team's first true scoring star. Playing at a wiry 5'-11" and 165 pounds, Pronovost was the first Penguin to score 50 goals and 100 points in a single season.

Born the 11th of 12 children, Jean Joseph Denis Pronovost grew up playing hockey on frozen ponds. Following older brothers Claude and all-star defenseman Marcel into the professional game, the young, high-scoring Jean developed a strong work ethic, playing solid defense as well as excellent offense.

A successful junior hockey player, Pronovost joined the talent-rich Boston Bruins organization, only to be overlooked and sold to Pittsburgh. Over the next 10 seasons, 1968-78, he emerged as a true star, team leader, and scoring champion.

Known for being the first on the ice and the last off, Pronovost passed, skated, and shot with near-perfection. As such, the team's 1968 Rookie of the Year led the team in scoring five times and points twice, netted 20 or more goals nine times—including 40 goals three times. A four-time All Star, and team captain, Pronovost's all-time Penguin statistics rank him third in games (753), third in goals (316), and fifth in points (603).

In 1978, Pronovost was traded to the Atlanta Flames. His last two NHL seasons were with the Washington Capitals.

A member of the Penguins Hall of Fame, Pronovost finished his career coaching Canadian junior hockey. In retirement, he and his wife Diane are active members of Athletes in Action, an inspirational Christian group.

Photographed by Mark Perrott, Qualters in his elements

Robert Qualters

Born March 13, 1934—McKeesport, PA

It was a dark time for Bob Qualters. Abstract expressionism—all those dreadful splatter paintings, all that pigment slathered on the canvas with a putty knife—was all the rage. What was he to do? Paint Pittsburgh? Especially in a wry, witty, nearly cartoonish way, just the way a poet and a dreamer would see it? The doyens of the art world deemed that idea impossibly gauche.

But Bob Qualters never lost faith, never gave up. He simply waited for Pittsburgh to come around to his way of seeing.

Born in 1934 in McKeesport, Robert Qualters studied at Carnegie Tech, took a hitch in the army, then split for San Francisco and the Catskills before returning home.

Painting the personal and the desperately familiar, the Qualters oeuvre runs the spectrum from Pittsburgh's grand vistas to the flotsam of life: Phipps Conservatory to the

Fort Pitt Bridge, street corners to luncheonettes to the inevitable steel mills. (His harrowing painting of the J&L steel mill on Hazelwood's Second Avenue, as colorful as it is ominous, is in the Carnegie Museum's permanent collection).

Often, but not invariably, Qualters' recognizable, immediately accessible visual images are complimented by words painted on the canvas, reflections, poetry, quotes. While Qualters has branched out into more abstract paintings of fog and other natural phenomena, of such artists as Rembrandt and Edward Hopper, of Rilke poems, he inevitably returns to Pittsburgh.

The 1985 Pittsburgh Center for the Arts Artist of the Year, he is the rare visual artist who has engaged in a series of collaborations, with poets Jane McCreery, Gail Ghai, Jan Beatty, Jay Carson, and Sam Hazo; photographer Mark Perrott; sculptor Nick Bubash; filmmaker Tony Buba, and musician Stephen Pellegrino; and others.

An accomplished outdoor muralist—in Oakland, Homestead, and Downtown—Robert Qualters lives in Squirrel Hill and works in his Homestead studio.

Zachary Quinto

Born June 2, 1977—Green Tree

At 11, he started acting with the CLO Mini Stars, playing summer roles in *Oliver!* and *The Wizard of Oz*. At Central Catholic, he played the Major General in Gilbert & Sullivan's *Pirates of Penzance* and won the Gene Kelly Award for best actor. Attending CMU, he appeared in the musical *Leaving Queens*, and performed in *Gross Indecency* and *Side Man* at City Theatre. Zachary Quinto is a young actor to watch.

Born in Green Tree, he trained at the CLO's school for young musical theatre performers. At 16, he was in a serious car accident that helped affirm his de-

sire to set out for the footlights. Upon graduating from CMU in 1999, he appeared in Marc Masterson's last production at City Theatre, 2000's *Side Man*, and took off for Hollywood, where his brother Joe is a professional photographer.

Since landing a first TV role as a car mechanic on *CSI*, he has had roles on *Touched by An Angel*, *Six Feet Under*, *Joan of Arcadia*, and a recurring role in the third season of *24*, playing the techie Andy Kaufman. He has also appeared often as Tori Spelling's gay companion on VH1's *So NoTORIous*. Now, Quinto has emerged from the shadows of the successful NBC series *Heroes* as Sylar, a brain-consuming evil-doer. He is slated next to star in his first film, another feature-length *Star Trek*, for which he will play young Spock.

Johann Georg Rapp

Born October 28, 1757—Württemberg, Germany
Died August 7, 1847—Economy, PA

From a small town in southern Germany, George Rapp immigrated to Western Pennsylvania and established one of America's most successful utopian communities.

Rapp began preaching around the age of 30, assembling a large following of separatists from the Lutheran church. He left Germany in 1803 to seek a new home where the group could have religious freedom. Two years later, on a site in Butler County along the Ohio River, "Father" Rapp and hundreds of his followers established the Harmony Society.

In accordance with Rapp's teachings, the "Harmonists" or "Rappites," as they were known, adopted communal living and celibacy in order to purify themselves for the Second Coming of Christ. Described by contemporary visitors as both a manipulative dictator and a simple yet powerful leader, Rapp was a revered patriarch who, as one account noted, held "an unbounded influence over his people." Under Rapp, the Society grew to nearly 1,000 members and became renowned for its agriculture and textile manufacturing.

After a brief relocation to Indiana in 1814, Rapp led the Society back to Pennsylvania in 1824, where they established Economy in Beaver County. Rapp's own belief in the looming millennium contributed to a schism in the Society in 1832 when, after the arrival of the mysterious German "Count de Leon," one-third of the Society left Economy.

The Harmonists would endure until 1905 when years of declining membership and economic struggle led to its dissolution. Rapp remained the spiritual leader until his death at age 90. He is buried in Old Economy's cemetery.

Richard S. Rauh, Helen Wayne Rauh and Richard E. Rauh

Love is a many splendored thing, and in mid-1930s Pittsburgh, it helped create a dynasty of theatre "angels." Because his fiancée might have left to trod the footlights of New York, Richard S. Rauh helped create the Pittsburgh Playhouse so Helen Wayne would have a local theater to show off her inestimable talents. In short order, after several years of marriage, they gave birth to little Dickie. And, today, Pittsburgh is blessed with the Rauh Theatre at the Pittsburgh Playhouse, the Helen Wayne Rauh Rehearsal Hall at Pittsburgh Public Theater, the Helen Wayne Rauh Studio Theatre at Carnegie Mellon University, the Richard S. Rauh Garden Room in Heinz Hall, the Richard E. Rauh Theater of Shady Side Academy, and the Richard E. Rauh Conservatory Program of the Pittsburgh Musical Theater.

First came Richard S. Rauh, a prominent Pittsburgh bachelor who was smitten by Helen Sisenwain when he saw her perform as a Carnegie Tech junior in a performance of *Three Cornered Moon* at the Schenley Hotel. Son of Enoch and Bertha, both of whom were civic leaders and who together supported the Pittsburgh Symphony and dozens of social and cultural organizations, Rauh was heir to the family's shirt business, and a long-term board member of the Symphony himself.

Helen, already a local celebrity, had her own weekly radio show on KDKA, *The Charm Lady*, by which she paid her college tuition. So popular was her show that producers at KDKA shortened her maiden name to Wayne, and promoted her as "Helen Wayne, the Sweetheart of the Air."

Not long after a formal introduction, Rauh promised to find a theatre for her if she promised not to leave for New York. They married.

Rauh then brought 15 of the city's amateur theatre groups to join forces to establish a single organization under the Pittsburgh Civic Playhouse, found performance space at The Frick School, hired a professional director and stage manager, organized a subscription campaign, and launched the Pittsburgh Playhouse, acquiring within the year (1937) a German social club and defunct synagogue on Hamlet Street in Oakland.

Helen Wayne Rauh performed regularly at the Pittsburgh Playhouse for 40 years, becoming "the First Lady of Pittsburgh Theatre." Richard died in 1954, but his son, then attending Shady Side Academy, was well on his way to supporting the arts in the manner of his parents and grandparents.

Richard E. Rauh has performed often on stage and in film. A Masters graduate of Carnegie Mellon, he was for 15 years the director of the popular Playhouse Film Series, wrote theatre reviews for the *Post-Gazette*, and has taught drama and film at Point Park University where he also serves as a trustee. Much credit is due him for the legacy and endowments his family name represents.

Eric Red

Born February 16, 1961—Pittsburgh

Were it for just one cult classic film he wrote, Eric Red might well fall to the obscurity of Pittsburgh trivia buffs. But the screenwriter, director, and producer affected and survived a real-life terror of gory carnage not unlike the film for which he is best known.

Born to C. Gerard "Neil" Durdaller, a renowned metallurgical engineer whose scientific writings on powder metals brought him to Pittsburgh in the mid-1950s, and Nancy Pickhardt, an actress long experienced in Shakespearean roles, the young Durdaller (whose name he later changed to Red) moved to Brooklyn to attend St. Ann's High School and, then, Overland College in Ohio. Eager to direct films, he lived in Austin, TX, to be near Tobe Hooper, famous for The *Texas Chainsaw Massacre*. There he wrote his first screenplay, *The Hitcher*, which was picked up in 1985 by HBO Pictures.

Starring C. Thomas Howell, Rutger Hauer, and Jennifer Jason Lee, the film follows Howell as he tries to escape Hauer's bloodlust rampage to frame Howell into committing suicide. Eighteen-wheelers plow into police cars, pick-up trucks splatter bystanders, and in the film's signature scene, Jason Lee is ripped apart when tied between two semis. The film raised the bar for gratuitous scenes of automotive gore.

So, too, have Red's other less favored films, the vampiric *Near Dark*, and the Frankensteinian *Body Parts*. But perhaps the most bizarre scenes related to Red happened for real on May 31, 2000. Then, according to an *LA Weekly* investigation by Paul Cullum, Red, driving his black Jeep Cherokee Laredo down Wilshire Boulevard in West Los Angeles, plowed into the rear of a Honda Accord waiting at a red light. When the driver stepped out of his car, Red's Jeep pushed the Accord into oncoming traffic, then veered left toward Qs Billiards, a popular open-air bar, crossing the median, knocking over a bus stop, and smashing through sidewalk tables to land almost upright inside the bar. According to witnesses, Red was awake behind the wheel. When he stepped out of the car, he reached for a piece of glass and swiftly slit his throat. One young law student Noah Baum died at the scene.

Red was taken to UCLA Medical Center and put under observation.

At 16, Red's father, Neil, then 46, was killed while stopped at a red light, rammed from the rear by another car.

In 2007, Intrepid Pictures remade *The Hitcher*, releasing it to a less-than-impressed audience. He currently has three more screenplays in production.

Vivian Reed

Born June 6, 1947—Hill District

Raised on Wandless Street in the Hill District, then Kedron Street in Homewood, Vivian Reed was singing at 3 for her parents, Clyde and Lucille. Clyde, a gospel singer of some repute, enrolled his daughter in the Pittsburgh Musical Institute, the once famed school whose students had included Billy Strayhorn and Walt Harper, when Vivian was just 8. She later attended Schenley High and there, before graduating, auditioned for the Julliard School of Music and was awarded a full scholarship.

She trained to be a dramatic soprano at Julliard. So, it was with some dismay that, having won her first audition to perform in *Green Pastures*, her teachers called the producers to ask that she not be cast. Reed prevailed, but was given an F for voice, and soon dropped out. On her own, she sang at the famed Apollo Theater, first appearing on the same bill as the equally green Bill Cosby. Then came *Don't Bother Me I Can't Cope*, a musical revue, which she first played in Chicago. Directed by Vinette Carol, the production came to New York where Reed next had the opportunity to audition for another musical revue, this a pastiche of black jazz from the 1920s and 1930s, *Bubbling Brown Sugar*. Reed, playing the role of Young Irene, was an instant success, winning the 1976 Drama Desk Award for Outstanding Featured Actress in a Musical, as well as a Tony© Nomination for Best Actress in a Musical.

Reed has appeared often in dozens of musical reviews, reprising her role in *Bubbling* with Pittsburgh's Kuntu Rep in 2005, and also performing the role of Lena Horne in Pittsburgh Ballet's original production of *Indigo in Motion*. Once a model and fashionable celebrity who has appeared in *Elle*, *Vogue*, *Paris Match*, *Time*, *Ebony*, *Jet*, and *People* magazines, she is an avid photographer.

Jacob Reese

Born in 1825—Wales
Died in 1907—Pittsburgh

It was 10-year-old Jacob Reese who lifted the furnace door as his father William, an iron monger, demonstrated a new boiling process for creating wrought iron to a Bellefonte, Pennsylvania, crowd. The 1835 event marked a significant advancement in manufacturing strong, yet malleable metal. Throughout his childhood, Jacob followed his father. A self-taught chemist and mechanic, Reese continued to advance the industry, acquiring over 175 patents in his lifetime including landmark innovations in the basic process of open-hearth steelmaking.

Jacob and his five siblings moved to Pittsburgh two years after their father's Bellefonte success. At the Birmingham Iron Works Jacob and hs father again introduced their boiling or "puddling" process.

As a young adult, Jacob Reese moved throughout Pennsylvania, consulting, managing, innovating, and profiting from the iron and emerging steel industry. He entered the petroleum refining business in 1860, and began a successful firm: Petrolite Oil Works. Struggling to find quality hoop iron for binding his oil barrels, Reese founded the Fort Pitt Steel Works, the Southside Rolling Mill and Tube Works, and a metallurgical testing plant in the Strip District where he patented many of his important innovations.

He and his first wife, Eliza Matthews, and their six children enjoyed an affluent lifestyle in Pittsburgh until 1877 when a fire, over-extended credit, and an explosion at the mill left the family bankrupt.

Andrew Carnegie, who was building his iron and steel empire, knew of Reese's innovative work in the industry and, in 1879, purchased two of his patents for the basic process of open-hearth steelmaking. An agreement to pay annual royalties to the inventor was later challenged by the Bessemer Association claiming that patents of a similar process by Sir Henry Bessemer were the first to introduce this method. After lengthy litigation, the Reese patents and his payments were honored, ostensibly naming this Pittsburgh puddler and innovator an inventor of the open-hearth steelmaking process.

Philip Reymer

Born June 27, 1824—Pittsburgh
Died March 3, 1893—Pittsburgh

Philip Reymer's candy empire fed Pittsburgh's sweet tooth for over a century.

His determination and keen business sense helped him turn his Wood Street-founded company into the region's premiere name in candy, with thousands of distributors for its chocolates and over a dozen retail locations around the city.

Reymer's grandfather was a German immigrant who served as a fifer during the Revolutionary War. Like his grandfather, Philip made a name for himself in the family's adopted home of Western Pennsylvania. One of 10 children, he was educated in Pittsburgh's public schools. He married Hannah Riter in 1859 and the couple had four children. The Reymers were longtime residents of Bidwell Street in Allegheny City.

In an early job at Hunker's candy factory in Pittsburgh, Philip honed the business and financial skills needed to start his own company. Success would not come without failure, however, as Reymer's first candy business—a partnership with fellow entrepreneur Joshua Rhodes—failed. Within a few years, however, he formed his next enterprise, the wholesale fruit and confectionary company of Reymer & Anderson. This one succeeded. The business prospered, and in 1861 Philip's brothers Jacob and Harmar Denny joined him. Over the ensuing decades the re-named Reymer & Brothers would grow by leaps and bounds, adding imported cigars to their fruit and candy sales as well as soda fountains and tea rooms throughout the region. Though his company is no more, Reymer's name lives on today through his famous Lemon Blennd drink.

DRINK Reymers' BLENND

Trent Reznor

Born May 17, 1965—Mercer, PA

About 60 miles due north of Pittsburgh, Mercer is home to the world's largest shoe store, the world's biggest candy store, and the world's most Industrial rocker, Trent Reznor, of Nine Inch Nails.

Born Michael Trent Reznor, he displayed an aptitude for music early on. He was playing the piano at the age of 5 and by his teens had discovered the saxophone and tuba. After his parents divorced, his sister stayed with their mom and he moved in with his grandparents. Isolated and lonely, music became Reznor's companion, escape, and sibling that he no longer had. He attended Mercer Area Junior and Senior High Schools where he was active in the school bands, and in theatre. Among his more memorable performances was Judas in *Jesus Christ Superstar*. Reznor attended Allegheny College in Meadeville, PA, where he briefly studied computer engineering, while also performing with the New Wave band, Option 30. Reznor dropped out to pursue music full time.

He landed in Cleveland, OH, first in the band The Innocent and then with Exotic Birds. By the late 1980s he was working at a local recording studio, while simultaneously producing demos for his new band, Nine Inch Nails. Their release, *Pretty Hate Machine,* debuted in 1989 and went triple platinum, in large part due to extensive touring, including the Lollapalooza Tour and a European tour with Guns n' Roses.

With their next release, Nine Inch Nails earned a reputation consistent with their dark and nihilistic themes. Enhancing that reputation was Reznor's choice of location for his follow-up release—the home where the Manson murders took place. In fact, several years later when the home was destroyed, Reznor purchased the front door for the entrance to his new recording studio. The product of that session was the 1994 release, *The Downward Spiral*, which debuted at number two on the Album charts and went on to sell in excess of five million copies, as well as win numerous awards.

Despite bouts with drugs and alcohol, relentless touring, and long periods between recordings, Nine Inch Nails released *The Fragile* in '99, *With Teeth* in '05 and most recently *Year Zero*, to very positive reviews. In addition to his work with Nine Inch Nails, Reznor has produced other projects including Marilyn Manson recordings and film scores such as *Natural Born Killers*.

Despite his dark and troubling persona, Reznor is a prodigious talent and multi-instrumentalist. His work has been covered by the likes of Johnny Cash and whose accolades are heralded by critics, fans, musicians, and publications such as *Time* magazine, which named Reznor one of the 25 most influential Americans in 1997.

Martha Rial

Born September 12, 1961—Murrysville, PA

Walking at dusk through Kibondo, perhaps the poorest town in Tanzania, her eyes burning from the cooking fires, Martha Rial was trailed by gangs of Hutu children calling "muzunga" (white person). Refugees from the deadly Rwandan civil war, many had never seen white skin. Most had never seen a camera.

One of only four native Pittsburghers to win a Pulitzer Prize for photography—with New Kensington's Eddie Adams (Vietnam), Natrona Heights' John Paul Filo (Kent State), and McDonald's Matthew Lewis (Washington)—Rial's 1998 award came for the largest body of work—and the only one by a woman.

Born in Murrysville in 1961, Rial graduated from the Art Institute, attended Ohio State, then worked as a staff photographer for Florida's *Fort Pierce Tribune* and Alexandria, Virginia's *Journal* Newspapers before joining the *Pittsburgh Post-Gazette* in 1994.

Shooting general assignment stories, Rial lobbied to go to Tanzania, where her sister Amy was a nurse with the International Rescue Committee. There, Rial said, she could photograph and report first hand on the terrible effects of the war which cost nearly one million lives.

When the *Post-Gazette* agreed, in late 1996, Rial traveled 9,000 miles to join her sister—and witness the incredible hardships faced by untold thousands of Burundian and Rwandan refugees.

Spending three harrowing weeks, Rial endured blistering heat, choking red dust, food poisoning, and a 104-degree fever to capture stark, brilliant images of a people suffering deadly dehydration, malnutrition, and malaria; dazed refugees snaking through the desert; mutilated women and the burial of children.

Trek of Tears, Rial's diary, and 45 photos won the Pulitzer, as well as a National Headliners Award, Scripps Howard Foundation Award for Photojournalism, and Pennsylvania Newspaper Photographer of the Year.

A veteran of essay-length assignments in Cuba, Northern Ireland, and the Balkans, Martha Rial joined the *St. Petersburg Times* in 2006.

Charles Owen Rice

Born in 1908—Brooklyn, NY
Died November 13, 2005—McCandless Twp.

He's often called Pittsburgh's labor priest, and he combined his ministry with leading the charge in social matters outside the traditional church role. The monsignor's brand of activism placed Rice squarely in the center of some of the most important issues of his time. It was a place that Rice relished as he moved outside the pulpit, often to the dismay of other clergy members.

He led protests in the 1930s, working to get fair pay and safe working conditions for labor. He railed against communism in the 1950s. He also marched with Dr. Martin Luther King, Jr., at the height of the Civil Rights movement and was a vocal opponent to America's involvement in the Vietnam War. For more than 70 years, Rice wrote stirring call-to-action pieces in *The Pittsburgh Catholic* newspaper, causing diocese bishop

Anthony Bevilacqua to joke about the sheer volume of mail Rice's pieces generated and the number of trees it took to feed it.

Rice, the son of Irish immigrants, was born in New York City in 1908. When his mother died four years later, he returned to Ireland to be raised by his grandmother. He returned to the states at age 11, with the goal to become a priest. Rice studied at Duquesne University and St. Vincent Seminary and was ordained. He would have posts at a variety of parishes in the diocese, including St. Joseph in Natrona, Immaculate Conception in Washington, PA, St. Anne's in Castle Shannon, and Holy Rosary in Homewood.

Even as a young priest, Rice felt the urge to do more than spread the gospel. In 1937, he helped found a Hill District shelter, St. Joseph House of Hospitality. That experience inspired him to give up his modest post ($33 a month plus room and board) to become the center's live-in priest, getting by on whatever he could raise. *Time* magazine chronicled the facility. That same year Rice found his first picket line at the H.J. Heinz Co. plant on the North Side. Rice's vocal support of the workers did not sit well with church leaders, particularly those whose parishes had been the recipients of Heinz's largesse. It did, however, gain the notice of other Pittsburgh labor leaders, including Father James Cox, John L. Lewis, and Philip Murray. It seemed that Rice was a fixture wherever there was a labor protest in the tri-state area, particularly in the steel industry.

Dr. Benjamin Spock, left, Dr. Martin Luther King, Jr., center, and Rice link arms in war rally, April 15, 1967.

It also led to Rice's ascension to the radio airwaves, where his thick Irish brogue offered fiery commentary on issues of the day. His one regret would be his activism in the anti-communism movement of the 1950s. Later in life he would say that driving communists out of the labor movement was "a crusade that did more harm than good."

The 1960s saw Rice turn his attention to the two most polarizing experiences of the decade—the Civil Rights movement and the Vietnam War. At an age when many protesters would be slowing down, he marched on the Pentagon. When big steel began to crash in the 1980s, he stood along with workers at the barricades outside the plants.

Rice summed up his accomplishments at his 90th birthday celebration, noting "I've only been a parish priest, and I haven't tried to be anything else, but as far as labor is concerned and the poor and the blacks, I kept the faith. I tried to help the downtrodden." He died in 2005 at age 96. Indiana University of Pennsylvania professor of labor relations Charles McCollester calls Rice, "the most important Catholic activist in 20th-Century Pittsburgh."

Dorothy Mae Richardson

Born in 1923—unknown
Died April 28, 1991—Pittsburgh

In 1968, in the aftermath of the riots triggered by the assassination of Dr. Martin Luther King, Jr., Dorothy Mae Richardson took a walk along Charles Street through her North Side neighborhood. Not surprisingly, she found ramshackle housing—broken windows, littered yards, crumbling foundations and two-story disasters waiting to happen—all at risk of demolition in the cause of urban renewal. But Richardson knew well that the cost to demolish a neighborhood was a fantastic sum compared to the simpler needs of her neighbors. The only problem was her community simply didn't have money for repairs.

Richardson, joined by Ethel Hagler and Isabelle Mike, asked how they could save their neighborhood. The answer they crafted in the course of a single night was so successful it has been copied by more than 240 community development organizations in 50 states. Known today as NeighborWorks® America, Richardson created the first local Neighborhood Housing Services, a long-term, low-interest circulating loan fund with a $15,000 cap. Dollar Savings Bank was an initial partner.

But she didn't stop there. The very same year, Richardson also created YOU, for Youth Opportunities Unlimited, a neighborhood program to train at-risk youth for productive employment. And the next year, she founded CASH, a grass roots movement for Citizens Against Slum Housing. In fact, for more than 30 years, Richardson tirelessly steered an entire generation of Northsiders—as well as civic policy wonks—to work together for a better community. There were few Charles Street residents in the 1970s and 1980s who didn't know Dorothy, Ethel or Isabelle by their first names.

In 1978, Congress formalized the purpose of Neighborhood Housing Services into a federal loan program under the Neighborhood Reinvestment Act. A recipient of dozens of awards locally and nationally, Richardson died at Allegheny General Hospital, just blocks from the neighborhood she saved.

George Richardson

Born in 1896—Georgetown, CO
Died in 1988—Pittsburgh

He's Pittsburgh's baron of bridges, serving as the design lead for the spans that have earned the city and region its reputation as the City of Bridges. The gifted designer/engineer with the Allegheny County Bureau of Bridges was the center point for what may be the golden age of bridge building in the 1920s and 1930s. Richardson's name is well-known among bridge aficionados (there's even an award named after him presented by *Roads and Bridges* magazine).

His credits include: The Three Sisters Bridges downtown (the only matching trio of bridges anywhere in the world); the George Westinghouse Bridge over Turtle Creek, (a magnificent span with five concrete arches, including a central arch that is the largest in the United States); The Homestead High-Level Bridge (now the Homestead Grays Bridge); the McKees Rocks Bridge over the Ohio River, (the county's longest bridge at about mile), and the Liberty Bridge over the Monongahela River.

The Colorado-born Richardson had dropped out of college in 1917 to serve as a cavalry lieutenant in World War I, before resuming his studies at the University of Colorado. After a teaching stint at the University of Pennsylvania, he made his way to Pittsburgh in early 1923 and quickly moved his way up the ranks of Allegheny County Department of Public Works. As assistant chief engineer of the department he led the fledgling bridge group and excelled at his work, trying new, bold designs. His West End Bridge was an engineering wonder, holding the record for more than 30 years as the nation's largest span with a tied steel arch.

But perhaps his crowning achievement was the Westinghouse Bridge, built to eliminate chronic bottlenecks on America's first superhighway, The Lincoln Highway, or Route 30. The bridge is a combination of great engineering—the longest reinforced concrete highway bridge in the Western Hemisphere—and aesthetics, with its decorative end pylons

that tell the story of industrialist George Westinghouse. It often garners comparisons to the era's other engineering masterpieces like the The Hoover Dam and The Holland Tunnel. Richardson described the bridge as "bringing order over the chaotic industrial valley."

Richardson launched his own firm in 1939. The company was built upon his reputation as bridge maker. Interestingly, one of his most inventive projects never left the drawing boards in Pittsburgh. He planned Skybus to be a mass-transit marvel that would revolutionize mass transit with its lightweight computer-controlled cars. It became a political boondoggle, though his firm did partner with Westinghouse to build similar systems in other cities. Another of Richardson's contributions to engineering happened outside the city of Pittsburgh. His firm came up with the procedure to build St. Louis' famed Gateway Arch, including developing the equipment needed to erect the edifice.

Harrison Richardson

Born June 16, 1919—Beaver, PA
Died July 17, 1999—Claiborne, MD

Harrison Holt Richardson became Peary's "polar opposite," exploring the South Pole with Admiral Richard Byrd in 1939 at the age of 19. He was the youngest member of Byrd's third expedition to Antarctica, serving as a dog sled driver and weather observer. He was paid $3.00 a week while living at the South Pole for two years. Later, as a Navy doctor he participated in expeditions to both the South and North Poles.

The young man heard Byrd speak of his two previous trips to Antarctica in a commencement address at Beaver College and was so smitten, he bombarded Byrd with pleas to join his next expedition. Byrd hired him, Richardson thought, for a summer job as a dishwasher on Byrd's 68-year-old wooden sailing ship, the *U.S.S. Bear*. Soon, he'd sent his parents a telegram saying, "See you in two years." A photography buff, Richardson used a 16mm movie camera to take the first color motion pictures of Antarctica and the U.S. base known as "Little America."

Occasionally, Richardson was invited to dine with the Admiral. "He didn't strike you as being a rugged individual and definitely didn't look like the outdoor type. But once he decided to do something, he'd do it come hell or high water."

The outbreak of World War II brought the expedition to an end, as German U-boats began patrolling nearby waters. Byrd later described Richardson as a "splendid and articulate young man of great intelligence. He is one of the best men I have ever had with me on one of my five expeditions." After that excursion, his intelligence got Richardson through Geneva College and the University of Pittsburgh Medical School. Still infatuated with the frigid ice caps at the ends of the earth, Richardson enlisted in the U.S. Navy as a medical officer and was assigned to U.S. military expeditions to both poles.

Upon leaving the Navy, he returned to Beaver County and was a radiologist for 30 years at Rochester General Hospital and the Beaver Valley General Hospital. Richardson's hard work and devotion to his patients made a lasting impression in Beaver County, as it had in Antarctica, where a rugged peak is named Mount Richardson.

Helen Richey

Born November 21, 1909—McKeesport, PA
Died January 7, 1947—New York, NY

The youngest of five children born to Amy and Joseph Richey, then superintendent of the McKeesport Schools, Helen at age 12 ran away to join the circus. By the time she had walked all the way to Uniontown, her father drove her back to their home in the 2000 block of Jenny Lind Street. Wanderlust was in her blood.

Though she graduated from McKeesport High, she lasted only a year at Carnegie Tech. In her idle hours, watching planes land across the river at Bettis Airfield, she convinced a friend to raise the money necessary for an impromptu flight to Cleveland in the steerage of a Waco biplane. Once arrived, Helen apparently had discovered her true calling and was eager to take lessons to pilot her own plane. It took a five-day stay in Cleveland before the weather cleared for her return. No sooner was she home than she started flying lessons.

At just 5' 4", she was a small but masterful pilot. In 1930, by the age of 20, Richey had earned her license (possibly from Bob Trader's Flying School) and almost immediately entered the barnstorming circuit. In 1932, she finished third in the Amelia Earhart Trophy Race and in 1933 set a 10-day endurance record staying aloft over the skies of Miami with co-pilot Frances Marsalis. Legend has it that during the contest, when the refueling plane's hose ripped her wing, she walked out on the wing, armed with needle and thread, and repaired the fabric in mid-flight.

Commercial airlines in the early 1930s competed ruthlessly for airmail contracts. Central Airline, based in Greensburg, was no different, except owner Dick Coulter went one step beyond all logic. In 1934, among a swirl of welcome publicity, he hired Richey to co-pilot flights between Washington and Detroit.

Richey thus became the first woman commercial pilot in the U.S.

The gig lasted only 10 months. She was barred from joining the all-male union, and her superiors would allow her to fly passengers only in favorable weather, and then, only in daylight. Realizing she was just a pawn for publicity, she resigned—but not before Amelia Earhart flew into Pittsburgh to protest. Soon, Richey earned jobs as an air-marking pilot, a flight instructor, an Army flight instructor, and as a ferry pilot for the RAF—all firsts for a woman. At the conclusion of World War II, upon the return of thousands of "more qualified" male pilots, she could find no work. She died from an overdose of sleeping pills at the age of 37.

© Associated Press

Tom Ridge

Born August 26, 1945—Munhall, PA

As Governor of Pennsylvania, Tom Ridge made Pittsburgh a priority. He pushed a $40-million program to create 21,000 jobs in a region suffering from the decline of the steel industry. He helped find $150 million for the city's David L. Lawrence Convention Center and sought millions more for improving local highways. State funds for PNC Park, Heinz Field, and the North Shore development were allocated during his tenure in Harrisburg. "His leadership at the state level probably had a bigger impact on Pittsburgh than that of any recent government official," said the former director of the governor's Pittsburgh office.

Ridge was born in 1945 in the Steel Valley community of Munhall along the Monongahela River, eight miles from downtown. Three years later, his father moved the family 125 miles northwest to Erie to take advantage of

public housing for World War II veterans. Ridge attended parochial schools in Erie and won a scholarship to Harvard, where he graduated with honors in 1967. Five years later, after a tour in Vietnam, he graduated from Dickinson School of Law in Carlisle.

Ridge returned to Erie and became an assistant district attorney. In 1982, he became the first enlisted man and decorated combat hero of Vietnam to be elected to Congress. He was sent back five more times. He ran for Pennsylvania governor, winning in 1994 and again in 1998, proving himself an exceptional vote-getter in a state where registered Democrats outnumbered Republicans by 500,000.

A friendship with fellow governor George W. Bush of Texas put him on a short list of Vice Presidential choices in 2000. A year later, President Bush hired Ridge to run the White House Office of Homeland Security following the 9/11 attacks. When Congress created the federal Department of Homeland Security, Bush appointed Ridge to be its first secretary. He implemented the color-coded terror alert system now in place and started a run on plastic sheeting and duct tape when his department suggested Americans use them to seal their homes in the event of chemical or biological attacks.

After 22 consecutive years in public office, Ridge stepped down in 2004 to start his own consulting business, Ridge Global. He also joined the corporate boards of Home Depot and The Hershey Company. Like so many officials who leave government, he wanted to spend more time with his family and prepare to pay college tuition for his two children.

Matthew Ridgway

Born March 3, 1895—Fort Monroe, VA
Died July 26, 1993—Fox Chapel, PA

For a man who left giant footprints on the world stage and introduced airborne invasions to military science, Ridgway's imprint on the Pittsburgh region pales by comparison. But he lived here—almost a third of his 98 years—leading a different kind of campaign.

Long before retiring as a four-star general, as the Army's chief of staff, and as a genuine hero of World War II and the Korean Conflict, he had led paratroop invasions of Sicily and Normandy. Under his command, U.S. troops crossed the Rhine and the Elbe

and linked with the Russians at the Baltic Sea. He is the only modern military figure who succeeded both Eisenhower and MacArthur, the iconic commanders who led America to victory in World War II. President Truman appointed Ridgway to replace MacArthur in Korea. Ridgway's tactical skills are credited with taking a U.S. Army in retreat and turning it around to drive the North Koreans and Communist Chinese troops back to the 38th Parallel, where a ceasefire was implemented.

Ridgway retired in 1955 from an Army career that started upon graduation from West Point in 1917. He then became chairman of the board of trustees of the Mellon Institute of Industrial Research, started by Pittsburgh's Mellon family. In 1967, seven years after Ridgway stepped down as chairman, the Mellon Institute merged with Carnegie Technical Institute to become Carnegie Mellon University.

Richard K. Mellon hired Ridgway. R.K. was known to admire Ridgway and dislike MacArthur. Pittsburgh military historian Donald Goldstein said the General believed there was a "right way, a wrong way, and a 'Ridgway.'" According to a Mellon family adviser, R.K. eventually concluded that Ridgway was trying to run an academic research institution like the army, and had become unpopular with the faculty and staff. When General Ridgway retired from the institute, Mellon assumed the chairman's job and title.

Ridgway received praise for enlarging the Institute's "fundamental" scientific research program at a time when the nation was focused on "applied" research. During his tenure, the institute's staff increased from 21 to 77, and federal grants rose in one year from six to 17.

Ridgway lived a quiet and lonely retirement in his Fox Chapel home, where he died at the age of 98.

Mary Roberts Rinehart

Born August 12, 1876—Pittsburgh
Died September 22, 1958—New York, NY

When it came to necessity being the mother of invention, Mary Roberts Rinehart literally wrote the book on it. Moving from near-rags to undreamt-of riches, she became one of the best-loved—and best-selling—American writers of the 20th Century.

Born Mary Roberts in 1876 in a small Arch Street house on the North Side, she published three short stories as an Allegheny High School student—and then gave up writing for a dozen years.

Studying at the Pittsburgh Training School for Nurses at Homeopathic Hospital, in 1896, Roberts graduated and married Dr. Stanley Marshall Rinehart. The couple had three sons: Stanley, Jr., and Frederick (with whom their mother would help begin the Farrar and Rinehart publishing house), and Alan.

With Stanley in medical practice, the family lived well enough until the 1903 stock market crash. Pressed for money, 27-year-old Mary returned to writing, producing an average of a short story a week for a year. By 1906 she had published her first significant mystery, *The Man in Lower Ten*, and in 1907 her masterpiece, *The Circular Staircase*, a national phenomenon, selling more than one million copies. In a century, it has never gone out of print.

Branching out from straight mysteries, Rinehart also wrote hospital fiction based on her nursing experiences. Combining the two, her Miss Pinkerton novels have both medical and detective aspects, one of the first series to do so.

With a firm and popular base, Rinehart also wrote comic women's fiction, notably her Letitia Carberry stories, in which Tish, a middle-aged spinster, does things forbidden to women of the time, including racing cars, piloting airships, and driving ambulances. A bit of a daredevil herself, Rinehart left Pittsburgh to serve as the first woman World War I correspondent on the Belgian front. Later, as a writer of serious women's concerns, her articles, including a ground-breaking account of her own bout with breast cancer, appeared in the *Saturday Evening Post*, the *Ladies Home Journal*, and other mainstream periodicals.

As her success grew, Rinehart branched out into other media, including collaborating with playwright Avery Hopwood on a number of Broadway comedies, such as 1909's *Seven Days*. *The Bat*, an adapatation of *The Circular Staircase*, enjoyed three different runs.

With more than three dozen adaptations of her work onto both the large and small screens, *The Bat* also had three versions, the last, in 1959, starring Vincent Price.

In a career lasting a half-century, Rinehart produced some 50 novels, an autobiography, eight plays, and hundreds of short stories. Remaining in Pittsburgh during her early success, she moved in the 1920s when her husband, who had enlisted in the army, was stationed in Washington. After his 1932 death, in 1935 she relocated to New York City.

By the early 1950s Rinehart retired from active writing—which she always did in longhand. In 1958, 82-year-old Mary Roberts Rinehart died in her 18-room Park Avenue apartment in New York City. She was buried next to her husband, Major Stanley Rinehart, in Arlington National Cemetery.

Dahl Ritchey

Born in 1910—Oakland
Died January 12, 2002—Pittsburgh

His masterpiece was never built.

Pittsburgh Stadium, as it was called in the early 1960s, was to be crescent-shaped, with a center field open to the Golden Triangle. With thousands of movable seats, and the football end zones positioned on the first and third base sides, America's first multipurpose stadium should have been a marvel. "It was way ahead of its time," remembered architect Louis Astorino, a one-time Ritchey intern. "Dahl was a visionary, an absolute visionary."

When the original idea proved too costly, Ritchey and his partners re-cast the stadium. Then did so again. The result was Three Rivers Stadium, which opened in 1970—and was imploded 31 years later.

The Civic Arena. Mellon Square. Allegheny Center. The University of Pittsburgh's Tower Dormitories and Trees Hall. Carnegie Mellon University's Donner Hall, Wean Hall, and Cyert Hall. Those and many more changed the Pittsburgh landscape forever.

Pittsburgh's first great native architect, Dahlen K. Ritchey was born in Oakland in 1910. Growing up on Parkview Avenue, Ritchey received a Carnegie Tech architecture degree, graduating in 1932.

After earning a Harvard master's degree, Ritchey designed windows at Kaufmann's. A decade later, he worked on Edgar Kaufmann's 1947 *Pittsburgh in Progress*, a vision of a redeveloped city.

Following his modernist bent—buildings with strong, sleek lines and gleaming surfaces—Ritchey's greatest achievement began as the Civic Auditorium, intended for the Civic Light Opera. Featuring a retractable stainless steel dome 417 feet in diameter and 109 feet tall, a 260-feet cantilever arm holds up eight 300-ton roof sections. Renamed the Civic Arena, it premiered in 1961 with another Pittsburgh first: the Ice Capades.

Jack Robin

Born October 15, 1912—Pittsburgh
Died May 11, 2000—Pittsburgh

He was called Pittsburgh's Robert Moses—after New York City's brilliant planner—and the comparison is apt.

A true Renaissance man with a seeming command of any subject—planning, law, history, politics, language, gastronomy, even baseball—he drew on his vast knowledge and extensive experience to serve four mayors and change the Pittsburgh landscape forever.

Voluble and good-humored, Robin was content to stay in the background, preferring that elected officials receive the accolades. "As long as the boss knew what I was doing and was satisfied," he summarized near the end of his life, "it was not necessary that I become a public figure. I did not have any family position or money to support me," he added. "I have done some satisfying things. Often I got by on sheer nerve."

Born John P. Robin, the son of a pharmacist, he was raised in Squirrel Hill. A Pitt zoology major, he left without a degree when offered a job with the *Post-Gazette*. When his 1935 exposé about conditions at the Pittsburgh Zoo received widespread attention, Mayor Cornelius Scully offered Robin a job on his staff.

Jack Robin was 23 years old, and for the succeeding 60 years never left public service.

Serving as Mayor Scully's executive secretary, 1935-43, in 1940 Robin began using his formidable literary talents to write speeches for then-Democratic Party state chairman David Lawrence. Mustered out of the army, in 1946 he became the new Mayor Lawrence's executive secretary. Two years later, in 1948, as an integral part of the Pittsburgh Renaissance team, Robin became the first executive director of the new Urban Redevelopment Authority, 1948-54, directing such landmark projects as Point State Park, Gateway Center, city-wide slum clearance and new housing, and the Penn-Lincoln Parkway (now I-376).

Moving to Harrisburg in 1955 as Commerce secretary, within nine months he returned to become president and first executive officer of the Regional Industrial Development Corporation. Seventeen months later, he went to Philadelphia, serving as president of The Old Philadelphia Development Corporation, heading the historic Independence Mall project.

Then Robin was tapped by the Ford Foundation to work on similar projects overseas. For the next 10 years he traveled the world, serving in Europe and South America, but primarily in Calcutta and Nairobi.

Returning to Pittsburgh in 1973 to take a Pitt chair in public affairs, Robin also served as an advisor to the Allegheny Conference. Mayor Caliguiri brought him back into city government in 1977. It was Robin who dubbed the new redevelopment efforts Renaissance II—even writing Caliguiri's first inaugural address on that theme.

Returning to the URA as chairman in 1978, and also chairing the Port Authority, Robin directed such major projects as PPG Place, the Martin Luther King Busway, and Light Rail Transit.

In 1983, the Civic Building, the URA's home at 200 Ross Street, was renamed in his honor, a rare tribute given to a living, non-elected public servant. Retiring in 1994, suffering from long-time heart ailments, he died, age 87, in 2000.

Robin shares laughs with Mayor Dick Caliguiri and URA Director Stephen George during an Urban Redevelopment Authority meeting, 1981, captured with autographs.

© UNDERWOOD & UNDERWOOD/CORBIS

Calbraith Perry Rodgers

Born January 12, 1879—Pittsburgh
Died April 3, 1912—Long Beach, CA

Cal Rodgers was the first man to fly across the continental United States. His flight from Long Island, NY, to Long Beach, CA, took only 84 days. The trip might have been quicker had Cal Rodgers not crash-landed 39 times in the process. The year was 1911. Orville had defied gravity just seven years earlier.

Very little is known about the Pittsburgh childhood of Cal Rodgers, but he attended Mercersburg Academy and, at the age of 32, was one of the Wright Brothers' first students. When William Randolph Hearst offered an unprecedented prize of $50,000 to the first person to fly coast to coast in less than 30 days, Cal headed straight to Dayton to buy a plane. Practiced in the delicate arts of cranking a four cylinder engine, changing oil gaskets, and following train tracks from an aerial height of 800 feet, Cal Rodgers' epic journey commenced on September 7, 1911, at Sheepshead Bay, NY.

He dubbed his plane the Vin Fiz Flyer, in contractual arrangement with the Armour Company of Chicago that had just launched a new grape soda they hoped would soon be available from coast to coast for just 5 cents. The aerial advertising subsidized the costs of a full rail car for his wife and mother, an accompanying rail car for a second plane (with extra parts), a Palmer-Singer automobile to tote his family from farm fields to nearby ho-

tels, and the assistance of not one, but two traveling mechanics.

In the air, Rodgers' only navigational aids were the sun and train tracks. Often flying in pouring rains, he barreled through lightning storms, landing only when out of daylight or petrol.

On November 5, 1911, he landed in Pasadena to a cheering crowd of 20,000. Long past the qualifying deadline to win the Hearst prize, Rodgers was still determined to prove his mettle. At long last, on December 10, Rodgers dipped his wheels in the Pacific Ocean at Long Beach, having flown some 4,000 miles. Rodgers became a national hero.

It was but a few months later, when, as a favor to his fans, he demonstrated his flying skills off the California coast. In the air, a flock of seagulls stormed his engine, and Cal Rodgers plummeted to his death—less than 500 feet from where he made history.

Rodgers is buried in Allegheny Cemetery.

1st AVIATOR TO CROSS THE CONTINENT

© UNDERWOOD & UNDERWOOD/CORBIS

HIS FATAL WRECK - LONG BEACH - CAL.

John Augustus Roebling

Born June 12, 1806—Muhlhausen, Prussia
Died July 22, 1869—Brooklyn, NY

It's no wonder the gullible were willing to buy the Brooklyn Bridge. Completed in 1883, it was an engineering masterpiece, the world's longest suspension bridge, spanning the East River to connect Manhattan and Brooklyn. The genius who designed it, John Augustus Roebling, also perfected the span's most significant component: 15-inch thick cables, each made up of 5,000 entwined wires that suspended the roadbed nearly 300 feet beneath the bridge towers.

Roebling was an engineer, architect, inventor, and philosopher—a protégé of Georg Hegel. In 1831, Roebling came to Western Pennsylvania from Prussia with his brother,

Karl, and others from their hometown, to settle in Butler County. They bought 1,600 acres from a larger parcel originally deeded to Robert Morris, the financier of the American Revolution. Roebling laid out a town he named Saxonburg and sold lots to his former Prussian neighbors who migrated to the U.S.

With a mind too restless for farming, Roebling developed an idea he saw in a German magazine: twisting strands of wire around a core to make a cable stronger than the hemp ropes used for bridges and inclines. That, in turn, allowed Roebling to implement his designs for a new suspension bridge, a concept he explored in his university thesis.

In 1841, Roebling put theory and invention into practice, engineering a suspension aqueduct to carry water across the Allegheny River. Four years later, he built a second Smithfield Street Bridge across the Monongahela River in Pittsburgh. (The original wooden one had burned in the city's Great Fire). Roebling's wire suspension bridge was in operation 40 years before it was replaced by the present truss bridge.

With his cable in worldwide demand, Roebling relocated to Trenton, NJ, to be closer to suppliers and East Coast ports. He had continued to design and supervise bridge construction, including a rail structure over the Niagara River, and the Cincinnati Bridge over the Ohio, each longer and more complicated than the previous one.

In 1869, Roebling injured his foot at the construction site of the Brooklyn Bridge. He refused regular medical treatment in favor of hydrology, continuously running cold water over his foot. But he died of tetanus, then known as lockjaw, 16 days later. His son carried on his work, supervising completion of the Brooklyn Bridge for 14 more years.

Ben Roethlisberger

Born March 2, 1982—Findlay, OH

This is supposed to happen only in movies. There's this 22-year-old kid quarterback, born in Columbus, 1982, raised in nearby Findlay, Ohio. He may be a beanpole wide-out early in high school, but he grows large—6'-5", 240. Not chucking the ball until his senior year, he plays at Miami of Ohio, hardly a football powerhouse. Tough, smart, and agile, Big Ben Roethlisberger sets a school record by throwing 84 touchdown passes—impressive enough for him to be taken by the Steelers in the first round of the 2004 draft.

He comes to the big club, to back up Tommy Maddox—Tommy Gun, one of the team's all-time leading passers. Things are going fine—until game two when Tommy Gun gets hurt.

Call in Big Ben, who finishes the game. Then Big Ben starts game three. And wins. And wins and wins—13 in a row, the team finishing 15-1, and Big Ben becoming Rookie of the Year. "Sure, we were surprised," says Coach Bill Cowher. "We didn't expect what took place because it's never been done. Ben did things far beyond what we expected a young player to do."

In 2005, Big Ben's sophomore year, the Steelers limp into the playoffs 11-5, no hope of success. With Big Ben in charge, the Steelers win three straight road games to face Seattle in Super Bowl XL.

And Big Ben becomes legend. With the Colts game on the line, Big Ben saves the season by making an impossible tackle—dubbed The Immaculate Redemption. Winning Super Bowl XL, the Steelers take their first championship in 26 years—and Big Ben becomes the youngest quarterback ever to do so. It matters little that 2006 is a bad dream—a motorcycle accident, and an emergency appendectomy. "What Ben's done is mind-boggling," Coach Cowher says. "And he's going to get better."

Fred Rogers

Born March 20, 1928—Latrobe, PA
Died February 17, 2003—Pittsburgh

If Pittsburgh is some place special, he was someone more so; a very real man affirming the interest (and allaying the fears) of very real children through the make-believe world of television.

Fred Rogers was born the only son to James and Nancy McFeely Rogers. Her father, Fred McFeely, was the founder of McFeely Brick Company of Latrobe, manufacturers of the very best industrial furnace bricks available in the U.S. So successful was the company his father ran, Fred was often left alone—to play with his retired grandfather. It was McFeely who first taught Rogers that he was—and every child is—special. A 1951 Music Composition graduate of Rollins College, he was hired by NBC in New York and, a year later, married college sweetheart Sara Joanne Byrd, also a talented pianist. Before returning to Pittsburgh, Rogers was an assistant producer on early TV shows like *The Kate Smith Hour*, *NBC Opera Theater*, and *Your Lucky Strike Hit Parade*.

In 1953, Rogers was hired by WQED, the first public education station, to develop programming. *The Children's Corner* was live, unscripted, and unrehearsed. Because Rogers had to make everything happen quickly behind stage, he discovered the benefits of wearing sneakers. At first rarely seen in front of the camera, Rogers' persona showed up in the animations of his many puppets.

In 1963, Rogers was hired by the CBC and moved with his then young family to Toronto where he created *MisteRogers*. He returned to Pittsburgh in 1965 where he began working on a half-hour program called *Mister Rogers' Neighborhood*, now in its 40th year on PBS. Many of the sweaters Rogers wore on the program were handmade by his mother.

Of all the lore surrounding his consistent lifestyle, message and program format—Rogers wrote every show, consulting with Dr. Margaret McFarland—this much is true: while he was an ordained Presbyterian minister, he also held a degree in Child Development from the University of Pittsburgh. He never smoked, never drank, never trained as a covert Navy Seal, nor had tattoos, but he did swim most every day. Above all, Rogers was true in every way. What children saw on television was the man he really was. A vegetarian—Rogers said, "I won't eat anything that had a mother." He died of stomach cancer in 2003.

Rob Rogers

Born May 23, 1959—Philadelphia, PA

In *Brewed on Grant*, his local comic strip set in a fictitious diner not far from the mayor's office, *Post-Gazette* editorial cartoonist Rob Rogers serves up weekly specials of skewered politicos and biting Pittsburgh satire. With the help of his original Pittsburgh icons, Rosie the Waitress and Vic the Steelers Fan, Rogers manages to lampoon everyone from hockey great Mario Lemieux to former County Coroner Cyril Wecht.

Deftly balancing wit and bite, Rogers' wry takes on international figures like Osama Bin Laden and George W. Bush have garnered more national acclaim than any other Pittsburgh editorial cartoonist since Cy Hungerford. His 1994 depiction of Newt Gingrich, "The Gingrich Who Stole Christmas," even graced the cover of *Newsweek* magazine.

Born in 1959 in Philadelphia, Rogers began cartooning as soon as he could hold a crayon, copying his favorite *Philadelphia Inquirer* comic characters, later enrolling in

Saturday art classes. In 1972 at age 13, Rogers and his family moved to Oklahoma, where, as a school project, he drew his first political cartoons—of Democratic Presidential candidate George McGovern.

While majoring in art at Oklahoma State University, Rogers began to draw political cartoons for the school paper. He returned to his home state to attend Carnegie Mellon, graduating in 1984 with a master of fine arts in painting. Rogers sent out a portfolio of editorial cartoons and was immediately hired by the *Pittsburgh Press*. Nine years later, when the *Post-Gazette* acquired the Press, Rogers joined that staff.

His cartoons gained immediate national attention and were soon picked up by United Feature Syndicate. Rogers' work regularly appear in America's top media outlets—the *New York Times*, *Washington Post*, *Chicago Tribune*, *LA Times*, *Philadelphia Inquirer*, *Newsweek*, and *USA Today*. Rogers and his cartoons have appeared alsoon NBC's *Today,* and CBS' *Face the Nation*.

A local as well as national award-winner, Rogers received the 1995 National Headliner Award and 2000 Overseas Press Club Award. In 1999, he was a Pulitzer Prize finalist.

In addition to his daily contributions to the editorial page, Rogers has become a national advocate for the profession of editorial cartooning, serving as the most recent president of, and organizing two national conventions for, the Association of American Editorial Cartoonists. He currently serves as board president for the Toonseum, a new museum of cartoon art in Pittsburgh.

George Romero

Born February 4, 1940—Bronx, NY

"'*Night of the Living Dead*' is probably the scariest film I ever made… All I see are the flaws. But I owe everything to that one. If it weren't for that, I'd be flipping burgers." Fifteen films later, George Romero is the maverick king of low-budget horror flicks. Films like *There's Always Vanilla*, *Hungry Wives*, or *Martin* may not be on horror fan's top 10 list, but more than many include at least one of his five "Dead" films: *Diary of the..*, *Land of the..*, *Dawn of the..*, *Day of the..*, and *Night of the Living…* (Apparently, after his first success, the oxymoron was no longer necessary).

Romero made his first film in Scarsdale, NY, using an 8mm Revere camera, borrowed from his uncle. The film, in which aliens invade the suburbs, was titled "The Man from the Meteor." He was 14, but already a sophomore high school student, having been advanced by two grades when a child growing up in the Bronx. Perhaps because of his younger age, he was a loner, and loved sneaking off to Times Square to watch films. After graduation, he attended Suffield Academy in Connecticut to fulfill a gap year before enrolling at Carnegie Tech in 1957. Five years of art classes later, but without sufficient credits to graduate, he and friends opened a production studio on Carson Street to shoot commercials. "Latent Image" did work for the Buhl Planetarium and Duke Beer—even shooting some Picture-Picture segments for *Mister Rogers' Neighborhood*—among other clients. The team raised enough cash—almost $100,000—to shoot a horror film. The year was 1968.

A black protagonist (actor Duane Jones,) no singular monster but many, no moralistic lessons behind the terror—just a relentless onslaught of zombies invading a rural farmhouse—conspired to create a cult classic. Drive-ins everywhere ran the black & white reels. Soon, Europe carried the distribution. According to the *Internet Movie Database*, *Night of the Living Dead* has grossed in excess of $42 million since its 1968 premiere.

Filmed primarily in Evans City, *Night* featured several local celebrities: Karl Hardman and Marilyn Eastman, husband and wife, who owned a successful recording studio, Bill Cardille, host of WIIC's *Chiller Theater*, played the news reporter, and Frank Doak, father of Pulitzer prize-winning author, Annie Dillard, played the scientist asked to explain the effects of radiation from a Venetian flying saucer that incites the dead to rise. Russ Streiner was the co-producer.

Though certainly not instantaneous, Romero's success advanced him production funds to shoot two more films. The first, *There's Always Vanilla*, was a 1960s psycho-socialism flop; *Martin* returned Romero to a more horrific plot in which a young man thinks himself to be a vampire.

From thence, the "Dead" trilogy commenced, though it is a pentalogy of sorts today. Romero's other successes have included *Monkey Shines, Creepshow* and TV work on *Tales from the Dark Side*. A re-make of *The Crazies* is due out in 2008 and a sequel to *Diary of the Dead* was announced in 2007.

But Pittsburgh must credit Romero with more than just creating a surprising cult classic, and a significant history of horror-genre hits, most of which were shot in Pittsburgh. What Romero truly created was a film industry within Pittsburgh. Special effects artists like Tom Savini and Greg Nicotero, logistics companies like Haddad's, film processing centers like WRS Motion Picture Labs, and scores of local actors, have fueled an industry that has brought to the local economy, since the inception of the Pittsburgh Film Office in 1990, more than $275 million in economic impact. Because of Romero's early success—because he proved that Pittsburgh had the production talent to staff feature films—more than 100 feature films have been filmed in the 'Burgh since his 1968 first.

Art Rooney

Born January 27, 1901—Coulterville, PA
Died August 25, 1988—Pittsburgh

If love is the recognition of virtue in others, there can be little wonder why Steelers founder, owner, and chairman Art Rooney was loved by so many. A gruff, tough guy, strong enough in his prime to knuckle the head of one of his coaches, he was also an extraordinarily kind man, and one with such a great gift of humanity that a simple hello affixed to a first name made a fellow glow for weeks.

Art Rooney, right, bought the Steelers franchise. His son, Dan Rooney, left, built a winning team.

Arthur Joseph Rooney, aka The Chief, was born in 1901, in nearby Coulterville. As a child, his father moved the family to the North Side, where young Art and his eight siblings were brought up on General Robinson Street, above the family saloon.

Art grew up as a champion amateur boxer and minor-league baseball and football player, anything that could draw a crowd or turn a buck. As a world-class horse player and small-time sports promoter, he ran a string of minor-league football clubs until 1933, when he bought a franchise in the new National Football League. Known as the Pittsburgh Pirates back then, the team was small potatoes compared to their legendary brothers of summer.

Through hard times, and mergers with Philadelphia and Chicago during World War II, Rooney made payroll—and not much more. After 1945, he built his franchise into respectability, displaying his legendary patience, watching the team's fortunes rise and fall, but never berating a coach, and never, never blaming the city or its fans. Forty years of losing and all he could do was chomp a little harder on his trademark cigar. Rain or shine, win or lose, he thanked his players for their efforts, often personally, often with unexpected bonuses.

As fans celebrate the Steelers' Super Bowl XL victory, January 5, 2006, they remember Rooney who had died some 18 years earlier.

Rooney, center in dark suit, joins his team in a prayer of gratitude after the Steelers won Super Bowl IX, January 12, 1975.

Then in the 1960s, fortune began to favor him. Legends like Bobby Layne and John Henry Johnson joined the team. And TV helped bring revenues no professional sport had previously realized.

In 1970, Three Rivers Stadium rose from the banks of the Allegheny, adding further to Steeler fortunes. Yet as the team grew, Rooney never lost touch with his roots. When grounds crews had to transform the field from baseball to football over cold Saturday nights, The Chief was there with them, hot coffee and sandwiches in hand. For such kindnesses, they made him an honorary member, an accolade he treasured all his life.

In the process, he saw his $2,500 investment transformed from something he could operate out of a hotel office—and a small pocket notebook—into a multi-million-dollar empire. The Pittsburgh Steelers became the literal toast—and definition—of the town. When he died in 1988, Art Rooney had become a Pro Football Hall of Famer, the father of Hall of Famer Dan Rooney, employer of numerous Hall of Famers, and proud possessor of four Super Bowl trophies.

In the end, though, his team, his city, and his humanity mattered far more than wins and losses—and accolades. "'Treat everybody the way you'd like to be treated,'" his son Art, Jr., recalled the Chief saying. "'Give people the benefit of the doubt. But never let anyone mistake kindness for weakness.' My father took the Golden Rule—and put a little bit of the North Side into it."

Dan Rooney

Born July 20, 1932—Pittsburgh

Great sports franchises are made, not born, and secure, consistent leadership is rare. As perhaps the most able, steady-handed steward of a pro team anywhere, in 2000 Dan Rooney deservedly joined his father as only the second father-son Pro Football Hall of Fame inductees. President and chairman of the most successful professional sports organization in Pittsburgh history, Rooney has made his club an exemplar of patience, dignity, and community spirit.

Born in Pittsburgh in 1932, a year before his fabled father purchased a National Football League franchise, Dan Rooney's earliest memories include being brought to Steelers training camp as a toddler. A quarterback at North Catholic High, he learned the organization literally from the ground up. By age 14 he was a ballboy, running errands for Jock Sutherland. In four short years Rooney was managing the camp, as well as signing players, selling program ads, working in the ticket office. Coming aboard in 1955, after graduating from Duquesne University, Rooney assumed day-to-day operations in 1964.

Working for a famous—make that legendary—father didn't make life any easier. Having had his own way for 30 years, Art Rooney had to contend with his son. Contend they did, fighting about something virtually every day. Finally, the Chief'd chomp a little harder on his trademark stogie, eye his very bright son, and snap, "OK, do it your way. Just don't make any mistakes."

Named president in 1975, and chairman in 2003, Rooney transformed a perennial laughingstock into preternaturally successful champion—while never forgetting where he was born. As he put it when the underdog Steelers went to Super Bowl XL, "it's something to pick up the town, the idea that we can do it. All over the world people are saying the Pittsburgh Steelers are in the Super Bowl. ...That's something above and beyond money."

Rosenberg's *Street by the Mill*, c. 1932, oil on canvas, H: 36 1/2 x W 40 3/4 in., Carnegie Musem of Art, Gift of Mr. and Mrs. Charles Dreifus, Jr., in memory of his father

Samuel Rosenberg

Born in 1896—Philadelphia, PA
Died 1972—Pittsburgh

It is said that he was Andy Warhol's favorite teacher at Carnegie Tech—perhaps because he saved the future auteur from certain expulsion. An enormously gifted, multifaceted artist who excelled at four different painting styles, Samuel Rosenberg enjoyed a six-decade career based on recognized talent, restless intelligence, and relentless innovation.

Born in Philadelphia in 1896, as a child Rosenberg moved to the Hill District where, by age 12 he was taking art classes at the Irene Kaufmann Settlement House. By age 19, in 1915, he was exhibiting his own work.

Initially drawn to realistic portraiture, Rosenberg's people display a deep sensitivity and a deft touch. By 1930, however, he had turned to social realism, portraying the Hill District's rich African-American and Jewish street life, as well as a rough, angular city defined by steep hills and dense smoke.

By 1942, as images of World War II began to play across America, Rosenberg again changed his focus, painting allegories of human suffering, redemption, and transcendence. By decade's end, Rosenberg had moved on again, to abstract expressionism, his extraordinary layers of color and glaze appearing almost as stained glass.

Throughout his career, Rosenberg exhibited nationally, including San Francisco's Golden Gate Exposition and New York City's 1939 World's Fair, Whitney biennials, and every Carnegie International, 1933-67. With his work shown at the Museum of Modern Art, the Corcoran, and the Pennsylvania Academy of Fine Arts, Rosenberg's complete oeuvre includes more than 500 paintings, 400 drawings, and 100 collages.

In addition, Rosenberg was a skilled art educator, the most famous of his time. Teaching for more than 40 years at Carnegie Mellon, where his students included Warhol, Pearlstein, and many others, Rosenberg also chaired the art department at Chatham College and taught at community art schools.

Rosey Rowswell

Born February 1, 1884—Pittsburgh
Died February 6, 1955—Pittsburgh

A radio pioneer—as well as a humorist, speaker, and widely published poet—Rosey Rowswell was the first Voice of the Pirates.

Born in Pittsburgh in 1884, Albert Kennedy Rowswell was a wry, gentle, unaffected man who translated a gift for folksy expressions and spinning yarns into the art of broadcasting baseball games.

Veteran of his own popular radio show, *Rosey Reflections,* Rowswell moved to the Pirates in 1936. At a time when remote radio broadcasts were unimaginable, Rowswell sat in a radio studio and, using the terse game  summaries from the Western Union telegraph ticker, re-created the games. As practiced early on by Rowswell—and other baseball announcers, including future President Ronald "Dutch" Reagan—the games inevitably featured lengthy stories, personal greetings, and colorful expressions—at which Rowswell excelled.

Pirate games, which were accompanied by the actual sound of the ticker, featured other primitive sound effects as well, chief among them breaking glass. When a Pirate hit a home run, Rowswell cried, "Raise the window, Aunt Minnie!" A moment later, Rowswell's broadcasting partner—first Jack Craddock, 1937-47; later, Bob Prince, 1948-54—dropped a box of broken glass. "Oh," Rowswell said, "I guess she didn't make it."

"Oh, my aching back," Rowswell moaned if a Pirate rally failed. In the Rowswell lexicon, a Pirates extra-base hit was a "doozie marooney," a strikeout was a "dipsy-doodle." When the bases were loaded Rowswell called them "FOB" (Full of Bucs).

Standing just 5'-6" and 120 pounds, Rowswell never drank anything stronger than water. A noted author and poet, Rowswell was also a popular after-dinner speaker, logging some 50,000 miles annually.

After 19 seasons with the Pirates, Rosey Rowswell died in 1955. More than 3,000 people came to his funeral at Samson Funeral Home. They lined the road to his burial in Allegheny Cemetery.

© /CORBIS

Charles Taze Russell

Born February 16, 1852—North Side
Died October 31, 1916—near Pampa, TX

Charles Taze Russell founded the religious order known today as the Jehovah's Witnesses. He was born into a Scottish-Irish Presbyterian family in Allegheny, PA, in 1852, but at a young age abandoned his religious upbringing in favor of his own unique beliefs. The core of Russell's theology argued that the Bible was the only source of truth and should therefore be meticulously studied. Russell also believed the end of the world was at hand. At the upcoming Battle of Armageddon, he taught, the forces of Good would defeat Satan resulting in the advent of the "Kingdom of Jehovah" in which his followers—known as "The Heavenly Classes"—would rule.

In the 1870s, Russell formed a Bible study group (later known as the Watchtower Bible and Tract Society) in Allegheny to spread his beliefs. Arguing that the only test of faithfulness was through missionary work, Russell inspired followers to embark on a campaign spreading his teachings door-to-door. Russell's charisma and oratorical skills also helped spread his ideas.

Failing to obtain support from established religions, which labeled him an eccentric, Russell dedicated his life to relaying his message independently, moving to Brooklyn, NY, in order to expand his following. He died in Texas in 1916 while returning from a west coast tour promoting his teachings. His body was returned to Western Pennsylvania.

Russell's Watchtower Bible and Tract Society eventually became the legal corporation of the Jehovah's Witnesses, a name adopted in the 1930s. Known for their pacifism, refusal to salute the flag, rejection of blood transfusions, and door-to-door solicitation, the Jehovah's Witnesses are still in existence today and number as many as six million.

Lillian Russell

Born December 4, 1861—Clinton, IA
Died June 6, 1922—Point Breeze

Lillian Russell was one of the most famous and beloved entertainers of the late 19th Century. Born Helen Louise Leonard, she was blessed with a fine singing voice and a mother determined to make the most of it. Nellie (as she was known) and her four sisters were all musically gifted.

Russell stated, "Our favorite game was 'opera' so it was natural when I heard my first opera, *Mignon*, I should decide I would become a grand opera singer."

© BETTMANN/CORBIS

Her mother Cynthia was a whirlwind devoted to suffrage for women and other progressive causes. She moved with two of her daughters to Chicago and then New York seeking greater opportunity for her own sphere of influence and her daughters' musical educations.

Russell made her Broadway debut in 1880 in Tony Pastor's revue. Light comic opera was her strong suit, and she toured the United States and England to rave reviews. Also known for her lavish lifestyle and hearty appetite, Russell married four times, but her true soul mate was railroad tycoon and gourmand Diamond Jim Brady. They became acquainted during Russell's singing engagement at the 1893 Columbian Exposition and remained fast friends until Brady's 1917 death.

As Russell aged and her singing voice diminished, she turned to acting and found success there as well. She honed her comedic skills with the famous vaudeville partners Joe Weber and Lew Fields with whom she worked for five years. In 1912 she announced her retirement from the stage and her engagement to Alexander P. Moore, publisher of the *Pittsburgh Leader*. The wedding was held June 12, 1912, at the Schenley Hotel (now the University of Pittsburgh Student Union) in Oakland. They made their home at 6744 Penn Avenue in Point Breeze.

Russell retired from the stage, but not from life. She wrote a beauty column, lectured on women's suffrage, and recruited for enlistment in World War I. She died shortly after returning from a trip overseas. The funeral was held at Pittsburgh's Trinity Cathedral on Sixth Avenue downtown, and she is buried in Allegheny Cemetery.

Rusted Root

The collaboration of Michael Glabicki and Liz Berlin, Rusted Root was formed in 1988 after the two met at a political rally in Pittsburgh. They began their collaboration acoustically but soon added Jim Donovan and Patrick Norman, classmates from an African drumming class that Liz had taken. A year later they added John Buynak on percussion and winds, who as a visual artist gave Rusted Root their strong visual imagery. Jenn Wertz, originally hired to photograph the band, was brought on to help with vocals. Quickly garnering a reputation as a great live jam band, Rusted Root gained much of their following through a heavy tour schedule, and eventually recorded their independently produced debut release *Cruel Sun* in 1992. When Jim DiSpirito, a percussionist who had studied music in India, joined the band in 1993, their sound was complete.

COURTESY OF DOYLE-KOS ENTERTAINMENT

Mercury Records signed the band and released *When I Woke* in 1994 to critical acclaim, selling to date over two million copies. Produced with Bill Bottrell, who produced for Tom Petty and Sheryl Crow, *When I Woke* generated their best known release, "Send Me on My Way." This and many of their releases have been featured in both movie and television soundtracks, including *Ice Age, Matilda, Twister, Alley McBeal,* and *Home for the Holidays* (requested specifically by the film's director, Jodi Foster).

Between 1996 and 2004, the band released *Remember, Rusted Root, Welcome To My Party*, and *Rusted Root Live*. In addition to a sizeable fan base, Rusted Root has toured with some of the biggest names in the industry, including The Allman Brothers, Grateful Dead, Jimmy Page and Robert Plant, the Dave Mathews Band, and Hot Tuna. The band's propensity for long jams and the members' abilities to play a multitude of instruments—in fact, they have been known to play as many as sixty different percussion instruments during a single concert—has made the Root a show not to miss.

In recent years Rusted Root has slowed its tour schedule as members pursue solo projects—from skate parks and drum clinics to political activism and new recording studios—but the distinctive sound that is Rusted Root is one of Pittsburgh's best known contributions to the "world beat" sound.

Salk reads *LIFE* magazine with his wife and three boys in Ann Arbor, MI, April 11, 1955.

Jonas Salk

Born October 28, 1914—New York, NY
Died June 23, 1995—La Jolla, CA

In the early 1950s, the University of Pittsburgh employed two little-known physicians who would have a powerful and lasting impact on the health of children. The names Spock and Salk were soon to become household words. Dr. Jonas Salk was a virus researcher from New York City who came to Pittsburgh in 1947 to help set up the university's Viral Research Lab in the basement of what was then called Municipal Hospital.

With an undergraduate degree from City College of New York and a medical degree

from New York University, the young doctor worked as a staff physician at Mt. Sinai Hospital in New York City. An interest in virology research led him to the University of Michigan, where, during World War II, he was on a team that succeeded in developing and providing influenza vaccine for American troops.

Starting at Pitt in 1947, Salk first continued his research in influenza. But infantile paralysis was a growing childhood epidemic and a source of angst, and sometimes hysteria, among the parents of youngsters. What intrigued Salk most in his research was the possibility of using an inactivated or dead poliovirus to trigger antibodies that would make the human body immune to the live poliovirus. The illness's high profile meant that research funding could be found. Salk and his team soon developed an effective vaccine.

Salk launched his first small field trial at the Arsenal Elementary School in Lawrenceville. Some 137 children there were to be the first of 10,000 Allegheny County public school children volunteered by their parents to get the vaccine. Salk later recalled how he had brought the vaccine, but had forgotten the lollipops he gave as a reward for the sting of the injection. With the success of the field trials confirmed, the nation could soon awaken from the polio nightmare. The disease declined from 18,000 reported cases in 1954 to only 61 in 1965. Its eradication earned Salk a Congressional Gold Medal for his work.

In 1963, the Salks left Pittsburgh for La Jolla, CA, where the Salk Institute for Biological Studies was under construction on a hillside with a breathtaking view of the Pacific Ocean. He closed his laboratory at the Institute in 1984, but continued working and writing until his death 11 years later, in 1995.

Bruno Sammartino

Born October 6, 1935—Pizzoferrato, Italy

Master of the feared and fabled Sammartino Slam, as well as the Standing Backwater and the Half Boston Crab, professional wrestler Bruno Sammartino is arguably the World Wide Wrestling Federation's (WWWF) all-time champion—and certainly Pittsburgh's most famous wrestling import.

Born Bruno Leopoldo Francesco Sammartino, his family hid in the mountains from the ravages of World War II. Emigrating to Pittsburgh as a skinny teenager in 1951, Sammartino attended Schenley High and worked

out at Pitt. Under the tutelage of coach Rex Peary, Sammartino became such an adept weight lifter that he placed on the 1956 United States Olympic team. By 1959, Sammartino had emerged as a 5'10", 285-pound professional wrestler, appearing locally on WIIC's *Studio Wrestling* for some 15 years, as well as in many national venues, including Shea Stadium and Madison Square Garden—the latter more than 200 times.

Achieving early notoriety by becoming the only man in wrestling history to lift—and slam—600-pound Haystacks Calhoun, by 1963 Sammartino had won the WWWF world heavyweight championship—a title which he held for nearly eight years, the longest single reign in professional wresting history. In late 1973, Sammartino regained his title, holding it for more than three years. All told, the so-called Italian Strongman was WWWF heavyweight champion for some 12 years, the longest combined reign in history.

Since retiring in 1987, Sammartino has publicly criticized professional wrestling for drug and steroid use. Still active in wrestling circles, he takes non-athletic parts in such events as *Ring of Honor* and *WrestleMania*. With his own line of documentaries, including *Bruno Sammartino's Legends Never Die*, he also has his own action figure.

A multiple award-winner in many wrestling categories, Sammartino is a member of the Professional Wrestling Hall of Fame and father of Pittsburgh-born professional wrestler David Sammartino.

Tom Savini

Born November 3, 1946—Bloomfield

He was just 10 when he saw *Man of A Thousand Faces*, starring James Cagney, at the Plaza Theatre in Bloomfield. The film, based on the life of Lon Chaney, was the spider's bite in Tom Savini's tarantella with horror films. He shined shoes in the neighborhood to earn cash for make-up, and he has confessed to stealing his mother's lipstick. While his friends were playing football, Tom could be found in the bathroom doing grotesque things to his face.

Known to thousands of horror fans worldwide, he is called the Master of Splatter, the Maestro of Mayhem and the Godfather of Gore. He learned his art from life. Just before auditioning for a small role in George Romero's *Night of the Living Dead*, Savini, who had enlisted in the Army, was called to service. In Vietnam, trained as a combat photographer, Savini was assigned to photograph the wounded. He learned firsthand the horror of a severed hand, a missing limb, and a decapitated torso.

An erstwhile actor, he performed often in repertory theatre in North Carolina where he was introduced to filmmaker Bob Clark, later of *Porky's* fame, but whose first genre was horror. Savini cut his teeth on 1972's *Deathdream*. In 1975, he met with Romero again

and was offered the job of special effects for *Martin*. The earlier success of "Night" of course led to its sequel, *Dawn of the Dead*, filmed entirely at the Monroeville Mall. Savini's work on "Dawn" was just the kind of realistic gore that the producers of an upcoming slasher film were hoping to recreate. The film, as much a modern classic as "Night," was *Friday the 13th*.

In addition to a huge string of horror hits, including Romero's *Creepshow* and Dario Argento's *Trauma*, Savini has had many successes as an actor, stuntman, and director. In 1995, he directed *Dracula* on stage for City Theatre. And every fall for the past eight years, he has produced *Terrormania*, a Pittsburgh haunted house experience created by students of his special effects and make-up school in Monessen. A proud resident of Bloomfield, his son Lon has a daughter named Chaney.

Chuck Scarborough

Born November 4, 1943—Pittsburgh

He still serves as the longest tenured news anchorman in New York City, having started at WNBC-TV4 in 1974, working alongside co-anchor Sue Simmons since 1980, making them the longest running news team in NY history. Only Bill Beutel has been on the air longer (though not with the same station) than Chuck Scarborough.

Born in Avonmore where his mother lived with her parents while his father flew B-17s in the war, Scarborough noted, "My childhood memories of Pittsburgh are restricted to arrivals and departures for visits to my grandparents' house, usually by train, occasionally by plane. Dr. & Mrs. Campbell loved spoiling their grandson. As a consequence, I equated the sulfurous smell of steel being smelted with unlimited childhood delights."

Growing up in Biloxi, he matriculated on the campus of the University of Southern Mississippi from whence he joined the Air Force and flew for four years. His professional career began at WLOX-TV in Biloxi, then WDAM in Hattiesburg from 1968 to 1969, following onto WAGA in Atlanta until 1972. In 2004, he celebrated his 30th year with NBC, having won 28 Emmys® for broadcast journalism.

As Mike Hoyt wrote in the *Columbia Journalism Review*, he "is as dependable as a toaster and nearly as neutral." Nearly, because, in 1996 the *New York Times* broke with a story about Scarborough's presidential campaign donations. He had donated $1,000 to Steve Forbes' campaign, and it was then soon discovered he, too, had contributed to the Bush-Quayle ticket, to Bob Dole and, like a good hometown boy, to Arlen Specter's re-election bid. WNBC quickly announced that he would not cover any more campaign stories, thus publicly slapping his wrist (no doubt the right one).

Scarborough is also the author of three suspense novels of which his most successful, 1991's *After Shock* about an earthquake centering on Manhattan, was turned into a made-for TV movie.

Fittingly, Scarborough and his wife live in the Carnegie Hill neighborhood of Manhattan's Upper East Side.

Mary Schenley

Born April 27, 1826—Louisville, KY
Died November 3, 1903—London, England

More than a century and a half before Paris Hilton captured the tabloid headlines with her exploits, Pittsburgh was home to another heiress supposedly gone wild. A granddaughter of Pennsylvania pioneer Gen. James O'Hara, Mary Schenley (nee Mary Elizabeth Croghan), all of 16 years old, shocked the nation with her elopement with Captain Edward W. Schenley of the British Army, a man 27 years her elder.

The elopement set off a bizarre chain of events. The federal government sent out boats in a vain attempt to intercept the vessel (which apparently had made a honeymoon stop in Bermuda). The boarding school from which the young heiress had eloped was forced to close after other fathers feared their socialite daughters would follow Ms. Croghan's lead. Her father reportedly had a stroke upon hearing the news of her marriage.

Newspapers had a field day with the story. The *Pittsburgh Dispatch*'s portrait of Captain Schenley was less than flattering: "His eyes had the hard glint of new dollars from the mint," it wrote. "While his character was not in question, he was considered by Croghan's friends as a fortune-hunting adventurer."

However, the story had a happy ending. The two seemed to be genuinely in love. And more importantly for Pittsburgh, Mary Schenley never lost her love for her birth city or her family's tract of land. In the late 1880s, there were rumors that land developers were planning to visit her in London to try to convince her to sell. When a young, enterprising Edward Bigelow, Pittsburgh's director of the Department of Public Works, heard about the potential land grab, he immediately dispatched a representative to pitch using the tract for parks and recreation.

The space race was on, with Bigelow's representative taking the train to New York and immediately boarding a steamer to England. He arrived two days ahead of the real estate developers and brokered a deal. Schenley would donate 300 acres and would give the city the option to purchase 120 more. Her caveats: The land could never be sold, and the area would be named after her. From that donation and purchase of the additional land, Pittsburghers for generations have enjoyed—and in perpetuity will enjoy—the splendor of Schenley Park and Schenley Plaza.

© 2007, THE TARTAN

Gladys Schmitt

Born May 31, 1909—Pittsburgh
Died October 3, 1972—Pittsburgh

"I can clearly trace my love of writing and my belief in myself as a writer to Gladys Schmitt's [Carnegie Tech] freshman English class," Pittsburgh novelist Iris Rainer Dart recalled. "Gladys Schmitt's appreciation of my work, her insightful comments on my papers, and her conviction that I had a writer's mind and gift gave me a large measure of confidence in myself. The way she talked to me as a writer made me feel I could be one."

Best-selling author, beloved teacher, Gladys Schmitt was a role model to students for three decades.

Born Gladys Schmitt in Pittsburgh in 1909, her talent emerged early. As a child she wrote verse plays; her high school essays merited a scholarship to the Pennsylvania College for Women—as Chatham was known. Transferring to Pitt, she placed a poem—"Progeny"—in *Poetry* magazine.

Working as a *Scholastic* magazine editor, in 1942 Schmitt scaled the twin peaks that defined her life: she came to teach English at Carnegie Tech and published her first novel.

The Gates of Aulis won the Dial Press Award for new fiction. Two years later, in 1944, her *David the King* became a Literary Guild selection, was translated into 10 languages, and sold more than one million copies.

Alexandra, a contemporary novel set in Pittsburgh, followed in 1947. *Confessors of the Name* (1952), *The Persistent Image* (1955), *A Small Fire* (1957), and *Rembrandt* (1961) led to Schmitt being named a Distinguished Daughter of Pennsylvania. After *Electra* (1965), in 1968 she founded Carnegie Mellon's creative writing program.

In 1972, her novel *The Godforgotten* became a Book-of-the-Month selection, and Schmitt received Carnegie Mellon's Ryan Award for Meritorious Teaching. That same year, 63-year-old Gladys Schmitt died of a heart attack in her Pittsburgh home.

In her memory, Carnegie Mellon created the Gladys Schmitt Creative Writing Center, a campus-based literary salon.

Marty Schottenheimer

Born September 23, 1943—Canonsburg, PA

One of the National Football League's all-time most successful coaches, Marty Schottenheimer is a member of the exclusive 200-win club. In addition, he has trained no fewer than eight NFL head coaches, including champions Bill Cowher and Tony Dungy.

Born Martin Edward Schottenheimer, he was an All-Western Pennsylvania linebacker and center on the Fort Cherry state championship basketball team.

© ASSOCIATED PRESS

At Pitt, the 6'-3", 225-pound Schottenheimer earned a 1965 English degree—and All-America linebacker honors. Taken in the 1965 draft by Buffalo, Schottenheimer played for the Bills, 1965-68, then the Boston Patriots, 1969-70. After two 1971 trades, Schottenheimer retired to sell real estate.

Returning in 1974 to the World Football League's Portland Storm, Schottenheimer was a player, then linebacker coach.

The following year, 1975, Schottenheimer became a New York Giants coach. After three years, in 1978 Schottenheimer moved to Detroit, then, in 1980, went to Cleveland.

Named Browns head coach during the 1984 season, over the next four years, Schottenheimer led Cleveland to three AFC Central titles and two AFC Championship Games.

Named Kansas City head coach in 1989, for the next decade, Schottenheimer's Chiefs went to the playoffs seven times, including the team's first AFC Championship Game.

In 2001, Schottenheimer became the Redskins head coach. After a season in Washington, he moved to the San Diego Chargers.

Over the succeeding five seasons, 2002-06, Schottenheimer's Chargers were twice Western division champs, including their first division title in a decade, 2004. Schottenheimer won multiple coach-of-the-year honors.

After another first-place finish in 2006, coupled with a playoff loss, Schottenheimer was fired. With his regular-season record, 1984-2006, standing as 200-126-1, he has a 61.3 percent winning percentage.

Married, the father of two, Schottenheimer is a skilled pilot who has flown with the Blue Angels and Air Force Thunderbirds.

Preston Schoyer

Born in 1911—Pittsburgh
Died in 1978—Stamford, CT

Pittsburgh's Pearl Buck, Preston Schoyer, wrote the book on China—literally.

Born in 1911, Schoyer grew up on Dunmoyle Street, Squirrel Hill, attended Peabody High, then Boston's Milton Academy. Taking a 1933 Yale degree, he became a teacher for the Yale-in-China Association, working in Changsa, Central China.

By 1937 Schoyer was in New York, wanting to write. When the words wouldn't come, he returned to China in 1938, to Yuanling, West Hunan. Writing in a cemetery during air raids, as he put it, Schoyer worked as a "teacher, ambulance driver, and coolie."

Leaving China, he wrote by oil lamps in Chinese inns, on buses bouncing along the Burma Road, in a Hanoi hotel, on a British steamer off the China coast, on an ocean liner across the Pacific, on the flight from Los Angeles, in Pittsburgh, and New York.

Back in New York in the early 1940s, Schoyer worked for the Institute of Pacific Relations, writing CBS Radio's *Spotlight on Asia*. Publishing his first novel in 1942, *The Foreigners* was a memorable portrait of contemporary China—its customs, characters, and conflicts.

With the United States in the war, by 1943 Schoyer was back in China, a major in Army Air Corps Intelligence, operating an underground railroad. It was dangerous, heroic work; by 1945 he had spirited some 1,000 downed allied flyers out of China, a feat for which he was decorated by the American and Chinese governments.

After World War II, Schoyer returned to Pittsburgh, writing 1947's *The Indefinite River*, the second of his four China novels. *The Ringing of the Glass* followed in 1950.

After another stay in China, 1951-55, Schoyer moved to Hollenden Place, Squirrel Hill, where he worked on his fourth and final novel, 1959's *The Typhoon's Eye*.

Having returned to New York, 67-year-old Preston Schoyer died in his Stamford, CT, home in 1978.

John Scull

Born in 1765—Chester, PA
Died in 1828—Pittsburgh

In 1786, Hugh Henry Brackenridge, Pittsburgh's pioneering lawyer-educator-writer, made 21-year-old John Scull an offer he couldn't refuse: if the Philadelphia printer and his partner Joseph Hall would haul their press over the Allegheny Mountains, they could have Pittsburgh—then little more than a 300-person village—and the entire Western frontier all to themselves.

So was born the *Pittsburgh Gazette*, the first newspaper west of the Alleghenies.

Born John Scull in 1765 in Chester, PA, he came from a Quaker family that had emigrated from Bristol, England, a century prior to his birth. Moving to Philadelphia to learn printing, Scull and Hall took Brackenridge's bait, moved west, and opened up shop at Water Street and Chancery Lane, near the Monongahela River ferry. On July 29, 1786, they printed the first edition of their 10 x 16, four-page, weekly newspaper.

Selling annual subscriptions at 17 shillings, six pence, it took a full 10-hour day to produce the paper. When Hall, also 21, died some four months later, Scull continued, printing the *Gazette*, pamphlets, even books (including, in 1793, the third volume of Brackenridge's novel *Modern Chivalry*, the first novel published in Pittsburgh. Scull also published the fourth and final volume in Pittsburgh in 1797).

Using such pseudonyms as Democritus, Vindex, Observer, and Farmer, Scull and Brackenridge used the *Gazette* to expound their political views. Brackenridge, for example, advocated transforming Pittsburgh into a major manufacturing center. For his part, Scull favored Federalism and Abolition—and a ban on horse racing.

In 1787, Brackenridge suggested that Scull partner with another Philadelphian, John Boyd. Two years later, Boyd hanged himself on what became the site of Duquesne University.

Retiring in 1816, Scull gave the *Gazette* to his son, John Irwin Scull.

In 1828, upon 63-year-old John Scull's death in Pittsburgh, his son sold the *Gazette* to Morgan Neville, severing the family connection.

Rick Sebak

Born June 5, 1953—Bethel Park, PA

No steelworker, politician, bartender, or cabbie can lay any more claim to the title of "Mr. Pittsburgh" than Rick Sebak. Western Pennsylvania's most credentialed ambassador of all things local and truly unique, he is recognized by millions of Americans as the jovial and passionate narrator/producer of more than 20 documentaries about Pittsburgh's proud past.

Born in Bethel Park as the second of four children to Charles and Peggy Sebak, he grew up doing the very things about which Pittsburghers love to wax nostalgic—spending hot sticky days at Kennywood, buying skyscrapers at Isaly's, daring to walk down the up escalator at Kaufmann's, and riding Shannon-Library streetcars to wherever they might take him. He sharpened his first pencil at St. Valentine's Elementary, learned knots in local Cub Scout Troop 225, and studied adolescent behavior at both Bethel Park's Junior and Senior Highs. There he also worked on experimental "Theatre 400" productions with Director Paul Mochnick. And after school his mother encouraged his brothers Skip and PK, and sister Denise, to join him in doing odd jobs at Stage 62 in the old Junior High on Park Avenue.

After his first year at the University of North Carolina, Chapel Hill, Sebak switched his intended theatre major to communications after participating in a weekend television workshop, and he soon landed an internship at South Carolina Educational Television. There he helped Josie Carey produce a daily half-hour children's program called *Wheee!* After a junior year of French food at the University of Lyon, he returned to earn his chops as the *Daily Tarheel*'s film critic and book reviewer. He also returned to SCETV and produced lots of local arts segments for its popular *Carolina Journal*, for which he also traveled to Australia. His *Slightly Wacky Aussie Doco* shot there may have convinced WQED to hire him. The prodigal son returned.

He won a Golden Quill Award for his very first QED documentary, *Transplant Town* (for which he puckishly laid down a musical bed of all "organ" music). That same year, 1987, he produced *The Mon, The Al and The O*, his first of the long-unfolding Pittsburgh History Series. By the time he produced *Things That Aren't There Anymore* in 1988, Sebak was earning some of the highest ratings for a locally produced show on any PBS station. When Philadelphia's WHYY copied his friendly documentary format, and even his title, the station earned over $1 million in pledges in one week. Within a year, more than 40 other PBS affiliates were copycatting the same "Things."

Sebak humbly calls his work "scrapbook documentaries" but he almost single-hand-

edly introduced America's public stations to an inexhaustible fountain of sentimental journeys. So popular are his many local videos that PBS itself has helped fund almost a dozen national programs with Rick's lighthearted narration and quirky insights. If you have appreciated amusement parks, beaches, cemeteries, diners, flea markets, hot dogs, ice cream, or sandwiches on TV, you've probably tasted his great work.

Danny Seemiller

Born June 13, 1954—Pittsburgh

Generally, diplomats wear striped pants and carry attaché cases.

Do they ever wear gym shorts and carry ping pong paddles?

In 1971 that's exactly what Danny Seemiller was—a ping pong diplomat opening up China.

It had been decades since Americans were permitted in the People's Republic. Because of a chance encounter between two players, the United States Table Tennis Team, visiting Japan, received a surprise invitation to play their counterparts in China.

Play, and tour, they did, the April visit going so well that a scant 10 months later, Richard Nixon visited China, a first for an American President.

Born in Pittsburgh in 1954, Danny Seemiller was a good enough baseball player to be scouted by the Pirates, and a competitive table tennis player by age 13. By 15, using an unorthodox style of holding the racket face down, and playing fore- and backhand with the same face (now a major style known as the Seemiller Grip), Seemiller had become the best junior in Western Pennsylvania. By 1971, he was a member of the United States Junior team, touring overseas.

Training 10-hour days, Seemiller skyrocketed from being just another interesting junior to a contender to a U.S. Open team champion. Winning his first big tournament in Toronto in 1973, Seemiller was the top-rated player in the United States from 1974-81. Winning five U.S. championships (1976-77-80-82-83), he played in tournaments all over the world, often competing in doubles matches

© LAWRENCE MANNING/CORBIS

with his brother Ricky. Passing his 40th birthday in 1994, Seemiller continued playing—and winning—as a senior.

A 1995 Table Tennis Hall of Fame inductee, Seemiller now lives with wife and family—including his son, Danny, Jr., also a competitive table tennis player—in New Carlisle, IN, where he serves as a table tennis coach at the South Bend Table Tennis Club.

© FILIPPO MONTEFORTE/EPA/CORBIS

Peter Sellars

Born September 27, 1957—Squirrel Hill

His career may well have started with a finger puppet he crafted in a third grade art class at St. Edmund's Academy. So enthralled was the tow-headed boy by animating his character that he soon volunteered to help Margo Lovelace produce children's shows for the Lovelace Marionettes. Of course, his career really may have started there, in that Margo Lovelace also produced some very esoteric puppet shows for adults, productions dealing with the eclectic modernism of James Joyce and the religious consciousness of Martin Buber. Just as likely, too, his career was born when he resigned in the midst of artistic differences while staging his first Broadway production, *My One and Only*, with Tommy Tune. Wherever its birth, Peter Sellars has become one of the most acclaimed (and criticized) directors, essayists, and iconoclasts of American and European dramatic arts.

Born in Squirrel Hill and raised on Northumberland Street, Sellars was a bright child, very much interested in snakes and turtles. His parents divorced when he was 11. He attended Phillips Academy in Andover, MA, and went on to Harvard. Within four years of his graduation, he became the directorial darling of resident theatres across the country, staging such revolutionary ideas as mixing George Gershwin with Maxim Gorski, or restaging Mozart's *Cosi Fan Tutti* in a neon-lit Cape Cod diner. He had also been named artistic director of the Boston Shakespeare Company. But in 1984, he was appointed Director of the American National Theater Company, based at the Kennedy Center. Although just 26, he was charged to create, recruit, manage, and direct a national theatre. It never happened because of—in a word—politics.

Just as he had left the Broadway stage to produce more revolutionary, and less commercially viable art, so, too, did he exit to Europe and, there, staged some of the most incredibly eclectic and controversial stagings of opera, theatre, dance, and symphony. A MacArthur Fellow, in 1998 he was awarded the Erasmus Prize for his work combining European and American cultural traditions in opera and theatre. Today he is currently a Professor of World Arts and Cultures at UCLA.

David O. Selznick

Born May 10, 1902—Pittsburgh
Died June 22, 1965—Hollywood, CA

Legend says that Lewis J. Selznick (Zeleznik) was a jeweler on Smithfield Street when he witnessed the opening of the Nickelodeon in 1905. So popular was the small movie house, Selznick closed up shop, booked a train to New York, walked in to Universal Film Manufacturing Co., and found an empty desk. Whatever the truth, Lewis Selznick did enter the film industry, beginning with the East Coast Universal Film Exchange, amassing an empire of several studios under the umbrella of World Pictures, and then losing his shirt in the film glut of 1923 when, overextended and having no market for his releases, his studio collapsed.

The Kiev-born pioneer had landed in Pittsburgh in the mid-1880s, married Flossie Sachs in 1896, and had four children, of which two sons were Myron and David. Both Myron and David attended Columbia University,

© JOHN SPRINGER COLLECTION/CORBIS

dropped out, and then worked briefly for their father. When the Selznick Pictures Company failed, they found work on their own.

David began anew as a script reader for MGM. He rose to become a production assistant, left to become an associate producer at Paramount, and jumped to RKO to become head of production. While there, he supervised one of Katharine Hepburn's first featured performances in *A Bill of Divorcement* and executive-produced *King Kong*.

In 1930, he married Louis B. Mayer's daughter Irene and three years later came to work, again, for the studio. *The Hollywood Reporter* famously headlined the story, "The Son-in-Law Also Rises."

At MGM, now one of four powerful producers including Irving Thalberg, whom he had once assisted, Selznick produced *Dinner at Eight*, *Reckless* (for which he wrote the script), *David Copperfield*, *Anna Karenina*, and *A Tale of Two Cities*. But Selznick, a micromanager who didn't wish to be managed himself, wanted to start his own studio, and with the help of his brother Myron, and a hefty investment from Thalberg, launched Selznick International Pictures. In 1937, at the pleading of his wife, he produced his first independent film, *A Star Is Born*, starring Janet Gaynor and Frederic March, winning the Oscar® for Best Story. Next came *The Prisoner of Zenda*, *Tom Sawyer,* and *Intermezzo*, starring a young Ingrid Bergman.

Always a reckless gambler, Selznick put it all on the line when, after 15 drafts, five directors, and a hard-fought deal in which he was loaned Clark Gable from MGM in exchange for the distribution rights and 50% of profits, he starred the unknown Vivien Leigh in his four-hour Civil War epic, *Gone With The Wind*. The investment was $4 million, but the film grossed $8 within two months. Although he is the only producer to have won back-to-back Best Picture Oscars, (which he did the following year by offering Alfred Hitchcock his American directorial debut with *Rebecca*,) Selznick was never able to top the success of *Gone With The Wind*.

Divorced in 1949 from Irene, he married actress Jennifer Jones the same year. Selznick died of heart complications in 1965.

Myron Selznick

Born October 5, 1898—Pittsburgh
Died March 23, 1944—Santa Monica, CA

The eldest son of silent filmmaking pioneer Lewis Selznick, Myron became the first talent agent in Hollywood, and forever established industry standards for representing artists, actors, directors, and film producers in the otherwise shady, backstabbing world of the early, big studios.

Upon dropping out of Columbia University, he went to work as a production supervisor for his father, who had bartered and sold several small studios into a risky, but flourishing empire he would later name Selznick Pictures. Prophetically, they promised "Quality, Not Quantity." The new studio's first picture, and the first produced by Myron, starred Olive Thomas, Pittsburgh's gift to the "world's most beautiful girls." The silent feature, 1919's *Upstairs and Down*, successfully led to Selznick Studio's next big film, *The Flapper*, also starring Thomas. The movie was a huge success and forever coined the stereotype of adventurous young women in the Roaring '20s. But the studio would crank out just 50 more pictures before folding under 1923's glut of new releases.

William Powell joins Selznick at the fights, October 1939.

At once, Myron Selznick started to represent the talent that was otherwise not tied to studio contracts or were popular overseas. Among his more famous clients were Alfred Hitchcock (whose leading lady Marjorie Daw he would later marry), Paulette Goddard, Katharine Hepburn, Carole Lombard, and Laurence Olivier. Indeed, as legend has it, Myron was responsible for inviting Olivier to the first day of shooting for *Gone With The Wind*. Because David O. Selznick had not yet cast Scarlett O'Hara, he decided to film the burning of Atlanta, for which he would only need the silhouette of the character. Olivier attended with his later wife, Vivien Leigh. When Leigh was introduced, Myron famously shouted to his brother, "Hey Genius. Meet your Scarlett."

Myron Selznick, who was much shorter, but altogether more "down to earth" than his younger brother, died at the age of 45. William Powell gave the funeral oratory.

Carol Semple Thompson

Born October 27, 1948—Sewickley, PA

Many athletes achieve early success by besting somebody better in the field.

However, rarely is one catapulted into the sports spotlight by beating one's own mother.

That's just how Carol Semple Thompson won her first golf championship, as a 16-year-old, playing against her mother Phyllis, in the Western Pennsylvania Women's Championship finals.

One of the greatest all-time American golfers, male or female, Carol Semple Thompson began with the bloodlines of a champion. Born in Sewickley in 1948, not only was her mother a champion amateur golfer, but her father Harton Semple was also a superb golfer—and United States Golf Association president from 1974 to 1975.

A veteran of some 100 USGA championship events, Semple Thompson has captured seven national titles—including the 1973 U.S. Women's Amateur Championship and four U.S. Senior Women's Championships—more than all but one other woman in American golf history. Competing a record 12 times in the Curtis Cup, Semple Thompson also enjoys a record 18 match victories.

Only the second woman to serve on the USGA Executive Committee (1994-2000), in 1991-92 she was president of the Pennsylvania State Women's Golf Association. A 21-time Pennsylvania amateur champion, in 1999 she became the first woman to compete in the U.S. Women's Open, U.S. Women's Amateur, U.S. Mid-Amateur, U.S. Senior Women's Amateur, and State Team Championship in a single year.

Having competed in five World Team Amateur Championships, Semple Thompson was a member of four victorious American squads (1974-80-88-94). Taking the 1974 British Ladies Open Amateur title, she was also low amateur finisher in three U.S. Women's Opens, 1978-88-94.

Simply revered by her fellow golfers, Semple Thompson's career accolades include the 2003 Bob Jones Award, the USGA's top honor for distinguished sportsmanship, the 2005 PGA First Lady of Golf Award, and her 2007 induction into the National Golf Coaches Hall of Fame.

© PHIL MCCARTEN/CORBIS

Shanice

Born May 14, 1973—McKees Rocks, PA

By the time she was 12 years old, her resume included starring in a KFC commercial with Ella Fitzgerald, winning twice on the Ed McMahon hosted talent show *Star Search,* and signing a record deal with A&M Records.

From McKees Rocks, PA, Shanice Lorraine Wilson, aka Shanice, has proven herself to be a multi-talented vocalist with a rare and impressive five octave range, ala Minnie Riperton's "Lovin' You." Born in 1973, Shanice showed her talents at a young age—in fact, 7 months young—when she would sing back to her mother the songs that had been sung to her. Her mother still has a tape of her infant child singing Chaka Khan's hit "Tell Me Something Good."

When Shanice was 8, her parents split up, so her aunt and mother packed up the car and the three drove 2,000 miles plus to the West Coast in search of greener pastures. Shanice was soon cast alongside Ella Fitzgerald, won

on *Star Search*, and landed her recording contract. For a time Shanice also played keyboards on the children's program *Kids Inc.*, while a young Fergie sang lead vocals. Her singing instruction was top shelf from early on, taking lessons from Seth Riggs, vocal coach to Natalie Cole, Prince, Kelly Clarkson, and Stevie Wonder. Shanice released her debut recording *Discovery* at the age of 14 and charted a couple of singles on the R&B charts. Shortly after the release, she was invited to be a guest on the popular children's sitcom *Family Matters*. Her star was already rising rapidly when her second release scored a number two hit in the country with *I Love Your Smile,* which also garnered her a Grammy® nomination for Best R&B Female Vocal performance.

Shanice performed for several months in the Broadway musical *Les Miserables*. She has been in demand for background vocal work as well, for artists like Babyface, Mary J. Blige, Whitney Houston, Usher, and Toni Braxton, and she has collaborated with artists as diverse as Kenny Loggins and Justin Timberlake.

In 2000 Shanice married actor/comedian Flex Alexander, with whom she has two children. Despite focusing on her personal life, Shanice released her fifth studio recording in 2006 and continues writing, producing, and collaborating with various artists, including Sheila E, who called Shanice "... one of the great voices of the 21st Century."

Paul Shannon

Born November 11, 1909—Crafton, PA
Died July 25, 1990—Lantana, FL

Were it not for the adoration of every cub scout den, brownie troop or 4-H club cheering in the bleachers of Paul's Rooters, or the countless generation of Pittsburgh children who tuned to Channel 4 every weekday afternoon from 1958 to 1975, Paul Shannon might be remembered only for his inventive humor. But Shannon, host of the local children's show *AdventureTime* can claim one great contribution to humankind, one singular selfless act which has forever enhanced American culture: he re-launched the careers of The Three Stooges.

In 1958, after 19 years of using his soft voice as an announcer on both WWSW and KDKA radio, Shannon was hired as a promotional announcer on fledgling WTAE, just

opening its new studios on Ardmore Boulevard. Nick Perry and Del Taylor were hired the same day. Shannon was given the assignment of creating a children's show, airing originally at 6:00 pm. He ran cartoons, played short clips of Shirley Temple or The Little Rascals, and started filling in the live scenes with characters like Mysto the Magician, Lippy the Leprechaun, and Randy Rocket, all of whom he played on tape (and then re-played to synchronize with his live retorts).

When letters poured in from fans wanting to visit his set, the show staff constructed bleachers and filled them every afternoon with church groups and scout troops. Reservations were booked a year in advance. To help his fans get their faces on screen, Shannon introduced a chroma-key effect and, suddenly, dozens of screaming kids, appearing through his player-piano doors, would say hello to Moms and Dads and Aunts and pets. To silence them, or to introduce a new segment, Shannon raised a Magic Sword and spoke these memorable words, "Down goes the curtain and back up again for... The Three Stooges."

Born in Crafton, one of five boys whose father, a janitorial supplier, once ran for Congress, Shannon graduated from Langley High and acted in small theatre groups. In 1937, he landed on the radio. His last appearance on *AdventureTime* was a Sunday afternoon show in March 1975. Father to four sons, he and his

wife June retired to Florida.

The details are not clear, but sometime in the late 1950s, when The Three Stooges were performing at a third-rate club in McKees Rocks, Shannon invited them on his show. The response was so positive, the Stooges were booked into the Holiday House, a first-rate club, and stayed on for a three-week run. Rediscovered, they went on to appear in six more feature films, of which the fourth *The Outlaws is Coming* features a cameo by Paul Shannon playing "Wild Bill Hiccup."

Saul and Frieda Shapira show off their garden, c. 1965.

Frieda Shapira

Born March 7, 1914—Hill District
Died July 7, 2003—Ligonier, PA

In 1912, Joseph Goldstein and Dora Bornstein made their living delivering wholesale groceries to small stores in Pittsburgh and the surrounding mill towns. They lived in rented rooms on Webster Avenue in the Hill District and, there, in 1914, Frieda Goldstein was born. In 1918, with Joe Porter and Ben Chait, Joe started the Eagle Grocery Company. They built the company from one small store in 1918 to 125 by 1928, at which time they sold it to Kroger. In 1931, teaming up with Hyman Morovitz and Morris Weizenbaum, Joe and his partners formed Giant Eagle.

In 1918, the Goldsteins moved to Edgerton Avenue in Point Breeze where Frieda attended Sterrett School. For her freshman year, she went to Peabody. (She would recall years later having swooned over a bare-chested Gene Kelly dancing on the school stage.) The Goldsteins then moved to Hobart Street in Squirrel Hill. At Allderdice for the next three years, she joined the swimming and volleyball teams and, standing a proud 5'-1/2" inch tall, was captain of the basketball team. Also a member of the Honors Society and VP of her senior class, she won the school's oratorical contest.

Although the families had lived near and known each other back in the Hill District, the Shapira's third child, Saul, didn't meet Frieda until Sunday School at B'Nai Israel as teens, and they didn't begin dating until they both attended the University of Pittsburgh. After graduating, they married. And moving to New York, he matriculated at Columbia Law and she at the School of Social Work. After graduation they returned to Pittsburgh, where he worked as an attorney and administrator for the Pittsburgh Housing Authority. As a social worker, Frieda worked first in New York, then in Pittsburgh, with neglected children. She stayed at home to raise their four children, David, Daniel, Ralph, and Edie. In 1945 Saul began to work at Giant Eagle, as the second generation representative of the Goldstein family.

But with her youngest child, Edie, then turning 11 in 1964, Frieda looked beyond her immediate family to see what good she could offer to her greater community.

And Frieda did many good things. In 1964, as President of the National Council of Jewish Women, Pittsburgh Section, she helped to organize the first free in-school lunch program, a forerunner of the first Head Start program in the country. Next, with an interfaith and interracial group she campaigned to have the nation's newly formed Job Corps training program include women. In 1967, she joined forces with Elsie Hillman as members of the Human Relations Commission. She advocated for diversity, for women, and for children.

Yet, some have said, not until Saul died swiftly from cancer in 1981, did Frieda kick into full gear. Just a short list of the organizations and boards she helped to steer include the Pittsburgh Foundation, Urban League, YWCA of Greater Pittsburgh, the United Way of Allegheny County, the Forbes Fund, Jewish Healthcare Foundation, CCAC, Beginning with Books, the United Jewish Federation, the University of Pittsburgh, WQED, and the American Jewish Committee. What Frieda accomplished in one month would take others years to achieve.

She was influential in a quiet way, but not shy. Fellow board members recall Frieda verbally blowing the whistle when programs ran amuck or redirecting precious funding from redundant programs—or challenging community boards to better reflect the community they served.

Said Esther Bush, president of the Urban League, upon her death, "Frieda was the community. She motivated and encouraged and mentored everyone she touched."

In 2004, the Bidwell Training Center, on whose board she had served, named a new hybrid orchid, the *Phalaenopsis Frieda Shapira*.

Jules Shear

Born March 7, 1952—Squirrel Hill

Although the concept of rock artists performing acoustic renditions of their hits was not necessarily groundbreaking, it certainly reached new heights with the MTV show *Unplugged*, thanks to Pittsburgh native, singer-songwriter Jules Shear.

His family lived on Rosemoor Street in Squirrel Hill. As a child Shear used to head downtown with his mom to watch the DJs at KQV spinning records. He began writing songs when he was a teenager, unaware of where that talent would lead him. He graduated from Taylor Allderdice High School in 1969 and then attended the University of Pittsburgh, where he would play local coffeehouses. He left Pitt and Shear headed to the West Coast to pursue his passion for music.

There he formed a band called The Funky Kings, along with Richard Stekol and Jack Tempchin (writer of Eagles hits "Peaceful Easy Feeling" and "Already Gone"). Billed as the next Eagles, and produced by legendary Doors and Janis Joplin producer Paul Rothchild, The Funky King's debut release, although critically successful, didn't fare well on the charts; the band was soon done. The album did include a modestly acknowledged song called "Slow Dancing," which Johnny Rivers turned into a top 10 hit.

Shear's next project was the popular cult band Jules and The Polar Bears who released three albums in the late '70s. Sales were tepid but they solidified the band's sizable cult following. Shear moved to New York and recruited the help of Todd Rundgren to produce his debut solo effort. That and subsequent releases were generally well-received but could never generate much sales momentum. What really clicked with Shear was the strength of his songwriting. Cyndi Lauper turned one of his songs, "All Through The Night" into a top five hit, Alison Moyet had a big international hit with "Whispering Your Name," and The Bangles had a top 40 hit with "If She Knew What She Wants." Shear's compositions have also been covered by The Band, 10,000 Maniacs, Art Garfunkel, and Tori Amos to name just a few. And Shear has had a wide variety of vocal partners including Margot Timmons (of the Cowboy Junkies,) Patty Griffin, Carole King, Roseanne Cash, and Paula Cole.

Shear had always had the idea of creating a venue where artists could perform acoustically—older more established artists accompanied by emerging artists—to foster a creative jam type session. In the early 1980s Shear pitched the idea to MTV, calling it *Unplugged*. The network liked the idea and Shear hosted the first 13 episodes.

Rolling Stone magazine has said of Shear's music: "Pop that's as literate as it is melodic."

Jim Shooter

Born September 27, 1951—Pittsburgh

A comic book legend, Jim Shooter is famous for his prodigious talent—and his controversial leadership style.

Born James C. Shooter in 1951 in Pittsburgh, he began his professional career at 13, writing *Legion of Super Heroes* stories for *DC*

Comics. Not only using existing heroes, but also creating new ones, "I worked my way through high school," Shooter says.

Moving to New York City, as a DC writer Shooter revolutionized comic technique by drawing entire stories then adding dialogue, rather than first creating prose scripts.

By the mid-1970s creative conflicts with DC editors caused Shooter to move to rival *Marvel Comics* as an assistant editor and writer. With the company in turmoil, by 1978 the 27-year-old Shooter became Marvel editor-in-chief. During the succeeding nine years, 1978-87, Shooter achieved great artistic and financial success. Setting deadlines, demanding artistic control, Shooter oversaw some of Marvel's greatest moments, including Spiderman's black costume, the X-Men's *Dark Phoenix Saga*, and writer Frank Miller's *Wolverine* and *Daredevil* series. At the time, Shooter himself scripted the 12-part *Secret Wars* series, which set sales records.

Despite all of Shooter's success—Marvel generally took three-quarters of all comics sales—his ongoing conflicts with writers and artists led to many departures. (Frank Miller created the popular *Dark Knight* for DC). Shooter was finally forced out.

Within two years, 1989, Shooter had founded *Valiant Comics*, where he co-created such critically acclaimed series as *Manowar*, *Shadowman*, and *Harbinger*, the latter rated as the most important comic series of the 1990s. Selling more than 80 million books in five years, nevertheless Shooter was again ousted—in part over artistic control.

In 1993, Shooter founded *Defiant Comics*, which folded after 13 months. His 1995 *Broadway Comics* met a similar fate, and the proposed *Daring Comics* did not materialize.

In his 50s, Jim Shooter continues to work in the comics-entertainment industry.

William Shoupp

Born October 12, 1908—Troy, OH
Died November 21, 1981—Pittsburgh

William Shoupp died as he lived, toiling on research for Westinghouse Electric Corp. The Edgewood resident had a long career here, starting in 1937 when he conducted research on photofission, the use of high-speed gamma rays to split uranium atoms into two equal parts, thus releasing a powerful burst of energy. It was heralded as a major step toward

developing nuclear energy and the atomic bomb. His work on radar and radar jamming during World War II made a significant contribution to American military successes.

Shoupp was a scientist with an uncanny foresight. In a 1966 speech to the Pennsylvania Electric Association, he predicted Americans would be living computerized lives by the year 2000. He said messages would be sent electronically, instead of by what we now call "snail mail." He predicted electronic devices would control heart rhythms and artificial limbs. He'd been able to base prediction of such futuristic devices on advanced research Westinghouse was conducting at the time.

In 1941, Shoupp worked on the development of what was variously called a "radium hound" or electric "detective" that traced radiation. It became known as the Geiger counter. He described how a hospital nurse accidentally disposed of $3,000 worth of radium that eventually made its way to a garbage dump. A search of the dump revealed nothing, until a herd of swine wandered through it, setting off the radiation detector. It was determined that one unfortunate hog had consumed the radium. "They found the radioactive pig and had him butchered to recover the radium," Shoupp explained.

A graduate of Miami University of Ohio in 1931, Shoupp received his MA and Ph.D. in physics at the University of Illinois before joining Westinghouse as a research fellow.

He rose to be vice president and general manager of the Westinghouse Research Laboratories and was a founder and president of the American Nuclear Society. He was honored for directing research that produced nuclear power plants for civilian and military uses. The engine of the first nuclear-powered submarine, the *U.S.S. Nautilus*, was designed by Westinghouse under Shoupp's leadership. So was the reactor that drove the first atomic power plant "devoted exclusively for peacetime purposes" in Shippingport, 25 miles west of Pittsburgh on the Ohio River.

Ronald Shusett

In space, no one can hear you scream. In Hollywood, without connections, it's much the same problem.

The 1970s found Ron Shusett spending much of his time (as he had spent much of that decade) in Hollywood, immersed in his own science fiction writing, hoping for that one great break to make a film—while starving in the process. And then one day, luck showed up—in the form of another down-at-the-heels filmmaker-wannabe, Dan O'Bannon, who had a proposal. O'Bannon would help Shusett develop a Philip K. Dick short story he had acquired (and was stagnating with) if Shusett would help flesh out a script he was working on that was likewise going nowhere. Neither man expected much out of the deal.

But as Shusett put it later, "Out of that meeting—here's two bums with no agent, no credibility—and out of that meeting came *Alien* and *Total Recall*."

Alien was the first to hit the screen, opening in 1979, earning in the years since a cult reputation as the best sci-fi horror film ever produced. A tight story-line coupled with startling special effects and an aching tension, the movie inspired countless copies and catapulted Sigourney Weaver into stardom.

Shusett didn't do so badly himself, snagging the credit as co-writer and executive producer of the multi-million dollar film. It also paved the way for a series of movies, including *Freejack*, *Total Recall,* and *Minority Report*, earning him the distinction as one of the most innovative filmmakers of his time.

Born in Pittsburgh, he refuses to disclose his age. And, in a recent phone interview, he stated he does not remember where he was born or in which neighborhood he lived. "Maybe that's why I wrote *Total Recall*," said he.

Raymond Simboli

Born December 26, 1894—Pescina, Italy
Died April 22, 1964—Neenah, WI

It's hard not to become an artist when your artist-father makes you his apprentice.

Born Raymond Stephen Simboli in 1894 in Pescina, Italy, the oldest of eight children to Angelina and Pietro (Peter) Simboli, a noted sculptor, painter, and muralist, Raymond emigrated to Pittsburgh with his family at age 6 in 1901. Growing up in Pittsburgh's East End, Simboli studied painting as a child, assisting his father in creating a number of city murals, in restaurants and churches, even the famed Nixon Theater.

Graduating from Peabody High in 1916, Simboli studied painting under the famed Arthur Watson Sparks at Carnegie Tech. Married in 1920, Simboli also accepted a position as a professor of painting and design at Carnegie Tech's School of Architecture—a posting he held for 42 years, until his 1962 retirement.

Living at 1270 North Negley Avenue, East Liberty, Simboli was a highly popular teacher. Aside from Carnegie Tech, Simboli also taught painting and drawing at Carnegie Institute, the Art Institute of Pittsburgh, Seton Hill College, Greensburg's Westmoreland Museum of Art—even his own Simboli School of Art.

An active Pittsburgh artist, Simboli was an Associated Artists multiple award winner, exhibiting at 41 annuals, 1916-62. The initial president of the Pittsburgh Watercolor Society, in 1946, he was named the Pittsburgh Center for the Arts Artist of the Year in 1955.

Exhibiting at four Carnegie Internationals, 1925-34, over time Simboli's work evolved from portraits to include Pittsburgh scenes, including Kennywood Park, the East Liberty Presbyterian Church, and Regent Square. With his architect brother William designing steel mills for Allegheny Ludlum, Simboli painted them, as well as other industrial sites, steelworkers, even labor strife.

Visiting a daughter in Neenah, Wisconsin, Simboli died in 1964, age 69. He was buried in Calvary Cemetery.

Herbert A. Simon

Born June 15, 1916—Milwaukee, WI
Died February 9, 2001—Pittsburgh

A scientist, scholar, and Nobel Prize winner, Herbert Simon's influence crosses many fields—economics, psychology, and computer science. Dr. Simon is often called the father of artificial intelligence, and his groundbreaking research helped move Carnegie Mellon University to the pantheon of academic institutions.

Born in 1916, the son of an electrical engineer turned patent attorney, as a youth Simon displayed a curiosity about choices that people made. "Since I was about 19, I have studied human decision-making and problem-solving," he told the *Pittsburgh Post-Gazette*. He earned a doctorate in Political Science at the University of Chicago in 1943 and joined the faculty at the Illinois Institute of Technology and the University of California, Berkeley. But Simon heard about a new school of industrial administration at Carnegie Tech, now Carnegie Mellon, and made the move to Pittsburgh.

That would begin a pathway that saw Simon move seamlessly among disciplines at the university, making a significant research mark at every stop. While in industrial administration, he turned his attention to incorporating his love of problem-solving to the social sciences, but soon grew frustrated that he was unable to provide hard numbers like those that could be used in math and science. However, at Carnegie Tech he would find a new tool that would help him in that quest— the computer.

During Christmas break in 1955, Simon, Allen Newell and programmer J.C. Shaw created Logic Theorist, a computer program that was capable of thinking, marking the beginning of what would become artificial intelligence. The program discovered proofs of geometric theorems. Soon, however, Herbert and his colleagues brought artificial intelligence to bear in using computer models to study human thought processes. He and Newell developed a theory that the human mind manipulates symbols in much the same way that a computer does. That discovery launched what is often called the cognitive revolution in the 1960s.

"When the computer came along, and more particularly when I understood that a computer is not a number cruncher, but a general system for dealing with patterns of any type," Simon recalled, "I realized that you could formulate theories about human and social phenomena in pictures and whatever you wanted on the computer, and you didn't have to go through this straitjacket of adding a lot of numbers."

Simon continued to be driven by his quest to understand decision-making. That led him to develop his economic theory of "bounded rationality," for which he was awarded the 1978 Nobel in economics. Simply stated, the theory turned economics on its head. For years economists had argued that people make rational choices based on finding the best commodity at the best price. But Simon countered that it was impossible. His theory said that people had too many choices and therefore too little time for analysis. For Simon, people chose the first option to meet people's needs.

With the Nobel, Simon's star power in the academic community continued to grow. His presence attracted the best and brightest to CMU, and his writings continue to be the benchmark in economics, cognitive theory, and in computer science. His school, adds Simon's colleague, Psychology Professor David Klahr, "should be named Carnegie Mellon Simon University."

Simon worked well into his 80s before dying of complications from cancer surgery. His legacy lives on at CMU, with the Newell-Simon Hall, that marks the contributions of two of the most important figures in the university's history.

The Skyliners

The song that defined the era of sock hops and drive-in theaters began in the halls of South Hills High School and made its way to Dick Clark's *Caravan of Stars*. The song was "Since I Don't Have You" and the group was The Skyliners.

The Skyliners began as an amalgamation of members from several area singing groups, including the Montereys, the El Rios, and the Crescents, adopting the name of the latter for a period before changing forever to The Skyliners. Local manager, writer, and promotion man Joe Rock, just 21 at the time, assembled the talents of Wally Lester, Jackie Taylor, Joe Versharen, Janet Vogel, and Jimmy Beaumont on lead vocals, an ensemble frequently described as the perfect harmonic vocal blend.

The lyrics to their breakout hit "Since I Don't Have You" were written by Joe Rock and are reputed to have been written at a traffic light after he had his heart broken by a girlfriend. Jimmy Beaumont, then just 17, wrote the melody and the group recorded a demo. After 13 rejections from major labels, the band was introduced to Calico Records, owned by local producers Bill Lawrence and Lou Caposi, and became a huge local hit, thanks to local DJs like Porky Chedwick and Art Pallan. Among the early disciples of the band was Dick Clark who invited them to join him on his *Caravan of Stars*, launching the band onto the national charts.

Credited with breaking down racial barriers at the time, "Since I Don't Have You" was the first single by a white group to hit #1 on the Cashbox R&B charts. And The Skyliners were among the first white artists booked to play the famed Apollo Theater in Harlem; legend has it the

promoters thought they were black.

The Skyliners had a number of chart scoring songs over the next several years and then scored big in 1975 with the song "Where Have They Gone." Tragically, Janet Vogel, the angelic voice hitting the high C at the end of "Since I Don't Have You," died in 1980 of an apparent suicide. Jimmy Beaumont and a new lineup of Skyliners continue to tour and perform today.

B. Smith

Growing up in small town Everson, PA, Barbara Smith considered Pittsburgh to be the center of her small universe. "I loved to visit museums, the flower show at Phipps Conservatory, home shows, and, of course, shopping in the large department stores." Accompanied by her parents William and Florence, and her three brothers Gary, Ronald, and Dennis, she was awed by the opportunities and, one day, noticed an ad in the *Post-Gazette* for the John Robert Powers Modeling School. "My father objected. I told him if he sent me to that school I would do the rest. This was in 1965. I signed up for every course they had and stretched out my classes over the next few years and graduated from 'JRP' about the same time I graduated from Southmoreland High School in June 1967."

B. Smith became a live-in companion to Bonnie Lewis, residing on Delmont Avenue in Beltzhoover. She was hired by TWA as a ground hostess at Greater Pittsburgh Airport, taught modeling at the Earl Wheeler School, and learned, above all, to multi-task. Her early personal triumphs in Pittsburgh were modeling for Alcoa, modeling wedding dresses for Lady Sarah and King Friday on *Mister Rogers' Neighborhood*, and winning the title of Miss Triad, Queen of the Three Rivers at Point State Park in 1969.

Few people have pursued as diverse or as many career goals as the young woman who is known in hundreds of thousand of households as B. Smith. Originally a Wilhelmina model who appeared on 15 different fashion magazine covers, she opened her first restaurant in 1986.

Today, she has been seen on *Oprah Winfrey*, *The Today Show,* and *The View*, while hosting her own syndicated TV show, *B. Smith with Style*. She operates and manages three B. Smith restaurants in NYC, D.C., and Sag Harbor, Long Island. Bed, Bath & Beyond promotes her "B. Smith with Style Home Collection" of bedding, bath furnishings, and serveware. She is the author of two lifestyle cookbooks, the spokesperson for Colgate Palmolive Oxy Plus, as well as for General Mills Betty Crocker Cornbread and Muffin Mixes, Pillsbury products, and more. Ms. Smith is also the first African-American woman to launch a national furniture collection, "At Home with B.Smith."

Clarence "Pine Top" Smith

Born January 11, 1904—Orion, AL
Died March 15, 1929—Chicago, IL

The term "boogie woogie" may not have been invented in Pittsburgh, but the first time it was ever vocalized in a song was right here in the 'Burgh—in Clarence Smith's "Pine Top's Boogie Woogie."

Clarence "Pine Top" Smith was raised in Birmingham, a self-taught piano player. He cut his chops playing house parties and vaudeville acts in his early teens. At the age of 16 he moved to Pittsburgh and played clubs along the vibrant Wylie Avenue in the Hill.

"Boogie" was a term used for the music played at rent parties (parties thrown to help friends raise money to keep from getting evicted). In the early 1900s, Boogie soon represented a style of music, evolved from ragtime. While in Pittsburgh, married and raising a family, Smith wrote and performed a number that he called "Pine Top's Boogie Woogie," the first time the words had been used together in a song. Cow Cow Davenport, fellow pianist and Alabama native, was appearing at the Star Theatre on Wylie Avenue, but stopped in at a club on Sachem Way and heard Smith play the tune. Upon his encouragement to head to Chicago and record it, Smith and his family packed their bags and landed at Vocalion Records where Smith recorded the classic tune.

Over the next year, Smith laid 10 more tracks with Vocalion, including "I'm Sober Now," "Nobody Knows When You're Down And Out" and "Pine Top Blues." Just a few weeks after his last recording session, Smith stopped at a club and was struck in the chest by a stray bullet. Clarence "Pine Top" Smith died at the age of 25.

Smith's legendary "Pine Top's Boogie Woogie" has been recorded by dozens of artists from Bing Crosby to Muddy Waters, influencing the likes of Jerry Lee Lewis, John Lee Hooker, Canned Heat, and ZZ Top.

Ethel Smith

Born November 22, 1902—Pittsburgh, PA
Died May 10, 1996—Palm Beach, FL

The First Lady of the Hammond Organ, her surprise hit "Tico Tico" went on to sell close to two million records and vaulted Ethel Smith to international stardom.

Ethel Smith was born Ethel Goldsmith in Pittsburgh, and she had three acute passions in her life: music, golf, and languages. Her musical training was at Carnegie Tech where she was instructed by Professor Caspar Koch, the official City of Pittsburgh organist from 1904 to 1954. While in school she studied multiple languages, including Italian, German, French, Portuguese, and Spanish. Her golf game, which was a lifelong love, was studied on the local municipal course, Schenley. But it was her musical prowess that made her an international phenomenon. Well, maybe her flamboyant costumes and spectacular hats helped a little, too.

Smith was working the pit of a local Shubert show when she was asked to go on the road for a 28-week engagement. Discovered by a now unknown Hollywood singer and endorsed by a Hollywood music store, she became the darling of the Hammond Organ company. Fluent in Spanish, and fascinated by South America, she became a delegate for the first Pan-American conference. There in 1940, she was offered an engagement at the Copacabana in Rio De Janeiro. Among the songs that she picked up way south of the border, was a native Argentinean number that would become her trademark, "Tico Tico."

World War II forced Smith's return to the states where she settled in New York at the St. Regis Hotel. She also landed a job on the popular radio show *Your Hit Parade* where she performed with stars like Frank Sinatra and Bing Crosby.

By now a Latin music craze was sweeping the nation and Smith's star power was huge. Hollywood came calling. Cast alongside stars like Xavier Cugat, Desi Arnaz, Lucille Ball, and Esther Williams, Smith put her organ skills to work in film, turning "Tico Tico" into a national hit and one of the best selling songs of the decade. At one point, Smith's hands were even insured by Lloyd's of London for $500,000.

Smith married actor Ralph Belamy but was divorced after two brief years, never marrying again. She spent much of the 1950s and 1960s touring, also playing the guitar almost as proficiently as the organ. An entrepreneur, she formed the Ethel Smith Music Corporation, publishing sheet music and Hammond instructional books. Smith was also active in community theatre.

She moved from Manhattan to Palm Beach in the 1970s where she continued to golf and entertain fans and friends on the Hammond. Her masterful rendition of "Tico Tico" can be experienced today on Youtube.com.

Nate Smith

Born February 23, 1929—Hill District

In the early 1970s, when *Ebony* magazine ran a story of the 100 most influential black Americans, among names like Jesse Jackson, Julian Bond and Barbara Jordon, appeared Nate Smith.

Above, Smith, center in dashiki, flanked by Rev. Jimmy Joe Robinson, left, and Byrd Brown, right, march, 1969.

Raised in the Hill District where he dropped out of school in sixth grade, his first job was cleaning a butcher's block on Wylie Avenue for just 25 cents a day. Smith ran away from home, shaved his head, and joined the Navy. At just 12 years old, he served as a captain's steward for two years until he let slip he was still not yet 15. Discharged, he returned to the streets of the Hill, took up boxing, and fought professionally whenever and wherever he could. One local sports writer even named him "Available" Smith. Edgar Kaufmann sponsored his professional training.

Only an occasional victor, but now married with children, he grew concerned about feeding his family. When an upcoming heavyweight bout sold out, Smith parlayed his prize contract for four ringside seats and gave them to a union boss in exchange for a Local 66 Operating Engineer's Union card. A week later he was working heavy equipment. But, at just 16, his fighting days weren't over.

Seeing so few blacks on job sites, Smith became a champion of a different ring. During construction of the U. S. Steel building, Smith forcibly persuaded his union leaders to hire more blacks. He staged demonstrations, organized marches, and, once, stared down a steamroller threatening to flatten him. Smith soon realized there might be more productive ways to create equal opportunities.

In 1967, he founded Operation Dig to train construction workers. Kaufmann and Republican organizer Elsie Hillman helped with funding. Within two years, armed with a federal grant of $10 million, he began the Pittsburgh Plan, a more formal jobs education program, ultimately training more than 10,000 minority candidates for steady employment. Smith became something of a celebrity, soon making the cover of *Jet* magazine. All through the 1970s, his program was replicated in dozens of American cities.

In 2007, Smith was mugged walking to his Homewood residence. Unshaken, at 87, he is President of Nate Smith Enterprises, still leading the charge for jobs training for youth at risk.

W. Eugene Smith

Born December 30, 1918—Wichita, KS
Died October 15, 1978—Tucson, AZ

It began in 1955 with a simple three-week photo assignment, a *Life* magazine veteran coming to Pittsburgh to shoot 100 photos. Two years and 17,000 images later, W. Eugene Smith had created the definitive portrait of a city in contrasts. In two years, Gene Smith's *Dream Street* had redefined Pittsburgh.

Born in Wichita in 1918, a professional photographer in his early teens, William Eugene Smith shot sports, aviation, and the Depression-era Dust Bowl for the *Wichita Eagle* and *Wichita Beacon*. By 1934, a Smith photo of the dry Arkansas River bed appeared in the *New York Times*. Briefly attending Notre Dame on a 1936 photographic scholarship, in 1937 Smith moved to New York City. Hired by *Newsweek*, then going free-lance, Smith's work appeared in *Collier's*, *Harper's Bazaar*, and the *New York Times*. By 1939 Smith was *Life* staff photographer, but resigned in 1941 over assignments.

In 1942, with America at war, Smith became a war correspondent, first for Ziff-Davis (*Flying* and *Popular Photography*), later for *Life*. In the bloody Pacific island-hopping campaign, Smith, invariably on the front lines, took part in 26 combat missions and 13 invasions, including Guam, Saipan, the Philippines, and Iwo Jima. Taking virtually any risk to get a photograph, Smith was badly wounded on Okinawa in 1945.

Spending two years recuperating, he took few photographs. One that survives: his two children in the famous *A Walk to Paradise Garden*, the final image in the *Family of Man* exhibition.

Back at *Life*, 1947-54, Smith shot a number of brilliant, evocative photo-essays, among them *Country Doctor*, *Spanish Village*, *Southern Midwife*, and *Man of Mercy*. The latter, about Albert Schweitzer, brought about Smith's second resignation from *Life*, over photo placement, for which Smith demanded complete control.

On his own again in 1955, Smith signed on with the Magnum photo group, which gave him a simple assignment: 100 photos for Stefan Lorant's *Pittsburgh: Story of an American City*, prepared for the city's 1958 bicentennial.

In Pittsburgh, Smith reveled in the city's duality: heavy industry and natural beauty, smokestacks and church spires, mill fires burning in workers' goggles, a melancholy woman at a street carnival, the grimy Love Street sign.

Taking some 17,000 pictures, Smith incessantly drove and walked through the city. Armed with a map and compass, he noted locations and optimum times for shots. The result, arguably the most complex and ambitious photo-essay ever created by a single photographer, bankrupted Smith, destroyed his first marriage, and, given his constant amphetamine use, nearly ruined his health. In the end, Lorant used only 64 images; in 1959 88 appeared in the *Popular Photography* Annual. Smith considered the published material a failure. (Currently, 175 photos are included in the book *Dream Street: W. Eugene Smith's Pittsburgh Project*).

After Pittsburgh, Smith shot many New York City photos, then in the 1970s worked on the harrowing *Minamata*, his study of mercury poisoning victims in a small Japanese fishing village.

Deteriorating health, combined with habitual drug and alcohol abuse, resulted in a fatal stroke in Tucson, 1978. W. Eugene Smith was 59 years old.

W.D. Snodgrass

Born January 5, 1926—Wilkinsburg

Perhaps it was his grandfather singing him Scottish songs and ballads. Perhaps it was his Quaker parents teaching him about the dignity and decency of life. Whatever the reason, by the time he was in his mid-20s W.D. Snodgrass emerged as one of the 20th Century's most powerful—and most powerfully personal—poets.

© Oscar White/CORBIS

Born William DeWitt Snodgrass, his studies at Beaver Falls' Geneva College were interrupted by World War II. Returning from Pacific naval duty in 1946, Snodgrass transferred to the University of Iowa, where he worked as a hotel clerk and hospital aide, and entered the prestigious Iowa Writers' Workshop.

Studying with such great poets as Randall Jarrell and Robert Lowell, Snodgrass' gestation was remarkably brief. Virtually eschewing the small magazines, reviews, and chapbooks that mark a fledgling poet's career, by 1951 the 25-year-old Snodgrass began publishing in such top-level outlets as *Partisan Review*, *The Paris Review*, *The Hudson Review*, and *The New Yorker*.

Torn apart by a divorce, and the loss of a daughter, Snodgrass poured himself into his poem "Heart's Needle." When five sections of it appeared in the 1957 anthology *New Poets of England and America*, the 29-year-old Snodgrass was widely acclaimed as one of America's strongest emerging voices in poetry.

Made the title poem of his 1959 book *Heart's Needle*, his raw emotions and powerful imagery won him a 1960 Pulitzer Prize—and made Snodgrass' career. Hailed for inaugurating the new school of confessional verse, Snodgrass followed his initial, startling success with some 40 years of publications, more than 18 books of poetry, plus essays, literary criticism, translations, anthologies, even plays. A distinguished professor, he has taught at such prestigious institutions as Cornell, Wayne State, Syracuse, Old Dominion, and the University of Delaware.

Retired since 1994, W.D. Snodgrass lives and writes in Upstate New York.

Benjamin Spock

Born May 2, 1903—New Haven, CT
Died March 15, 1998—La Jolla, CA

The Pittsburgh years were pivotal in the life and career of Benjamin Spock. Yet in his own autobiography, *Spock on Spock,* he makes only brief mention of them. His biographer, Thomas Maier, devotes 14 of 460 pages to the four years, from 1951 to 1955, Spock spent on the faculty of the University of Pittsburgh School of Medicine. But those years marked the ascent of his colorful and controversial public career.

Spock graduated from Yale and got his medical degree from Columbia. He completed residencies in pediatrics and psychiatry at Cornell Medical School. With the help of his wife, Jane, Spock wrote *Baby and Child Care* while in the Navy during World War II. The book was first published in 1946 and gradually won worldwide acclaim. Expected to sell 10,000 copies, more than 750,000 were sold in just the first year. In the fall of 1951, as a new professor of child development at Pitt, Spock began to promote the book—and himself— more aggressively.

Pittsburgh held promise. Spock was comfortably in middle age, his popular book had come out in paperback, and the university position offered the twin pleasures of teaching and practicing pediatrics. In time, he would help found the Arsenal Family and Children's Center in Lawrenceville, still operating today. Ben and Jane Spock and their two sons lived in a spacious three-story, red-brick Georgian home near the campus.

© Bettmann/CORBIS

The Spocks, both tall and elegant, became part of the city's social scene, until Jane was hospitalized for the first time in a lifelong battle with alcoholism and mental illness. That, and some internecine battles within the medical school led to their abrupt departure for Cleveland and Spock's new position at Case Western Reserve University.

In the 1960s, the now-famous baby doctor enlisted in political causes. President Kennedy had won Spock's endorsement and sought his counsel. Spock became a spokesman for the National Committee for a SANE Nuclear Policy; he marched with the Rev. Martin Luther King Jr. in Vietnam War protests. In a hopeless but symbolic gesture, he allowed himself to be the Presidential nominee of the radical People's Party in 1972. Having failed at electoral politics, Spock continued to enjoy fame on the lecture circuit while continuously updating the book that made him famous and resisting old age by marrying a second wife 40 years his junior.

Ray Sprigle

Born in 1886—Akron, OH
Died in 1957—Pittsburgh

The Post-Gazette's Ray Sprigle was Central Casting for the investigative reporter, successfully posing as a coal miner, mental patient, black market racketeer—even an African-American—to expose cruelty, corruption, and Jim Crowism. For his 1937 revelation that President Roosevelt's new Supreme Court appointee, Hugo Black, was once a member of the Ku Klux Klan, Sprigle won the 1938 Pulitzer Prize—the city's first.

Born Martin Raymond Sprigle, he attended Ohio State, 1905-06, then picked up a newspaper job in Columbus. Bouncing to Lansing, Little Rock, and St. Louis, Sprigle landed in Pittsburgh in 1911, where he was a newsman for the next 46 years.

Instantly recognizable in the office, with his wide-brimmed Stetson and corncob pipe, in the field Sprigle went anywhere, did anything, was anybody. Posing as a 1920s coalminer, he wrote of coal-mine abuses—and helped end the reign of the dreaded Coal

Police. Following Nellie Bly, Sprigle went into Dixmont and Mayview state hospitals—as a patient, 1931, then as an attendant, 1947, painting a terrifying portrait of neglect and abuse. In 1940, like Edward R. Murrow, Sprigle put himself in harm's way by reporting on the Battle of Britain—when the night skies brought a deadly barrage of bombs.

In 1948 Sprigle, posing as an African-American, wrote a 21-part series "I Was a Negro in the South for 30 Days." Presaging John Howard Griffin's *Black Like Me* by 11 years, Sprigle's stories ran in 14 newspapers. Turned into the book *In Jim Crow Land* in 1949, it appeared the same year that Sprigle reported on the dreadful conditions in Displaced Persons camps in Germany.

In 1957, covering a trial, 71-year-old Ray Sprigle's taxi was hit by a car. Taken to Allegheny General, he died eight hours later. In his memory, Pittsburgh's top reporting honor is awarded in his name.

Squonk Opera

The scene: Rosebuds in the Strip, 1993. **He** enters, wearing pantyhose over his head, having just performed on stage for a raucous crowd. **She**, seated, suggests that perhaps his stage act might benefit from more music. Right then and there, **He** and **She** decide to make beautiful music together. And wacky theatre. First as Girdle and Clutch, then as Identical Twins (think Patty Duke), next as The Ways & Means Committee, then finally, in a junkyard under the Glenwood Bridge—when 500 people come to watch a rock tango of bulldozer and crane—forever as Squonk Opera.

Characters: **She**, Jackie Dempsey, born on Hawthorne Street in Swissvale to a steelworker-turned-master plumber and a Holiday House waitress, starts playing piano at 8 years

of age. Graduating "10th in my class" from Plum High School, she matriculates at Washington University earning her masters in music, and—almost—a Ph.D. in "metaphorical music theory." A year's sabbatical teaches her that waiting tables and teaching piano at Pitt are just as rewarding.

He, Steve O'Hearn, born in Kabul, Afghanistan, to a Gulf Oil chemist and a homemaker, moves to Gibsonia, age 4, attending Hance Elementary, then Pine-Richland. His academic tenure is short. A non-reader, "I wind up at Penn-Circle Academy where our teachers smoke bongs and chant Hare Krishna." Hitchhiking across America, studying the "classics" in New Mexico, and playing flute in Ireland are his educational foundation. Fortunately, many Saturdays earlier, Joe Fitzpatrick's Tam O'Shanter class has instilled in him some confidence in art and design. So, belatedly, he pursues a degree in industrial design at Rhode Island School of Design, and becomes the wunderkind of architecture firm RTKL in Baltimore. Industrial design then gives way to set design, at CMU.

Action: The year is 1995. Dempsey and O'Hearn get a call from Marc Masterson at City Theatre to assemble a September production of *Night of the Living Dead: The Opera*. A monstrous success, George Romero and fellow zombies attend. The now-five Squonkers start touring, rather unprofitably. A last minute cancellation during a convention of theatre technicians at the Westin William Penn affords them the kind of exposure years of touring would never promise. And they create *Bigsmorgasbordwunderwerk* at P.S. 122 Off-Broadway. The NY critics go wild. The intimate show lands at Broadway's vast Helen Hayes stage, then bombs. But the singular credit and the collective credibility of many new collaborators help make Squonk Opera a touring sensation in Scotland, Belgium, Germany—even South Korea—and at dozens of theatre festivals worldwide.

More recently, *Pittsburgh: The Opera* has been "metro-morphed" in more than six other cities. Thanks to more and more significant national grants, Dempsey and O'Hearn, adoring partners (but only professionally,) mount a new production about every two years. In 2008, a new out-of-this-world production is due to land on the North Shore.

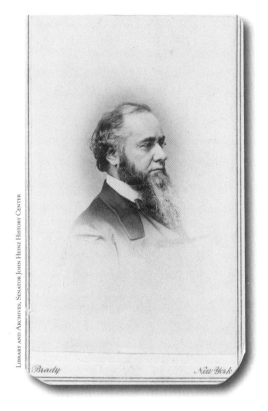

Edwin Stanton

Born December 19, 1814—Steubenville, OH
Died December 24, 1869—Washington, D.C.

A native of Steubenville, but longtime resident of Pittsburgh, Edwin M. Stanton served as President Abraham Lincoln's Secretary of War from 1862 to 1865.

Prior to the Civil War, Stanton had developed a national reputation as a brilliant young lawyer, using his training to climb to high ranks in the federal government. After graduation from Kenyon College in Ohio, he moved to Pittsburgh in 1847 and opened a successful law practice in the city. While living in Pittsburgh, he earned national attention for arguing an interstate commerce case for the Commonwealth of Pennsylvania before the Supreme Court. After nearly 10 years, he moved his practice to Washington, D.C. His first notable governmental post was as Attorney General to President James Buchanan

from 1860-1861. Abraham Lincoln named Stanton as his Secretary of War at the height of the Civil War. One of his most important tasks was to enforce the federal draft. The idealistic Secretary argued against a congressional provision that exempted drafted men if they paid $300 or furnished a substitute. His protests were unsuccessful, however, and wealthy men often avoided military service.

After Lincoln's assassination, Stanton remained Secretary of War in the administration of President Andrew Johnson. His relationship with Johnson soured, however, and Stanton emerged as a leading advocate of his impeachment. In 1869, he was selected by President Ulysses Grant to serve on the U.S. Supreme Court, although he died only days after his appointment.

Willie Stargell

Born March 6, 1940—Earlsboro, OK
Died April 9, 2001—Wilmington, NC

"The umpire," he famously commented, "says 'play ball,' not 'work ball.' "

A fierce competitor on the field, a gentleman—and gentle leader—off it, Willie Stargell led the Pirates during their greatest sustained success in team history. Playing 21 seasons, 1962-82, he was captain in the 1970s, when the club won an unprecedented—and unmatched—four National League Eastern Division titles and two World Championships, 1971 and 1979.

Raised in Alameda, CA, Wilver Dornel Stargell was signed by the Pirates out of high school, came to the majors at age 22 as a power-hitting leftfielder, and within two years was an All Star—the first of seven times.

Playing at 6'-2" and 225, Stargell set all-time team marks for home runs (475) and RBIs (1,540), while leading the major leagues in home runs for the 1970s. Leading the National League twice—48 in 1971, 44 in 1973—many of Stargell's home runs were tape-measure shots, including four upper-deck blasts at Three Rivers Stadium and two completely out of Dodger Stadium, one traveling 500 feet.

Nicknamed Pops for his elder statesman role, Stargell liberally pasted gold stars on his teammates' caps for exemplary plays—and on civilians who helped his efforts to raise awareness for sickle-cell anemia, a favorite charity. With his most memorable year coming in 1979, Stargell swept the league's Most Valuable Player awards—regular season, playoffs, and World Series, batting .400 in the Fall Classic with three home runs.

After his 1982 retirement, Stargell held positions in both the Pittsburgh and Atlanta baseball organizations, and was elected to baseball's Hall of Fame in 1988. In 2001, at age 61, he died of a stroke in Wilmington—ironically the day a 12-foot statue in his honor was unveiled at PNC Park.

Thomas Starzl

Born March 11, 1926—Le Mars, IA

At one point in his early years, Thomas Starzl believed he had received a call to enter the priesthood. The death of his mother from breast cancer, disintegrating the Starzl family just as he was completing college, galvanized his decision to pursue a new mission. He decided to leave the saving of souls to others, while he dedicated his career to saving lives.

Born to a prominent publishing family in Iowa, Thomas enlisted in the U.S. Navy immediately after high school with the intent of joining World War II. He was sent to Westminster College in Fulton, MO, for officer's training. But, upon his discharge from the Navy, he returned to the college and earned a degree in biology. From there, he began to train with leaders in neuroanatomy and surgical advances at the University Medical School in Chicago, earning additional medical degrees, surgical training, and deep admiration from his peers along the way. Johns Hopkins followed as did a stint at the University of Colorado School of Medicine.

It was in the Denver area that he performed the first of 1,000 kidney transplants and began ground-breaking research in liver transplantation. Indeed, in 1963 he performed the first human liver transplant and in 1967 the first *successful* liver transplant. Pioneering techniques in the field, he reportedly once worked three days straight to perform a surgery

for which he was the only surgeon capable.

Fourteen-hundred miles away, however, he would earn the reputation as the 20th century's greatest surgeon, and recast Pittsburgh as the transplant capital of the world.

He arrived in 1981, joining the staff of the University of Pittsburgh School of Medicine as a professor of surgery. For the next 10 years, he oversaw the largest transplant program in the world, served as the director of the Pittsburgh Transplantation Institute (PTI), and developed the clinical usage of critical anti-rejection drugs and protocols without which patients could not routinely expect positive outcomes with their new organs. The drug discovery also made possible the ability to transplant organs formerly impossible to consider, including the pancreas, lungs, and intestines. He also continued to tackle the cases no one else would—or could. The first simultaneous heart and liver transplant on 6-year-old Stormie Jones in 1984 was notably among them. He was called the Father of Transplantation.

In 1996 the PTI was renamed the Thomas E. Starzl Transplantation Institute. In 2004, President George W. Bush tapped him to receive the National Medal of Science, the nation's highest honor for the discipline. Now retired from active surgery, he continues research in critical areas of transplantation.

Dakota Staton

Born June 3, 1930—Homestead
Died April 10, 2007—New York, NY

In the early 1950s Dakota Staton, a young girl from Homestead, was being discovered in a Harlem nightclub by a producer from Capitol Records. It was soon after that *Down Beat* magazine would award her with the "Most Promising New Comer Award." Within two years Staton would have the number four song in the country, with "The Late Late Show".

Staton's meteoric rise to fame was no fluke. She had received comparisons to the great Dinah Washington and Sarah Vaughan, and incorporated elements of R&B and Blues into the jazz framework for which she was known. She was singing and dancing at the age of 4 and by her mid teens, graduating from Westinghouse High School, she was enlisted as the vocalist for the popular Pittsburgh band The Joe Westray Orchestra.

Staton followed her musical dreams to Detroit and then Canada, Indianapolis, Minneapolis, St. Louis, Cleveland, and ultimately New York where her talents were discovered singing in Harlem. She was signed to Capitol Records and by 1957 had her first and biggest hit, the crossover number "The Late, Late Show." She continued to record for Capitol, producing a number of fine releases with her arranger and collaborator Sid Feller (who was well known for his work with greats Ray Charles, Nancy Wilson, and Dean Martin).

Dakota Staton never attained the same notoriety as some of her peers. But she continued to entertain legions of fans well into her 60s, including a performance in Pittsburgh during the Mellon Jazz Festival in 1996.

Dakota Staton passed away in April 2007, at the age of 76.

Lincoln Steffens

Born April 6, 1866—San Francisco, CA
Died August 9, 1936—Carmel, CA

Rarely did a writer spend so little time in Pittsburgh yet have such an enormous impact.

Many authors had come and written about the city—Charles Dickens, for example, in *American Notes*, and journalist James Parton, who described Pittsburgh as "hell with the lid off." However, no one made Pittsburgh as famous—or infamous—as muckraking journalist Lincoln Steffens, whose 1904 exposé *Shame of the Cities* put Pittsburgh on the national map.

Born Joseph Lincoln Steffens, he was raised in Sacramento and graduated from the University of California, Berkeley. Working at *McClure's* magazine, Steffens wrote in-depth, investigative articles about political corruption in St. Louis, Minneapolis, Philadelphia, Chicago, New York—and Pittsburgh.

Steffens began positively. "Pittsburg," he wrote, using the old spelling, "is an unpretentious, prosperous city of tremendous industry and healthy, steady men."

After that praise, however, Steffens in-

troduced a rich cast of characters: political bosses, crooked contractors, price-fixers. Led by Christopher Magee and William Flinn, their ring controlled Pittsburgh—from patronage jobs to asphalt specifications, building stones to trolley lines. "Boss Magee's idea was not to corrupt the city government," Steffens wrote, "but to be it."

Thorough and detailed, "the Pittsburg article had no effect in Pittsburg," Steffens lamented. "We Americans may have failed. We may be mercenary and selfish. Democracy with us may be impossible and corruption inevitable, but these articles, if they have proved nothing else, have demonstrated beyond doubt that we can stand the truth; that there is pride in the character of American citizenship."

By 1910 Steffens was looking abroad, covering the Mexican Revolution, visiting the Soviet Union in 1919. "I have seen the future," he famously said of Bolshevism, "and it works."

By the 1930s, after widespread Stalinist purges, Steffens recanted. A member of the California Writers Project, 70-year-old Lincoln Steffens died in Carmel, CA, in 1936.

Gertrude Stein

Born February 3, 1874—Pittsburgh
Died July 27, 1946—Neuilly-sur-Seine, France

Gertrude Stein, whose Paris salon nurtured famous ex-patriot American writers, and whose famous line about Oakland, CA— "there is no there there"—has become an American slogan, was born in Allegheny, as Pittsburgh's North Side was known.

Born Gertrude Stein in 1874, she was the daughter of a streetcar executive whose real estate investments made the family wealthy. Taken out of Pittsburgh at age 3, Stein moved with her family to Vienna, then Paris, and finally to Oakland, CA. Later, when asked about Pittsburgh, she quipped that she'd only seen it from the air.

From 1893-97, Stein studied with renowned psychologist William James at Radcliffe, then enrolled at Johns Hopkins Medical School, which she left in 1901 without graduating.

Moving to Paris in 1903, she lived with her brother Leo for 11 years. Together, they encouraged and enabled the emerging modern art movement, assembled one of the world's first—and finest—collections. Befriending such young talents as Georges Braque, Henri Matisse, and Pablo Picasso, Stein both bought their works and posed for portraits. A staunch patron of the arts, Stein maintained that it was sitting beneath a Cezanne portrait that influenced the modernist writing style of her 1906 novel *Three Lives*.

A prolific author—Stein's oeuvre extends to more than two dozen volumes of fiction, non-fiction, plays, and poetry; her *Autobiography of Alice B. Toklas* was an international bestseller—she is nevertheless best known for her Saturday salons, 27 Rue de Fleurus, Paris, where she encouraged the young men she dubbed the Lost Generation: Sherwood Anderson, Paul Bowles, F. Scott Fitzgerald, Ernest Hemingway, Ezra Pound, and Thornton Wilder, among others.

Living with her lifelong companion Alice B. Toklas (of the cookbook and cannabis brownies fame), Stein continued her salon and writing until her 1946 death at age 72, from stomach cancer at Neuilly-sur-Seine. She was buried in the Père Lachaise Cemetery, Paris.

William Steinberg

Born August 1, 1899—Cologne, Germany
Died May 16, 1978—New York, NY

In the Pittsburgh Symphony's 23 years under the direction of William Steinberg, it reached an artistic apex that established the PSO as one of the world's truly great orchestras. But beyond that, it was a collaborative relationship between conductor and orchestra filled with love, respect, and beautiful music.

Piano virtuoso Arthur Rubinstein clowns around on the keyboard to the amusement of Steinberg, date unknown.

Born Wilhelm Hans Steinberg in Cologne, Germany, William Steinberg was a gifted musician who was composing cantatas at the age of 13. Playing violin and piano, he studied at Cologne Conservatory and upon graduation accepted a position as an assistant alongside Otto Klemperer with the Cologne Opera. He would eventually become their principal conductor when Klemperer left. In 1929, Steinberg became musical director of the Frankfurt Opera but left the post, and Germany, when the Nazis removed him from the Frankfurt Opera and only permitted him to conduct all-Jewish orchestras. He was invited by Arturo Toscanini to join the Palestine Symphony Orchestra, today known as the Israel Philharmonic Orchestra, and then invited by Toscanini to become the associate conductor with the NBC Orchestra in the U.S., which he did from 1938 to 1940. His next assignment was with the Buffalo Philharmonic until 1952 when he began his illustrious tenure with the Pittsburgh Symphony Orchestra.

By the end of Steinberg's first decade conducting the PSO, attendance had increased a remarkable 250 percent. Additionally, the PSO was the only American orchestra to completely sell out, all at the hands of season ticket holders. In August 1964, Steinberg and the PSO set out on a world tour across 14 nations, helping to elevate the cache of the Pittsburgh Symphony Orchestra and the entire city. During the tour, Queen Elizabeth specifically chose the PSO's first performance as her only appearance at the Edinburgh Festival in Scotland. In 1971, Steinberg also presided over the PSO during the move from the Syria Mosque to the acoustically superior Heinz Hall in downtown Pittsburgh.

The bond that existed between Steinberg and his musicians can't be overstated. Pittsburgh is the city where he became a great conductor, and it was under Steinberg's direction that the Pittsburgh Symphony became an even greater orchestra. Said Raymond Marsh, retired violinist with the PSO, "Steinberg excelled at taking us to a different level, to a magical sort of place for the few moments of that specific symphony."

Stella's *Collage No. 8*, c. 1922, paper, paint and mud on paper, H: 16 5/16 x W 11 in., Carnegie Musem of Art Print Purchase Fund

Joseph Stella

Born June 13, 1877—Muro Locano, Italy
Died November 5, 1946—Astoria, NY

Although painter Joseph Stella is best remembered for his 1919 futurist rendering, *Brooklyn Bridge*, his first great artistic breakthrough came a decade before, in the early years of the 20th Century. During Stella's 1908 visit to Pittsburgh, he drew more than 100 stunning scenes of dusky industrial might— and hard-edged industrial life. "In sheer technical brilliance," the Whitney Museum's John Baur wrote, "they surpassed anything of the kind in America at that time."

Born in 1877 in Muro Lucano, a mountain town in southern Italy, in 1896 Stella emigrated to New York, ostensibly to study medicine. Studying painting instead, Stella drew fellow immigrants, laborers, down-and-outers on New York's Lower East Side.

His work received so much attention that by 1905 Stella was drawing for *The Outlook*, a popular reformist weekly. His *Americans in the Rough, Ellis Island Immigrants* published in *The Outlook*, led to other such commissions. In 1907, for example, *Charities and Commons* sent Stella to West Virginia to cover a mine disaster.

The following year, 1908, *The Survey* sent Stella to illustrate *The Pittsburgh Survey*, an exposé of steelworker life. In such sections as *Skunk Hollow: A Pocket of Civic Neglect in Pittsburgh* and *Thirty-Five Years of Typhoid*, Stella captured Pittsburgh's astounding industrial might—as well as its dangerous working conditions, dreadful living places, and careworn workers.

The haunting, compelling works, some of which Stella exhibited at the 1910 Carnegie International, cemented his standing as a first-rate American artist. Returning to Pittsburgh in 1918, Stella changed modes, producing stunning pastels, notably the memorable *Night Fires*, with a fiery sky framing a steel mill's raw energy.

Although his career had many turns— Stella, proclaiming his artistic independence, often changed styles and modes—his oeuvre never surpassed his stark, brilliantly rendered Pittsburgh series.

Kaye Stevens

Born July 21, 1932—Lawrenceville

Vivacious, swingin', effervescent, and electrifying were all common buzzwords used to hype the best 1960s nightclub entertainers, but perhaps none were applied more often than to singer Kaye Stevens. A brassy redhead with a better comedic sense than most, Stevens followed the likes of Anita Ekberg, Jayne Mansfield, and the ever-present Anita Bryant on Bob Hope's USO World tours. She made a few films, sang in hundreds of clubs, and cut a few records, but her long association with Hope won her a doctor of humane letters from Brewer Christian College in 1995.

Born in Lawrenceville, Stevens attended the Arsenal School kindergarten, but left Pittsburgh at age 6 because her father found better work as a car mechanic in Cleveland.

After selling cemetery plots there, she was billed as "Cleveland's Edith Piaf," and headed west. Though she traveled the U.S. many times over, she always exclaimed to have been born a Pittsburgher. "Gosh, it's good to be home," she announced from the stage at the Holiday House in 1966, just several months after releasing her latest album, *Ruckus at the Riviera.* Stevens was a standard in Vegas, once billed with Sinatra and his Rat Pack at Caesar's Palace.

Her many early appearances on *The Ed*

Sullivan Show, and many subsequent guest gigs on *Hollywood Palace*, *The Dean Martin Show*, and *the Tonight Show with Johnny Carson*, brought her smaller guest roles on popular TV shows, like *CHiPS*, and *Days of Our Lives*, and many stints on popular game shows. She toured often, too, in Broadway productions. More recently, she has dedicated her career to singing Christian and Gospel music, for which she has an online ministry at *www.kayestevens.com*.

Jimmy Stewart

Born May 20, 1908—Indiana, PA
Died July 2, 1997—Hollywood, CA

In dozens of legendary films, he never swore, never played the villain, and refused to accept any role in which he, as the underdog, would not triumph. Even in his personal life, he kept things clean and did his duty for God and country. Jimmy Stewart was the quintessential American "everyman" whom audiences worldwide adored.

Of course, he grew up in idyllic small-town America—Indiana, PA—to which he often returned. His 1940 Oscar® for *The Philadelphia Story* sat in the window of his father's hardware store on Philadelphia Street for 25 years. On his 50th birthday, celebrated in his hometown, he said, "I've settled down 3,000 miles from Indiana. I've traveled to points in the world three times that distance. At times I've stayed away several years at a stretch, but I somehow have never felt that I was very far from here ... somehow I don't feel that I have ever been away." Little wonder then that in 1995 the town assembled a museum honoring his life's work. A visit is worth much more than the admission price.

Stewart attended Mercersburg Academy and graduated from Princeton in 1932. He spent two years doing summer stock in Falmouth, MA, and landed a role in *Journey By Night* on Broadway where he was "discovered" for film. His first movie, 1934's *Art Trouble*, featured Shemp Howard of The Three Stooges. In 1936 he played the brother of Jeanette McDonald in *Rose Marie*. And, in the same year, he appeared with William Powell in *After The Thin Man*.

The 1930s and 1940s were prolific years for Hollywood, churning out films as fast as a studio could. So when an actor appears in a string of hits, studios take note. Such was the case with Stewart whose first film classic was in George S. Kaufman's 1938 screen adaptation of *You Can't Take It With You*, the first film in which Stewart was directed by Frank Capra. The two teamed up again the following year with *Mr. Smith Goes to Washington*, another classic that gave Stewart his first top billing and forever painted his persona with American values. In the same year, however, Stewart starred with Marlene Dietrich in *Destry Rides Again*, perhaps the most risqué of all of his work. Follow that with *The Shop Around The Corner*, another classic, in which he starred with Margaret Sullavan and a young William Tracy. Of three more Stewart films released in 1940, *The Philadelphia Story* earned him his first and only Oscar®.

Even before Pearl Harbor, Stewart enlisted in the Army, making his way into the Army Air Force. He refused special treatment, but earned his wings, flying 25 bombing missions over Europe.

After five years in the service, he returned to the screen, without seemingly missing a beat. His first post-war film was *It's A Wonderful Life*, his third Capra collaboration, and the film he often claimed as his favorite.

Not until 1949 did Stewart marry. He was 41 when Gloria McLean came to the chapel with two sons from a previous marriage. After filming the immortal *Harvey* as Elwood P. Dowd, he and Gloria had fraternal twin girls, Judy and Kelly, in 1951.

By then, Stewart had become one of the first Hollywood stars to command a percentage of the film's gross receipts. But Stewart, other than dining in his select booth at Chasen's, eschewed much of the glitz and materialism of the Hollywood scene. He did care passionately about the scripts and directors and casts he played with, and he carried major clout. Of his work in the 1950s and 1960s, he generated long-term revenues with directors like Alfred Hitchcock in *Rope*, *Rear Window*, and *Vertigo*, and with John Ford in *The Man Who Shot Liberty Valance*, *How The West Was Won*, and *Cheyenne Autumn*. Such lists overlook the breakthrough characterizations he gave to *The Glenn Miller Story*, *The Spirit of St. Louis*, and *Anatomy of a Murder*.

By the 1970s, he had his own short-lived TV show, and started appearing regularly on *The Dean Martin Show*, and *The Tonight Show with Johnny Carson*, often reading poetry to mask suspected memory loss. Stewart barely survived the emotional loss of his wife in 1994, and died from pulmonary embolism in 1997.

David Stock

Born June 13, 1939—Pittsburgh

Perhaps more than any other person, David Stock has ensured that Pittsburgh's classical music fans are exposed to modern, often challenging works rather than a safe and steady diet of Brahms and Beethoven. Founder and music director of the Pittsburgh New Music Ensemble, Stock was instrumental in building an audience for new compositions.

His works have been played all over the world, including "Kickoff" which premiered during the famed New York Philharmonic's 150th anniversary season and his "Violin Concerto," debuted by his hometown Pittsburgh Symphony.

However, Stock's stock was not always so high in Pittsburgh. When he moved back to the city in 1975 he was struggling to find a job let alone a musical niche. "I had no prospects and three kids," he recalls. "I went around to everyone in Pittsburgh and said I wanted to start a new music ensemble, and everyone said I was crazy, but I couldn't afford not to do it."

That dedication brought avant garde, contemporary works to town with the formation of the PNME. Working with classical music station WQED-FM, Stock spread the gospel of contemporary classical music. It was a long, slow climb, with Stock reckoning that he could only afford to pay himself about $1,000 in the PNME's first season. In artistic terms, it was "if you build it, they will come." Soon composers from all over the world were sending in works.

And Stock's work was gaining notice as well. He received a Guggenheim Fellowship, five fellowship grants from the National Endowment for the Arts, and five fellowships from Pennsylvania. He served as conductor in residence with the Pittsburgh Symphony Orchestra and picked up the baton for orchestras in Australia, China, Europe, and Mexico.

By 1999, Stock turned to education. He left the PNME and continued composing, also joining Duquesne University as a professor of music, where he continues to conduct the university's Contemporary Ensemble. There have also been teaching stints at Carnegie Mellon University, the Cleveland Institute of Music,

September 1, 1945, Stewart with his parents shortly after returing from service overseas, at the St. Regis Hotel, New York.

and Brandeis University. Stock also has proved to be an ambassador for modern works. As host of *Da Capo*, a weekly public-radio series, he showcases new composers.

That dedication was a key factor in The Pittsburgh Cultural Trust awarding him a coveted Creative Achievement Award for Outstanding Established Artist in 1992.

Maurice Stokes

Born June 17, 1933—Rankin, PA
Died April 6, 1970—Cincinnati, OH

"I feel like I'm going to die," he told a teammate. Hours later, he was paralyzed for life.

Of all the tragic tales in sports, basketball star Maurice Stokes' may be the saddest. Born in Rankin, in 1933, moving to Homewood at age 8, by the time Big Mo played for Westinghouse High he was basketball royalty. When 'House won back-to-back city championships, 1950-51, Stokes received multiple scholarship offers. Choosing Saint Francis, in nearby Loretto, the 6'-7", 240-pound Stokes became a national star. As a junior, 1953-54, he led his tiny college to a 22-9 record and into the National Invitational Tournament. The following year, 1954-55, St. Francis returned to the NIT. Named MVP, Stokes also captured All-American honors.

The number-two 1955 national draft choice, Stokes played two years for the Rochester Royals, 1955-57, then a year in Cincinnati when the team relocated, 1957-58. The 1956 Rookie of the Year, and a three-time All Star, Stokes was a powerhouse, averaging more than 17 rebounds a game. He was a strong, accurate passer, among assist leaders every year.

The end began during the last game of the 1957-58 regular season. In Minneapolis, Stokes, driving to the basket, was hit, fell, and lay unconscious. Three days later, after a 12-point, 15-rebound playoff performance in Detroit, Stokes fell into a coma.

With a brain injury that left him paralyzed and unable to speak, for the succeeding dozen years he underwent extensive physical therapy, gaining minimal movement.

Dying of a heart attack at 36 in 1970 in Cincinnati, he was buried on the Saint Francis campus, where the Stokes Athletic Center was named in his memory.

In 1973, his story was made into the film *Maurie* (*Big Mo* in video release), starring retired football player Bernie Casey.

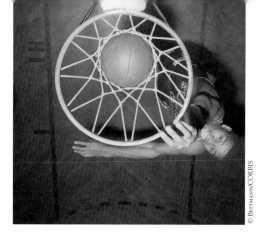

In 2004, Maurice Stokes was posthumously inducted into the Basketball Hall of Fame.

Sharon Stone

Born March 10, 1958—Saegertown, PA

The irony of Sharon Stone's rise to fame as one of Hollywood's more erotic personas is the fact that she left Saegertown High School to be enrolled as a freshman at Edinboro University when she was just 15. A brilliant, bookish child, said to have an IQ of 154, Stone was more likely destined to become a writer. She has said of herself "I was a nerdy, ugly duckling who sat in the back of the closet with a flashlight and read. I was never a kid. I walked and talked at 10 months. I started school in the second grade when I was 5, a real weird, academically driven kid, not at all interested in being social."

The second of four children born to Joseph and Dorothy, Stone grew up on RD#3 in Saegertown, PA. Self-conscious about her youth and good looks, she was dared to enter a beauty contest and won the title of Miss Crawford County. While competing for the title of Miss Pennsylvania, she realized a new career in modeling, and, in 1977, she dropped out of Edinboro University to sign with the Eileen Ford Agency in NY.

Her first film was Woody Allen's *Stardust Memories* in which she played the unspoken role of "pretty girl on train." Wes Craven then cast her in *Deadly Blessing*. TV roles followed in shows like *Silver Spoons*, *Remington Steele,* and *Magnum, P.I*. But no parts of real import came to pass until she played Arnold Schwarzenegger's wife in *Total Recall* (1990). The following year she starred in *Basic Instinct*, the film that launched her to stardom as the novelist whose true crime story is uncovered by infatuated lover Michael Douglas. The police interrogation scene was not the first glimpse of Stone's sexual mystique—nor the last.

1993's *Sliver*, *The Last Action Hero*, and *The Quick and the Dead* never matched the success of her first Golden Globe nomination for *Basic Instinct*. But, 1995's *Casino*, the Martin Scorsese hit, won her the Golden Globe for Best Actress as the cocaine addicted wife of Vegas mob boss Robert DeNiro. The film also won her an Oscar® nod. The following year, she landed in Pittsburgh to film *Diabolique* with Isabelle Adjani in Squirrel Hill. The film, a remake of the French classic, failed Hollywood's expectations.

Stone has since sustained a more modest career as a sex symbol. She produced and starred in a sequel of *Basic Instinct* in 2006 that decidedly bombed. However, her role as the hairdresser of the Ambassador Hotel in *Bobby* that same year was a standout.

Said the actress who recovered from a horrific car accident in 1998, as well as a brain aneurism in 2001, "After you've been through all that stuff, the rest of this is just kid's stuff. As Winston Churchill says, when you're going through hell, keep going.'"

In 2007 Stone returned home to be honored with a doctorate in philosophy from Edinboro in recognition of her commitment to funding AIDS research.

Billy Strayhorn

Born November 29, 1915—Dayton, OH
Died May 31, 1967—New York, NY

Everyone knows the jazz classic "Take The A Train," Duke Ellington's signature song. But what many don't know is that it was written by the brilliant arranger, composer, pianist—and Duke's main collaborator for almost 30 years—Billy Strayhorn. Although born in Dayton, he was raised on Tioga Street in Homewood.

William Thomas Strayhorn was anything but an ordinary child. Billy moved to Pittsburgh when he was 5 because his family was looking for better opportunities. His love of music started very early; so passionate was he, while still in grade school, he worked to raise money to buy an upright piano. As a student at Westinghouse High School, Strayhorn was involved in numerous musical pursuits and even composed a Concerto for his high school graduation. Still a teen, Strayhorn composed one of his signature pieces, "Lush Life," a song that possesses the insights and observations of a seasoned veteran. Indeed, it has been recorded by a multitude of jazz greats from Nat King Cole to John Coltrane.

Introduced to the likes of Art Tatum and Earl "Fatha" Hines, Strayhorn took to playing jazz and studied music theory at the Pittsburgh Musical Institute. He played locally with a group called the Madhatters. In 1938, Strayhorn was able to meet Duke Ellington while in town playing a concert at the Stanley Theatre. After hearing him play his song "Lush Life," Duke invited Strayhorn to join him in New York. There he would later accept Ellington's offer to join him as a collaborator. Their relationship grew for 28 years during which time the two wrote some of the world's best known classics. Said Ellington of Strayhorn, "he's my right arm, left foot, eyes, stomach, and soul."

Above, photographed by Teenie Harris, dancer Honey Coles gets a leg up on Duke Ellington and Strayhorn.

Strayhorn's genius shone brightly with Ellington's orchestra. In 1941 when ASCAP imposed a ban on performing any songs it represented, including Ellington's own compositions, the Orchestra's current tour was threatened. Strayhorn rose to the occasion. Called to Ellington's side to write and arrange a new repertoire of non-ASCAP songs, Strayhorn completed the task during a frantic train ride from New York to California. Arriving exhausted, Strayhorn unloaded a bag of hits: "Johnny Come Lately," "Chelsea Bridge," and the song that would become Duke Ellington's signature number, "Take The A Train."

For the rest of his career, Strayhorn served as an inspiration to Ellington, collaborating on songs, concerts, suites, and musicals. Additionally, Strayhorn worked on solo projects including a musical revue for a Harlem-based fraternal organization called the Copasetics. And he wrote songs for his close friend Lena Horne. In 1967, after many years of heavy smoking, Billy Strayhorn died of esophageal cancer at just 51.

Since his death, Strayhorn's bittersweet musical arrangements, often masked by Ellington's powerful stage presence, have come forward from the shadows of Strayhorn's many unimposing and unspoken relationships. His contribution to American jazz is still yet untold.

A constant companion and contributor to Duke Ellington, Strayhorn's influence was pervasive and pivotol.

Bill Strickland

Born August 25, 1947—Manchester

It was 1963, and Bill Strickland was 16 and feeling out of sorts. Wandering around Oliver High, on the North Side, he spied an art teacher at a pottery wheel.

The malleability of the clay, the creativity of the moment, the sense of possibility, changed his life.

Born in Manchester in 1947, William E. Strickland, Jr., felt he was going nowhere—until that day at Oliver. Becoming a skilled potter, he graduated in 1965, going on to earn a 1969 Pitt history degree.

But he had never left the neighborhood—where he lived then, and lives now. In 1968, he founded the Manchester Craftsman's Guild in a shabby row house, encouraging neighborhood kids to become artists. Within three years a moribund vocational program, Bidwell Training Center, asked him for help.

Becoming what Harvard has since termed a social entrepreneur, Strickland articulated a simple message: give people the tools they need, treat them with respect, and watch them perform miracles.

Over four decades, his two down-at-the-heels programs have blossomed into the Manchester Bidwell Corporation. Headquartered in its own signature 1815 Metropolitan Street building, MBC teaches roughly 1,000 inner-city teens and adults real-life skills every year, horticulture to computer programming, college prep to culinary arts.

As president and CEO, Strickland guides the operation, as well as developing a greenhouse for orchids and hydroponic tomatoes and a medical technology complex. In the original facility, there's also a 350-seat music hall housing America's longest-running jazz subscription series. In more than 20 years, MCG Jazz has produced more than 1,200 concerts, has its own recording label, and has won three Grammys®.

Exporting MBC philosophy, Strickland has partnerships in Cincinnati, San Francisco, Baltimore, and other cities. His numerous accolades include a MacArthur "Genius" Grant, as well as seats on the National Endowment for the Arts, University of Pittsburgh Board of Trustees, and Carnegie Institute.

David Strickler

Born in 1881—Latrobe, PA
Died in 1971—Latrobe, PA

Among those responsible for the inventions of boxed chocolates, greeting cards, and cheap paperbacks, David Strickler's name ranks heads above as the creator of the American drugstore's most treasured guilty pleasure: the three-scoop banana split.

A master study in subtle complexities—one scoop each of chocolate, vanilla, and strawberry ice creams, cradled by a single banana sliced lengthwise and crowned with various toppings—the split cost twice as much as any other concoction at its debut in 1904. Few cared as they readily plunked down their 10 cents.

Ostensibly working as an apprentice pharmacist at the Tassel Pharmacy in Latrobe, 23-year-old Strickler nevertheless found time to tinker at the store's soda fountain. Ultimate inspiration, it's said, came during a trip to Atlantic City. Returning home, he tinkered some more and pitched the final product to students at nearby Saint Vincent College. They, in turn, spread news of the cool treat far and wide, gaining fans as well as challengers who claimed they, too, had invented the split. Doubtful, say historians. In fact, the National Ice Cream Retailers Association has certified the banana split's birthplace is Latrobe.

And, just for the record, Strickler also gets credit for designing the split's special elongated glass dish he called the "banana boat." The Westmoreland Glass Co. order form, dated 1905, is on permanent display at Latrobe's historical center.

Though much has been made of his role in ice cream history, Strickler lived modestly. He eventually bought the Tassel Pharmacy—Strickler's Pharmacy he renamed it—and earned the nickname "Doc" as the town's optometrist.

Maxine Sullivan

Born May 13, 1911—Homestead, PA
Died April 7, 1987—New York, NY

She was the daughter of a barber from Homestead who would go on to become the first black jazz artist to have a weekly coast-to-coast radio show.

Marietta Williams was born in 1911 in the steel town of Homestead. On the family's old phonograph young Maxine would listen to the records of Bessie Smith, Ethel Waters, and Fletcher Henderson. She had a smooth and likeable delivery that won her local contests and would eventually earn her a spot singing in her Uncle Harry's band. While still in her teens she landed a job in a speakeasy called The Benjamin Harrison Literary Club where she was discovered and encouraged to take her talents to New York. She was given the name "Sullivan" because of the many Irish clubs she played at the time,

and it stuck with her for the rest of her career. Her first recording was of an old traditional Scottish folk song that would become her signature, "Lock Lomond."

Pianist Gladys Mosier heard Sullivan perform and urged her to head to New York. After saving her money for six months, Sullivan moved to New York and became the vocalist at the Onyx Club where she met and married bassist John Kirby. In 1940, Sullivan and Kirby also teamed up on the nationally broadcast radio program *Flow Gently Sweet Rhythm*, making them the first black jazz artists to have their own national radio show.

Sullivan went on to act and tour, and she enjoyed success throughout the U.S. and Europe. She retired from the music scene on several occasions, once to pursue a nursing career. Always resurfacing, Sullivan became a staple on the jazz festival circuit enjoying a second wind of sorts during the 1970s and 1980s.

Sullivan was one of only three women included in 1958 when Art Kane snapped his famous shot "A Great Day In Harlem," which features some of jazz's greatest musicians.

Maxine Sullivan died in April 1987 and in 1998 was inducted into the Big Band and Jazz Hall of Fame.

Jock Sutherland

Born March 11, 1889—Coupar Angus, Scotland
Died April 11, 1948—Pittsburgh

A coach of such high standing that friend and foe alike called him Doctor, John Bain "Jock" Sutherland set the gold standard for Pitt football—and in two brief years with the Steelers arguably saved the franchise.

Born in Scotland, in 1889, the dour, unmarried Sutherland honed single-wing football to unparalleled success. An All-American lineman for legendary Pop Warner's Pitt Panthers, Sutherland starred on national championship teams, 1915-16.

After graduation and a dentistry degree, Sutherland left town to coach. By 1924 he was back, replacing his mentor to lead the Panthers. For the next 15 seasons, through 1938, Sutherland racked up a school-record 111 wins—more than any coach in Pitt history—going undefeated four times, taking the national title in 1937, along with four shared titles. A three-time Rose Bowl loser, Sutherland's 1936 Panthers trounced Washington 21-0.

The only way to top that victory was not to return. Invited the following year, Sutherland turned down the honor, saying that his squad had already played in Pasadena and he preferred to spend Christmas at home.

Sparring with Pitt Chancellor John Bowman over the place of the football program, Sutherland left after '38 to coach the pro football Brooklyn Dodgers. In 1946 he returned to coach the Steelers. With attendance soaring, that year the Steelers went 5-5-1. While it was a great success for the previously inept team, it was Sutherland's only squad not to have a winning season. The next year, 1947, the Steelers tied the Eagles for first place—their best finish until the 1970s.

People expected 1948 to be even better. Suffering from headaches, Sutherland collapsed on a spring scouting trip. Rushed back to Pittsburgh, he died of a brain tumor. "He gave Pittsburgh fans the kind of teams they were looking for," Art Rooney recalled. "If it hadn't been for the Doctor, I never would have been able to continue in pro football."

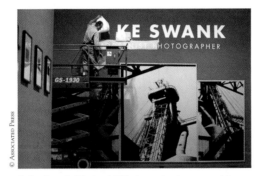

Luke Swank: Modernist Photographer is prepared for a major exhibition at the Carnegie Museum of Art, 2005.

Luke Swank

Born in 1890—Johnstown, PA
Died in 1944—Pittsburgh

Photographer Luke Swank was the quintessential late bloomer.

Born in Johnstown in 1890, as a young man Swank did virtually everything other than heft a camera: studied horticulture at Penn State, bred cattle, trained police dogs, worked in the family hardware store, and managed an auto dealership.

He may have tinkered with a camera in the 1920s, but it wasn't until 1930, when Swank was 40, that he began to take pictures seriously, of Johnstown's Bethlehem Steel plant, stark, unyielding, images of industrial might. Within a year, Swank was looking to exhibit his work nationally. Within three, 1933, he had a one-man show at a New York art gallery, and placed a stunning 12-foot steel mill photomural at New York's Museum of Modern Art (MOMA). By the following year, 1934, Swank was regularly exhibiting in San Francisco as well as New York.

Moving to Pittsburgh in 1934, Swank was hired by Chancellor Bowman as the University of Pittsburgh's official photographer, where, from his Cathedral of Learning studio, Swank taught the nation's first college-level photography courses.

Leaving Pitt two years later, 1936, to open his own downtown studio, Swank worked for many industrial clients, including ALCOA, Calgon, and Heinz, illustrating cookbooks, ads, and articles. Working also for department store magnate Edgar Kaufmann, Swank's Fallingwater photos were exhibited at MOMA, 1938.

Publishing in national outlets such as *Vogue, House & Garden, Fortune, Life*, and *The New York Times*, Swank relished the tough, gritty side of life. Indeed, many of his surviving 4,000 images are sharply contrasted studies of urban life, rural architecture, and steel mills.

During World War I, Swank, assigned to a poison gas facility, suffered an accident that chronically affected his health. That, combined with high blood pressure, resulted in the heart attack that took Swank's life in Pittsburgh in 1944, age 54—ending his brief but brilliant 14-year career.

Lynn Swann

Born March 7, 1952—Alcoa, TN

The epitome of the graceful, acrobatic athlete, Steeler Lynn Swann played just nine seasons, 1974-82, but not only helped the team achieve unprecedented success, he also changed the game. "Swann reshaped football," Myron Cope said. "He changed expectations about what is catchable."

Lynn Curtis Swann grew up in California. A star athlete and honor student at San Mateo's Junipero Serra High, where he was a state-champion long jumper, Swann was an All-American wide receiver at the University of Southern California. Drafted number one by the Steelers in 1974—the same class as Hall of Famers Jack Lambert, John Stallworth, and Mike Webster—Swann played on four Super Bowl champions. Gifted with extraordinary leaping ability and concentration, plus an uncanny ability to deliver the big play, Swann credited dance lessons, "ballet, tap, and jazz," he said. "They helped a great deal with body control, balance, a sense of rhythm, and timing."

Playing at a lithe 5'-11" and 180, Swann's showcase was Super Bowl X, where his MVP performance included four catches for 161 yards, then a record, including a spectacular 64-yard catch—one, along with Franco Harris' 1972 Immaculate Reception, that stands as the centerpiece of every all-time Steeler highlight film.

For his career, Swann had 336 catches for 5,462 yards and 51 touchdowns. A three-time Pro Bowler, he was elected to the College Football Hall of Fame in 1993 and the Pro Football Hall of Fame Class of 2001.

The married father of two sons, and former chairman of the President's Council on Physical Fitness and Sports, Swann lives in Sewickley Heights. "I was determined that I would go back to southern California," he said. "But Pittsburgh became home. I could not have chosen a better place."

An ABC Sports broadcaster since 1976, Swann resigned in 2006 to campaign unsuccessfully for Pennsylvania governor.

Jane Gray Swisshelm

Born in December, 1815—Pittsburgh
Died in 1884—Pittsburgh

Jane Grey Swisshelm was a journalist, abolitionist, and women's rights advocate in the mid-1800s. She served as freelance writer, editor, and publisher of four newspapers that advocated for the abolition of slavery and women's rights and authored several books. She was influential in passing a bill through the Pennsylvania legislature granting women property rights.

Jane Grey was born in December 1815, in Pittsburgh. After her 1836 marriage to James Swisshelm, they moved to Kentucky where she encountered slavery first hand. In 1839, against the wishes of her husband, she moved back to Pittsburgh to care for her mother. Upon her mother's death, she used inheritance money to start her own paper, the *Pittsburgh Saturday Visiter*, in 1848. Her passionate editorials promoted the abolition of slavery, women's rights, and temperance.

Several years later she was hired by Horace Greeley to write a weekly political commentary article for the *New York Tribune*. She endured years of unhappiness in her marriage, which fueled much of her writing on women's rights, before leaving James and moving to Minnesota with her daughter. The mother and daughter settled in St. Cloud

where Jane became editor of the *St. Cloud Visiter*. She continued to promote anti-slavery and women's rights issues as well as attacking many of the local Democratic leaders. In retaliation, her newspaper office was set on fire and her printing press thrown into the Mississippi River. Never one to be intimidated, she managed to raise enough money for another press and stepped up her tirades for social reform in the *St. Cloud Democrat*.

She played a formative role in the organization of the Minnesota Republican Party. In the early 1860s she traveled to Washington D.C. to speak with the President on her Indian policy views. While there she encountered another native Pittsburgher, Edwin Stanton, then Secretary of War, who offered her a clerkship in the government. She sold her Minnesota paper and moved to D.C. where she worked in the government and served as a nurse for Union soldiers during the Civil War.

After the war, Swisshelm started her final newspaper, *The Reconstructionist*, in which she critiqued President Andrew Johnson's reconstruction policy, which eventually caused her to lose her government post and paper. After a successful legal fight with her ex-husband over their land in Swissvale she moved back to their farm where she wrote her 1880 autobiography, *Half a Century*. She died in 1884 and was buried in Allegheny Cemetery. The city of Pittsburgh neighborhood of Swisshelm Park, near Swissvale, is named in her honor.

Lyle Talbot

Born February 8, 1902—Pittsburgh
Died March 2, 1996—San Francisco, CA

One of the 24 founding members of the Screen Actors Guild, Lyle Talbot was known to his peers as "Mr. Hollywood," not because he was a legend of the silver screen (though he appeared in many more films than his more famous contemporaries), but because his middle name was Hollywood—literally.

Talbot had a long and somewhat distinguished career, first performing as a magician's assistant and then taking the stage in a number of local theatre groups. He formed his own Lyle Talbot Players, and while touring in Houston, was invited to audition for the silver screen. The year was 1932. Asked in a 1984 interview by the *Los Angeles Times* to what he owed his success, Talbot replied, "It's really simple. I never turned down a job, not one...ever."

Indeed Talbot appeared as a character actor in hundreds of B movies, and a solid handful of A's. Of his better known films, he appeared with Humphrey Bogart and Bette Davis in *Three on a Match*, the original *42nd Street*, *20,000 Years of Sing Sing* with Spencer Tracy, and *Go West Young Man* starring Mae West.

But what is so endearing to those who remember his career are the roles that might have made him a cult figure. Talbot was the original Lex Luthor in the Kirk Alyn *Superman* serials, Commissioner Gordon in the original *Batman & Robin* serials, and he was cast in two of the worst Ed Wood, Jr., films ever made, *Glen or Glenda* and *Plan 9 from Outer Space*. Indeed, these classics will out-

Tanner's *Sand Dunes at Sunset, Atlantic City* hangs in the Green Room of the White House.

© Associated Press

live any Carole Lombard or Barbara Stanwyck film as there are many in which he appeared.

Talbot was also known to television fans as Joe Randolph, the distrustful neighbor of *Ozzie and Harriet*, airline pilot friend of Robert Cummings on *Love that Bob*, and he was seen frequently on *Burns and Allen*, *The Danny Thomas Show*, and *The Lucy Show*.

Born the only child of parents who performed on the many showboats streaming through Pittsburgh in the early 1900s, he was raised by his grandmother for most of his childhood. It was her last name he took as his stage name.

Tanaghrisson

Born Unknown
Died October 4, 1754—Harrisburg, PA

Although very little is known about his early life, Tanaghrisson is thought to have been a Catawba Indian by birth captured at a young age and raised by the Seneca. In the 1740s he resided with members of the Iroquois Nation on the banks of the Ohio River at a place then known as Logstown—present-day Ambridge. He likely earned the title "Half King" because of his dual role as diplomatic spokesperson between the Iroquois and the British forces throughout the region.

Forced to walk a delicate line between the French and the British troops, Tanaghrisson nonetheless aided the British cause on numerous occasions. He accompanied George Washington in his travels to French outposts in Western Pennsylvania in 1753 with the intent of demanding they leave the area. The mission was unsuccessful and hostilities between the French and British escalated to violence.

In retaliation to the French construction of Fort Duquesne, George Washington was dispatched to regain British control over the region. Accompanied by Tanaghrisson, Washington's troops engaged and defeated the French on May 28, 1754, in what is now known as the Battle of Jumonville Glen. After the battle, Tanaghrisson reportedly killed the captured French leader Jumonville during interrogation by George Washington. This battle was an early conflict in the escalating French and Indian War In North America.

Seeking refuge from the hostilities, Tanaghrisson subsequently moved his people east into central Pennsylvania where he lived out the remainder of his days. He died in 1754.

Henry Ossawa Tanner

Born June 21, 1859—Hill District
Died May 25, 1937—Paris, France

In the 1990s, the painting *Sand Dunes at Sunset, Atlantic City* became the first work by an African-American artist in the White House collection.

For Henry Ossawa Tanner, it was only the latest in a long line of firsts.

The oldest of nine children, son of an African Methodist Episcopal minister, Tanner was born in 1859 in the Hill District. Five years later, in 1864, the Tanner family moved to Philadelphia, where by 13 Henry decided to become an artist.

Enrolling in the Pennsylvania Academy of Fine Arts in 1879, Tanner studied with Thomas Eakins. In 1886 he opened his own Philadelphia studio, which failed. Moving to Atlanta, Tanner opened a photography studio, which similarly failed, then taught drawing at Clark College.

By 1891, Tanner had traveled to France, where he studied at the Academie Julian. Returning to Philadelphia, in 1893 Tanner painted *The Banjo Lesson*, and in 1894 *The Thankful Poor*, the first major, dignified renditions of African-American life by an African-American artist.

Tanner then left America permanently—and eschewed such subjects in favor of religious tableaus. In 1895, his *Daniel in the Lion's Den* won an honorable mention in the Paris Salon. Two years later, *Resurrection of Lazarus* took third prize. Purchased by the French government, it was exhibited at the Luxembourg Gallery, then became part of the Louvre collection.

In 1900, *Daniel in the Lion's Den* was awarded a silver medal at Paris' Universal Ex-

position; the following year, it received a second silver medal, at Buffalo's Pan-American Exhibition.

Elected a member of the National Academy of Design in 1910, in 1927 Tanner was made a full academician, the first African-American so awarded. In 1923 he became an honorary chevalier in France's Legion of Honor.

Henry Ossawa Tanner died in Paris in 1937 at age 77. In 1973 his likeness appeared on an American postage stamp.

Paul Taylor

Born July 29, 1930—Edgewood, PA

The son of a widow remarried briefly to a physicist (who worked for Westinghouse,) living briefly in Edgewood, Paul Taylor was born into an unusually lonely childhood, reared as best could be by three half-siblings, the youngest of which, Bettie, was 16 years his elder. Taylor and his mother, whom he called Mammy, lived during the Depression in the Brighton Hotel on California Street in Washington, D.C. She worked constantly in the kitchen. He roamed the halls, entertaining himself by playing with imaginary friends. Still, they were extraordinarily close.

From childhood, Taylor was a prodigy of the visual arts, learning to draw and paint during classes at the Corcoran. When informed by his instructor that the young Taylor showed immense talent, Mammy cancelled his lessons; she had no time to raise a genius. Nevertheless, Taylor studied painting at Syracuse University and while there was partnered in a modern dance recital. Soon he received a dance scholarship at Julliard, then another at Connecticut College. Upon performing at the

American Dance Festival, he was spotted by Martha Graham and invited to study with her School. The year was 1952.

In 1954, Taylor, while performing as a soloist for Graham, formed his own dance company, beginning a long portfolio of dances he choreographed to spotlight the beauty of ordinary human movement and—in one memorable "dance"—non-movement. The "action" of waiting for a bus, or checking one's watch, were common gestures made uncommonly dramatic in typical Taylor fashion. Sometimes chided as a minimalist, Taylor embraced simple, everyday expressions through body language, and has created some 90 dances, of which his masterpieces are included in the repertoires of many of the world's finest ballet and dance companies.

Taylor, in air, Bettie De Jong, and Renee Kimball rehearse the "insects and heroes" routine from their performance at London's Shaftesbury Theatre, December 3, 1964.

Not just a master choreographer, Taylor was a dancer of incredible strength and passion who performed up until 1975. Of his many students, he claims Twyla Tharp, Laura Dean, Dan Wagoner, and Sentra Driver as protégés. Taylor's company has performed in more than 300 U.S. cities, and toured overseas more than 40 times, performing in more than 50 countries. Celebrating its 50th anniversary in 2004, the Paul Taylor Dance Company continues to tour across the U.S., while its founder lives reclusively on Long Island. His 1987 autobiography, *Private Domain*, reprinted in 1999 by the University of Pittsburgh Press, received wide critical acclaim.

Jimmy Thackery

Born May 9, 1953—West View

Growing up not too far from West View Park, one of Thackery's earliest memories was his father making him ride the Dips roller coaster. The experience was so frightening for the young boy that he has since been unable to climb into a coaster. The family moved to Pittsburgh from Ohio after his father accepted a position with the Labor Relations Board. When he was 5, Thackery moved several times, finally landing in Washington D.C.

His musically educated mother was an important force. He first learned the piano but soon found the guitar to be much more interesting, and a better vehicle for picking up girls. Much of the music that caught his ear as a youngster were the twangy sounds of movie and TV theme music, arrangements like those by Henry Mancini.

Longtime buddies with David Raitt, Bonnie Raitt's brother, the two played in a band together in high school. Raitt helped broaden Thackery's musical horizons when he introduced him to the legendary blues guitarist Buddy Guy. A second life-transforming experience was watching Jimi Hendrix perform as the opening act for the Monkees.

In 1974 Thackery was introduced to harmonica player Mark Wenner. The two soon became half of the hard-driving blues workhorse known as The Nighthawks. Local bluesman Billy Price met and befriended Thackery while Price was touring with Roy Buchanan. He invited The Nighthawks to play back in Pittsburgh and reunited Thackery with his old town. During their 13 years and 20 albums together, The Nighthawks were one of the most respected, hard-working and popular blues bands in the nation, and it gave Thackery the opportunity to play with some of the greats, like Otis Rush, Muddy Waters, and Buddy Guy. After growing weary of playing 300 nights a year, in 1987 Thackery struck out on his own, producing some of the best material of his professional career, exploring acoustics, jazz, and R&B in addition to his straight ahead electric blues.

Thackery currently lives in the Ozarks and is still active in the blues world touring and recording extensively.

Harry K. Thaw

Born February 12, 1871—Pittsburgh
Died February 22, 1947—Miami, FL

Some say the phrase "brain storm" was first used to excuse Harry Thaw's actions on the night of June 25, 1906, when he shot and killed the famous New York architect Stanford White.

Born in Pittsburgh to William Thaw, a prominent railroad executive and Mary Copley Thaw, a socialite, Harry grew up in affluence on Fifth Street. He was no doubt a spoiled child, demanding and prone to fits of rage. His bratty behavior followed him to Harvard, where he was a self-proclaimed student of poker, ultimately getting expelled for chasing a fleeing cab driver with a shotgun.

In 1901, he became infatuated with Evelyn Nesbit, a 16-year-old *Floradora* chorus girl.

Showering her with flowers when she was convalescing in a New York Hospital, Thaw won her attention. While traveling together overseas, Nesbit confessed to Thaw that she was not a virgin but that an unfortunate night with Stanford White was not her fault. Harry's rage toward Stanford manifested itself in brutal beatings of Evelyn, but despite his cruel treatment, they were married in 1905. A full year later, ever loathing White, on the night of June 25, 1906, during a performance of *Mamzelle* at Madison Square Garden, Thaw approached White's table and shot him three times at close range.

Enjoying a catered breakfast from Delmonico's restaurant, Thaw awaits trial in his jail cell, circa 1906.

Thaw's first trial caused a media frenzy, but ended in a deadlocked jury. It was during his second trial that Dr. Britton D. Evans described him as suffering from "a severe brain storm" as is common in people who have gone through "an explosive or fulminating condition of mental unsoundness." Thaw was found not guilty by reason of insanity and spent five years in a state hospital. Released in 1915, he divorced Evelyn a short time later denying all paternity claims to the child she bore while he was incarcerated.

Through the years, Thaw could not escape his violent past. After a suicide attempt, he served another six years in an asylum. He was unsuccessful in all of his business endeavors and spent the last years of his life traveling. Before his death, he wrote a memoir of his murder trials, titled *The Traitor*. Thaw is buried in Allegheny Cemetery.

Olive Thomas

Born October 20, 1894—Charleroi, PA
Died September 10, 1920—Neuilly-sur-Seine, France

Whether it was murder, suicide, or accident, the death of Olive Thomas was the talk of tinsel town for decades and, more recently, the subject of a 2002 book which mourns the tragic death of this young silent film beauty.

Olive Duffy was born in Charleroi. She likely attended the local elementary school but whether or not she attended any post-secondary school, even the sketchiest of biographies affirm that she was an inquisitive girl, bold and forthright. At 17, she married a Kaufmann's store clerk, Bernard, and took his last name, Thomas.

While visiting an aunt in New York, she accepted an invitation to pose for the popular magazine artist, Harrison Fisher, who, like Charles Dana Gibson, was famous for depicting the quintessential beauty of the *American Girl*. Whether by favor or request, Fisher introduced Olive Thomas to Florenz Ziegfeld. She became widely popular on the Broadway stage.

A year after her divorce from her first husband, she met and married Jack Pickford, younger brother to Mary, the first million dollar contract star of silent Hollywood. "I had seen her often at the Pickford home, for she was engaged to Mary's brother, Jack," noted the screenwriter Frances Marion in her autobiography, *Off With Their Heads*. "Two innocent-looking children, they were the gayest, wildest brats who ever stirred the stardust on Broadway. Both were talented, but they were much more interested in playing the roulette

of life than in concentrating on their careers."

Pickford had long been signed to film contracts, playing Dicken's Pip and Twain's Sawyer in hugely successful features. Thomas signed with Triangle Pictures in 1917. Their shooting schedules often separated them for long months. And, in 1918, Jack entered the Navy. By 1920, the still young newlyweds sailed to Paris for a second honeymoon. Some say they were madly in love; others, that their marriage was on the rocks.

On the night of September 9, 1920, having checked into the Hotel Ritz in Paris, the young couple returned to their bedroom at 3:00 a.m. after hours of touring the local bistros. Olive ingested a handful of tablets of bichloride of mercury, prescribed for Jack's syphilis (that Olive, too, had certainly contracted). She died four days later of the violent poisoning. She was just 26.

More famous dead than alive, Olive Thomas was one the first film stars to have been mourned through mass media.

Jack married twice more, but died of his disease at 36.

Kenneth Thomson

Born January 7, 1899—Pittsburgh
Died January 26, 1967—Hollywood, CA

Born just blocks away from Mercy Hospital on Marion Street in the old Sixth Ward, Kenneth Thomson was a handsome, young actor who rose to some acclaim as an early contract player under Cecil B. DeMille. Although he was trained as a stage actor—in fact, most Hollywood performers in the 1920s

had earned their stripes on the Great White Way—he was one of few to actually leave a Broadway career expressly for work in the tiring, workaday heat of the sound stage. Yet, in 1926, the idea of a "sound"stage was not yet realized. Perhaps, the bewilderment of 1927's first talkie *The Jazz Singer* was inspiration.

A student of Carnegie Tech's School of Drama, Thomson was compelled to enlist in the Marine Corps, aided, as a 1933 *Pittsburgh Press* story relates, by Lillian Russell, a then prominent Pittsburgh lady whose late husband was Ambassador A.P. Moore. This is some indication that Thomson was raised in higher society, but in truth, his mother, widowed when Thomson was 7, found work as a concert manager and thus may have met the famous Russell through her work. In any case, Thomson served as a gunner on the *U.S.S. Frederick* before returning to Pittsburgh to pursue his degree at Carnegie Tech.

His career on Broadway was significant if only for having performed with Ethel Barrymore in *Declasse*. But as a young upstart, with experience few other returning soldiers could offer, Thomson was assured a theatrical career. While performing in Galsworthy's *The Rivals* on Broadway, he was spotted by DeMille and offered a year's contract in Hollywood. Thomson eagerly accepted.

December 31, 1942, left to right, Mr. and Mrs. James Cagney, Thomson, and Joan Blondell enjoy a star-studded New Year's Eve dinner.

From 1926 to 1937, he appeared in more than 65 films. As was the custom in the early studios, he was cast often for his type, that of the lascivious playboy, a role he first played in 1929's *The Broadway Melody*.

But what brought Thomson real credibility in the lore of Hollywood was not his solid acting career. In 1933, he and his wife Alden Gay, a more famous model than actress, convened a meeting in their living room under a cloak of absolute secrecy. That night—and no date was ever recorded—Thomson and 17 fellow screen actors, including Pittsburgh's own Lyle Talbot, formed the Screen Actor's Guild, ensuring certain protections for actors engaged in movies which the studios could not produce fast enough. Thomson served as the first Secretary of SAG, retiring in 1943.

Dick Thornburgh

Born July 16, 1932—Rosslyn Farms

Born to Charles Garland Thornburgh and Alice Sanborn Thornburgh, the youngest child of four, Thornburgh attended Rosslyn Farms Elementary, Carnegie High, Mercersburg Academy and Yale,  graduating in 1954 with a degree in Civil Engineering. By his own admission, he was not a great student, but an elective class in law prompted his interest in going to Pitt's Law School where he graduated in 1957. Married in 1955 to Ginny Hooten, a high school sweetheart, the two soon had three boys—John, David, and Peter —by the time Thornburgh had joined the fledgling law firm of Kirkpatrick & Lockhart.

In 1960, Ginny Hooten Thornburgh, while driving with her three children, was killed in a head-on collision. All three boys were injured, but Peter, the youngest son, suffered lasting brain damage. Three years later, Thornburgh married Ginny Judson, and together they had a son, Bill. Ginny, like her husband, has been a tireless advocate for the elderly and disabled.

In 1966, Thornburgh entered his first political race, running for U.S. Representative, and lost. In 1969, Nixon appointed him to serve as U.S. Attorney for Western PA. Five years later, Ford appointed him Assistant Attorney General. And, in 1978, Thornburgh ran for Governor of PA, fending off his opponent Mayor Pete Flaherty. No sooner had he taken office than the crisis of Three Mile Island— and the wholly coincidental release of *The China Syndrome*—placed Thornburgh in the national spotlight. As Governor, he steered a tight ship, creating a "rainy day" fund of $350 million in state surpluses. He also helped champion the State System of Higher Education with K. Leroy Irvis.

Upon concluding his two-term governorship, Thornburgh became Director of the John F. Kennedy School at Harvard. In 1988, Reagan appointed him Attorney General and George H.W. Bush retained him in the same office. But Thornburgh resigned in 1991 to run for the Senate seat vacated by the death of John Heinz, losing it to Harris Wofford. He then served two years as undersecretary at the UN, and is once again employed by Kirkpatrick & Lockhart, known today as K&L Gates, in Washington D.C.

Willie Thrower

Born March 20, 1930—New Kensington, PA
Died February 20, 2002—New Kensington, PA

"I felt like the Jackie Robinson of football," Willie Thrower said, but for the first African-American to quarterback an NFL team, it was only a brief, shining moment.

While Jack Roosevelt Robinson went on to have a celebrated, Hall-of-Fame career, Willie Lawrence Thrower played in two games and faded into obscurity.

Born in 1930 in New Kensington, Thrower played high school halfback, leading New Kensington to back-to-back WPIAL Class AA championships, 1946-47. Standing just 5'11" and a flyweight 182 pounds, Thrower was signed by Michigan State's legendary coach Clarence "Biggie" Munn. Seeing Thrower's rifle arm, Munn converted his young protégé into the Big Ten's first black quarterback—a valued member of the 1952 national championship team.

As an undersized, black, non-starter, Thrower was not taken in the 1953 NFL draft. However, George Halas signed Thrower to his Chicago Bears for $8,500. On October 18, when another Western Pennsylvania quarter-

back—George Blanda—came out of the game, Thrower was called off the bench. His first play made history.

Completing three of eight passes for just 27 yards, Thrower played in one more game before Halas gave him his unconditional release.

Not finding another NFL berth—it was 1954, and African-Americans had to wait 14 years for another African-American to quarterback a National Football League team, then two more for one to start—Thrower bounced around Canadian football for three years until a shoulder separation sidelined him in 1957. He was 27 years old and out of football for good.

Suffering from diabetes, 71-year-old Willie Thrower died of a heart attack in 2002. Four years later, in 2006, a statue in his memory was erected near Valley High.

Franklin Toker

Born April 29, 1944—Montreal, Canada

Although he calls himself "a dedicated nonspecialist," architectural historian Franklin Toker has written definitive studies of both Pittsburgh architecture and Pittsburgh's most famous building, Frank Lloyd Wright's masterpiece, Fallingwater.

Born in Montreal in 1944, Toker took fine arts degrees at McGill, Oberlin, and Harvard before coming to Pitt to teach art and architecture. Garnering worldwide recognition for his decade-long archaeological excavations below Florence's Santa Maria del Fiore Duomo, his award-winning 1971 *The Church of Notre-Dame in Montréal* introduced him as a significant writer and historian.

Turning his attention to Pittsburgh, Toker's next three books were benchmarks of scholarship and style. An exhaustive look at virtually every significant building in the city, Toker's award-winning 1986 *Pittsburgh: An Urban Portrait*, which has enjoyed multiple printings, is simply the region's one indispensable handbook for assessing Pittsburgh's built environment.

Toker spent 18 years researching America's most famous house, Fallingwater, including the collaboration of department store magnate Edgar Kaufmann and architect Frank Lloyd Wright. Exhaustive, exacting, brilliantly written, Toker's 2003 *Fallingwater Rising: Frank Lloyd Wright, E.J. Kaufmann, and America's Most Extraordinary House* has similarly enjoyed multiple printings—and has become the standard text in the field.

In 2008 the University of Pittsburgh Press will publish Toker's study of Pittsurgh's highly varied neighborhoods.

Regis Toomey

Born August 13, 1898—Pittsburgh
Died October 12, 1991—Woodland Hills, CA

The 1930's film *Shadow of the Law*, a Paramount-Publix production, may represent best the kind of odd influence Pittsburgh had on Hollywood. Not only did the film feature Regis Toomey, the young University of Pittsburgh graduate who stayed here even after his East Ender parents moved to Upland, CA, the crime film also starred William Powell and Natalie Moorhead.

A graduate of Peabody High School, the son of Mr. and Mrs. Francis X. Toomey, he was recommended by a Dean at Pitt to the C.A. Turner Company of Third Avenue, downtown, to accept a sales position in the mining supply industry. Although he never considered himself to be a successful salesman, he did know he had a great smile. But, once while visiting a girlfriend in New York, he determined to try his hand at theatre. After all, he had been a leading player in productions of the Cap & Gown Society, often playing women's roles because, as captain of the Pitt track team, his legs were lean and slender.

He got his first bit part in the chorus of *Rose Marie* on Broadway, married the dance captain, and followed the production to London. There he enjoyed a lengthy run in George M. Cohan's *Little Nelly Kelly*. Several years later, now stateside and touring California, he was cast in his first film, *Alibi*, in which he played, not the lead, but the pivotal character, Danny McGann, an undercover agent who dies a tragic death at the film's end.

That was the first of many. Noted *People* magazine in a 1991 obituary, "Toomey died so

© John Springer Collection/CORBIS

frequently in movies that he once joked he should be voted 'the mortician's man of the year' and began refusing roles in which he would be killed off."

In all, Toomey appeared in more than 200 films, and in his later TV career played Gene Barry's sidekick in *Burke's Law*, as well as Dr. Stuart on *Petticoat Junction*. Films of note include *The Big Sleep*, *Mighty Joe Young*, *The High & The Mighty*, *Guys and Dolls*, *Dakota Incident*, and *Voyage to the Bottom of the Sea*.

Marie Torre

Born June 17, 1924—Brooklyn, NY
Died January 3, 1997—Wilmington, DE

Before arriving in Pittsburgh in 1962, Marie Torre had attained national recognition by refusing to divulge a confidential news source to a Federal Court hearing a defamation suit brought by Judy Garland. An undisclosed source, a prominent CBS executive, had been quoted as telling Torre that Garland was likely balking at signing a TV contract because she feared she was too fat.

Just 34 and a seasoned reporter for the *New York Herald Tribune*, Torre served her 10-day sentence at the Hudson County Jail. She was the first reporter, male or female, to apply First Amendment rights to defend the freedom of the press.

© Getty Images

Married with two small children, she took a job as news reporter and co-anchor at KDKA-TV2 where she was immediately hailed as one of few women anchors "doing hard news" in local broadcast. Here she joined Bill Burns for the noon news and Al McDowell for the city's first half-hour evening news program. She also produced an afternoon interview program called *Contact*.

In 1977, widowed, she left for New York where she enjoyed successive contracts at WABC and WCBS. But she adopted Pittsburgh as her hometown, returning often to lecture here and, in 1991, to co-produce a series, *Pittsburgh Profiles*, with her daughter Roma Torre, on WQEX.

Born Marie Torregrossa in Brooklyn, she attended New York University. Her legend says she broke into journalism by pretending to interview the editor of the *Herald Tribune*.

Upon her death from lung cancer in 1997, by her own wishes, she requested to be interred in Pittsburgh at Jefferson Memorial Park in Pleasant Hills.

William Tracy

Born December 1, 1917—Pittsburgh
Died July 18, 1967—Hollywood, CA

One of the more popular character actors of his time, William Tracy was the chubby-cheeked, high-pitched delivery boy, the officious army sergeant, or the effervescent "gee whiz" neighbor from down the street. Although he had successful roles in several mainstream films

of the 1930s and 1940s, his greatest body of work is found in his squeaky portrayal of Terry Lee in the Saturday matinee serial, *Terry and the Pirates*.

Although born in Pittsburgh, his academic career is unknown until he went to New York to train at the Academy of Dramatic Arts. He was first cast as a replacement in the role of Misto Bottome in the stage comedy, *Brother Rat*, which ran on Broadway for 557 performances in 1937. Tracy was just 19. It was a role he would replay the next year on film, with newcomers Ronald Reagan and Jane Wyman. (Eddie Albert played the lead in both stage and film versions). Tracy's other significant movie roles included the delivery boy in *The Shop Around the Corner*, the younger Pat O'Brien in *Angels with Dirty Faces*, and the hillbilly son in *Tobacco Road*.

As Terry Lee in Milton Caniff's 1939 serialized film version of his popular comic strip, Tracy played the wide-eyed adventurer searching for the lost civilization of Wingpoo, the cache of gold buried by the evil Dragon Lady, or the mysterious Temple of the Dawn, all while fending off crazed gorillas, spear-throwing natives, or the treachery of his arch nemesis, Master Fang. The cliffhanger shorts, like many produced by Republic Pictures, were the inspiration for the *Indiana Jones* adventures of the 1980s and 1990s.

Tracy was popular, too, for reprising his role as Sergeant Dodo Doubleday in a series of wartime comedies like *Tanks A Million* or *Fall In*. Ultimately, like many teen stars whose opportunities and popularity fade, Tracy segued his diminishing film career into lesser character roles in early television, appearing often as Hotshot Charlie, in the 1953 TV version of *Terry and the Pirates*. Tracy died in obscurity at age 50.

Pie Traynor

Born November 11, 1899—Framingham, MA
Died March 16, 1972—Pittsburgh

The man many consider one of the all-time greatest third basemen, Pie Traynor played on two Pittsburgh World Series teams, 1925 and 1927, later leading the Pirates as the player-manager of good, but ultimately unsuccessful, Depression-era ballclubs.

As a fine-fielding third baseman, with excellent reflexes, quick hands, and a strong, accurate arm, Harold Joseph Traynor—nicknamed Pie for his favorite dessert—was born in 1899 in Framingham, MA. Scouted by the Pirates, Traynor was signed and brought up to Pittsburgh in 1920. Seeing limited action 1920-21, he became a regular in 1922, hitting .338 and leading the National League in triples. Playing full seasons through 1934, when he also accepted managerial duties, in 13 years (plus 1920-21 and limited appearances in 1935 and 1937), Traynor hit .320, batting .300 10 times, including a career-high .366 in 1930.

Taking over the managerial reins in 1934, Traynor guided the Pirates through 1939, including the heart-breaking 1938 season, when Chicago barely edged the Bucs for the National League pennant.

After retiring, Traynor worked as a Pirate scout and spring-training instructor; popular raconteur and after-dinner speaker; KQV sportscaster, 1945-66; and studio wrestling host with WIIC's Bill Cardille. A popular TV pitchman, Traynor's 1960s' spots for American Heating—with the oft-imitated tagline "Who can? Ameri-can!"—became part of Pittsburgh's cultural landscape.

Elected to the baseball Hall of Fame in 1948, Traynor died of emphysema in Shady-side Hospital, in 1972 at age 72. He is buried in Homewood Cemetery.

Agnes Sligh Turnbull

Born October 14, 1888—New Alexandria, PA
Died January 31, 1982—Livingston, NJ

"I feel that there are more good people in the world than bad," best-selling novelist Agnes Sligh Turnbull answered her critics who claimed her historical sagas were too sentimental, "and that it is just as realistic to write of the former as the latter—and much more satisfying."

Born Agnes Sligh in 1888 in New Alexandria, Westmoreland County, the daughter of an immigrant Scots father and Pennsylvania-Scots mother, she attended the village school, learning from Appleton's readers. Because New Alexandria did not have a high school, Sligh was sent to boarding school, then to Indiana State Teachers College (now Indiana University of Pennsylvania), graduating in 1910.

Teaching high school English until 1918, she left to marry James Turnbull—who, a month after their wedding, went to World War I France. After his return, by 1920 Agnes Sligh Turnbull was writing and publishing short stories. Moving to Maplewood, NJ, in 1922, for the next decade she was strictly a short-story writer, selling widely.

In 1936 Turnbull turned to novels and published the first of 15 books (10 novels, four juvenile novels, and one memoir). Writing about her roots, *The Rolling Years* centered around three generations of Scots who settled Westmoreland County—and who steadfastly

maintained their Presbyterian faith against the growing tide of secularism. Selling in the millions, Turnbull's other Pennsylvania-Scots novels include *Remember the End* (1938), *The Day Must Dawn* (1942), *The Gown of Glory* (1950), and *The Nightingale* (1960).

While her 1963 *The King's Orchard* discusses George Washington's landmark 1753 expedition to Western Pennsylvania, the main character is James O'Hara, the Irish émigré army officer and businessman who served at Fort Pitt, then went on to invest successfully in iron, glass, brewing, and real estate.

In 1982, two years after publishing her last novel, *The Two Bishops*, 93-year-old Agnes Sligh Turnbull died in Livingston, NJ.

Stanley Turrentine

Born April 5, 1934—Hill District
Died September 12, 2000—New York, NY

Stanley Turrentine was surrounded by significant musical mentors growing up in the Hill District; his father and mother both played instruments, his brothers Tommy and Marvin played, and his neighbors were among the most influential names in jazz, including Ray Brown, Art Blakey, Kenny Clarke, Joe Harris, and Ahmad Jamal. His youth was all about music. Whether it was the talk around the dinner table or listening to jazz on the radio, while his father frequently quizzed them, "who's playing third trumpet," the family were all jazz junkies.

Turrentine began first with the piano and, at 7, could sit down and play by ear what he had heard on the radio. He picked-up the saxophone around the age of 11 and quickly

© Associated Press

Tommy Turrentine

**Born April 22, 1928—Hill District
Died May 17, 1997—New York, NY**

He was the older brother and a very talented musician, but he always played in the shadow cast by the stagelights on his younger brother, Stanley.

Tommy was given his first trumpet by an aunt when he was in grade school His father, Tommy Turrentine, Sr., and younger brother Stanley both played saxophone. Tommy, Sr., worked construction to feed his family. His mother cleaned homes. Their youngest brother Marvin was killed in Vietnam.

Tommy joined local Musician's Union 471 when he was just 15 years old while attending Herron Hill Jr. High School. Legend has it that when musicians came to town, they had to pass the "Turrentine Test," administered by Tommy himself, to gain the respect of the locals. Just a year later he quit school and went on the road with Snookum Russell's Band, as had fellow Pittsburgh musician Ray Brown. At 18 he had joined Benny Carter's big band and was soon touring with George Hudson's orchestra (that included Ahmad Jamal).

Throughout the years, Tommy Turrentine played with a who's who of jazz greats including Dizzy Gillespie, Count Basie, Billy Eckstine, John Coltrane, Horace Parlan, Sonny Clark, and of course his brother, Stanley. In the late 1990s Tommy's health forced him into retirement and he died in May 1997, of cancer.

became proficient. His first band was called Four Bees and a Bop and he would play at local dances and an occasional basketball game. Later he played the Perry Bar with his older brother Tommy. Turrentine attended Herron Hill Jr. High School and Schenley High. At 16 years old he received a call from the musician's union (Local 471) telling him that blues guitarist Lowell Fulson and his band (also including pianist and vocalist Ray Charles) were in town looking for a sax player—and for more than just one gig.

Despite his mother's tearful pleas, Turrentine hit the road with the band. He returned home for a short spell before relocating to Cleveland with his brother. In 1953, he was hired to fill the shoes of John Coltrane departing Earl Bostic's band. But just as his music career was beginning to sprout wings, Turrentine was drafted. He served two years.

After his release from Army duty, he was called to fill in for Max Roach's band playing at the Crawford Grill. His tenure with Roach helped get Turrentine in front of bigger audiences, placing him in the forefront of the New York jazz scene. There he would meet two of his most legendary collaborators, his soon-to-be wife (and organist) Shirley Scott and popular jazz organist Jimmy Smith.

With Smith, Turrentine recorded several critical albums including *Back At The Chicken Shack, Midnight Special,* and *Prayer Meeting.* Now a staple on the respected Blue Note jazz label, Turrentine had a run of successful releases through the 1960s. After a move to Philadelphia and a divorce from his wife in 1971, Turrentine was signed to CTI and released his crossover hit "Sugar" and a string of commercially successful records. Though jazz purists questioned his motives, Turrentine's success in pop, R&B, and funk allowed him to reach a wider audience—and pay his bills.

Recording again on the Blue Note label in the 1980s and 1990s, Turrentine's soulful sound and bluesy approach are much revered by jazz aficionados worldwide.

Turrentine died of a stroke at the age of 66, and is buried in Allegheny Cemetery.

Pete Henderson, Tommy Turrentine, Chuck Austin and an unknown fourth trumpeter stand behind Will Smith on bongos in a photograph by Teenie Harris, date unknown.

Charles "Teenie" Harris Collection, Gift of Heinz Family Fund © 2008 Carnegie Museum of Art

Tuskegee Airmen

Even before the Japanese attack on Pearl Harbor, the Army sought every means of preparation before entering the European theaters of 1941. As an experiment to determine if blacks could pilot airplanes successfully, the Army Air Corps recruited academically qualified African-Americans from many of the more populated college campuses to create what would be called the 99th Pursuit Squadron, an all-black corps of cadet pilots, engineers, and mechanics. Better known today as the Tuskegee Airmen, this elite squad, eventually numbering as many as 1,500, included dozens of men from Pittsburgh.

BUY WAR BONDS

January 1945, singer Lena Horne poses in the cockpit with men from the Tuskegee Airbase, Tuskegee, AL.

Heavyweight champ Muhammad Ali and Chauncey Eskridge leave U.S. District Court, March 29, 1967.

Chauncey Eskridge

Born in 1918—Homewood
Died January 18, 1988—Chicago, IL

Raised on Tioga Street in Homewood, Chauncey Eskridge earned the rank of Lieutenant as a member of a secondary class of black pilots trained at Tuskegee. After his discharge, he graduated from the University of Chicago Law School and later became legal counsel to the Southern Christian Leadership Conference.

On April 4, 1968, he was awaiting Dr. Martin Luther King, Jr., outside his Memphis hotel room, when the hopes of a nation were slain by a single bullet. Just three years later, Eskridge was in the headlines, again, when he won an appeal before the U.S. Supreme Court, granting boxer Muhammad Ali the status of conscientious objector before the Selective Service Board.

Wendell Freeland

Born February 27, 1925—Baltimore, MD

Wendell Freeland first trained at Tuskegee Institute in 1942. Absent his sophomore year at Howard University, he was given flying instructions under the Civil Air Patrol program. Trying his hands in a Piper Cub, his instructor warned him that the pedals on the floor were not brakes, but rudders. Freeland remembers assuring his instructor he wouldn't know what they were because he "didn't even know how to drive a car."

Freeland, though accomplished as a pilot, navigator, and bombardier, never saw action. But he did make history. In 1945, when relocated with his squad to Freeman Field, IN, he entered the all-white officers club in defiance of the base commander's Jim Crow regulations. Refusing to sign orders that would acknowledge his disobedience, he and 68 fellow black officers were placed under arrest and individually tried for insubordination.

Freeland single-handedly typed every one of 69 letters formally posting their grievances. When all of their cases but one were acquitted, and the commanding officers deposed, Freeland realized victory. Many historians of the civil rights movement point to Freeman Field, not Rosa Park's Montgomery bus ride, as the first battle of the long-fought campaign.

Freeland, Baltimore-born, moved to Pittsburgh in 1950. A founder of Hill House, community activist, and esteemed attorney, Freeland considers the Freeman Field victory "one of the high points of my life."

William R. Thompson

Born January 26, 1916—Hill District
Died April 15, 2006—Chicago, IL

William R. Thompson was among the first of 28 officers commissioned under Lt. B. O. Davis, Jr., the famed black commander of the 99th.

Thompson grew up near Wylie Avenue, the son of a former railroad chef who founded the New Life Baking Company at the corner of Wylie Avenue and Junilla Street. His father eventually owned the Smith & Hahn Catering Company, too. As a widower—his wife having died two weeks after giving birth to William—he made certain his children were well attended.

Upon moving to Dithridge Street, young Thompson attended the Frick International School in Oakland. Inspired by Lindbergh's sensational 1927 transatlantic flight, Thompson made hundreds of model planes and pursued his singular interest at Schenley High School. Upon graduating, he sought enrollment in the Army Air Corps, but was rejected. He attended Hampton University, where he graduated in 1940, and again sought enlistment. His timing coincided with the newer interests of the Pentagon, and upon landing at the uncompleted airstrip near Tuskegee for training, was named one of the first officers of the 99th. Thompson later earned the rank of lieutenant and armament officer.

James Wiley

Born c. late 1920s
Died year unknown

The first of four pilots to fly under the newly formed emblem of the 99th, James Wiley successfully bombed the Island of Pantelleria between Libya and Sicily on June 2, 1943.

Although the 99th had been formed almost two years earlier, well-trained pilots like Wiley were consistently held back from active duty due to evident racism of the time. Yet Wiley saw action, was among the very first to risk his life as an elite pilot of the 99th, and became a local hero mobbed by his hometown.

Wiley grew up on the North Side and earned a scholarship to Pitt where he majored in physics. Many of his classmates were accepted into "classified" assignments working on the Manhattan Project, but Wiley was rejected. He attended Carnegie Tech for graduate work and there enrolled in civilian pilot training. After earning his wings as an exceptionally talented flyer, he was directed to enlist at Tuskegee.

In 1944, returning from his pioneering tour of duty, Wiley was honored by throngs of civilians at Kennard Field in the Hill District.

Above right, Wiley poses for photographer Teenie Harris upon his return to Pittsburgh after active duty with the 99th Pursuit Squadron. Below, Wiley is feted by crowds attending a ceremony at Kennard Field, circa 1944, also photographed by Harris.

Other known Western Pennsylvanian veterans of the several flying corps collectively honored as Tuskegee Airmen include:

James Addison	William Hunt
George Allen	Abram Jackson
Lee Archer	Allan Jackson
William Bailey	Frank Jackson, Jr.
Arthur Barnes, Jr.	Hampton Johnson
Brack M. Barr	Robert Johnson
George Bivins	William Johnston
George Bolden	Vernol Leaphart
Curtis Branch	Rafael Lee
Milton Brooks	Robert Lucas
Forest Bryant	Jake Lytle
Allen Carter	Andrew McCoy
Marcus Clarkson	Henry McCullough
Calvin Corbin	Luther McIlwain
John Cundiett	William Morgan
William Curtis	Maurice Moss
Claude C. Davis	Robert Nelson
William Dorsey, Sr.	Sylvester Parrish
Ellis Edwards	Roscoe Perkins, Jr.
William Edwards	Walter Person
Charles Ellison	Charles Proctor
Marshall Fields	John Rector
William Gilliam	Roosevelt Richardson
Robert M. Glass	Charles Ross
Cornelius P. Gould, Jr.	William Rucker
George Greenlee	Calvin Smith
Thomas Gunn	Charles Tate
Frank Hailstock	Elmer Taylor
Edward Harris	Frank Thomas
William Hicks	William Tyler
Mitchell Higginbotham	Charles Williams
Robert Higginbotham	Carl Woods, Jr.
Lynn Hooe	James H. Wright

Abraham Twerski

Born October 6, 1930—Milwaukee, WI

Coming to Pittsburgh in 1959 for a Western Psych residency, he met a woman who gave him pause. The daughter of a Christian clergyman, she had become an alcoholic prostitute. "I wondered what motivated her to make such a drastic change," Rabbi Dr. Abraham Twerski recalled. "I had never heard anything about alcoholism. They didn't teach it in medical school or psychiatry."

So he had to teach it to himself.

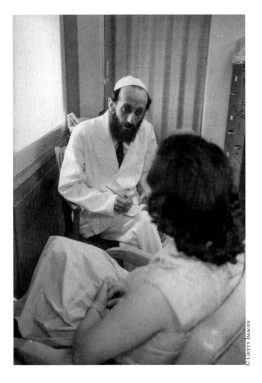

© GETTY IMAGES

Born in Milwaukee in 1930 to a dynastic Chassidic family, Abraham Joshua Twerski was chosen to succeed his father as the head of the Hornosteipler congregation, which had fled Soviet persecution in the 1920s. Watching people come to his father's study for counseling, the young man wanted to pursue that sort of rabbinate. But by the 1950s, he found that professional life had largely become performing religious rituals.

Preferring counseling, he pursued psychiatry at Marquette University medical school. After his residency, Dr. Twerski remained in Pittsburgh, serving as St. Francis Hospital's psychiatric director for some 20 years. When he came, he found programs for detox and in-hospital AA, but none to help people stay sober. Developing programs based on self-esteem, Dr. Twerski saw countless patients—and became internationally recognized as an authority on substance abuse.

Opening Gateway Rehabilitation Center in Center Township, Beaver County, since 1972, Dr. Twerski and his staff have helped some 45,000 people. Now expanded into some 20 regional centers, Gateway continues to draw people from all walks of life, and from as far away as Finland, Japan, and Brazil.

A tireless author, Dr. Twerski has produced some six dozen books, innumerable articles, and countless e-mail answers on Jewish and self-help topics. Teaming with the late Charles Schultz, the two combined *Peanuts* characters and messages of self-esteem.

Currently Gateway's medical director emeritus, he maintains residences in Monsey, NY, and Efrat, Israel, visiting Pittsburgh frequently.

Johnny Unitas

Born May 7, 1933—Pittsburgh
Died September 11, 2002—Baldwin, MD

He's the all-time greatest Steeler who never played a game for Pittsburgh.

A skinny, crew-cutted kid, picked in the ninth round of the 1955 draft, he was a preseason cut by the Steelers because they had too many quarterbacks. Married, a father, he was working construction and getting $6 a game playing for the semi-pro Bloomfield Rams, until, signed as a free agent by the Baltimore Colts, Johnny Unitas went on to become one of the greatest quarterbacks in NFL history.

John Constantine Unitas grew up on Mount Washington and played for St. Justin High. At 6'-1" and a mere 145 pounds when he went to play college ball at Louisville, in 1956 Unitas went to Baltimore as a back-up quarterback. Two years later, the man with the trademark crewcut, drooping shoulders, bandy legs, and black hightops had filled out to a robust 194 pounds—and led the team to a fabled league championship.

© ASSOCIATED PRESS

In a game still rated by many as the all-time best, the 1958 Colts-Giants championship was not only the first sudden-death overtime game in NFL history, it was also classic Unitas. Performing brilliantly under pressure, he drove the Colts down the field, throwing seven straight completions to set up a game-tying field goal. Then, in overtime, Unitas' 80-yard drive brought the title to Baltimore.

In 18 seasons, 1956-73, Unitas won another championship in 1959, Super Bowl V in 1970, played in 10 Pro Bowls, and was a three-time MVP. Elected to the Hall of Fame in 1979, he finished with 2,830 completions, 40,239 yards, and 290 touchdowns. Between 1956-60, he threw touchdown passes in 47 consecutive games, a record that is likely to remain unbroken.

While exercising at a physical therapy facility in Baldwin, Maryland, he died of a heart attack in 2002, age 69.

Robert L. Vann

Born August 27, 1879—Ahoskie, NC
Died October 24, 1940—Pittsburgh

In 25 years, Robert L. Vann propelled the *Pittsburgh Courier*, which began as a small-town weekly, into the nation's most influential African-American newspaper, publishing 14 editions and enjoying a circulation of more than 250,000.

Born Robert Lee Vann, he was the son of a cook, Lucy Peoples, herself the daughter of former slaves. As was the slave custom, she gave her child the name of the family for whom she worked.

A gifted child, Vann graduated valedictorian of his grammar school, worked his way through high school, then won a scholarship to Western University of Pennsylvania at Pittsburgh (as Pitt was known). Working in a boarding house, and as a night waiter on the B&O Railroad, Vann excelled at oratory, debate, and journalism. Editor of the student newspaper, the *Courant* (forerunner of the *Pitt News*), Vann graduated in 1906, entered Pitt law school, and graduated in 1909.

Opening law offices in 1910, Vann's rising profile in the city netted him a post as assistant city solicitor, 1917-31, then, after campaigning for Franklin Roosevelt, special assistant to the attorney general, 1933-40.

At the same time, an aspiring writer named Edwin Harleston began publishing the *Pittsburgh Courier* in 1907. Three years later, Harleston asked Vann about incorporation. Interested, Vann agreed to help, expanding his role to include financial and editorial duties. Within two years, he was the editor.

Not only reporting the news, Vann's *Courier* tirelessly championed African-American advancement. Fighting slum housing, discrimination, and Jim Crow laws, the *Courier* attracted some of the era's greatest African-American writers, including W.E.B. DuBois, Marcus Garvey, James Weldon Johnson, and Zora Neale Hurston, and published special editions in Texas, Louisiana, Ohio, and New York.

In 1940, 61-year-old Robert L. Vann died in Shadyside Hospital, and was buried in Homewood Cemetery. A Pittsburgh school was renamed in his memory.

Tom Vilsack

Born December 13, 1950—Pittsburgh

The first Democratic governor to be elected to the state of Iowa in 30 years (as well as the second Democrat to announce his intention for the 2008 U.S. presidency,) he began his life far east of the prairie corn fields.

Known as Kenneth for the first 5 months of his life, Tom Vilsack, the 40th governor of the Hawkeye state, was placed in a Pittsburgh Roman Catholic orphanage at birth. Bud and Dolly Vilsack, heirs to the Iron City Brewery, adopted the boy, raising him in an environment of privilege and service. Shady Side Academy offered him his first taste of political success when he was elected class vice president. Though he would not formally enter politics for another two decades, so obvious were his interests that he reportedly introduced himself to his future wife with the line, "Are you a Humphrey or Nixon supporter?" Whatever her answer, she said, "yes" to his proposal of marriage, and after completing their studies at Hamilton College, and he studying law in New York, the two moved to her home town of Mount Pleasant, IA. There, Vilsack worked as an attorney in his father-in-law's law firm.

Ten years later, following the murder of Mount Pleasant's mayor, Tom ran for and was

elected to the office. In 1992, he was elected to the state senate by a very narrow margin. Six years later, he earned another narrow electoral victory, this time as governor of Iowa, an office he held for two terms. As a middle-of-the-road Democrat, he led the war on methamphetamines and built a high-tech $50-million crime lab among his most notable achievements.

Though little-known beyond Iowa, in late November 2006, at a community potluck dinner in Mount Pleasant, Tom announced his candidacy for U.S. President. Among a field that included eight other candidates, Tom ended his campaign four months later, endorsing U.S. Senator Hillary Rodham Clinton. Though his run was brief, his extensive use of social media—viral video clips and personal blogs—helped take modern politics to a new level.

Today, Tom continues his ties to Pittsburgh as a member of the board of directors for Carnegie Learning, a publisher of math curricula for secondary school students.

Bobby Vinton

Born April 16, 1935—Canonsburg, PA

Back in 1964 as American music was screaming, "The British are coming, the British are coming," one song made its last stand at the top of the charts before being unceremoniously dethroned by The Fab Four—Bobby Vinton's "There I've Said It Again."

Bobby Vinton was born Stanley Robert Vintula, Jr., in Canonsburg, PA. Bobby's father, Stan Vinton, was a popular local big bandleader in the area. As an only child born into a musical family, Bobby was encouraged to pursue music and did so with vigor.

Graduating from Duquesne University with a degree in Music Composition, Bobby served in the U.S. Army, where he was inspired to write a couple of his biggest hits, "Mr. Lonely" and later "My Melody of Love." Upon

his discharge, he toured the country playing back-up music for teen idols like Fabian and Frankie Avalon. Guy Lombardo asked Bobby and his band to play on his *TV Talent Scouts* show, a forefather to today's *American Idol*. As a result of his appearance, he was signed to Epic Records as a bandleader. Their first two albums *Dancing at the Hop* and *Young Man with a Big Band* received lackluster responses. Epic was about to cut him loose when Vinton asked if he could try his hand at a little song called "Roses Are Red." It climbed to number one on the charts, eventually selling over four million copies. The album spawned another Vinton hit, "Mr. Lonely."

Between the years of 1962 and 1972, Vinton scored a total of 28 Top 40 songs, including one of his most memorable hits, "Blue Velvet." In the mid-1970s Epic terminated its recording contract with Vinton. Seven major record labels turned down Vinton's next new song—one he sang partially in Polish—before ABC Records took a chance. "My Melody of Love" was a multi-million selling single that made it to number one on the Adult Contemporary charts and was embraced by Polish Americans as their new national anthem.

Vinton hosted his own variety show for CBS from 1975 to 1978, starred in two John Wayne movies, *Big Jake* and *The Train Robbers*, and was honored with his own bronze star on the Hollywood Walk of Fame. Vinton also owned, operated, and performed in his own Blue Velvet Theatre in Branson, MO, until he sold it in 2002. Over the course of his illustrious career, Bobby Vinton, Pittsburgh's adopted "Polish Prince" has sold more than 75 million records.

The Vogues

It seemed like one minute Bill Burkette was running a lathe at Westinghouse Air Brake (WABCO), the next fending off screaming fans as a teen heart-throb and member of a national chart-topping band. One of the hottest bands of the 1960s was made up of Turtle Creek High School buddies Don Miller, Hugh Geyer, Chuck Blasko, and Bill Burkette, better known as The Vogues.

They formed a singing group called the Val-Aires back in 1960 and got the attention of local manager, producer and record label owner Elmer Willett. A couple of their early singles received airtime from local DJs, including Porky Chedwick, and they opened for some of the national acts passing through town, but nothing much happened outside of Pittsburgh. Then, the Val-Aires found a Petula Clark song called "You're The One" and went into Gateway Studios to lay down the vocal tracks. At the suggestion of a friend, the Val-Aires adopted a new name, which was a shortened version of their friend's McKeesport Club, The Vogue Terrace. In the autumn of 1965, the four friends from Turtle Creek hit it big with the number four song in the country. Within months The Vogues were back in the studio recording a follow-up song called "Five O'Clock World." That song also went to number four on the national charts. During the next several years The Vogues were in vogue, making appearances on shows like *American Bandstand*, *The Ed Sullivan Show*, *The Tonight Show*, and *The Red Skeleton Show*, fueled in large part by their million-selling 1968 song "Turn Around, Look At Me."

The whirlwind of fame was a bit much for the quartet from East Pittsburgh and slowly the band began to pull back and refocus on their family and friends. The musical landscape had also begun to change, and vocal groups weren't garnering the success that rock-influenced bands were.

After several management changes, the trademark name of The Vogues was sold to another party. Legal proceedings resulted and it was ruled that the original four members of The Vogues could only perform as "The Vogues" in 14 counties of Western Pennsylvania. The purchaser of the trademarked name The Vogues, continues to tour outside of this region. Chuck Blasko has lobbied Congress for better trademark laws to prevent groups from misrepresenting themselves as the original artists.

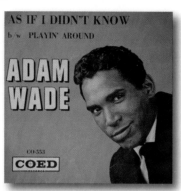

Adam Wade

Born March 17, 1937—East Liberty

East Liberty native Patrick Henry Wade, better known as Adam Wade, stormed the pop charts in the early 1960s. Among his biggest influences as a young aspiring star were Johnny Mathis and Nat King Cole. In fact, Adam's sound bore an uncanny resemblance to Mathis, so much so that it may have hindered his music career.

Wade attended Virginia State College where he worked briefly as a lab assistant with Dr. Jonas Salk's team. In his early 20s Wade headed to New York to find stardom. He was picked-up by CoEd Records, famous for its Doo Wop acts, and had a couple of moderate hits. He became a regular on the nightclub circuit, including the famous New York Copacabana. In 1961 Wade hit it big with three top 10 hits, "Take Good Care Of Her," "The Writing On The Wall," and "As If I Didn't Know." He left CoEd Records and signed with Epic but, with the exception of a mildly successful remake of Elvis Presley's "Crying In The Chapel," his chart-topping days were over.

Wade found work doing voiceovers, including Gizmo Man on the *Super Harlem Globetrotters* cartoon, as well as acting gigs and cameos in "blaxploitation" classics *Shaft*, *Come Back, Charleston Blue*, and *The Education of Sonny Carson*. Soaps and sitcoms soon folllowed, growing his impressive re-

sume, with appearances on *Adam 12, Police Woman, Sanford & Son, The Jeffersons, As The World Turns,* and *The Guiding Light* to name only a few. Then in 1975, Wade became the first African-American to host a national television game show, called *Musical Chairs*.

Today Wade is a speech and theater adjunct professor at Long Island University and Bloomfield College where he and his wife are very active in theatre.

Honus Wagner

Born February 24, 1874—Carnegie, PA
Died December 6, 1955—Pittsburgh

"Just throw the ball," rival manager John McGraw told his pitchers about Pirate short-stop Honus Wagner, "and duck!"

One of five initial players elected to baseball's Hall of Fame in 1936, from 1900-17 Wagner led the Pirates to 14 consecutive first-division finishes. A quiet man, 5-11 and 200 pounds, with bowed legs and broad shoulders, a barrel chest, long arms, and powerful hands, he was one of five sons of a Bavarian coal miner.

The consummate natural, with range, power, and speed, John Peter Wagner, nicknamed The Flying Dutchman, was born in 1874 in Mansfield (later Carnegie), discovered throwing rocks at railroad cards, and

WAGNER, PITTSBURG

whisked off to Louisville—where in 1897 he batted .344, his first of 17 straight .300 seasons.

In 1900, when the National League slimmed down from 12 to eight teams, Wagner came home to Pittsburgh, where the Bucs won four National League pennants and played in the first World Series in 1903. In 1909, playing in the new Forbes Field, the team won an all-time 110 games, taking the World Series from Ty Cobb's Detroit Tigers.

Playing 21 seasons (1897-17), Wagner won eight batting titles—a National League record tied 86 years later—the lifetime .327 hitter had 3,415 hits, a record which stood until Donora's Stan Musial broke it in 1962. It's still good for seventh all time.

Retired in 1917, he returned to the Pirates, 1933-52, as a coach, hitting instructor, and goodwill ambassador.

In 1955, just before Wagner's death, a life-sized statue atop a 12-foot pedestal was erected outside Forbes Field. Since that time, it has moved with the Pirates to Three Rivers Stadium and PNC Park.

The first player to have his signature branded into a Louisville Slugger bat, his rare 1909 baseball card has sold for a record $2.8 million.

Joe Walker

**Born February 20, 1921—Washington, PA
Died June 8, 1966—Edwards, CA**

At Mach 3, the spoken word cannot be understood. For Joe Walker, the first human to experience supersonic speed and survive, the meaning was clear enough: man was no longer fettered to Earth's bonds. It was a fact he worked to underscore, additionally becoming the first person to pass the 50-mile altitude—the demarcation to outer space. Twice. The year was 1963, and these "space-plane" flights remained singular events until repeated in 2004 by SpaceShipOne.

Joe was a farm boy. Typical of his time, he performed his chores early in the morning on the family spread in Washington before taking up his studies in a one-room schoolhouse a few miles away. Though he won a scholarship to Washington and Jefferson College in the fall of 1938, he was not marked for much special, save for a career off the farm. During his senior year, he enrolled in the civilian pilot training program, a proving and training ground for young pilots gearing up to enter

World War II. He would never make it, he was told. His instructors deemed him too cautious and by-the-book. Joe decided to rewrite the story, however, taking his aviation cadet examination and earning the highest score of any cadet in the Pittsburgh region.

Indeed, he did go to war, flying 58 reconnaissance missions and taking the Distinguished Flying Cross and the Air Medal with seven oak leaf clusters in the process.

© BETTMANN/CORBIS

Returning stateside, he continued to prove his mettle. He joined the National Advisory Committee for Aeronautics' Aircraft Engine Research Laboratory in Cleveland as a physicist, becoming an experimental test pilot known for pushing the physical barriers of space and sound. In 1951, he transferred to the High-Speed Flight Research Station in Edwards, California, as a research pilot and chief test pilot for the X-15, the plane that took him higher and faster than any human before him.

In 1966, Joe was killed in a mid-air collision during a publicity photo shoot. Thirty-nine years later he received his astronaut's wings.

William Coventry Wall

**Born in 1810—Oxford, England
Died in 1886—Pittsburgh, PA**

When he emigrated from England, age 11, William Coventry Wall could scarcely have imagined that he would begin a family fine art dynasty that would carry on for more than a century.

The son of William Wall, a painter and sculptor, William Coventry Wall was born in 1810, in Oxford, England. In 1821, the family came to the United States, first to Mount Pleasant, PA, then in 1835 to Allegheny, where Wall's father worked as a carver, stone cutter, and gilder.

Interested in art from an early age, in his 20s Wall opened an art supply store to help support his increasing interest in art. But it

would be another decade before Wall got his big break. After Pittsburgh's 1845 Great Fire, Wall made lithographs of two scenes he had made of the city. When they sold well, Wall's reputation was assured.

Although never formally trained, Wall became a skilled landscape painter, developing a pleasant, highly detailed style that best depicted Western Pennsylvania's natural beauty and frontier lifestyle.

While his myriad paintings alone would have made Wall a memorable Pittsburgher, he is also notable for being part of the region's largest, and longest-lived, artistic families. Wall's American-born brother Alfred (1825-96), and Alfred's son A. Bryan (1861-1935), were also landscape artists of note. A portrait painter as well, Alfred Wall became not only a highly respected consultant to Pittsburgh's emerging art collectors, but also one of the initial trustees of Carnegie Institute. In turn, A. Bryan Wall not only took his father's place as a Carnegie Trustee, he was also something of a prodigy, exhibiting his work at the National Academy of Design at age 18. Skilled at still life as well as portraiture, A. Bryan Wall is largely remembered for his many pastoral renderings of sheep.

William Coventry Wall died in Pittsburgh in 1886 and was buried in Allegheny Cemetery.

W.C. WALL, *Winter Landscape*, COURTESY OF OWNER

Joseph Wambaugh

Born January 22, 1937—East Pittsburgh, PA

Joe Wambaugh was just another hard-bitten cop with a dream—until *The New Centurions*, his first fictionalized account of L.A.'s Finest, brought him instant success, and changed police writing forever.

Born Joseph Aloysius Wambaugh, Jr., in East Pittsburgh in 1937, he was the son of a police officer who enlisted in the marines right out of high school. After serving a three-year hitch, 1954-57, Wambaugh headed west, earning a Chaffey College associate's degree before joining the Los Angeles Police Department in 1960.

Rising through the ranks from patrolman to detective sergeant in his 14-year tenure, Wambaugh also attended California State University, Los Angeles, earning both Bachelor's and Master's degrees.

He also wrote tough, real-life accounts of police officers and police work. When *The New Centurions* appeared in 1971, to virtually universal praise, the *National Review* called it "incomparably the best revelation of the lives and souls of policemen ever written."

Still a working police officer, Wambaugh followed immediately with three more best-sellers, *The Blue Knight* (1972), *The Onion Field* (1973), and *The Choirboys* (1975). *The Onion Field*, Wambaugh's first non-fiction book, told the story of two police officers' kidnappings, one's execution, and the second's lifelong guilt; it won numerous awards.

Turning to writing full-time, Wambaugh produced a significant body of work, including nine other novels and four non-fiction accounts of murders in England and Philadelphia, serial arson, and patrolling the Mexican border.

As creator of *Police Story*, the landmark television show showing real-life police problems, Wambaugh paved the way for such later dramas as *Hill Street Blues* and *NYPD Blue*.

In addition, Wambaugh's screen adaptations have hosted a Hollywood who's who, including James Garner (*The Glitter Dome*), William Holden (*The Blue Knight*), Stacey Keach and George C. Scott (*The New Centurions*), and James Woods (*The Onion Field*).

Joseph Wambaugh lives and works in Los Angeles.

Paul and Lloyd Waner

Paul: Born April 16, 1903—Harrah, OK
Died August 29, 1965—Sarasota, FL

Lloyd: Born March 16, 1906—Harrah, OK
Died July 22, 1982—Oklahoma City, OK

They were 150-pound Oklahoma farm boys, earning nicknames Big Poison and Little Poison, becoming the only playing brothers to be inducted into baseball's Hall of Fame.

Growing up in Harrah, Oklahoma, Paul and Lloyd Waner weren't big, but farmwork made them strong. Encouraged by their father, a ballplayer who claimed his farm during the Oklahoma land rush, they developed incredibly quick wrists by swinging at corncobs.

Older brother Paul Glee Waner, born in 1903, came to Pittsburgh in 1926. Hitting .336 as a rookie, he topped the National League the next year, hitting .380, winning the first of three batting titles and a Most Valuable Player award.

That year, 1927, the Pirates brought up younger brother Lloyd James Waner, born 1906, to play centerfield, next to Paul in right. While Paul hit more, and with more authority, Lloyd slapped the ball around with the best of them, hitting .355, collecting 223 hits his rookie year, including 198 singles, still a record.

That was a good year when the Waners and their Pirates went to the World Series. Facing the Yankees, while the Pirates lost in four games, the Waners actually out-hit Babe Ruth and Lou Gehrig.

"Pretty easy, this baseball," Lloyd said. "We'll be back in the World Series next year."

It was not to be. They played through 1945, but never saw another Fall Classic.

Overall, Paul hit over .300 14 times, finishing with a .333 lifetime average and 3,152 hits, good for a 1952 Hall of Fame berth. Lloyd's .316 lifetime average and 2,459 hits were good enough for 1967 enshrinement. Together, they hold the career record for hits by brothers, 5,611.

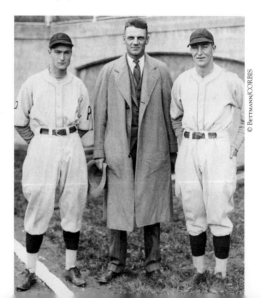

Hugh Ward

Born in year unknown
Died in year unknown

History is never linear; never straight up, across, or diagonal. In fact it took something of a circuitous route when Hugh Ward of Hazelwood first appeared in the mid-ways of Pennsylvania carnivals during the 1920s, encouraging enterprising folk to play a little something he called "Bingo." Ward maintained he first saw the game in action when visiting the Toronto Exposition in 1916 and witnessed several Canadian soldiers playing a game of chance they inexplicably called "Horsey-horsey." Using beans to mark their cards, lucky winners would shout out "Beano!" Whether due a linguistic corruption or a sensibility rarely seen on the boardwalk, "beano" became "bingo," and the rest became schoolroom fodder and senior center history.

It almost didn't happen.

Ward's version of the game was based on 75 number combinations, reduced from the Canadian version of 109. He developed an official rulebook, some marketing equipment, and hit the road in 1924, taking it nationwide and enjoying moderate success. He also attracted a fair number of folk who likewise laid claim to developing the game. Among them an Edwin S. Lowe, whom history gives some tolerance to his insistence that the game got its start after he played a round of Beano in Georgia—in 1929—a full five years after Ward took to the road with his own version, as his loyalists like to point out.

For the record, however, the courts weren't quite so loyal to Ward. In 1933, one of his rivals, a Massachusetts manufacturer who claimed *he* had developed the game Beano and now expected Bingo residuals, decided to press the matter before a judge. He won his suit, but in a bittersweet judgment, his victory was limited to the exclusive right to all things Beano.

Ward meanwhile continued Bingo success unchallenged, spawning a world that has brought "quickies" and "speed" among other variations of the game to thousands of charity and religious organizations. Along the way, it has earned more than 60 million worldwide followers, who wager more than $10 billion a year.

1927, former Pittsburgh Pirates player Max Carey, center, then of Brooklyn, with the Waner brothers, Lloyd, left, and Paul, right

Andy Warhol

**Born August 6, 1928—Oakland
Died February 22, 1987—New York, NY**

In the end, he was famous for far more than his predicted 15 minutes, creating a multimedia empire and inspiring his own signature museum that have far outlasted him.

Elevating the banal, obsessed with fame, Andy Warhol defined 1960s American Pop Art—and caused a revolution in how people both appreciate and evaluate art.

The man who defined himself as "a deeply superficial person" was born Andrew Warhola in Pittsburgh, 1928. The son of Slovakian immigrants, Warhol lived in Oakland, on Dawson Street, and attended St. John Byzantine Catholic Church.

Sickly as well as noticeably talented as a child, Warhol drew in bed—and collected photos of movie stars. Graduating Schenley High in 1945, and Carnegie Tech in 1949 with a Bachelor of Fine Arts degree, Warhol moved to New York City, where he shared an eighth-floor St. Mark's Place walk-up apartment with fellow Tech grad Philip Pearlstein. Pursuing a career in commercial art, Warhol quickly became a successful magazine illustrator for *Vogue* and *Harper's Bazaar*, among others. One specialty: ink drawings of I. Miller shoes, which Warhol exhibited as early as 1952. By 1956, his work had appeared in New York City's Museum of Modern Art.

Frustrated by the disconnect between his commercial work and artistic aspirations, in the early 1960s Warhol merged the two. Focusing on the superficial in popular culture, Warhol began to make paintings and sculptures of such famous American products as Campbell's Soup cans, Brillo boxes, and Coca-Cola bottles—and silkscreens of such pop icons as Marilyn Monroe and Elvis Presley, Jackie Kennedy, and Troy Donahue.

Achieving immediate notoriety for his efforts, Warhol quickly branched out into other arts, including film, music, and publishing.

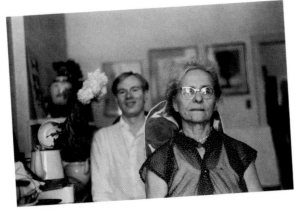

Surrounding himself with artists and collaborators, his Manhattan studio, which he called The Factory, mass-produced his art works. Simultaneously, from 1963-68 Warhol's Factory produced some five dozen films. Featuring his so-called Superstars, such films as *Chelsea Girls* and *Poor Little Rich Girl* presented Edie Sedgwick, Viva, Nico, Billy Name, Baby Jane Holzer, and Ultra Violet, among many others.

In addition, Warhol published various works of literature, produced the rock band The Velvet Underground (featuring Lou Reed), and created *Interview* magazine.

Warhol's life took a bizarre turn in 1968 when a marginal Factory figure shot and seriously wounded him. The freewheeling Factory days were effectively over.

In the 1970s, Warhol became, if anything, even more entrepreneurial, largely focusing on celebrity portraits—Mick Jagger, for example. By the 1980s, Warhol was collaborating with established and emerging artists, including Keith Haring and Jean-Michel Basquiat.

In 1987, after routine gallbladder surgery in New York City, the 58-year-old Warhol died of a sudden heart attack. After his funeral at the Holy Ghost Byzantine Catholic Church, on Pittsburgh's North Side, Warhol was buried next to his parents in Bethel Park's St. John the Baptist Byzantine Catholic Cemetery.

Seven years later, in 1994, the Andy Warhol Museum opened on the North Side. The world's largest art museum dedicated to a single artist, the Warhol collection includes more than 12,000 works, including all of his films, videos, and extensive archives.

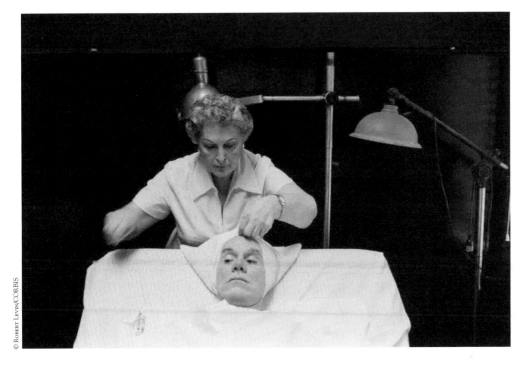

Above, Tom Sokolowski, director of the Andy Warhol Museum, passes by a self-portrait of Warhol in the Croatian capital Zagreb's Art Pavilion on Tuesday, September 11, 2001.

Center, Duane Michals' *Andy Warhol and his mother Julia Warhola,* 1958, gelatin silver print, H: 11 x W: 14 in., Carnegie Museum of Art, Gift of the Henry L. Hillman Fund

The Warner Bros.:
Harry, Albert, Sam, and Jack

Harry: Born December 12, 1881—Poland
Died July 25, 1958—Hollywood, CA

Albert: Born July 23, 1883—Poland
Died November 26, 1967—Miami, FL

Sam: Born August 10, 1887—Baltimore, MD
Died October 5, 1927—near Los Angeles, CA

Jack: Born August 2, 1892—London, ON
Died September 9, 1978—Hollywood, CA

Long before Harry Davis and John P. Harris opened their Nickelodeon on Smithfield Street, motion pictures were staple entertainment in beer halls and traveling tent shows. Thomas Edison had made it all possible by inventing the kinetograph camera and then the kinetoscope, first a magnified peepshow of flipping photographs and, later, an electric lamp capable of projecting moving images from a reel of film.

Around 1902, Sam Warner, the second youngest child of Ben and Pearl Eichelbaum's eight children—the eldest two of whom, Harry and Albert, immigrated from Krasnostow, Poland, to Youngstown, Ohio—purchased an Edison Kinetoscope Model "B" projector with his family's savings of $1,000. Along with baby brother Jack, the four Warner brothers toured Western Pennsylvania and exhibited

silent shorts wherever they could draw a paying crowd. They had to travel far and wide—their inventory of films was small. Back in 1902, itinerant exhibitors had to purchase their films, mainly from "distribution exchanges," all based either in New York, Paris, or Berlin.

But in 1904, the four Warner brothers founded the Duquesne Amusement & Supply Company to distribute regionally-licensed films in Baltimore, Pittsburgh, Norfolk and Atlanta. The successful business, of which very little is known, may have employed Lewis J. Selznick, father of David and Myron, or Harry M. Berman, father of Pandro S., among others whose careers later coalesced to create the major studios of Hollywood. (So specialized

was the film distribution business from 1904 to 1906, it would be implausible these men did not know each other professionally—even if as competitors.)

In 1907, the brothers Warner began to think bigger. Adjacent to Cascade Park, New

Castle's splendid trolley park, they opened the 99-seat Cascade Theatre to exhibit the very same films they licensed to other exhibitors—like Davis and Harris. The Warner Brothers had long known that the film industry possessed more than one profit center.

Two years later, however, Edison—who, too, understood the vertical opportunities his inventions had created—imposed patent protections on most all motion film technology and, thus, on film distributors, too, effectively shutting down the Duquesne Amusement Company overnight.

The four Warner brothers began to make their own films. The first two, forgotten by time, were quiet flops. Determined to recapture the business lost to Edison, Harry sent his younger brothers to California to make films outside of Edison's reach, while he and Albert would stay in the east to distribute them in uncontested markets.

Although they found success idealizing Broadway's *Gold Diggers,* as well as the heroic actions of a German Shepherd by the name of Rin Tin Tin, Warner Bros. Studios never proved truly successful until 1927. Sam, the same son who first purchased the used kinetoscope, oversaw the development of a new "Vitaphone" technology contributed by Western Electric and the Bell Telephone Company. On October 6, in New York's Warner Theatre, *The Jazz Singer* premiered and forever changed the American film industry.

Sadly, less than 24 hours before, Sam died of a cerebral hemorrhage. Brother Jack became the legendary studio boss, while brothers Harry and Albert, the consummate operators.

Above, a billboard on the side of Warners' Theatre in New York advertises *The Jazz Singer,* the first "talkie," in 1927.

Center, November 10, 1969, Jack Warner, center, at his retirement party with Warner Bros.' chief executive officer, Ted Ashley, left, and Jack Valenti, President of the Motion Picture Association of America

May 11, 1965. Jack Warner, Harry Warner, and Albert Warner began their movie careers in 1902 in their hometown, New Castle, PA, by purchasing a projector and renting a vacant store to open their first theater.

Pop Warner

Born April 5, 1871—Springville, NY
Died September 7, 1954—Palo Alto, CA

"Pro-gram!" the hawkers bellowed. "Program here! Can't tell the players without a program!"

Legend has it the first time that plaintive cry was heard was at Forbes Field, the Pitt Panthers' home prior to Pitt Stadium. Why? Among his many innovations, Pitt head football coach Pop Warner had sewed numbers on his players' jerseys.

Warner, who coached at Pitt for nine extraordinary seasons, 1915-23, left a name synonymous with fair play, visionary change, and youth football.

Born Glenn Scobey Warner in 1871 in Springville, New York, he acquired his lifelong nickname as a 21-year-old Cornell guard. Older than his teammates, 1892-94, the team captain was called Pop—and it stuck.

After graduation, and a brief Buffalo law practice, in 1895 Warner was hired by the University of Georgia as head football coach. Receiving the princely sum of $34/week, the 24-year-old Warner went on to coach for 44 years, amass 337 wins, and re-cast football.

After coaching at Georgia, Iowa State, Cornell, and Carlisle, in 1915 Warner moved to the University of Pittsburgh, where he coached the Panthers to 33 straight victories, including three national championships, 1915-16-18. His aggregate record: 60-12-4.

Moving to Stanford in 1924, Warner finished his career at Temple in 1938. While in

Philadelphia, an existing football program was re-named—and re-cast—in his honor. Pop Warner football still requires students to earn good grades in order to play.

During his four decades, Warner wrought incalculable change to football, including the screen pass, single- and double-wing formations, shoulder and thigh pads, huddles, crouched blocking, and many others.

Inducted into the College Football Hall of Fame in 1951, three years later Warner underwent surgery for removal of a tumor. Never fully recovering, he died in Palo Alto in 1954 at age 83. In 1997, Pop Warner was honored with a U.S. postage stamp.

Jeff "Tain" Watts

Born January 20, 1960—Hill District

Jeff "Tain" Watts is one of the leading drummers in contemporary jazz as well as one of the most in-demand drummers in the world.

Watts isn't the typical story of a child prodigy who picks up drum sticks at 9 months and is soloing at age 3. It wasn't until the fourth grade that Watts beat on his first snare drum and that was only after they told him his teeth weren't right to play trumpet. He played in the East Allegheny High School band for a few years but didn't focus on jazz until his brothers turned him on to artists like Herbie Hancock, The Mahavishnu Orchestra, and Chick Corea's *Return To Forever*. But even then, Watt's focus was predominantly classical percussion.

At Duquesne University he played tympani and was interested more in opera and musicals, preparing to be a symphonic percussionist. Watts transferred to Berklee School of Music in Boston and quickly fell in with a prodigious crowd of young musicians, including Branford Marsalis, Kevin Eubanks, and Marvin "Smitty" Smith.

Between 1981 and 1989 Watts was a member in bands led by Wynton Marsalis, George Benson, Harry Connick, Jr., McCoy Tyner, and Branford Marsalis. In fact, Watts was known as *the* drummer for brothers Wynton and Branford Marsalis, two of the most prominent figures in jazz. For several years Watts was based on the West Coast and was the drummer for *the Tonight Show* band when Branford became its director. Spike Lee came calling and cast Watts in the role of Rhythm Jones for his film *Mo Better Blues*. In 1995 he joined bop saxophonist Kenny Garrett's band and has since played with everyone from Michael Brecker and B.B. King to Jack McDuff and Sonny Rollins. The saying "you are the company you keep" is especially fitting for Watts, who has been asked to drum for some of the best musicians in jazz.

Watts has been a part of five Grammy® Award-winning recordings as a sideman and has received critical acclaim for his releases as a leader, too.

Frederick Way, Jr.

Born February 17, 1901—Sewickley, PA
Died October 3, 1992—Sewickley, PA

Shades of Huck Finn and Mark Twain's *Life on the Mississippi*, shades of Annie Dillard's father hightailing it down the Ohio and Mississippi to New Orleans, Sewickley's Fred Way was an adventurer, author, and authentic river boat captain.

Born Frederick Way, Jr., in 1901 into what was then a century-old Sewickley river family (the first Way house dates from 1810; the second from 1838), he was a teenaged mud clerk (unskilled hand), then a mate, master, and, finally, at age 22 in 1923, a licensed pilot. Two years later, Way had his own wood-hulled river packet, the vintage 1880s *Betsy Ann*, which he piloted between Pittsburgh and Cincinnati.

In 1933, Way turned his life on the Ohio into his first of nine successful books, *The Log of the Betsy Ann*. Nine years later, in 1942, he published his first of four directories of steamboats, towboats, and packets, along with *Pilotin' Comes Natural* (1943).

In 1948, Way embarked on his greatest river adventure, captaining the flat-bottomed, stern-wheeling *Delta Queen* from San Francisco, down the Pacific coast, through the Panama Canal, across the Gulf of Mexico, finally up the Mississippi and Ohio Rivers to Neville Island's Dravo shipyards, where it received a thorough retrofit. Way's 1951 *The Saga of the Delta Queen* aptly re-tells the tale.

Off and on the rivers, Way was an active writer, photo collector, and supporter of inland waterways; his contributions to such publications as the *Inland River Record* and *S&D Reflector* added greatly to river lore. As a river activist, his successful 1939 effort to form the Sons and Daughters of Pioneer Rivermen led in turn to the creation of Marietta's Ohio River Museum.

A member of the National Rivers Hall of Fame, 91-year-old Fred Way died in Sewickley in 1992. In his memory, the *Delta Queen* sounds its whistle every time it passes his home.

Fritz Weaver

Born January 19, 1926—Schenley Farms

Born the first son of John Weaver on Bryn Mawr Terrace in Schenley Farms, Francis William Weaver attended the Falk School until 1939, and Peabody High School, graduating in 1943. His father was a one-time radio host and a leader of the Georgist Movement, advocating a single property tax in lieu of all others. (The Henry George Foundation of America was established in Pittsburgh in 1926 by many of the then-local progressive Democrats of Allegheny County).

Upon graduating from Peabody at the outset of World War II, Weaver declared himself a conscientious objector and entered the Civilian Public Service, spending five years in service to his country at the Big Flats, New York, CPS Camp.

Despite his father's public persona, Fritz demonstrated no interest in speech, theatre or the performing arts, except for an early inkling to write plays. As he stated in a 1970 *Post-Gazette* interview, "I wrote two bad plays." While attending the University of Chicago, however, he decided he might write better plays if he knew what actors must understand about building a character, and there, he caught the acting bug.

In 1955 Weaver made his debut on Broadway in *The Chalk Garden*, produced by Irene Mayer Selznick, winning the Theater World Award as well as a Tony® nomination for best featured actor. His career was launched, and he appeared in dozens of early dramatic TV shows like *Studio One*, *Playhouse 90,* and the *United States Steel Hour*, while also playing leads in successive Broadway productions. In 1964, he was cast in his first film, Sidney Lumet's doomsday nail-biter, *Fail-Safe*. Meanwhile, Weaver was also seen in such regular TV adventures as *Combat!*, *Rawhide*, *The FBI*, *Gunsmoke,* and *Mission Impossible*. His next big lead on Broadway had him in a deerstalker cap, smoking a meerschaum in *Baker Street*, a musical comedy that ran the full season in 1965. Throughout the 1960s, Weaver was a constant guest artist seemingly appearing in at least one episode of every successful detective show on the tube.

In 1970, he won the Tony for best actor in Robert Marasco's *Child Play*. And, on television, he appeared in countless more series like *Cannon*, *Quincy M.E.*, *The Streets of San Francisco,* and *Hawaii 5-0*.

In 1982, he returned to Pittsburgh to shoot George Romero's *Creepshow*, playing the part of a catatonic professor who has escaped the clutches of a once-caged monster in the school laboratory.

Living in California, with two grown children, Lydia and Anthony, Weaver can be heard often as the voice of *The History Channel*. His older sister Mary, a theatrical set designer who graduated from Carnegie Tech, married Jack Dodson.

April 19, 1970, Cleavon Little, Lauren Bacall, Tammy Grimes, and Weaver pose for winning unrelated Tony© Awards at the Mark Hollinger Theater, New York.

Cyril Wecht

Born March 29, 1931—Bobtown, PA

As a boy, growing up in the Hill District, Cyril Wecht indulged in an odd pastime. Lured by what he could not say, he enjoyed sneaking past distracted sentries at the city morgue to view bodies as they waited for attention. To this day, the fascination with death remains—now parlayed into a career of more than four decades as a world-renowned medical-legal expert, forensic pathologist—and occasional television drama inspiration.

Indeed, Wecht has made a living out of meeting the dead. Long after they've left the land of the living, he's befriended them, studied them, and delivered conclusions regarding their demises at turns unsettling, comforting, and sometimes downright challenging.

Members of the Warren Commission might have slept a little sounder had Wecht not disputed their single-magic-bullet theory about President John F. Kennedy's assassina-

tion. Likewise, Elvis Presley might be remembered to this day as a clean-living entertainer with an improbable, premature death.

Cable viewers globally recognize him for his running commentary of the O.J. Simpson murder trial and for his firm insistence that Jon Benet Ramsey's death, though tragic and criminal, was largely accidental. Even those who aren't familiar with his distinctive features will likely have heard of his television alter ego: Jack Klugman's *Quincy, M.E.*, a long-running drama purportedly based on Wecht's career.

"Murder, accidents, suicide, people killing, people being killed … My God, there's nothing that comes near it on a steady basis," the *Pittsburgh Post-Gazette* has quoted him. And nothing that comes close to Wecht, either.

With a fascinating personality that embraces both the good dirty joke and the tumbling grandchild, Wecht has no difficulty courting and flaunting controversy. His youth as a minority Jew in Uptown gave him an intolerance for discrimination of any sort, and his determination to live a life marked by overachievement provided him the means to be able to do something about it.

In addition to his Pittsburgh-based career in high-profile forensics, Wecht has tried his hands in politics, too, winning the office of Allegheny County Medical Examiner from 1970 to 1980 and again from 1996 to 2006, and losing his quest to be Allegheny County's first County Executive. In 2000, he also established the Cyril H. Wecht Institute of Forensic Science and Law, which offers a graduate degree and professional certificate programs in forensic science.

George Westinghouse

Born October 15, 1846—Central Bridge, NY
Died March 12, 1914—New York, NY

To some, George Westinghouse was America's greatest industrialist, to others a prolific inventor with 361 patents, while others revere him as a leading engineer. He was also a successful businessman who started 60 companies, and his name continues to grace appliances worldwide.

Westinghouse saw the potential in ideas. One was using air to stop a train, and so when he was just 23 years old, in 1869, the Westinghouse Air Brake Company was born. Westinghouse also saw potential in electricity and formed the Westinghouse Electric Company two years later. A rivalry heated up with Thomas Edison—the "Battle of the Currents"—with Westinghouse favoring alternating current, Edison direct current. The 10-year scuffle ended in 1895 when Niagara Falls was harnessed by three 5,000-horsepower Westinghouse alternating current generators. After this success, the world was electrified with Westinghouse's A/C.

When natural gas was discovered in Murrysville, PA, Westinghouse thought it might make a good fuel for his plants. He even drilled a well in the back yard of his home, Solitude, in Homewood, where he struck a huge vein of gas. He created a steam heater for railroad passenger cars and invented the automobile air spring, known today as a car's shock absorber.

© Bettmann/CORBIS

There was never a strike at a Westinghouse company while he was in control (this during a heightened period of strife between "labor" and "capital"). In fact, Westinghouse was the first major employer in the country to grant workers a "half holiday" on Saturdays. Doctors and nurses provided immediate care for workers if they were injured at the plant, and there was a cafeteria for workers. Homes built by Westinghouse were sold, not rented, to the workers with payments deducted on a monthly basis from their checks. These houses were insured so wives and children had a home if the family breadwinner was killed or passed away.

Upon his 1914 death, Westinghouse's pall bearers were eight of his oldest workers, honoring a great man and a great innovator.

A Civil War veteran, he was buried in Arlington National Cemetery.

Randy White

Born January 15, 1953—Pittsburgh

Quick, tough, smart, durable, and hardworking, Dallas Cowboy ironman Randy White played All Pro football for 209 regular-season games, missing just one game in 14 years.

Nicknamed Manster, for half-man, half-monster, Randy Lee White was born in Pittsburgh in 1953. Playing scholastic football at Thomas McKean High in Wilmington, Delaware, he played his college ball at the University of Maryland. Beginning as a full-

© Associated Press

back, White moved to defensive tackle as a sophomore. Blossoming on the defensive line, White's 1974 senior year was its own trophy shelf, garnering him such national honors as the Outland Trophy, Lombardi Award, Atlantic Coast Conference Player of the Year, along with a half-dozen other awards. Although his Terrapins lost the 1974 Liberty Bowl, White was named the game's Most Valuable Player as well as a Consensus All-American.

Taken by the Dallas Cowboys second in the nation in the 1975 NFL draft, standing 6'4" and 257 pounds, White enjoyed a stellar 14-year career, 1975-88. A linebacker for his first two seasons, in 1977 White was moved to defensive tackle where he became a nine-time All Pro. His best season came the following year, 1978, when White recorded 123 tackles and 16 sacks and was named NFC Defensive Player of the Year.

An integral part of the great Dallas teams of the 1970s, White played in three Super Bowls—X, XII, and XIII. Named the co-MVP of Dallas' victorious Super Bowl XII, White also played in six NFC Championship Games.

He was named NFL Defensive Lineman of the Year, 1982. For 14 seasons White racked up more than 1,100 tackles (701 solo) to go with 111 sacks.

Named to the Pro Football Hall of Fame, College Football Hall of Fame, and the Dallas Cowboys Ring of Honor in 1994, he owns Randy White's Hall of Fame Barbeque in Frisco, Texas.

Byron "Whizzer" White

Born June 18, 1916—Fort Collins, CO
Died April 15, 2002—Denver, CO

It was time to give the Same Old Steelers—then called the Pirates—a little respectability. After five years in the fledgling National Football League, the team couldn't seem to win the coin toss—much less real games.

Clever promoter that he was, before the 1938 season, team owner Art Rooney signed a bona fide star. Colorado's All-American Byron Raymond "Whizzer" White was the NFL's first big money player, one who was great on the field and Gibraltar-solid at the gate. Playing tailback in a single-wing offense, White led the league in both rushing and salary. Racking up 567 yards, he earned $15,000—triple what the NFL's best were getting elsewhere.

Nevertheless, having the league star in

© Associated Press

the backfield didn't really help the team: the Steelers still went 2-9. Of the team's 10 touchdowns, White had four.

Born in 1916 in Fort Collins, scholarship student White's speedy, heady play netted him the Whizzer tag, which he hated. Graduating valedictorian, he earned a Rhodes Scholarship to Oxford University, an honor he deferred for a year to play for the Steelers. He returned to this country in 1940 and played two seasons for the Detroit Lions, leading the league in rushing in 1940.

World War II took him to the Navy, where, as an intelligence officer, he wrote the report on Lieutenant John Kennedy's 1943 PT-109 sinking. In 1962 President John Kennedy appointed White to the United States Supreme Court, a post he held until his retirement in 1993.

Elected to the College Football Hall of Fame in 1954, Whizzer White remains the lone NFL veteran ever to sit on the Supreme Court. Arguably the all-time smartest Steeler, one of the rare bright spots in the 1930s squads, Mr. Justice White died in 2002 at age 85, in Denver.

Whitfield, right, plays a store clerk held hostage by Jack Nicholson in Nicholson's first film, *Cry Baby Killers*, produced by Roger Corman, 1958.

Jordan "Smoki" Whitfield

Born August 3, 1918—Pittsburgh
Died November 11, 1967—Los Angeles, CA

Scant little is known about the off-screen life of Jordan Whitfield, the man who appeared in more B-movie jungle films than perhaps any other. Either he was a true pioneer among African-Americans in the matinee days of Hollywood or, just as probable, he was one likable and able actor who was sure to be available when the casting agent needed a doorman, cabbie, porter, or witch doctor. Whitfield played them all, and often.

Most frequently seen in the many sequels to Johnny Weismuller's *Tarzan* films, Whitfield was almost consistently cast as Eli, a jungle native to Johnny Sheffield's *Bomba, The Jungle Boy*. In the first of the series, Whitfield was no ordinary loin-clothed native; he serves the plot handily arguing with his white hunters to avoid the retributions of tribal leaders; then later, divulges to Bomba the circumstances of his orphanage to the jungle. In the last of the series, Whitfield plays an evil native who is entrusted to keep Bomba tied to a tree. Whitfield played significant roles in eight of the 12 Monogram Pictures.

Even before his success with Bomba, Whitfield played opposite George Reeves (who would later forever be tied to the role of TV's *Superman*) as Oolonga, the Witch Doctor. (Whitfield would later appear in several *Superman* episodes.) And he had a small role as a servant in Lillian Hellman's *Another Part of the Forest* (1948).

In 1950, he played a bootblack in a memorable scene with Broderick Crawford in *Born Yesterday* and, in 1953, he could be seen as a chauffeur to Fred Astaire in *The Band Wagon*. Neither role was credited.

For trivia buffs, Smoki Whitfield had the distinction of appearing in Jack Nicholson's first film, *The Cry Baby Killers*, in which he is held hostage by the then 20-year-old future star.

© Associated Press

Clearly, Whitfield was much appreciated by the more established studios. With consistent work in dozens of films, he earned yet another regular gig in 1960 as Oscar Marlon in Disney's historic series, *The Swamp Fox*. More, but less frequent, TV roles ensued until Whitfield died from a heart attack in November 1967.

William "Red" Whittaker

Born April 10, 1948—Camp Hill, PA

Meltdown is not a word to inspire confidence, and in 1979, after a partial core nuclear meltdown at the Three Mile Island Nuclear Generating Station, few sensible people would agree to spend any meaningful time in the damaged facility to perform critical clean-up.

William "Red" Whittaker, roboticist and research professor of robotics at Carnegie Mellon University, grew up in Hollidaysburg, PA. With a budget of $1.5 million, he and his team at CMU researched and built thinking machines—robots—to inspect and perform repairs at the facility. Far from the automated robots that are traditionally tasked with performing a series of rote actions, Red's creations responded autonomously to changing situations. In short, they "thought." In addition to helping secure the toxic reactor, they ushered in a new era of robotics, led Red and his team to establish the Field Robotic Center at CMU, and cemented their creator's reputation as a robotics rock star.

With Red's contributions and leadership, he has helped design and build machines that take human intellect to places no human can easily go: to the ice fields of Antarctica, to the active volcanoes in Alaska, to the surface of Mars.

Today, in addition to serving as the director of the Field Robotics Center, he is also the founder of the National Robotics Engineering Consortium at CMU and the chief scientist of RedZone Robotics. His robotics team is also recognized as one of the fiercest competitors (and as of 2007 the first place winner) of the The Defense Advanced Research Projects Agency (DARPA) Challenge, an event that looks like a robot road rally but is internationally recognized as the best place to witness the most sophisticated robotics in action.

Next stop: the moon. Excited by the prospect of the public domain returning to the moon before any government agency does it first, Red has entered the Google Lunar X PRIZE. The idea is to send a privately funded rover to the moon that will be capable of completing several missions, relaying information back to Earth. The purse is $2 million with more than $30 million in incentives along the way. The money looks nice, but as Red himself puts it, robotics is simply the field "[that] I was born for."

James Widdoes

Born November 15, 1953—Squirrel Hill

The original spokesman for Son of a Gun blow dryers, once president of the notorious *Delta House*, then head of household with *Charles in Charge*, James Widdoes is one of the busiest, if not the most prolific, directors of television sitcoms today.

He grew up on Dunmoyle Place at the top of Negley Hill, attending St. Edmund's first, then Shady Side Academy. Dad Pete was a commercial realtor and Mom Barbara was the first director of the Three Rivers Arts Festival. An enthusiast of all things theatrical, she would encourage her young son to perform even at parties. Widdoes, never shy, learned to dazzle his audience. He attended prep school in Connecticut, went to Skidmore College for a year, then spent two more at NYU. He might have graduated if his roommate, Michael O'Keefe (later of *The Great Santini*,) hadn't proved there was money to be made as a professional actor. Theatre enticed. After a quick Don Brockett road show, he performed Off-Broadway in *Wonderful Town*, and on Broadway in *The Caine Mutiny Court Martial,* and 1981's *Is There Life After High School?* for which he won a Theatre World Award.

Widdoes performed in a slew of hip commercials for Aunt Jemima, Freshen-Up Gum, and Montgomery Ward, and learned his craft

early in a competitive world. It all paid off when he was asked to audition for a *National Lampoon* film, spoofing college and slated to star John Belushi as well as a fraternity of young budding actors. Widdoes landed the role of a lifetime as Robert Hoover, the ineffectual but spirited president of *Animal House*.

The success of the movie spawned an ABC-TV sitcom, *Delta House*, featuring newcomer Michelle Pfeiffer. Even she couldn't save it. But Widdoes was now a formidable talent, and soon after appeared in 22 episodes of *Charles in Charge*, the Scott Baio sitcom for CBS in which he plays the ineffectual, but spirited father.

Soon, Widdoes was directing, too. *Just the Ten of Us*, *Anything But Love*, *Harry and the Hendersons*, and *Home Free*, led to a more frequent contract directing and executive producing *Dave's World*. Of hundreds of sitcom episodes the more popular series he has directed and/or produced since 1995 include: *The King of Queens, All About the Andersons, 8 Simple Rules.., According to Jim,* and *Two and a Half Men*. Currently, Widdoes is the frequent director of Fox's *'til Death* and TBS's *The Bill Engvall Show*.

John Edgar Wideman

Born June 14, 1941—Washington, D.C.

A much-awarded novelist who sees life as beset by what he terms "Greek gloom and inevitability," John Edgar Wideman writes about African-Americans' "haunted history," deliberately tackling society's—and his own family's—most deep-seated problems.

Born in Washington, D.C., in 1941, Wideman's family moved to Homewood when he was an infant. An outstanding student and championship basketball player at Peabody High, Class of '59, Wideman attended the University of Pennsylvania. An award-winning collegiate writer and member of Phi Beta Kappa, Wideman was also an All-Ivy League basketball player. Good enough to consider a professional basketball career, his relatively short stature—Wideman stands 6-feet-two-inches—convinced him to pursue an academic and writing career.

Subject of a *Look* magazine article "The Astonishing John Wideman," he graduated Penn in 1963, and became the second African-American to win a Rhodes scholarship. Studying literature at Oxford University, Wideman found time to play pickup basketball with fellow student Bill Bradley, future New York Knick and United States Senator.

In 1966, Wideman attended the prestigious Iowa Writers' Workshop, where he completed his first novel, *A Glance Away*, published in 1967.

Other novels followed, most set in Homewood, all dealing with race. By the mid-1980s, three of Wideman's books—*Damballah*, *Hiding Place*, and *Sent for You Yesterday* (which won the 1984 PEN/Faulkner Award)—were packaged as the Homewood Trilogy.

Over his career, Wideman's novels and story collections have offered a "notion of history [that] is not linear," he has said, "but much more like traditional, indigenous versions of history—African, American Indian, Asian—that see time as a great sea. Everything that has ever happened, all the people who have ever existed, simultaneously occupy this great sea. It fluctuates, and there are waves, and ripples, so, on a given day, you are as liable to bump into your great-great-great-great-grandmother, as you are to bump into your spouse.

"The notion of progress is crazy in many ways," he added. "Beneath our certainties, there's always chaos."

Nowhere are his theories of time, technique, and repeated theme of racial oppression used to greater advantage than in his 1990 *Philadelphia Fire*, which also won an unprecedented second PEN/Faulkner Award. Based on the 1985 firebombing of a West Philadelphia row house owned by the radical cult Move, the novel details the tragedy that took 11 lives and burned 60 homes. Along the same lines, Wideman's 1996 *The Cattle Killing* re-creates the infamous 1793 Philadelphia yellow fever epidemic, when African-Americans helped the victims—then were blamed for the plague and killed.

Saving his most personal narratives for his non-fiction, Wideman's 1984 *Brothers and Keepers* dissects his brother Robby's 1976 murder conviction and subsequent life prison sentence. Similarly, Wideman's 1994 *Father-along: A Meditation on Fathers and Sons, Race and Society* painfully examines Wideman's own complex family—and forces the reader to confront American racial tensions.

A distinguished university professor, he has taught at Howard, Penn, Wyoming, Massachusetts, and Brown. The recipient of a MacArthur "Genius" Grant, John Edgar Wideman lives and works on New York City's Lower East Side.

Earl Wild

Born November 26, 1915—Pittsburgh

Considered by many to be one of the greatest pianists of the 20th Century and held in such regard that he has played for six different Presidents, Earl Wild is a musical legend of the greatest magnitude.

Wild's story is a fairly typical one of a child prodigy; his parents exposed him to classical music at an early age and by 3 he was reciting overtures note for note. Wild was reading music by the age of 6 and before he was a teenager was studying with some of the best instructors that money could buy. While most kids his age were playing stickball in the alley, Wild was getting music instruction at Carnegie Tech in a program for gifted children.

Wild performed his music on KDKA radio, alongside their orchestra, and made such an impression that he worked for the station for eight years. Under the direction of Otto Klemperer, the Pittsburgh Symphony hired Wild, then just 14, to play the piano and celeste.

© Associated Press

At the age of 22, Wild was hired as a staff pianist at NBC where he stayed for the next seven years. Among his many highlights were being the first artist to perform a piano recital on U.S. television and being the featured pianist in an NBC radio broadcast of Gershwin's "Rhapsody in Blue," immediately vaulting him into a national spotlight.

Wild served in the U.S. Navy as a musician and in 1961 was the featured pianist during the Inaugural Concert for the newly elected John F. Kennedy. ABC hired Wild as their staff pianist where he remained until 1968, all the while performing concerts with orchestras from all over the world. For several years Wild worked with Sid Caesar on a number of TV skits for his popular *Caesar Hour*.

In addition to Wild's many musical contributions, perhaps his most important is the knowledge and experience that he continues to share at the university level. Wild holds the title of distinguished visiting artist at his alma mater, Carnegie Mellon University and has taught at Julliard, Penn State University, Ohio State University, University of Rochester's Eastman School of Music, Manhattan School of Music, and in Tokyo, Beijing and all over the world. At the tender age of 82, Wild took home a Grammy® Award for "Best Instrumental Soloist Performance without Orchestra."

Wild is considered to be among the last of a line of great virtuoso pianist/composers. He resides in New York.

William Wilkins

Born December 20, 1779—Carlisle, PA
Died June 23, 1865—Homewood

William Wilkins helped construct bridges, build libraries, improve river navigation, and bring Western Pennsylvania issues to the forefront in national politics.

William, the first of four boys, was born in Carlisle, PA, to John Wilkins, one of the seven delegates from Pennsylvania to go to the 1776 Constitutional Convention in Philadelphia. After graduating from Dickinson College, he was admitted to the Pittsburgh bar in 1801. In 1814 Wilkins was elected the first president of the Bank of Pittsburgh, the first of numerous civic appointments. He was also president of the Monongahela Bridge Company, the Greensburg and Pittsburgh Turnpike Company, and the Vigilant Fire Company. He directed the Permanent Library Company and served as a member of the Pittsburgh Common Council, which was responsible for Pittsburgh's transition from a borough to a city.

Wilkins was not satisfied with only serving Pittsburgh on a civic level and in 1819, was elected to his first term in the state legislature. From there, he accepted a judgeship on the U.S. District Court for Western Pennsylvania, serving for seven years until 1831 when

he was elected to the U.S. Senate. During his tenure, Wilkins chaired numerous committees, fought for the construction of the turnpike, improved Pennsylvania tax guidelines, and safeguarded Pennsylvanian African-Americans from kidnapping and sale into slavery. He was also a staunch supporter of Jacksonian politics, a position that often set him up for criticism and debate.

After a brief candidacy for Vice President in 1832, Wilkins accepted the ministership to Russia, which he held for two years. Wilkins' service in government culminated with his appointment to Secretary of War in 1844 under President John Tyler, which he held until the end of Tyler's presidency.

Wilkins was elected for one last term as senator in 1855, and actively supported the Union in the Civil War as brigadier general of the Home Guards. He died at age 86 at his Homewood estate and is buried in Homewood Cemetery, named for and located on part of the property that used to be his home.

Mary Lou Williams

Born May 8, 1910—Atlanta, GA
Died May 28, 1981—Durham, NC

On the piano she was a master of all styles: blues, be-bop, boogie-woogie, swing, and stride. She is considered by many music historians to be one of, if not *the*, most influential female musicians in jazz. Born Mary Scruggs in Atlanta in 1910 (eventually taking the name of her first husband John Williams), Mary Lou Williams moved to East Liberty when she was just a young girl. "The Little Piano Girl," as she was known around her East End neighborhood, used to sit on her mother's lap while she played the pump organ. One day she beat her mother to the keys and played a melody, sending her parents scrambling for the neighbors to come and listen. A child prodigy, she was soon involved in jam sessions with local musicians, among them Earl "Fatha" Hines.

She earned money for her family when her stepfather would smuggle her into after-hours gambling joints along Pittsburgh's Wylie Avenue. She also was hired to play for some of the area's wealthiest families, such as the Mellons and the Olivers. It's ironic that she would later in life be responsible for founding the Pittsburgh Jazz Festival, later to become the Mellon Jazz Festival. In speaking of playing for the Mellons she said: "They were won-

derful! They'd send a chauffeur out for me and I'd play their private parties. Once they gave me $100. My mother almost fainted. She wanted to know if the lady drank. She even called the people to see if they made a mistake."

In her early teens Mary Lou hit the road when school was out as the fill-in pianist in a vaudeville act. The leader of the act was Johnny Williams, soon to become Mary Lou's first husband when she was just 16. After some personnel changes, the band appointed Andy Kirk as the leader, and the band became The Dark Clouds Of Joy (later becoming The Clouds Of Joy) and made Kansas City their home where Mary Lou was entrenched in

Kansas City swing. By then, in addition to her exceptional piano dexterity, Mary Lou became an accomplished arranger and composer for the bands of Jimmy and Tommy Dorsey, Louis Armstrong, Jimmy Lunceford, and Benny Goodman. Her chart successes with Kirk and her marriage to Williams lasted until the early 1940s. For a while Mary Lou wrote for Duke Ellington and even traveled with a group that included Art Blakey when he was just a teenager.

Mary Lou next moved to New York, where her small Harlem apartment became the popular hangout for a who's who of jazz greats, including Miles Davis, Dizzy Gillespie, Kenny Clarke and Art Blakey, Sarah Vaughan, Thelonious Monk, and Charlie Parker. She was at the heart of the sound that became Be-bop. She had a long-standing gig at Café Society, New York's first integrated jazz club.

In 1952, what was supposed to be a short trip to Europe turned into a two-year relocation. There Mary Lou suffered a breakdown and withdrew from the jazz world. What followed was a spiritual rebirth, a conversion to Catholicism, and a rededication of her music to serving the church. Additionally she spent much of her time raising money for the poor and struggling musicians who had fallen on hard times. In 1977, Mary Lou Williams relocated to Durham, NC, and spent her remaining years as artist-in-residence at Duke University.

Mary Lou Williams' musical legacy is enormous. Her piano style spanned virtually every form of jazz; she wrote for and recorded extensively with many of jazz's greatest musicians; she wrote a mass commissioned by the Vatican; she performed at the White House; she wrote over 350 musical compositions, taught and lectured extensively, eventually withdrawing at the height of her career to focus on her spirituality and care for the needy. A life well served.

Next page, top, Constanza Romero, left, wife of August Wilson, Azula Carmen Wilson, second from left, and Sakina Ansari, right, daughters of Mr. Wilson, and Rocco Landesman, President of Jujamcyn Theaters, attend the dedication ceremony of the August Wilson Theatre, Sunday, October 16, 2005, in New York.

Next page, left, Wilson and his daughter Azula Carmen outside the Virginia Theatre, later to be renamed the August Wilson Theatre, in New York, prior to the opening of *King Hedley II*, Sunday, April 29, 2001

and Yale Rep director, within two years the play was on Broadway. Directed by Richards (who took five additional Wilson plays to Broadway), it won the New York Drama Critics Circle Award for Best Play.

Nine more plays followed, each encapsulating the African-American experience in a decade of the 20th Century. With all but *Ma Rainey* set in the Hill District, the plays were dubbed The Pittsburgh Cycle and won one Tony© Award, two Pulitzer Prizes, three American Theatre Critics Awards, and seven New York Drama Critics Circle Awards. Wilson's most popular play, *Fences* (1985), starred James Earl Jones and grossed $11 million its first year (then a Broadway record for a non-musical). *The Piano Lesson* (1990) was made into Wilson's only film: shot entirely in Pittsburgh, it starred Alfre Woodard.

August Wilson

Born April 27, 1945—Hill District
Died October 2, 2005—Seattle, WA

Pittsburgh's greatest autodidact, August Wilson was a high school dropout who became a two-time Pulitzer Prize winner and the greatest American playwright of his era.

Born Frederick August Kittel in 1945 in the Hill District, the son of an African-American cleaning woman and German-American baker, he was raised with five siblings in a two-room apartment above Bella's Grocery, 1727 Bedford Avenue. By age 5, he was abandoned by his father; by 15 he had dropped out of high school (three high schools, really: Central Catholic, Connelly, and Gladstone). Completing his education by reading voraciously at Carnegie Library—from which he was later given an honorary high school diploma, the only one in its history—by age 18 he was working odd jobs. Called Freddy by his family, and Youngblood by the railroad men with whom he spent time at Pat's Place, a Hill District cigar store, after his father's 1965 death,

he changed his name to August Wilson, for his mother's family, and, with the purchase of a $10 typewriter (which he frequently pawned) set out to be a poet.

By 1968 he had turned his attention to drama, working with playwright Rob Penny to create the Black Horizon Theater. Moving to St. Paul in 1978, Wilson wrote scripts for the Science Museum of Minnesota. By 1982, an early version of *Jitney* debuted in Pittsburgh; entirely rewritten, its full-scale 1996 premiere was at the Pittsburgh Public Theater.

Submitting plays to Connecticut's Eugene O'Neill Theater, in 1982 Wilson's *Ma Rainey's Black Bottom* was accepted. Working closely with Lloyd Richards, the O'Neill

From *Joe Turner's Come and Gone* (1984) through *Radio Golf* (2005), with *Gem of the Ocean* (2003), *Seven Guitars* (1995), and *Two Trains Running* (1990) in between, the plays, Wilson said, "exalt and celebrate a common humanity."

Moving to Seattle in 1990, Wilson never lost touch with Pittsburgh. Indeed, the 1999 world premiere of *King Hedley II* opened the Pittsburgh Public Theater's new O'Reilly Theater.

In 2005, at age 60, August Wilson died of liver cancer at Seattle's Swedish Medical Center and was buried in Greenwood Memorial Park, O'Hara Township. Among his tributes were declaring his Bedford Avenue home a state landmark, naming the August Wilson Theatre on Broadway, and announcing the August Wilson Center for African-American Culture in downtown Pittsburgh.

Above, Sakina Ansari-Wilson leads a dedication ceremony for a state historical marker outside the birthplace of her father, August Wilson, Wednesday, May 30, 2007.

Jonathan Wolken

Born July 12, 1949—Shadyside

The phenomenon that is Pilobolus is two-fold. First, it's a phototropic fungus that can launch its spores at speeds of 45 miles per hour. Secondly, it's a dance company that for 35 years has startled audiences worldwide, not so much for its creative movement than for its weight-sharing human sculptures. One of the founders of Pilobolus, Jonathan Wolken, often visited his father's laboratory at Carnegie Tech to help him research the photoreceptive mechanisms of this minute form of fungi.

Pilobolus dancers perform *Megawatt*, July 13, 2005.

Born from a dance class led by Allison Chase at Dartmouth in the late 1960s, four students—Moses Pendleton, Robby Barnett, Michael Tracy, and Wolken—created Pilobolus in 1972. Said Wolken in a *Time* magazine feature story in 1978, "None of us had the dance background, and we didn't feel secure alone, so we developed a kind of linked moment."

Pilobolus is internationally reknowned for its astonishingly unorthodox interpretation of creative movement. The company mastered gravity-defying forms of humans-in-balance, as seen most recently during the 2007 Academy Awards®, long before Cirque de Solei ever came along. Pilobolus has been hired for television commercials for Mobil, Toyota, and Bloomingdale's, and in 2002 was the subject of the popular documentary, *Last Dance*, in which they collaborated with illustrator and writer Maurice Sendak.

Wolken grew up in Shadyside, the second of four siblings. He attended the Falk School and Peabody, graduating in 1967. He earned a B.S. in philosophy from Dartmouth. Like many of his collaborators, he resides in Wasington Depot, CT, where he lives with his wife, JoAnne, and their four daughters.

Otis Cook, a Pilobolus principal dancer, hails from Mt. Pleasant, PA.

John Woodruff

Born July 5, 1915—Connellsville, PA
Died October 30, 2007—Fountain Hills, AZ

At the 1936 Berlin Olympics, even while Adolf Hitler denounced him as one of America's "black auxiliaries," 21-year-old John Woodruff won a Gold Medal in the 800-meter race.

Born John Youie Woodruff in 1915 in Connellsville, the son of illiterate parents and grandson of former slaves, he began his athletic career as a high school football player. But when practice got in the way of his chores, chopping wood and hauling coal, his mother made him quit.

Standing 6'-3", the whip-thin "Long John" Woodruff had impossibly long strides—some nine feet—and fierce determination. The following spring, he ran half-mile and mile races—and won. By the time he graduated Connellsville High in 1935, Woodruff had set school, county, district, and state records.

With a Pitt track scholarship, in 1936, after his freshman year, Woodruff won the Allegheny Mountain 880, advanced to the Olympic semi-finals at Harvard. Winning there, and at Randall's Island, he earned a trip to Berlin.

In Germany, running 800 meters, Woodruff crushed the early competition, beating his closest contenders by 20 yards.

In the finals, deliberately boxed in by the other runners, Woodruff stopped, was spiked, then dashed to the outside and swept the pack.

Some 10,000 people jammed his Connellsville welcome-home parade. Back at Pitt, among his honors Woodruff took three national half-mile championships and set a new American 800-meter record.

Graduating in 1939, earning a 1941 NYU Masters, Woodruff enlisted in the army. Serving in Korea as well, Woodruff later worked as a New York City teacher and parole officer.

In 1936, every Olympic medalist received a Black Forest oak sapling. Woodruff planted his at Connellsville's football stadium, where it stands more than 60 feet high—over the John Woodruff 5-K run held every year in his honor.

His legs amputated due to diabetes, John Woodruff died at the age of 92.

Lewis Woodson

Born January 1806—Greenbrier, WV
Died circa 1877

A minister and important leader in the African Methodist Episcopal Church, Lewis Woodson campaigned for education and equal opportunity for African-Americans. His convictions led him to found reform-minded organizations and institutions as both an educator and business person.

The oldest son of Thomas and Jemima Woodson, Lewis was born in 1806. The family settled in Chillicothe, OH, where Woodson was educated by Quakers. Later involved in the establishment of the AME church in the town, Woodson became a minister and in 1827, founded the African Education and Benevolent Society.

Woodson quickly involved himself in causes linking the church, education, and the quest for freedom. In 1829 he authored a letter printed in the newspaper *Freedom's Journal*, which argued against emigration to Africa and instead for 'colonization' in the United States. He joined the dialogue occurring within the AME Church, serving as secretary for the AME Conference in Ohio and attending the first Negro Convention in 1830 at Mother Bethel AME in Philadelphia.

Woodson and his wife Caroline relocated to Pittsburgh that year where he served as minister in the Bethel AME Church. In Pittsburgh, he also established a school for African-American children while working as a barber to support his growing family.

A founding member of the Pittsburgh African Education Society, Woodson became a vocal advocate for education, encouraging the 1833 AME Ohio Conference to ratify an amendment to establish or assist, "common schools, Sunday schools and temperance societies." In partnership with other leaders of the African-American community in Pittsburgh, such as John Vashon and Martin Delany, who had been his student, Woodson wrote, taught, and served as an advocate for political and economic opportunity. He joined with others to author the 1837 Pittsburgh Memorial, a document stating that blacks should retain voting rights in the state.

Involved in the founding of Wilberforce University in 1856, Woodson's life stands in testament to his belief in the importance of educational institutions in both teaching and furthering the cause of freedom.

Jock Yablonski

Born March 3, 1910—Philadelphia, PA
Died December 31, 1969—Clarksville, PA

He began working in the mines at the age of 15, boasting later in life that "Jock Yablonski can go anywhere in the coal fields." He died some 44 years later, well above ground, having spent his final days fearful of a more horrific demise. When death came, it was in face-to-face combat with a hired assassin who ultimately bettered him with five bullets. His wife and daughter were murdered too as they cowered under their bed sheets.

Yablonski's violent death was the capstone to a life fiercely led. Prompting zealous devotion or deep hatred, his own passions lay in confronting what he perceived to be gross negligence among the leadership of the United Mine Workers (UMW), an organization to which he claimed steadfast allegiance and membership. It was under a banner of righteous indignation that he both shocked and energized members of the rank and file, launching the first insurgency in the organization since 1926.

For airing his claims that union headquarters in Washington, D.C., had patently ignored workers' demands for stricter health and safety procedures, he attracted many new loyalists, including Ralph Nader, John D. Rockefeller IV, and Walter Reuther. He also attracted the enmity of then-current UMW President W.A. "Tony" Boyle, who grew infuriated at Yablonski's public denunciations as well as his accusations of mismanagement and embezzlement.

March 19, 1973, outside an Erie, PA, courtoom, A. Tony Boyle confronts the media before testifying in the trial of William Prater, convicted as one of three murderers of Yablonski and his family, and whom Boyle was later convicted of hiring to commit the murders.

Yablonski lost the election but not before Boyle lost his temper. He arranged for Yablonski's death in June 1969, delaying it until after the election to avoid suspicion.

Months later, investigating Boyle's activities, the FBI came to the same conclusion of who and what motive had cost Yablonski his life. In 1971, Boyle was indicted for fraud and misuse of union money that included paying $20,000 for the New Year's Eve hit on the Yablonski home in Greene County. Found guilty, he died while serving three life terms in 1985 at the age of 83.

Molly Yard

Born July 6, 1912—Shanghai, China
Died September 21, 2005—Pittsburgh

Born in 1912 to Methodist missionaries working in China, Molly Yard's birth could hardly have evoked less local enthusiasm. Upon her arrival, an empathetic male friend of her father presented him with a beautiful brass bowl—less as a baby gift and more as a consolation prize. As the family's third daughter, Molly was considered rather redundant.

Once on the scene, however, she was hard to ignore. Her reputation as one of America's most vocal feminists and social activists was fearsome. Like-minded colleagues sometimes threatened opponents by suggesting, "You can deal with us now or Molly later." Most, it is suggested, took the first option, rather than tangle with the woman who became the National Organization of Women's (NOW) two-term president.

Her political and social passions began in the 1930s during her political science studies at Swarthmore College. While the curriculum challenged her intellect, it was the anti-Semitic discrimination she recognized in her own sorority that prompted her to abolish all sororities on campus and served as her life long battle call to activism. Personal experience of gender inequality, meanwhile, kept her acutely mindful of what was at stake.

Having married a Swarthmore classmate

in 1938, she and her husband Sylvester Garrett tried to open a joint checking account. That she had elected to keep her maiden name rather than adopt her husband's surname rendered the task impossible. If only Ms. Yard had been Mr. Garrett's mistress, bank employees explained, it would have been no problem at all.

An active member of the Democratic Party in the 1940s and 1950s, she developed a reputation for challenging old-school politics and, having moved from California to Pittsburgh in 1953, worked to help elect David L. Lawrence as the governor of Pennsylvania.

It was as a resident of Squirrel Hill that she became an active member of NOW in 1974. Thirteen years later, she became its president. Upon taking office, she made it her personal goal to defeat President Ronald Reagan's nomination of Judge Robert H. Bork to the U.S. Supreme Court. The man she called "a Neanderthal" was soundly rejected by the U.S. Senate.

She suffered a stroke while seated at her desk in 1991, and resigned that year. In 2005, she died in her sleep at a Beechview nursing home.

Mr. Yuk

Born March, 1971—Oakland

The realization came to Children's Hospital medical researchers in 1971 that the traditional skull and crossbones, the age-old symbol of poison to generations of adults, meant almost nothing to children. Likewise, the octagonal red stop symbol. Ditto any kind of red-slashed icongraph. When a boy participating in the research study pointed to the now familiar green face with the down-turned tongue, he said, "He looks yukky." A new Pittsburgher was born.

Mr. Yuk, now 37 years old, is known internationally as a warning to children and a help aid to adults needing immediate information about poison prevention. Answering calls 24/7, the Pittsburgh Poison Center at Children's Hospital responds to over 150,000 phone calls every year, peopling its database of product ingredients with clinical toxicology nurse specialists. On average the Center assists callers with some 30 actual poison episodes every day. Cleaning products are the most commonly ingested toxins by children, while drug interactions and overdoses are most common with the elderly.

Free Mr. Yuk stickers are available by mail. Go to: www.chp.edu/chpstore/poisonprev.php for the PPC's current address. (Children's Hospital will be moving to Lawrenceville in 2009).

In October 2007, UPMC sued a Minneapolis politician for using a Mr. Yuk-like symbol on lawn signs protesting a proposed amendment to the city's charter.

George Zambelli

Born in 1924—New Castle, PA
Died December 25, 2003—Pittsburgh

Known to thousands of clients as "Boom Boom," "Mr. Fireworks," or "The Great Zambelli," George Zambelli, Sr., was the pyrotechnic genius who helped make New Castle, PA, the fireworks capital of the world. Though he may not have engineered the chemistry of his rockets, nor introduced later advances in computer timing, he is credited as having been the first pyrotechnician to choreograph displays to music. Today, the "1812 Overture," one of Zambelli's favorites, is often staged as the finale in many of the 3,500 shows produced by Zambelli Fireworks Internationale every year, more than half of which occur on the same day, July 4th.

Zambelli's father, Antonio, actually brought the business to New Castle in 1893. A native of Caserta, Italy, he and his wife Maria Geuseppe, were determined to raise their family in America, opening a small hotel in their adopted town. Antonio and Maria raised seven children and put them to work, cooking, cleaning, and waitressing in their popular restaurant. On the side, the children also learned to make fireworks. At 7 years of age, George, the fifth born child, rolled firecrackers.

Graduating in 1946 from Duquesne University with a degree in accounting, George garnered the faith of his siblings and father to take over the fireworks business in earnest. In that his father never learned to speak English, young George knew that he could communicate the opportunities for growth and sales that his father never understood.

George Zambelli was a tireless businessman, often described by his children as a person who arose at 5:30 every morning and didn't retire until 11 at night. His work was his life, and he parlayed his salesmanship into diplomatic liaisons with world leaders. In fact, Zambelli was acquainted with more than seven U.S. Presidents, and launched dozens of shows at the White House, even as late as 2001 when President Bush entertained Mexican President Vincente Fox.

Today, the New Castle facility, situated on 400 acres at Nashua Port, is the world's largest fireworks assembly plant. The company owns warehouses in seven cities across the U.S.

George Zambelli died from complications of influenza at West Penn Hospital on Christmas day, 2003. Said his daughter, Marcy, one of his and devoted wife Connie's children, "It's ironic. The one day each year he didn't work was Christmas Day."

June 1, 1998, Zambelli Fireworks Internationale's father and son team George Zambelli and George Jr. celebrate their home town.

Fritzie Zivic

Born May 8, 1913—Lawrenceville
Died May 16, 1984—Pittsburgh

Thumbs up? How about a thumb in your eye? Or a blow below the belt? That's what a fighter getting in the ring with Fritzie Zivic could expect—and more. Dubbed the world's dirtiest fighter, and maybe the quickest. Anybody complained, Fritzie'd just growl, "You're boxing, you're not playing the piano."

Dust-ups came naturally to The Croat Comet. Born Ferdinand Henry John Zivcich in the Ninth Ward (Lawrenceville) in 1913, Fritzie was one of five brothers known as the Fighting Zivics. As he put it about growing up tough in a tough part of the city, "you either had to fight or stay in the house. We went out."

Go out Zivic did, turning featherweight pro at 18, in 1931, fighting for the next 18 years, finally retiring in 1949 at age 36. His enviable record rated him a spot in the International Boxing Hall of Fame: 158 wins (including a teeth-rattling 80 knock-outs), 64 losses, nine no-decisions. His biggest bout: besting Hammering Hank Armstrong in Madison Square Garden, 1940, to cop the world welterweight crown. Holding the title for the next eight months, Zivic lost it to battler Red Cochran, 15 rounds, July 29, 1941, Newark, NJ.

Over his rough-and-tumble career, Zivic faced such feared rivals as Pittsburgher Billy Conn, Jake "Raging Bull" LaMotta, and Sugar Ray Robinson—seven future Hall of Famers and nine world champions, all told.

After he left the ring, and down on his luck, Zivic ran his own boxing school for a bit, then tried his hand at promoting and managing, but nothing worked out. For the next 30-odd years, he did turns as a steelworker, liquor salesman, bartender, county laborer, and, finally, boilermaker.

Surrounded by part of the floor show's chorus, the irrepressible Zivic mastered the ceremonies at an unidentified Pittsburgh night club, February 9, 1944.

Elected to the Hall of Fame in 1973, Fritzie Zivic died of Alzheimer's Disease in 1984, age 71, at the Aspinwall VA hospital.

Vladimir Zworykin

Born July 30, 1889—Murom, Russia
Died July 29, 1982—Princeton, NJ

According to AC Nielson, by the time the average American turns 65, he will have spent nine years of his life watching a television screen. For all that time, very few know that Vladimir Zworykin helped invent it in 1923.

What little most Americans know about how television actually works is the function of two geographically separate parts: the TV camera and the cathode-ray tube. Zworykin invented both—at least the parts that count the most. First known as the Iconoscope, the TV camera rapidly scans the image its lens captures, then feeds these pulses to a radio transmitter. The second, originally the kinescope, receives this transmission then fires the same pulses at the inside of a large vacuum tube in which multiple lines of phosphorescent cells react to the targeted charges. That's the basic principle.

Zworykin first worked on lesser principles of wired tele-transmissions in St. Petersburg as early as 1910. First a student of Boris Rosing at the Imperial Institute of Technology, he was lured to Paris to study X-rays before serving in the Russian Signal Corps during World War I, after which he emigrated to the United States in 1919. He joined Westinghouse in 1920, worked in the East Pittsburgh laboratories on radio tubes and photocells, and concurrently studied at Pitt to earn his Ph.D. in physics.

While at Westinghouse, after-hours and late at night, Zworykin returned to his interests in tele-transmissions, now using the newer technology of radio. In 1925 he demonstrated his 50-line kinescope to his superiors. They were not impressed—at least not with the commercial viability of Zworykin's radical improvements. Of course, he nor they had any vision of television being the entertainment medium it is today. (Fortunately, David Sarnoff of RCA did and, by 1929, hired Zworykin away to work in Camden, NJ.) No, Zworykin had had this ridiculous idea that someday his camera might show earthlings the other side of the moon.

In fact, popular for denouncing the crime and violence depicted on TV, Zworykin, often called the "Father of TV," watched very little of it. No doubt, he was too busy. Among his 120 U.S. patents, he created traffic guidance systems for cars, night-vision devices, garage door openers, an electric acupuncture system, and many invaluable contributions to the electron microscope. Awarded the National Medal of Science in 1967 he was also inducted into the National Inventors Hall of Fame in 1977.

The History Makers

Each year, the Senator John Heinz History Center hosts the History Makers Award Dinner, an event which began in 1992 to honor people who have made a contribution of historic significance to the culture and community of Western Pennsylvania. Recipients are nominated annually from the fields of *Arts & Letters, Business & Industry, Community Service, Education, Government, Humanities, Leadership, Literature, Medicine & Health, Social Sciences,* and *Sports & Entertainment.*

Born or bred in Western Pennsylvania, these individuals—together and individually—represent a legacy of innovation, work ethic, community pride, and civic spirit. Each are "change makers to the world" and embody the best that Pittsburgh has to offer our region and the world.

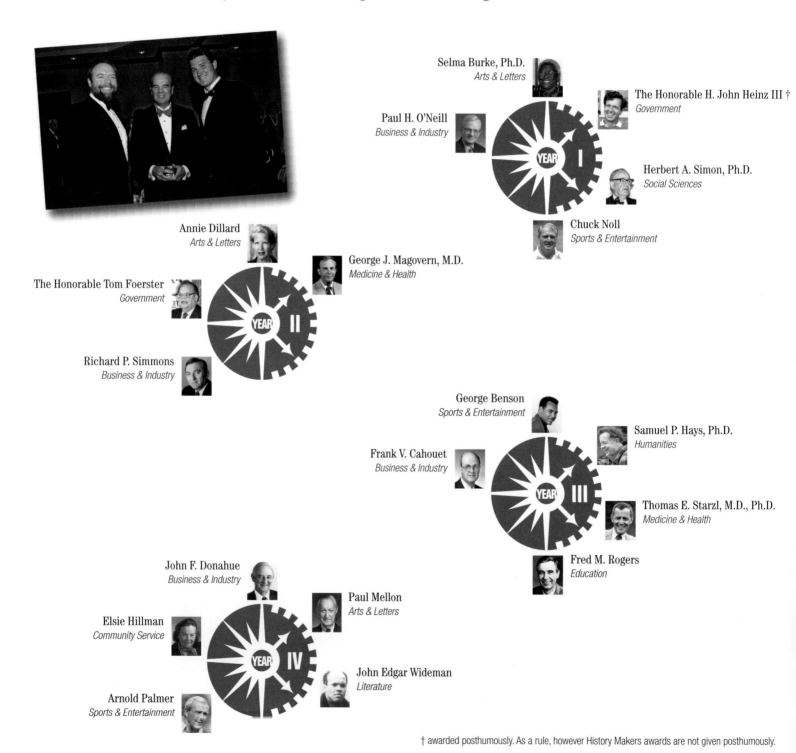

Selma Burke, Ph.D.
Arts & Letters

The Honorable H. John Heinz III †
Government

Paul H. O'Neill
Business & Industry

Herbert A. Simon, Ph.D.
Social Sciences

YEAR I

Chuck Noll
Sports & Entertainment

Annie Dillard
Arts & Letters

George J. Magovern, M.D.
Medicine & Health

The Honorable Tom Foerster
Government

YEAR II

Richard P. Simmons
Business & Industry

George Benson
Sports & Entertainment

Samuel P. Hays, Ph.D.
Humanities

Frank V. Cahouet
Business & Industry

YEAR III

Thomas E. Starzl, M.D., Ph.D.
Medicine & Health

Fred M. Rogers
Education

John F. Donahue
Business & Industry

Paul Mellon
Arts & Letters

Elsie Hillman
Community Service

YEAR IV

John Edgar Wideman
Literature

Arnold Palmer
Sports & Entertainment

† awarded posthumously. As a rule, however History Makers awards are not given posthumously.

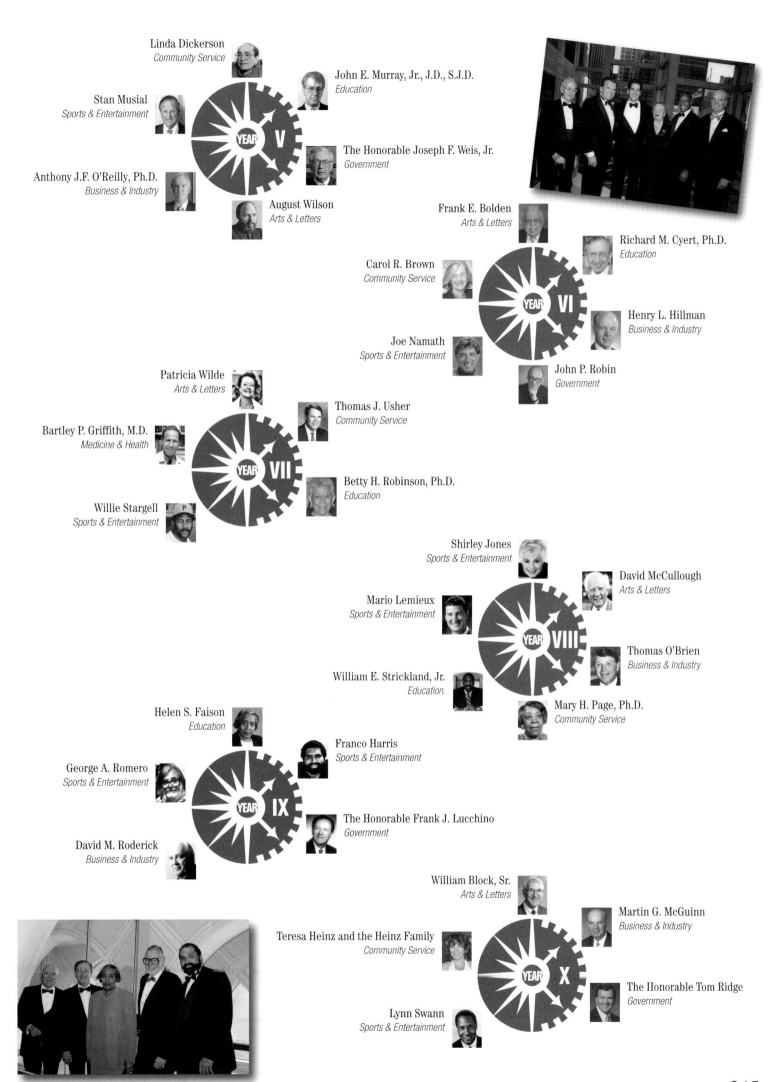

Linda Dickerson
Community Service

Stan Musial
Sports & Entertainment

Anthony J.F. O'Reilly, Ph.D.
Business & Industry

John E. Murray, Jr., J.D., S.J.D.
Education

The Honorable Joseph F. Weis, Jr.
Government

August Wilson
Arts & Letters

YEAR V

Frank E. Bolden
Arts & Letters

Carol R. Brown
Community Service

Joe Namath
Sports & Entertainment

Richard M. Cyert, Ph.D.
Education

Henry L. Hillman
Business & Industry

John P. Robin
Government

YEAR VI

Patricia Wilde
Arts & Letters

Bartley P. Griffith, M.D.
Medicine & Health

Willie Stargell
Sports & Entertainment

Thomas J. Usher
Community Service

Betty H. Robinson, Ph.D.
Education

YEAR VII

Shirley Jones
Sports & Entertainment

Mario Lemieux
Sports & Entertainment

William E. Strickland, Jr.
Education.

David McCullough
Arts & Letters

Thomas O'Brien
Business & Industry

Mary H. Page, Ph.D.
Community Service

YEAR VIII

Helen S. Faison
Education

George A. Romero
Sports & Entertainment

David M. Roderick
Business & Industry

Franco Harris
Sports & Entertainment

The Honorable Frank J. Lucchino
Government

YEAR IX

William Block, Sr.
Arts & Letters

Teresa Heinz and the Heinz Family
Community Service

Lynn Swann
Sports & Entertainment

Martin G. McGuinn
Business & Industry

The Honorable Tom Ridge
Government

YEAR X

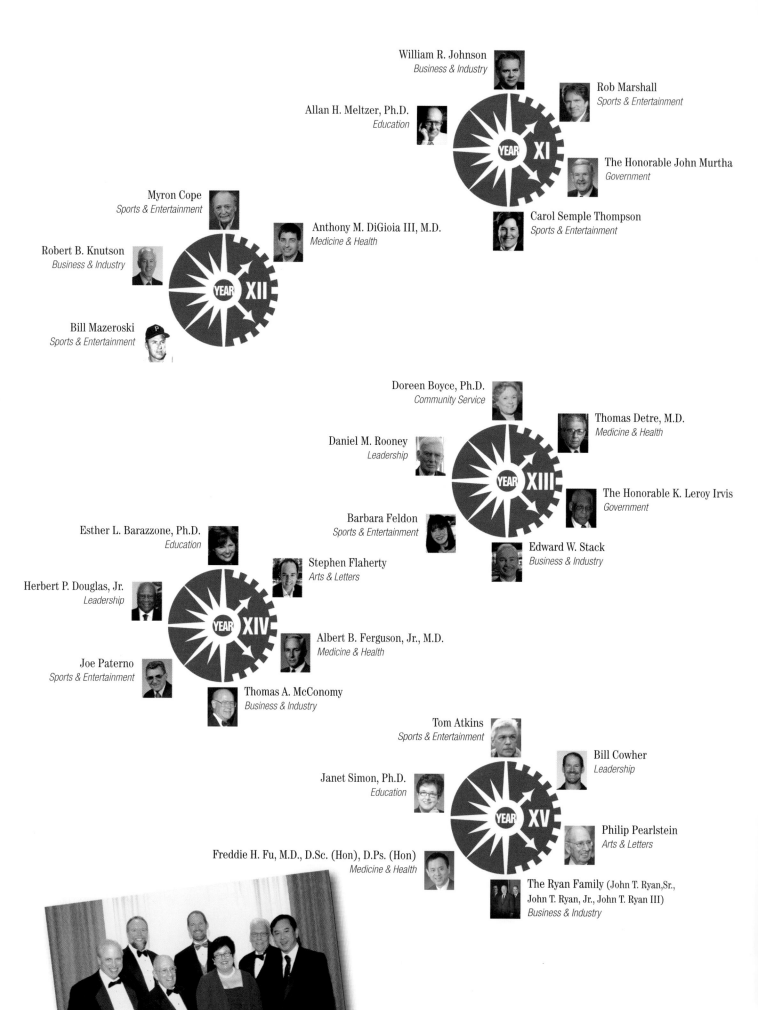

William R. Johnson
Business & Industry

Rob Marshall
Sports & Entertainment

Allan H. Meltzer, Ph.D.
Education

The Honorable John Murtha
Government

YEAR XI

Carol Semple Thompson
Sports & Entertainment

Myron Cope
Sports & Entertainment

Anthony M. DiGioia III, M.D.
Medicine & Health

Robert B. Knutson
Business & Industry

YEAR XII

Bill Mazeroski
Sports & Entertainment

Doreen Boyce, Ph.D.
Community Service

Thomas Detre, M.D.
Medicine & Health

Daniel M. Rooney
Leadership

The Honorable K. Leroy Irvis
Government

YEAR XIII

Barbara Feldon
Sports & Entertainment

Edward W. Stack
Business & Industry

Esther L. Barazzone, Ph.D.
Education

Stephen Flaherty
Arts & Letters

Herbert P. Douglas, Jr.
Leadership

YEAR XIV

Albert B. Ferguson, Jr., M.D.
Medicine & Health

Joe Paterno
Sports & Entertainment

Thomas A. McConomy
Business & Industry

Tom Atkins
Sports & Entertainment

Bill Cowher
Leadership

Janet Simon, Ph.D.
Education

YEAR XV

Philip Pearlstein
Arts & Letters

Freddie H. Fu, M.D., D.Sc. (Hon), D.Ps. (Hon)
Medicine & Health

The Ryan Family (John T. Ryan,Sr.,
John T. Ryan, Jr., John T. Ryan III)
Business & Industry

Allegheny Conference on Community Development

Incorporated in 1944 as an effort to transform the city.

It was a time when Pittsburgh was as tough as gristle, all steel and smoke, when the Point was a jumble of railroads and warehouses, when Frank Lloyd Wright famously growled "abandon it."

Edgar J. Kaufmann, William P. Snyder, III, then President of the Allegheny Conference; Leland Hazard, and Stefan Lorant study plans for the first Point State Park project, 1954.

Allegheny Conference Board Members convene to resolve regional issues of the '60s.

But it was also a time of giants, when financier Richard King Mellon and politician David Leo Lawrence used their clout to back the effort not to abandon but transform a city.

In so doing, they reinvented the way corporations handle civic matters, and how government works with business. Out of Pittsburgh's cauldron of need they forged something entirely new, a public-private partnership, the highest-level of business working in the public interest to re-shape a region. Pittsburgh became a national model, and still serves as a template for how American regions effectively grow and change.

That public-private partnership had a striking arm: the Allegheny Conference on Community Development. Incorporated in 1944, its own history is nothing less than Pittsburgh's proud record of accomplishment over the past 60 years.

Brokering an agreement for smoke control, the Conference helped rebuild Downtown. With Equitable Life Assurance investing in Gateway Center, Downtown's keystone economic revitalization project, the Conference also worked to develop Point State Park. Influential in its creation, the Conference also played a major role in Point State Park's revitalization some 60 years later, demonstrating an enduring interest not only in the region, but in many individual projects as well.

Other contemporary Conference projects included dams on the Allegheny and Monongahela Rivers, such highways as the Penn-Lincoln Parkway (now I-376), public parking authorities and the creation of Port Authority Transit of Allegheny County.

In the 1960s-70s, the Conference expanded its focus, from bricks-and-mortar projects to a greater social agenda by instituting programs to aid the growth of minority-owned businesses.

Through the 1970s and '80s, the Conference helped transform the 14-block Penn-Liberty Corridor into Pittsburgh's glittering Cultural Dis-

trict. It launched Strategy 21, enabling public and private agencies to work together when requesting state funds. Highly successful, Strategy 21 resulted in the new Pittsburgh International Airport, the Andy Warhol Museum, and other projects.

In the '90s, the Conference broadened its leadership base across the 10-county Pittsburgh region, strengthened regional economic development through brownfields legislation and helped create the Regional Asset District, a national model for funding civic and cultural institutions and municipal services. It supported efforts to improve local government, education and the region's workforce.

Schenley Plaza – the renovated gateway to Schenley Park – was a key initiative of the Conference's Oakland Investment Committee.

In 2000, the Pennsylvania Economy League—Western Division, the Greater Pittsburgh Chamber of Commerce and the Pittsburgh Regional Alliance combined with the Conference as the region's umbrella civic leadership organization to continue to advance the region's economy and quality of life.

In 2006, the Conference was once again recognized as a national model for its civic leadership accomplishments by the Alliance for Regional Stewardship.

Today, as the region's premier private-sector leadership organization with more than 300 Regional Investors, the Conference continues its work.

Today, Conference chairman Jim Rohr and Conference board member Michele Fabrizi of MARC USA ask many to "imagine what you can do here" in promoting the Pittsburgh region.

American Bridge

Founded in 1900 as a J. P. Morgan merger.

In 1993, when Bob Luffy was recruited to rejoin American Bridge Company after a 17 year hiatus, it was barely recognizable.

From the world's leading bridge company as recently as the 1980s, American Bridge was down to 25 employees, had no production facility, and took in just $30 million annually.

Luffy was not the man to let that situation stand. After earning a civil engineering degree from the University of Pittsburgh in 1972, and joining American Bridge, he had worked on West Virginia's New River Gorge Bridge, then the world's longest steel-arch bridge.

Although he left in 1976, Luffy returned to breathe life into what was once—and is again—one of America's top construction, engineering, and manufacturing companies. Now, with 2008 revenues projected at $550 million, and some 1,000 highly skilled employees, Luffy's work speaks for itself.

It also mirrors American Bridge's extraordinary history. Founded in 1900 as a J.P. Morgan-engineered merger of 28 bridge and structural companies, the company operated on an unprecedented scale. With roots reaching to the American Bridge Works, that was founded in Chicago in 1870, Morgan's new combine had four Pittsburgh-based companies, including Andrew Carnegie's Keystone Bridge Works. During that early period of purchase, consolidation, and growth, the main operations were moved to Ambridge, formerly Economy. When the plant was completed in 1903, its capacity was triple that of the previous record holder, and equal to American Bridge's five largest acquisitions.

A painter paints suspender cables on the San Francisco Oakland Bay Bridge in 1936.

Tagus River Bridge, Lisbon, Portugal, built 1962-1966

One of American Bridge's fifteen major New York water crossings, the Verrazano-Narrows Bridge's 4,260 feet made it the world's largest suspension bridge, 1964-81. Now seventh world-wide, it still stands as the largest in the United States.

In Vancouver, British Columbia, Lions Gate, a suspension bridge carrying 70,000 cars a day, is 5,890 ft. (1823 m) long.

Carrying nearly 300,000 cars every day, the new earthquake-proof version of the San Francisco-Oakland Bay Bridge runs 8.4 miles over picturesque San Francisco Bay.

Operating as a part of US Steel from 1901-87, American Bridge played a significant role in the creation of global railroads; supplied more than 600,000 tons of fabricated steel for the construction of New York City's subway system; and constructed more than 55 crossings of the Mississippi River and its tributaries, 14 crossings of the Columbia River & tributaries, and 13 crossings of the Hudson/Harlem/East River system.

American Bridge constructed what were, at the time, the longest suspension bridges in North America, Europe, and South America. It also erected renowned landmarks such as the Empire State Building, the San Francisco-Oakland Bay Bridge, the Mackinac Straits Bridge, the Verrazano Narrows Bridge and many of the nation's notable buildings, including the Woolworth Building, Chrysler Building, United Nations Secretariat, Rockefeller Center, Sears Tower, Louisiana Superdome, and many others. In addition, American Bridge played a major part in the construction of the Kennedy Space Center, Panama Canal, and Alaska Pipeline.

During World War II, the company constructed 119 LSTs in 942 days, turning out a 328-foot, 1,625-ton ship every eight days—in addition to fabricating hundreds of thousands of tons of structural steel for aircraft and other defense applications.

In 1987, US Steel sold American Bridge; in 1989 current ownership purchased the company. Since 1993, major bridge project successes, marine construction, and a greater involvement in complex concrete construction, have all served to diversify and modernize the company.

In 1999 American Bridge bought 32 acres on the Ohio River in Coraopolis and opened a modern steel fabricating plant. That facility, opened in 2000, was followed by a new headquarters complex in 2002, and a specialized steel painting facility in 2003. The most recent addition to the campus is a state of the art Training Facility, completed in 2008, which will train new generations of engineers in the company's craft of the construction of the world's most complex structures.

In the past decade, American Bridge has proudly regained its status as one of the top bridge builders in the world, witnessed by contracts including the Woodrow Wilson Bridge replacement in Washington, DC, the world's largest movable bridge, and the $1.43 billion Self Anchored Suspension Span for the San Francisco-Oakland Bay Bridge, among numerous others.

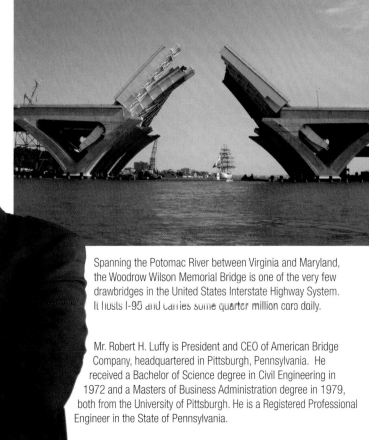

Spanning the Potomac River between Virginia and Maryland, the Woodrow Wilson Memorial Bridge is one of the very few drawbridges in the United States Interstate Highway System. It hosts I-95 and carries some quarter million cars daily.

Mr. Robert H. Luffy is President and CEO of American Bridge Company, headquartered in Pittsburgh, Pennsylvania. He received a Bachelor of Science degree in Civil Engineering in 1972 and a Masters of Business Administration degree in 1979, both from the University of Pittsburgh. He is a Registered Professional Engineer in the State of Pennsylvania.

ATI

ATI's parent corporation was founded in 1938.

One of the world's largest, most diversified specialty metals producers, Allegheny Technologies Incorporated (ATI) supplies a wide range of specialty metals for growing, global markets such as aerospace and defense, chemical processing, oil and gas, electrical energy, medical, automotive, food equipment and appliance, machine and cutting tools, and construction and mining.

In November 2006, ATI and Boeing hosted a community awareness event at the Heinz History Center in Pittsburgh, PA. Pictured at the event are (L) Pat Hassey, Chairman, President and CEO of ATI; and Scott Carson, President and CEO of Boeing Commercial Airplanes.

Throughout ATI's history, it has been an innovator. For aerospace and defense, ATI developed high-performance titanium alloys used since the 1940s. By the mid-1950s, ATI specialty metals were used in the Boeing 707, the nation's first commercial jet airplane.

For chemical processing, ATI was the first industrialized producer of zirconium, a critical alloy used in this industry. In the late 1980s, for oil and gas, an ATI alloy was used for the first high-strength firewalls in a North Sea oil facility.

For nuclear power generation, in the late 1950s ATI zirconium was used in the nation's first full-scale commercial power plant, Shippingport, Pennsylvania.

In the 1920s ATI stainless was used in the Chrysler Building, a New York City icon. In 1929, ATI stainless was used on the Ford Model A. And in 1965, ATI titanium was used for the Gemini 4 spacecraft.

Today, with some 9,700 employees throughout the United States, Europe, and Asia, ATI is Building the World's Best Specialty Metals Company™ by focusing its industry-leading technologies on meeting the ever-increasing demands of global customers.

ATI titanium is being used on the new Boeing 787 Dreamliner. Also ATI is a world leader in the production and development of premium high performance alloys critical for commercial and military jet engine applications.

ATI also provides corrosion-resistant alloys for offshore oil and gas applications, high-performance alloys for chemical plant applications, stainless alloys for ethanol and LNG (liquefied natural gas) applications, and tungsten carbide components for drilling.

One of the many specialty metals manufactured by ATI is 6-4 titanium alloy (shown in this color photomicrograph at 50x magnification) for use in airframe and jet engine applications, medical and dental devices, chemical processing equipment, and numerous other applications.

Throughout ATI's history it has been an innovator in the specialty metals industry. ATI solutions enable enginners the freedom to design products that help build a better quality of life for the world. Gary Hibner, pictured here, is a lab technician at ATI's technical and commercial center in Natrona Heights, PA.

ATI's titanium castings have been used in commercial and military applications since the late 1950s.

ATI is a leading supplier of specialty metals for coal, natural gas, nuclear and wind energy.

For medical applications, ATI specialty metals are used for knees, hips, and other prosthetics; in stents to support collapsed or clogged blood vessels; and as surgical screws.

As ATI Chairman, President, and CEO, L. Patrick Hassey says, "ATI is an integrated enterprise with unsurpassed manufacturing capabilities. Our broad product portfolio and deep technical competency enable our customers to design products that help improve the quality of life for people throughout the world."

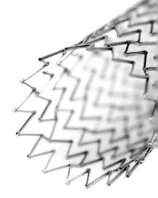

ATI's nickel-titanium shape memory alloy is for use in stents to support collapsed or clogged blood vessels.

ATI's specialty metals are used in today's most innovative airplane designs, such as the new super-efficient Boeing 787 Dreamliner shown in this ad titled 'There's a little bit of Pittsburgh all over the World.'

ATI works to drive operating performance and customer service through the ATI Business System, an integrated business system based on the principles: (1) Make to Use, (2) Elimination of Waste and (3) People Connect the System. The ATI employees pictured are from its Washington, PA, facility.

ATI's stainless is used in the roof of the David L. Lawrence Convention Center in Pittsburgh, PA. Photo courtesy of the David L. Lawrence Convention Center.

Alpern Rosenthal

Providing personalized and innovative CPA and business advisory services since 1961.

For more than 45 years, Alpern Rosenthal has been a leading accounting firm providing accounting, tax and consulting services to a wide array of businesses, not-for-profits, and individuals in Western Pennsylvania.

Founded in 1961 as Alpern, Rosenthal & Company by entrepreneurs Ed Alpern and Irving Rosenthal, both of whom grew up in Squirrel Hill and attended Allderdice High School, the company employed just one accountant and one secretary. However, when revenues doubled in the firm's second year, it was clear that Alpern Rosenthal's inventive solutions and dedicated personnel were meeting a vital need in the Pittsburgh region.

Chairman Emanuel DiNatale and President Alexander Paul

Alpern Rosenthal is located in Heinz 57 Center, Downtown

As Irving Rosenthal, a graduate of the University of Pittsburgh, led the firm into the 1990s, Alpern Rosenthal continued on its path of growth and innovative, personal service. As the firm grew by strengthening its internal structure, adding shareholders, and expanding into new offices, so did its industry expertise and resources. Indeed, by the 1990s Alpern Rosenthal's industry practice groups included construction, investment companies, manufacturing, medical, not-for-profit, professional services, real estate, retail and wholesale distribution services.

During the late 1990s, firm management transitioned to the current leadership team of Chairman Emanuel DiNatale and President Alexander Paul, both of whom graduated from Peabody High School. Mr. DiNatale is a native of Pittsburgh's East End and a graduate of Robert Morris College. Mr. Paul grew up in Stanton Heights and attended the University of Pittsburgh.

In 1999, a merger with Kaplan Sipos & Associates expanded another rapidly growing service—business valuation/litigation support, which remains one of Alpern Rosenthal's fastest-growing areas.

Within the last five years, Alpern Rosenthal has continued to expand its array of services to clients, both for privately held and publicly traded companies. In addition to such practice areas as employee benefits, and mergers and acquisitions, the firm offers services in high tech, internal audit and Sarbanes-Oxley compliance, wealth management advisory, state and local tax and international taxation.

As a member of the Leading Edge Alliance, Alpern Rosenthal also has access to the resources of an international network of many of the largest independently-owned accounting and consulting firms in the world. As many of Alpern Rosenthal's clients either have national operations or are foreign-owned, Alpern Rosenthal is able to provide both international audit, tax services and consulting through its network of more than 300 worldwide offices.

In 2007, Alpern Rosenthal again moved strategically by merging with with Cass, Levy & Leone of West Palm Beach and Stuart, Florida. Through this most recent merger, Alpern Rosenthal has expanded its industry expertise into the hospitality and family office sectors.

Enjoying its ranking as one of Pittsburgh's—and the nation's—largest accounting and business advisory firms, Alpern Rosenthal proudly employs over 200 employees in its signature 54,000-square-feet offices in Downtown Pittsburgh's Heinz 57 Center, in addition to some 30 employees in its Florida offices.

Alpern Rosenthal continues where it began, offering a full array of creative, effective services to its clients—who know that with Alpern Rosenthal, their future is filled with leading-edge solutions.

Bayer

The Bayer Pittsburgh story begins in 1958.

As Pittsburgh celebrates its 250th anniversary in 2008, Bayer is celebrating a major milestone of its own: 50 years of calling Pittsburgh home. The Bayer Pittsburgh story begins in 1958 when Mobay Chemical Company, a joint venture of Bayer and Monsanto Chemical Company, relocated from St. Louis to Pittsburgh. The rest, as they say, is history.

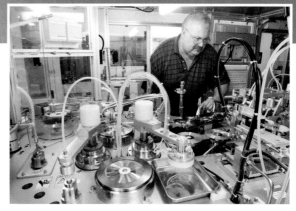

Bayer's Optical Media Lab allows Bayer researchers to stay on the leading edge of technology developing materials to meet demanding industry requirements.

Since then, Bayer has been an integral part of the Pittsburgh community. And just as Pittsburgh has evolved from the Steel City to America's Most Livable City, so too, Bayer's businesses—and name—have evolved over the years, with several mergers and acquisitions leading to the creation of Bayer Corporation in 1995. Pittsburgh serves as the headquarters of Bayer Corporation, Bayer Corporate and Business Services LLC and Bayer HealthCare affiliate MEDRAD, Inc., as well as the NAFTA headquarters for Bayer MaterialScience LLC.

The company's mission statement —Bayer: Science For A Better Life— underscores Bayer's willingness as an inventor company to help shape the future and its determination to develop innovations that benefit humankind. As such, the expertise and products of Bayer's three North American subgroups—Bayer CropScience LLC, Bayer HealthCare LLC and Bayer MaterialScience LLC—help diagnose, alleviate and cure diseases; improve the quality and adequacy of the global food supply; and contribute significantly to an active, modern lifestyle.

A Bayer volunteer works with students at the Bayer campus wildlife habitat.

More specifically, Bayer CropScience is one of the world's leading crop science companies in the areas of crop protection, non-agricultural pest control, seeds and plant biotechnology. Bayer HealthCare focuses on discovering and manufacturing innovative products that will improve human and animal health. For example, its Pittsburgh-based MEDRAD affiliate is a leading provider of medical devices and services that enable and enhance imaging procedures of the human body. Bayer MaterialScience is one of the largest producers of polymers and high-performance plastics in the world. Its developments in coating, adhesive and sealant raw materials, polycarbonate, polyurethane and thermoplastic polyurethane elastomers enhance the design and functionality of products in a wide variety of markets. Bayer Corporate and Business Services provides business-critical services to these three North American subgroups.

Throughout Bayer's evolution, a constant has been and continues to be the organization's strong commitment to the Pittsburgh community. Today, Bayer is part of the chemicals industry that generates some $3.4 billion in the local economy. Bayer has roughly 2,700 employees in the Pittsburgh area—1,500 on its suburban campus and 1,200 at MEDRAD. While this is vital to the region, Bayer's influence in the Pittsburgh area goes beyond job creation and economic impact.

Bayer is a major supporter of community initiatives. Employees enhance the community with their personal involvement in many local volunteer and service opportunities, such as the United Way; American Heart Association; and BASIC (Bayer Association for Science in Communities), an employee volunteer program in Pittsburgh that is part of Bayer's award-winning *Making Science Make Sense*® science literacy initiative. Bayer also spearheaded the nationally known science program, ASSET Inc. (Achieving Student Success Through Excellence in Teaching), which has grown from two pilot districts to approximately 40 member school districts, charter and private schools serving approximately 1,800 teachers and 125,000 students in 5,000 classrooms in six Western Pennsylvania counties.

Bayer takes its role as a socially and ethically responsible corporate citizen seriously. The Pittsburgh campus features a 40-acre wildlife habitat, certified by the Wildlife Habitat Council—a testament to Bayer's ongoing commitment to sustainability.

Pennsylvania Governor Ed Rendell engages in hands-on science activities with Pittsburgh elementary school students, using an ASSET Inc. science curriculum kit. Governor Rendell has rolled out ASSET statewide in Pennsylvania.

Carlow University

Values. Scholarship. Vision.

The Carlow University story begins in 1831, on Baggot Street in Dublin, Ireland, when Sister Catherine McAuley founded the Sisters of Mercy. Having inherited a large fortune some seven years prior, Sister Catherine built a large house in Dublin where she and several other women provided educational, religious, and social services for needy women and children. This building, called the House of Mercy, became the first Mercy convent. "No work of charity can be more productive of good to society or more conducive to the happiness of the poor than the careful instruction of women," Catherine McAuley later wrote.

Sister Catherine McAuley founded the Sisters of Mercy in 1831 and later opened the House of Mercy for needy women and children.

In 1843, Mother Frances Warde and six Sisters of Mercy left Carlow, for Pittsburgh.

Six years later, in 1837, Father Andrew Fitzgerald, President of St. Patrick's College at Carlow, welcomed the Sisters of Mercy, where they established a convent and also opened a school for girls and young women.

In 1843, as their work flourished, Mother Frances Warde and six Sisters of Mercy left Carlow for Pittsburgh. Thus, America's first Mercy community was formed, and its impact on Pittsburgh was quickly noticed. In fact, Mother Frances Warde, at the Pittsburgh bicentennial, was named one of the 10 outstanding women in the city's history, though she had been in Pittsburgh just seven years.

The Sisters of Mercy opened Saint Mary Academy in 1844, a K-12 school. In 1894, the Sisters purchased a 14-acre site in Oakland. Then, in 1929, seeing the need for college-level women's education in a Catholic setting, especially in the fields of nursing and education, the Sisters of Mercy opened Mount Mercy College.

Despite the Depression, Mount Mercy grew. In 1936 Aquinas Hall was built to house the library and administrative offices. Five years later, Trinity Hall opened as the science center. Antonian Hall was built in 1948, followed by Frances Warde Hall and Grace Library. Tiernan Hall is home to The Campus School of Carlow University (pre-K-eighth grade).

Carlow's original Women of Spirit®: Sisters Flynn, Grace, Dougherty, Tiernan, Ragen, and Curran.

Renamed Carlow College in 1969 to honor the founding Sisters' Irish heritage, the school kept pace with the times, expanding its women's studies program and actively recruiting both traditional and non-traditional students. In 2004, Carlow was granted university status. Now Carlow University, it stands as Pennsylvania's first Catholic, women-centered liberal arts university.

Since becoming a university, Carlow has launched an MFA program, an MBA program, and its first doctoral program in counseling psychology. It is also home to the Women of Spirit Institute® and the Grace Ann Geibel Institute for Justice and Social Responsibility. In addition to its main Oakland campus, Carlow offers classes in Greensburg, Cranberry's Regional Learning Alliance Conference and Learning Center, and in Downtown Pittsburgh. A short walk from other universities, libraries, and hospitals, Carlow's Oakland campus is 10 minutes from Downtown's arts, commerce, and sports activities.

With an enrollment of 2,200 and a student-faculty ratio of 12-1, Carlow students enjoy small classes and individual instruction.

Carlow University prepares students, primarily women, for effective leadership and compassionate service in personal and professional life.

The St. Agnes Center of Carlow University is located on Fifth Avenue.

Carlow University's Oakland campus extends for 14 acres in the heart of Pittsburgh's Oakland neighborhood—home to numerous institutions of higher learning, including the University of Pittsburgh and Carnegie Mellon University.

Carnegie Library

In 1895, Andrew Carnegie donated $1 million for a "free public library."

You never know how far an act of kindness will reach.

In the case of Carnegie Library of Pittsburgh, one man's helping hand to an immigrant boy became the region's single-most visited asset.

More than a century ago, Saturday nights in Allegheny meant that Colonel James Anderson opened his personal 500-volume library to working boys—including a young messenger named Andrew Carnegie. Borrowing, reading, growing, Carnegie re-made himself—and encouraged others to do the same.

By 1881 he was a millionaire many times over – and as one arm of his philanthropic efforts he sought to repay Colonel Anderson's favor, offering to donate $250,000 for a free public library, provided that the city donate the land and appropriate $15,000 annually for library operations. By 1890 Carnegie had increased his investment to $1 million for a Main Library and five neighborhood branches. (Carnegie would go on to establish more than 2,500 libraries worldwide.)

Three years later, in 1893, ground was broken, and the flagship Oakland facility opened in 1895. By the end of 1896, the library, headed by Edwin H. Anderson, boasted a 19-person staff—and 27,000 books.

By the turn of the century, Carnegie opened five additional branches, Lawrenceville, West End, Hill District, Mt. Washington, and Hazelwood; an East Liberty branch came on board in 1905. Four years later, 1909, the South Side Branch became the last Pittsburgh library to be financed from Carnegie's original gift. In

Carnegie Library of Pittsburgh, Public Affairs Room, 1951

One of the region's finest resources, the Pennsylvania Room

A place for everyone: the Wylie Avenue Children's Room

Mr. Carnegie's grand edifice, Oakland, 1908

1910, the Library's Homewood Branch became the eighth and last of the Carnegie-financed branches, and the last branch erected in Pittsburgh until 1964, when the city began its building program.

As one of the first public library systems in the United States, Carnegie Library has observed such milestones as:

First storytime, 1899
First organized children's department, 1899
First training class for children's librarians, 1900
First science and technology department, 1902
Services to the blind, 1907
Depository for Library of Congress catalogue cards, 1908

Since opening, the Library has built an extensive collection of materials about Pennsylvania. In 1928 the materials were consolidated into one unit, the Pennsylvania Department, with resources on history, biography, law, economics, sociology, and demographics. The Pittsburgh Photographic Library contains more than 100,000 images of Pittsburgh.

Today, with 19 locations, Carnegie Library provides more than 8,000 free programs, classes, and other learning and training opportunities. With the proliferation of new technologies, library resources can be accessed at any time from any location using any type of electronic device. And those resources, in excess of 5.5 million items, include publications, audio and visual materials, downloadable video, eBooks, newspapers and journals, eAudio, streaming music and spoken word.

With the Library facing the challenge of adapting 19th-century buildings for 21st-century requirements, newly renovated libraries reflect community needs—more computers, more meeting rooms, even coffee bars! Nevertheless, just as it did more than a century ago, the Carnegie Library of Pittsburgh continues to be a cornerstone of society, a gathering place, and a promoter of literacy and lifelong learning.

One of Carnegie Library's many innovations: the Teen Reading Room

The latest books are always on display in the Carnegie Library of Pittsburgh Main Branch first floor.

Girls share a moment in the Squirrel Hill Branch's Window Alcove

Ready to meet the 21st Century, Carnegie Library is online

Carnegie Mellon University

In 1900, a small school started preparing students for a revolution.

That revolution never ends. For more than 100 years, Carnegie Mellon University has been carrying on a tradition of generating innovations with global impact by combining systematic analysis and problem solving with entrepreneurial creativity and hard work. These remain the distinctive values of Carnegie Mellon today. That's what enables our faculty, students and alumni to consistently see beyond the curve and change the world.

Carnegie Mellon's seven colleges include:

College of Fine Arts (CFA)

College of Humanities & Social Sciences (H&SS)

David A. Tepper School of Business (Tepper)

H. John Heinz III School of Public Policy and
　Management (Heinz)

Mellon College of Science (MCS)

School of Computer Science (SCS)

Carnegie Institute of Technology (CIT)

1900 Founding Industrialist Andrew Carnegie founded Carnegie Technical Schools as a gift to the city of Pittsburgh as a school for the education of steel-mill workers' children.

1905 Uniting Arts and Technology The first classes began in 1905 in industries and applied arts. The Margaret Morrison Carnegie College offered classes for women.

1912 Becoming Carnegie Tech The school was renamed as Carnegie Institute of Technology and baccalaureate degrees were offered. In 1919 the first PhD was awarded.

1947 The Carnegie Plan President Robert Doherty led the creation of "the Carnegie Plan," a new standard for engineering education.

1948 Transforming Management Education William Larimer Mellon supported the creation of a new school focused on a systematic analysis and practical application of the principles of management. The curriculum devised at the new Graduate School of Industrial Administration (now the Tepper School of Business) revolutionized on business education everywhere.

1956 The Birth of Computing An IBM 650 was installed in the basement of the business school beginning collaboration among the business, mathematics, engineering, and psychology departments. Professors Herbert A. Simon and Alan Newell saw the new "thinking machine" as a way to understand intelligence itself and they created artificial intelligence as a new field of study.

1967 Carnegie Mellon University Carnegie Tech merged with the Mellon Institute, a private industrial research laboratory that the Mellon family had founded in 1911.

1968 Impact on Policy In response to concerns about urban poverty and racial tensions in America, the Richard King Mellon Foundation supported the creation of the School of Urban and Public Administration, changed in 1991 to the H. John Heinz III School of Public Policy and Management (Heinz School).

2002 Beyond Pittsburgh The university expanded its presence beyond Pittsburgh to campuses in Doha, Qatar and Silicon Valley, along with partnerships and degree programs around the world.

An autonomous vehicle, "Boss" was developed by the Carnegie Mellon Tartan Racing Team, winners of the 2007 Urban Challenge.

Quick Facts

Private Research University
President: Jared L. Cohon
Campuses: Pittsburgh, Qatar, Silicon Valley
Faculty: 1,426
Undergraduate students: 5,758
Graduate and doctoral students: 4,644
Alumni around the world: 72,496
Degree Programs in 10 Countries
15 Nobel Laureates
Listed in "The Top 100 Global Universities"
    by *Newsweek*

Carnegie Technical School establishes the School for Apprentices
and Journeyman in 1907.

Photo courtesy of Carnegie Mellon University Archives

Carnegie Mellon.
www.cmu.edu

Children's Hospital of Pittsburgh of UPMC

A Healthy Place To Be

For nearly half of Pittsburgh's 250 years, Children's Hospital of Pittsburgh of UPMC has been the only hospital in western Pennsylvania devoted solely to the care of infants, children and young adults.

More than 600 board-certified physicians and 2,800 staff combine science with compassion to provide premier care at its main facility in Oakland; at ambulatory care centers east, north and south of the city; and at regional locations throughout western Pennsylvania. Additionally, Children's Community Pediatrics — more than 100 pediatricians affiliated with Children's — provides primary pediatric care at 27 locations throughout western and central Pennsylvania. Children's also shares its world-renowned expertise in a number of specialty areas such as pediatric transplantation and cardiothoracic surgery with physicians, patients and families across the country.

A Standard of Excellence

Children's Hospital has helped establish the standards of excellence in pediatric care. The hospital consistently is at the forefront of advanced patient care, biomedical research and medical education. The hospital's international reputation for high-quality clinical services is complemented by its commitment to the practice of family-centered care, advanced nursing practices, innovative technology and patient safety. As a result, Children's is designated consistently as among the best pediatric hospitals in the United States by a number of elite lists of pediatric health care facilities.

Since the first 15-bed hospital opened in Oakland in 1890, Children's Hospital has been the site of major medical innovations.

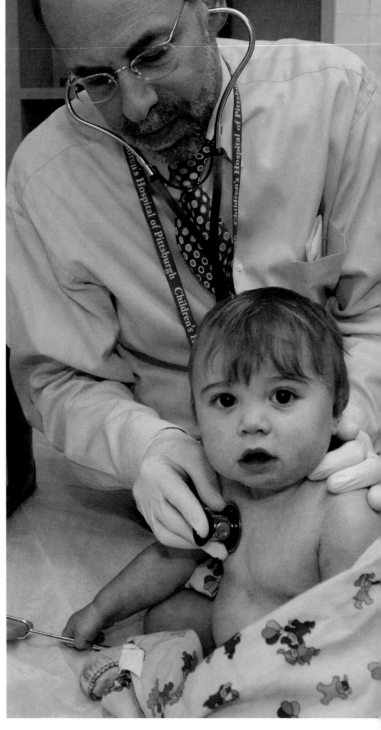

A medical staff of more than 600 board-certified physicians provide care to the patients who make more than 400,000 visits to Children's various locations each year.

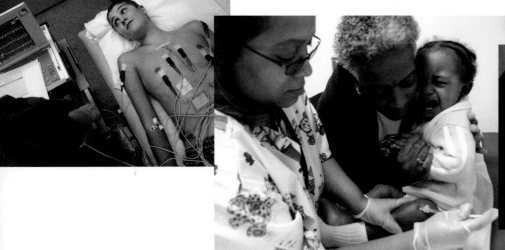

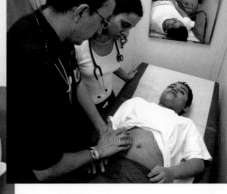

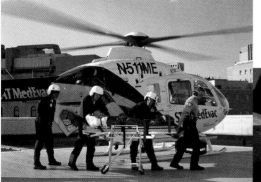

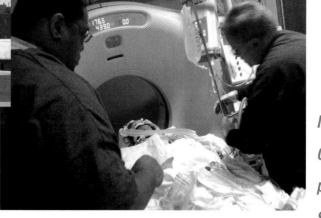

Children's Benedum Pediatric Trauma Program is a Level I Regional Resource Pediatric Trauma Center accredited by the American College of Surgeons — one of only three in Pennsylvania.

Additionally, the National Institutes of Health (NIH), whose funding to Children's research has risen from less than $4 million to more than $20 million during the past 20 years, recognized the hospital's stature by selecting Children's Hospital as a Center of Excellence for training the nation's future pediatric researchers — making it one of only 20 such NIH-funded Child Health Research Centers nationwide.

In fiscal year 2007, Children's Hospital provided approximately $31.8 million in free care.

Medical Advancements and Innovations

As the site of one of the fastest growing pediatric research programs in the country, Children's is committed to the same type of high-impact research that resulted in Dr. Jonas Salk's development of the polio vaccine here in the 1950s.

Children's Hillman Center for Pediatric Transplantation, which was the nation's first pediatric transplantation center, offers innovative immunosuppression protocols and achieves among the highest pediatric outcomes for single-organ and complex multi-organ transplant cases in the nation. Some of the hospital's most notable transplant advancements include performing the first pediatric heart-lung and pediatric heart-liver transplants, and curing the rare Maple Syrup Urine Disease through liver transplantation.

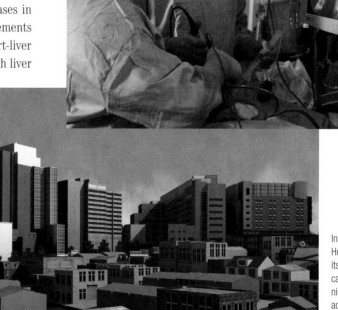

Among the many innovations pioneered by the physicians at Children's is a minimally invasive neurosurgical technique that enables surgeons to remove tumors as large as baseballs through the nasal passages using narrow scopes and surgical tools — some of them developed by the surgeons themselves.

Growth for the Future

To help accommodate the growing need for space for new and expanding clinical services and research efforts, Children's Hospital will move in spring 2009 to a new 10-acre campus in Lawrenceville. Planners incorporated an innovative design process to seek input from physicians, nurses and patients and their families in order to meet the need for a preeminent facility that is efficient, yet comfortable.

In 2009, Children's Hospital will move to its new Lawrenceville campus, which includes nine clinical and administrative buildings situated on 10 acres.

Additionally, Children's new campus will be a benchmark for quality built on the principles of family-centered care, patient safety and technological sophistication. The new hospital is designed to promote human and environmental health. It will be an environmentally sustainable "green" building with ample natural light, better air quality and reduced noise levels.

Through its strong commitment to finding the best approaches to quality patient care, Children's Hospital of Pittsburgh of UPMC is positioned to support the health and well-being of children now and for generations to come.

Generous contributions from the Hillman Foundation and the Richard King Mellon Foundation, as well as many other Pittsburgh area foundations, corporations and residents, enable Children's to improve the health and well-being of children through excellence in patient care, teaching and research.

Photos: Steven Adams, Terry Clark, Bill Exler, Ron Fontana, Lisa Kyle, Kathryn Komperda, Jim Schafer
Rendering: Astorino

Cohen & Grigsby

For more than 25 years, advice and action with a difference.

It was March, 1981 when nine lawyers, all working at a prestigious, old-line Pittsburgh law firm, decided they want to do things differently. Specializing in corporate and securities, taxation, labor, and civil litigation, they came together as Manion, Alder & Cohen.

Charles C. Cohen, co-founder and chairman of the board, Cohen & Grigsby, P.C.

This newly formed law firm differed from other firms in that the founders wanted to offer an intellectual work product equal to—or better than—their peer law firms, but doing so with better service and pricing more favorable to their clients. They formulated a plan to accomplish these objectives. In matters of recruitment, they paid scrupulous attention to credentials, character, and competency; in matters of promotion and compensation, to performance and industriousness.

Most importantly, they paid scrupulous attention to overhead and operating costs.

Novel philosophies when they were adopted, they remain differentiating factors, because Cohen & Grigsby has consistently translated these ideas into managerial action.

Another distinguishing characteristic: from the beginning, Cohen & Grigsby decided to take on client engagements only when they were confident that, when the engagement was completed, they would achieve excellence. Striving to be the best at what they did, they did not hesitate to introduce a client to another lawyer or law firm, even a competitor, if there was reason to believe that it would be best for the client.

Growing to 24 lawyers during the firm's first four years meant success—and separation. Because of differing desires, seven of the 24 left in 1985. Adding Robert Grigsby, a top area trial lawyer and, briefly, a Common Pleas judge, changed the nature and the name of the firm, to Alder, Cohen & Grigsby. Three years later, in 1988, the firm became Cohen & Grigsby.

cohen&grigsby®
progressive law.

625 Liberty Avenue, the new home of Cohen & Grigsby, in Pittsburgh's Cultural District. © Ed Massery.

Now at 130 lawyers, the firm is led by Jack Elliott, president and CEO of the firm; and Charles Cohen, chairman of the board. The practice areas have expanded to include international, estates & trusts, employee benefits, environmental, and intellectual property. Attesting to the firm's overall excellence, 27 of 40 full partners were voted by their peers to appear in Best Lawyers in America.

As Cohen & Grigsby looks forward to its fourth decade, it prospers not only because of the quality of its attorneys, but also because it has created an environment in which its support staff is valued, regarded as colleagues and not subordinates. Eschewing stratification and rigid job classifications, Cohen & Grigsby enables—and encourages—all staff members to function to the limits of their abilities. An economic consequence is that the proportion of non-lawyers to lawyers is relatively low, and turnover is far lower than normal.

As Chuck Cohen says, "We are proud of the fact that everybody goes to the same holiday party in December. And we are proud of the fact that our staff members are, by and large, very happy."

While Cohen & Grigsby has attracted a considerable volume of clients, transactions, and cases not linked to western Pennsylvania, nevertheless, the firm intends to retain its Pittsburgh identity, fulfilling its role as a solid and respected local institution. Cohen and Grigsby also maintains offices in Naples, FL, and Bonita Springs, FL.

Jack W. Elliot, president and CEO, Cohen & Grigsby, P.C. This photo taken by Joe Wojcik appeared in the November 24, 2006 issue of the Pittsburgh Business Times.

CONSOL Energy

As early as 1750, Pittsburghers were unearthing the rich coal of Western Pennsylvania.

Their names are lost to history, hardened individuals, pioneers, miners who endured the worst conditions to dig relentlessly in the earth for the hard black gold that ignited mills and cities and an Industrial Revolution that re-shaped the world.

Using highly sophisticated equipment, today's smart, skilled coal miners enjoy excellent advancement opportunities and long-term careers.

Coal mining was never easy, but the early pioneers in the field had it particularly difficult —digging by hand and hauling with mules.

They began as far back as 1750, in woods, on hills, in backyards, mining the rich coal seam that lies under Western Pennsylvania—the Pittsburgh seam, the world's most valuable ore deposit, some 160 miles square. From Coal Hill in Pittsburgh, to Clarksburg in West Virginia, they found America's largest indigenous energy resource, one that will last into the next century and beyond.

By 1860, several small Western Maryland coal mining firms had merged into Consolidation Coal Company; four years later, with demand incessant, and the Civil War raging all around them, Consolidation Coal incorporated.

By 1927, Consolidation Coal had become America's largest bituminous coal producer, a distinction it retains today. Merging with Pittsburgh Coal in 1945, 21 years later, in 1966, Continental Oil Company (Conoco) acquired Consolidation Coal. From 1981 through 1999, when CONSOL Energy stock began to be traded on the NYSE as CNX, Conoco, along with its subsidiary, Consolidation Coal, underwent a series of ownership changes by DuPont and RWEA.G.

Steady, positive growth continued. In 2000-02, for example, CONSOL purchased extensive coalbed methane reserves, facilities and pipelines in southwestern Virginia. The company is also a majority shareholder in one of the largest U.S. producers of coalbed methane, CNX Gas Corporation. Collectively, coal and gas fuel two-thirds of all U.S. power generation. CONSOL Energy's reserves of both fuels are located mainly east of the Mississippi River, making CONSOL Energy a major fuel supplier to the electric power industry in the northeast quadrant of the United States.

On the rivers, CONSOL's fleet of 22 vessels and 600 barges annually hauls nearly 25 million tons of coal.

To better utilize its vast land holdings—a half-million surface acres, some $4 billion of land, plants and equipment—CONSOL Energy has brokered industrial and retail development projects and oversees timber sales and forestry management activities.

CONSOL Energy, a member of the S&P 500, has annual revenues of about $3.8 billion. The company was named one of America's most admired companies in 2005 by Fortune magazine. It received the U.S. Department of the Interior's Office of Surface Mining national Award for Excellence in Surface Mining for the company's innovative reclamation practices in 2002, 2003 and 2004. Also, in 2003, the company was listed in Information Week magazine's "Information Week 500" list for its information technology operations. In 2002, the company received a U.S. Environmental Protection Agency Climate Protection Award.

Yet, for all its record-setting production, CONSOL Energy also sets

the pace for safety, with an incident rate that's nearly twice as good as the national average.

Finally, as a good neighbor and better corporate citizen, CONSOL averages $1 million annually in charitable donations, with an additional $400,000 going toward scholarships and grants to colleges and universities

One of the biggest changes in coal mining over the last century is the improvements in safety and environmental concerns. Pictured here is a CONSOL Mine Rescue Team.

Davison's Inventionland

George Davison
"Creative Genius"
Entrepreneur magazine, January 2008

More than getting his feet wet, George Davison and Inventionland create 240 new products every month.

As a boy, dreaming in his Oakmont tree house, George Davison knew that he wanted to do something unique. He achieved that with the creation of his innovative product development company, Davison, and Inventionland—the world's most unique workspace. "As long as I can remember," Davison says, "I've always done things differently than most people."

Born in 1963, Davison is a fourth-generation Pittsburgh business leader. In 1854, his family formed Davison Sand and Gravel, which over 125 years grew into Western Pennsylvania's largest company of its type. With dredge, truck, and plant operations, Davison built roads and foundations under many steel mills.

Following his family's entrepreneurial spirit, Davison spent two years after graduation from Allegheny College developing a product to kill toothbrush germs—only to be discouraged when someone beat him to the market. That's when Davison figured there must be a better way to design, develop, and bring new products to market.

His answer: to come up with a way to get ideas designed, developed, and prepared for licensing in one place. Now, Davison's exclusive development process—of creating new or improved products by de-

George M. Davison, Gordon Davison and their mother Moira.

signing for manufacturers in a timely, efficient manner—drives his company.

To pursue this goal, in 1989 he started Davison in his grandfather's Eighth Street home, one of the oldest homes in Oakmont.

Making prototype molds, working with customers, and developing a process that would help the company grow, by 2001, with multiple area operations, Davison united under one roof at 595 Alpha Drive in RIDC Park, O'Hara Township. The 36,000-square-foot facility remains the home of Davison's corporate, sales, and administrative headquarters.

In 2006, the design division moved next door into Inventionland, a creative

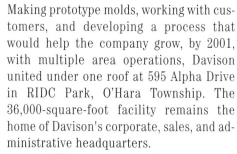

Working by trial and error, Davison began his career in this Oakmont home, 1989.

workspace. Occupying more than 60,000 square feet, Inventionland is unlike any other workspace, as new products come to life in 16 themed sets.

Toy designers' ideas set sail on the deck of the pirate ship Discovery, electronics designers build electric gadgetry inside a giant robot, and designers of automotive products

Davison Sand and Gravel helped pave Western Pennsylvania.

New product designers work on gadgets and gizmos inside of Inventron 54.

let their minds race in the Motor Speedway.

Davison also has traded in his ordinary office in the neighboring building for an office in the Treehouse, from which he can look out at the waterfalls of the cavern and the turrets of Inventalot Castle. He and his team often brainstorm on the deck, think-

Following the family tradition of entrepreneurship and innovation, George Davison leads teams of designers, engineers, and marketers in creating new ways to bring products to store shelves.

ing up the products of the future. Entrepreneur magazine January 2008 issue said it best. They said, "There's nothing like a little fantasy to get imaginations —and business—moving."

In the fall of 2007, Davison received extraordinary recognition when Inventionland was featured in *Ripley's Believe It or Not!, The Remarkable... Revealed*.

The secret entrance to Inventionland is hidden in Edison's Lab, a room that highlights the evolution of the company and its product successes. The room also is a tes-

Davison's process takes a product from idea to licensing, with many engineering and assembly steps in between.

tament to Davison's inspirational heroes, Thomas Edison, Walt Disney and Henry Ford.

Metalworking, woodworking, molding, laser cutting, prototyping, circuit board construction, and more take place in a state-of-the-art product sample construction facility. In all, more than 240 new products are created there every month, delivering a constant flow of innovative products to companies wanting to stay ahead of their competitors.

Recognized by the industry, Davison awards include a 1993 bronze Industrial Design Excellence Award (IDEA) from the Industrial Design Society of America for the Oil Filter Gripper, which eliminates the

Davison's team of talented employees design and construct client projects in-house.

struggle and mess of removing an oil filter. In 2006, Davison designers won two more IDEAs, for the Hover Creeper and the Bike-Board, a unique hybrid bicycle-skateboard.

Turning ideas into products. Davison-designed products have sold in stores nationwide.

With plans for steadily growing his company, Davison plans to expand Inventionland and continually improve the process of developing ideas. "I'm hoping we can do for product development what Disney did for family entertainment."

Sailing the creative seas. Davison's crew of designers develops ideas on the pirate ship Discovery.

Duquesne Light

Powering homes and businesses since 1880

Thanks to the work of the employees of Allegheny County Light, Pittsburgh became the most electrified city in America by 1896.

For more than 125 years, Duquesne Light has been delivering Pittsburgh energy. From the early industrial age to the emerging technology era, Duquesne Light has been an integral part of this region's growth.

Duquesne Light's roots run deep. In 1880, nine Pittsburgh businessmen—including Christopher Magee, future U.S. Senator George Oliver, and city councilman Hugh McNeill—pooled $90,000 and formed the area's first electric utility. Called Allegheny County Light, the fledgling firm caught the eye of one of the region's pre-

Formed in 1880, Allegheny County Light—and George Westinghouse—changed the face of the city.

mier inventors and futurists—George Westinghouse, who brought ideas about alternating current.

With the Pennsylvania Railroad as the new company's first private customer, Allegheny Light lit the dark —and thief-infested—railroad yards. Then, with public safety paramount, Allegheny Light power plants went up all around the city. One milestone: in 1888, industrialist Henry Clay Frick had his East End mansion Clayton wired for the new flameless light.

The company successfully fought off a challenge from proponents of direct current, with Thomas Edison and Westinghouse agreeing to pool patents in 1896. By then, Pittsburgh had gone so electric that some felt it was the most electrified city in the country.

Acquired by the Philadelphia Company, Allegheny Light seemed destined to control all the region's power until 1903, when a consortium of 150 smaller companies—some as small as a single generator operating only at night—banded together to fight for its share of the market. Called Duquesne Light, and headed by Robert Hall, an investment broker, it was headquartered at 238 Fourth Avenue, in the heart of Pittsburgh's financial district. With its main plant in East Liberty, Duquesne Light signed up so many customers that the two companies merged in 1912—with the Duquesne Light name enduring.

Power use soared, from 5,000 customers in 1905 to more than 200,000 in 1925 —with no end in sight.

In 1915 Duquesne Light began creating the first high-tension transmission ring to surround a major city, a 66,000-volt line that by 1920 would cover some 800 high-tension towers and use more than 9,000 miles of wire.

Powering the nation's military factory during World War II, Duquesne Light helped Pittsburgh build tanks, airplane parts, and landing craft. During Pittsburgh's 1950s Renaissance, Duquesne Light doubled its capacity in just nine years. In 1957, Duquesne Light opened the nation's first full-scale commercial nuclear power plant. Shippingport, President Eisenhower said, "put the atom to work for the good of mankind."

In the 1970s, Duquesne Light pioneered environmental protection at its coal-fired power stations.

With electric energy more profoundly affecting modern life than any other product, Duquesne Light helped transform the way people live, delivering extraordinarily reliable energy for more comfort and leisure, faster communications and transportation, business prosperity, improved health care—indeed, virtually every facet of life.

Under CEO Morgan K. O'Brien, Duquesne Light has achieved all-time high customer satisfaction ratings, improved service and reliability, and instituted a more than $500 million infrastructure investment program. Today, the company continues its longstanding role as a committed community partner while delivering a safe, reliable supply of electricity to more than 585,000 homes and businesses.

Duquesne Light created the first high tension power ring around a city.

Sunshine or snow, Duquesne Light delivers.

Gateway Clipper Fleet

In 1958, the Gateway Clipper sailed her Maiden Voyage.

In 50 years, the Gateway Clipper Fleet has grown from a one-boat, 100- passenger operation to the five-boat, 2,500-passenger fleet of today. Sailing all year from the Southern Bank of the Monongahela River at Station Square, the Gateway Clipper Fleet offers a wide variety of dining, sightseeing, and entertainment cruises.

Although today the Three Rivers are clean, for the first half of the 20th Century they were polluted. By the 1950s, civic leaders agreed that something had to be done.

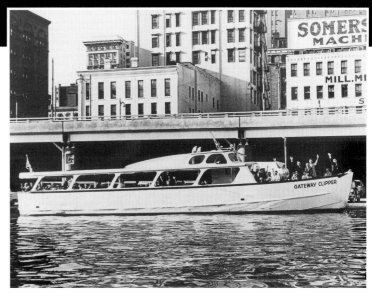

The original Gateway Clipper plies the Monongahela on one of her early voyages.

In 1955, John E. Connelly was appointed treasurer of ALCOSAN, the agency tapped to clean the rivers. Perhaps more than anyone else, Connelly saw the rivers' potential – "these rivers are the lifeblood of the city," he said. Aside from cleanliness, he believed that the rivers needed an excursion boat to showcase the city.

Enlisting his nephew, Captain Jack Goessling, to help him find the right vessel, in Erie they found a fishing boat that seemed right. Excited about the prospect of purchasing a boat, Connelly jumped into his car so quickly that he forgot to bring money – or even a check! After haggling over the boat's value, and losing a coin toss to decide the price, Connelly gave the man all the money in his pocket – $50 – as a down payment.

Then came a truly Herculean task – bringing a riverboat from Lake Erie to Pittsburgh. Beginning in April, 1958, over four weeks Goessling traveled some 2,200 miles, from Lake Erie to the Detroit River, across Lake St. Clair to Lake Huron, through the Straits of Mackinac to the Illinois River, to the Mississippi, finally to the Ohio River and Pittsburgh. On May 17, 1958, the renamed Gateway Clipper sailed from the Monongahela Wharf – with the YMCA as its first chartered pleasure cruise.

A success from the start, the Gateway Clipper sailed just four months that maiden season, hosting more than 25,000 passengers. The following year, 1959, two more 100-passenger boats were added, Gateway Clipper II and the Good Ship Lollipop. Through the years, more than 20 boats have been members of the fleet.

In 1982, the Gateway Clipper Fleet moved across the river to Station Square. Under the leadership of Terry Wirginis, Connelly's grandson, the Gateway Clipper Fleet "keeps changing, adapting, and adding cruises to keep up with the needs of our customers," Wirginis says.

In 1987, for example, Gateway Clipper added the largest boat ever to sail with the fleet. The 277-foot, 1,000-passenger Majestic leads a line including the 600-passenger Party Liner, 400-passenger Liberty Belle and Keystone Belle, and 150-passenger Good Ship Lollipop — all authentic reproductions of antique riverboats.

Boasting 70 full-time and 300 seasonal employees, the Gateway Clipper Fleet sails all year long. "As the nation's largest inland riverboat fleet," Wirginis says, "we are a model for the excursion boat industry."

And as Pittsburgh's number-one attraction, in a half-century more than 25 million passengers have sailed the Three Rivers — and beyond.

"Our growth potential is limited only by our own creativity," Wirginis says. "Our future is filled with incredible promise."

From it's early days, a Clipper voyage was a fun adventure for the whole family.

Who hasn't sailed the Gateway Clipper fleet and asked the captain to ring the boat's bell?

Giant Eagle

In 75 years, Giant Eagle has grown from a single store into a regional retail chain.

It all began in 1931 when five families—who all still own the company—combined to form Giant Eagle. What began as a dream is now a company with approximately 36,000 employees working in 350 stores throughout Pennsylvania, Ohio, West Virginia, and Maryland.

Giant Eagle's success arises in part because it has been able to change with the times. In the 1930s, the era of the Great Depression, the store remained strong, giving customers quality products at good prices. In the '40s, as able-bodied men joined the war effort, women employees became a permanent part of the working society—and the Giant Eagle staff.

From the first, Giant Eagle gave good quality at good prices.

As the century turned, Giant Eagle continued to grow. Most recently, the company expanded further by launching two new store concepts, Market District and Giant Eagle Express.

Expanding its presence in Ohio, Giant Eagle opened retail locations in Columbus and Toledo. Aside from moving into Maryland, Giant Eagle also entered the fuel and convenience store business, by mid-decade operating nearly 100 GetGo outlets.

In more than 75 years, Giant Eagle's growth has been based on fair pricing, outstanding value, and superior service. And for nearly a century, Giant Eagle's valued customers and hard-working employees have been the measure of the company's success.

During the 1950s and '60s, the average size of Giant Eagle stores grew to 15,000 square feet and were designed to offer more products and variety. Giant Eagle again kept up with the times, introducing overall price lowering along with store remodeling.

The 1960s also saw Giant Eagle acquire the former Kroger warehouse in Lawrenceville, doubling the retailer's total available storage area. When the South Hills Giant Eagle opened, as the company's first 20,000-square-foot supermarket, it heralded a new era of variety and value.

To help customers with inflation-related issues of the 1970s, Giant Eagle introduced generic products as well as its Food Club line, lower-priced private label products. This decade also saw Giant Eagle open its doors on Sundays, and introduce open-code dating, allowing customers to determine products' freshness.

In the 1980s, Giant Eagle celebrated its 50th birthday—with 52 stores, including its first 50,000-square-foot location. In an ongoing effort to offer more services to Giant Eagle's loyal customers, some stores included on-site bakeries, pharmacies, florists, automotive and houseware departments, paperback books and greeting cards, photo processing, and video rentals.

During the 1990s, Giant Eagle became the market leader in Western Pennsylvania, Eastern Ohio, and Northern West Virginia.

As the 1990s drew to a close, Giant Eagle acquired Cleveland's Riser Foods, adding 53 stores to the company.

The Giant Eagle Advantage Card®, introduced in 1994, became the area's first frequent shopper card. At the same time, the Eagle's Nest, an in-store supervised learning and activity center staffed with trained childcare workers, was opened to help both shoppers and staff.

Giant Eagle has approximately 36,000 employees in more than 350 retail stores.

GSK Consumer Healthcare

For more than 150 years, medicines that make a difference.

As consumers take increasing responsibility for managing their own healthcare, Moon Township-based GlaxoSmithKline Consumer Healthcare is working to ensure they have broader access to the medicines they need to do more, feel better and live longer.

George Quesnelle, President & CEO

The GSK Consumer Healthcare medicine chest boasts more than 30 popular, long-trusted consumer brands such as Aquafresh, Sensodyne, PoliGrip, Abreva, Tums, Os-Cal, Goody's and BC Powders and Citrucel as well as ground breaking over-the-counter solutions for two of the toughest healthcare challenges consumers face: weight loss and smoking cessation.

In 2007 GSK Consumer Healthcare launched the only FDA-approved OTC weight loss product, alli. Consumers responded strongly to this launch because they are hungry for a more effective weight loss therapy. Also, for more than a decade, the GSK has led the smoking cessation category with its Nicorette, NicoDerm CQ and Commit products. An estimated 7.6 million adults have successfully quit smoking since these brands, previously available only by prescription, became available over-the-counter.

Pittsburgh has been home to GSK Consumer Healthcare for 31 years, and more than 600 of the firm's 1,400 North American employees are based here. Parent company GlaxoSmithKline is based in the United Kingdom and is midway through its second century helping people around the globe, not only with over-the-counter medicines and oral care products, but also life-saving vaccines and prescription therapies for diseases such as HIV, cancer and malaria. GSK sales were $45 billion in 2006, including $6 billion contributed by GSK Consumer Healthcare globally.

alli is GSK's newest remedy for weight gain.

GSK's strong track record in delivering products that resonate with consumers dates back to 1842 when Thomas Beecham introduced his Beecham's Pills products in the United Kingdom. The products were widely successful and led to the world's first factory opened exclusively for the production of medicines.

Founded in the UK, Thomas Beecham introduced his pills in 1842 to grateful consumers.

GSK's Pittsburgh presence began in 1977 when the Beecham Group, a predecessor company, purchased Calgon Consumer Products from Merck & Co. and added Sucrets and Calgon household products to its brand portfolio. Within a year, the company introduced Aquafresh toothpaste.

The Pittsburgh-based organization continued to grow through acquisition and innovation as it led the industry in the switch of previously by-prescription-only products to over the counter brands. In 1995, GSK Consumer Healthcare became the only company to have three product switches in one year as it launched Tagamet HB, Nicorette and NicoDerm CQ. Abreva followed in 2000 and is the only non-prescription cold sore medicine approved by the FDA.

Looking ahead, GSK is committed to providing consumers with even more drug choices that will help them live longer, healthier lives.

"The GSK Consumer Healthcare story is rich with brand successes. By ensuring the consumer's needs are met, we become partners with our retailers, our associates and healthcare professionals, as well as the communities in which we operate, in 'doing well by doing good.'" —George Quesnelle

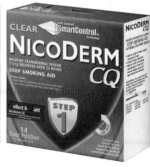

GSK's smoking cessation products have helped millions of consumers kick the habit.

H.J. Heinz Company

Heinz has grown from a horse-and-wagon vegetable business to the worldwide purveyor of processed foods.

It's a story as American as apple pie, or, in this case, tomato ketchup. It's the story of the son of German immigrants who transformed through sheer will a horse-and-wagon vegetable business into a global pure foods pioneer, setting new standards for product quality, safety and promotion along the way.

Heinz on the go: a marketing genius, Heinz invented 57 Varieties, the Heinz Pickle Pin, and the factory tour.

A student of agronomy, a born salesman and a master of marketing and public relations, Henry John Heinz began his life in the food business at age 12, peddling the produce of his family's garden in the hamlet of Sharpsburg, along the banks of the Allegheny River. By 1869, the 25-year-old Heinz was shredding his own signature horseradish, shrewdly bottling it in clear glass to demonstrate its purity, using the Pennsylvania keystone as his product symbol.

After horseradish came pickles, sauerkraut, vinegar and many other varieties, all delivered by horse-drawn wagons to Pittsburgh grocers. In 1876 Heinz introduced a product which would revolutionize the American diet—tomato ketchup—followed quickly by chili sauce, mustard, olives, baked beans, and the first sweet pickles ever brought to market.

By 1890, Heinz had begun constructing what would become a 17-building factory complex on the North Side. Dubbed the "Prince of

Paternalism," Heinz provided his workers clean clothes daily, installed indoor plumbing and running water, and ordered weekly manicures for food handlers.

Always thinking promotion, at the 1893 Chicago World's Fair Heinz dreamed up the pickle charm—later a pin—which became the world's most successful promotional item. Four years later, riding a New York City elevated train, he saw a sign advertising 21 "styles" of shoes. Captivated by the concept, he settled upon "57 Varieties" for his slogan. He kept thinking big. By 1900, Heinz had erected New York City's first electric sign, with 1,200 incandescent bulbs.

When Howard Heinz succeeded his father in 1919, he had already introduced modern quality control into all company factories. After H. J. Heinz II became president in 1941, the company acquired companies in the Netherlands, Italy, Portugal, Mexico, and the United States. In 1965, Heinz transformed Ore-Ida from a regional business into America's leading retail frozen potato.

Now, with more than 110 locations worldwide, such Heinz brands as Ore-Ida, Smart Ones, Bagel Bites, and Classico are market leaders on six continents.

Heinz Chairman Jack Heinz (right), grandson of the founder, ladles soup at a new plant in Australia in 1955 while Australian Prime Minister Sir Robert Menzies (second from right) looks on.

Under R. Burt Gookin, named CEO in 1966, acquisitions and growth quickened. By 1972, Heinz had reached the billion-dollar mark in sales.

International expansion reignited under Anthony O'Reilly, who became president and CEO in 1979, leading Heinz into South Africa, Russia, the Czech Republic, Hungary, South Korea, China, India, and Egypt.

Under the strong leadership of William R. Johnson, Chairman, President and CEO since 2000, Heinz continues to market healthy, convenient, and great tasting foods focused on a basket of 15 powerful brands that deliver approximately 70 percent of sales, with a strong presence in the world's major developed markets and a growing business in emerging markets.

With approximately $10 billion in annual sales, Heinz pleases palates of every age around the world, both in the home, and in restaurants and on-the-go.

CEO William R. Johnson inspecting Heinz's latest hybrid tomato varieties with Director of Global Tomato Research and Supply Reuben Peterson.

From the original homestead to factories around the world, Heinz quality has always come first.

Henderson Brothers

For more than a century, Henderson Brothers has served Pittsburgh's insurance needs.

The brawny town of Pittsburgh began as a river city, a fort and a trading post on America's western frontier.

Offices, Fort Duquesne Boulevard, Downtown

Then came black gold—coal, oil, iron ore. As business exploded, so did river traffic—moving materiel down the world's greatest steel production line, shipping finished product to markets domestic and foreign. By the end of the 19th Century, nearly 10 million tons passed through the Port of Pittsburgh every year.

Where there was trade, there were riches. And where there were riches, there was risk. And the management of risk.

By 1893 two brothers—Alexander Henderson and his brother James, a captain in the U.S. Army Corps of Engineers—saw the need for an insurance agency to serve Pittsburgh's thriving river industry. Their new Henderson Brothers agency placed insurance for the maritime industry, initially concentrating on longshoremen and harbor workers coverage.

By the 1920s, John J. "Jack" Kelly and his sister Rosalie E. Kelly had joined the Hendersons, along with Ralf E. Simpson. Smart, strong-willed, ahead of her time, by the early 1930s the woman who became Rose McMinn came to serve as the firm's Secretary & Assistant Treasurer on the Board of Directors, holding her post through 1961.

Dan and Tom Grealish

That same year, 1961, Thomas E. Grealish joined the firm as Vice President & Secretary, assuming the Presidency shortly thereafter. A member of the larger Kelly family, he and other family members—including John Philbin, who joined the firm as Vice President in 1963— assumed leadership roles, along with Leon F. Zinger as Vice President in 1965, and Doug Reichert as Vice President in 1967.

Dan and Tom Grealish with a painting of their father, Tom, Sr..

By 1978 Dan Grealish had joined his father and his family, along with Anthony Michael in 1981 and Tom Grealish in 1983. The following year, 1984, Dan and Tom's mother, Peg Grealish, joined the Board as Assistant Secretary.

Then tragedy struck, such profound tragedy that it would have destroyed a weaker firm. In 1986, Tom Grealish, Sr. died of cancer in April, Tony Michael died of lymphoma in July, Leon Zinger died of heart attack in October, and Peg Grealish died of a heart attack in November. In extraordinarily difficult circumstances, the Henderson Brothers moved forward, growing the business, continuing to serve clients. Made of sterner stuff, Dan and Tom Grealish were blessed to work with the gifted, skilled professional team that they had built at Henderson Brothers.

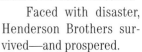

At Henderson Brothers, the business of insurance has always been a family affair.

Faced with disaster, Henderson Brothers survived—and prospered.

In 1961, for example, there were but six employees. By 1985, there were 25. In the 21st Century, there are more than 100.

Much like the region, Henderson Brothers grew from an insurance agency for river business to a full service insurance broker. Today, the firm serves the needs of all types of regional businesses, including design custom benefit packages, succession planning, strategic planning, crisis/disaster planning, workers compensation, and more.

While ownership may have passed from Henderson Brothers some 70 years ago, the firm has remained family-owned—decidedly so. Fiercely independent, when presented with difficult situations Henderson Brothers works together, works hard, and prevails.

Remembering their maritime origins, the Henderson logo on ice

Heyl & Patterson, Inc.

The world's finest bulk handling and thermal processing equipment since 1887.

It wasn't merely steel and coal that made Pittsburgh. It was handling the ore, and the ingots, that transformed a frontier trading post specializing in beaver pelts into the world's steel capital. That's where Heyl & Patterson came in.

Founded in 1887 by William J. Patterson and Edmund W. Heyl, the firm was an immediate impact player. Made of engineers, fabricators, and erectors, with offices on the former Monongahela riverside Water Street, and a factory on the North Side, Heyl & Patterson set the industry standard for world-class heavy bulk materials handling equipment. Bridges transferring ore at steel mills, cranes lifting entire railroad cars; towers unloading barges filled with ore, coal, sand, and slag; corrugated steel coal preparation plants cleaning and classifying coal; giant loaders for seafaring ships—for more than a century, they've been designed, fabricated, erected, serviced by Heyl & Patterson.

The business booming, by 1918, Messrs Heyl and Patterson had hired a young accountant named Harry Edelman, Jr. Rising through the ranks, he, his son, and grandsons, have led Heyl & Patterson nearly a century. Maintaining a strong tie to the past, they carefully preserve their original drawings, servicing their equipment, supplying replacement parts for century-old applications—using their own worldwide service teams that operate 24/365.

As times change, successful corporations like Heyl & Patterson change with them. Where the company's effective radius once stretched from Pittsburgh to Canada, now Heyl & Patterson's effective reach covers North and South America, Asia and Australia, serving such industries as chemical, food, pharmaceutical, power, port, mining, minerals, and more. Still a specialty engineering company designing and constructing bulk transfer and thermal processing equipment, Heyl & Patterson's twin divisions—Bulk Transfer and Renneburg—combine innovation and experience.

Offering consulting and field service, Heyl & Patterson designs, fabricates, installs, and services the highest-quality, custom-engineered equipment. As such, the Bulk Transfer Division designs and manufactures rotary railcar dumpers, including C-shaped rotary dumpers, closed and open-sided turnover dumpers, single and multiple car

Heyl & Patterson has succeeded for more than a century because of its outstanding core of engineers, designers, fabricators—and marketers.

dumpers, as well as such railcar moving devices as train positioners, train indexing equipment, CUB, and so on. Bulk Transfer also offers such material handling equipment as barge unloaders with both grab and continuous bucket designs, and related specialty machinery.

The Renneburg Division handles thermal processing of powders and bulk solids, offering a full complement of advanced chemical, mineral, and environmental processing equipment, including dryers, coolers, calciners, agglomerators, presses and mixers. While Heyl & Patterson has been making thermal processing dryers since the 1950s, in 1985 Heyl & Patterson expanded its thermal processing capabilities by acquiring the Edw. Renneburg & Sons Co. of Baltimore. Today, the division delivers innovative thermal processing technology tailored to the environmentally sensitive and production-minded needs of the powder and bulk solids, and chemical and mineral thermal processing industries.

For more than a century, from the early days of coal and steel to today's state-of-the-art bulk transfer equipment and advanced thermal processing, Heyl & Patterson has evolved with the industries it serves—combining cutting-edge technology and a wealth of experience to create products and services that preserve the past – while embracing the future.

The muscle that moves the material: Heyl & Patterson has it.

Only with the dedication of its employees, by 1921, Heyl & Patterson became the standard of its industry.

Working fast and working smart, by 2007, Heyl & Patterson combined a century of experience with cutting-edge technology to face the future.

Highmark Blue Cross Blue Shield

For more than 70 years, Highmark Blue Cross Blue Shield has worked to meet Pittsburgh's ever-changing health care needs.

During the Great Depression, as the nation swung toward Social Security and other policies, physicians and medical administrators began to consider ways to create workable insurance systems to provide health coverage for millions of unemployed workers.

Growing numbers of subscribers and claims put pressure on the staff responsible for billing and claims processing.

In 1935, Abe Oseroff, an executive at Pittsburgh's Montefiore Hospital, took up the challenge. He convened a meeting of top hospital administrators to develop a system to ensure funds would be available to pay for hospital and medical services. Within two years, the groundwork was laid for the formation of Blue Cross of Western Pennsylvania.

Across the state, Dr. Chauncey L. Palmer presented a similar idea to Pennsylvania Medical Society delegates in 1938. It was a voluntary plan with free choice of physicians. Approved by the legislature in 1939, Pennsylvania Blue Shield grew during World War II, and got a big boost in 1951, when it signed steelworkers at $1.50 per employee per month.

These were unique organizations from the outset —nonprofit corporations that were structured along traditional business lines. To this day, the company remains the "insurer of last resort." This represents an important distinction be-

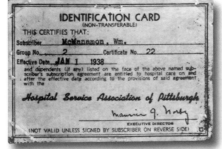

Each subscriber received a numbered membership card.

tween Highmark and for-profit competitors when it comes to shouldering the risk of underwriting health care coverage programs for at-risk populations.

To greater serve Pennsylvanians, Blue Cross of Western Pennsylvania and Pennsylvania Blue Shield consolidated in 1996 to create Highmark, a leader in health insurance, offering affordable, high-quality health care to more than 4.2 million people across the state.

In the first decade since its founding, Highmark has continually refined its mission and its strategies to meet emerging community needs. In fact, in 1985, the Highmark Caring Foundation teamed with community and business leaders to create the Caring Program for Children, to offer free and low-cost insurance coverage to children whose families did not have health insurance. In 1992, the Caring Program for Children became the model for the Pennsylvania Children's Health Insurance Program (CHIP). Highmark continues today as a lead administrator of the CHIP Program.

Caring Cub, the mascot of the Highmark Caring Foundation until 2004, was created to respond to the health care needs of children of the unemployed.

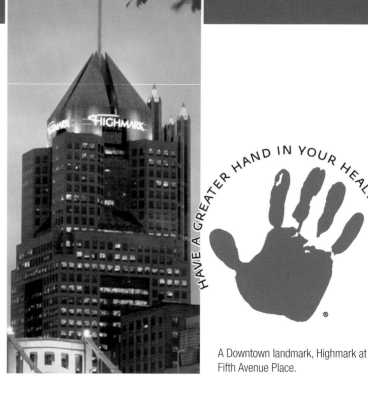

A Downtown landmark, Highmark at Fifth Avenue Place.

Healthy living is also a major Highmark focus. Providing opportunities for people to finds ways to change behaviors and create healthier habits is the core of wellness programming offered through Highmark and supported by corporate grantmaking in the community. In addition, Highmark has stepped forward to improve people's quality of life as the first health insurer in the country to both provide and pay for the Dr. Dean Ornish Program for Reversing Heart Disease, a year-long, non-invasive treatment option that can slow, stop and even reverse the progression of heart disease.

Along the same lines, Worksite Wellness is an employer-driven approach to enhance employee health through initiatives based at the worksite as well as in employee communities and homes. Such activities include awareness education, behavior modification and lifestyle change, as well as creating a supportive environment. Personal Wellness Profiles help to identify an individual's health risks and establish goals to improve health.

As yet another aspect of Highmark's commitment to healthy communities, the company made $100 million available in 2006 to create Highmark Healthy High 5, an initiative of the Highmark Foundation designed to address children's health promotion. Key areas of the initiative's focus include nutrition, physical activity, bullying, self-esteem and grieving with Highmark Healthy High 5 programs available at schools and in the community.

Highmark's predecessors helped Pennsylvanians pay for health care. Today, Highmark's mission is unchanged to provide access to affordable, quality health care, enabling individuals to live longer, healthier lives.

Hill House

Scion of 19th-century settlement houses, Hill House began as a 1960s' solution to changing community needs.

It begins in the 19th Century, with teeming immigrant populations flooding these shores. At Chicago's Hull House (1889), at New York City's Henry Street Settlement (1893), new Americans were acclimated to life in the New World. Child care, nursing services, English lessons—settlement houses helped transform so-called greenhorns into citizens.

It was no different in Pittsburgh, where by the turn of the 20th Century the population had increased sevenfold in just a few decades. With Eastern European Jews streaming into the Hill District, by 1895 the Council of Jewish Women had established a settlement house on Townsend Street. Some 14 years later, in 1909, department store magnate Henry Kaufmann donated a large, new building in memory of his daughter, the Irene Kaufmann Settlement.

Standing for 48 years at 1835 Centre Avenue, free and non-sectarian, the IKS, as it became known, helped untold thousands of people, free milk to art classes. Renamed in 1957 for Anna B. Heldman (1873-1940), a Castle Shannon-born, Hill District visiting nurse for 38 years, by the 1960s the building—as well as its settlement vision—had outlived its purpose.

And, according to planners, so had the Lower Hill. To build the Civic Arena, and a planned but never completed arts complex, between 1956-61 some 8,000 people were displaced—a fifth of the population, 1,500 families, 400 businesses.

Over four decades, Hill House thrived. Providing care and support for more than 500,000 children, adults, and seniors, Hill House averages 70,000 people a year touched by its programs. Serving clients through five strategic program areas— early learning and child development, senior services, and neighborhood development—Hill House also offers health and human services through multiple agencies that reside on the Hill House campus, now six buildings.

Because of Hill House, young people participate in science, arts, and recreation programs; high school graduates choose careers instead of the street; families participate in safe, high-quality childcare; and seniors enjoy warm winters and full cupboards.

From toddlers to seniors, Hill House provides a wealth of community services. President and CEO Evan Frazier is a hands-on leader.

Within a year, it was clear that the once-thriving Hill District desperately needed help. In 1962, the Allegheny County Health and Welfare Association initiated a study on the needs of the African-American community. Two years later, there came a clear mandate to create a new kind of agency to address changing community needs.

In 1964, three long-lived agencies, the Anna B. Heldman Center, Hill City Youth Municipality, and the Soho Community Center, joined forces into a new entity, the Hill House Association. Within eight years, in 1972, it had it own signature space, a modernist structure on the site of the former Heldman Center.

More than a half-million children and adults have found a safe haven—and the strength to grow—at Hill House.

Marsh

Since 1845.

For more than a century, Pittsburgh businesses have trusted Marsh to deliver exceptional risk and insurance services and solutions.

Marsh's Pittsburgh Office Managing Directors

Marsh and its preceding companies opened the company's Pittsburgh operation in 1929; however Marsh has provided risk and insurance advice to Pittsburgh clients, including its oldest client, a Fortune 500 Pittsburgh-based corporation, since 1901.

In Pittsburgh, Marsh services over 100 clients, including many with multi-state and international locations. Serving businesses primarily in Western Pennsylvania and West Virginia, Marsh's Pittsburgh office advises companies in a number of industries, including steel, mining, power and utilities, manufacturing, construction, education, health care, financial institutions, and transportation.

Marsh has the depth of expertise to address not only traditional property and casualty coverage but also such risk issues as emergency response planning and business continuity, product liability, directors and officers liability, safety, natural hazards, and mass tort. Marsh's Pittsburgh office is also a regional leader in aviation insurance and surety.

One key aspect of Marsh's client-oriented philosophy is dedication to risk education through Marsh's Academy of Risk. First established in Pittsburgh, Marsh's Academy offers Marsh clients and future clients the opportunity to learn more about risk.

Marsh's Pittsburgh Office Department Managers

Marsh is devoted to finding opportunity in risk. As Pittsburgh businesses increasingly grow globally, facing a myriad of differing cultures and legal landscapes, they come to Marsh for help identifying risks others may not see, earmarking opportunities others may not grasp.

Marsh's Risk Analyst Program Graduates 2001-2007

Ably led by Managing Director/Head of Office Michael Barbarita, Marsh is dedicated to making a difference in the Pittsburgh community. Locally, more than 80 percent of Marsh colleagues support regional cultural and charitable organizations, donating time and money. The firm locally sponsors its own women's organization, Women Making a Difference, which comprises a team of colleagues from Marsh and Mercer. Also, Marsh's Risk Analyst broker trainee program is dedicated to developing the next leaders in risk management. Through these programs, Marsh is cultivating the next generation of leaders at Marsh and within the greater Pittsburgh business community.

The Women Making a Difference group of Marsh and Mercer

Marsh is part of the family of MMC companies, including Kroll, Guy Carpenter, Mercer, and the Oliver Wyman Group (including Lippincott and NERA Economic Consulting). Its sister companies complement Marsh's capabilities, providing advice and solutions in risk, strategy, and human capital. Working with large and mid-size businesses, public entities, organizations, and private clients in more than 100 countries, Marsh's experience helps clients to transform risk into competitive advantage.

Marsh is extremely proud to be a part of the Pittsburgh business community for more than a century and to celebrate Pittsburgh's 250th Anniversary.

Congratulations Pittsburgh!

MARSH

MMC   MARSH   MERCER   KROLL
GUY CARPENTER   OLIVER WYMAN

The Bank of New York Mellon

Through its rich history, vision and performance, this financial services company helped to lead Pittsburgh's evolution.

In 1869 Thomas Mellon and his sons, Andrew W. and Richard B., founded T. Mellon & Sons' Bank in Pittsburgh. Built on the foundation of integrity and hard work, overlaid with a sense of vision, the company went on to grow into one of the world's great financial institutions. In the 139 years that followed the company's founding, the local T. Mellon & Sons' Bank went through several transitions and eventually grew into the global company, Mellon Financial Corporation, known today as The Bank of New York Mellon.

Thomas Mellon, a retired judge, founded T. Mellon & Sons' Bank. Together with his sons, Andrew and Richard, he built what would later become Mellon Financial Corporation, known today as The Bank of New York Mellon.

A Rich History

A look back through history clearly reveals how the company's leadership was a key part of Pittsburgh's evolution. As one of the driving forces behind the industrial revolution, the company helped to finance many modern aluminium, oil, consumer electronics and financial companies.

At the end of World War I, Mellon embarked on a tradition of employing mergers and acquisitions as a springboard to growth. Through the 1920's, Mellon grew to a point where it had only one serious Pittsburgh competitor—Union Trust, which was also controlled by the Mellon family. After surviving the 1929 stock market crash and resulting economic crisis, Mellon expanded its geography of retail banks while also expanding its institutional offerings. Mellon and Union Trust merged in 1946, creating a bank with the size, scale and expertise to compete with the nation's largest banks.

It was the first bank to acquire and install its own computer, setting the foundation as a technology leader. And, it was one of the first banks to automate clearing house operations and teller stations and introduce automated teller machines.

In 1955, Mellon was the first bank to buy and install a computer. The two-and-a-half-ton machine took up a large room and helped to bring banking into the electronic age.

In the 1980s and 1990s Mellon completed a series of acquisitions and merged with one of the country's oldest and largest mutual fund companies: The Dreyfus Corporation. Then, in 2001, Mellon shed its retail banks to sharpen its strategic focus. In 2007, Mellon's asset management businesses topped $1 trillion in assets under management.

Later that same year, Mellon Financial Corporation merged with The Bank of New York to become the world's largest securities servicing provider and a top asset management firm globally.

Contribution to the Community and the Arts

While the name is new, The Bank of New York Mellon is a long-standing and integral part of Pittsburgh. As an active leader in the community, it supports economic development initiatives, including affordable housing and workforce development programs, with a specific focus on helping the Pittsburgh communities to be welcoming places to live and work.

The company also supports the arts as critical to total economic development efforts. From the support for the Carnegie International to longstanding jazz programming in the city and its neighborhoods, The Bank of New York Mellon remains committed to the communities it serves.

Growing into the Future

The Bank of New York Mellon has begun the 21st Century with vigor. Through a powerful combination of expertise and collaboration, the company is poised to broaden its global reach while delivering exceptional results and long-term value to clients. And, The Bank of New York Mellon remains committed to continuing its rich tradition of excellence—in Pittsburgh, and around the world.

THE BANK OF NEW YORK MELLON

2007

T. MELLON & SONS BANK			MELLONBANK	Mellon Bank	Mellon
1869	1909	1946	1972	1981	1999

Over the years, the logos that Mellon has used to represent the company have evolved along with the company.

PIAD

In 1967, PIAD Precison Casting had one coke-fired furnace and two employees.

This is a story of pluck, determination, and grit; of engineering savvy and entrepreneurial spirit; of success the old-fashioned, Pittsburgh way, through hard work, attention to detail, and manufacturing excellence.

.   When 28-year-old Karl Schweisthal came to this country from Germany in late 1967, he had planned on a three-year career boost, honing his English skills, then returning home.

That was 41 years ago, when PIAD Precision Casting had one coke-fired furnace and two employees.

Today the German-owned, Greensburg-based company manufactures in a 59,000-square-foot foundry and a 28,000-square-foot machine shop, and sells $35 million of precision castings annually.

PIAD today has 175 employees, has built dies for 2,850 parts and sells to 245 customers.

PIAD CEO's Karl Schweisthal, right, and his son, PIAD President Holger Schweisthal, continue to grow the precision casting company that enjoys $35 million in annual sales.

Using the chill casting permanent mold process which was developed by Piel & Adey, the German parent company, PIAD makes functional components for many different industries, such as the electrical power distribution industry; transportation industry; mining industry; marine-based hardware industry; valve and pump industry and packaging machines industry.

When Schweisthal came to America, PIAD started as a joint venture with Ringsdorff Carbon Corporation which was located in East McKeesport.

At the beginning Ringsdorff provided sales and administrative support. PIAD started manufacturing its first castings in a rented building in Export, PA. Schweisthal provided the technical directions of the business; conducted sales training; did all quotations; hired employees; purchased equipment; designed molds and supervised the operation.

As hands-on engineers, father and son supervise all casts, molds, and all-important quality control.

PIAD Corporation facilities in Greensburg employ 175 workers in a 59,000 square-foot foundry and 28,000 square-foot machine shop.

An engineer in PIAD's original casting facility in Export, PA.

PIAD Foundry

PIAD began exploring hi-end computerization in the late 1990s and continues to advance its automated processes today.

In 1979 still operating as a joint venture with Transtech Corporation (previously Ringsdorff Carbon Corp.) PIAD purchased six acres of land in an industrial park in Greensburg and built a state of the art new foundry and started manufacturing in the new facility in 1982.

In 1989 reacting to demands in the market place, PIAD started its own machining facility enabling it to provide a complete product to its customers including silver and tin plating.

In 1996 PIAD bought out its American partner and became a wholly owned subsidiary of Piel & Adey, a German company.

What started in 1968 with a coke fired furnace and manual manipulation of the dies has developed into a state of the art foundry utilizing electric induction smelting and electric resistance holding furnaces and semi-automatic gravity casting machines developed in Italy with design input from PIAD. PIAD now counts as its customers all major electrical equipment manufacturers in the United States such as Square D, G.E., Siemens, ABB, and Eaton Cutler Hammer.

Helped by its value-added oriented business model, PIAD has continued to grow while the foundry industry in the United States has been shrinking.

PIAD is now guided by the second Schweisthal generation; Karl Schweisthal still serves as CEO and Holger Schweisthal, his son, as President and General Manager.

PIAD engineers cost-effective precision castings for a variety of industrial applications.

PNC Financial Services Group, Inc.

Since 1852, a Pittsburgh financial leader

Like many Pittsburgh stories, PNC's begins with steel—and land once owned by William Penn (and sold by his heirs for $90.00.)

In 1852 steel magnates B.F. Jones and James Laughlin began a new venture, Pittsburgh Trust and Savings. Within months, the company moved to Wood Street, one door from the corner of Fifth Avenue. In 1858, it acquired the corner lot, once owned by Penn (and afterward used for a church, Masonic Lodge, even the Mansion House Hotel, where Lafayette stayed in 1825.) The company, and its successors, have been doing business there ever since.

PNC Firstside Center: A leader in environmentally friendly building, PNC possesses more certified green buildings than any other publicly traded company in the world.

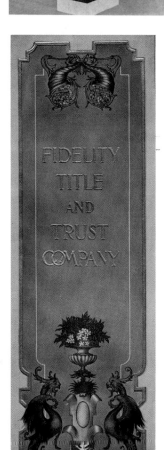

Within a decade, their treasurer, John Scully, had helped the federal government create legislation that revolutionized banking—and coincidentally made possible the sale of bonds to finance the Civil War. Applying for a charter under the National Banking Act of 1863, Pittsburgh Trust became the First National Bank of Pittsburgh.

At the same time, other PNC forerunners were established, including People's Savings, 1866; Fidelity Title, 1886; and the Pittsburgh Trust Company, 1893. After some 60 years of mergers, Pittsburgh National Bank was formed in 1959.

Across the state, Philadelphia's Provident National Corporation similarly dates back to the mid-19th century. In 1982, when Pennsylvania law allowed statewide banking, Pittsburgh National and Provident National were the first two banks to act on the new legislation, affecting what was then the largest bank merger in American history. Taking the shared initials of their holding companies, in 1983 they created a new entity, PNC Financial Corporation.

Growth and acquisition have continued to this day. In 1986, PNC merged with an out-of-state bank, Citizens Fidelity Corporation of Louisville, Kentucky. Shortly thereafter, PNC acquired the Central Bancorporation of Cincinnati and the Bank of Delaware. In 1991, PNC purchased First Federal Savings and Loan Association of Pittsburgh, making PNC Pittsburgh's largest bank and largest bank holding company.

Between 1991 and 1996, PNC acquired nine financial institutions in northern Pennsylvania, Philadelphia, Cincinnati, northern Kentucky, and Pittsburgh. In 1995, PNC entered New Jersey by merging with Midlantic Corporation.

PNC's growing wealth management business was bolstered by two bank acquisitions in the '90s: the Massachusetts Company, Boston, the country's oldest trust company, dating from 1818 and counting John Quincy Adams, Daniel Webster, and Henry Wadsworth Longfellow among its clients; and Indian River Federal Savings Bank of Vero Beach, FL, which added private banking capabilities to PNC's existing Florida trust business.

Always a premier employer: PNC's award-winning softball team

BlackRock became a part of PNC's asset management business during the mid-1990s, and is currently one of America's largest investment managers.

Also in 1999, PNC's steady transformation into a diversified company with national reach was further strengthened with the addition of First Data Investor Services Group to PNC's PFPC subsidiary, a leading provider of services to mutual funds and other investment vehicles. In 2005, PNC acquired Riggs National Corporation, gaining entry into Washington, D.C., Maryland, and Virginia.

In 2002, PNC became a leader in sustainability with a program to build environmentally friendly branches it trademarked as "Green Branch" locations. It made a further investment in its community in 2004 by creating PNC Grow Up Great, a 10-year, $100 million initiative to help prepare young children for school and life.

By the end of 2007, PNC had added Mercantile Bankshares Corporation, extending its reach into Baltimore. It operated more than 1,100 retail branches in eight states and the District of Columbia, with operations across the United States and Europe.

Now one of America's most admired companies, PNC competes on a regional, national and international basis. But it still maintains its headquarters in Pittsburgh at the corner of Fifth and Wood, as it has for more than 150 years.

For decades, PNC employees have been among the Pittsburgh area's most active volunteers. PNC is a leading corporate citizen.

From an original green lithograph of its once signature bank building to an architecturally green design of a new retail branch office, PNC serves every client wisely.

PPG Industries

PPG Industries was founded in 1883 when Captain John B. Ford and John Pitcairn built the first commercially successful plate glass factory in the United States in Creighton, PA. Known as Pittsburgh Plate Glass Company, Ford and Pitcairn's enterprise focused on innovation and quality. And 125 years later, PPG Industries is still successful because of those early values.

PPG Place, a landmark six-building complex that reshaped Downtown

By 1883, John Ford and John Pitcairn had re-branded their company as Pittsburgh Plate Glass

During the company's first decade, PPG expanded its flat glass production operations rapidly through new facilities and acquisitions.

PPG diversified its business in 1899 with the construction of an alkali plant in Barberton, OH, to ensure supply of raw materials for glassmaking. This plant would serve as the precursor to PPG's chemicals businesses. A year later, PPG would begin building its coatings business with the acquisition of Wisconsin-based Patton Paint Company. Glass and paint provided continued growth to the company in the 1920s, as the automotive industry and construction of skyscrapers expanded.

In the early 1940s, PPG entered the optical products business with the introduction of CR-39® optical monomer. Still widely used today in prescription lenses, CR-39® optical monomer was the forerunner to a business that has evolved to provide a broad array of specialty optical lens materials.

In 1952, recognizing the potential of another type of glass product, PPG established its continuous strand fiber glass business.

As a result of its diversification, growth and rapidly developing global presence, the company changed its name to PPG Industries in 1968. In the ensuing decades, the company gave new emphasis to innovation, the development of specialty products, process efficiency and accelerated global expansion in Europe, Latin America and Asia-Pacific.

Today, PPG is a global supplier of paints, coatings, optical products, specialty materials, chemicals, glass and fiber glass. Its products are used in a wide variety of applications. PPG's well-known brands include Pittsburgh®, Lucite®, and Olympic® Paints. PPG coatings appear on airplanes, golf balls, circuit boards, packaging, appliances, wood flooring, automobiles, bridges and buildings. PPG's chemicals help purify water. Its Transitions® optical lenses help protect eyes from harmful UV rays. And PPG's glass appears as windows in houses, office towers, and as windshields in automobiles and aircraft.

With 2007 sales of $11.2 billion, PPG Industries has more than 150 manufacturing facilities and equity affiliates and has 44,000 employees operating in more than 60 countries.

From horsepowered days to the space age, PPG has had an unwavering commitment to scientific innovation.

125
1883 - 2008

A global company producing a wide array of products, PPG is an industry leader in coatings, optical products, chemicals, glass and fiber glass.

As PPG celebrates its 125th anniversary in 2008, the company holds true to the spirit of its founders—Ford and Pitcairn—and enters its next 125 years by continuing to offer innovative solutions to its customers.

With four Pittsburgh tech centers, PPG is the region's largest employer of scientific personnel.

Beginning in Creighton, PA, PPG burned coal to create the world's finest plate glass. Now, using glass to create energy, PPG and joint venture partner Devold's glass-fiber reinforcement fabrics are used in wind turbine blades.

Respironics

Gerald E. (Jerry) McGinnis transformed his luck, vision, and kitchen equipment into a world leader in sleep and respiratory therapy.

It seemed that nothing could stop Jerry. Even when his business burned to the ground in 1977, he kept experimenting with respiratory masks, baking them in his wife's (Audrey) oven. He, of course, achieved success—while ruining her favorite home appliance.

Born in Illinois, Jerry came to Pittsburgh in 1958 to work at Westinghouse. After 11 years and such milestone work, including an artificial heart and medical devices, it was time for the manager of the bioengineering department to move on. For the next two years he headed surgical research at Allegheny General Hospital, working with famed cardiothoracic surgeon Dr. George Magovern. Then, in 1971, with a mind full of ideas and the determination to be out on his own, Jerry founded Lanz Medical Products, named for his wife, Audrey Lanz. Over the next five years his understanding of the respiratory health market grew. He learned in depth about asthma, SIDS and sleep apnea, along with some 80 identifiable sleep disorders and numerous pulmonary conditions. In 1976, he founded Respironics.

Respironics' world headquarters, Murrysville, home of a $1 billion corporation.

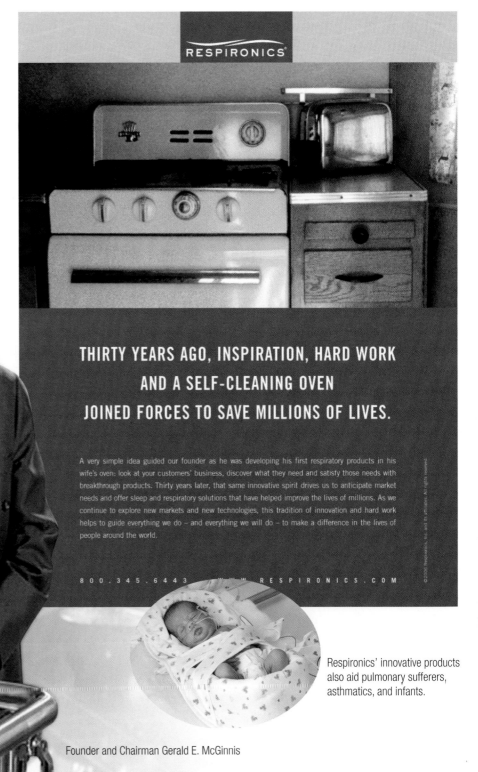

RESPIRONICS

THIRTY YEARS AGO, INSPIRATION, HARD WORK AND A SELF-CLEANING OVEN JOINED FORCES TO SAVE MILLIONS OF LIVES.

A very simple idea guided our founder as he was developing his first respiratory products in his wife's oven: look at your customers' business, discover what they need and satisfy those needs with breakthrough products. Thirty years later, that same innovative spirit drives us to anticipate market needs and offer sleep and respiratory solutions that have helped improve the lives of millions. As we continue to explore new markets and new technologies, this tradition of innovation and hard work helps to guide everything we do – and everything we will do – to make a difference in the lives of people around the world.

800.345.6443   WWW.RESPIRONICS.COM

Respironics' innovative products also aid pulmonary sufferers, asthmatics, and infants.

Founder and Chairman Gerald E. McGinnis

With able, steady leadership, Respironics is positioned to prosper in the 21st Century.

NASDAQ Tower—30th Anniversary

At first he worried about making payroll. Thirty years later his company employed more than 5,000 people (called associates) worldwide and enjoyed sales of more than $1 billion. As a leading provider of innovative solutions for the global sleep and respiratory markets, the success of Respironics can be traced to a history deeply rooted in ingenuity and a passion to deliver solutions to those in need.

By 1982, the company was expanding manufacturing operations overseas. In 1985, Respironics released the world's first commercially available Continuous Positive Airway Pressure (CPAP) device, thereby providing relief for millions of sufferers of sleep apnea and other respiratory disorders. Respironics continued to refine its processes and garner additional patents. In 1988, Respironics began trading on the NASDAQ as a public company. In 1990, the same year the company was named by *Forbes* magazine as one of America's best small companies, Respironics opened its manufacturing facility in Murrysville, Pennsylvania.

Respironics continuously grew through product developments and business acquisitions, including the 1998 acquisition of Healthdyne Technologies. It was during the Healthdyne acquisition that the company inherited a dynamic young sales and marketing senior vice president, John Miclot. Rising through the ranks at Respironics, he became President and CEO in 2003, with Jerry continuing as Chairman.

Currently organized into three primary groups—the Sleep and Home Respiratory Group, the Hospital Group, and the International Group—Respironics' decentralized business structure helps to ensure that resources are channeled efficiently to meet specific market needs. With each group having a comprehensive understanding of its market, they each can plot a course from present day healthcare to future opportunities for emerging technologies. With primary facilities in California, Georgia, Connecticut and New Jersey, and facilities abroad in the United Kingdom, the Philippines, and China, Respironics' products are marketed in more than 141 countries.

Always expanding, in late 2007, Respironics broke ground on a new $32 million, 165,000-square-foot, suburban Pittsburgh manufacturing facility focusing on sleep therapy devices. As John Miclot commented, "our associates have helped to build a culture of accomplishment, commitment, and pride that continues to flourish throughout our organization. The milestones that we have achieved, and those to come, are due to the hard work and dedication of Respironics' global team of associates."

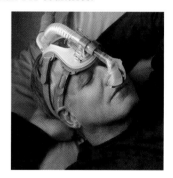

Respironics' Continuous Positive Airway Pressure device brings relief to millions of sufferers from sleep apnea and other sleep disorders.

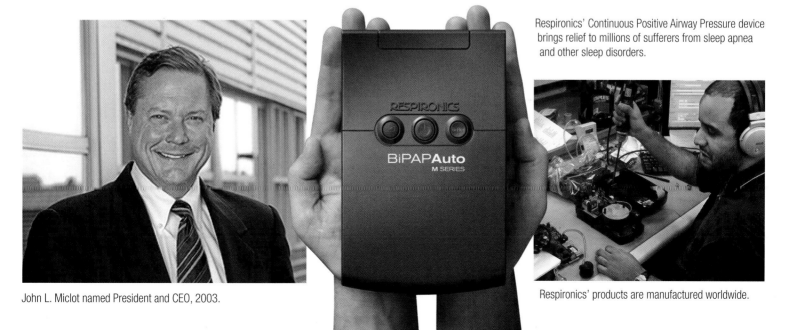

John L. Miclot named President and CEO, 2003.

Respironics' products are manufactured worldwide.

Robroy

A Scottish immigrant, Peter McIlroy began the Enameled Metals Company in Etna in 1905.

The Robroy Industries story begins in 1878, in the little town of Addiewell, Scotland, with the birth of Peter McIlroy. One of six children, the teenaged Peter and a brother came west, seeking their fortunes. Landing in Philadelphia, they eventually moved to McKeesport, where Peter went to work in a steel mill.

Threading pipe, bending pipe, coating pipe, Peter McIlroy eventually patented more than 30 separate processes.

Working 12-hour days, earning five cents an hour, the smart lad found a way to double his output. When he asked for a commensurate raise, and was given but a penny, he protested—so vociferously that he was fired, then blacklisted as a troublemaker.

Taking a job as a night watchman in a bankrupt factory, he looked at the black-enameled ceiling and began experimenting, dipping samples of steel pipe into enameling vats. One thing leading to another, Peter McIlroy discovered a way to enamel steel conduit, then the breakthrough technology for housing electric wires.

In 1905 McIlroy founded the Enameled Metals Company in the Allegheny River mill town of Etna. Buying pipe from a local mill, McIlroy cut, threaded, and enameled it, sending his first shipments by horse and buggy to McCullough Electric. Eventually patenting some 30 processes, McIlroy developed the technology to bend pipe, making conduit that could be installed around corners. With black enameling giving way to galvanizing, McIlroy made both electro-galvanized and hot-dipped galvanized conduit.

Buffeted by Depression, flooded in '36 (the waters running 18 feet high in Etna), scorched by fire in '48, Enameled Metals survived—and prospered. With Peter's son Robert becoming president in 1952, the company changed its name to Pittsburgh Standard Conduit to better identify with its product.

Opening a plant adjacent to U.S. Steel's Fairless Works in Morrisville, Pittsburgh Standard embarked on a 50-year modernization program, at first using an automated conveyer system for cleaning and pickling the steel, adopting new hot galvanizing, and shifting from rail to truck transport.

By 1958, Pittsburgh Standard had opened a plant and modern offices in Verona, and in 1961 moved manufacturing operations to Texas, expanding into plastics, using an extruder for fabricating PVC conduit.

Adopting the name Robroy Industries in 1967, within a decade it had purchased Stahlin, a Belding, Michigan, fiber-glass electrical enclosure manufacturer. With Stahlin, and Plasti-Bond coated conduit products, Robroy again adapted to meet the future.

By 1980, the third generation held sway, as Peter McIlroy II became president. Named CEO in 1988, and Chairman in 1993, he piloted Robroy's further modernization as well as acquisition of plants manufacturing oil-industry-dedicated corrosion-resistant pipe. By 1995, with facilities in Kansas, Oklahoma, Texas, and New Mexico, Robroy decentralized, leaving Verona as the corporate headquarters. "Today," Peter McIlroy says, "we could be anywhere, but our roots are in Pittsburgh. We're staying here."

Now with the fourth generation of McIlroys in Robroy leadership positions, the company has never been stronger. "In 2008 we're 103 years old," Peter McIlroy says, "more than a century of one-family ownership. Only four percent of businesses survive that way. And we're operating at record levels. This an exciting time for us. The future looks bright."

Employee loyalty has spawned generations of smart, skilled labor.

Above: Chairman, CEO and President, Peter McIlroy II. For more than a century, four generations of McIlroys have led RobRoy Industries.

United States Steel Corporation

For more than a century, visionary steel leadership.

When they gathered at New York's University Club on a December night in 1900, 80 moguls hardly thought they'd be facing the future—but that's the surprise Andrew Carnegie had prepared for them.

Today's steelmaking facilities focus on safety and utilize the latest technology.

Andrew Carnegie's company became a vital part of U. S. Steel.

Standing, Charles Schwab presented an idea so bold, so revolutionary, that J.P. Morgan himself simply stared, unlit cigar hanging from his mouth.

Let us meet the new century by creating a united front against foreign competition, Schwab said. Let us band together, cooperating not competing, in one large corporation.

That's how U. S. Steel was born. Incorporated the following February, it was a confederation of nearly a dozen steel companies. With one bold stroke, United States Steel became the largest company ever launched, with authorized capital of $1.4 billion.

While Charles Schwab articulated that original vision, the principal architect was Judge Elbert H. Gary, the first chairman of a corporation so powerful that in its first year, U. S. Steel made 67 percent of all domestic steel. As a leader, Gary set the gold standard not only for business, but also for conducting business. Espousing honesty, fairness and openness, he initiated such now-common practices as annual meetings (the first, Feb. 17, 1902, in Hoboken, N.J.), a code of ethics,

Steel made by U. S. Steel employees has been used to build and defend our nation for more than 100 years.

even annual reports (the 1902 edition was 40 pages). Along the way, Gary's new company invented the slogan "Safety First."

Handling America's big jobs, U. S. Steel supplied products that were used in the construction of New York City's Empire State and Chrysler Buildings, the Panama Canal, Rockefeller Center, the Hoover Dam, St. Louis' Gateway Arch, and Chicago's Picasso statue. The company also produced much of the steel that was used by our armed forces in two world wars.

In the 1980s, U. S. Steel diversified its holdings by branching into the energy market with the acquisitions of Marathon Oil and Texas Oil & Gas. In 1986, the company changed its name to USX Corporation. In 2001, USX reorganized its holdings, spinning off its steelmaking assets on Dec. 31, 2001, and renaming the new company United States Steel Corporation.

By that time, the company's leaders had already begun to explore growth opportunities through acquisitions. In 2000, the company purchased Slovak steelmaker VSZ a.s. In 2003, U. S. Steel acquired certain assets of National Steel in the United States as well as Serbian steel company Sartid a.d. Four years later, the company bought Dallas-based tubular products maker Lone Star Technologies, Inc. and Canadian steelmaker Stelco.

Today, more than a century after its founding, U. S. Steel remains the largest integrated steel producer headquartered in the United States and is the fifth largest steelmaker in the world. The company manufactures high value-added steel products for the automotive, appliance, container, construction, industrial equipment and energy industries and has an annual raw steelmaking capability of 31.7 million net tons. U. S. Steel operates steelmaking facilities in the United States, Canada, Slovakia, Serbia, and, of course, right here in Pittsburgh. The company produces coke and iron ore pellets, operates three research and development facilities—including one near Pittsburgh, and is involved in a number of other ventures. Today, U. S. Steel's high-tech, efficient operations are capable of making more than 1,500 different kinds of steel, some of which didn't even exist just a few short years ago.

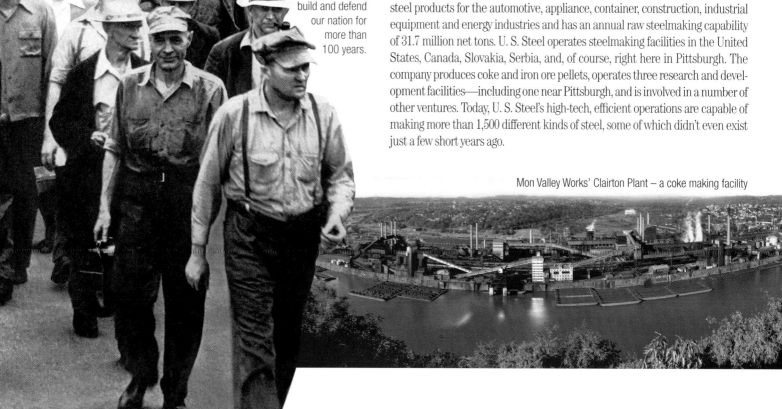
Mon Valley Works' Clairton Plant – a coke making facility

University of Pittsburgh

Founded in 1787 as the Pittsburgh Academy, the first major school west of the Alleghenies was designed to create statesmen.

When Hugh Henry Brackenridge founded the Pittsburgh Academy—today's University of Pittsburgh—in a log cabin in 1787, he hoped it would serve as a "candle lite in the forested wilderness."

Novelist, lawyer, publisher, legislator, and educator Hugh Henry Brackenridge established the Pittsburgh Academy, today's University of Pittsburgh, in 1787.

That hope of enlightening our region was realized quickly. By 1819, renamed the Western University of Pennsylvania, the school had moved to Allegheny City—today Pittsburgh's North Side—and had grown to include engineering, pharmacy, economics, dentistry, medicine, and law. By 1908, the University of Pittsburgh, starting down the path to becoming one of America's great research universities, had moved to Oakland, which it has called home for 100 years.

Today, Mark A. Nordenberg, Pitt's 17th chancellor, oversees a 132-acre Pittsburgh campus of 16 undergraduate, graduate, and professional schools—as well as four regional campuses—all committed to enhancing the human experience through the power of education. "A community of intellectuals is, by definition, committed to the power of the mind and is bound together by its interest in ideas. Certainly that is one important dimension of life at Pitt," says Nordenberg. "But a university also should be an institution with a heart—an institution that values nothing more than the potential that exists within its people."

Ground was broken for the University's Cathedral of Learning in 1926, and the building was dedicated in 1937. Contributors to the campaign for the Cathedral included more than 97,000 schoolchildren, who each contributed a dime in exchange for a certificate testifying that they were "Builders of the Cathedral of Learning."

Transplant pioneer Thomas Starzl developed surgical techniques and antirejection drugs that have given better—and longer—lives to thousands of patients.

The visionary behind the Cathedral of Learning, Chancellor John Bowman wanted students to "find wisdom here and faith—in steel and stone, in character and thought—they shall find beauty, adventure, and moments of high victory."

Pitt undergraduates are a testament to that potential. Since 1995 alone, they have won two Rhodes—back to back in 2006 and 2007—six Marshall, four Truman, four Udall, one Churchill, and 29 Goldwater scholarships and three Mellon Humanities Fellowships. Pitt's more than 250,000 alumni have an outstanding record of achievement, receiving the National Medal of Science, the John Fritz Medal for engineering, the Pulitzer Prize, Olympic gold medals, Nobel Prizes, the Presidential Medal of Freedom, and other prestigious awards.

From its proud past, with Samuel Langley's experiments with flying machines and the world's first unmanned flight in 1896 to Jonas Salk's 1955 vaccine that prevented polio to Thomas Starzl's pioneering work in human organ transplantation in the 1980s and '90s, Pitt faculty and alumni have always looked for

Pitt athletic greats—the Rev. Dr. James J. "Jimmy Joe" Robinson, Heisman Trophy winner Tony Dorsett, and Olympian Herb Douglas—are but three of the athletes who have graced the school's playing fields.

ways to better the human condition. In 1906, Reginald Fessenden made the first trans-Atlantic broadcast of the human voice, using research he developed at Pitt; in 1932, Charles King isolated vitamin C; in 1948, Philip Hench first used cortisone in the treatment of rheumatoid arthritis; in the 1950s, Peter Safar pioneered cardiopulmonary resuscitation (CPR) and established the first intensive care unit (ICU); and in the 1960s, Paul Lauterbur started the work that would develop magnetic resonance imaging (MRI). They are all Pitt people who changed the world.

Today, the University continues as a center for innovation and discovery with its work in Alzheimer's disease, biotechnology, transplantation, materials science, nanotechnology, and dozens of other areas of pioneering inquiry. This excellence in research is recognized by Pitt's being ranked sixth in the nation among academic institutions in funding from the National Institutes of Health, receiving $447 million in research support.

At the heart of the University complex stands the more than 80-year-old Cathedral of Learning, symbolizing the grand ascent and the great power of knowledge. A 42-story Gothic tower, it houses 26 one-of-a-kind Nationality Rooms and is a beacon of the University's shining accomplishments. The "candle lite" of the city's namesake University now shines brighter than ever.

Chancellor Mark A. Nordenberg with Pitt alumnus Wangari Maathai, leader of the Green Belt Movement in Kenya and winner of the 2004 Nobel Peace Prize "for her contribution to sustainable development, democracy, and peace."

Cathedral of Learning

Pitt medical school faculty member Jonas Salk's vaccine changed medicine by preventing polio.

All-American quarterback and Pittsburgh native Dan Marino took Pitt to four bowl games, set numerous NFL records, and is a member of both the College Football and Pro Football halls of fame.

Former Girl Scouts of the USA CEO Frances Hesselbein received the Presidential Medal of Freedom in 1998.

Westinghouse Electric Company

George Westinghouse

Born in 1846, the son of a New York machine shop owner, George Westinghouse was just 19 when he invented a rotary steam engine.

When he was 22, his railroad air brake made his fortune—and changed the world.

George Westinghouse

Turning to electricity, he built a practical alternating current network. By 1886, Westinghouse had formed the Westinghouse Electric & Manufacturing Company. By 1895, Westinghouse had installed the first AC generators at Niagara Falls.

In the 20th Century, Westinghouse (as a corporation) had such accomplishments as:

The first commercial radio broadcast, Pittsburgh's KDKA (1920)

The first diesel-electric rail car (1929)

The first industrial atom smasher (1937)

The electronic amplifier to improve X-ray images (1948)

The first commercial pressurized nuclear plant, Shippingport (1957)

Additionally, Westinghouse technology enabled the world to watch the first walk on the moon, 1969.

Westinghouse's comprehensive service center near Madison, PA, houses major nuclear components for training, certification and robotics development.

Proud of its reputation for innovation, research and development, during the 20th Century Westinghouse scientists were granted more than 28,000 American patents, third in the nation.

After that century of unparalleled growth—in broadcasting, consumer goods (when the slogan "you can be sure...if it's Westinghouse" was the gold standard for product reliability), electric generation, nuclear energy, and more—there came a decade of divestment. Today, Westinghouse Electric Company is exclusively in nuclear energy, and is majority-owned by Toshiba since 2006.

Currently, Westinghouse offers a wide range of nuclear plant products and services to utilities throughout the world, including fuel, spent fuel management, service and maintenance, instrumentation and control, and advanced nuclear plant designs.

Continually strengthening its position in and commitment to the worldwide commercial nuclear power industry, in April, 2000, Westinghouse purchased the nuclear businesses of ABB. This acquisition, and a recent hiring program, brings Westinghouse's worldwide employment to more than 10,000

The control room for the AP1000™ nuclear power plant is designed to provide operators with prompt, relevant information to further improve upon already-high levels of safety and efficiency.

In the United States, Westinghouse technologies power more than 60 existing nuclear power facilities. The Westinghouse AP1000 has been selected as the supplier and technology of choice for a combined total of 12 probable new plants.

As the world's population rises, so does its reliance on electricity. An additional two billion people are expected to need energy by 2020. Led by Westinghouse Electric, a new generation of safe, plentiful, economical, clean nuclear power is at hand.

Westinghouse has trained and recertified more than 10,000 nuclear plant operators from the Americas, Europe and Asia.

Today, well over 40 percent of the world's 440 operating commercial nuclear plants were provided by either Westinghouse or its licensees, clearly giving Westinghouse the world's largest installed base of operating plants.

In South Korea, Westinghouse is actively involved in the construction of new nuclear plants, helping to bring a new plant on line at essentially the rate of one per year. The Westinghouse AP1000™ nuclear power plant is emerging as the world's choice in nuclear plant technology. This simplified, standard design is pre-fabricated and able to be

built in a shipyard, then assembled on site in as little as three years. As such, in 2006, China's State Nuclear Power Technology Company selected Westinghouse to provide four new AP1000s, with the first to come on line in 2013.

Westinghouse technicians service and maintain nuclear power plants throughout the world, working in a variety of disciplines, including fuel design and manufacture, refueling services, maintenance, inspection and repair.

Westinghouse will begin moving into its new headquarters building north of Pittsburgh in Cranberry Woods beginning in 2009.

A century-and-a-half of medical innovation, healthcare, and community service.

For more than 150 years, West Penn Allegheny Health System has provided the region's finest healthcare. Together, its hospitals have been distinguished by excellence and innovation, pioneering technology, groundbreaking research, and exceptional medical talent.

They also have the region's deepest medical roots. When Dr. Henry Sellers convened a meeting in the Odeon Building on March 19, 1847, to create the Western Pennsylvania Hospital, Pittsburgh's first non-sectarian healthcare facility, he insured that there would be care for the entire community—regardless of ability to pay.

With each member contributing $100, within two years West Penn had more than 200 subscribers—in 1848 becoming Pittsburgh's first chartered public hospital. With Harmar Denny and William Croghan (Mary Schenley's father) donating land, in 1853 the four-story hillside edifice, in what is now Polish Hill, was completed, and began admitting patients.

In 1862, West Penn became the first area hospital to serve Civil War veterans. Dispatching two hospital steamers, the *Hailman* and *Marengo*, to Shiloh, they retrieved some 400 wounded men, 70 brought to Pittsburgh. By October 1865, nearly 3,000 Union soldiers had been treated at West Penn.

In 1883 West Penn opened the area's first medical college. Within two years, the school had its own four-story building—and 55 students. By century's end, West Penn boasted 300 students, a faculty of 50, and Pittsburgh's first X-ray machine.

Aided by such luminaries as Mellon, Frick, Carnegie, Heinz, and Fisher, West Penn opened its Bloomfield facility in 1912. The new building boasted 650 rooms, including accommodations for 500 patients. By 1959, it had the city's first intensive care unit.

Across the Allegheny River, in 1886 Allegheny General began in two Stockton Avenue buildings. Within a year AGH had treated nearly 400 patients—and opened a children's wing.

West Penn in Bloomfield was the first chartered public hospital in the city.

By 1904 AGH had grown into a new building with 405 beds. By 1925, plans for a new hospital were drawn up, but financial hardships prevented its opening for 11 years. Finally, on June 24, 1936, the new, $8 million, 1,300-room, 20-story building debuted; at 300 feet high, it became an instant Pittsburgh landmark. Dubbed the Skyscraper Hospital, it stood as America's tallest medical facility.

Today, WPAHS features some of the oldest and best-known names in health care in western Pennsylvania. Comprised of two tertiary and four community hospitals, WPAHS includes Allegheny General Hospital and The Western Pennsylvania Hospital, both in Pittsburgh; Alle-Kiski Medical Center in Natrona Heights; Canonsburg General Hospital in Canonsburg; The Western Pennsylvania Hospital–Forbes Regional Campus in Monroeville; and Allegheny General Hospital–Suburban Campus in Bellevue.

Rising 300 feet, Allegheny General is the North Side's most commanding landmark.

From the region's leading burn center to its first helicopter transport service, WPAHS provides a complete range of comprehensive care for patients who need trauma and emergency care.

WPAHS has one of the most comprehensive cancer diagnosis and treatment programs in the region.

WPAHS has a strong commitment to medical research and education and is dedicated to training future generations of health-care professionals.

The treatment of brain and nervous system diseases and disorders is an area of excellence within WPAHS and is recognized both nationally and internationally.

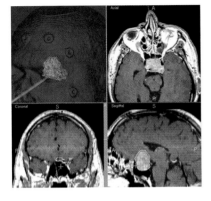

WPAHS delivers over 4,500 babies annually and has accredited Level III Neonatal Intensive Care Units at both AGH and West Penn.

Offering a comprehensive range of medical and surgical services, the hospitals serve Pittsburgh and the surrounding five-state area, house nearly 2,000 beds and employ more than 13,000 people. Together, the WPAHS hospitals admit more than 78,000 patients each year, log over 200,000 emergency visits and deliver more than 4,000 newborns. Combined, the hospitals are among the leaders in percentages of total surgeries, cardiac surgeries, neurosurgeries and cardiac catheterization procedures performed throughout the region.

The hospitals have won—and continue to win—both national and international recognition for their programs in numerous specialty areas. Supporting both a charitable and an academic mission, WPAHS has a strong commitment to medical research and education and is also dedicated to training future generations of health-care professionals. Allegheny General serves as the western Pennsylvania campus for the Drexel University College of Medicine in Philadelphia, and West Penn serves as the western Pennsylvania campus for Temple University School of Medicine in Philadelphia.

WPAHS physicians are the official medical provider for the Pittsburgh Pirates. In addition, they provide sports medicine services and programming for numerous area school districts and coaches.

Innovative, outstanding heart care is a hallmark of WPAHS. For more than a half century, our physicians have been on the national forefront of treatment and clinical research.

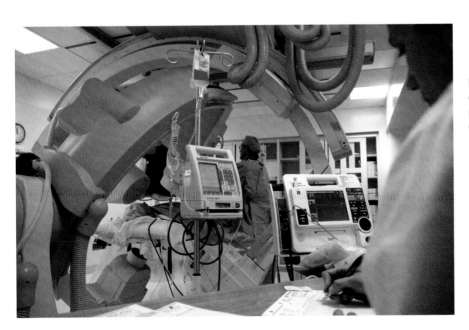

WEST PENN ALLEGHENY
HEALTH SYSTEM

The Pittsburgh 250th Anniversary Commission thanks the many individuals and organizations that have made the celebration possible.* Without their support it would not have been possible to transform Point State Park, complete the Great Allegheny Passage, publish *Pennsylvania's Forbes Trail: Gateways and Getaways along the Legendary Route from Philadelphia to Pittsburgh*, organize one-of-a-kind events that have touched seven states and the District of Columbia, and to initiate grassroots activities across 14 counties of Southwestern Pennsylvania.

ABARTA, INC
AHRCO
Alcoa Foundation
Allegheny Conference on Community Development
Allegheny County
Allegheny County Airport Authority
Allegheny Technologies, Inc.
Allegheny Trail Alliance
American Bridge Company
American Eagle Outfitters, Inc.
Andy Warhol Museum
Anonymous
Arch Street Management, LLC
ASKO Inc.
Arby's
Astorino
Atlas Energy Resources LLC
Bayer Corporation
Berner International Corporation
Broadhurst Family Trust
Buchanan Ingersoll & Rooney
Buhl Foundation
Burns & Scalo
Canadian Consulate General
Carlow University
Carnegie Mellon University
Carnegie Museums of Pittsburgh
Carnegie Science Center
Chaska Property Advisors
Chatham University
Chester Engineers, Inc.
Citizens Bank of Pennsylvania
City of Pittsburgh
Colcom Foundation
Columbia Gas of Pennsylvania
Community Foundation of Armstrong County
Community Foundation of Fayette County
Community Foundation of Greene County
Community Foundation of the Alleghenies
Community Foundation of Western Pennsylvania & Eastern Ohio
Community Foundation of Westmoreland County
Consol Energy
Del Monte Foods

Diebold
Discover Pittsburgh Country
Dollar Bank
Donald & Sylvia Robinson Family Foundation
Duquesne Light Company
Duquesne University
Eat 'N Park Hospitality Group, Inc.
Eaton Electrical, Inc.
Equitable Resources
Family Communications
FedEx Ground
Fifth Third Bank
First Commonwealth
First Energy
Gateway Clipper
Gateway Financial Group, Inc.
Giant Eagle, Inc.
H.J. Heinz Company
Hefren-Tillotson Inc.
Heyl & Patterson Inc.
Highmark Healthy High 5™
Hillman Foundation
Howard Hanna Real Estate
Housetrends Magazine
Huntington Bank
Idearc
iGate Corp.
Independence Blue Cross
Jewish Healthcare Foundation
K&L Gates
Katherine Mabis McKenna Foundation
KDKA-TV
KDKA-AM
Kennametal Inc.
Koppers Inc.
KPMG LLP
Lamar, Inc.
Lanxess Corporation
Leslie Sansone In-Home Walking
Lord's International
Manchester Bidwell (MCG)
MARC USA
McDonald's

McKesson Automation, Inc.
MEDRAD Inc.
Meyer Unkovic & Scott LLC
Michael Baker Corporation
Mine Safety Appliances
National City
NiSource
Norfolk Southern
Nova Chemicals Corporation
Oxford Development Corporation
P.J. Dick-Trumbull-Lindy
Pennsylvania Department of Community & Economic Development
Pennsylvania Department of Conservation and Natural Resources
Pennsylvania Department of Transportation
Pennsylvania Museum and Historical Commission
Pennsylvania House of Representatives
Pennsylvania Senate
Pennsylvania State Police
Pennsylvania Turnpike Commission
Pitt Ohio Express
Pittsburgh Ballet Theatre
Pittsburgh Business Times
Pittsburgh Cultural Trust
Pittsburgh Downtown Partnership
Pittsburgh Magazine
Pittsburgh Penguins
Pittsburgh Pirates
Pittsburgh Post-Gazette
Pittsburgh Quarterly
Pittsburgh Steelers Sports Inc.
Port Authority of Allegheny County
Port of Pittsburgh Commission
Progress Fund
Point Park University
PPG Industries
Pressley Ridge
Reed Smith LLP
Respironics
Richard King Mellon Foundation
Robert Morris University
Saint Vincent College
Seagate
Senator John Heinz History Center
Schneider Downs
Seton Hill University
Snavely Forest Products

Sony Technology Center—Pittsburgh
Staley Capital Advisers, Inc.
Steel City Media
Sunoco, Inc.
The Bank of New York Mellon
The Buncher Company
The Claude Worthington Benedum Foundation
The Grable Foundation
The Heinz Endowments
The Hillman Company
The Laurel Foundation
The Members of the Allegheny Conference Regional Investors Council
The Pittsburgh Foundation
The Pittsburgh Foundation Funds:
Elmer G. and Gladys Schade Klaber Fund
The Clarence G. Koepke Memorial Fund
Ray H. Kohl Fund
Phillip M. LeMaistre Fund
Fannie A. Lawrence Fund
The Lois Tack Thompson Fund
William Christopher and Mary Laughlin Robinson Fund
The PNC Financial Services Group, Inc.
The PNC Foundation
Thorp Reed & Armstrong LLP
TRACO
Twentieth Century Club
US Airways
Union Switch and Signal, Inc.
United States Steel Corporation
University of Pittsburgh
UPMC Health System
Value Ambridge Properties, Inc.
Verizon Wireless
VisitPA
VisitPittsburgh
Wal-Mart
West Penn Allegheny Health System
Westinghouse Electric Company
Williams Coulson
WDUQ-FM
WPGH-TV
WPXI-TV
WQED Multimedia
WTAE-TV
XEROX
Zambrano Corporation

*Supporters as of February 24, 2008

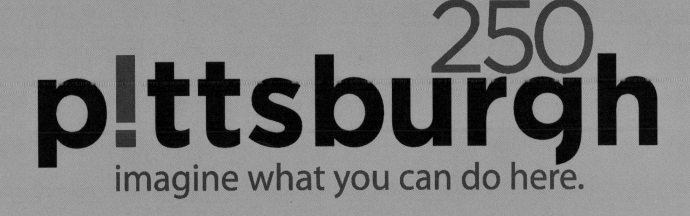

Index by Name or Venue

Index by School

Index by Cemetery

Destined for another flea market, Mendelson, Orr, and Clarke await more amusements and thrilling discoveries.

PHOTO BY SARAH REED

Acknowledgments

From Andy Masich, President and CEO, Senator John Heinz History Center:

On behalf of The History Center and the Pittsburgh 250 Publications Committee, a debt of gratitude is owed to the authors, Prentiss Orr, Abby Mendelson, and Tripp Clarke for their inspiration to conceive this project and for their tireless efforts to see it through to successful completion. Many thanks also to the Pittsburgh 250 Publications Committee for their active support and valuable suggestions.

From C. Prentiss Orr, Editor, who principally covered the performing artists, leaders, and pioneers:

My wife made me promise her a long time ago that should I have the great fortune to win an Academy Award®, or just as improbably a Tony®, I would thank her three times in my acceptance speech. I haven't won any awards, but now may be my one shot to thank her in front of an audience. So first, to my patient, supportive spouse, I thank you from the bottom of my heart. As we said in the preface, this has been one heck of a ride. Thanks for sharing the dips of realization and peaks of discovery. Equal thanks go to my children who have been tolerant, to say the very least.

Others who deserve my gratitude are Andy Masich, Betty Arenth, Brian Butko, Sherrie Flick and dozens of eager History Center associates who have been as enthusiastic in the last few weeks as they were the first. Historically significant thanks go to Don Riggs who first gave this idea wings; to Marion who helped hatch the idea long before anyone else was talking about a 250th anniversary; to the librarians of the Penn-

sylvania Room who pulled more files for this one project than they did for fifty others of far higher academic pursuit; to the many History Center writers who captured the spirit and souls of those people who called Pittsburgh home before 1900; to William Daw at the Curtis Collection for expert assistance; to Mary Louise for suffering through some pretty dull movies just to appease my interest in obscure Pittsburgh actors; to Boris Weinstein for corroborating our claim that the Hollywood sign rightfully should stand on Mount Washington; to the kind folks at Pitt, CMU, Chatham and Duquesne who helped search a lot of photos and transcripts; to Lee who got the first folders filled with solid research; to Terry who has a great eye for design; to Charlie for all the alphabetizing and indexing; to all of our corporate sponsors who made this history (and, frankly, most all of Pittsburgh's history) happen; to Barry for taking charge of my other obligations; to the many, truly humble people whose contributions to our culture and community are of epic proportion (yet allowed us to compress their life-long largesse to less than 300 words); to Dan who hung in there the whole way; to Greg who was willing to track down the most reclusive stars and ask questions only the most lunatic fan might ask; to Fred, Sr., and Fred, Jr., of Attic Records in Millvale for allowing us into their stacks and for letting us continue the legacy of plugging a deserving record store; and, finally, to Lulu—did I mention my wife?—with whom I look forward to sharing some cold potato vodka.

From Abby Mendelson who wrote the profiles of athletes, writers, and visual artists:

As with any book, there are far too many people to thank, especially the hundreds of friends and colleagues who bravely cheered on

this project, or allowed me to intrude on their lives with endless interviews and fact-checking.

However, a few individual thanks are in order. First, to Judy Mendelson, who, since the propitious day she married me, has graciously accepted my long hours in the shop and has freely given much-needed advice. Next, to my sons Elie Mendelson, who consulted on design and set up the all-important ftp site, and Jesse Mendelson, who lent his encyclopedic sports knowledge. Along those lines, I must also offer a tip of the stick to Jed Cohen, for his sage advice on hockey.

For all these profiles, my own extensive files and resources were simply insufficient. Without the help of the incredibly knowledgeable and infinitely patient folks at the Carnegie Library's Pennsylvania Room, this book would not exist. I thank them all.

From Tripp Clarke, author of the many and diverse musician profiles:

Pittsburgh's contribution to the musical landscape of our country is enormous. There are great musicians from Pittsburgh who are properly celebrated and there are great musicians from here that deserve more acknowledgement than they have received. My hope is that this book honors both.

I couldn't have accomplished the herculean task of identifying all of the significant "players" from our area without the help of the veteran music community—to help tell the stories, cut through the muck and fill in the gaps ... oh yeah, and double-check my work. I am very grateful to them for sharing their time, their knowledge, their lunch hour, their stories, and their friendship.

Among the many people who helped me identify and tell the stories of these great people were Chuck Austin, Joe Bonadio, Joe Negri, George Heid, Bob Studebaker, Tom Wendt, Chris Fletcher, Harold Betters, Dick Kay and Fred Bohn. Thanks to Jack for listening. Thanks also to the superb staff at the Carnegie Library of Pittsburgh and the Historical Society of Western Pennsylvania. A very special thanks to my wife Katie and my three children, Evan, Will and Catlin for putting up with the many hours spent with my laptop instead of with them. Special thanks to Catlin for the shoulder squeezes... .

The authors, researchers and the more famous folk of Pittsburgh will be grateful for your comments, corrections and recollections addressed to pghbornpghbred@gmail.com